Careful Reading,
Thoughtful Writing

A GUIDE WITH MODELS
FOR COLLEGE WRITERS

Richard J. Prystowsky

Irvine Valley College

 HarperCollins*CollegePublishers*

Senior Acquisitions Editor: Patricia Rossi
Developmental Editor: Lynne Cattafi
Project Coordination, Text and Cover Design: Interactive Composition Corporation
Cover Photograph: Steve Thornton
Electronic Production Manager: Eric Jorgensen
Manufacturing Manager: Hilda Koparanian
Electronic Page Makeup: Interactive Composition Corporation
Printer and Binder: RR Donnelley & Sons Company
Cover Printer: Phoenix Color Corp.

For permission to use copyrighted material and photographs, grateful acknowledgment is made to the copyright holders on pp. 394–396, which are hereby made part of this copyright page.

Careful Reading, Thoughtful Writing: A Guide With Models for College Writers

Library of Congress Cataloging-in-Publication Data

Prystowsky, Richard J. (Richard Jay), 1956–
     Careful reading, thoughtful writing: a guide with models for college
writers / Richard J. Prystowsky. — 1st ed.
          p. cm.
     Includes bibliographical references and index.
     ISBN 0–06–501412–X (Student Edition)
     ISBN 0–06–501413–8 (Instructor's Edition)
     1. English language—Rhetoric. 2. College readers. I. Title
PE1408.P775 1996
808'.0427—dc20   95–2757
                                                                             CIP

95 96 97 98 9 8 7 6 5 4 3 2 1

In memory of Doris E. Miles,

WHOSE SOUL IS LOVE

"Imitation is natural to man from childhood, one of his advantages over the lower animals being this, that he is the most imitative creature in the world, and learns at first by imitation."

ARISTOTLE
Poetics

"Ever since he began writing, Norbert Kosky followed the precepts of F. L. Lucas: 'In fine, there is much to be said for the principle "Write in haste; and revise at leisure." And revision is usually best when one has had time to forget what has been written, and comes back to it with fresh eyes.'"

JERZY KOSINSKI
The Hermit of 69th Street

Annotated Contents

1

Thinking About Writing 1

Highlighting the notion that writing is a process-oriented activity, this chapter discusses some of the ways in which students can become (and remain) good, confident, seriously committed writers.

READINGS

SHERWOOD ANDERSON, *Certain Things Last: A Writer Warms to His Story*

A famous author—or a created author-narrator?—explains his own struggles to write a book. 12

KEVIN MULLEN, *"Writing: A Leap of Faith," Model Essay and Commentary*[1]

A student writer movingly writes about the ways in which his struggles to write are intertwined with his life struggles and then, in his commentary, attempts to explain why this essay turned out to be "one of the most difficult that [he had] ever written." 17

2

Critical Thinking: An Introduction 21

This chapter introduces a number of key aspects of critical thinking and explains how students can apply them to their writing.

READINGS

AESOP, *The Shepherd Boy and the Wolf*

This is the famous story of a shepherd boy who abuses the kindness of his fellow citizens. 31

---

[1] Each contributing author produced work in response to the featured assignment found in the appropriate chapter.

4

This chapter introduces three common prewriting techniques and a sample first draft in an attempt to help students see how predrafting ideas can lead to promising draft material.

READINGS

ELIE WIESEL, *Why I Write*

One of the most well-known Holocaust survivors offers a clear and painful articulation of his personal commitment to writing, telling us, among other things, that he writes in order to "wrench [the] victims [of the Holocaust] from oblivion[,]," to "help the dead vanquish death."

JAY JULOS, *"Why I Write," Model Prewriting, First Draft, and Commentary*

After doing some freewriting, charting, and clustering, this chapter's student author constructs both a first draft of an essay, in which he explains why he enjoys writing, and a commentary, in which he explains how his use of predrafting techniques helped him to organize his thoughts for a first draft.

CLAUDE LANZMANN, from *Shoah*

In this official Nazi document, cited in Lanzmann's book on the Holocaust, we see how a perpetrator of Holocaust crimes uses language both to reveal and to conceal the truth about a particular atrocity that he helped to commit.

FRED E. KATZ, *A Sociological Perspective to the Holocaust*

An insightful sociologist teaches us something about the bureaucratic aspects of the Holocaust, focusing particularly on the ways in which "'ordinary' human behavior can be harnessed in the service of 'extraordinary,' and monstrous, objectives."

CHRISTOPHER R. BROWNING, *Ordinary Men*

An acclaimed historian provides a historical framework within which we can view otherwise ordinary men acting as agents of terrible human destruction.

ABRAM L. SACHAR, *The Carob Tree Grove: Christian Compassion*

A distinguished scholar and university administrator highlights the heroism displayed during the Holocaust by some Christians who, at great risk to themselves and their families, refused to stand idly by while their fellow human beings suffered.

5

Ideas and Strategies for Revising and Moving Beyond the First Draft

This chapter explores various aspects of revision, including those concerning thesis development, in order to help students see how they might move beyond their initial drafts. It also briefly covers some important aspects of paragraphing.

READINGS

LOUIE CREW, *Thriving As An Outsider, Even As An Outcast, In Smalltown America*
SELECTION

Documenting what happened when he and his spouse—who form "a gay, racially integrated couple"—tried "living openly in [a] small town," the author shows how he and his partner triumphed over the hatred expressed towards them.

SHEHLA YAMANI, *"The Dilemma," Model Rough Drafts, Revisions, and Commentary*
RESPONSE

In her drafts and revisions, a foreign-born student writes with pain and insight both about her being an outsider in the United States and about her efforts to practice "Jihad against ignorance and misinformation". In her commentary, she explains, among other things, how the writing process itself helped her to discover that she was caught in a rather uncomfortable "dilemma" concerning victims and victimizers.

SIGMUND FREUD, *The Sexual Aberrations*
The father of psychoanalysis explores the psychoanalytic dimensions of "normal" and "abnormal" sexuality in a way that both explains the significance of and yet undermines some common notions about this issue.

BURTON M. LEISER, *Evaluating the "Unnaturalness Argument" Concerning Homosexuality*
A philosopher shows us the problems that arise when people use the terms "natural" and "unnatural" to discuss the topic of sexual orientation.

DAVID GELMAN, ET AL., *Born or Bred?*
Some journalists report on recent scientific work investigating whether or not—and, if so, to what extent—all of us might be genetically or biochemically programmed for a particular sexual orientation, despite whatever social influences might also affect our sexual behaviors.

7

This chapter tries to help students understand some important differences between personal writing and traditional academic writing so that they can put together a strong essay of the latter variety.

READINGS

8

Covering a number of important topics, such as the students' need to be careful about drawing general conclusions from their personal experiences, this chapter tries to help students see how they might meet the sometimes difficult demands of the sort of academic writing project that calls for them to invest themselves in their nonpersonal analytical work.

READINGS

Thematic Contents

Sexual Orientation: Concepts, Conflicts, (Re)Solutions

Religion and Spirituality

Childhood and Young Adulthood

Ethics, Judgment, Conduct

Foreword

I have long been committed to the idea that the best way to learn to write well—with style as well as with clarity—has been to read and become imbued with the ways of words and sentences, of sounds and subtleties and rhythms, in many fine texts, past and present. I was persuaded to this idea many years ago, as I became aware of the process by which my own master teacher became the fine writer he was. Coming from another country with little mastery in English, he had much to learn if he was to take his place in the philosophical and literary discussions in the academy in the United States. So for some years he read—and read and read—in a wide variety of writers, not in order to become a copier or disciple of any of them but to immerse himself in the vibrations of the language usage that gave the texts the qualities he sensed. And gradually he came to take on his own style and, ultimately, to join his work to the extended sequence of distinguished writings in the language.

Some years afterwards I was able to repeat his experiment with a specially favored student of mine. Though he was, almost instinctively I felt, a sensitive student of literature, he went to Vietnam without graduating High School and was afterwards in the university and in my class only through veterans' rights and a patient community college system. His insights were superb, his writing sub-literate. So under my guidance he went to work as my teacher had, reading and re-reading one well selected text after another, and thinking about what it was in them that would shape how he himself would go about his work. How proud I was of the person and the method as I saw him develop into a young and productive scholar, with a completed doctoral dissertation and a good number of impressive publications to his credit.

So, even as I admire many of the more recent revolutions in the teaching of writing courses, I have maintained my faith in the extraordinary benefits to the fledgling writer in the study of exemplary texts. And this book indicates that my student, Richard Prystowsky, has had that faith transmitted to him. He now wants to pass it on to his readers.

Thanks to the recent explosion of electronic technology, we are being increasingly bombarded—almost to the exclusion of everything else—by an endless stream of visual images. We are in danger of forgetting an abiding element in how we define who we are: as philosophers have long told us, what constitutes us as human is the fact that the human is, primarily, a speaker of words and, subsequently, a writer of texts. The pages that follow will make students much better at being both of these.

— MURRAY KRIEGER

To the Instructor

There are three main premises underlying this book: one, that thoughtful writing often derives from careful reading; two, that people become adept at doing things largely by learning from and often by imitating others who are good at doing them; and three, that all writing, including that which is contained in final drafts, is writing-in-progress. Every aspect of this book has been created in an attempt to match the integrity of these principles.

In this text, your students will be able to study and learn from two sources of good writing: that produced by professional writers whose work is highlighted in *featured* and *related* reading selections, and that produced by student writers in their model essays, which were written in response to the featured writing assignments. Seeing how fellow student writers produce good responses to the same (kinds of) assignments with which your students will be working ought to help your students determine how *they* might best use the writing process in order to produce personally meaningful, academically sound papers. That is the intention behind this book's inclusion of the contributing authors' work.

Let me say, too, that when I talk about your students' imitating the work of other writers, I am not referring to slavish copying of preconceived, static, so-called masterful writing. The contributing authors provide *examples* of good writing. But like the book's instructional material in general, these examples are not meant to be ends in themselves. Rather, they are offered as means to ends, good instructional roads on which your students might travel in their search for their own paths to good thinking, reading, and writing.

The Layout of the Text

This book's first two chapters are intended to be *very* introductory in nature. Chapter One has a threefold purpose: (1) to help your students see that they need not fear writing; (2) to help them develop a healthy attitude about writing; and (3) to help them "set up shop" so that they will have the space and time within which to pursue their writing.

Chapter Two should help your students understand what will be expected of them as critical thinkers. The chapter includes two light-hearted readings rather than any serious argument-based ones so that students have an opportunity to practice critical reading with some ease.

Since writing always constitutes an act of reading (even if writers are their own readers), and since, more often than not, good writers are also good, active readers, this book devotes an entire chapter—Chapter Three—to showing students how they might read a text closely by interacting with and responding to it. To help your students see how different readers approach the same text, this chapter presents the work of two readers/writers; their work includes their annotated versions of the featured reading selection, their comments on the selection, and their commentaries on their reading experiences. The chapter also includes the supporting apparatuses that you'll find in the remaining chapters (see below).

Each of the text's remaining chapters is devoted to teaching your students some process-oriented, often stage-specific writing ideas and techniques. Chapters Four and Five take them through the phases of prewriting, drafting, and revising.

If you decide to rearrange the order in which the instructional material in this book is presented, you might want to keep in mind that the instructional material contained in Chapters Six, Seven, and Eight presupposes that your students already understand something about the substantive matters discussed in Chapters One through Five. Though also process-oriented, the book's final three chapters concentrate on helping students learn how to write three common types of college essays: a personal narrative, a traditionally academic analysis, and an essay in which the writer combines "the personal" and "the academic."

The Characteristic Features of the Book's Chapters

Each of Chapters Three through Eight includes a featured reading selection as well as related readings thematically akin to that featured selection. Each featured assignment either derives from or in some way responds to the issues highlighted in the chapter's featured reading and thus is meant to be undertaken in connection with some study of this selection. Students who study the chapter's instructional component ought to find that the information presented there helps them do the featured assignment.

For each reading selection in Chapters Three through Eight, students will find a close-reading tip, followed, when necessary, by a reference to some relevant textual passages. These close-reading tips are meant to be useful points of departure, hints of important interpretive possibilities that your students might want to watch for and consider. You might encourage your students not only to use these close-reading tips for their own extended analyses of the readings in question, but also, if appropriate, to take issue with what is said in some or all of them. If they make these moves, then they'll *surely* be reading *actively*!

Chapters Three through Eight also contain pre-reading and post-reading questions, which are meant to help your students understand that, since all reading, like all writing, is context-specific, it follows that no one ever reads in a vacuum. Put differently, these apparatuses are intended to help your students engage in active reading by helping them to see how, as readers and writers, they always work within and in response to situation-specific demands—for example, the demands imposed upon them in an assignment or on an exam—and how their efforts are always informed, to some extent at least, by the ideas that they bring to and take away from their reading and writing activities. These apparatuses can help your students become increasingly better readers by helping them to see both how and why good readers try to understand (1) the issues and ideas that they bring to their readings of texts, (2) those that they derive from their having read and thought about the texts, and (3) the relationship between their pre- and post-reading thoughts and experiences.

The book contains one more supporting apparatus: suggestions for hands-on activities. I strongly believe that, in the final analysis, the lasting value of a college education has little to do with what a student produces in class, and much to do with the ways in which that student can take her or his college learning experiences out of the classroom and apply them to her or his other life experiences.

Used to its fullest advantage, this book ought to help your students become confident, competent, and perhaps even highly committed readers, thinkers, and writers.

Acknowledgments

During the course of this book's progress, many, many individuals—students, teachers, colleagues, family, and friends—gave me their help and support. Though space does not permit me to name all of these people, they know who they are. To them, I give my sincere thanks. And, with a feeling of deep gratitude, I give an extra bit of such thanks to my parents, Rose and Milton Prystowsky, and to my father-in-law and late mother-in-law, Elmore and Doris Miles.

Though the task of writing and rewriting a manuscript of this nature is never easy, my job was greatly facilitated by the efforts of the reviewers who read different versions of the manuscript. The feedback that I received from these individuals was, in a word, invaluable. Besides offering kindly and more than helpful advice, they showed a tremendous generosity of spirit. I humbly thank the following reviewers for their efforts: Patricia Bridges, Mount Union College; Irene Lurkis Clark, the University of Southern California; David Jolliffe, the University of Illinois at Chicago; Dennis Lebofsky, Temple University; Lisa J. McClure, Southern Illinois University at Carbondale; Carol S. Olsen, Valparaiso University; Karen Rodis, Dartmouth College; Meryl F. Schwartz, the University of Hartford; and Dean Stover, Arizona State University.

Though I warmly thank everyone at HarperCollins who assisted me, I want to give special thanks to the following three people: Lynne Cattafi, my senior editor's assistant, who helped me above and beyond the call of duty during the final phases of this project; Marisa L'Heureux, my former developmental editor, who displayed uncanny patience and gave me hours and hours of help; and Patricia Rossi, my senior editor, whose gracious belief in this book helped insure that this project reached fruition.

I feel deeply humbled to have had the opportunity to learn from a number of outstanding teachers, many of whose theories, practices, and teachings I have tried to incorporate into my own teaching and writing. Among my many fine teachers, five have given me very special gifts and thus will always remain near to my heart: Professor John Moore, who helped me discover the soul of poetry; the late Professor C. A. "Dean" Patrides, who helped me see the poetry of the soul; Professor Sandor Goodhart, who has given me the gift of a cherished, long-standing friendship; Professor Hal Toliver, who has shown me incredible kindness and generosity; and Professor Murray Krieger, who continues to show me that profoundly wise teachers are also humble and compassionate human beings. To all of these great men, I remain deeply grateful and give my heartfelt thanks.

Finally, I offer my deepest thanks and profoundest love to the members of my family, who, in both the best and the worst of times, not only put up with my occasional (!) ill humor, but also offered me encouragement, hope, and love. My daughter Cyleste, a psychology major at the University of California at Riverside, read parts of the manuscript and, in our many discussions, helped keep me focused on the needs of my students. My daughter Sami and my son Cobby, the two "little ones," patiently let me work even during those times when we all would rather have been playing together. In addition, they continually taught me that the most meaningful learning begins in the heart, mind, and will of the learner, and that teachers would do well to allow themselves to learn from their students as much and as often as possible. And finally, Charlie, my wife, lover, and best friend, never stopped believing either in me or in this project. Furthermore, she continually helps me to see how the best teaching is that which directly engages the teacher with his or her own learning needs. But most important, her love remains the wellspring of our individual and yet intimately connected spiritual growth and synergistically engaged destiny.

— RICHARD J. PRYSTOWSKY

"No matter where you fall on the anxiety axis, you can be sure there is a writer in you. Every person has ideas and feelings to share. Only the proper subject, occasion, and impetus are needed to draw them out."

Barbara Lounsberry
The Writer in You

Thinking About Writing

IN AN ESSAY concerning the writing of her now-famous book *The Color Purple,* Pulitzer Prize-winning author Alice Walker has this to say about her struggles to put words on paper:

> When I was sure the characters of my new novel were trying to form (or, as I invariably thought of it, trying to contact me, to speak *through* me), I began to make plans to leave New York. Three months earlier I had bought a tiny house on a quiet Brooklyn street, assuming—because my desk overlooked the street and a maple tree in the yard, representing garden and view—I would be able to write. I was not. ("Writing *The Color Purple*" 356; author's italics)

Unfortunately, even after moving to a more rural environment in northern California—to a place that she and her lover "could afford and that [her] characters liked" (357)—Walker experienced "days and weeks and even months when nothing happened. Nothing whatsoever" (358).

In fact, Walker's experiences are not unique. From time to time, all writers have trouble coming up with things to say. Moreover, at one time or another, *all* writers have felt bad about *some* of their writing, have felt like scrapping this or that project, have doubted their abilities to say what they needed or wanted to say. A la characters in T. S. Eliot's famous poem "The Love Song of J. Alfred Prufrock," all writers have at least occasionally made the following sorts of comments about their work: "And how should I presume?"; "And how should I begin?"; "It is impossible to say just what I mean!"; "'That is not what I meant at all.'"

In short, writing is a messy business, one entailing many starts and stops, visions and revisions, good luck and bad. Moreover, as the excerpt from Walker's essay intimates, writing represents a *process,* and not just a final *product. Good* writing, at least, does not simply pour out of the pens of good writers like water tumbling over the falls of Niagara—effortlessly, and with a force that commands the reader's attention and respect. Though a great writer often produces final products that give the illusion of their having been produced naturally and effortlessly—much as Mikhail Baryshnikov and Cynthia Gregory's ballet performances might lull us into fancying that these dancers simply and naturally dance well, that they never have to rehearse, and that they never make mistakes—experienced writers such as your instructor know the truth about smooth writing: in the words of Alexander Pope, the great eighteenth-century English poet, "True Ease in Writing comes from Art, not Chance, / As those move easiest who have learn'd to dance" ("An Essay on Criticism," II.362–363).

Thus, whatever else writing might be (a means of self-discovery, for example, or a way for one to make sense of her world), it is always an *activity.* And *good, powerful, meaningful* writing almost always derives from the pens of writers who have put much time and energy into performing this activity as well as possible. Like their counterparts in fields such as athletics, music, and medicine, seriously committed writers practice their craft often and consistently and keep practicing it after others less committed to being good at their work would have called it quits.

Having or Developing a Good Attitude About Writing

Notwithstanding writers' bursts of inspiration and creative energies, good writing, then, does not simply materialize out of thin air; instead, it results from a process of writing and rewriting. That fact helps to explain why the success or failure of any one of your papers might have little or no relationship to your general aptitude or inaptitude as a writer. What *does* bear on this general aptitude or inaptitude, though, is your attitude about yourself as a (non-)writer. If you are intent upon writing well, you will need to have or develop a positive attitude before you begin tackling your various writing tasks, and you'll need to maintain this attitude throughout the writing process.

Of course, some students have trouble producing decent papers despite their also having a good attitude about their writing. But why *begin* with a handicap if you can avoid doing so? You yourself probably know from experience that your ability or inability to perform a given activity well (playing basketball, riding a horse, playing the piano, taking the SATs) often depends, at least in part, not only on your desire or lack of desire to do well in this activity, but also on your attitude about your ability or inability to do well in it. Attitudes are not divorced from either the processes of performance or, by extension, the final outcomes or products of these performances.

Thus, even if you know something about the process of writing, you will probably have at least some trouble writing a good paper if as you write you keep telling yourself that you've never been good at writing and that you don't like writing. Although space does not permit even a cursory attempt to explain *why* you might have such an attitude and how you might begin changing this attitude, we can at least acknowledge the obvious: if you give yourself negative messages about yourself as a writer, then, for you, writing might very well turn out to be the sort of painful, unrewarding activity that you've already determined it to be. On the other hand, if you give yourself positive messages about yourself as a writer—even, and perhaps *especially,* when you might be having some trouble with your prose—you might stumble upon some hitherto unknown and unexplored intellectual and emotional rewards that the writer in you had been hoping and waiting to discover.

Getting Down to Business

In practical terms, having a good attitude about yourself as a writer is useful or valuable only to the extent that you actually write. Since good writing inevitably involves a process of careful writing and rewriting, thinking and rethinking, envisioning and revising, you'll need to commit yourself to having the space and time within which to write—consistently, often, relatively undisturbed, and for relatively long stretches of time—if you want to produce good work. And then you'll need to stick by that commitment.

Among other things, consistent practice in writing should help you work through difficulties that inevitably will surface as you write your papers. Road-blocks and their attendant frustrations are simply part of the territory in writing, just as missed steps and false starts inevitably occur during dance rehearsals. But writers can help keep themselves from becoming rusty in their writing and can aid their efforts to work through their writing difficulties if they write consistently rather than sporadically. If you want to get into and stay in shape and be able to work through exercising difficulties even on an off day, then you'll need to exercise more than once a month. Pinch hitters committed to hitting well take batting practice regularly, not sporadically.

By the same token, you will greatly aid your writing efforts if you set up what I like to call, for psychological effect, "writing blocks," that is, blocks of time in which you plan on either writing or doing writing-related activities (such as reading, working on grammatical or stylistic problems, and so on). If you don't keep in shape as a writer by writing consistently and faithfully, and, in the worst case scenario, if you begin your essay the night before it is due, you increase the chances that you'll be unable to work your way out of that *other* sort of writer's block, the one with which all writers are quite familiar. At the very least, you will make the task of writing your paper that much harder, and probably less enjoyable, if you delay starting your essay until the last minute.

Setting Up a Writing Schedule

Many people write better, or at least feel more comfortable writing, at certain times and in certain places than they do at other times and in other places. Some people, for example, write better in the morning; others find themselves better able to write in the afternoon or evening. Many a professor has trouble writing in her office at school, though she can write for ten or 12 hours a day in her study at home. Some people like to write late at night; if there is an all-night restaurant on or near your campus, you'll probably discover some students and instructors there writing into the wee hours of the morning. Many, many writers set up shop at the dining room table. Others need to write at a desk—sometimes, at a *particular* desk set up in a *particular way*. Although there is no universally "right" place at which or time within which to write, if you want to maximize your writing efforts, you'll need to decide when and where you generally feel most comfortable writing, set up a writing schedule that allows you to take full advantage of your own writing proclivities, and then *write*.

To help yourself determine the writing schedule that will work best for you, follow these three simple guidelines: (1) outside of class, devote at least two to three hours to your writing for every hour that you spend in class; (2) allow yourself, for now, at least two consecutive hours within which to write, gradually increasing these writing blocks to four or five consecutive hours, if possible; and (3) write at least three days a week. Though you might be able to dash off a decently penned note or letter to a friend, you will find it difficult to dash off a quality paper for a college class, especially one for a writing class, in which—let's face it—writing counts. When you are putting together a paper for a class, you need time to read, think about what you're reading, write, stop writing, think, read, reread, jot down notes, make outlines, write some more, read some more, think some more, and so on. If you are not used to spending many hours at a time reading and writing, you probably shouldn't block out too much writing time initially, any more than you would want to begin exercising for three or four hours a day if you are unaccustomed to exercising for long stretches of time. Otherwise, you might become frustrated and, eventually, give up or skimp on your reading and writing tasks altogether, just as many a would-be exercise enthusiast stops exercising because he or she tries too hard to get into shape right away.

Arrange your schedule so that you can write both where you're most comfortable writing (and where you're not likely to be disturbed) and when you are free and most able to write. And then keep your writing appointments, even if you think that you have nothing to write during those times. Be honest with yourself. Don't say, "Well, I have free time every day between three and six a.m., so I'll set up my writing blocks then," unless you really plan to write every day between three and six a.m. Ordinarily, you wouldn't make a doctor's appointment that you knowingly can't or won't keep, so why make a writing appointment that you plan to miss?

If during a particular writing block you find yourself staring for too long at a blank piece of paper that seems to be doubling as a place mat or at a blank document that seems to be doing little more than covering up the icons and folders on your computer screen, you can always first read material that is directly related to your present writing task and that you think might help you generate some ideas for writing and then write in response to what you've just read. Sometimes, reading and then writing informally about texts *not* directly related or even completely *unrelated* to your writing task might help you generate ideas for writing, too. You might also make notes for a present or future writing project, write about why you are or seem stuck and how you can move beyond your problem, work on isolated writing tasks, such as those involving grammatical or stylistic problems that continue to plague your writing, write papers for other classes, write in your personal journal or diary, do some freewriting or engage in some other prewriting activity (see Chapter Four for a detailed discussion of prewriting), and so on. Don't simply give up and do something else. Anything short of your making and fulfilling at least a relatively respectable commitment to your writing might eventuate in otherwise preventable difficulties for you and your written college work.

The following sentence-level and paragraphing exercise is an example of the sort of writing activity that you might want to do during a writing block.

Remember that this exercise is only one of many that you might want to do. Taking control of and responsibility for your own writing, you should create and engage in activities that suit your own particular writing needs.

1) Write a hefty paragraph (6–8 sentences) in which you describe what you consider to be your dominant personality trait.

2) Highlight the paragraph's subjects, verbs, direct objects, and subject complements.

3) Try replacing state of being verbs with action verbs (and vice versa) and then try changing the voices of verbs from passive to active and from active to passive. Then write informally (in your personal journal, for example) about whether or not your writing reflects the ways in which you see yourself and whether or not, by revising your prose, you necessarily rethink these self-reflections.

4) Write about what you learned from your having engaged in this writing activity.

5) Jot down some ideas concerning what you might want to work on during your next writing block. (If you want to extend the parameters of this particular exercise, you might decide that, during your next writing block, you'll first write a paragraph in which you describe what you imagine *others* see as your dominant personality trait and then do steps two through four, above. During yet another writing block, you might write an extended journal entry in which you reflect on the thoughts that you had and the feelings that you experienced while you engaged in these other two writing activities.)

Reader-Based Versus Writer-Based Prose

Throughout the semester, you will engage in a number of writing activities in which you construct what many composition theorists and instructors call **writer-based prose,** such as diary or personal journal entries, personal notes to yourself, and class notes, all of which constitute writing done primarily or exclusively for you yourself (have you ever had trouble deciphering a classmate's notes?). As long as *you* can understand what you are saying when you do such writing, fine. In fact, you might even write some of your writer-based prose in such a way that would-be readers who stumble upon your writing will have trouble deciphering what you have said.

For those pieces of writing—such as the bulk of your college papers—that will be written for eyes other than yours, however, you'll need to write so that someone other than you will understand what you are saying. When you write for others, you are engaged in writing what we call **reader-based prose,** that is, prose meant for the eyes of a reader. If your instructor, peer editor, or someone else for whom you are writing doesn't quite understand what you are trying to say in your reader-based work, you can't legitimately reply, "But *I* understand what I mean here." If your writing has left your *intended* reader confused, then you won't win any points by making such a statement, for your job was to have made your writing understandable *precisely to that reader.*

As the previous paragraph suggests, writers write for *intended* readers, not for *all* readers, however different their intended readers are from one another. In other words, writers write for specific audiences, even if those audiences are more or less heterogeneous. You'll serve your writing interests well if whenever you write you bear in mind this crucial distinction between "intended readers" and "readers." If you are writing for your peers, then you need to express your thoughts so that your *peers* will understand what you are saying. If you are writing for an instructor, then you need to write so that *she or he* will understand what you are saying. If you are writing for your mother, then you need to write so that *she* will understand what you are saying. And if you are writing for all three groups, then you need to write so that they *all* will understand what you are saying.

To help yourself write good, understandable reader-based prose, you might try incorporating one or more of the following performance-oriented techniques into your writing process: playing the role of both author and intended reader, deliver your paper while you are standing in front of a mirror; imagine and then analyze the facial expressions and body language of audience members hearing you present your material to them at a meeting; picture and hear yourself responding to questions that your intended readers would likely ask you about your ideas. If you become petrified at the mere thought of your having to give a speech, then you might wish, instead, to try visualizing and then interpreting the reactions of an intended reader engaged in the act of reading your work. Additionally, and regardless of your fears, at various stages of the writing process you might find it quite helpful to tape-record your thoughts for writing and then play them back.

In trying to decide how you might communicate most effectively to your intended readers, remember that your goal is not to use a particular technique, but rather to maximize your writing's strengths and minimize its weaknesses. Try an approach that you think might work. If it does work, exploit it; if it doesn't work, discard it and choose another.

Finding a Topic Worth Writing About

To some extent, reader-based and writer-based prose overlap. Indeed, writers of reader-based prose often write about issues that are close to their own hearts, a fact that might help explain why a number of professional writers say that they write for themselves, notwithstanding their desires to have others read their works. William Zinsser, a noted expert on writing, goes so far as to say that "[w]riters of every age will write better and more confidently if they are allowed to write about what they care about. Affection for the subject is a tonic" (240). The passion and insight that infuse the works of great writers such as James Baldwin, E. B. White, Alice Walker, and Virginia Woolf, for example, derive not simply from these authors' deep understanding of their material, but also—and maybe even largely—from the profound personal interest, the high personal stake, the significant personal investments that they have in the subject matter about which they write. Perhaps when the stakes are high enough for you personally, you yourself write with a strong commitment to your writing task and produce meaningful work.

Though for most or all of your college papers you might have little or no choice concerning the general topic on which you are asked to write, you can almost always incorporate into your writing some aspect of your own interests. When you receive a writing assignment, then, ask yourself what the subject matter represented in the assignment means to you personally. Don't force the issue, but do try to generate pertinent ideas that also hold *your* interest. If you can't find anything of interest in the assignment, you should probably talk with your instructor to see if he or she can help you in this matter. Otherwise, you might find your writing task an onerous, tedious affair. There's a world of difference between your struggling to make a meaningful assignment work and your struggling merely to get through an assignment that bores you or for which you can find no relevance to your own life. Keep in mind that, if you are bored with your writing, you might generate prose that reflects this boredom and, consequently, that bores your reader, too. Think about how you would feel having to sift through such prose, and then take special care not to produce that sort of writing for your intended readers, who probably share your feelings.

Writing as Learning

Writers write for many reasons: to entertain, to make money, to carry out a work-related task, to teach, and so on. In addition, many writers write at least partly to learn—to help themselves understand an idea or to help clarify their own views concerning an issue, for example. You might find your writing experiences particularly enjoyable if you treat your writing assignments as learning experiences. Of course, by its very nature, learning is personal. Though you can learn *from,* you cannot learn *for* someone else. You can learn only *for yourself.* In this sense, even the best reader-based prose has significant writer-based meaning.

At times, however, your ability to learn from your own reader-based writing projects might be compromised if you are so close to the material that you cannot see the weak spots in your writing and thinking as clearly as an intended outside reader can see them. But you can help yourself avoid getting into this dilemma or, once in it, help yourself escape it if, as suggested later in this book (see Chapter Five, p.128), you always write your reader-based papers *as a reader*—in other words, if you write them *with a reader's eyes.* Doing so, you'll help yourself become your own reader-critic, a move that experienced writers strive to make.

Even if you work hard at accounting for your readers' needs, though, you might discover that some members of your intended audience don't quite understand what you are saying—a rather frustrating situation that all writers face at one time or another. Sometimes, you might know what you want to say but for some reason will have trouble clarifying your points to your intended readers. At other times, however, you might discover that, in fact, you *don't* know or *aren't quite sure* what you want or mean to say.

Discussing your work with your instructor, you should be able to determine rather easily which, if either, of the above two situations you are in. If your instructor doesn't know what you mean at a given moment in your paper and you feel confident that you understand what you are attempting to say, try to explain your ideas to him as clearly and concisely as possible. If you find yourself able to do so relatively easily, then perhaps all you need do is give more examples, change some of your wording, or add clarifying phrases and clauses. During office visits, your instructor ought to be able to help you determine the sorts of changes that you need to make. (It's another matter altogether if your instructor is responsible for having misunderstood a point that you had made in your paper.)

If, on the other hand, you find yourself fumbling for the right words as you attempt to explain to your instructor those ideas that *you* think you have conveyed clearly in your writing but that *he* honestly doesn't understand, you might be discovering that you aren't in control of your ideas as much as you had originally thought. In this case, you'll likely need to do some rethinking and rewriting.

One way to see whether or not you do in fact need to return to the drawing board is to look carefully at your paper's writing *per se*. In particular, take a close look at any "problem" areas to see whether or not a close relationship exists between the troublesome nature of your writing and the obscurity or dubiousness of your ideas. If, for example, your paper contains lots of sentence fragments, unconnected sentences, and vague expressions, its ideas might very well appear fragmented, disjointed, and vague. Rather than wondering how you should "fix" these sorts of problems cosmetically so that your writing looks or sounds "right," you should try to understand how these writing problems manifest troubled thinking and then see how you might revise both your thinking and your writing so that in the end you will have produced a paper whose good, clear prose reflects good, clear ideas. *However, always be prepared to accept the strong possibility that, even under the best of circumstances, at least some of your points in some of your papers will remain unclear to at least some of your intended readers.*

Ultimately, and ideally, all of your reader-based writing tasks should afford you an opportunity to teach as you learn and to learn as you teach. You'll help increase your chances of successfully reaching both of these goals if you allow yourself to learn from the processes of reading and writing about your material, whether you write about matters concerning which you already have some knowledge or about those concerning which you yourself are in the process of learning. And remember: a writer sincerely committed to writing meaningful prose is a writer willing to revise her ideas if, during the processes of reading, writing, and learning, she discovers that personal honesty and integrity compel her to do so.

Seeking Advice During the Writing Process

Perhaps, like some students, you think that you will need to see your writing instructor only if the paper on which you are working receives a "bad" grade. However, you should be aware that you might be unnecessarily risking the outcome of your work if you hold off seeing your writing instructor until she has finished grading your paper; indeed, waiting until then to confer with her is a little like holding off consulting with your accountant until the IRS has finished examining your tax returns. Instead, taking control of and responsibility for your writing, try to meet regularly with your writing instructor so that you can discuss your work with her. Even if you don't always follow your instructor's advice or agree with her views, you'll often find that throughout the writing process she can help you brainstorm and generate ideas, organize these ideas in thematically sound ways, and revise your prose so that it says what you really want it to say. Of course, you yourself must decide what you will finally say in any given paper and how you will say it, but at least you will have had the benefit of receiving, in advance, advice from one of your most important intended readers (if not *the* most important one).

Additionally, if you regularly discuss your writing with your instructor, you will help her become familiar with your writing style, your writing voices, and your manners of interpretation, and thereby increase the chances that she will give you the benefit of the doubt when she has a question about your work. At the very least, you'll increase the chances that she will be able to fill in blanks should they appear in your papers.

Though perhaps you'll also want to obtain advice from, say, dormmates who aren't in your class, friends from high school who are attending other colleges, or family members, keep in mind that these people might not be quite up to speed with the requirements of college academic writing in general and might have little or no understanding of your present writing tasks in particular. College academic writing is a special class of writing, and most or all of your assignments will be class-specific. Since the requirements for class-specific, college-level papers differ in both degree and kind from the requirements of other sorts of writing, you should always exercise due caution whenever you obtain advice about your writing from well-meaning people who nevertheless might be either unfamiliar with or not well informed about the *particular* needs of *your specific* college-level writing tasks.

At various points during the semester, you'll probably seek advice from your classmates. Sometimes you might be asked to do so during activities such as in-class peer group work, and sometimes you might do so simply as a matter of course, since you and they know from the inside what you are all expected to produce in your papers. However, with respect to their assistance, too, you should probably exercise some caution; at the very least, check with your instructor before committing to paper any substantial advice that your classmates offer you. For, as helpful as their ideas might be, most of your classmates will not have nearly the amount of experience with college-level writing that your instructor has. Not infrequently, as many a student has sadly come to discover, some classmates will give each other bad advice despite their good intentions. This problem might not amount to much if you are working within a cooperative learning environ-ment in which you and your classmates help grade each other's work. But if you are working within a traditional classroom setting—even one in which your classmates are your intended audience—chances are that, whether your class-mates judge your work more generously or more harshly than does your instruc-tor, your instructor will have the last "official" word on evaluating your papers.

Some Final Thoughts

There's an old joke that goes something like this: How many psychiatrists does it take to change a light bulb? One, but the light bulb really has to want to be changed. No writing text, no writing instructor, and no writing course can help you become a self-confident writer of meaningful prose if you yourself are unwilling to work hard at becoming such a writer or to make use of those writ-ing talents that you already have. You need to decide whether or not you are will-ing to make this sort of commitment to yourself, for, in the final analysis, you and you alone are ultimately responsible for your writing. *You* control whether or not your papers demonstrate your good-faith endeavors to seek and gain knowledge about the subject matter under consideration. *You* decide whether or not—and, if so, how and to what extent—your writing manifests your sincere good efforts to express your ideas so that your intended readers can understand and perhaps even benefit from them. During office visits and perhaps class discussions, only you can decide whether or not you want to show yourself to be the sort of student who is interested in the processes as well as in the products of learning—that is, the kind of student who wants to grow as a reader, writer, and thinker, and thereby as a human being.

Indeed, serious, meaningful writing involves more than the mere act of one's saying things on paper. One of writing's most powerful attributes is that it has the potential to empower the *writer,* to give her real choices in her ways of thinking and behaving, to help her decide what is and isn't meaningful for *her.* In its most pro-found dimensions, writing constitutes an act in which the writer welds together her freedom to write and her responsibility to make meaningful choices about her life. If you do decide to commit yourself to being and remaining a serious writer, then you will need to devote a fair amount of time and energy to your writing tasks not only because doing so will help you reach your goal, but also—and more impor-tant—because a personal quest of this nature demands nothing less from you.

. . .

As you engage in the work presented in this book's remaining chapters, you will be learning how to think critically, read closely, draft and revise your papers, and so on. For now, in the spirit of thinking about writing, spend some time con-templating what you consider to be the general worth of the material that you've just read and the applicability of this material to your own experiences. Then, try doing the following **featured assignment:**

FEATURED ASSIGNMENT

Part I: Write a brief essay in which you describe both your past experiences with and your present attitude towards writing. Be as explicit as possible. If necessary, quote from or otherwise refer to Anderson's essay (see below).

Part II: Write a brief reflective commentary on what you experienced, thought, and/or felt while doing this assignment.

To help prepare yourself for this writing task, peruse the following piece, entitled "Certain Things Last: A Writer Warms to His Story," written by Sherwood Anderson (1876–1941), a widely-respected American author whom a number of writers and critics consider a writer's writer. As you read this piece, think about those moments when you yourself have had problems coming up with ideas to write about or finding precisely the right phrase to use (at one point, Anderson talks about a woman who "had on a dress of some soft clinging stuff" [paragraph 28]), as well as those times when your writing clicked. And think about those of your successes in writing that derived from or were inspired by otherwise seemingly mundane moments.

After reading Anderson's essay, study the contributing author's response to the featured assignment, but remember that your paper need not resemble his. As an experienced writer tries to do, strive to be true to your *own* writing voices. . . . And welcome to the club.

Certain Things Last: A Writer Warms to His Story

SHERWOOD ANDERSON

Sherwood Anderson (1876–1941) produced much of his finest work after "Winesburg, Ohio," the 1919 cycle of short stories for which he is best known. The following story, probably written in the early 1920's, is an example of a kind of writing that Anderson pioneered, part story, part credo, in which the narrator is and is not Anderson himself. It was found among his papers and appears here in print for the first time, a half-century after his death. [Headnote to the original publication.]

1   For a year now I have been thinking of writing a certain book. "Well, tomorrow I'll get at it," I've been saying to myself. Every night when I get into bed, I think about the book. The people that are to be put between its covers dance before my eyes. I live in the city of Chicago, and at night motor trucks go rumbling along the roadway outside my house. Not so very far away there is an elevated railroad, and after 12 o'clock at night trains pass at pretty long intervals. Before it began I went to sleep during one of the quieter intervals, but now that the idea of writing this book has got into me I lie awake and think.

2   For one thing, it is hard to get the whole idea of the book fixed in the setting of the city I live in now. I wonder if you, who do not try to write books,

perhaps will understand what I mean. Maybe you will, maybe you won't. It is a little hard to explain. You see, it's something like this. You as a reader will, some evening or some afternoon, be reading in my book and then you will grow tired of reading and put it down. You will go out of your house and into the street. The sun is shining and you meet people you know. There are certain facts of your life just the same as of mine. If you are a man, you go from your house to an office and sit at a desk where you pick up a telephone and begin to talk about some matter of business with a client or a customer of your house. If you are an honest housewife, the iceman has come, or there drifts into your mind the thought that yesterday you forgot to remember some detail concerned with running your house. Little outside thoughts come and go in your mind, and it is so with me too. For example, when I have written the above sentence, I wonder why I have written the words "honest housewife." A housewife, I suppose, can be as dishonest as I can. What I am trying to make clear is that, as a writer, I am up against the same things that confront you, as a reader.

3   What I want to do is to express in my book a sense of the strangeness that has gradually, since I was a boy, been creeping more and more into my feeling about everyday life. It would all be very simple if I could write of life in an interior city of China or in an African forest. A man I know has recently told me of another man who, wanting to write a book about Parisian life and having no money to go to Paris to study the life there, went instead to the city of New Orleans. He had heard that many people lived in New Orleans whose ancestors were French. "They will have retained enough of the flavor of Parisian life for me to get the feeling," he said to himself. The man told me that the book turned out to be very successful and that the city of Paris read with delight a translation of his work as a study of French life, and I am only sorry I can't find as simple a way out of my own job.

4   The whole point with me is that my wish to write this book springs from a somewhat different notion. "If I can write everything out plainly, perhaps I will myself understand better what has happened," I say to myself and smile. During these days I spend a good deal of time smiling at nothing. It bothers people. "What are you smiling about now?" they ask, and I am up against as hard a job trying to answer as I am trying to get under way with my book.

5   Sometimes in the morning I sit down at my desk and begin writing, taking as my subject a scene from my own boyhood. Very well, I am coming home from school. The town in which I was born and raised was a dreary, lonely little place in the far western section of the state of Nebraska, and I imagine myself walking along one of its streets. Sitting upon a curbing before a store is a sheepherder who has left his flock many miles away in the foothills at the base of the western mountains and has come into our town, for what purpose he himself does not seem to know. He is a bearded man without a hat and sits with his mouth slightly open, staring up and down the street. There is a half-wild, uncertain look in his eyes, and his eyes have awakened a creepy feeling in me. I hurry away with a kind of dread of some unknown thing eating at my

vital organs. Old men are great talkers. It may be that only kids know the real terror of loneliness.

6   I have tried, you see, to start my book at that particular point in my own life. "If I can catch exactly the feeling of that afternoon of my boyhood, I can give the reader the key to my character," I tell myself.

7   The plan won't work. When I have written 5, 10, 1,500 words, I stop writing and look out my window. A man is driving a team of horses hitched to a wagonload of coal along my street and is swearing at another man who drives a Ford. They have both stopped and are cursing each other. The coal wagon driver's face is black with coal dust, but anger has reddened his cheeks and the red and black have produced a dusky brown like the skin of a Negro.

8   I have got up from my typewriter and walk up and down in my room, smoking cigarettes. My fingers pick up little things on my desk and then put them down.

9   I am nervous like the race horses I used to be with at one period of my boyhood. Before a race and when they had been brought out on the tracks before all the people and before the race started, their legs quivered. Sometimes there was a horse got into such a state that when the race started, he would do nothing. "Look at him. He can't untrack himself," we said.

10   Right now I am in that state about my book. I run to the typewriter, write for a time and then walk nervously about. I smoke a whole package of cigarettes during the morning.

11   And then suddenly I have again torn up all I have written. "It won't do," I have told myself.

12   In this book I am not intending to try to give you the story of my life. "What of life, any man's life?—forked radishes running about, writing declarations of independence, telling themselves little lies, having dreams, getting puffed up now and then with what is called greatness. Life begins, runs its course and ends," a man I once knew told me one evening, and it is true. Even as I write these words, a hearse is going through my street. Two young girls, who are going off with two young men to walk, I suppose, in the fields where the city ends, stop laughing for a moment and look up at the hearse. It will be a moment before they forget the passing hearse and begin laughing again.

13   "A life is like that, it passes like that," I say to myself as I tear up my sheets and begin again walking and smoking the cigarettes.

14   If you think I am sad, having these thoughts about the brevity and insignificance of a life, you are mistaken. In the state I am in, such things do not matter. "Certain things last," I say to myself. "One might make things a little clear. One might even imagine a man, say a Negro, going along a city street and humming a song. It catches the ear of another man, who repeats it on the next day. A thin strand of song, like a tiny stream far up in some hill, begins to flow down into the wide plains. It waters the fields. It freshens the air above a hot stuffy city."

15   Now I have got myself worked up into a state. I am always doing that these days. I write again, and again tear up my words.

16   I go out of my room and walk about.

. . .

17   I have been with a woman I have found and who loves me. It has happened that I am a man who has not been loved by women and have all my life been awkward and a little mixed up when in their presence. Perhaps I have had too much respect for them, have wanted them too much. That may be. Anyway, I am not so rattled in her presence.

18   She, I think, has a certain control over herself, and that is helpful to me. When I am with her I keep smiling to myself and thinking, "It would be rather a joke all around if she found me out."

19   When she is looking in another direction, I study her a little. That she should seem to like me so much surprises me, and I am sore at my own surprise. I grow humble and do not like my humbleness either. "What is she up to? She is very lovely. Why is she wasting her time with me?"

20   I shall remember always certain hours when I have been with her. Late on a certain Sunday afternoon, I remember, I sat in a chair in a room in her apartment. I sat with my hand against my cheek, leaning a little forward. I had dressed myself carefully because I was going to see her, had put on my best suit of clothes. My hair was carefully combed and my glasses carefully balanced on my rather large nose.

21   And there I was, in her apartment in a certain city, in a chair in a rather dark corner, with my hand against my cheek, looking as solemn as an old owl. We had been walking about and had come into the house and she had gone away, leaving me sitting there, as I have said. The apartment was in a part of the city where many foreign people live, and from my chair I could, by turning my head a little, look down into a street filled with Italians.

22   It was growing dark outside, and I could just see the people in the street. If I cannot remember facts about my own and other people's lives, I can always remember every feeling that has gone through me, or that I have thought went through anyone about me.

23   The men going along the street below the window all had dark, swarthy faces and nearly all of them wore, somewhere about them, a spot of color. The younger men, who walked with a certain swagger, all had on flaming red ties. The street was dark, but far down the street there was a spot where a streak of sunlight still managed to find its way in between two tall buildings and fell sharp against the face of a smaller red-brick building. It pleased my fancy to imagine the street had also put on a red necktie, perhaps because there would be lovemaking along the street before Monday morning.

24   Anyway, I sat there looking and thinking such thoughts as came to me. The women who went along the street nearly all had dark-colored shawls drawn

up about their faces. The roadway was filled with children whose voices made a sharp tinkling sound.

25   My fancy went out of my body in a way of speaking, I suppose, and I began thinking of myself as being at that moment in a city in Italy. Americans like myself who have not traveled are always doing that. I suppose the people of another nation would not understand how doing it is almost a necessity in our lives, but any American will understand. The American, particularly a Middle American, sits as I was doing at that moment, dreaming, you understand, and suddenly he is in Italy or in a Spanish town where a dark-looking man is riding a bony horse along a street, or he is being driven over the Russian steppes in a sled by a man whose face is all covered with whiskers. It is an idea of the Russians got from looking at cartoons in newspapers, but it answers the purpose. In the distance a pack of wolves are following the sled. A fellow I once knew told me that Americans are always up to such tricks because all of our old stories and dreams have come to us from over the sea and because we have no old stories and dreams of our own.

26   Of that I can't say. I am not putting myself forward as a thinker on the subject of the causes of the characteristics of the American people or any other monstrous or important matter of that kind.

27   But anyway, there I was, sitting, as I have told you, in the Italian section of an American city and dreaming of myself being in Italy.

28   To be sure, I wasn't alone. Such a fellow as myself never is alone in his dreams. And as I sat having my dream, the woman with whom I had been spending the afternoon, and with whom I am no doubt what is called "in love," passed between me and the window through which I had been looking. She had on a dress of some soft clinging stuff, and her slender figure made a very lovely line across the light. Well, she was like a young tree you might see on a hill, in a windstorm perhaps.

29   What I did, as you may have supposed, was to take her with me into Italy.

30   The woman became at once, and in my dream, a very beautiful princess in a strange land I have never visited. It may be that when I was a boy in my Western town some traveler came there to lecture on life in Italian cities before a club that met at the Presbyterian church and to which my mother belonged, or perhaps later I read some novel the name of which I can't remember.

31   And so my princess had come down to me along a path out of a green wooded hill where her castle was located. She had walked under blossoming trees in the uncertain evening light, and some blossoms had fallen on her black hair. The perfume of Italian nights was in her hair. That notion came into my head. That's what I mean.

32   What really happened was that she saw me sitting there lost in my dream and, coming to me, rumpled my hair and upset the glasses perched on my big nose and, having done that, went laughing out of the room.

33   I speak of all this because later, on that same evening, I lost all notion of the book I am now writing and sat until 3 in the morning, writing on another

book, making the woman the central figure. "It will be a story of old times, filled with moons and stars and the fragrance of half-decayed trees in an old land," I told myself, but when I had written many pages, I tore them up too.

34 "Something has happened to me or I should not be filled with the idea of writing this book at all," I told myself, going to my window to look out at the night. "At a certain hour of a certain day and in a certain place, something happened that has changed the whole current of my life.

35 "The thing to be done," I then told myself, "is to begin writing my book by telling as clearly as I can the adventures of that certain moment."

Excerpted from *Certain Things Last: The Selected Short Stories of Sherwood Anderson*, edited by Charles L. Modlin and published by Four Walls Eight Windows.

Writing: A Leap of Faith

KEVIN MULLEN

[Editor's note: Asked to submit a brief autobiographical statement from which I would glean material for an introduction to his work, Kevin Mullen sent me a creative, thought-provoking paragraph whose language and content, in my view, will help the reader better understand the person behind the following model essay than would any revised statement that I might devise. Thus, I offer Kevin's autobiographical statement to you, the reader, in its original, unedited form.]

"I was born in the ethnic crucible of Brooklyn, New York, in 1959. Shortly thereafter my family moved to Staten Island, a convenient labor storehouse cast between Manhattan's monolithic skyscrapers and New Jersey's grinding factories. As a young witness to overt racism, an unpopular war, counterculture movements, government intrigue, a failing economy, and "Dirty Harry" role models, I unknowingly developed a *don't trust anyone over thirty* attitude. Today, in my thirties, I am a junior student of philosophy and classics at the University of California, Irvine. My youthful skepticism has been slightly modified by my studies in the humanities, finding expression in the maxim *Question authority!* My short-term goal is to expose the diffuse yet deadly authority of popular opinion and common practice to the light of critical thinking. My long-term goal is to help construct the kind of world that John Lennon once asked us to *Imagine*."

RESPONSE

PART I   Essay

The night struggles to maintain its serenity as the steam
rolls off my coffee. In the other room my wife is going
through her pre-dawn ritual, lying in bed, anticipating the

alarm clock, and wishing that her life were different, very different. Eighteen demeaning years of secretarial subordination has taken its toll. She dies a little every day, and I watch. Her silent struggle echoes, the night slips away, and I am left with only rage. A last sip of coffee and I brace myself for battle. It is time to hurl words, time to fire sentences, time to explode paragraphs. It is time to change the world.

I began college in 1988 not with fiery notions of changing the world, but with hazy notions of obtaining a diploma. The writing requirement, I soon discovered, hovered over me like a dark and threatening cloud. A typical short paper shackled me to the computer for fifty hours a week. I buried myself in writing texts, learned the mechanics, but still struggled desperately with my papers. Writing would get easier with time, I had thought, but it didn't. Within a year I had considered changing my major to mathematics, and I almost dropped out of school. The diploma was not worth the effort.

Despite my difficulties, and my desire to run, something had taken firm hold of me. There was more to writing than just writing: there was content. I was writing about poetry, racism, history, religion, logic, sexism, art, politics, love, economics, hate, culture, life, and death. To write about these things I needed to read about them and to think critically about them. Somewhere between Pico's Oration and Hitler's SS I had become emotionally involved. Writing, once a dark and narrow corridor leading to a diploma, became a bright and open frontier expanding to the unknown. Like a hungry explorer I journeyed deeper and deeper into a vast new world. I didn't know what to expect, but there was no turning back.

Now, after five years of exploration, I often wish that I had turned back. The content of my writing had originally given me wings, but that same content has now sent me crashing to the ground. After five years of reading, writing, and thinking about western culture, I have learned that the bloodshed far outweighs the beauty. Socrates asked for truth nearly twenty-five centuries ago and he received hemlock; Martin Luther King asked for love nearly twenty-five years ago and he received a bullet. These tragic heros mark western civilization's bloody trajectory, one which has moved from the slow production of swords to the mass production of nuclear bombs.

All along I have been writing about my own audience. I have been writing mostly about conquest, slavery, cunning, sacrifice, persecution, intrigue, torture, deceit, murder, fraud, and malice of every kind. For every one Gandhi I find one thousand Stalins. Indeed, I have written, I have learned, and I have lost faith in my audience: humanity.

So here I sit, a writer without an audience. For whom now should I fabricate a psychologically-satisfying conclusion (in a world so psychologically dissatisfying)? Shall I find faith in denial? Shall I applaud Athenian democracy and overlook Athenian slavery? Shall I marvel at the Roman aqueducts and ignore the Coliseum? Shall I bathe in Dante's Paradisio and extinguish his Inferno? Shall I laugh with Chaucer and banish Machiavelli? Shall I soar with Michelangelo and escape the Inquisition? Shall I pretend that Beethoven compensates for Hiroshima? For whom should I feign sanity in a world gone mad?

Once again the night struggles to maintain its serenity, the steam rolls off my coffee, and my wife goes through her pre-dawn ritual. Once again I find myself here, before my computer, a writer without an audience. I sulk, I brood, and I nearly turn off the computer. But a voice calls to me, perhaps Homer's voice ringing through the millennia. It implores me to find faith, to find strength, and to get back into the battle and write. Outside the moon hangs low on the horizon, the same moon that had aided the first farmers, puzzled the ancient philosophers, inspired the romantic poets, and ignored the victims of Auschwitz. Down the hallway I hear my wife's footsteps. Somehow she has found the strength to face another day. I gaze into the moon, I gaze into myself, and somehow I find the strength, somehow I find the words: Yes, today I will change the world.

PART II   Commentary

This paper was without doubt one of the most difficult that I have ever written. An example reveals why it was so difficult. I once wrote a paper about a survivor of the Nazi's Sobibor death camp. The survivor recalled how he regularly witnessed guards killing infants: tearing them apart at the legs, tossing them alive into burning pits, and using them for target practice. At the time I had recounted these events in my paper. During revision, however, I found myself correcting spelling and punctuation, choosing appropriate verbs, and eliminating unnecessary prepositional phrases so as to describe these unspeakable events in just the "right way."

Now what was I supposed to do with this past experience in relation to the current assignment? Should I have swept it under the rug, pretending that I had never had it (so as to expedite the paper)? To write about my experiences with writing, therefore, I needed (once again) to think about infants being torn apart, burned alive, and shot to pieces, and what it had been like when I had squeezed such images into the rhyme and reason of literary convention (for a letter grade). How should I have described that experience in the current assignment? My point, here, is not to answer that question, but to flush out the difficulties that were involved in writing about my experiences with writing.

Moreover, writing about my attitude toward writing was equally difficult. Why? In responding to the first part of the assignment, I was forcefully reminded that my experiences with writing have nearly destroyed my faith in humanity. So why should I communicate with humanity? Why should I write to humanity? It's a waste of time. That is my attitude toward writing, and the nature of this assignment constantly reminded me of that attitude. Accordingly, I constantly wanted to shut off the computer. To hell with humanity, and to hell with this paper, is what I kept thinking.

And what have I learned from this assignment? I have learned everything that my paper suggests. I have learned that something keeps me going despite my dismal view of our species. I have learned that I cannot walk away from writing. I have learned that I cannot walk away from humanity.

"*As* the years went by, little Wahss grew wise in all the secrets of the forest. She learned the good of every plant. She learned that goodness lies sometimes in the leaves, sometimes in the seeds, sometimes in the roots. She learned that some medicines are cooked and that some are not. She learned that there was much more to learn. That meant that she was really learning. When one thinks there is no more to learn, he knows next to nothing."

MELICENT LEE
Indians of the Oaks

"'What good fortune for those in power that people do not think.'"

ADOLF HITLER
quoted in Alice Miller's
For Your Own Good

Critical Thinking: An Introduction

A S INTIMATED IN the previous chapter, the process of writing is intimately tied to the process of thinking. That is, in the process of writing and rewriting a paper, you'll likely find yourself thinking and rethinking your ideas; in turn, as you rethink your ideas, you might want to revise your writing so that it reflects your new thoughts. Like writing, thinking is a process-oriented activity; and like good writing, good thinking requires you to work patiently and diligently with your material.

The sort of thinking referred to above, a kind of active, process-oriented thinking, has come to be known as "critical thinking." If you conscientiously practice your critical thinking skills, you should help yourself arrive at good views concerning the issues which you will be studying and on which you will be writing. But keep in mind that, as suggested above, critical thinking, like writing, involves *both* an end product *and* a process that leads to that product. In other words, critical thinking involves not only *what* you think, but also your attempts to *think about thinking*. In the final analysis, your opinions—on matters such as abortion or gun control, for example—will only be as good as will be the thinking that leads you to form these opinions.

Critical Thinking Defined

Broadly defined, critical thinking involves people's engaging in the free exchange of ideas with the intent to establish the best possible positions on given issues or to arrive at the best solutions to the problems under investigation. To these ends, critical thinking will entail your careful evaluation of data (evidence) in the service of your finding the "truth" about or, failing that, the best possible explanation of these data. Critical thinking might best be understood, then, as a process, methodology, or mechanism of thinking, by means of which you will try to form opinions that are *reasonable* and that *follow from evidence*.

Here are some examples of critical thinkers at work: An analytic philosopher applies the rigorous principles of logic to the construction and evaluation of arguments. A literary critic applies an understanding of the relationship between metaphor and meaning to analyze a poem or short story. A police detective working in the homicide division evaluates the facts in a murder case in order to determine first whether or not the case does indeed involve murder, and then, if she finds that it does, who committed the murder, how it was committed, and so on. A geologist analyzes rock strata to determine the geological age of a given land mass. A physician evaluates a patient's signs and symptoms in order to determine both the latter's ailment and the best course of treatment for him. A student writes a personal narrative in which she explains why she never enjoyed writing until she took a freshman composition class. Though all of these people know that chance sometimes plays a role in their decision-making processes and thus helps determine the outcomes of their efforts, in their critical thinking endeavors they usually try not to leave too many matters to chance.

Sometimes, critical thinking involves a questioning of standard or accepted methods and practices rather than an application of them. Many composition theorists and instructors, for example, continually revaluate methods of writing instruction to see if these methods really do help students become better, more self-confident writers. Musicians and artists routinely question standard musical and artistic practices, experimenting with new ways to achieve desired effects in their own work. Whether they are using or questioning a particular methodological approach, people engaged in careful critical thinking are practicing active, analytical thinking in their pursuit of knowledge.

Three Common Misconceptions About Critical Thinking

1. Viewpoints and opinions are personal possessions. In our everyday speech, we often talk about someone's "having" an opinion or a point of view; we might say, for example, that Fred "has" a legitimate opinion, or that Ethel's point of view is strong. Though such talk provides us with a convenient way to communicate with one another, it also lends subtle support to the quite erroneous proposition that a person can *own* a point of view. Not uncommonly, people who see their viewpoints as personal possessions seem to feel that they need to guard their ideas at all costs.

Generally, when you are dealing with a problematic viewpoint in which you have little or no personal investment, you might not have much trouble accepting the idea that no one, including you, owns a point of view, and that you yourself should abandon a troublesome opinion. When the stakes are high for you personally, though, you might have difficulty evaluating your and others' views honestly and fully, and you might find it hard to sever your ties to "your" views. But even if you feel comforted by your opinions, you ought to be ready to give up comfort in return for analytical soundness if in the face of solid, well-founded criticism of your views, you need to alter or even discard them. Indeed, even if your beliefs are entirely sincere, you will serve your thinking well if you keep in mind that, in terms of proving or supporting a point of view, sincere but troublesome beliefs are simply no match for views derived from sound thinking. From the standpoint of critical thinking, keeping a flawed but comfortable perspective at the expense of a sound but uncomfortable one is a poor bargain.

2. Different points of view about an issue represent nothing more than mere differences of opinion. This common misconception seems to derive, at least in part, from *another* common misconception: to wit, that everyone's right to hold an opinion on a given issue implies that all opinions on that issue should be accorded equal weight.[1] True, some differing or opposing views *are* weighty enough to be considered of relatively equal worth. But some views are verifiably stronger than others, even though the latter might still hold some promise. And after having been carefully evaluated, other views are of such little value (or are of no value at all) that

---

[1]And *this* misconception seems to derive, in part, from the erroneous view that personal opinions are on the order of personal tastes. However, although both opinions and tastes can be either informed or uninformed, opinions, unlike tastes, can also be demonstrably right or wrong.

they prove to be not worth having and thus can be dismissed without further consideration.

For the sake of convenience, we might use the phrase "the democratization of ideas **fallacy**" to refer to the troublesome proposition that, "since everyone has a right to have an opinion concerning whatever issue or topic is under discussion, all points of view concerning this issue or topic are necessarily to be accorded equal weight" (a fallacy is simply an error in thinking). The person who commits this fallacy "democratizes" all ideas about a specific issue or topic, seeing them as partaking in a kind of "one view, one vote" system of analysis. In a democracy, everyone's vote is equal to everyone else's vote; analogously (though problematically), in a world in which the "democratization of ideas fallacy" holds sway, everyone's view about a given issue or topic is considered to be of equal worth to everyone else's view concerning that issue or topic.

To see the dangers inherent in the democratizing of ideas, imagine that a friend of yours, watching you read this book, ardently tries to convince you that the tail of a giant, pink gopher is resting on your book, keeping it from flying off into outer space. Not wanting merely to dismiss his view, you ask him to explain his reasons for having his opinion. He tells you that he believes that the gopher likes to help people, that it has a particular affinity for helping students, that it told your friend to watch today for a signal of its beneficence, and so on. After evaluating his argument, you reject his view, offering in its stead a view suggesting that, among other things, the force of gravity keeps this book from flying off into outer space. Now, are we *really* talking about nothing more than a difference of opinion here? Should your view and your friend's view really be accorded equal weight? Does his right to hold a given point of view—including an absurd one—necessarily guarantee that his view ought to be taken seriously?

3. All issues, topics, and points of view are open to debate. Perhaps because they want to be fair and open-minded—an admirable goal, to be sure—many people who harbor the common misconception that all issues, topics, and points of view are open to debate find it almost offensive for anyone to think otherwise. And yet, the problematic proposition that all issues, topics, or points of view are debatable sometimes leads to anything but fairness and open-mindedness. Would someone *really* be acting fairly and open-mindedly were he to insist that the Holocaust, the enslavement of African Americans, the nonflatness of the earth, or his own "coming into being" by means of natural or artificial conception are topics open to debate? If in fact we are obligated to debate absolutely everything, including indisputable facts, then we might legitimately wonder why we should bother trying to think carefully at all. Of what value is careful thinking if it is reduced to such absurdity?

Holding the position that not every issue is open to debate represents a profound respect for fairness and a deep commitment to the free exchange of ideas. It is important to remember that freedom is not the same as license. Freedom entails limits and restrictions. An American cannot simply say whatever she wants, for example, even though in the United States we recognize one's freedom of speech; there is such a thing, after all, as libel. License, on the other hand, denotes a kind of freedom without restriction; a licentious person, for instance, is one who is morally or sexually unrestrained. The free exchange of ideas, then, does not denote a sort of opinion appreciation exercise, in which people can get away with saying anything at all about the issue under discussion, nor does it imply that people freely exchanging ideas with one another are obligated to accept and value whatever anyone says about this issue.

Advising that you not debate verifiably indisputable facts which are obviously not open to debate, I am not thereby suggesting that you avoid trying to find out whether or not something is a fact if you need to do so. For example, if you don't know that the Nazis and their collaborators systematically murdered millions of Jews, or that racism and sexism continue to be major problems in the United States, or that Columbus grossly mistreated Native Americans, you wouldn't simply want to *assume* that the reality of these phenomena is open to debate. Instead, being intellectually honest and in good faith, you first would want to do some relevant research, after which you would want to pose relevant, meaningful questions that might lead you to make inferences about the obvious facts that (one hopes) you will have discovered. By their very nature, inferences are always open to legitimate, good-faith debate. On the other hand, verifiably indisputable facts are not.

Critical Thinking and Careful Writing

Critical thinking is meant to be used, and not just studied; its purpose is ultimately practical, not theoretical. Thus, it will only be as valuable as will be your use of it. People familiar with the principles and practices of good critical thinking know (or should know) that no methodological approach to analysis can match well-executed critical thinking in rigor, fairness, and interpretive precision. Indeed, people engaged in serious thinking are doing far more than memorizing and regurgitating facts, participating in contests of rhetorical or semantic wit, or playing silly games of trivial intellectual pursuit.

Similarly, writers using good thinking in their papers are doing far more than attempting to achieve grammatical correctness and stylistic elegance. Using her critical thinking skills, the careful writer documents her evaluation of pertinent evidence in order to show her reader that a given point of view follows from a careful analysis of this evidence and stands to reason. To be sure, she might help her case by couching her ideas in clear prose. But just as a well-argued case expressed in unclear prose might be little more than a well-argued case waiting to be discovered, so a badly argued case expressed in clear prose might not be much more than a case that one can clearly see is bad.[2]

---

[2]For detailed discussions of the nature and function of arguments, take a look at one or more of the following three texts: Irving M. Copi's *Introduction to Logic,* his *Informal Fallacies,* and Alex C. Michalos' *Improving Your Reasoning.*

Ten Tips and Guidelines Concerning Critical Thinking

You can employ good critical thinking skills to help you write all of your papers, whether or not those papers are argumentative in the strictest sense of that term. For example, you might use critical thinking to help you understand and write about the meaning of a recurring dream—yours or someone else's—or the significance of your feelings concerning a poem that you read for a class, or your reasons for wanting to write or avoid writing a particular paper for your composition or biology class. Whatever your writing tasks, the following ten tips and guidelines should help you see how you might use critical thinking to your best advantage.

1. Read texts closely. Throughout this book, you'll notice that much attention is given to the notion of "close" (or careful) reading. That is because, whether you are directly or indirectly using material from a text in your papers or are simply trying to come to terms with the textual material that you are studying, you need to know what a text actually says and what it implies before you can draw any reasonable conclusions about it or engage in worthwhile interpretations of it. (See Chapter Three for a fuller discussion of close reading.)

2. Take serious issues seriously, approaching discussions of them humbly and carefully. Be honest about what you know and what you don't know. Recognize that we all have limits to our knowledge. And keep in mind that, when we are dealing with complicated issues, complexity and messiness are often the order of the day. If you can find no other reason to write a given paper, use the assignment to discover the limits of what you know, of what you want to and can learn about yourself and others, and, perhaps, of what you are unwilling to know.

3. Remain in good faith. There's nothing wrong with your having to admit that, like everyone else on the planet, you, too, have intellectual stumbling blocks. Problems will occur, though, if you pretend to be open-minded when you are not. Even if you generally value ideas and the search for truth—whether that truth is universal or personal—if while working on a particular writing assignment you think and write in bad faith, you'll not likely gain much (if any) self-enlightenment, nor will many (if any) of your serious, intended readers likely be receptive to your work. If you maintain that you are interested in discovering the "truth" but end up calling out your ideas from behind a shield, then in effect you are telling your readers that you are on guard—and that they shouldn't approach!

4. Keep your goal(s) in mind. Why are you writing your paper? Are you interested in teaching the reader anything? Are you interested in teaching *yourself* anything? Are you trying to protect your views, or are you willing to modify or give up some of your beliefs if the need arises? Will you be upset with a reader who disagrees with or doesn't understand you? Will you assume that someone who disagrees with you either is close-minded or represents your enemy? Reread tip #2.

5. Know your audience. Always try to determine how much information you need to explain to your readers so that they will understand your points. And ask yourself if the readers for whom you are writing will likely agree with or question your assumptions. But be careful here. A reader's acceptance or rejection of your views and assumptions indicates neither their obvious acceptability nor their clear unacceptability. In trying to size up your audience's thinking, you are merely trying to discover points of departure for the discussion and to see which of your ideas you need to explain and which you can take for granted while writing for *this* audience. (Subsequent chapters contain more information on the topic of writing for a particular audience.)

6. *Keep in mind that conclusions ought to derive from reasons and square with pertinent evidence.* Whether you are writing personal narratives or impersonal analytic essays, always be sure to let evidence and reasoning guide you to your conclusions.[3] The philosopher Friedrich Nietzsche disparagingly but accurately characterizes the opposite approach to sound analytical thinking: "When someone hides something behind a bush and looks for it again in the same place and finds it there as well," Nietzsche writes, "there is not much to praise in such seeking and finding" (85).

7. *Always try to ask good questions.* One mark of a good, careful thinker is that she knows how to ask good questions, or at least that she tries to ask such questions. Good questions, like good statements, tend to open rather than close discussions and investigations. Not uncommonly, they help lead both the writer and the reader to new insights. If, for example, you read a short story and find yourself troubled by the narrator's troubles, don't just end the matter there. Instead, ask, "Why does the narrator seem so bothered, and why am I bothered by her anxiety?" If you remain in good faith in your efforts to understand what is going on in the story and in your own mind, who knows to what depths of insight these deceptively simple inquiries might lead both you and, through your writing, *your* readers?

As you engage in more and more serious critical thinking endeavors, don't be surprised if you discover that you end up with more questions than answers. Though in your papers you'll often need to solve problems or provide answers to questions, you sometimes might find that your writing will be best served if you raise questions, explain their significance, offer a few possible answers, and then let the questions remain as questions. Those of your readers who approach their work as seriously as you do should understand that some questions must be asked but cannot be fully answered. "Why do so many men hate women?" "How can we explain the fact that so many supposedly God-fearing U.S. soldiers slaughtered so many Native Americans?" "Why do I feel the need to write about such-and-such an event from my childhood?" These are excellent questions. And though your attempts to answer them might yield you and your readers excellent insights, these kinds of questions have no definite, final answers. Should you try

---

[3]Similarly, when you are evaluating someone else's point of view, concentrate on analyzing the reason or reasons that (supposedly) lead(s) to her or his conclusion rather than focusing on the acceptability or unacceptability of the conclusion itself.

offering such answers to them anyway, you might very well end up writing papers whose ideas seem rushed, forced, or reductive—not at all the kinds of ideas that match the integrity and maturity of your inquiries.

8. *Maintain a self-critical position with respect to your ideas.* Assess and reassess your general understanding of whatever issue you are studying, and be willing to be wrong. If you write only in order to justify your current ways of thinking, you might find yourself writing in bad faith. At the very least, you'll not likely advance the cause of your own intellectual growth, nor will you probably do much to help your readers learn much from you. Testing your views, you might discover some meaningful insights that you might not have come upon otherwise. If nothing else, you ought to find that, by remaining in good faith in your critical thinking endeavors, and by using good critical thinking in order to take some intellectual risks and to expand the boundaries of your knowledge, you'll be in the company of other serious thinkers who are as committed as you are to an honest—even if sometimes painful—pursuit of truth and understanding.

9. *Keep in mind that it will be perfectly normal, and perhaps even reasonable, for you to become defensive, frustrated, or upset when your views are challenged.* You should not ignore such feelings, since doing so could keep you from understanding why you are having trouble dealing with the issue(s) under discussion. However, do remember that, in order for you to be intellectually honest and humble—requisite conditions for you to be able to learn and (intellectually) grow as much as possible—you probably will have to move beyond these kinds of feelings. If you find yourself unable to move beyond them, you might have to pull back and do some (re)thinking. Hopefully, you'll discover that writing has the potential to help you see either how to make such a move or why, perhaps, you ought not to continue evaluating those of your views that are under consideration.

10. *Determine the boundaries and test the limits of your own intellectual integrity.* As intimated earlier, the litmus test of your commitment to critical thinking probably won't be your investigating an issue, concern, or idea about which you have moderate, little, or no personal investment, but rather your investigating an issue, concern, or idea about which the personal stakes for you are quite high. But remember that critical thinking is not a game in which you will either win, lose, or draw; it is a methodological process by means of which you can carefully evaluate and arrive at points of view. Valuing both truth and its pursuit, as well as intellectual honesty and integrity, more often than not, with enough practice, you should be able to avoid the pitfalls of bad thinking and to enjoy the fruits of good thinking.

Whatever else you do to keep tabs on your thinking, always try to determine the limits of your willingness to test your ideas. When you are engaged in a critical thinking task, ask yourself how much you really *are* willing to find out about your thinking. Do you want to know how well or fully your assumptions, conclusions, and other ideas explain the evidence pertinent to your investigation? Are you willing to be patient with the evidence that you are interpreting so that you can discover where it leads you, that is, so that you can determine what conclusion, if any, to draw from a careful examination of the evidence—whether or not you feel comforted by the conclusion that you are led to draw? If necessary, are you willing to concede that you don't know enough about a particular matter under investigation to formulate an informed opinion about this matter? Put differently: Are you willing to have no view at all rather than having an uninformed or a misinformed view? Are you willing, able, and ready to live with more questions than answers and, at times, more paradoxes than resolutions? Are you willing to learn and grow? And, perhaps most important, are you *really* willing to be wrong?

Some Possible Risks and Some Personal Goals and Rewards of Careful Critical Thinking

From time to time, you might find it helpful to remind yourself that many racists and sexists (for example) don't simply say and do bad things; rather, they often ground their actions in ideas and arguments about race and gender—*misguided* ideas and *bad* arguments, to be sure, but ideas and arguments nonetheless. As you pursue your critical thinking tasks, you might occasionally confront such people. Acting in bad faith, these kinds of people often disregard or deny good evidence that undermines what they want to believe, maintain a position of committed unfamiliarity with or hostility to careful thinking, or, even worse, are seriously committed to intellectual fraud. Save yourself some grief by not engaging in critical thinking tasks with such people, for you will not likely convince them easily (if you can convince them at all) that their thinking or behavior is problematic and that they would be intellectually and perhaps morally better off were they to use good critical thinking skills in order to evaluate, discriminate between or among, and arrive at points of view. People can only *meaningfully* arrive at and believe in this approach to thinking on their own, when they themselves are ready to do so.

Instead of being intellectually codependent by trying to catch others in, and feeling at least partly responsible for, their bad thinking endeavors, act in the spirit of attaining self-realizations by setting as your primary goal the strengthening of your *own* thinking abilities. Indeed, some of the greatest benefits of critical thinking are not public, at least not immediately so. This is not to say that decisions derived from good critical thinking haven't directly and immediately affected the public: for example, in 1954, the United States Supreme Court Justices relied upon sound principles of critical thinking when they voted unanimously to desegregate public schools in this country. Nevertheless, the serious critical thinker knows that the most immediate benefits of his engaging in critical thinking tasks are personal. Thus, he knows that his first task is not to get everyone else's critical thinking house in order, but, instead, to get his own in order. And once he is engaged in *this* pursuit, he will be on his way to attaining what the great ancient Greek philosopher Socrates has taught us is the most important, most fundamental knowledge of all: *self-knowledge*.

Self-knowledge is not the same as self-indulgence or self-aggrandizement. In fact, a serious quest for self-knowledge undertaken along the route of careful critical thinking should ultimately lead you to *humility*, if not also to inner peace (which, of course, you might also achieve outside of the realm of critical thinking). As it turns out, humility also represents an intellectually important starting point for any serious critical thinking endeavor. As paradoxical as this idea might seem right now, don't be surprised if you discover that the more you learn about a particular matter which you are studying, the less you understand it. Driven perhaps to learn even *more* about your subject matter, you should gain greater knowledge about and insight into the material than you had gained previously; but, if all goes *well*, this increase in knowledge will only reconfirm for you your previous insight that, in the grand scheme of things, you know very little. In turn, this reconfirmation should keep you engaged in the cycle of what we might call "humble learning."

At some point in their lives, many great thinkers come to a similar realization about the state of their own knowledge. Perhaps no one expressed more profoundly and memorably the nature of this self-revelation than did Socrates, when he explained what he had discovered in his attempts to understand why he was considered the wisest man in the world. Puzzled by what he took to be this rather strange rumor about him, Socrates conversed with many people who he thought might help him understand the nature and the cause of this dubious accolade. After analyzing these conversations, he finally concluded that, in fact, he *was* the wisest man in the world. However, far from intending this conclusion to reflect a self-adulatory position, Socrates meant for it to reflect a profound criticism of both himself and others. What he says in comparing himself to another person also thought to be quite wise bespeaks his general view on this entire matter: "It is only too likely that neither of us has any knowledge to boast of, but he thinks that he knows something which he does not know, whereas I am quite conscious of my ignorance. At any rate[,]" Socrates continues, "it seems that I am wiser than he is to this small extent, that I do not think that I know what I do not know" (*Socrates' Defense [Apology]* 7–8).

For you, then, a serious, good-faith thinker, critical thinking is not an *option*, but an *expectation*, a *requirement*, at least when you are investigating issues or attempting to solve problems. And though you probably will notice the payoffs sooner than you might think, from time to time you might find yourself quite personally challenged in your critical thinking tasks. But if you remain in good faith in your intellectual endeavors, take full advantage of the opportunities afforded you by your classes and your written assignments to expand the boundaries of your knowledge, and commit yourself to taking some intellectual risks, you will have joined a relatively small but highly respectable community of serious, committed thinkers who, like you, understand why a person who values thinking and right moral conduct tries to seek truths in a world so hostile to their discovery. Use your critical thinking skills to your best intellectual advantage, and reap the rewards of your thinking and writing tasks well done.

. . .

Like most of the critical thinking tasks that you will undertake in your college courses, the critical thinking tasks that you will engage in as you work with the readings and assignments in this book will be rather serious. Sometimes, though, the best way for someone to see whether or not she understands a body of concepts is to apply her understanding of them to non-serious or less than serious matters (even if these matters have a serious underpinning). In the spirit of this way of thinking, try your hand (or, rather, your mind) at critical thinking by having some fun interpreting the following two reading selections.

The first selection is that famous fable concerning the boy who cried wolf. Written in the sixth century B.C.E. by Aesop, a slave in ancient Greece, "The Shepherd Boy and the Wolf" describes what happens when a shepherd who had signaled a number of false alarms eventually signals a real need for help. From the villagers' decisions to the moral of the story, Aesop presents a nice testing ground on which readers can practice and sharpen their critical thinking skills. As you read this piece, see what you make of the characters' and narrator's reasoning, and then think about how you might have reasoned and what you might have done (and why) had you been in any of their places.

The second selection, "Who Stole the Tarts?" is an excerpt from Lewis Carroll's *Alice's Adventures in Wonderland*. ("Lewis Carroll" was actually the pen name of Charles Lutwidge Dodgson [1832–1898], an English clergyman, mathematician, author, and teacher.) In this excerpt, the King and Queen of Hearts are holding trial to determine who stole the tarts. As you read through this material, evaluate the thinking that the different characters use. How do their arguments strike you? How do the characters deal with evidence? If you were on trial, would you want any of them representing you, serving on the jury, acting as judge? There's much to observe here, even though you're not yet looking into—or is that through?—the looking glass. . . . Or are you?

The Shepherd Boy and the Wolf

AESOP

1   Every day the shepherd boy was sent with his father's sheep into the mountain pasture to guard the flock. It was, indeed, a lonely spot at the edge of a dark forest, and there were no companions with whom he could pass the long, weary hours of the day.

2   One day, just to stir up some excitement, he rushed down from the pasture, crying "Wolf! Wolf!" The villagers heard the alarm and came running with

clubs and guns to help chase the marauder away, only to find the sheep grazing peacefully and no wolf in sight.

3   So well had the trick worked that the foolish boy tried it again and again, and each time the villagers came running, only to be laughed at for their pains.

4   But there came a day when a wolf really came. The boy screamed and called for help. But all in vain! The neighbors, supposing him to be up to his old tricks, paid no heed to his cries, and the wolf devoured the sheep.

. . .

Moral: Liars are not believed even when they tell the truth.

Who Stole the Tarts?

LEWIS CARROLL

1 ... The King and Queen of Hearts were seated on their throne when they arrived, with a great crowd assembled about them—all sorts of little birds and beasts, as well as the whole pack of cards: the Knave was standing before them, in chains, with a soldier on each side to guard him; and near the King was the White Rabbit, with a trumpet in one hand, and a scroll of parchment in the other. In the very middle of the court was a table, with a large dish of tarts upon it: they looked so good, that it made Alice quite hungry to look at them—"I wish they'd get the trial done," she thought, "and hand round the refreshments!" But there seemed to be no chance of this; so she began looking at everything about her to pass away the time.

2   Alice had never been in a court of justice before, but she had read about them in books, and she was quite pleased to find that she knew the name of nearly everything there. "That's the judge," she said to herself, "because of his great wig."

3   The judge, by the way, was the King; and, as he wore his crown over the wig (look at the frontispiece if you want to see how he did it), he did not look at all comfortable, and it was certainly not becoming.

4   "And that's the jury-box," thought Alice; "and those twelve creatures," (she was obliged to say "creatures," you see, because some of them were animals, and some were birds,) "I suppose they are the jurors." She said this last word two or three times over to herself, being rather proud of it: for she thought, and rightly too, that very few little girls of her age knew the meaning of it at all. However, "jurymen" would have done just as well.

5   The twelve jurors were all writing very busily on slates. "What are they doing?" Alice whispered to the Gryphon. "They ça'n't have anything to put down yet, before the trial's begun."

6   "They're putting down their names," the Gryphon whispered in reply, "for fear they should forget them before the end of the trial."

7   "Stupid things!" Alice began in a loud indignant voice; but she stopped her-self hastily, for the White Rabbit cried out "Silence in the court!" and the King put on his spectacles and looked anxiously round, to make out who was talking.

8   Alice could see, as well as if she were looking over their shoulders, that all the jurors were writing down "Stupid things!" on their slates, and she could even make out that one of them didn't know how to spell "stupid," and that he had to ask his neighbour to tell him. "A nice muddle their slates'll be in, before the trial's over!" thought Alice.

9   One of the jurors had a pencil that squeaked. This, of course, Alice could *not* stand, and she went round the court and got behind him, and very soon found an opportunity of taking it away. She did it so quickly that the poor lit-tle juror (it was Bill, the Lizard) could not make out at all what had become of it; so, after hunting all about for it, he was obliged to write with one finger for the rest of the day; and this was of very little use, as it left no mark on the slate.

10   "Herald, read the accusation!" said the King.

11   On this the White Rabbit blew three blasts on the trumpet, and then unrolled the parchment-scroll, and read as follows:—

"The Queen of Hearts, she made some tarts,
All on a summer day:
The Knave of Hearts, he stole those tarts
And took them quite away!"

12   "Consider your verdict," the King said to the jury.

13   "Not yet, not yet!" the Rabbit hastily interrupted. "There's a great deal to come before that!"

14   "Call the first witness," said the King; and the White Rabbit blew three blasts on the trumpet, and called out "First witness!"

15   The first witness was the Hatter. He came in with a teacup in one hand and a piece of bread-and-butter in the other. "I beg pardon, your Majesty," he began, "for bringing these in; but I hadn't quite finished my tea when I was sent for."

16   "You ought to have finished," said the King. "When did you begin?"

17   The Hatter looked at the March Hare, who had followed him into the court, arm-in-arm with the Dormouse. "Fourteenth of March, I *think* it was," he said.

18   "Fifteenth," said the March Hare.

19   "Sixteenth," said the Dormouse.

20   "Write that down," the king said to the jury; and the jury eagerly wrote down all three dates on their slates, and then added them up, and reduced the answer to shillings and pence.

21   "Take off your hat," the King said to the Hatter.

22   "It isn't mine," said the Hatter.

23   "*Stolen!*" the King exclaimed, turning to the jury, who instantly made a memorandum of the fact.

24 "I keep them to sell," the Hatter added as an explanation. "I've none of my own. I'm a hatter."

25 Here the Queen put on her spectacles, and began staring hard at the Hatter, who turned pale and fidgeted.

26 "Give your evidence," said the King; "and don't be nervous, or I'll have you executed on the spot."

27 This did not seem to encourage the witness at all: he kept shifting from one foot to the other, looking uneasily at the Queen, and in his confusion he bit a large piece out of his teacup instead of the bread-and-butter.

28 Just at this moment Alice felt a very curious sensation, which puzzled her a good deal until she made out what it was: she was beginning to grow larger again, and she thought at first she would get up and leave the court; but on second thoughts she decided to remain where she was as long as there was room for her.

29 "I wish you wouldn't squeeze so," said the Dormouse, who was sitting next to her. "I can hardly breathe."

30 "I ca'n't help it," said Alice very meekly: "I'm growing."

31 "You've no right to grow *here*," said the Dormouse.

32 "Don't talk nonsense," said Alice more boldly: "you know you're growing too."

33 "Yes, but *I* grow at a reasonable pace," said the Dormouse: "not in that ridiculous fashion." And he got up very sulkily and crossed over to the other side of the court.

34 All this time the Queen had never left off staring at the Hatter, and, just as the Dormouse crossed the court, she said, to one of the officers of the court, "Bring me the list of the singers in the last concert!" on which the wretched Hatter trembled so, that he shook off both his shoes.

35 "Give your evidence," the King repeated angrily, "or I'll have you executed, whether you are nervous or not."

36 "I'm a poor man, your Majesty," the Hatter began, in a trembling voice, "and I hadn't begun my tea—not above a week or so—and what with the bread-and-butter getting so thin—and the twinkling of the tea——"

37 "The twinkling of *what*?" said the King.

38 "It *began* with the tea," the Hatter replied.

39 "Of course twinkling *begins* with a T!" said the King sharply. "Do you take me for a dunce? Go on!"

40 "I'm a poor man," the Hatter went on, "and most things twinkled after that—only the March Hare said——"

41 "I didn't!" the March Hare interrupted in a great hurry.

42 "You did!" said the Hatter.

43 "I deny it!" said the March Hare.

44 "He denies it," said the King: "leave out that part."

45 "Well, at any rate, the Dormouse said——" the Hatter went on, looking anxiously round to see if he would deny it too; but the Dormouse denied nothing, being fast asleep.

46   "After that," continued the Hatter, "I cut some more bread-and-butter——"

47   "But what did the Dormouse say?" one of the jury asked.

48   "That I ca'n't remember," said the Hatter.

49   "You *must* remember," remarked the King, "or I'll have you executed."

50   The miserable Hatter dropped his teacup and bread-and-butter, and went down on one knee. "I'm a poor man, your Majesty," he began.

51   "You're a *very* poor *speaker*," said the King.

52   Here one of the guinea-pigs cheered, and was immediately suppressed by the officers of the court. (As that is rather a hard word, I will just explain to you how it was done. They had a large canvas bag, which tied up at the mouth with strings: into this they slipped the guinea-pig, head first, and then sat upon it.)

53   "I'm glad I've seen that done," thought Alice. "I've so often read in the newspapers, at the end of trials, 'There was some attempt at applause, which was immediately suppressed by the officers of the court,' and I never understood what it meant till now."

54   "If that's all you know about it, you may stand down," continued the King.

55   "I ca'n't go no lower," said the Hatter: "I'm on the floor, as it is."

56   "Then you may *sit* down," the King replied.

57   Here the other guinea-pig cheered, and was suppressed.

58   "Come, that finishes the guinea-pigs!" thought Alice. "Now we shall get on better."

59   "I'd rather finish my tea," said the Hatter, with an anxious look at the Queen, who was reading the list of singers.

60   "You may go," said the King, and the Hatter hurriedly left the court, without even waiting to put his shoes on.

61   "——and just take his head off outside," the Queen added to one of the officers; but the Hatter was out of sight before the officer could get to the door.

62   "Call the next witness!" said the King.

63   The next witness was the Duchess's cook. She carried the pepper-box in her hand, and Alice guessed who it was, even before she got into the court, by the way the people near the door began sneezing all at once.

64   "Give your evidence," said the King.

65   "Sha'n't," said the cook.

66   The King looked anxiously at the White Rabbit, who said, in a low voice, "Your Majesty must cross-examine *this* witness."

67   "Well, if I must, I must," the King said with a melancholy air, and, after folding his arms and frowning at the cook till his eyes were nearly out of sight, he said, in a deep voice, "What are tarts made of?"

68   "Pepper, mostly," said the cook.

69   "Treacle," said a sleepy voice behind her.

70   "Collar that Dormouse!" the Queen shrieked out. "Behead that Dormouse! Turn that Dormouse out of court! Suppress him! Pinch him! Off with his whiskers!"

71   For some minutes the whole court was in confusion, getting the Dormouse turned out, and, by the time they had settled down again, the cook had disappeared.

72   "Never mind!" said the King, with an air of great relief. "Call the next witness." And he added, in an undertone to the Queen, "Really, my dear, *you* must cross-examine the next witness. It quite makes my forehead ache!"

73   Alice watched the White Rabbit as he fumbled over the list, feeling very curious to see what the next witness would be like, "—for they haven't got much evidence *yet*," she said to herself. Imagine her surprise, when the White Rabbit read out, at the top of his shrill little voice, the name "Alice!"

Alice's Evidence

74"HERE!" cried Alice, quite forgetting in the flurry of the moment how large she had grown in the last few minutes, and she jumped up in such a hurry that she tipped over the jury-box with the edge of her skirt, upsetting all the jurymen on to the heads of the crowd below, and there they lay sprawling about, reminding her very much of a globe of gold-fish she had accidentally upset the week before.

75   "Oh, I *beg* your pardon!" she exclaimed in a tone of great dismay, and began picking them up again as quickly as she could, for the accident of the gold-fish kept running in her head, and she had a vague sort of idea that they must be collected at once and put back into the jury-box, or they would die.

76   "The trial cannot proceed," said the King, in a very grave voice, "until all the jurymen are back in their proper places—*all*," he repeated with great emphasis, looking hard at Alice as he said so.

77   Alice looked at the jury-box, and saw that, in her haste, she had put the Lizard in head downwards, and the poor little thing was waving its tail about in a melancholy way, being quite unable to move. She soon got it out again, and put it right; "not that it signifies much," she said to herself; "I should think it would be *quite* as much use in the trial one way up as the other."

78   As soon as the jury had a little recovered from the shock of being upset, and their slates and pencils had been found and handed back to them, they set to work very diligently to write out a history of the accident, all except the Lizard, who seemed too much overcome to do anything but sit with its mouth open, gazing up into the roof of the court.

79   "What do you know about this business?" the King said to Alice.

80   "Nothing," said Alice.

81   "Nothing *whatever?*" persisted the King.

82   "Nothing whatever," said Alice.

83   "That's very important," the King said, turning to the jury. They were just beginning to write this down on their slates, when the White Rabbit interrupted: "*Un*important, your Majesty means, of course," he said, in a very respectful tone, but frowning and making faces at him as he spoke.

84   "*Un*important, of course, I meant," the King hastily said, and went on to himself in an undertone, "important—unimportant—unimportant—important——" as if he were trying which word sounded best.

85   Some of the jury wrote it down "important," and some "unimportant." Alice could see this, as she was near enough to look over their slates; "but it doesn't matter a bit," she thought to herself.

86   At this moment the King, who had been for some time busily writing in his note-book, called out "Silence!" and read out from his book "Rule Forty-two. *All persons more than a mile high to leave the court.*"

87   Everybody looked at Alice.

88   "*I'm* not a mile high," said Alice.

89   "You are," said the King.

90   "Nearly two miles high," added the Queen.

91   "Well, I sha'n't go, at any rate," said Alice; "besides, that's not a regular rule: you invented it just now."

92   "It's the oldest rule in the book," said the King.

93   "Then it ought to be Number One," said Alice.

94   The King turned pale, and shut his note-book hastily. "Consider your verdict," he said to the jury, in a low trembling voice.

95   "There's more evidence to come yet, please your Majesty," said the White Rabbit, jumping up in a great hurry: "this paper has just been picked up."

96   "What's in it?" said the Queen.

97   "I haven't opened it yet," said the White Rabbit; "but it seems to be a letter, written by the prisoner to—to somebody."

98   "It must have been that," said the King, "unless it was written to nobody, which isn't usual, you know."

99   "Who is it directed to?" said one of the jurymen.

100   "It isn't directed at all," said the White Rabbit: "in fact, there's nothing written on the *outside*." He unfolded the paper as he spoke, and added "It isn't a letter, after all: it's a set of verses."

101   "Are they in the prisoner's handwriting?" asked another of the jurymen.

102   "No, they're not," said the White Rabbit, "and that's the queerest thing about it." (The jury all looked puzzled.)

103   "He must have imitated somebody else's hand," said the King. (The jury all brightened up again.)

104   "Please, your Majesty," said the Knave, "I didn't write it, and they ca'n't prove that I did: there's no name signed at the end."

105   "If you didn't sign it," said the King, "that only makes the matter worse. You *must* have meant some mischief, or else you'd have signed your name like an honest man."

106   There was a general clapping of hands at this: it was the first really clever thing the King had said that day.

107   "That *proves* his guilt, of course," said the Queen: "so, off with——"

108   "It doesn't prove anything of the sort!" said Alice. "Why, you don't even know what they're about!"

109   "Read them," said the King.

110   The White Rabbit put on his spectacles. "Where shall I begin, please your Majesty?" he asked.

111   "Begin at the beginning," the King said, very gravely, "and go on till you come to the end: then stop."

112   There was dead silence in the court, whilst the White Rabbit read out these verses:——

"They told me you had been to her,
And mentioned me to him:
She gave me a good character,
But said I could not swim.

He sent them word I had not gone
(We know it to be true):
If she should push the matter on,
What would become of you?

I gave her one, they gave him two,
You gave us three or more;
They all returned from him to you,
Though they were mine before.

If I or she should chance to be
Involved in this affair,
He trusts to you to set them free,
Exactly as we were.

My notion was that you had been
(Before she had this fit)
An obstacle that came between
Him, and ourselves, and it.

Don't let him know she liked them best,
For this must ever be
A secret, kept from all the rest,
Between yourself and me."

113   "That's the most important piece of evidence we've heard yet," said the King, rubbing his hands; "so now let the jury——"

114   "If any one of them can explain it," said Alice, (she had grown so large in the last few minutes that she wasn't a bit afraid of interrupting him,) "I'll give him sixpence. *I* don't believe there's an atom of meaning to it."

115   The jury all wrote down, on their slates, "*She* doesn't believe there's an atom of meaning in it," but none of them attempted to explain the paper.

116   "If there's no meaning in it," said the King, "that saves a world of trouble, you know, as we needn't try to find any. And yet I don't know," he went on, spreading out the verses on his knee, and looking at them with one eye; "I

seem to see some meaning in them, after all. '—*said I could not swim*—' you can't swim, can you ?" he added, turning to the Knave.

117 The Knave shook his head sadly. "Do I look like it?" he said. (Which he certainly did *not*, being made entirely of cardboard.)

118 "All right, so far," said the King; and he went on muttering over the verses to himself: "'*We know it to be true*'—that's the jury, of course—*If she should push the matter on*'— that must be the Queen—'*What would become of you?*'— What, indeed!—'*I gave her one, they gave him two*'—why, that must be what he did with the tarts, you know——"

119 "But it goes on '*they all returned from him to you,*'" said Alice.

120 "Why, there they are!" said the King triumphantly, pointing to the tarts on the table. "Nothing can be clearer than *that*. Then again—'*before she had this fit*'—you never had *fits*, my dear, I think?" he said to the Queen.

121 "Never!" said the Queen, furiously, throwing an inkstand at the Lizard as she spoke. (The unfortunate little Bill had left off writing on his slate with one finger, as he found it made no mark; but he now hastily began again, using the ink, that was trickling down his face, as long as it lasted.)

122 "Then the words don't *fit* you," said the King looking round the court with a smile. There was a dead silence.

123 "It's a pun!" the King added in an angry tone, and everybody laughed. "Let the jury consider their verdict," the King said, for about the twentieth time that day.

124 "No, no!" said the Queen. "Sentence first—verdict afterwards."

125 "Stuff and nonsense!" said Alice loudly. "The idea of having the sentence first!"

126 "Hold your tongue!" said the Queen, turning purple.

127 "I won't!" said Alice.

128 "Off with her head!" the Queen shouted at the top of her voice. Nobody moved.

129 "Who cares for *you*?" said Alice (she had grown to her full size by this time). "You're nothing but a pack of cards!"

130 At this the whole pack rose up into the air, and came flying down upon her; she gave a little scream, half of fright and half of anger, and tried to beat them off, and found herself lying on the bank, with her head in the lap of her sister, who was gently brushing away some dead leaves that had fluttered down from the trees upon her face.

131 "Wake up, Alice dear!" said her sister. "Why, what a long sleep you've had!"

132 "Oh, I've had such a curious dream!" said Alice. And she told her sister, as well as she could remember them, all these strange Adventures of hers that you have just been reading about. . . .

3

"If we read differently, we do differently—reading better, we do better."

JAMES R. KINCAID, "WHO GETS TO TELL THEIR STORIES?" *The New York Times Book Review, May 3, 1992*

Careful Reading

H AS THE FOLLOWING ever happened to you? You're talking with a friend or parent about something that is very important to you, when suddenly you realize that this person doesn't seem to be listening. Frustrated, you say, "Hey, you're not listening to what I'm saying," only to have this person respond, "Yes, I am. I heard every word that you said." Maybe so. The problem, though, is that your friend or parent was listening *passively,* not *actively,* and thus could not have been listening very *carefully.*

Something similar can be said about passive readers, too. Like passive listeners, who superficially hear the words of a conversation, passive readers might indeed read the words of a text, but they do so without fully attending to its details. As a result, they often miss various subtleties that the text has to offer and might even overlook some important connections that the author has worked hard to create. In short, passive readers are almost never careful readers, and, in the world of academics—which is the world that you entered when you enrolled in your college courses—readers who do not read carefully are readers who might have trouble with their work. This chapter is intended to help you steer clear of such trouble by helping you become an ever more careful, active reader.

Though no chapter in a book can fully launch you on your way to becoming such a reader, this one should at least help get you started. The featured reading selection, Sandra Cisneros' short story "My Name," provides the sorts of images and details that whet readers' appetites by inviting readers into a story and, in the process, making them curious about the author's choice of certain words and phrases. In particular, Cisneros—an experienced fiction writer—creatively shows us how the relationship between one's name and one's identity can be both complicated and quite telling. More generally, Cisneros' presentations of the narrator's attitudes and feelings concerning the latter's name ultimately make us stop and think about how that which is personal and familiar can contain stores of enlightening information—for us as well as for others.

To gain some practice in the art of close reading, pay careful attention to those textual details in Cisneros' story that strike you as being important, that are repeated elsewhere in the story, that are confusing, stimulating, challenging, and so on. The following four tips, intended to help you see how you might keep track of your reactions to Cisneros' text, can be applied to any close-reading activity that you pursue:

- Underline or otherwise highlight textual details—words, phrases, and even whole passages—that you think deserve special attention now and that you feel might be important to review when you read the story again.

- In the margins of your book, comment on these textual details, indicating why, for personal or other reasons, you see them as somehow standing out. Ask questions about them, comment on their significance in and of themselves and to the story as a whole, and note similarities and differences between these and other relevant details in the story.

- In the margins of your book, in a reading journal, or, if applicable, in the blank space at the end of the reading selection, challenge the writer, argue with her, take issue with those of her points that you feel are troublesome, underdeveloped, underexplained, or just plain wrong. Conversely, indicate your agreement with those of her points that you think make sense. In either case, briefly note *why* you feel as you do.

- In a reading journal or the blank space at the end of the reading selection, comment on your general reactions to the text, noting anything specific (the implications of certain words and phrases, for example) that influences or is otherwise relevant to your interpretation of the reading selection.

If you haven't done much or any **annotating** of a text before, you might not be sure exactly how much of the text to mark up (or how to mark it up) or precisely what sorts of comments you should make in the margins. The truth is, there are no absolute rules in this area. On the other hand, there are some useful guidelines. For example, you should avoid the extremes—underlining nearly everything, for instance, or underlining next to nothing. When she rereads the material, the reader who annotates nearly every textual detail often finds her annotations more distracting than helpful. By the same token, the reader who makes few or no annotations—thereby giving herself a sparse record or no record at all of how she read and responded to the material— often finds herself at a disadvantage both when she reviews the reading selection and when she tries to cite relevant textual evidence in a paper. You yourself will need to decide how to achieve the proper balance between these two extremes.

You'll probably discover that your personal reaction to a text has much to do with the ways in which you understand that text. If you annotate those passages that you find especially noteworthy, you'll help yourself track your interpretive moves. Using the margins of the text to note major themes in the reading material should prove especially helpful, since, when rereading the text, you'll be able to see at a glance the text's major ideas, the order in which it presents them, how often it returns to them, how it explicates them, and the like. In this sense, commenting in the margins will often prove more profitable than will highlighting or underlining key words and passages, since the latter techniques will merely help remind you that certain words or passages are important and that, consequently, you'll want to look at them again. Your marginal comments, however, will help you recall specific details of the text, make associations between or among these details, and so on (you might find it useful to reserve the right-hand margins for certain kinds of comments and questions and the left-hand margins for others). Besides, you'll likely end up rereading those parts of the text you highlighted or underlined.

. . .

To ease yourself into the annotating game, you might try annotating only minimally at first—by putting a check mark or an exclamation point beside a particularly important or interesting passage, for example, or by making a simple marginal note concerning a passage's content. If necessary, you can then add more details to your annotation (or even annotate your annotation!) during a subsequent reading of the text. On the other hand, if right from the start you find it helpful to make lengthy annotations or to mix lengthy and sparse ones, then by all means do so. Though not unlimited, the techniques and practices used in careful, active reading are indeed many and varied.

Suffice it to say that reading tends to be a fluid activity, and not a static one. All texts are open to the different approaches of different—and even the same—readers. To prepare yourself for any reading activity, plan on using those annotating strategies that you think might aid your ability to read actively. Give yourself permission, though, to alter your plans so that whatever reading habits you develop and put into practice best meet your own reading needs. Whether or not, in any given reading situation, you decide to make note of repetitions, cross-reference similar or dissimilar items, ask questions, raise objections, make connections, and underline or in some other way highlight what you consider to be noteworthy words, phrases, clauses, whole sentences, or even whole paragraphs, *always adopt the system of annotating that works best for you at the time.*

A final word concerning the *substance* as opposed to the *form* of your annotations. By annotating the text with your various comments, questions, agreements, and disagreements, you'll be actively *dialoguing* with the text. In class, you'll probably discuss some methods for determining which of your textual interpretations are substantively strong, which are substantively weak, and which fall somewhere in between. Before you start on your interpretive journeys, though, consider the following pre-reading tip, which ought to help you prepare to partake meaningfully in your forthcoming conversations with texts: always think about the *kind* of text that you are about to read, because you'll need to interpret different kinds of texts differently.

If, for instance, you are about to read a Dr. Seuss book, in which you know you will find fantastic characters involved in fantastic adventures, you probably will prepare yourself to see, among other things, how the author uses fantasy to make points about reality (of course, a child might actively read the same book with an entirely different reading agenda). It is unlikely that you will first expect to read a true story in a Dr. Seuss book and then judge the author's work according to whether or not his text meets such an expectation. On the other hand, if you are about to read a historical account of the Battle of the Little Bighorn, you probably will prepare yourself to see not the extent to which the author uses fantasy to help us understand reality, but rather the extent to which he presents well-informed interpretations of historical facts. If you discover that for no apparent reason he completely ignores historical data and writes instead that Native Americans badgered government soldiers by trying to get them to eat green eggs and ham, you undoubtedly will judge his work harshly in light of your pre-reading expectation.

But what if, instead of completely disregarding historical data, the author were to use material from Dr. Seuss' books in order to explain historical events by way of analogy? Under this circumstance, you might give the author some leeway, even if you believe, say, that a historical text should "stick to the facts." Thus, even though you always want to be as prepared a reader as possible by knowing *something* about the nature of the text that you are about to read—Is it a historical document? A personal letter? A diary entry? A short story?—you should take care that you don't decide in advance how you'll approach a given text and then stick to your presuppositions no matter what. Unless you are a very unusual reader, you'll sometimes find that your pre-reading expectations are off the mark and need to be rethought in the light of your reading experiences.

In short, then, you want to know something about the sort of text that you'll be reading so that you can read the text with care. On the other hand, you want to strive to judge others' texts as you would have them judge yours—fairly, honestly, and as open-mindedly as possible.

Finally, before we move on to the featured reading selection and the featured assignment, let me say a word or two about the modeled responses prepared by Ellen K. Miles and Susan McKenzie, this chapter's contributing authors. Don't worry if, as you evaluate your work in light of theirs, you discover that your responses differ from theirs. Though Miles and McKenzie are indeed careful readers, their annotations and written responses represent only *two* readers' active participation in a close-reading activity. Miles and McKenzie offer excellent *examples* of close reading and insightful writing, but they certainly do not offer the *only* good examples of such reading and writing. Ultimately, as this book consistently intimates, you must construct your own models of active, careful reading and meaningful, thoughtful writing.

FEATURED ASSIGNMENT

Part I: Read Cisneros' story, annotating those passages that you think are significant or that you simply like. Then, reread the story, making additional annotations if necessary. Next, in a reading journal, in the space provided at the end of the story, or in both, make some summary comments concerning the meaning or significance that the story holds for you. If you wish, reread the story again, reexamining and perhaps revising your annotations and summary comments.

Part II: Write a brief reflective commentary on what you experienced, thought, and/or felt while doing this assignment.

READING AND WRITING

This chapter's reading selections should help us understand something about the intimate connections among our personal names, our ideas of who we are, and our feelings of belonging to or being outside of a particular community, culture, family, or ethnic group. Whether we like them, have always hated them, or never thought much about them, our personal names play a part in how we and others see us. Each of this chapter's readings suggests as much, teaching us, among other things, how the notion of "personal identity" both marks and is marked by notions of "difference." Taken together, however, these readings also reinforce the point that sometimes what is personal, particular, and familiar is also universal and shared.

F E A T U R E D   R E A D I N G

My Name

SANDRA CISNEROS

"The daughter of a Mexican father and a Mexican-American mother, and sister to six brothers," Sandra Cisneros (1954–) "is nobody's mother and nobody's wife" (*The House on Mango Street* [1991 ed.] 111). Cisneros was graduated from the prestigious Iowa Writers Workshop and has received two National Endowment for the Arts fellowships. During one of these fellowships, she completed *The House on Mango Street*, a collection of short stories which won the American Book Award from the Before Columbus Foundation and from which the featured reading selection is taken. Others of her works include *Bad Boys* (1980), *The Rodrigo Poems* (1985), *My Wicked, Wicked Ways* (1987)—all works of poetry—and, recently, another collection of short stories, entitled *Woman Hollering Creek and Other Stories* (1991). A former college recruiter and arts administrator, Cisneros has also taught writing at various colleges as well as at an alternative high school for dropouts. At this high school—located in Chicago, the city of her birth—she "always tried to prove to her students that 'art is in all of us'" (*The House on Mango Street* [1984 ed.] 103). [Most of this biographical information has been gleaned from the two editions of *The House on Mango Street* noted parenthetically, as well as from Susan M. Trosky, ed., *Contemporary Authors*, vol. 131, p. 109.]

PRE-READING QUESTIONS:

1) Do you have any thoughts or feelings about personal names that are culturally or ethnically different from yours? If you do, keep these thoughts and feelings in mind as you read Cisneros' story, watching to see whether or not—and, if so, how,

why, and to what extent—they affect your understanding of or reactions to her piece.

2) Do you like your name(s)? Has any of your names ever given you trouble or brought you joy? Will your thoughts about and experiences with your name(s) likely guide you in choosing names for your children?

3) What is the origin, meaning, or significance of your names in terms of your culture, family, and/or ethnic group?

4) Knowing that you are about to read a short story, do you have any expectations concerning the nature of the writing that you will encounter? For example, do you expect the writer to make her points similarly to or differently from the way in which, say, a political analyst writing for a newspaper might make *her* points?

CLOSE-READING TIP

Like other talented creative writers, Cisneros often "defamiliarizes the familiar" in her works by describing everyday matters or common feelings in such a way that careful readers cannot help but take a second look at what she is saying. When you come upon such descriptions in "My Name," see what *you* make of them; when you discuss the story in class, see if your classmates react to or understand these descriptions as you do. Consider, for example, some relevant descriptions in paragraphs 1, 3, and 4.

CISNEROS SELECTION **My Name**

1   In English my name means hope. In Spanish it means too many letters. It means sadness, it means waiting. It is like the number nine. A muddy color. It is the Mexican records my father plays on Sunday mornings when he is shaving, songs like sobbing.

2   It was my great-grandmother's name and now it is mine. She was a horse woman too, born like me in the Chinese year of the horse—which is supposed to be bad luck if you're born female—but I think this is a Chinese lie because the Chinese, like the Mexicans, don't like their women strong.

3   My great-grandmother. I would've liked to have known her, a wild horse of a woman, so wild she wouldn't marry until my great-grandfather threw a sack over her head and carried her off. Just like that, as if she were a fancy chandelier. That's the way he did it.

4   And the story goes she never forgave him. She looked out the window all her life, the way so many women sit their sadness on an elbow. I wonder if she

made the best with what she got or was she sorry because she couldn't be all the things she wanted to be. Esperanza. I have inherited her name, but I don't want to inherit her place by the window.

5   At school they say my name funny as if the syllables were made out of tin and hurt the roof of your mouth. But in Spanish my name is made out of a softer something like silver, not quite as thick as sister's name Magdalena which is uglier than mine. Magdalena who at least can come home and become Nenny. But I am always Esperanza.

6   I would like to baptize myself under a new name, a name more like the real me, the one nobody sees. Esperanza as Lisandra or Maritza or Zeze the X. Yes. Something like Zeze the X will do.

POST-READING QUESTIONS:

1) Did any of the thoughts or feelings that you discussed in your response to the first pre-reading question affect your understanding of or help shape your reactions to Cisneros' story? Did her story cause you to reexamine your reasons for having these thoughts and feelings?

2) In your view, did the sorts of textual details alluded to in the close-reading tip detract from or add to the meaning and significance of the story? Did they do both? What other textual details did you find particularly noteworthy, and why did they seem important to you?

3) Did your understanding of or feelings concerning the story change as a result of your having read and thought about the piece a second time?

4) Do your summary comments about this story coincide with your annotations of the piece? Did you revise any of these comments or annotations?

5) Having read and thought about this story, do you want to change or rethink any of your responses to the first three pre-reading questions?

6) Did Cisneros' story fulfill your expectations of it *as* a short story? Did these expectations affect your reading of the story? Did reading the story cause you to rethink these expectations?

A Close Reading of Cisneros' Story: Annotations and Comments

ELLEN K. MILES

Four years after she began college as a 25-year-old single mother, Ellen K. Miles—a member of Phi Beta Kappa (a prestigious academic honors organization)—received her B.A. in Spanish in 1981 from the University of California, Irvine, from which she was graduated *magna cum laude*. After attending graduate school for two years, she withdrew in order to care full-time for her children. Describing herself now as a "professional mother," Ellen believes that nurturing the lives of children is as challenging, demanding, and worthwhile a professional activity as is any other. A vocal advocate for children's rights, she homeschools her two youngest children and volunteers as a leader in La Leche League, an international, nonprofit, nonsectarian organization devoted to promoting breastfeeding and supporting breastfeeding mothers.

PART I RESPONSE **Annotations and Comments**

Spanish concept of Time → personal connotations

esperanza in Spanish means hope + waiting

(1) In English my name means hope. In Spanish it means too many letters. It means sadness, it means waiting. It is like the number nine. A muddy color. It is the Mexican records

Double meaning in Spanish.

my father plays on Sunday mornings when he is shaving, songs like sobbing.

Family heritage Name = traits = great-grandmother = narrator

(2) It was my great-grandmother's name and now it is mine. She was a horse woman too, born like me in the year of the horse—which is supposed to be bad luck if you're born female—but I think this is a Chinese lie

Narrator wants strength

because the Chinese, like the Mexicans, don't like their women strong.

horse woman v/s wild horse woman v/s Chandelier = object

(3) My great-grandmother. I would've liked to have known her, a wild horse of a woman, so wild she wouldn't marry until my great-grandfather threw a sack over her head and carried her off. Just like that, as if she were a fancy chandelier. That's the way he did it.

(4) And the story goes she never forgave him. She looked out the window all her life, the way so many women sit their sadness on an elbow. I wonder if she made the best with what she got or was she sorry because she couldn't be all the things she wanted to be. Esperanza. I have inherited her name, but I don't want to inherit her place by the window.

Turning her to a chandelier demonstrates how she became lifeless, waiting.
Narrator ≠ great-grandmother

cultural bias

⑤ At school they say my name funny as if the syllables were made out of tin and hurt the roof of your mouth. But in Spanish my name is made out of a softer something

metallic sounds

like silver, not quite as thick as sister's name Magdelena which is uglier than mine. Magdalena who at least can

Nicknames

come home and become Nenny. But I am always Esperanza.

Names reflect - identify

⑥ I would like to baptize myself under a new name, a name more like the real me, the one nobody sees. Esperanza as Lisandra or Maritza or Zeze the X. Yes. Something like Zeze the X will do.

Desire to be free.

without culture → exotic

narrator
The ~~author~~ is burdened by her Hispanic heritage, but also by being a woman. The grandmother's burden was that as a female, she ha to become passive to the male.
The ~~author~~ narrator will parent herself —re-name herself to show her identity,
Identity→ in the world she could be different from the identities assumed for her by others,-classmates and family.

PART II   Commentary

I immediately became aware of the tension that Cisneros creates in the first two lines between ethnic "realities." These two perspectives, which are so subjective, emerge from the contrast between English and Spanish as languages that shape perception and give rise to some of the differences between Mexican and North American culture. She tells us that her name, which translates simply into English as "hope," means many things in Spanish. In this language of her family, her heritage, this concept of "hope" also points to a lack of fulfillment, an emptiness which she emphasizes by using words like "sadness," "waiting," "muddy," and "sobbing."

Each time I have read the piece, my understanding and appreciation of it as a whole has grown. Initially, I was drawn to the issue of naming. Thinking about how important names and naming have been in my life helped me to be sensitive to the way that names shape our perception of reality and identity. The cultural and familial implications of names and the way that ethnic names mark an individual as "other" to the dominant culture shape the Cisneros story. I was surprised to realize, on my fifth or sixth reading, that she doesn't mention her name, "Esperanza," until half-way through the piece.

Equally important as the narrator's ethnic identity is her vision of herself as a woman. She contrasts the idea of a "wild horse of a woman" who might bear the name "Zeze the X," with a passive conception of woman who can be captured tamed and "carried. . . off. . . as if she was a fancy chandelier." This is her challenge, to confront the burden of her past and to forge an identity all her own. Most of us, especially those of us who are women, can probably identify with the need to be free and wild, and to escape the predetermined vision of ourselves imposed by our families.

A Close Reading of Cisneros' Story: Annotations and Comments

SUSAN MCKENZIE

A first-generation American (her family is from Jamaica), Susan McKenzie is a 24-year-old African American who attends Irvine Valley College, in Irvine, California. Susan was born and raised in New York City, a circumstance that, in her view, gave her the distinct advantage of socializing, in her late teens, with people of different races. Susan feels that this exposure prompted her interest in learning about and trying to understand the differences among people. Pursuing this interest, she plans to receive her B.A. in Development Studies—a field of studies focusing on the political, social, and economic situations in underdeveloped countries—and then to become an international lawyer.

RESPONSE

PART I

Annotations and Comments

My name means "Lily" in Hebrew.

My name came from a 16 yr old girl my mother knew at the teenage pregnancy home in N.Y. My mother told me she was strong, mentally.

In English my name means hope. In Spanish it means too many letters. It means sadness, it means waiting. It is like the number nine. A muddy color. It is the Mexican records my father plays on Sunday mornings when he is shaving, songs like sobbing.

It was my great-grandmother's name and now it is mine. She was a horse woman too, born like me in the year of the horse—which is supposed to be bad luck if you're born female—but I think this is a Chinese lie because the Chinese, like the Mexicans, don't like their women strong.

— My great-grandmother. I would've liked to have known her, a wild horse of a woman, so wild she wouldn't marry until my great-grandfather threw a sack over her head and carried her off. Just like that, as if she were a fancy chandelier. That's the way he did it.

This to me may symbolize men's domination of women, something seen in many cultures.

And the story goes she never forgave him. She looked out the window all her life, the way so many women sit their sadness on an elbow. I wonder if she made the best with what she got or was she sorry because she couldn't be all the things she wanted to be. Esperanza. I have inherited her name, but I don't want to inherit her place by the window.

In my culture, I've seen the women "sit their sadness" in their eyes, which look deceivingly strong.

I wonder the same about my mother who while trying to finish High School had to worry about two children to feed.

At school they say my name funny as if the syllables were made out of tin and hurt the roof of your mouth. But in Spanish my name is made out of a softer something like silver, not quite as thick as sister's name Magdelena which is uglier than mine. Magdalena who at least can come home and become Nenny. But I am always Esperanza.

I was always teased in school about my name because it wasn't "Black." "What was your mother thinking when she named you" they would say.

I would like to baptize myself under a new name, a name more like the real me, the one nobody sees. Esperanza as Lisandra or Maritza or Zeze the X. Yes. Something like Zeze the X will do.

I wished once to rename myself but I thought there is no name which could describe me. Right then I knew I was unique. A name is just a small way to identify me and I would not be limited by it.

PART II Commentary

My thought while reading "My Name" was if Cisneros liked her name. She refers to her name as an inheritance which I presume is unwanted. It seems her name Esperanza stigmatizes her. From reading this I think it's hard for her to see a name is sometimes just a name.

R E L A T E D   R E A D I N G S

from **Black Elk Speaks**

BLACK ELK, AS TOLD THROUGH JOHN G. NEIHARDT

An Oglala Sioux warrior and medicine man, Black Elk (1863–1950) is one of the most significant figures in Native American history. He was a great and eminently gifted teacher, a seer and holy man who seemed to understand instinctively both the necessity and the way for humans to live at peace with one another, with other living beings, and with the planet as a whole. He was also a moving oral chronicler of his people's history. Concerning the aftermath of the massacre at Wounded Knee, for example, he says that "[t]he snow drifted deep in the crooked gulch, and it was one long grave of butchered women and children and babies, who had never done any harm and were only trying to run away. . . . I can see that something else died there in the bloody mud," he adds, "and was buried in the blizzard. A people's dream died there. It was a beautiful dream" (*Black Elk Speaks* 223 and 230).

The excerpts that follow—which recount some of the promise and pain associated with that dream—are from the book *Black Elk Speaks,* John G. Neihardt's "re-creation in English of the holy man's account of his life and vision" (*Black Elk Speaks* 236; Black Elk spoke no English). "An adopted member of the Oglala Sioux" (ibid.), Neihardt published his first book, *The Divine Enchantment* (1900), when he was only 19 years old. His major work, *A Cycle of the West* (a collection of five epic songs begun in 1912), is "'designed to celebrate the great mood of courage that was developed west of the Missouri River during that period which began in 1822 and ended in 1890 [when the massacre at Wounded Knee occurred]'" (*Black Elk Speaks* 237). Born near Sharpsburg, Illinois, Neihardt (1881–1973), also known as "Flaming Rainbow," was a teacher, editor, and writer who could claim among his many awards and honors the distinction of being named Nebraska's official Poet Laureate. A recognized "authority on [the] traditions and customs" of the Omaha Indians, he was "chosen by Black Elk as heir to the seer's mystic powers" (ibid. 237 and 236). [Biographical information on Neihardt was taken from *Black Elk Speaks* 235–238.]

PRE-READING QUESTIONS:

1) Have you formed any opinions concerning Native American culture or history? If so, keep these opinions in mind as you read Black Elk's narrative, watching to see whether or not they influence your understanding of or reactions to his ideas.

2) Knowing that you are about to read a historical narrative—in particular, the narrative of a Native American holy man told by an "adopted member of the Oglala Sioux"—do you have any preconceptions concerning the sort of writing that you'll encounter?

3) If you were asked to identify both yourself and those who are close to you, how would you do so?

4) Does your family have any unusual or surprising stories concerning the naming of children?

CLOSE-READING **TIP**

As you read through this selection, note the frequency with which Black Elk uses some form of the verb "to be" (am, is, are, was, were, be, been, being) in the context of explaining who people are, what they are called, and how they were named. Think about why he might use such verbs in these contexts and whether or not the meanings of his sentences might change were he to replace these verbs with action verbs (and revise the sentences accordingly). Consider, for example, relevant sentences in paragraphs 1, 3, and 10.

1   I am a Lakota of the Ogalala band. My father's name was Black Elk, and his father before him bore the name, and the father of his father, so that I am the fourth to bear it. He was a medicine man and so were several of his brothers. Also, he and the great Crazy Horse's father were cousins, having the same grandfather. My mother's name was White Cow Sees; her father was called Refuse-to-go, and her mother, Plenty Eagle Feathers. I can remember my mother's mother and her father. My father's father was killed by the Pawnees when I was too little to know, and his mother, Red Eagle Woman, died soon after.

2   I was born in the Moon of the Popping Trees (December) on the Little Powder River in the Winter When the Four Crows Were Killed (1863), and I was three years old when my father's right leg was broken in the Battle of the Hundred Slain.[1] From that wound he limped until the day he died, which was about the time when Big Foot's band was butchered on Wounded Knee (1890). He is buried here in these hills.

3   I can remember that Winter of the Hundred Slain as a man may remember some bad dream he dreamed when he was little, but I can not tell just how much I heard when I was bigger and how much I understood when I was little. It is like some fearful thing in a fog, for it was a time when everything seemed troubled and afraid.

4   I had never seen a Wasichu[2] then, and did not know what one looked like; but every one was saying that the Wasichus were coming and that they were going to take our country and rub us all out and that we should all have to die fighting. It was the Wasichus who got rubbed out in that battle, and all the people were talking about it for a long while; but a hundred Wasichus was not much if there were others and others without number where those came from.

---

[1] The Fetterman Fight, commonly described as a "massacre," in which Captain Fetterman and 81 men were wiped out on Peno Creek near Fort Phil Kearney, December 21, 1866. [Neihardt's note.]

[2] A term used to designate the white man, but having no reference to the color of his skin. [Neihardt's note.]

5   I remember once that I asked my grandfather about this. I said: "When the scouts come back from seeing the prairie full of bison somewhere, the people say the Wasichus are coming; and when strange men are coming to kill us all, they say the Wasichus are coming. What does it mean?" And he said, "That they are many."

6   When I was older, I learned what the fighting was about that winter and the next summer. Up on the Madison Fork the Wasichus had found much of the yellow metal that they worship and that makes them crazy, and they wanted to have a road up through our country to the place where the yellow metal was; but my people did not want the road. It would scare the bison and make them go away, and also it would let the other Wasichus come in like a river. They told us that they wanted only to use a little land, as much as a wagon would take between the wheels; but our people knew better. And when you look about you now, you can see what it was they wanted.

7   Once we were happy in our own country and we were seldom hungry, for then the two-leggeds and the four-leggeds lived together like relatives, and there was plenty for them and for us. But the Wasichus came, and they have made little islands for us and other little islands for the four-leggeds, and always these islands are becoming smaller, for around them surges the gnawing flood of the Wasichu; and it is dirty with lies and greed. . . .

8   Afterwhile we came to the village on Powder River and went into camp at the downstream end. I was anxious to see my cousin, Crazy Horse, again, for now that it began to look like bad trouble coming, everybody talked about him more than ever and he seemed greater than before. Also I was getting older.

9   Of course I had seen him now and then ever since I could remember, and had heard stories of the brave things he did. I remember the story of how he and his brother were out alone on horseback, and a big band of Crows attacked them, so that they had to run. And while they were riding hard, with all those Crows after them, Crazy Horse heard his brother call out; and when he looked back, his brother's horse was down and the Crows were almost on him. And they told how Crazy Horse charged back right into the Crows and fought them back with only a bow and arrows, then took his brother up behind him and got away. It was his sacred power that made the Crows afraid of him when he charged. And the people told stories of when he was a boy and used to be around with the older Hump all the time. Hump was not young any more at the time, and he was a very great warrior, maybe the greatest we ever had until then. They say people used to wonder at the boy and the old man always being together; but I think Hump knew Crazy Horse would be a great man and wanted to teach him everything.

10   Crazy Horse's father was my father's cousin, and there were no chiefs in our family before Crazy Horse; but there were holy men; and he became a

chief because of the power he got in a vision when he was a boy. When I was a man, my father told me something about that vision. Of course he did not know all of it; but he said that Crazy Horse dreamed and went into the world where there is nothing but the spirits of all things. That is the real world that is behind this one, and everything we see here is something like a shadow from that world. He was on his horse in that world, and the horse and himself on it and the trees and the grass and the stones and everything were made of spirit, and nothing was hard, and everything seemed to float. His horse was standing still there, and yet it danced around like a horse made only of shadow, and that is how he got his name, which does not mean that his horse was crazy or wild, but that in his vision it danced around in that queer way.

11   It was this vision that gave him his great power, for when he went into a fight, he had only to think of that world to be in it again, so that he could go through anything and not be hurt. Until he was murdered by the Wasichus at the Soldiers' Town on White River, he was wounded only twice, once by accident and both times by some one of his own people when he was not expecting trouble and was not thinking; never by an enemy. He was fifteen years old when he was wounded by accident; and the other time was when he was a young man and another man was jealous of him because the man's wife liked Crazy Horse. . . .

POST-READING QUESTIONS:

1) Did you find that your pre-reading opinions about Native American culture or history influenced your understanding of or helped shape your reactions to Black Elk's narrative? Did his narrative cause you to reexamine your reasons for having these opinions?

2) Do these excerpts read like passages in standard history texts? Did the *style* of writing used here influence your understanding of or reaction to the excerpts' contents? How would you evaluate your response to the second pre-reading question in light of your present reading experience?

3) How would you compare the ways in which you identify yourself and those close to you with the ways in which Black Elk identifies himself and those close to *him*?

4) Do you see any relationship between Black Elk's descriptions of people and the history that he relates concerning his tribe's conflicts with the Wasichus? Do you find any special interpretive significance in Black Elk's descriptions of or references to dates, events, and places?

5) Were you surprised by Black Elk's explanation of how Crazy Horse received his name? How does this story compare to those that you cite in your response to the fourth pre-reading question?

from **The Gospel According to Matthew**

MATTHEW

Though "The Gospel According to Matthew" is presented as the first book in the Christian New Testament, it might very well have been written second, after Mark's Gospel. Be that as it may, Matthew's text remains among the most educational and systematic of the texts in the Christian New Testament. Sometimes referred to as "'the teaching Gospel,'" it "[n]ot only. . . give[s] prominence to Jesus' ministry as a teacher. . . , but. . . also has proved to be so admirably arranged for teaching purposes that it has remained the most widely used of the four Gospels" (Ferguson 589).

One of the Twelve Apostles, Matthew seems to have written his Gospel around the middle of the first century C.E. Although he is commonly understood to be the tax collector who knew and followed Jesus, many biblical scholars now question his status in that regard. Reminding us that "Matthew's text alone. . . defines Matthew as a tax collector and substitutes Matthew's name for Mark's Levi" (according to Mark, Jesus used the name "Levi" to refer to the tax collector who followed him [*Mark* 2:14]), one scholar argues emphatically that "Matthew's Gospel was not written by an eyewitness disciple" (Fox 128–129). Among other things, this scholar says, Matthew's text excludes "the independent witnessing or memoirs which a close disciple would have contributed" (129). Whether or not your appreciation of Matthew's text is affected by this controversy is another matter altogether, of course. [The following two texts provide almost all of the details presented above: Everett Ferguson, ed., *Encyclopedia of Early Christianity,* pp. 588–589, and Robin Lane Fox, *The Unauthorized Version: Truth and Fiction in the Bible, passim.*]

PRE-READING QUESTIONS:

1) Do you have any positive or negative preconceptions about religion in general or about Christianity in particular? If you do, do you think that these preconceptions enhance or undermine your ability to appreciate and understand religious texts? Do you feel that you can interpret or judge the merits of such texts objectively?

2) Do you tend to read religious texts similarly to or differently from the ways in which you tend to read other sorts of texts (such as newspaper articles or works of detective fiction, for example)? What sorts of expectations, if any, do you have prior to your reading a religious text? Do you have similar expectations prior to your reading other kinds of texts?

3) What do you make of the scholarly claims that "[t]he Jesus who was called *Christos,* 'Anointed,' took his title from Middle-Eastern savior-gods like Adonis and Tammuz, born of the Virgin Sea-goddess Aphrodite-Maria (Myrrha), or Ishtar-Mari

(Hebrew Mariamne [*sic*])" and that there were "[e]arlier biblical versions of the same hero" (B. Walker 464)?

CLOSE-READING TIP

Matthew very carefully traces what he sees as Jesus' familial/religious genealogy. Think about why Matthew might cite certain names in this lineage. Consider, for example, the names contained in the following passages: 1:1, 1:2, 1:5–6, 1:15–16, and 1:20–21.

---

1   The book of the genealogy of Jesus Christ, the son of David, the son of Abraham.

2   Abraham was the father of Isaac, and Isaac the father of Jacob, and Jacob the father of Judah and his brothers,

3   and Judah the father of Perez and Zerah by Tamar, and Perez the father of Hezron, and Hezron the father of Ram,[a]

4   and Ram[a] the father of Ammin'adab, and Ammin'adab the father of Nahshon, and Nahshon the father of Salmon,

5   and Salmon the father of Bo'az by Rahab, and Bo'az the father of Obed by Ruth, and Obed the father of Jesse,

6   and Jesse the father of David the king.
And David was the father of Solomon by the wife of Uri'ah,

7   and Solomon the father of Rehobo'am, and Rehobo'am the father of Abi'jah, and Abi'jah the father of Asa,[b]

8   and Asa[b] the father of Jehosh'aphat, and Jehosh'aphat the father of Joram, and Joram the father of Uzzi'ah,

9   and Uzzi'ah the father of Jotham, and Jotham the father of Ahaz, and Ahaz the father of Hezeki'ah,

10   and Hezeki'ah the father of Manas'seh, and Manas'seh the father of Amos,[c] and Amos[c] the father of Josi'ah

11   and Josi'ah the father of Jechoni'ah and his brothers, at the time of the deportation to Babylon.

12   And after the deportation to Babylon: Jechoni'ah was the father of She-al'ti-el,[d] and She-al'ti-el[d] the father of Zerub'babel,

13   and Zerub'babel the father of Abi'ud, and Abi'ud the father of Eli'akim, and Eli'akim the father of Azor,

---

[a]Greek *Aram* [b] Greek *Asaph* [c] Other authorities read *Amon* [d] Greek *Salathiel* [f] Other ancient authorities read *of the Christ*
1.1–17: Lk 3.23–38. 1.3–6: Ruth 4.18–22; 1 Chron 2.1–15. 1.11: 2 Kings 24.14; Jer 27.20. 1.18: Lk 1.26–38. 1.21: Lk 2.21; Jn 1.29; Acts 13.23. 1.23: Is 7.14
[These notes appear in the Revised Standard Version of the Bible.]

14 and Azor the father of Zadok, and Zadok the father of Achim, and Achim the father of Eli'ud,

15 and Eli'ud the father of Elea'zar, and Elea'zar the father of Matthan, and Matthan the father of Jacob,

16 and Jacob the father of Joseph the husband of Mary, of whom Jesus was born, who is called Christ.

17 So all the generations from Abraham to David were fourteen generations, and from David to the deportation to Babylon fourteen generations, and from the deportation to Babylon to the Christ fourteen generations.

18 Now the birth of Jesus Christ[f] took place in this way. When his mother Mary had been betrothed to Joseph, before they came together she was found to be with child of the Holy Spirit;

19 and her husband Joseph, being a just man and unwilling to put her to shame, resolved to divorce her quietly.

20 But as he considered this, behold, an angel of the Lord appeared to him in a dream, saying, "Joseph, son of David, do not fear to take Mary your wife, for that which is conceived in her is of the Holy Spirit;

21 she will bear a son, and you shall call his name Jesus, for he will save his people from their sins."

22 All this took place to fulfil what the Lord had spoken by the prophet:

23 "Behold, a virgin shall conceive and bear a son, and his name shall be called Emman'uel" (which means, God with us).

24 When Joseph woke from sleep, he did as the angel of the Lord commanded him; he took his wife,

25 but knew her not until she had borne a son; and he called his name Jesus. . . .

POST-READING QUESTIONS:

1) Did you find that any of your preconceptions about religion in general or about Christianity in particular affected your ability to appreciate and understand this excerpt from *Matthew*? Were you able to view this text objectively? In light of your present reading experience, do you want to rethink your response(s) to the first and/or second pre-reading questions?

2) Did this selection confirm or alter your understanding of the name "Jesus Christ"? Did it cause you to rethink your response to the third pre-reading question? Did the information contained in or your response to that question affect your reading of this excerpt? In your view, would it have mattered had the Emmanuel who took the names "Jesus Christ" not taken them and, instead, kept his own name, which, according to Matthew, means "God with us" (*Matthew* 1:23)?

3) Why do you think that Matthew begins his gospel by tracing Jesus' (supposed) genealogy? Does this genealogy seem significant either in and of itself or in relation to others found in the Bible (compare, for example, this genealogy to the one in *Genesis* 10:1ff.)?

4) In terms of the importance of names and naming, how would you compare Matthew's text to (or with) Black Elk's?

---

from **The Law of Return**
ALICE BLOCH

"Barbara Bloch, my younger sister, died of leukemia on June 22, 1973, at the age of twenty. Among the things she left me were. . . some of her imagination and spunk, a huge wad of grief, a hole in my life where she had been, and an unfinished project: an article we had planned to write together, describing our experiences during her illness" (ix). So writes Alice Bloch (1947–) in the preface to her book *Lifetime Guarantee* (1981), the completion of (or substitute for?) the "unfinished project" that she and her sister had planned to carry out. Two years after she had published *Lifetime Guarantee,* Bloch published her second book, *The Law of Return,* from which the following reading selection is taken. Also deeply personal, *The Law of Return* is "an autobiographical novel" having to do with the struggles faced by a "devoutly religious Jewish lesbian" who leaves her homeland, the United States, to live in Israel (Em L. White 61). In fact, in 1969 Bloch had interrupted her graduate work in romance studies at Cornell University to live in Israel, where she found both promise and pain, fulfillment and frustration. (N.B.: The "Law of Return" was "[t]he very first law passed by the Knesset [Israel's Parliament] after Israel[ ]" became a state. . . . This law "guarantees all Jews the right to emigrate to Israel and claim immediate citizenship" [Telushkin 333].)

Presently a technical writer who has also "published articles, commentaries, and poetry in several feminist and lesbian periodicals[,]" Bloch has not produced another book since 1983, though she is currently working on a novel (White 61). If the quality of the writing in this forthcoming novel matches that which we find in her previous books, then once again Bloch will have given us the pleasure of reading a text whose words—with their "'unusual richness and texture'" (Beck, qtd. in White 63)—remind us that we are in the presence of a truly gifted writer.

PRE-READING QUESTIONS:

1) Have you ever thought much about why a person might want to change her or his given name(s)? Have you yourself ever wanted to change your name(s)? Keep your reflections in mind as you read the following excerpt, watching to see whether or not—and, if so, how, why, and to what extent—they affect your understanding of or reactions to Bloch's text.

2) Have you ever felt that you didn't quite fit in where you live, that perhaps you belonged somewhere else?

3) In terms of cultural and ethnic diversity, do you consider the United States a melting pot, a quilt, or something else altogether?

4) In your view, does the act of naming have the same significance for women as it has for men? Might this matter be culture-specific?

5) Knowing that you are about to read an excerpt from a novel, are you expecting to take what you read with the proverbial "grain of salt"?

CLOSE-READING TIP

As you read this excerpt, you'll come across passages which directly or indirectly address how the main character thinks and feels about people who either influence or intimidate her. Try to see whether or not an understanding of these passages helps you better understand the character's struggles with her personal identity. Consider, for example, representative passages in paragraphs 3, 28, 32, 34, and 39.

---

1 . . . A young woman hugs her parents goodbye at the Pittsburgh airport. "See you next month," she says. She boards an El Al airplane.

2   It is 1969, so the young woman still thinks of herself as a girl. She has just graduated from the University of Wisconsin, with a B.A. in French, and has been accepted for graduate school at Berkeley. She has saved enough money from summer jobs to take this summer trip to Israel.

3   Israel never interested her much until a year ago, when a boyfriend told her she should go to Israel, she would like it there. The same boyfriend told her she should go to Berkeley, she would like it there too. She had never gone to bed with anyone else, so he had a certain power over her at the time. He soon moved on to a new girlfriend, and she retaliated by finding someone else to go to bed with, and then someone else, so that the first affair would seem less important—but nonetheless, she is on her way to Israel for the summer.

. . .

4   She is in Jerusalem, city of stone and light, narrow cobbled streets and walls within walls. A wall of sound surrounds her: *sh* and *tz* and *kh* and *im,* all around her the strange noises and familiar voices. The voices holler and grate and whisper and complain and praise and *shekket Shekket SHEKKET!* a shriek from a window over the café where she sits. She is afraid. What does *shekket* mean? go to hell goddamn brat police divorce? The waitress laughs: "She shouts for quiet. *Shekket.* Such a noisy word."

5   A noisy word, a noisy world. The intimate new voices mimic her ancestors, initiate her to a landscape of rough sound and sleek vowel, rough stone and smooth tile floor, clay and sandstone consonants sticking in the

ear, straining her throat when she tries to imitate these sounds without meaning, guttural and sheer, nonsense syllables of rock and rough bark and golden scrolls, vowels of braided bread and consonants of goat cheese, vowels of *shabbat* and consonants of *ḥol,* a week of magic in every word, not even words yet the sounds rise and fall without separation, a song of creation and origin, the first marsh of sound before separation of light from dark, before separation of water from water, before separation of water from land, before names and meanings, before the braided candles of *havdalah.* The original language, nothing but sound, the swirling music of air.

. . .

6 That language, that city pulled on me like gravity. I needed to learn Hebrew, I needed to live in Jerusalem. The longing I felt was as simple and instinctive as my longing, a year earlier, for a lover to touch my body.

7 For me, at that time, there was no separating the land, the language, and the religion. I wanted all three, and to me they were one. *Sliḥa,* the solemn word of atonement, the word of Yom Kippur, the prayer for forgiveness: I learned to say this same word when I bumped into someone in the street. To use Biblical words everyday made everyday life holy, made me want to acknowledge every day's holiness through my people's ancient religious practices, in my people's ancient city, in my people's ancient tongue.

8 I saw no contradiction, no inconsistency then. It was simple, this religious urge of the senses, as simple as the need for body against body.

. . .

9 "You are Jewish?"

10 "Yes."

11 "You can be a citizen right now, under the Law of Return, or you can be a temporary resident for a maximum of three years, and then you must become a citizen. Which do you want?"

12 "Temporary resident, please."

13 "Last name?"

14 "Rogin."

15 "First name?"

16 "Ellen."

17 "Ellen? You don't have a Hebrew name, maybe, from when you were born?"

18 "Yes. Elisheva. But everyone has always called me Ellen, even my parents."

19 "Everyone *here* will call you Elisheva." The clerk looks at her an instant, his eyebrows raised—if she wishes to protest, this is the opportunity; then he writes something on her identity card. "Father's first name?"

20 "Arthur. Wait. . . Asher in Hebrew."

21   "Asher. *B'seder.*" He passes the card across the desk. "Now you must sign at the bottom."

22   She stares at the card. She can read nothing, recognizes only the cheap photograph of her own face at the top: hair hanging limp and straight, partially covering one eye; the other eyebrow puny, from the time she overplucked, and the hairs never grew back, so that she now looks perpetually surprised; the white sunglass ridge over the nose; the nose itself, already burned darker than the rest of the face, as if singled out by the strong sun of Israel; the cheeks rounder than she would like; the half-smile she wears when she is uncertain what is expected of her.

23   "I can't sign my name in Hebrew."

24   "So sign in the other alphabet."

25   "How do you spell 'Elisheva'?" She signs letter by letter, as he spells for her. The result, her own name in her own handwriting, looks like what it is: a word she is learning to spell.

. . .

26   "You are Jewish?"

27   Nowhere else in the world is it safe to answer that question. I think I knew it even then, knew I was the first Rogin to feel no fear when an immigration official asked that question.

28   As for the Lowenthals, my mother's family—well, the Israeli clerk asked nothing about them. Did I notice at the time? Or did I accept as normal his exclusive interest in Asher/Arthur/Dad? Perhaps I noticed but was glad he didn't ask Mother's name, Clara, because I had no Hebrew alternative to offer, the American Lowenthals having been American for so many generations. And as for the European Lowenthals, the stubborn ones who hadn't crossed a border since the Middle Ages, who tarried in Berlin until there was no leaving by choice: I must assume they had reasons more powerful than the fear of Ellis Island inspectors.

29   It was one of those Ellis Island fellows who bestowed the name Rogin on my grandfather. In Lithouania the name had been Roginsky. A volunteer interpreter spelled the name in American letters for the inspector, and at "n" the inspector said, "That's long enough."

30   So I probably could have taken back Roginsky while I was at it, but what was the point? "Roginsky" was the whim of some other Christian official, a few hundred years ago when all the Jews were suddenly required to take last names. One Christian official gives a name and another takes part of the name away: what does any of it have to do with me?

31   But Elisheva, the name I didn't even know how to spell in English or Hebrew—this name goes all the way back to the Torah; this name has been in my father's family as long as anyone can remember. I was named after my father's sister, who died in 1946; she was named after her grandmother, who died in 1910; she was named after her aunt, who died in 1845.

32   Nowhere else in the world has an immigration official ever restored a Jew's original name, her claim to history. Nowhere else in the world, when she has answered "yes" to the question "Are you Jewish?" does the man behind the desk reply, "In that case you must become a citizen."

. . .

33   Assimilation has scarred me more than I ever imagined. Parts of name lopped off like the nose job I never had. Elisheva to Ellen, Roginsky to Rogin (the next step is Rogers). Ah yes, the last name has its significance, too. "Sky" is what they removed. They took the whole goddamn sky away from us.

34   Those girls in the cafeteria line at school, talking about whether Jews are damned to hell. Yes, they decided. I just listened.

35   I wish I'd had the name Elisheva then. It would have done them good to try to pronounce it. Those girls, and Mrs. Gallagher the French teacher who couldn't even pronounce French, let alone Hebrew, and Billy Williams Jr., my first date.

36   "Rogin. What kind of name is that?"

37   "Jewish."

38   They always looked surprised when I said it straight out. After my grandfather died I considered going back to Roginsky in his honor. I told Mrs. Gallagher of my intention. She was my favorite teacher, accent or no, and her job was to introduce Americans to a foreign culture. I thought she might understand.

39   "Oh, I don't think you should change your name, Ellen," she said. "People will have trouble. . . remembering it."

40   Well sure, none of them are used to having to remember anything. No other language or two or three from a couple of generations ago. No other language to learn for prayers except the Catholics. I recall thinking, maybe that's why the Protestants name their kids after themselves when the parents are still alive: so they won't have to memorize a new name. And Billy Williams Jr. even had the same name first and last, no strain at all.

41   I thought such things, but I knew better than to say them. To say them would mean I was conceited, obnoxious, improper, loud. In short, too Jewish.

42   And then later I was glad I hadn't said those things about poor Billy, who enlisted in the Marines and never came back from Vietnam. If only he'd waited a few years, gone to college like my brother Neil. By the time Neil was up for the lottery, I was a draft counselor and he got out on a trumped-up medical exemption. I would have been glad to help Billy too, even though I never went out with him again after that one date.

43   I suppose in some grotesque way, Billy lives on in my eyebrows. It was for the date with Billy that I plucked out the bushy centers, which I thought looked too Jewish, and in plucking, I permanently damaged the roots. . . .

POST-READING QUESTIONS:

1) Did the ideas that you articulated in your responses to the first and fifth pre-reading questions affect your understanding of or help shape your reactions to

Bloch's text? Did this reading selection cause you to reexamine these or others of your pre-reading ideas or expectations?

2) Given your understanding of her ideas about culture and ethnicity, how do you think that Ellen/Elisheva would answer the second and third pre-reading questions? Before answering this question, reflect upon Ellen/Elisheva's feelings about living in Israel rather than in America and consider that, earlier in the chapter from which this excerpt is taken, she says, "America is my birthplace, Israel my homeland, nowhere my home."

3) Does the reading selection seem either to support or to undermine the idea expressed in the quotation cited at the end of the previous post-reading question? Does it both support and undermine this idea?

4) How do you think that Ellen/Elisheva might evaluate your responses to some or all of the pre-reading questions?

5) How do you think that Cisneros, Black Elk, Matthew, and Bloch might evaluate each other's ideas concerning both the significance of names and naming and the relationship among personal names, personal identity, and cultural or ethnic identity?

HANDS-ON ACTIVITY:

While working on this chapter in an attempt to improve upon your ability to read carefully, you probably experienced at least some moments of frustration. You can imagine, then, how those people must feel who on a daily basis are reminded of their inability to read *at all,* let alone *carefully.* Lacking even the most basic reading skills, many of these functionally illiterate people cannot read the simplest signs—such as those in department store windows—that you yourself can probably read in a matter of seconds. To help such people overcome their often devastating problem of illiteracy, volunteer to work for a literacy project in your community. You can probably obtain information on such a project from either your school's library or your community's public library.

"You don't wait all day for a freeway to clear when there are other roads that will get you to your destination. The point of commuting is to get there, not to worry about the best route."

WILLIAM STRONG
Writing Incisively

Prewriting Your Way to a First Draft

WHEN ASKED TO identify their anxieties about writing, many students respond that, among other things, they worry that they will have nothing—or nothing of value—to say. In the world of academics, this fear cannot be taken lightly, since so much of a student's work involves writing. Fortunately, though, most cases of writer's block—often writer's paralysis—can be prevented or cured. This chapter is intended to help you either avoid having this problem or, if you do run into it, move beyond it.

More important than anything else, keep in mind that, like Rome, your final essay product need not be built in a day. And know that, at some point during the writing process, all writers struggle to generate ideas. Commonly, though, writer's block occurs at the beginning of the writing process, during the **predrafting** phase (some composition instructors refer to this period as the **precomposing** phase), when the writer is collecting ideas for writing but hasn't actually begun to create any written drafts yet. All such reading, thinking, and writing that you'll do in this initial phase of the writing process comes under the banner of **prewriting**, a term denoting primarily the thinking, reading, and writing that a writer does prior to actually writing a paper (though one can prewrite during any phase of the writing process). We might say that prewriting allows writers to think and write their way into the drafts of their papers.

Prewriting activities can be as formal as the making of a formal outline or as informal as the devising of shorthand notes. And they can be creative: you might find that you get your writing juices flowing by writing a sequel to a short story that you are reading or by writing a letter to someone who somehow is connected to or figures prominently in the project about which you are going to write. For example, you might write to the author of a novel that deeply moved you or the writer of a newspaper article whose content riled you; in some circumstances, you might even decide to send your letter to the person in question. Prewriting can even involve nothing more than your (1) thinking about what the writing assignment calls for and what you *might* want to say in response to it and (2) jotting down some thoughts concerning what items of interest you can find in the material, how you react to this material, and how much you know or need to find out about the subject matter.

Not all writers use the same prewriting techniques, and often the same writer might use certain prewriting techniques at one time and others at another time. Many writers keep a notebook or journal containing ideas for writing; some of these notebooks, such as those kept by the philosopher Friedrich Nietzsche in the early 1870s, are filled with such important and relatively complete information that they've been published as texts in and of themselves. Isaac Bashevis Singer, a Nobel laureate in literature, used to keep a small note pad with him, in which he would jot down ideas as they came to him; later, he would see how he might use some of these ideas in his formal writing. Most experienced writers generate ideas in whatever way strikes them at the moment—however the inspiration hits them.

In short, there are no rules governing how writers should collect ideas for writing. But in some way all writers *do* collect ideas for writing, whether they do so in the margins of their books, in their notebooks, on scraps of paper, on a restaurant's paper napkins, in reading journals, in diaries or personal journals, on tape, on pads of writing paper, at their typewriter, at their computer, or in their heads. Part of the writing process, then, involves the writer's consciously *thinking as a writer* as much as possible, collecting and stowing away an ever-expanding set of prewriting ideas. When you look at the sky, think about how you would describe and write about what you see (or don't see), and perhaps how you might use this bit of information in a hypothetical or real paper. When you are riding on a bus, imagine how other passengers could become models for characters in a short story. Whether or not your description of the sky or of the characters on the bus yields fruit later, engaging in such ongoing prewriting activities will help you keep yourself practiced at the art of reading the world, enabling you to see it as textual material for your own prose. Writers are forever prewriting. Why not join the club?

Don't worry if you come up with far more material than you'll ever use in your papers, or if some of what you come up with amounts to little more than clichés, hyperbole, and the like. From time to time, all writers think of less-than-profound ideas, and all writers accumulate material that they hope no one will ever see. That's just part of the territory in writing. In your college papers, you probably will use some of your ongoing collection of ideas and disregard others. But even if you can put pen to paper only three or four days in a given week, if you think as a writer more or less all of the time—if, in effect, you are more or less always prewriting—you will be collecting information that you otherwise might have overlooked and that might benefit your work. The more comfortable you become with prewriting, the more confident you should feel about writing and revising your essays. And that confidence should lead you, in turn, to accept the following threefold notion that probably *all* experienced writers accept: that writing is always writing-in-progress; that at some point you simply have to let go of your writing, even if you feel dissatisfied with it and have invested yourself in it; and that a "finished product" sometimes represents little or nothing more than the best that the writer could produce under the circumstances.

As you experiment with using different predrafting techniques, you might find that one technique works well in one instance but does not work quite so well in another. Don't be alarmed if this happens, for sometimes even the most skilled writers discover that they must employ different predrafting techniques at different times, depending upon their moods, their reasons for writing, the nature of the material, the extent of their knowledge about or interest in the subject matter, and so on. Writers need room to write, both physically and psychologically; as much as they need a place in which to write comfortably and undisturbed, they need to feel free to choose whatever predrafting techniques will help them generate ideas so that they can explore the depths of their own creativity, interests, and knowledge.

As a writer, then, you should feel free to use whichever technique proves most valuable at the time. If, while moving from one phase of the writing process to another, you discover that using a particular writing tool impedes rather than helps your efforts to produce good work, toss it aside and replace it with an apparatus that facilitates your attempts to write a good paper. Focusing on *formally* "getting things right" with a prewriting or writing technique can harm your writing as much as, at the beginning of the writing process, focusing too much on the final product can. In both cases, you'll likely compromise your ability to write a good essay. In the final analysis, prewriting and writing techniques are useful only to the extent that they help you become a better, more confident writer.

In sum, whether they are writing a work of fiction or of nonfiction, writers tend to use whatever prewriting (and writing) techniques inspire them at the time to generate and expand upon their ideas. Like reading, writing is a fluid activity, one open to and often made exciting because of the different approaches that different writers bring to it. Short of engaging in illicit or otherwise troublesome behavior, during any phase of the writing process you should feel free to do any kind of prewriting activity that you think will help you write.

. . .

Whenever you write, try not to move from one phase of the writing process to another until you feel ready to do so. Somewhat like an athlete who knows what could happen were she to play before she had a chance to warm up, ideally you don't want to engage in later-phase writing until you feel at least relatively secure about the work that you've accomplished in previous phases (hence, all the *more* reason to begin your writing tasks as early as possible!). To show you how you yourself might carefully work through some initial phases of your own writing projects, I'll play the role of "Eddy," a college student who, faced with a dilemma in response to which he needs to carry out a common writing task, uses **freewriting, charting,** and **clustering**—three relatively easy-to-use predrafting techniques—to help him generate and organize some ideas for his writing. (Remember that these and other prewriting techniques might prove useful both at the beginning of and throughout the writing process.) After Eddy completes his prewriting work, he'll create a first draft whose contents are based upon his predrafting ideas.

Rather than produce an academic essay, Eddy will eventually write a personal letter. I've selected a non-classroom-based writing task as the focal point of our study for two reasons: (1) you'll have a chance to see how a writer prewrites his way into a first draft of a classroom-oriented writing task when you study the work of this chapter's contributing author; and (2) I want to stress the point that writing is neither essentially nor exclusively classroom-based. What's important is that you begin to understand how, using the *process* of prewriting, you can help yourself gain insight into your material so that you can successfully reach the destination of a final writing *product*, whether that product is a formal essay, a business report, or even a personal letter. In fact, once you feel comfortable using prewriting techniques, you might discover that they can help you generate ideas for nonwriting tasks, too, such as some talks that you might want to have first with your dormitory assistant and then with your dormmates concerning the latter's playing of loud music during quiet hours. The point is not that you yourself necessarily *should* use prewriting to help you think through your non-classroom-based work, but that you *can* do so, and that doing so could often turn out to be more helpful than you initially might have thought. As suggested earlier in the chapter, writers prewrite even when they don't have immediate plans to use their prewriting material.

Freewriting

Of the many convenient and easy ways for people to **brainstorm** their ideas, students seem to favor none more than freewriting. Among the reasons explaining this common feeling, perhaps the simplest is that, when one freewrites, one cannot really make a mistake, for even mistakes are considered appropriate in freewriting. Thus, one who freewrites should be able literally to write *freely*, which means that, everything else being equal, one should be able to come up with *something* to say.

Perhaps you'll understand the nature and function of freewriting most easily if you consider it analogous to the psychoanalytic technique of free association. When he free-associates, an "analysand"—that is, a person in analysis—is either given a series of words to respond to as briefly and quickly as possible or is asked merely to talk freely about an issue, a problem, a dream, and so forth (sometimes, analysands are asked to do some combination of both approaches). Presumably, the process of free-associating will help the analysand avoid running into the barriers erected by his unconscious, whose psychological censoring apparatus purportedly blocks his ability to reach the depths of his feelings and, subsequently, to understand what these feelings mean.

Similarly, people engaged in freewriting write without interruption and without worrying about matters of form, style, grammar, organization, the development of their ideas, and the like. Freewriting thus allows the writer to create and develop thoughts that might have been impeded had she worried about such matters. Though at a certain point the writer must think carefully about what she wants and needs to say or avoid saying in her paper, if at the beginning of the writing process she worries too much about whether or not she's "getting things right," then, like the analysand, she might miss opportunities to generate the very ideas—often seemingly insignificant or unrelated at first—that she needs to analyze, develop further, connect, or otherwise investigate (and perhaps revise).

On the other hand, although you will want to avoid self-censure when you freewrite, you'll need to set up *some* guidelines for yourself before you begin freewriting. For one thing, you'll need to decide whether you will write in freehand or use a typewriter or computer (if at all possible, always choose the mode of transcribing your thoughts and feelings that will allow you to freewrite most easily). And since you'll not be able to freewrite indefinitely, you'll also need to decide upon a minimum page or time limit. Though you'll want to give yourself permission to write freely for as long as necessary, until you are used to doing this activity you shouldn't try freewriting for too long; otherwise, you might become frustrated and decide to quit. Generally, you should be able to write fairly easily for a page or so or for about five minutes; as you freewrite, allow yourself more space or time if you need to keep writing, but don't hold yourself to a prearranged plan whose projected outcomes might very well be beyond your present capabilities. Here's a good rule of thumb: Before you freewrite, plan on doing less; as you freewrite, strive to do more.

Additionally, you should decide in advance either to freewrite without stopping or to pause *briefly* from time to time to collect your thoughts. If you do the latter, don't pause for too long or make too many corrections and changes, or else you'll be doing something other than freewriting. As much as possible, you'll want to **keep writing,** copying words and sentences over and over again if necessary. Sometimes, you'll easily tap into your store of ideas or break through your resistances in order to reach more hidden thoughts and feelings. At other times, you'll have difficulty sounding the depths and probing the limits of your ideas and emotions. In either case, when freewriting, you should always **push on** as much as possible. Your goal should be to finish the freewriting journey itself, for this journey in and of itself might very well prove to be an integral part of your writing project's promise and fulfillment.

Finally, to free up your store of ideas, you might freewrite without *any* prompt whatsoever, or you might begin your freewriting by free-associating about a specific term or by providing an extended, uninterrupted (even if disjointed) answer to a particular question related to the writing task. For instance, if for your history class you need to write an essay in which you analyze the meaning(s) of the clause "all men are created equal," you might decide simply to begin freewriting and then see what ideas you produce, or you might decide to freewrite for a page or so or for about five minutes in response to the terms "men," "sexism," "patriarchy," "democracy," "feminism," "founding fathers," and so on. Or, you might begin with a question such as "Was Jefferson referring to both men and women when he wrote the *Declaration of Independence*?" and then proceed to answer this question by freewriting according to a predetermined time or page limit.

When you are engaged in freewriting, you ultimately ought to discover that, with the usual constraints lifted, you can generate ideas and make connections rather easily, even if these ideas and connections seem disorganized or chaotic at best. What you eventually do or don't do with this mass of ideas and associative connections is another matter. Perhaps your freewriting will eventuate in very promising and fruitful writing; perhaps it will remain among the remnants of a writing task that ended in midstream. Maybe you'll freewrite more than once for a particular writing task and in your subsequent prewriting or writing activities use selected material from some or all of your freewriting efforts. If nothing else, after you have produced some freewriting, you will have in front of you a sheet or more of paper clearly showing that, your other worries about writing notwithstanding, you do in fact have something to say.

Let's now consider Eddy's dilemma and then take a look at the actual freewrite that I (acting as Eddy) produced in response to a relevant prompt. Recently, Eddy received a letter from his parents asking that he accompany them on this year's family vacation—a trip to Tahiti—which they have scheduled for the middle of October, when Eddy is still in school. They've asked him to write to them in a week or so to let them know whether or not he will join them; legitimately, they want to purchase the cheapest airline tickets, be sure that the hotel can accommodate everyone in their party, and so on. Eddy wants to make the right decision, but he isn't entirely sure what the right decision is. Experiencing a rush of sometimes confusing and conflicting ideas and feelings, he decides to freewrite for about five minutes in response to the prompt "Should I or Shouldn't I Go? That is the Question."

Freewriting

"Should I or Shouldn't I Go? That is the Question."

O brother, I'm really glad I get tho have this particular choice now. I'm really cglad that I' was consulted about what to do, where to go, when to go , etc. Okay. I need to get down to business. What if i go? What would happen if that happens? I mean, I don'[t want to hurt their feelings, but what if, o I cannot miss that many classes. What i am I saying? Of course, on the other hand, the chance to go to Tahiti is probpably once in a lifetime, whell, not really once in a lifetime, but I'd really like to go. I[d like to be with the family, but i would really rather not. Of course, the really important matter at this point is the fact that i would be forced to miss too many clases. How can i do that? Why didn';t they think of that/ are they really asking me honestly or do they think that they're just having ot ask me and then their responsibility is ove with Im not sure anyway back to the question there are lots of pros and cons well, actually there are really more cons than pros a I think, anyway, i would like to see this place and to see if it for free is really a special treat, I don[t know when I'll have this chance again. Once I start med school, who knows? Med school! Are you kidding:? If I go on this trip, I'll miss my exams, and that will mean that' I'll flunk out of school, or at least that I'll fail my courses, and that will mean that I can kill kiss my GPA goodbuy and that will mean bonkers for me. Okay, it's pretty clear that I am not gooing to be able to go, so how do I break the news to them? Am i or should -i say it in a way How can I say it without hurting their feelings?

. . .

What you see above is a freewrite that I produced in about five minutes. Looking it over, I see that I've made quite a lot of typographical errors and offered quite a few revealing insights into my own struggles with this issue. Additionally, I can see without any trouble that my sentences are not exactly models of great grammar and style. In advance, I decided that I would allow myself to pause only briefly, if necessary, and that I would delete as little as possible during the freewrite (in fact, I revised only a few words as I typed). Knowing that I might uncover insights if I pushed on, I decided just to let the freewriting take its course. Thus I created—and *allowed myself to create*—more or less uncontrolled, disorganized, and unfocused writing reflecting a thought pattern that resembles the kind of free-flowing, stream-of-consciousness, tangential thinking that we normally do from moment to moment rather than the sort of controlled, organized, focused thinking that I strive for when I revise my writing.

But none of this worries me, because I know that the intent of this freewriting exercise was merely to help me generate some early, predraft ideas concerning the issue at hand, ideas that I can then organize and develop (or dismiss altogether) in subsequent phases of the writing process. At this point, I'm unconcerned about the substance or appearance of the paper's final or even first draft, for I'm not yet in the drafting phase of my writing project. Nor am I concerned that I don't yet have a **thesis**—that is, a main assertion concerning the subject matter, in this case the point that I'll try to put forth and defend in my letter—since I don't yet know how I'll form my ideas into a reasonable response. What I do know is that whatever revised, relatively "cleaned-up" final product I might eventually produce will in many ways be an illusion of my actual *thinking* concerning the issue under consideration. The prewriting that I've shown you above, besides being quite telling for me personally, rather honestly represents the *process* of my present free-flowing thinking and writing about this issue.

Charting

Charting is another predrafting technique that helps writers generate and organize their ideas for writing. Although it can be used instead of, in addition to, prior to, or after freewriting, somewhat arbitrarily I decided in advance that I would use it after I had done some freewriting. I felt that, by charting the ideas produced in (and by) my freewriting, I might help my thinking begin to achieve a sense of cohesion, organization, and direction; of course, I also could have engaged in additional freewriting both to generate more ideas and to see if any of my present ideas would change. As expected, you yourself will have to experiment not only with different prewriting techniques, but also with using different prewriting techniques at different times and in different chronological arrangements in order to find out both the techniques and the combination and arrangement of prewriting strategies that work best for you.

Charts come in many forms. If you studied biology in school, you probably used rectangular or square charts to discover the likelihood of a child's being born with particular genetic traits such as hair or eye color. If you've ever dieted, most likely you've seen more than your share of charts concerning food groups, calorie intake, percentages of fats from certain foods, and the like—not to mention the various goals that you might want to set for yourself according to any number of charted factors. Indeed, from work schedules to appointment calendars to product labels, charts seem to be everywhere.

The particular kind of chart that we're going to focus on here might best be understood as a **comparison chart**; its chief function is to allow the person constructing it to see at a glance how different items compare with (or to) each other. This is the sort of chart that you might use when you draw up a list of pros and cons, strengths and weaknesses, and so on. Let's take a look at the following comparison chart to see how it helps me organize some of the ideas that I produced in my freewrite, ideas that, I'm beginning to sense, Eddy might want to focus on in his letter:

PROS	CONS
a paid vacation	will miss classes
a beautiful place to visit	will miss exams
might be only chance to see Tahiti	
a chance to be with family	will be with family
might meet someone with whom I can have fun	if my girlfriend finds out. . . !

Now, to be sure, this is only one charting possibility, and an incomplete one at that. But it should suffice to help you see how you might use charting to (1) generate and organize your thoughts either before you begin drafting them or while you are in the process of drafting them and (2) begin organizing selected material from a previous prewriting activity such as freewriting. When using a technique such as charting to help you with your writing, don't worry about getting the form "right." Notice that the first two pro and con items in my comparison chart are not parallel, but that the last two are. I'm not at all concerned about this configuration, because I am merely trying to see whether or not *any* sort of thematic organization, *any* pattern of ideas, is emerging from my thinking.

To develop some of these charted thoughts further, I could continue literally charting the course of my decision; I could freewrite; I could create an informal, annotated outline; in short, I could employ any number of prewriting strategies (of course, I could also begin drafting my letter, prewriting if and when necessary during the drafting phase of my writing). However, Eddy is becoming a bit restless. Wanting to see how he might expand upon and further organize some of his ideas in order to develop them into a cohesive whole, he has decided to use the prewriting technique known as clustering, which is tailor-made for the job.

Clustering

Like charting, clustering can be used at any phase during the writing process to help writers generate and organize their ideas (and like all prewriting techniques, it need not be used exclusively in the service of classroom-based writing projects). When writers use clustering, they configure spatial groupings or extensions of ideas in order to see which ideas go together, which are plentiful and related enough to hold promise for an extended analysis, and so on. Clustering is akin to the prewriting activity of freewriting, in that it involves something on the order of free-associating, though the free-associating that writers do while clustering their ideas is usually less spontaneous and more controlled than is the free-associating that they do during their freewrites. Clustering also is akin to the prewriting technique of charting, which tends to help writers both generate and organize their ideas (brainstorming techniques such as freewriting often prove to be more helpful as *generative* rather than as *organizational* activities). Given clustering's multiple uses, some writing instructors and students find it to be a marvelous prewriting technique. Other instructors and students, however, find clustering a confusing activity; in fact, a number of people with poor spatial orientation feel disoriented by this method of predrafting. In the worst cases, they feel as if they have a writing equivalent of the bends. As usual, you yourself will have to judge how effective this technique is for *you*.

Its possible downside notwithstanding, let's find out if, by using the technique of clustering to extend the thinking that manifests itself in the comparison chart displayed above, Eddy can literally see whether or not he should accept his parents' invitation. Though he could create a cluster for each item listed in this chart, as well as for any items that result from, that branch off from, such clustering, he has decided to cluster some ideas around one major concern that surfaced in the two previous prewriting activities and that, he is strongly hinting to me, seems to be central to his decision-making:

As you can see, clustering is something on the order of spatially configured language. Considering what we observe in *this* clustering of ideas, you and I might reasonably infer (or induce) that, being a conscientious student, Eddy has probably decided not to join his family on this year's family vacation. Now, the question is, what will he tell his parents? How can he use the material derived from the prewriting activities to help him put together a good letter to them? In other words, how would a letter reflect the ideas that these prewriting techniques have helped him generate and begin to organize?

Writing a First Draft

In a sense, a first draft is similar to a formal freewrite. Like a freewrite, a first draft gives the writer the freedom to lay out some ideas for writing without also obliging her to produce the sort of cohesive, coherent prose that she'll hope to construct in a final draft. On the other hand, whereas in a freewrite the writer might not worry about collating any ideas, in a first draft she'll at least want to collate them loosely. Further, although in a freewrite she might omit conventional paragraphing and not pay the slightest heed to grammar and syntax, in a first draft she'll probably—even if roughly—separate different ideas into different paragraphs and concentrate a bit on formal sentence structure. In other words, her first draft probably will cohere to some degree, even if many of its ideas, like many of the ideas in her freewrites, seem a bit scattered.

Remember that, as suggested at the beginning of this chapter, ordinarily you shouldn't have to complete a writing project in one day—at least not if you've allocated your time well. Under normal circumstances, then, you should construct your first draft merely with the intention of creating a *working* rather than a *final* draft of your ideas. Though you would obviously suit your writing interests well were you to create a first draft containing grammatically correct and stylistically elegant prose, as well as fully developed, coherent, and unified paragraphs, you shouldn't pressure yourself to achieve such results right away. Everything else being equal, you'll not likely damage your chances of writing a good final draft if you wait until a later phase of the writing process to work on creating sophisticated sentences and paragraphs.

On the other hand, even in this early drafting phase, you'll want to begin narrowing your focus and creating some sort of narrative flow. Though you don't want to restrict your field of vision too much, by the same token you don't want to begin drafting your paper with so wide a field of vision that you leave yourself feeling out of control with your writing. If you aren't sure how to begin focusing your essay for the first draft, then perhaps you should do some more predrafting, which, again, is meant to help you both generate as many ideas as possible *and* begin organizing these ideas into a coherent mass. Eddy wouldn't want to begin his letter to his parents, for example, with unwieldy and ultimately extraneous material that he is then obligated to talk about, such as the wonder of modern travel; historical meetings or clashes between culturally different peoples; the nature of parental guidance and support; or some version of the "ever since the beginning of time" disease, which has proved fatal to many otherwise promising pieces of writing. Such commentary will hardly meet the reading needs of his parents, who are his intended audience. At best, it will likely do little, if anything, to help them see the *substantive* value of his letter; at worst, it could make them suspicious of both his motives and his ideas.

If you feel ready to do so, try offering a thesis in your first draft and then try proving or supporting this thesis throughout the rest of the draft. Think about the dominant point for which you want to argue—that's your thesis. Try to organize the rest of your points around this dominant idea, keeping your paper focused as narrowly as possible. If as or after you write your first draft you discover that you need to change your thesis or to rethink or reorganize your ideas, feel free to do so. Remember that you are simply trying to create a blueprint of a paper that, however roughly sketched, begins to configure your perspective on the important matters at stake. You have full authority to redesign this drafting document as often as necessary, or at least until the deadline for submission arrives. (Note: If for your first draft you will be offering a thesis and then at least *attempting* to support or prove it, you might find it helpful to read the section in Chapter Five entitled "Deriving your main point from your close examination of evidence" [p. 135] before you begin composing your initial draft.)

Let's take a look at the first draft of Eddy's letter to his parents, one whose contents derive, at least in part, from the material that he generated by doing the above prewriting activities. As you yourself will probably want to do in at least some of your papers, he tries to ease his audience into the letter's overall theme. Then, after telling them his decision, he offers them reasons that he hopes will convince them that his thinking is sound (whether or not they are entirely comfortable with his decision is another matter altogether). He tries to narrow the letter's focus, concentrating on developing and expanding upon one principal point (I must confess, though, that I'm unsure whether or not he also offers a clearly stated thesis. See what you think.) Here, then, is the next product of Eddy's work-in-progress:

Dear Mom and Dad,

I want to thank you for your generous and tempting offer to take me with you and the family to Tahiti. I always wanted to go there, and I don't know when I'll have the chance to go—if ever—if I don't go there with you in October. Such a beautiful place! And a free vacation (just kidding—not really, though). But, unfortunately, I'm going to have to say no. As much as I'd like to go, I just can't afford to miss that many classes. Besides, I have exams that week, and my profs. won't let us make up missed exams. "Too bad," they said. "If you're that bad off that you have to miss an exam, you should probably drop out of school." Nice folks, huh? Anyway, if I miss my exams, then I'll fail my courses, and my GPA will be ruined—and you will have wasted your money.

You see, I'm beginning to realize that in college you're expected to attend classes or take your lumps. One of those lumps is that we can't make up missed exams. And if I miss my exams, then I probably can kiss med school good-bye. Besides, my profs. won't write letters for me if I flake off in their classes, which is how they'll judge me if I miss their stupid exams.

Sorry, Mom and Dad! I know how into family vacations you are, but I also know how much you want me to do well in school. So, I'm hoping that you'll understand my decision. If you don't, I'm sure you'll let me know.

Anyway, gotta go now. Give my love to Susie, and tell her that I'll write to her soon—the little squirt!

Love,
Eddy

When Eddy looks this letter over to see whether or not he should revise it (and, if so, *how* he should change it), maybe he'll decide to drop the part about his parents' wasting their money. Maybe he'll decide to say more about the consequences that would likely follow were he to miss his classes and exams. Maybe he'll lessen the melodrama about his GPA, adopt a different tone of voice, wear a different persona mask, and the like. The point is, he now has the beginnings of a working draft of his letter, and he still has lots of predrafting material waiting in the wings.

The next chapter explains in some detail what you'll need to think about when you are ready to move beyond a first draft. Ultimately, you might decide to use prewriting techniques such as freewriting, charting, and clustering to refine the thinking and writing that you'll produce in your second and subsequent drafts. For now, though, you will accomplish quite enough if you try your hand at using these or other prewriting techniques, including those of your own devising, in an attempt to develop a good, working, first draft of a paper, letter to your parents, letter to the editor, or other piece of writing. Though the steps in writing are not straightforward, you would do well to try taking them one at a time.

READING AND WRITING

This chapter's reading selections center on a horrendous event known as The Holocaust. Increasingly, this term is used to describe any number of catastrophes of monumental proportions, such as the slaughtering of the Armenians and Cambodians, for example, and the slaughtering of billions of animals in the food industry. One local newspaper in Southern California even used the term to describe the widespread devastation caused by the fires that ravaged Southern California in 1993. However, the word's primary meaning in the modern age (the word is actually quite old)—the meaning invoked in this chapter—has to do with the Nazis' attempts to destroy European Jews and Jewry. Understood as such, the Holocaust predates the Second World War, with which, nonetheless, it is obviously intertwined. It began in 1933, when Hitler became chancellor of Germany and the first laws and decrees against German Jews were issued, and ended in 1945, when the Allies' defeat of Germany helped put a halt to the systematic persecution of those Jews who had come under Nazi control (though Jews were persecuted even after the war had ended).

The readings that follow touch upon a number of complex and painful issues concerning the Holocaust, forcing us to ask many difficult questions: Why did it occur? How could it have happened? Who was responsible, and how did those responsible feel about what they did? Did anyone try to help? Did anyone resist? What can we say about the victims who died? What can we say about—or to— those who survived? Who *were* the victims? What does the Holocaust teach us about other major tragedies? About the world we live in? About *us*?

Taken together, these readings bring us a bit closer to answering these and similar questions. They also help us to understand, in general, something about victimizers, victims, and their relationship to each other; about people who help create and control social evil and those who are conditioned and controlled by such evil; and about people who oppose evil, sometimes suffering as a result. After studying these pieces, one wonders about the degree to which we ourselves, who inhabit the same world as the victims and perpetrators of the Holocaust, might already be or at some point become like them. In the eyes of many survivors, scholars, and students of the Holocaust, that is perhaps the most frightening question of all that the Holocaust has left in its wake.

FEATURED ASSIGNMENT

Part I: Read Elie Wiesel's essay "Why I Write" and then freewrite for about five minutes on why *you* either (like to) write or don't (like to) write (poetry, diary entries, essays, and so on). Then, use a comparison chart, clustering, or both to help you organize your most important reasons for writing or not writing. Afterwards, construct a first draft of an essay explaining why you (like to) write or don't (like to) write.

Part II: Write a brief reflective commentary on what you experienced, thought, and/or felt while doing this assignment.

FEATURED READING

Why I Write

ELIE WIESEL

Born in 1928 in Sighet, a small Jewish village located in Transylvania, Elie Wiesel spent much of his youth in serious religious study (he remains a profoundly religious person). In 1944, he was deported to Auschwitz, an infamous death, labor, and concentration camp complex. Later, he was transported to the concentration camp Buchenwald, from where American soldiers liberated him and others in April 1945. Having written and worked as a journalist for many years, Wiesel is now the Andrew Mellon Professor in the Humanities at Boston University. A frequent lecturer, he has also written approximately three dozen books, including the award-winning novels *The Testament* and *The Fifth Son*, the scholarly works *Sages and Dreamers* and *A Jew Today*, and his best known work, *Night*, an autobiographical account of his Holocaust experiences. Already honored in 1984 by the United States and French governments, in 1986 Wiesel traveled to Norway to receive one of the highest distinctions in the world: the Nobel Peace Prize, in the citation for which he is described as "a messenger to mankind" whose "message is one of peace and atonement and human dignity."

PRE-READING QUESTIONS:

1) Do you have any thoughts or feelings about whether or not survivors of the Holocaust or other tragedies should talk about their own and their fellow victims' experiences? If you do, keep these thoughts and feelings in mind as you read Wiesel's essay, watching to see whether or not—and if so, how, why, and to what extent—they affect your understanding of or reactions to his ideas.

2) Why do you think that some professional writers write essays explaining their reasons for writing? Have you ever felt the need to explain either why you write or why you try to avoid writing?

3) Do you think that you did enough writing in high school? Should all courses—both in high school and in college—require writing?

4) Does your knowing that Wiesel is a Holocaust survivor affect the way in which you are about to read his essay? If Wiesel had been a guard at a concentration camp, would you approach his essay with different expectations from those that you now are bringing to his piece? Would you approach his essay differently if you thought that it was a work of fiction?

CLOSE-READING **TIP**

As you read Wiesel's essay, pay particular attention to those moments when Wiesel directly addresses his role as a writer, his reasons for writing, and his feel for, relationship to, and general understanding of language *per se*, especially his understanding of its rhythms, powers, and limitations. See if you can determine whether or not, for Wiesel, these various matters are causally or emotionally linked.

SELECTION

WIESEL   Why I Write

1   Why do I write? Perhaps in order not to go mad. Or, on the contrary, to touch the bottom of madness.

2   Like Samuel Beckett, the survivor expresses himself "en désespoir de cause,"[1] because there is no other way.

3   Speaking of the solitude of the survivor, the great Yiddish and Hebrew poet and thinker Aaron Zeitlin addresses those who have left him: his father, dead; his brother, dead; his friends, dead: "You have abandoned me," he says to them. "You are together, without me. I am here. Alone. And I make words."

4   So do I, just like him. I also say words, write words, reluctantly.

5   There are easier occupations, far more pleasant ones. But for the survivor, writing is not a profession, but an occupation, a duty. Camus calls it "an honor." As he puts it: "I entered literature through worship." Other writers said: "Through anger, through love." Speaking for myself, I would say: "Through silence."

6   It was by seeking, by probing, silence that I began to discover the perils and power of the word.

7   I never intended to be a philosopher, or a theologian. The only role I sought was that of witness. I believed that, having survived by chance, I was duty-bound to give meaning to my survival, to justify each moment of my life. I knew the story had to be told. Not to transmit an experience is to betray it; this is what Jewish tradition teaches us. But how to do this? "When Israel is in exile, so is the word," says the Zohar. The word has deserted the meaning it was intended to convey—impossible to make them coincide. The displacement, the shift, is irrevocable. This was never more true than right after the upheaval. We all knew that we could never, never say what had to be said, that we could never express in words, coherent, intelligible words, our experience of madness on an absolute scale. The walk through flaming night, the silence before and after the selection, the monotonous praying of the condemned, the Kaddish of the dying, the fear and hunger of the sick, the shame and suffering, the haunted eyes, the demented stares. I thought that I would never be able to speak of them. All words seemed inadequate, worn, foolish, lifeless, whereas I wanted them to be searing. Where was I to discover a fresh vocabulary, a primeval language? The language of night was not human; it was primitive, almost animal—hoarse shouting, screams, muffled moaning, savage howling, the sound of beating. . . . A brute striking wildly, a body falling; an officer raises his arm and a whole community walks toward a common grave; a sol-

---

[1] "As a last resource." (Ed. note)

dier shrugs his shoulders, and a thousand families are torn apart, to be reunited only by death. This is the concentration camp language. It negated all other language and took its place. Rather than link, it became wall. Could it be surmounted? Could the reader be brought to the other side? I knew the answer to be negative, and yet I also knew that "no" had to become "yes." It was the wish, the last will of the dead. One had to break the shell enclosing the dark truth, and give it a name. One had to force man to look.

8   The fear of forgetting: the main obsession of all those who have passed through the universe of the damned. The enemy counted on people's disbelief and forgetfulness. How could one foil this plot? And if memory grew hollow, empty of substance, what would happen to all we had accumulated along the way?

9   Remember, said the father to his son, and the son to his friend. Gather the names, the faces, the tears. If, by a miracle, you come out of it alive, try to reveal everything, omitting nothing, forgetting nothing. Such was the oath we had all taken: "If, by some miracle, I emerge alive, I will devote my life to testifying on behalf of those whose shadow will fall on mine forever and ever."

10   This is why I write certain things rather than others: to remain faithful.

11   Of course, there are times of doubt for the survivor, times when one would give in to weakness, or long for comfort. I hear a voice within me telling me to stop mourning the past. I too want to sing of love and of its magic. I too want to celebrate the sun, and the dawn that heralds the sun. I would like to shout, and shout loudly: "Listen, listen well! I too am capable of victory, do you hear? I too am open to laughter and joy! I want to stride, head high, my face unguarded, with out having to point to the ashes over there on the horizon, without having to tamper with facts to hide their tragic ugliness. For a man born blind, God himself is blind, but look, I see, I am not blind." One feels like shouting this, but the shout changes to a murmur. One must make a choice; one must remain faithful. A big word, I know. Nevertheless I use it, it suits me. Having written the things I have written, I feel I can afford no longer to play with words. If I say that the writer in me wants to remain loyal, it is because it is true. This sentiment moves all survivors; they owe nothing to anyone, but everything to the dead.

12   I owe them my roots and memory. I am duty-bound to serve as their emissary, transmitting the history of their disappearance, even if it disturbs, even if it brings pain. Not to do so would be to betray them, and thus myself. And since I feel incapable of communicating their cry by shouting, I simply look at them. I see them and I write.

13   While writing, I question them as I question myself. I believe I said it before, elsewhere: I write to understand as much as to be understood. Will I succeed one day? Wherever one starts from one reaches darkness. The killers' sneers, their victims' tears, the onlookers' indifference, their complicity and complacency, the divine role in all that: I do not understand. A million children massacred: I shall never understand.

14   Jewish children: they haunt my writings. I see them again and again. I shall always see them. Hounded, humiliated, bent like the old men who surround them as though to protect them, unable to do so. They are thirsty, the children, and there is no one to give them water. They are hungry, the children, but there is no one to give them a crust of bread. They are afraid, and there is no one to reassure them.

15   They walk in the middle of the road, like vagabonds. They are on the way to the station, and they will never return. In sealed cars, without air or food, they travel toward another world; they guess where they are going, they know it, and they keep silent. Tense, thoughtful, they listen to the wind, the call of death in the distance.

16   All these children, these old people, I see them. I never stop seeing them. I belong to them.

17   But they, to whom do they belong?

18   People tend to think that a murderer weakens when facing a child. The child reawakens the killer's lost humanity. The killer can no longer kill the child before him, the child inside him.

19   Not this time. With us, it happened differently. Our Jewish children had no effect upon the killers. Nor upon the world. Nor upon God.

20   I think of them, I think of their childhood. Their childhood is a small Jewish town, and this town is no more. They frighten me; they reflect an image of myself, one that I pursue and run from at the same time—the image of a Jewish adolescent who knew no fear, except the fear of God, whose faith was whole, comforting, and not marked by anxiety.

21   No, I do not understand. And if I write, it is to warn the reader that he will not understand either. "You will not understand, you will never understand," were the words heard everywhere during the reign of night. I can only echo them. You, who never lived under a sky of blood, will never know what it was like. Even if you read all the books ever written, even if you listen to all the testimonies ever given, you will remain on this side of the wall, you will view the agony and death of a people from afar, through the screen of a memory that is not your own.

22   An admission of impotence and guilt? I do not know. All I know is that Treblinka and Auschwitz cannot be told. And yet I have tried. God knows I have tried.

23   Did I attempt too much or not enough? Out of some fifteen volumes, only three or four penetrate the phantasmagoric realm of the dead. In my other books, through my other books, I try to follow other roads. For it is dangerous to linger among the dead; they hold on to you, and you run the risk of speaking only to them. And so, I forced myself to turn away from them and study other periods, explore other destinies and teach other tales: the Bible and the Talmud, Hasidism and its fervor, the *Shtetl* and its songs, Jerusalem and its echoes; the Russian Jews and their anguish, their awakening, their courage. At times, it seems to me that I am speaking of other things with the sole purpose of keeping the essential—the personal experience—unspoken. At times I won-

der: And what if I were wrong? Perhaps I should not have heeded my own advice and stayed in my own world with the dead.

24 But then, I have not forgotten the dead. They have their rightful place even in the works about Rizhin and Koretz, Jerusalem and Kolvillàg. Even in my biblical and Midrashic tales, I pursue their presence, mute and motionless. The presence of the dead then beckons in such tangible ways that it affects even the most removed characters. Thus, they appear on Mount Moriah, where Abraham is about to sacrifice his son, a holocaust offering to their common God. They appear on Mount Nebo, where Moses enters solitude and death. And again in the Pardés, where a certain Elisha ben Abuya, seething with anger and pain, decided to repudiate his faith. They appear in Hasidic and Talmudic legends in which victims forever need defending against forces that would crush them. Technically, so to speak, they are of course else where, in time and space, but on a deeper, truer plane, the dead are part of every story, of every scene. They die with Isaac, lament with Jeremiah, they sing with the *Besht*, and, like him, they wait for miracles—but alas, they will not come to pass.

25 "But what is the connection?" you will ask. Believe there is one. After Auschwitz everything brings us back to Auschwitz. When I speak of Abraham, Isaac, and Jacob, when I evoke Rabbi Yohanan ben Zakkai and Rabbi Akiba, it is the better to understand them in the light of Auschwitz. As for the Maggid of Mezeritch and his disciples, it is to encounter the followers of their followers, that I attempt to reconstruct their spellbound, spellbinding universe. I like to imagine them alive, exuberant, celebrating life and hope. Their happiness is as necessary to me as it was once to themselves. And yet.

26 How did they manage to keep their faith intact? How did they manage to sing as they went to meet the Angel of Death? I know Hasidim who never vacillated; I respect their strength. I know others who chose rebellion, protest, rage; I respect their courage. For there comes a time when only those who do not believe in God will not cry out to him in wrath and anguish.

27 Do not judge either. Even the heroes perished as martyrs, even the martyrs died as heroes. Who would dare oppose knives to prayers? The faith of some matters as much as the strength of others. It is not ours to judge; it is only ours to tell the tale.

28 But where is one to begin? Whom is one to include? One meets a Hasid in all my novels. And a child. And an old man. And a beggar. And a madman. They are all part of my inner landscape. The reason why? Pursued and persecuted by the killers, I offer them shelter. The enemy wanted to create a society purged of their presence, and I have brought some of them back. The world denied them, repudiated them, so let them live at least within the feverish dreams of my characters.

29 It is for them that I write.

30 And yet, the survivor may experience remorse. He has tried to bear witness; it was all in vain.

31 After the liberation, illusions shaped one's hopes. We were convinced that a new world would be built upon the ruins of Europe. A new civilization was to

see the light. No more wars, no more hate, no more intolerance, no fanaticism anywhere. And all this because the witnesses would speak. And speak they did, to no avail.

32   They will continue, for they cannot do otherwise. When man, in his grief, falls silent, Goethe says, then God gives him the strength to sing of his sorrows. From that moment on, he may no longer choose not to sing, whether his song is heard or not. What matters is to struggle against silence with words, or through another form of silence. What matters is to gather a smile here and there, a tear here and there, a word here and there, and thus justify the faith placed in you, a long time ago, by so many victims.

33   Why I write? To wrench those victims from oblivion. To help the dead vanquish death.

Translated by Rosette C. Lamont

POST-READING QUESTIONS:

1) Did you find that any of your thoughts or feelings about survivors or their testimonies affected your understanding of or helped shape your reactions to Wiesel's ideas? Did his essay cause you to reexamine your reasons for having these thoughts and feelings, especially those that you discuss in your response to the fourth pre-reading question?

2) What do you make of Wiesel's reasons for writing? Also, what do you make of his paradoxical idea that, although he needs to write, no words seem adequate for explaining what happened during the Holocaust? Have you ever tried to explain something and found yourself either at a total loss for words or at a loss for the exact words that you wanted or needed?

3) Why do you think that Wiesel often uses such clipped sentences, that is, short, direct sentences devoid of flowery style?

4) Did reading Wiesel's essay help clarify for you why you do or do not like to write? Does his approach to and understanding of language help you revaluate your ideas about the value of your own written work?

5) Do you want to amend any of your responses to the pre-reading questions in light of your understanding of Wiesel's essay? Why or why not?

"Why I Write": Prewriting and First Draft

JAY JULOS

A native Californian, Jay Julos (1963-) continues to live in "the Golden State." A former history major at Irvine Valley College as well as a self-employed consultant for manufacturing companies in the water purification industry, he is now a student at the University of California at Santa Cruz, from which institution he hopes to earn a degree in Russian history. Asked to describe himself and his interests, he says that he "plays softball, drinks nonalcoholic beer, and enjoys spending time at quaint cafés and coffee houses, reading and observing the ebb and flow of people as they make their way through the circuitous course of everyday life." He also has an intense interest in and commitment to Holocaust Studies; in fact, he helped found and was the first president of the Irvine Valley College Holocaust Studies Group. And as you will probably gather from reading the following prewriting and drafting materials, he also enjoys writing. Indeed, these materials seem to help verify Jay's certainty that writing will be one of his "lifelong avenues for personal growth."

PART I
RESPONSE

Freewrite, Chart, Cluster, and First Draft for my essay, "Why I Write"

I have sometimes thought about being a writer but have never really sat down and throuhgt about why i like to write I think that most of the time when i was younger thhat have thought anout why I dont like to write. Why/ immature? this mates sens e to me because in the pas t i probably have tended to think about negative things rather thatn good things such as how writing class and grammar class was such a drag. but now actually in the past severa; years I have begun to change my thinking habits to concentrate on the good things in life rahter than the bad. like how enjoyable and useful good writing skills can be. But of corse this does not answer why I like to write yet.

I think that I like to write because I simple enjoy it. because maybe it comes easy to me? of course, the more i learn about writing the more that I find how difficult it is at times. maybe because I think that I 'm good at it? sure, I think that we like to do things that we are good at. one of the reasons that I like to write isbecause it makes me think about whatever that I am writhing about. I think that I can learn more about a subkjet when I write anout itr ather than jsut reading about it and thinking and conversing about it although those parts are integral to writing about it. writing for me takes organizing thoughts into good structure and I try to make sence to the reader as nuch as possible. by doing so, I naturally learn more about the subject.

I think that writing isa great way to relax although I can think of times when writing was not relaxing at all, more like pulling my own teeth or standing in the DMV line; it was very frustrating at times. but I can also think of times then it was very relaxing espceiallywhen I was understanding what I was writing about, or at least thought or enjoyed waht I was writing about and sometimes I would find that I learned greatly about was I was writing about, so maybe I just like to write because it is sometimes relaxzing. I think that writing can be a great way to get to know myself better. Such as when I take on a subject that I don't know too much about or that I think that I know a lot about anf then find out that I knew little. I mean that sometimes, actually most of the time I know less that I thought I did. Writing seems to humble me when I investigate my facts and figures,.. while writing I learn about how others think and how their thoughts effect mine. It is rewarding to learn about something that at one time I thought one way and after researching it, I change my way of thinking about it. and then the new thought or way of thinking that I develop is usually stronger I'm also better able to explain it to others and even defend it when needed. Writing is a way for me to express my inner feelings. I think of times when I am in class and I choose not to talk about something, because I cant feel completely comfortable about getting my complete thought across to the others. But when I am able to set down and write about it, I can feel comfortable that I am giving my sort of complete reasoning about it. Writing also enables me to dodge the arrows and bullets launched from others at least for a little while, until they read it. And them, when they read it, at least I have been able to present my reasoning to them in somewhat of a complete fashion,., This makes me think of how I long for organized conversation rather than what normally happens in the class room that of arguing.

I also like to write for the art content that writing has. I like to explore ways of saying things in differebnt manners and forms.. When it comes to argumentative writing, I like to write analytically and as clear as possible, but when I write about personal experience and things that have emotive content, I like to be creative I guess that that is creative writing, which I like to do as well. It seems that most of my writing however is other than creative,

---

CHART: WHY DO I LIKE WRITING?

Reasons why I like to write	Reasons for not writing
I enjoy writing for other peoples enjoyment.	Sometimes the material may make them sad or angry.
I like to generate thought in my audience.	I don't enjoy controversy, unless it results in defining the truth.
I enjoy clearly expressing ideas. It helps me to better understand the subject, and helps me to communicate better orally.	It's time consuming (requires thinking and rethinking)
I enjoy reading what I have written in the past to see what my thinking was like when I wrote it (have I changed? improved?)	Thoughts are private, but written words may not be.

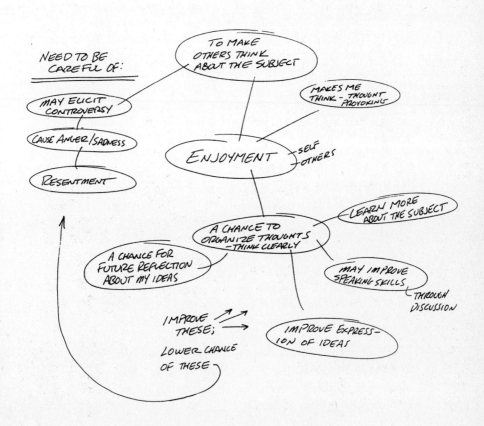

I enjoy writing for many reasons, and nearly all of them find their genesis in self-expression. I like to express my feelings, my opinions, and even my questions. I especially enjoy writing when the reader enjoys my work—don't we all! If I'm watching the reader while they are reading my work, and they smile, I smile with them. If they look sad or moved, I feel with them. When the material that I'm writing about is close to my heart, I enjoy evoking questions in the reader to help them see my points of view, to explore my feelings, and what is more important to discover their own emotions.

I once wrote an essay about an event from my childhood. I enjoyed the responses that I received from those who read it. Most of the readers told me that the story reminded them of happy events in their childhood, and how they enjoyed those times. Their response made me feel good. However, I have found that writers are not always the harbinger of glad tidings. The same story that brought memories of childhood fun and adventure to my happy readers, brought sadness to a close friend and made her cry. That made me feel sad. Fortunately, we talked for a while, and she felt better. I couldn't be happy writing to make people sad (surely I don't have aspirations of being a "Romance" writer!).

On the other hand, I have written about controversial subjects that have elicited strong disagreement and debate. Although I enjoy "non-debatable" writing more, I enjoy writing of this kind because, if done properly, it enables me to better understand the subject matter. I have to be careful with the material, because once I commit it to writing and send it to my audience, it is laid wide open and bare to the whip of the opponent. I don't mind entering into argumentation as long as the parties involved are willing to work towards the truth.

I would have never believed it if someone had told me that writing would improve my oral communication skills, but it certainly has. Writing has, and continues to enlarge my vocabulary and the way I use those words. I find that writing helps me to organize my thoughts and presenting them to the reader helps me to do the same when verbally presenting information. Writing has helped my critical thinking process, which is certainly important when speaking to an audience.

I find that writing is very time consuming, and can be very frustrating at times, but when the process is "flowing," I don't mind. When I'm writing well, I enjoy the process of discovering new thoughts, of learning, of solving problems, of answering questions, and the pleasing flow of thoughts and expression into the work. If this "writer's flow" could be captured or synthetically manufactured, it would probably replace caffeine as the writer's stimulant.

[conclusion]

PART II   **Commentary**

This predrafting exercise truly helped me in preparing my rough draft by organizing my initial thoughts and keeping my thinking on the right track throughout the writing. I tend to be the kind of person that refuses to read an instruction manual when assembling something. I often get ahead of the steps and may even leave some out, only to return to the instructions later and realize how important they were. By then I'm thoroughly frustrated and the family Bar-B-Que becomes a gardenia planter. My writing has often suffered the same mistreatment. I would anxiously jump into the writing and thunder along on a weak thread of ideas leading to poorly developed paragraphs, which lack unity and conformity.

Using predrafting techniques, I was able to explore and discover thoughts in my mind, capture them in the "freewrite" and place them on a "comparison chart" for organization. I remember so many times just trying to get started writing and becoming more frustrated as the minutes and hours passed away. As mentioned above, once I did get started, I was off to the races, but usually madly out of control. The freewriting exercise helped me to get started writing right away. I thought it was a little funny at first, writing without regard for grammar, spelling, or even making sense. I was tempted to fix the errors that I was making, but then I relaxed and just let the thoughts come to the surface. I noticed after a few minutes of freewriting, that important thoughts were coming to my mind and flowing right through my fingers and onto the screen (I use a computer for writing, which I find invaluable). After a few more minutes of freewriting,

I found that I had covered most everything that I could think of about the subject matter.

I then analyzed the resulting page and a half of text and highlighted the main thoughts and ideas. I was able to sort and combine those thoughts according to their importance and similarity and create a "cluster chart" with them. An interesting facet of the cluster chart that I immediately found useful was how I could link the thoughts together, and form a common thread between some of them. I was able to use this feature to maintain a certain emphasis within the overall theme of the writing. A common problem that I have had in my writing has been veering off on harmful sidetracks. By following the predrafting aids, I was able to stay focused on the subject. I also found that while organizing the key thoughts, intermediate or connecting thoughts surfaced and became useful material for the first draft.

While I was writing the first draft, I used these aids as guides. By referring to them, I was able to address all of the important thoughts and ideas in an organized and even relaxed manner. I did not have to rely on my memory to recover them. They were right there in the form that they first came to my mind. Thus, I could concentrate on each idea and develop it as fully as possible without thinking about what I needed to cover next.

I found that this writing experience was enjoyable due to the predrafting techniques that I used. I feel confident that I covered all of the points that I initially intended to cover. Without the organizing help of the predrafting aids, my work would have been less satisfying.

RELATED READINGS

from Shoah

CLAUDE LANZMANN

The excerpt that follows is taken from *Shoah: An Oral History of the Holocaust*, a book by Claude Lanzmann (1926–) which presents the text of Lanzmann's epic, nine-and-a-half-hour documentary film *Shoah*. Unlike other filmmakers who have treated the theme of the Holocaust, Lanzmann doesn't use archival film footage. Instead, he spends the bulk of his film interviewing an array of individuals associated with the Holocaust, including leading officials of death camps, ordinary bureaucrats, train engineers, and others, all of whom actively participated in the destruction of Jews; survivors who had performed "special" jobs during the Holocaust (such as burning the bodies of recently killed victims) or who had engaged in "unusual" activities (such as working for a resistance movement); and bystanders, who, through their indifference to or tacit support of Nazi efforts, indirectly helped the Nazis achieve their aims. Additionally, in various ways Lanzmann helps us to understand how official documents—such as the one that follows—shed light on the mechanistic nature of the massive tragedy which we call The Holocaust.

Prior to making *Shoah*, Lanzmann had been a minor filmmaker, as well as a journalist, a student of philosophy (he was friends with both Jean-Paul Sartre and Simone de Beauvoir, two highly respected French philosophers), and, during World War II, a resistance fighter. Without question, though, his fame rests on his extraordinary accomplishment in the form of his film *Shoah*, a "sheer masterpiece" (de Beauvoir vi), which he spent 11 years making and which was released in 1985. Perhaps the most fitting tribute to both Lanzmann and his film comes from Pope John Paul II, who "lauded Lanzmann for [the latter's] 'conscientiousness . . . that human conscience may never . . . become accustomed to . . . racism and its abominable ability to exterminate'" (Van Biema 66; author's ellipses). A native of Poland, where much of the destruction of European Jewry occurred during the Holocaust, the Pope speaks poignantly of a tragedy with which he is painfully familiar. [Some of the information contained in this headnote is from David H. Van Biema's 1986 article in *People Weekly* magazine, entitled "Filmmaker Claude Lanzmann Devotes 11 Years of His Life to a Biography of Death."]

PRE-READING QUESTIONS:

1) Ordinarily, what sorts of expectations do you have when you are about to read a business letter or form letter that has been sent to you? Do you have similar expectations when you are about to read a personal letter that a good friend has sent to you? Keep your response in mind as you read the following business letter, watching to see whether or not your pre-reading experiences and expectations affect the way in which you interpret and feel about this document.

2) Do you think that it's ever proper or right, or at least acceptable or understandable, for one to use euphemisms? Is it ever clearly improper, wrong, or unacceptable for one to do so? Have you yourself ever talked or written euphemistically? If so, why did you feel the need to do so, and how would you evaluate the results of your having done so?

3) If you ever have been treated as if you were not a person or have treated someone else in this way, how would you describe and explain your and the other person's (or people's) motives, actions, and reactions?

CLOSE-READING **TIP**

This letter's language is rather deceptively specific and telling. As you read this document, pay attention to certain words, phrases, and even whole sentences to see if you notice anything unusual about them.

1   Geheime Reichssache (Secret Reich Business)
Berlin, June 5, 1942
Changes for special vehicles now in service at Kulmhof (Chelmno) and for those now being built

2   Since December 1941, ninety-seven thousand have been processed (*verarbeitet* in German) by the three vehicles in service, with no major incidents. In the light of observations made so far, however, the following technical changes are needed:

3   The vans' normal load is usually nine per square yard. In Saurer vehicles, which are very spacious, maximum use of space is impossible, not because of any possible overload, but because loading to full capacity would affect the vehicle's stability. So reduction of the load space seems necessary. It must absolutely be reduced by a yard, instead of trying to solve the problem, as hitherto, by reducing the number of pieces loaded. Besides, this extends the operating time, as the empty void must also be filled with carbon monoxide. On the other hand, if the load space is reduced, and the vehicle is packed solid, the operating time can be considerably shortened. The manufacturers told us during a discussion that reducing the size of the van's rear would throw it badly off balance. The front axle, they claim, would be overloaded. In fact, the balance is automatically restored, because the merchandise aboard displays during the operation a natural tendency to rush to the rear doors, and is mainly found lying there at the end of the operation. So the front axle is not overloaded.

4   2. The lighting must be better protected than now. The lamps must be enclosed in a steel grid to prevent their being damaged. Lights could be eliminated, since they apparently are never used. However, it has been observed that when the doors are shut, the load always presses hard against them [against the doors] as soon as darkness sets in. This is because the load naturally rushes toward the light when darkness sets in, which makes closing the doors difficult. Also, because of the alarming nature of darkness, screaming always occurs when the doors are closed. It would therefore be useful to light the lamp before and during the first moments of the operation.

5   3. For easy cleaning of the vehicle, there must be a sealed drain in the middle of the floor. The drainage hole's cover, eight to twelve inches in diameter, would be equipped with a slanting trap, so that fluid liquids can drain off during the operation. During cleaning, the drain can be used to evacuate large pieces of dirt.

6   The aforementioned technical changes are to be made to vehicles in service only when they come in for repairs. As for the ten vehicles ordered from Saurer, they must be equipped with all innovations and changes shown by use and experience to be necessary.

7   Submitted for decision to Gruppenleiter II D, SS-Obersturmbannführer Walter Rauff.

8   Signed: Just

POST-READING QUESTIONS:

1) Did your pre-reading experiences and expectations affect the ways in which you read and *felt while reading* this document? In turn, does this letter help you better understand your pre-reading experiences and expectations? Might you think about this letter and your reaction to it the next time that you are about to read a business letter or form letter?

2) At what point in your reading were you able to determine the precise nature of the operation to which this letter refers? What tipped you off? Are you still confused about this letter's contents and meaning(s)?

3) Why do you think that the letter writer uses euphemistic language in a letter that was "Secret Reich Business," even though he also uses proper names (Saurer and Walter Rauff), including his own (Just)? Here's a related question: What would you say to Just were he to tell you that he's not really responsible for what happened to the Jews murdered in the killing vans since he himself did not *directly* kill them?

4) How would you compare the verbs used in the excerpt from *Black Elk Speaks* (p. 52) with those used in this letter? Does the question of *context* come into play in your comparative analysis?

5) Do you want to rethink and/or amend your response to any of the pre-reading questions in light of your understanding of this document?

A Sociological Perspective to the Holocaust

FRED E. KATZ

Fred E. Katz (1927-) was born in a village in southern Germany. In 1939, he left Germany as a child refugee of the Holocaust and spent the war years in England (tragically, his parents and brother, unable to escape, were killed in the Holocaust). In 1947, Katz came to the United States, where he earned a doctorate in sociology from the University of North Carolina at Chapel Hill. He has taught at a number of universities, including the University of Missouri, the State University of New York at Buffalo, Johns Hopkins University, Tel Aviv University, and the University of Toronto. He has authored a number of articles and books, the latter of which include *Autonomy and Organization: The Limits of Social Control* (1968), *Structuralism in Sociology: An Approach to Knowledge* (1976), and, most recently, *Ordinary People and Extraordinary Evil: A Report on the Beguilings of Evil* (1993).

PRE-READING QUESTIONS:

1) In your view, is the world basically a good or bad place, or, perhaps, something in between? Think about your view as you read Katz's essay, watching to see whether or not—and, if so, how, why, and to what extent—it helps shape your understanding of or reactions to his piece.

2) How would you define the term bureaucrat, and how, in general, would you describe a bureaucrat's (or a bureaucratic) job? If you read the previous reading selection, do you think that what you learned from studying it has influenced the way in which you want to respond to this question?

3) What does the expression "a package deal" mean to you? In what circumstances have you heard this expression used, or, if you've never actually heard someone use it, in what circumstances do you think that it might be used?

4) If you were told that the following reading selection—a scholarly essay published in a scholarly journal—had been written for your school newspaper, might you approach it differently from the way in which you are about to approach it now?

CLOSE-READING TIP

Katz divides his essay into individual sections, which, taken as a whole, are meant to help us understand "how evil can be *routinized*[,]. . . how 'ordinary' human behavior can be harnessed in the service of 'extraordinary,' and monstrous objectives" (author's italics). This claim seems to reflect, if not capture, Katz's **thesis**, that is, his main assertion or main point (a detailed discussion of a thesis can be found on pp. 135–138). As you read his essay, try to determine whether or not the specific examples and explanations that Katz uses support the points that he tries to make in each subdivision, whether or not the material offered in these subdivisions helps support Katz's overall thesis, and whether or not Katz's method of organizing his material helps make his essay more readable.

I n her recent book, *The Holocaust and the Historians*, Lucy Dawidowicz draws attention to historians' neglect of the Holocaust.[1] She points out that textbooks on modern history as well as specialized works by respected scholars give scant attention to it.

---

[1] L. Dawidowicz, *The Holocaust and the Historians* (Cambridge [Mass.], 1981).

2   To a sociologist Dawidowicz' book strikes a timely note. Sociologists, too, have been reluctant to study the Holocaust. Not long ago it was noted in a sociology journal that "there is no sociology of the Holocaust."[2] This may be doing an injustice to recent work by Helen Fein, who compared the persecution of Jews in different countries that had been occupied by the Nazis[3] and to Irving Horowitz' analysis of genocide in relation to national political systems.[4] But by and large sociologists have concentrated far more on anti-Semitism, ethnic issues and extremism bearing on Jewish life in the English-speaking countries[5] than on the Nazi Holocaust itself. Given the large number of Jewish sociologists, this remains somewhat of a riddle. Perhaps Hannah Arendt's quasi-sociological work on the banality of Eichmann's evil left a bad aftertaste—particularly its claim, met by much outrage, that the victims heavily contributed to their own demise. Perhaps, too, the trauma of the Holocaust that affects all Jews, including Jewish sociologists, has substituted grief for intellectual inquiry, where dispassionate analysis is the last thing on anyone's mind. A prominent Jewish sociologist recently told me: "The most profound thing anyone can do about the Holocaust is to be silent; but I wish you luck in not being silent."

3   The upshot of sociologists' silence is that distinctive sociological contributions to knowledge of the Holocaust remain relatively untapped. Such contributions would not be duplications of historians' explanations of why and how the Holocaust happened. They would, instead, clarify wherein the Holocaust was unique and wherein it was generalizable, utilizing existing widespread propensities for evil; and, wherein lie human routines that might again be tapped for massive extremes and wherein lie countervailing forces to extremism.

4   In this paper I want to take a step in this sociological direction by discussing the Holocaust as a way of routinizing monstrous behavior. . . .

5   The vast scale on which the Holocaust operated means that, to a considerable extent, the killings and torture were routinized. This was so particularly during the latter stage. In the early stage, by contrast, during the mass killings on the Russian front, the non-routinized nature of mass killings produced considerable protest by German military personnel.

6   Much of the Holocaust was carried out as part of the "ordinary" day-to-day routines of government machinery. Much of it became part-and-parcel of "ordinary" career patterns of civil servants, of military personnel, and of many persons in the civilian, private sector of European nations. Much of it relied on

---

[2]B. M. Dank, Review of "On the Edge of Destruction," in *Contemporary Sociology*, 8, 1 (1979), p. 129.

[3]H. Fein, *Accounting for Genocide* (New York, 1979).

[4]I. L. Horowitz, *Taking Lives: Genocide and State Power* (New Brunswick, [N.J.], 1980).

[5]For example, S. M. Lipset and E. Raab, *The Politics of Unreason* (Chicago, 1978); G. J. Selznick and S. Steinberg, *The Tenacity of Prejudice* (New York, 1969); C. Y. Glock and R. Stark, *Christian Beliefs and Anti-Semitism* (New York, 1973); W. Kornhauser, *The Politics of Mass Society* (New York, 1959).

a specially trained staff of concentration camp administrators, persons who were human extermination specialists. . . .

7   It is crucial to know how the Holocaust came to be routinized. Sociologically, routinization means that complex social objectives—such as public elementary and secondary education, the collection of taxes, the incarceration of criminals, and the conduct of wars—are so organized that they can be carried out in an orderly fashion, even when they involve personal suffering and extreme disruption of life.

8   A nation's bureaucracies tend to play a major role in such routinization. Bureaucracies are social machineries for accomplishing complex objectives in relatively orderly fashion. They often operate with moral blinders.[6] The individual bureaucrat typically focuses on a particular task, without considering wide implications, including broader moral issues.[7] Means, rather than ends, are the main concern.[8] The possibility that one's actions may be evil is often beyond the day-to-day level of awareness.[9] So it comes about that when the bureaucrat organizes the transportation of Jews (and Gypsies and others deemed undesirable) to extermination camps, or arranges for the "efficient" use of slave labor in the Ruhr's munitions factories, the immorality of killing people is not taken into account.[10] Morality or immorality may simply be outside the bureaucrat's range of concern. Technological issues—the availability of trains, for example—are apt to prevail.

9   One feature of the routinization process that is especially important is that relatively "ordinary" people participated in the murderous Nazi bureaucracy, and did so with enthusiasm and innovativeness. Of particular interest are people at the middle levels of the Nazi hierarchy, not ideological or government leaders. How were they involved? Before turning to one of these, it is important to be explicit about the theory to be used. The theory will try to go beyond the conventional wisdom about bureaucrats, namely that bureaucrats are extreme examples of two common syndromes: (1) Obedience to authority; (2) the modern era's pursuit of specialization. Both of these have been used by Nazi officials to attempt to be absolved from responsibility for their actions. Both have, in addition, presented scholars with the tantalizing and perverse view that, to some extent, "we are all Nazis."[11]

---

[6]M. Weber, *The Theory of Social and Economic Organization*, trans. T. Parsons (New York, 1947); R. K. Merton, *Social Theory and Social Structure* (New York, 1968); H. C. Kellman, "Violence Without Moral Restraint," *Journal of Social Issues* 29, 4 (1973), pp. 25–61; M. Silver and D. Geller, "On the Irrelevance of Evil: The Organization and Individual Action," *Journal of Social Issues*, 33, 4 (1978), pp. 2561.

[7]S. Milgram, *Obedience to Authority* (New York, 1974).

[8]R. K. Merton, *Social Theory and Social Structure* (New York, 1968).

[9]M. Silver and D. Geller, *op. cit.*; H. C. Kellman, *op. cit.*

[10]F. E. Katz, "Implementation of the Holocaust: The Behavior of Nazi Officials," *Comparative Studies in Society and History* 24, 3 (July, 1982).

[11]H. Ashkenazy, *Are We All Nazis?* (Secaucus [N.Y.], 1978).

1. Incremental Processes

10 The Nazi movement, like many other extremist movements, did not have a fully spelled out program to which it adhered. The extermination of the Jews, for example, developed in a step-by-step incremental manner after the Nazis came to power in 1933. It had not been specified in detail beforehand.[12]

11 Before the systematic physical annihilation began in 1942, the Nazi persecution of Jews included numerous *ad hoc* harassments of individual Jews and a highly orchestrated propaganda campaign of vilification of Jews. But its major device consisted of a series of increasingly repressive laws against Jews.[13] Through this device Jews were deprived of an ever-larger number of civil rights. Hence, in a technical sense, much of the persecution of Jews was done "legally", that is, through the existing legal machinery of the state. The mass persecution was grafted onto the existing legal machinery of the German nation. No separate legal system was created—no separate system of courts, no separate judiciary staff was employed. The systematic persecution of Jews (and others the Nazis considered undesirable) was being carried out with a minimal attention to its *newness*. After all, the existing machinery of the state was carrying it out. Persecution had become an expression of the will of the state, operating within the established and trusted mechanisms of the state. For an individual bureaucrat, accustomed to executing rather than initiating policy, the challenge of Nazism might not be fundamentally new. This would be especially true when the bureaucrat has become accustomed to Nazi policies in small, incremental installments.

12 The incremental, step-by-step character of the repressive laws not only contributed to hiding its novelty. It also obscured the degree of persecution that was being implemented. In the 1930's few people, even among the Jewish victims, could believe that total annihilation of European Jews was a real prospect. To many Jews individual laws, such as the requirement for Jews to get identification cards or adopt a Jewish-sounding name, were isolated acts. Surely, many believed, this did not presage wholesale murder of Jews. Incrementalism contributed to camouflaging the true direction of the process of persecution. When the final secret order came, in 1942, to actually kill all Jews in German-occupied lands,[14] this was but a further increment in what had become a publicly evolving course of action. It was not out-of-character with what had gone on before. In short, by disguising the extremes and newness of the persecutions, the incremental process contributed to making the persecutions acceptable to the German population.

13 There is another sense in which incremental processes aided the Nazi cause. It relates to the manner in which individuals come to participate in a career. How did Nazi functionaries come to join and participate in the Nazi movement? Many, perhaps most, Nazi bureaucrats did not start out as professional

[12]Y. Bauer, *The Holocaust in Historical Perspective* (Seattle, 1978).

[13]L. Dawidowicz, *The War Against the Jews, 1939–1945*, (New York, 1975); R. Hillberg. *The Destruction of European Jews* (Chicago, 1961).

murderers. Yet, how could they exhibit so much zeal for carrying out programs of extermination of human beings? For some people the choice of an occupational career and, later, one's participation in a career, are not based on one major decision that will set the course of one's occupational life. Instead, it is based on a series of small, localized decisions. Each of these "small" decisions is apt to deal with an immediate problem one is currently facing. Thus, a choice of major field in college may be based on solving certain immediate economic or interpersonal problems.[15] Such *incremental* processes, comprised of a series of localized decisions, may make up the career path throughout one's adult occupational life.

14 A crucial aspect is that by concentrating on such localized decision-making an individual may become engaged in a course of action to which he has little commitment. A person may become a physician without a commitment to healing; a person may become a teacher without commitment to teaching. This may seem paradoxical, particularly if one assumes that because a person has gone through a program of training in medicine that person becomes committed to healing; because a person has gone through a program of educational studies that person becomes committed to teaching; that, in short, "socialization" takes place in the course of education, especially in the education of professionals. This is far from proven in the existing sociological literature. A person may become a physician, and carry out some of the demands of the role of physician *very fully and enthusiastically*, and still have little commitment to some other dimensions of the role of physician, including a primary concern for healing.[16]

15 The history of the Nazi bureaucrats exemplifies these patterns very clearly. Studies of a variety of S.S. officers by Merkl, of early Nazis by Dicks, and of Eichmann by Arendt suggest that many became immersed in Nazism incrementally.[17] Eichmann, for example, joined the Nazi movement because it seemed a "sociable" thing to do. He evidently began with little commitment to extreme anti-Semitism. In the course of his S.S. service he became extremely committed to, and innovative in, the murder of Jews. However, there is a good deal of indication that his zeal for this murderous behavior owed every bit as much to a commitment to a career in the Nazi state machinery as it did to personal commitment to anti-Semitism. Of course, this does not absolve him of responsibility for mass murder. (I shall return to this point under the section on Autonomy.) But it gives a glimmer of understanding that goes beyond the conception that only blind hatred can induce monstrous behavior.

---

[14]K. A. Schleunes, *The Twisted Road to Auschwitz: Nazi Policy Toward German Jews, 1933–1939* (Urbana [Ill.], 1970).

[15]F. E. Katz and H. Martin, "Career Choice Processes," *Social Forces*, 41 (1962), pp.. 149–153.

[16]F. E. Katz, *Autonomy and Organization: The Limits of social Control* (New York, 1968), Part II.

[17]H. Arendt, Eichmann in Jerusalem: A Report on the Banality of Evil (New York, 1976); H. Dicks, *Licensed Murder: A Socio-Psychological Study of Some S.S. Killers* (New York, 1972); P. H. Merkl, *Political Violence Under the Swastika: 581 Early Nazis* (Princeton [N.J.], 1975).

16   In and of themselves, incremental processes are neither good nor bad. They are part of the repertoire of many *ordinary* patterns of social behavior. They are very typical of features of ongoing social systems. In the present political system of the United States much national policy is made in an incremental manner. For example, policy decisions regarding unemployment and inflation are being influenced by current perceptions about forthcoming congressional elections. New laws are commonly created through *ad hoc* deliberations, often based on compromises among competing factions and interest groups. Many an actual law as finally formulated may not represent the ideal version of any one group. It is the end product of a series of local, incremental decisions.

17   Let us return to individual Nazis. Officials, such as Eichmann and his superior, Himmler, sometimes expressed distaste for aspects of the extremes of mass murder activities in which they were engaged. Yet they engaged in them enthusiastically and innovatively. How does one explain this apparent anachronism? The easiest explanation is to disbelieve their claims of distaste for their actions, to suggest that they were lying, be it to themselves or to a wider audience. Another explanation, at least as plausible, is that their whole-hearted commitment was to the Nazi cause *in toto*. That cause was a culmination of historic German nationalism which emphasized that (1) the German nation was not only different from the other nations; it was superior to them. And, (2) the individual obtains his ultimate personal fulfillment by subordinating himself to the nation.[18]

18   The murder of Jews, and other designated undesirables, was part of one's duty toward the total, grand cause represented by the Nazi Reich. Himmler, in a message to S.S. members who seemed to recoil from some of the horrors of their own deeds, told them to say to themselves: "What horrible things do I have to witness while carrying out my sacred duty."[19] Commitment was not just to a particular set of deeds, such as the execution of Jews, but to a larger cause. One might find some of one's deeds abhorrent while still regarding them as a positive contribution to a larger, acceptable cause. This cause was comprised of a *package* of programs.

2. The Packaging of Nazism

19   Nazism was made up of a number of different programs. These included extreme anti-Semitism (a greatly expanded version of long-existing anti-Semitism),[20] heightened nationalism (including the plan to recapture land Germany had surrendered because of its loss of the First World War), ethnicism (based

---

[18]Lucy Dawidowicz, *The Holocaust and the Historians* (Cambridge, Mass., 1981), p. 45; Georg Iggers, *The German Conception of History: The National Tradition of Historical Thought from Herder to the Present* (Middletown [Conn.], 1968).

[19]H. Dicks, *op. cit.*; E. Crankshaw, *Gestapo* (Moonachie [N.J.], 1977).

[20]L. Dawidowicz, 1975, *op. cit.*, p. 220.

on old themes in German culture, that Germans were a master race),[21] and economic revitalization (which would bring jobs and income to the currently unemployed, as well as renewed growth and prosperity for the nation's industry). Although these programs addressed very different issues, they were amalgamated into one composite. The Nazi movement combined them into one *package* in its propaganda and in its political actions.

20   Stated differently, the Nazi movement's diverse programs appealed to very diverse groups within Germany. They appealed to unemployed workers as well as industrialists, to military career officers and many a civil service careerist, to anti-Semites and nationalists, to name just a few. Since Nazi Germany was a highly coercive dictatorship, the diverse constituencies could not exercise separate power as "interest groups", as they might in a more loose-knit Western democratic nation. Nazism was one *package*.

21   Three important characteristics flow from this situation. One, individual Nazis were apt to be attracted to Nazism by one or another of its programs. They need not be drawn by all of its programs. Two, due to the amalgamation of the Nazi programs into a cohesive package, individual Nazis were very apt to be engaged in helping to implement the entire Nazi package, even those components to which they had no strong personal commitment. And, given a strong allegiance to the Nazi package, *as a total entity*, they were apt to help implement the entire package with considerable zeal, *even those components items to which they had little commitment*. Three, a cohesive package serves to *contextualize* an individual's activities. It places them in a particular context that has a degree of immunity from other contexts. Horrendous deeds are justified in the name of that one context. Other contexts—such as traditional ethical and religious contexts—are eliminated from consideration.

22   These features are highlighted in the exasperating claim by some Nazi and S.S. officials, such as Eichmann, that they were not anti-Semitic.[22] Given their zealously murderous activities against Jews, such a claim is hard to believe. Are they simply lying, to deceive others and/or themselves? Correlatedly, are they exhibiting a characteristically Western culture pattern, wherein anti-Semitism often exists but is hidden from public view and acknowledgment? Although these explanations are plausible, yet another explanation must be entertained. It is that some Nazi functionaries were really not committed to anti-Semitism; that the zealous pursuit of the murder of Jews was being carried out by individuals whose primary commitment might be to other things, such as careerism within the Nazi movement. This could take the form of focusing obsessively on one's sacred "mission" within the Nazi package of programs. In the case of Eichmann that sacred mission was the annihilation of Jews. (To be sure there were Nazis, such as Julius Streicher, whose explicit and primary commitment within the Nazi package probably was to anti-Semi-

---

[21]H. W. Koch, *The Hitler Youth: Origins and Development, 1922–1945* (New York, 1975).

[22]R. Hilberg, *op. cit.*; H. Arendt, *op. cit.*

tism.) In the analysis of anti-Semitism the "non-committed" anti-Semites must be taken very seriously. Their proficiency in things other than anti-Semitism, notably in bureaucratic efficiency, may make them more dangerous anti-Semites than the professed and "committed" anti-Semite. In some ways they may have greater autonomy to practice and implement anti-Semitism than the single-minded anti-Semite. Also, because of the particular package in which their murderous anti-Semitism is contextualized, they may be unreachable through other contexts, such as the context of Judao-Christian [*sic*] canons of the sanctity of human life.[23]

3. The Question of Autonomy of Nazi Officials

23   How much autonomy did Nazi officials have? As noted earlier, much of the persecution, of Jews and others, was carried out through the existing German state's administrative bureaucracies. This fact was used as an excuse by many a Nazi at the Nuremberg and other post-war trials. They claimed that they were merely following orders; they were officials sworn to obey the laws of the state; they were military officers sworn to obey the authority of their superior officers; they were holding positions which were subject to very clear lines of authority. Surely, they claimed, the individual has little discretion under such conditions. Consequently, given their lack of discretion, they bore no responsibility for the character of many of their actions.

24   All this omits from consideration the fact that bureaucracies operate on a dual track, control and *autonomy*. A bureaucratic organization is not only a mechanism for controlling people's behavior. It is also a mechanism for giving a measure of autonomy to the people who participate in it in order to carry out policies. Stated differently, a bureaucracy is not only an organization that demands service from its functionaries. It also provides these functionaries with the opportunity to pursue a career.[25] The manifestations of the career can take the form that the individual, over time, receives increasing income and other positional perquisites, receives advancement within the bureaucratic hierarchy of positions, or receives both. To be entitled to such rewards the bureaucrat is expected to do more than merely obey instructions. He/she is ordinarily expected to make independent contributions, to use initiative. This can only be done through relatively autonomous activity.

25   From the perspective of the individual who occupies a position within an organization, this involves what Max Weber called "status honor."[25] An individual derives honor from an organization, such as the S.S., because of the

---

[23]The mechanism of *contextualization* seems to be basic to explaining Milgram's well-known findings. (Milgram, *op. cit.*, 1974) Milgram found that persons were willing to inflict serious pain on innocent persons when requested to do so in a laboratory situation. Here was a context in which the canons of supposedly pure science prevailed, shutting out other countervailing contexts.

[24]H. H. Gerth and C. W. Mills (trans. and edd.), *From Max Weber: Essays in Sociology* (New York, 1958).

[25]*Ibid.*, pp. 186–187.

status-position he occupies in it. However, what Weber and other social scientists have not clarified is that the individual can also contribute to (or detract from) the honor of his status. He does so through his conduct while he occupies that status. Contributing to the honor of one's status, and through it to the honor of the S. S., to other Nazi organizations and to the larger Nazi cause for which they stand, was a major factor in the behavior of individual Nazi officials. Such contributions to his status honor was typically based on how the bureaucrat used his autonomy, the discretion available to him.

26   Bureaucrats have considerable autonomy. This has been discovered in sociological research.[26] But it is also well known by the general public. Anyone who has had dealings with bureaucrats knows that the individual bureaucrat not only "knows" rules. He or she typically has much autonomy to *interpret* rules. A given bureaucrat may interpret the rules so literally that they destroy the spirit of the rules, the ideals for which the rules stand. Conversely, a bureaucrat may bend the existing rules in order to conform to the spirit of the rules, as he or she interprets their spirit. In the political realm, this goes far to explaining why a new Administration often finds its efforts to introduce change frustrated by the middle and lower levels of the existing bureaucracy, even after new officials have been installed at the top. As a result, after a relatively short period of publicly proclaiming change and innovation a government agency is apt to pursue the same practices and policies it did before the change of Administration.

27   Let it not be assumed that this only applies to American bureaucracies, such as the State or Defense Department's policies and practices toward the Middle East. It applies amply to Germany in the Nazi era. Nazi bureaucrats, from Gauleiters to other party functionaries, were masters at protecting themselves and using their own autonomy in bureaucratic infighting.[27]

28   Individual S.S. officials directing the mass murders found ways to exercise autonomy while carrying out the government's orders for ultimate destruction of the Jews. There was S.S. General Otto Ohlendorf (an *Einsatzgruppe* Commander) who, in the Nuremberg trials, admitted killing over 90,000 persons on the southern front in Russia. However, he was proud to claim that he used his personal initiative—his autonomy—to make these killings as "humane" as possible. He did so, he claimed, by introducing methods and procedures that speeded up the process of killing, so that both the victims and the military personnel who carried out the killings had a minimum amount of mental anguish beforehand.[28]

29   It is important to realize not only that individual functionaries have autonomy, in that they have options available to them and that their behavior is not completely predetermined by their position in a hierarchy of a bureaucracy. It is also important to see how the autonomy is being used. In the case of General Ohlendorf, autonomy was used to accomplish two different objectives. One, he

---

[26]P. M. Blau, *The Dynamics of Bureaucracy* (Chicago, 1955); F. E. Katz, 1968, *op. cit.*

[27]Cf., A. Speer, *Inside the Third Reich* (New York, 1970).

[28]E. Crankshaw, 1977, *op. cit.*

used his own autonomy to implement the Nazi extermination policy. He did so by being inventive in developing methods and procedures for mass killing, thereby speeding up the killings. Two, he used his autonomy to reconcile the killings with some of the traditional German values. He did so by developing methods which supposedly introduced a degree of "humanity" into the inhumane process. Complaints from German soldiers had been reaching back home about German atrocities on the Russian front and the strains this produced among the soldiers. Such reports produced some pressure toward "humanizing" the inhumane acts at the front. It is not clear whether Ohlendorf was responding to these pressures or whether he was acting entirely on the basis of his own reactions. At any rate, in *his* view, he was catering to a German value placed on some regard for the quality of human life.

30   Both of these uses of autonomy—innovating ways to speed up killings and finding ways to reconcile the killings with existing values—contributed to *making the Nazi policies work*. They are self-initiated contributions by a Nazi official toward making Nazi policies a reality. It is not at all clear whether the Nazi extermination policies could have been accomplished as fully had there not been many such contributions, initiated locally at many points within the system.

31   A contrasting use of autonomy, of deliberately not taking part in the killings, also existed. At the Eichmann trial it was brought out that ". . . it was possible for an S.S. officer to obtain transfer if he felt himself unable to take part in the murder of Jews—without thereby losing rank or status."[29] Even persons under Ohlendorf's command were transferred in this manner.[30]

32   Perhaps the best documented case of how an individual's autonomy was used to promote the Nazi annihilation process is that of Eichmann.[31] He manifested considerable zeal and innovativeness to bring about the mass murder of Jews. Indeed, there is every indication that the extermination of Jews became a near-obsession for Eichmann. He used all his autonomy to achieve it. For example, toward the end of the war, when Germany was losing the war and when there was a considerable shortage of trains, Eichmann insisted on getting trains to transport Jews to the extermination camps. This led to conflict with his own superiors, who insisted the trains be used for the transportation of troops. At one point Himmler, Eichmann's superior as head of the S.S., ordered Eichmann to stop transporting Jews to the camps. Eichmann managed to sabotage this order and continued to send Jews to the camps.[32]

33   Eichmann's actions display a bureaucrat's autonomy. He can interpret orders with zeal and he can subvert orders. He can marshal resources in many ways that are not officially spelled out in the existing rules that govern the bureaucracy. The existing rules and orders are typically formulated very broadly. They permit much interpretation by the bureaucrat who implements

[29]M. Pearlman, *The Capture and Trial of Adolf Eichmann* (New York, 1963), pp. 401ff.

[30]*Ibid.*, p. 404.

[31]H. Arendt, *op. cit.*; M. Pearlman, *Ibid.*

[32]M. Pearlman, *Ibid.*, pp. 195, 353, 366–367.

them. All this points to areas where the individual has autonomy and, there-from, culpability for his actions. How the bureaucrat uses his or her autonomy is crucial, both for the success of reaching the bureaucracy's goals and for demonstrating the bureaucrat's personal responsibility. . . .

Conclusion

34   The Holocaust remains abhorrent, but it need not remain a mystery. Much of the Holocaust can be seen as a by-product of modern bureaucratization.[33] Indeed, much of it relied upon the sort of orderliness found in modern political and industrial bureaucracies. This paper has focused on the bureaucratic processes involved by concentrating on three facets of their operation: (1) The nature of *incremental* career decision-making and personal participation in bureaucracies, particularly by Nazi functionaries; (2) The *packaging* of diverse political programs into one cohesive entity, particularly the packaging of the Nazi programs; (3) The *autonomy*, in the sense of discretionary behavior, of bureaucrats, particularly the autonomy enjoyed by Nazi functionaries. Each is integral to the process as a whole. . . .

35   Above all, the sociological lesson to be learned from a study of. . . [the] SS. . . is how evil can be *routinized*. For [members of the SS] show us how "ordinary" human behavior can be harnessed in the service of "extraordinary," and mon-strous, objectives.

POST-READING QUESTIONS:

1) Did you find that any of your thoughts or feelings about the nature of the world affected your understanding of or helped shape your reactions to the material that Katz presents? Does his essay cause you to reexamine your reasons for having these thoughts and feelings?

2) Did your notion of what a bureaucrat is and does square with Katz's explanations of Nazi bureaucrats and Nazi bureaucracy? If you read the excerpt from *Shoah* (p. 92), also discuss whether or not Just's letter helps you better understand Katz's essay, and vice versa.

3) Do the subheadings that Katz uses effectively prepare you for the material contained in the essay's subdivisions, and do the latter adequately reflect the ideas articulated in the former? Do the subdivisions work well on their own? Do they work well together? Do they, as a group, seem to provide enough material to support Katz's thesis? Do you feel that Katz's thesis is other than that suggested in the close-reading tip?

4) After reading Katz's essay, are you (further) convinced that anyone—Jew or non-Jew—can be either a victim or a victimizer? Can you use Katz's ideas to help explain other social phenomena, tragic or otherwise? If you've read Stanley Milgram's "The Perils of Obedience" (p. 276), how do you think that Milgram might respond to Katz's essay (and vice versa)?

---

[33]R. L. Rubenstein, *The Cunning of History* (New York, 1978).

Ordinary Men

CHRISTOPHER R. BROWNING

Christopher R. Browning (1944–) is a professor of history at Pacific Lutheran University in Tacoma, Washington, where he has taught since 1974. He pursued his undergraduate studies at Oberlin College, in Ohio, from where he was graduated *summa cum laude* in 1967. In 1975, he received his Ph.D. from the University of Wisconsin-Madison. He is the author of numerous scholarly articles, as well as the following four books: *The Final Solution and the German Foreign Office* (1978), *Fateful Months: Essays on the Emergence of the Final Solution* (1985), *Ordinary Men: Reserve Police Battalion 101 and the Final Solution in Poland* (1992), and *The Path to Genocide* (1992). A well-recognized scholar and well-respected teacher, Browning is the recipient of various awards and fellowships, including the Faculty Excellence Award at Pacific Lutheran University (1992) and a Fulbright senior research fellowship in Israel (1989). His book *Ordinary Men*, from which much of the following excerpt is taken, received the National Jewish Book Award, for the Holocaust category, in 1993. A former member of the Institute for Advanced Studies at the Hebrew University of Jerusalem, he is currently writing one volume for a multivolume comprehensive history of the Holocaust to be published by Yad Vashem, Israel's world-renowned Holocaust Studies museum and institute.

PRE-READING QUESTIONS:

1) Would you say that most people are basically good, essentially bad, or something in between? What do you make of the fact that good people sometimes do bad things and that bad people sometimes do good things? As you read the following excerpt, see if Browning's material strengthens or poses a challenge to your views on these matters.

2) Have you ever been asked to do something that you thought was wrong or repugnant? If so, did you do it anyway? If you've never been placed in such a situation, how do you think that you'd respond if someone were to ask you to do something that went against your moral values or that you thought was repugnant?

3) Do you consider yourself a basically good or bad person? Do you think of yourself as being ordinary or extraordinary? Do you think that others see you as you see yourself?

4) Do you have any particular expectations of Browning's material, in light of its being the work of a historian? Do you expect Browning's work to meet certain standards? Do you expect Browning, as a historian, to adhere to any special principles in his work? Would your expectations be different were you about to read a poem or an excerpt from a novel?

CLOSE-READING TIP

In a section of his work not reprinted here, Browning says, ". . . [A]s self-conscious as I have tried to be, at times I undoubtedly made purely instinctive judgments without even being aware of it. Other historians looking at the same materials would retell these events in somewhat different ways." As you read through the explanatory part of his material, which precedes the narrative telling us what happened, pay attention to those moments in which Browning seems to make or rely upon judgments, instinctive or not, and think about whether or not these judgments add to, take away from, or leave unchanged the historical record that follows. Consider, for example, some of Browning's statements in paragraphs 4–8.

1   In mid-March 1942 some 75 to 80 percent of all victims of the Holocaust were still alive, while 20 to 25 percent had perished. A mere eleven months later, in mid-February 1943, the percentages were exactly the reverse. At the core of the Holocaust was a short, intense wave of mass murder. The center of gravity of this mass murder was Poland, where in March 1942, despite two and a half years of terrible hardship, deprivation, and persecution, every major Jewish community was still intact, and where eleven months later only the remnants of Polish Jewry survived in a few rump ghettos and labor camps. In short, the German attack on the Jews of Poland was not a gradual or incremental program stretched over a long period of time, but a veritable blitzkrieg, a massive offensive requiring the mobilization of large numbers of shock troops. This offensive, moreover, came just when the German war effort in Russia hung in the balance—a time period that opened with the renewed German thrust toward the Crimea and the Caucasus and closed with the disastrous defeat at Stalingrad.

2   If the German military offensive of 1942 was ultimately a failure, the blitzkrieg against the Jews, especially in Poland, was not. We have long known how the Jews in the major ghettos, especially Warsaw and Lódź, were murdered. But most Polish Jews lived in smaller cities and towns whose populations were often more than 30 percent Jewish, and in some cases even 80 or 90 percent. How had the Germans organized and carried out the destruction of this widespread Jewish population? And where had they found the manpower during this pivotal year of the war for such an astounding logistical achievement in mass murder? The personnel of the death camps was quite minimal. But the manpower needed to clear the smaller ghettos—to round up and either deport or shoot the bulk of Polish Jewry—was not.[1]

3   My search for the answers to these questions led me to the town of Ludwigsburg near Stuttgart. Here is located the Central Agency for the State Administrations of Justice (Zentrale Stelle der Landesjustizverwaltungen), the

Federal Republic of Germany's office for coordinating the investigation of Nazi crimes. I was working through their extensive collection of indictments and judgments for virtually every German trial of Nazi crimes committed against the Jews of Poland when I first encountered the indictment concerning Reserve Police Battalion 101, a unit of the German Order Police.

4 Though I had been studying archival documents and court records of the Holocaust for nearly twenty years, the impact this indictment had upon me was singularly powerful and disturbing. Never before had I encountered the issue of choice so dramatically framed by the course of events and so openly discussed by at least some of the perpetrators. Never before had I seen the monstrous deeds of the Holocaust so starkly juxtaposed with the human faces of the killers. . . .

5 Ultimately, the Holocaust took place because at the most basic level individual human beings killed other human beings in large numbers over an extended period of time. The grass-roots perpetrators became "professional killers.". . .

6 In recent decades the historical profession in general has been increasingly concerned with writing history "from the bottom up," with reconstructing the experiences of the bulk of the population ignored in the history of high politics and high culture hitherto so dominant. In Germany in particular, this trend has culminated in the practice of *Alltagsgeschicte*—"the history of everyday life"—achieved through a "thick description" of the common experiences of ordinary people. When such an approach has been applied to the era of the Third Reich, however, some have criticized it as an evasion—a way to shift attention from the unparalleled horrors of the Nazi regime's genocidal policies to those mundane aspects of life that continued relatively undisturbed. Thus, the very attempt to write a case study or microhistory of a single battalion might seem undesirable to some.

7 As a methodology, however, "the history of everyday life" is neutral. It becomes an evasion, an attempt to "normalize" the Third Reich, only if it fails to confront the degree to which the criminal policies of the regime inescapably permeated everyday existence under the Nazis. Particularly for the German occupiers stationed in the conquered lands of eastern Europe— literally tens of thousands of men from all walks of life—the mass-murder policies of the regime were not aberrational or exceptional events that scarcely ruffled the surface of everyday life. As the story of Reserve Police Battalion 101 demonstrates, mass murder and routine had become one. Normality itself had become exceedingly abnormal.

8 Another possible objection to this kind of study concerns the degree of empathy for the perpetrators that is inherent in trying to understand them. Clearly the writing of such a history requires the rejection of demonization. The policemen in the battalion who carried out the massacres and deportations,

---

[1]Raul Hilberg estimates that more than 25 percent of the victims of the Holocaust died in shootings. More than 50 percent perished in the six major death camps equipped with gassing facilities, and the remainder under the terrible conditions of ghettos, labor and concentration camps, death marches, etc. *The Destruction of the European Jews* (New York, 1985), 1219.

like the much smaller number who refused or evaded, were human beings. I must recognize that in the same situation, I could have been either a killer or an evader—both were human—if I want to understand and explain the behavior of both as best I can. This recognition does indeed mean an attempt to empathize. What I do not accept, however, are the old clichés that to explain is to excuse, to understand is to forgive. Explaining is not excusing; understanding is not forgiving. Not trying to understand the perpetrators in human terms would make impossible not only this study but any history of Holocaust perpetrators that sought to go beyond one-dimensional caricature. Shortly before his death at the hands of the Nazis, the French Jewish historian Marc Bloch wrote, "When all is said and done, a single word, 'understanding,' is the beacon light of our studies."[2] It is in that spirit that I have tried to write [my own study]. . . .

. . .

9   Shortly before dawn on 13 July 1942 a convoy of trucks carrying more than 450 men from Reserve Police Battalion 101 halted before the Polish village of Jozefów some sixty miles south of the district capital of Lublin.[3] The reserve policemen, middle-aged family men mostly of working-class background from the city of Hamburg, were considered too old to be of use to the German army—their average age was thirty-nine—and they had been drafted into reserve units of the Order Police instead. They had arrived in Poland less than three weeks earlier. This was to be their first major action, but they had not yet been told what to expect.

10   The battalion commander was Major Wilhelm Trapp, a fifty-three-year-old career policeman affectionately known by his men as "Papa Trapp." As daylight was breaking, he assembled the men in a half-circle. With choking voice and tears in his eyes, he visibly fought to control himself as he explained the battalion's assignment. They had to perform a frightfully unpleasant task, he said, that was not to his liking, but the orders came from the highest authorities. If it would make their task any easier, they should remember that in Germany the bombs were falling on women and children, that the Jews had instigated the American boycott against Germany, and that these Jews in the village of Jozefów supported the partisans.

11   Trapp proceeded to explain the assignment. The battalion was to round up the Jews in Jozefów. The males of working age were to be separated and taken to a work camp. The remaining Jews—the women, children, and elderly— were to be shot by the battalion.

12   Trapp then made an extraordinary offer: if any of the older men among them did not feel up to the task that lay before him, he could step out. After some moments one man stepped forward from Third Company. His captain, one of only two career SS officers in the battalion, began to berate him. The

---

[2]Marc Bloch, *The Historian's Craft* (New York, 1964), 143.

[3]This account is drawn from my *Ordinary Men: Reserve Police Battalion 101 and the Final Solution in Poland* (New York: Aaron Asher Books, HarperCollins, 1992).

major silenced the captain, and ten or twelve other men stepped forward as well. They turned in their rifles.[4]

13   Major Trapp, who was seen "weeping like a child" during much of the day, then met with the company commanders and gave them their respective assignments. First and Second companies were to round up the Jews, while Third Company cordoned off the village. Then First Company was to form firing squads in the woods, while Second Company was to guard the Jews assembled in the marketplace and load them on the trucks which shuttled to and from the forest. Any Jew trying to escape or hide was to be shot on the spot; anyone too sick or frail to walk to the marketplace, as well as infants, were also to be shot on the spot.

14   Before departing for the woods, the men of First Company were given a quick lesson in the gruesome task that awaited them. The battalion doctor traced the outline of a human figure on the ground and showed the men how to use a fixed bayonet placed between and just above the shoulder blades for aiming their carbines. Several men approached the First Company Sergeant, one of them confessing that he found the task "repugnant"; they were released from the firing squad and reassigned to accompany the trucks.

15   Totally inexperienced in organizing firing-squad procedures that would maximize detachment between shooter and victim, the First Company Sergeant formed two groups of about thirty-five men, which was roughly equivalent to the number of Jews loaded into each truck. In turn each squad met an arriving truck at the edge of the forest. The individual squad members paired off *face-to-face* with the individual Jews they were to shoot, then marched their victims into the forest. The Jews were forced to lie face down in a row. On signal the policemen fired their carbines at point-blank range into the necks of their victims. A noncommissioned officer had to deliver so-called mercy shots, because many of the men, some out of excitement and some intentionally, shot past their victims. By midday alcohol appeared from some-where to "refresh" the shooters. After the shooting started, a group of men approached the First Company captain, the other career SS officer in the bat-talion, and pleaded that they were fathers with children and could not con-tinue. The captain curtly refused their plea. Subsequently, however, the First Company Sergeant released them and a number of other older men as well.

16   By midmorning it had become apparent that the rate of execution was too slow for the task to be completed by nightfall. Third Company was called in from its outposts around the village to take over close guard of the market-place, and the men of Second Company were informed that they had to join the shooters in the woods. At least one sergeant once again offered his men the opportunity to report if they did not feel up to it. No one took up his offer.

---

[4]The afternoon before, when Trapp had informed the officers of this assignment, one man had indicated that, as a reserve lieutenant and Hamburg businessman, he could not participate in such an action in which defenseless women and children were shot. He asked for a different task and was assigned to guard the work Jews to be taken to Lublin.

17   Unlike First Company, Second Company received no instruction on how to carry out the shooting. Initially bayonets were not fixed as an aiming guide. Thus many of the men did not give neck shots but fired directly into the heads of their victims at point-blank range. The victims' heads exploded, and in no time the policemen's uniforms were saturated with blood and splattered with brains and splinters of bone. Though alcohol made its appearance in Second Company as well, the dropout rate among its shooters was even greater than among First Company.

18   As one policeman remembered: "I myself took part in some ten shootings, in which I had to shoot men and women. I simply could not shoot at people anymore, which became apparent to my sergeant. . . because at the end I repeatedly shot past. For this reason he relieved me. Also other comrades were sooner or later relieved, because they simply could no longer continue." Another recalled:

> The shooting of the men was so repugnant to me, that I missed the fourth man. It was simply no longer possible for me to aim accurately. I suddenly felt nauseous and ran away from the shooting site. I have expressed myself incorrectly just now. It was not that I could no longer aim accurately, rather that the fourth time I intentionally missed. I then ran into the woods, vomited, and sat down against a tree. To make sure that no one was nearby, I called loudly into the woods, because I wanted to be alone. . . My nerves were totally finished. I think that I remained alone in the woods for some two to three hours.

19   In the confusion of men coming and going around the trucks, some men evaded shooting altogether.

> It was in no way the case, that those who did not want to or could not carry out the shooting of human beings with their own hands could not keep themselves out of this task. No strict control was being carried out here. I therefore remained by the arriving trucks and kept myself busy at the arrival point. In any case I gave my activity such an appearance. It could not be avoided that one or another of my comrades noticed that I was not going to the executions to fire away at the victims. They showered me with remarks such as "shithead" and "weakling" to express their disgust. But I suffered no consequences for my actions. I must mention here, that I was not the only one who kept himself out of participating in the executions.

20   Most of the men, however, continued to shoot all day. The forest was so filled with dead bodies that in the end it was difficult to find places to make the Jews lie down. Around 9:00 P.M., some twenty-nine hours after Reserve Police Battalion 101 had arrived in Jozefów, the last of approximately 1,500 Jews was shot. After the men had returned to their barracks, they were given extra rations of alcohol. They were depressed, angered, embittered, and shaken. They talked little, ate almost nothing, but drank a great deal. One policeman expressed the sentiments of many, when he said: "I'd go crazy if I had to do that again." But

in fact it was only the beginning of Reserve Police Battalion 101's involvement in the Final Solution, which was to stretch over many months. . . .

POST-READING QUESTIONS:

1) Did Browning's material strengthen or pose a challenge to the views that you offered in your response to the first pre-reading question? Have your thoughts about the other readings in this chapter influenced your thinking about the men of Reserve Police Battalion 101?

2) Do you feel that Browning's historical narrative bears traces of the author's personal judgments? If so, do you feel that these judgments compromise and/or bolster the integrity of the narrative? In your view, *can* a reader *entirely avoid* judging the material that she/he is analyzing?

3) Has Browning's material caused you to want to emend any parts of your responses to the second or third pre-reading questions?

4) Why do you think that Browning says, "in the same situation [in which the men of Reserve Police Battalion 101 found themselves], I could have been either a killer or an evader. . . " (paragraph 8)? Do you think that, in the same situation, you, too, could have been either a killer or an evader? Might you have answered either of these questions differently had you not read any of this chapter's other reading selections, especially Katz's?

5) Did Browning's material meet your expectations of what a historical account should be like? How would you compare your reception of his ideas to your reception of Black Elk's (see p. 52) or Esperanza's (cf. p. 46)? Do you think that you might have interpreted the data that Browning presents differently had he presented them in a poem rather than in a historical account? How about if a *poet* had presented these data, either in a poem or in a historical account?

The Carob Tree Grove: Christian Compassion

ABRAM L. SACHAR

Aside from being a well-respected scholar, Abram Leon Sachar (1899–1993) was an extraordinarily gifted and well-recognized higher education administrator. The first president (and only chancellor) of Brandeis University, which was named for Louis Brandeis, the first Jew appointed to the United States Supreme Court, Sachar ". . . built a world-renowned university from the dreams of the American Jewish community. . . . He won recognition world wide as the driving force behind the molding of Brandeis into the youngest major private research university in the United States" (quotation taken from the program notes for Sachar's memorial service). And at the University of Illinois, where he had taught history for 24 years prior to his becoming president of Brandeis University, Sachar "was one of the pioneers of the Hillel Foundation and for nearly two decades was the international director of B'nai B'rith Hillel Foundations and later served as chairman of the Hillel Commission of B'nai B'rith" (memorial service program notes; named after an ancient and most revered rabbi, "Hillel" is an organization for Jewish college students). The recipient of numerous national and international honors—including "honorary degrees from more than 30 American colleges and universities" (program notes)—Sachar is also the author of many books, including *A History of the Jews* (1938), *The Course of Our Times* (1972), *A Host At Last* (1976), and *The Redemption of the Unwanted* (1983), from which this chapter's final reading selection is taken.

PRE-READING QUESTIONS:

1) How would you characterize either the historical relationship between Judaism and Christianity or particular relationships (yours or others', perhaps) between Jews and Christians? See if your pre-reading thoughts and feelings help determine the ways in which you respond to the material that Sachar presents.

2) In your view, what constitutes an act of heroism? Can you think of any people whom you consider heroes or heroines? If so, who are they, what acts of heroism did they engage in, and why would you consider these acts heroic?

3) What thoughts come to mind when you hear the phrase "Righteous Gentiles"? In your view, are these words redundant? Can there be an *un*righteous Gentile? Does the phrase "Righteous Gentile" seem offensive?

4) Sachar presents several vignettes, which comprise a sort of anecdotal history. Given this information, do you have any expectations concerning the ways in which you might judge the facts that the author will present?

CLOSE-READING TIP

Though fairly straightforward, the accounts of bravery that Sachar describes do contain some rather telling ironies. As you read about the accounts of heroism discussed in this reading selection, watch for these ironies and, when you notice them, think about how they underscore both our understanding of and our consternation about the Holocaust. You'll find representative passages in paragraphs 11, 15, and 27ff.

1 In August 1953, the Israeli Knesset authorized the creation of the Yad Vashem Research Institute, to be housed on Memorial Hill in Jerusalem.[1] It was to devote itself to an analysis of all aspects of the Holocaust, based on

---

[1]The designation came from the Prophet Isaiah (56:5): "I will give them an everlasting name which shall be not be cut off." [Sachar's note.]

scrupulous scholarship. Article 9 of the resolution mandated that the research should include the identification of concerned Christians who had risked harassment, imprisonment, torture, reprisals against loved ones, even death, to save Jewish lives. The names and the nationalities of those chosen were to be inscribed at the base of individual carob trees that would become a Grove of the Righteous. The plantings, lovingly attended, flourished to remind beholders that each of the Righteous, named in gratitude, "is like a tree planted by streams of water that yields its fruit in its season and its leaf does not wither" (Psalms 1:3). The carob tree was chosen because of its endurance, resisting the hot, gusty summer and bitter winter winds of the highest hills of Jerusalem. There was felicitous symbolism too in the decision, for the fruit of the carob recalled the ministry of John the Baptist, to whom it was "The staff of life." Indeed, it is sometimes known as St. John's bread.

2   In the thirty years since the first plantings, about a thousand trees, in double rows, have grown up to shade the avenue leading to the Yad Vashem headquarters and museum. Each tree commemorates an individual man or woman or a community whose acts of heroic concern have been identified and confirmed. The number seems pathetically small, given the fact that the names have been drawn from throughout Europe. Nor is the grove likely to acquire many more trees in the future. As the survivors of the Holocaust themselves grow older and die, it becomes more difficult to validate the courage, at great personal risk, that challenged the Nazis.

3   Nevertheless, those few daring spirits who did emerge, and whose actions can be authenticated, stand out, in Milton's phrase, "Godlike erect with native honour clad." The overwhelming majority of the Righteous seem to have arisen from among the common folk—a humble parish priest here, a minister there, a Mother Superior of a convent, a modest housewife, a shopkeeper or small businessman, the people of a feisty French village, a mini-company of laborers, a group of students. Many of the stories have been detailed in histories and biographies; others, documenting deeds as daring and sacrificial, have remained in the files of the Yad Vashem. In an overview of a period that challenges human values, it seems appropriate to include a sampling of the known and the comparatively unknown, to recall that there were valiant spirits, however rare, whose actions pierced the Stygian darkness.

. . .

4   Anna Simaite, a Lithuanian whose wholesome peasant face would scarcely be associated with intrigue, became a conspirator when the choice for her was to break man's law or God's. As a youthful radical when czarist Russia controlled the Baltic States, she had managed to stay clear of the police and became a teacher in a high school in Riga. Her charges were mainly waifs from the poorest families and she spent several years in Moscow to prepare for more intensive service among them. During World War II, though the Germans invested Lithuania, she managed to secure a post as a junior librarian at the University of Vilna. Many of those who frequented the library were Jewish children and she loved them dearly. But the Germans soon drove all Jews into an overcrowded ghetto

area, and, as she wrote later, she knew then that her own well-being would have to be subordinated to a more compelling call.

5 Non-Jews were forbidden to enter the ghetto lest they be tempted to succor those whom they knew. Anna defied the order. She was admitted by the guards when she explained that her girls had been omnivorous readers and, since many of the books in the library had been taken into the ghetto, she hoped to ferret them out. Occasionally she secretly provided extra food. The coupons allocated to Aryans entitled her to obtain margarine and cheese, and she saved them for the children, who subsisted on potato peelings and cabbage. She rescued some rare books and sacred documents hidden in the synagogues and even some Torah scrolls that she stored under the floor of her lodgings and in the vaults of the university library. From the ghetto she would gather up lice-infested clothing to be disinfected, washed and ironed, and smuggled back to the owners. Occasionally when the guards' vigilance relaxed, she was able to spirit very young children out of the ghetto. Soon Anna became bold enough to bring in small arms obtained from the Partisan underground, to be hoarded for the day when the break for freedom would come. She encouraged the children to write scraps of diaries so that their experiences could be preserved; she hid the papers on her person and brought them out for deposit in the vaults of the university library.

6 Such subversion could not, of course, go long unnoticed. The Gestapo, using threat and coercion on weaker souls, eventually caught up with her. Anna was arrested in the summer of 1944 and tortured to reveal what she had done, and where her Jewish children were hidden. She did not break her silence and was sentenced to immediate execution; but unknown to her the university officials had interceded by bribing a Nazi guard, and she was dispatched to Dachau. There, by another quirk of luck, she was at the last moment reprieved and deported to a camp in southern France. The American invasion set her free.[2]

7 In the postwar world Anna's ministrations, which she did not discuss, were long in coming to light. She earned a bare livelihood in Toulouse as dishwasher, seamstress, and ultimately, once again, as a librarian. During the early 1950s her Vilna experiences became known through some of the families she had rescued. The Society of Lithuanian Jews in America came to her assistance. A home was found for her in Paris. Soon she was besieged by letters from some of the children, "her children," who had settled in Israel and pleaded that she join them. Anna resisted until 1953, when she agreed to accept a little farm in Petach Tikvah, and a pension from the government. . . .

. . .

8 After Hitler came to power, the Protestant churches in Germany were brought under the control of Nazi-appointed officials espousing "the Aryan

[2]Shammai Golan, *The Holocaust*, cited in Bauer, *A History of the Holocaust*, p. 288.

paragraph" of the Nazi platform. Many of the Protestant pastors resisted this assault upon their conscience and they organized a schismatic wing, the Confessional Church: by 1936 it could claim the adherence of 9,000 pastors, about 40 percent of all the Protestant canons and clerics. Martin Niemöller, who had performed brilliantly as a naval officer in World War I and then chosen a career in the ministry, was one of the founders, for he was convinced that the Nazi party was going far beyond a resurgence of nationalist fervor.

9   As the number of Jewish victims mounted into the millions, Niemöller could not carry his dissidence silently. His preaching, always eloquent, "spoke poignards and every word stabbed." Though he came from an important Evangelical family and had a distinguished war record, his defiance could not remain unchallenged. He was arrested and sent to one of the concentration camps, ultimately to Dachau, where he shared imprisonment with the former French Prime Minister, Léon Blum, who had been transferred from Theresienstadt.

10   Niemöller survived to return to his ministry, never ceasing to regret that he had not spoken out sooner before the Nazis had acquired their unlimited power. "We let God wait ten years," he declared. "These things happened in our German name and in our world. . . . I regard myself as guilty as any SS man."[3] Since for a while he had been a member of the Nazi party, no carob tree was planted for him by Yad Vashem. But the retribution for moral neutrality was never better stated than in one of his deepest felt charges to the German people: "They went after the Jews, but I was not a Jew, so I remained unconcerned. Then they went after the Catholics, but I was not a Catholic so I remained unconcerned. Then they went after the Communists, but I was not a Communist, so I remained unconcerned. Then they went after the Protestants and there was no one left to be concerned.". . .

. . .

11   Perhaps no more shining example of national courage was offered in the teeth of Nazi occupation than that of Denmark. Itself tiny among the peoples of Europe, it had a Jewish population in 1940 of about 7,300, three-fourths of whom had migrated there from Germany and other European countries in the years between the two world wars. There were also some seven hundred non-Jews who had married Jews. These people were mainly centered in Copenhagen, where they savored every opportunity for participation in Danish life. The one cloud, and it was then no larger than a man's hand, appeared in Schleswig-Holstein, the disputed province on the southern border of Germany which Bismarck had usurped in mid-nineteenth century. Schleswig-Holstein had been returned to Denmark after World War I. Fifty thousand Germans still lived in the province and occasional rumblings of anti-Semitism were heard from there, but were not taken too seriously either by the general population or by the Danish Jews.

---

[3]Philip Friedman, *Their Brothers' Keepers*, pp. 30–32.

12   When Hitler came to power after 1933, Nazi irredentism grew bolder. The effort to stimulate disaffection angered the Danes and their leaders. Indeed, on April 22, 1940, King Christian X attended the centennial celebration of Copenhagen's main synagogue, and spoke eloquently of Jewish contributions to Danish national life. This was a fortnight after Hitler had launched his attacks on the lands that he coveted; Denmark, along with Poland and the Baltic States, was rapidly occupied. Sweden was permitted the status of neutrality and escaped attack when it did not resist the flight of Nazi aircraft over its territory to complete the subjugation of Norway.

13   At first the Nazis made little attempt to bring the Danes into the Fascist fold, content to dictate economic policy and to strip the land of its rich dairy products and foodstuffs. Jew-baiting, however, began at once. The German ambassador to Denmark, Werner Best, drew up a master plan for the deportation of Danish Jews to the death camps, expecting, for this purpose, to rely upon the normal machinery of government. He requested the Danish Parliament to enact the appropriate legislation. Parliament refused.

14   Meanwhile, Danish writers—no mean force in so literate a society—demonstrated their defiant solidarity through an ingenious historical parallel. When the centennial of George Brandes, a Jewish intellectual and revered Danish literary critic, was observed in February 1942, the literati staged a series of celebrations. Selections from Brandes' writings were read aloud at public meetings, all chosen for their appositeness in the prevailing climate. Ernest Renan's prayer to Athena was intoned and acquired a rare popularity: "The world will only be saved by returning to you and thus shaking off the barbarism in which it finds itself." The Nazis fumed. Nevertheless, they bided their time until August 1943 when, the war going against them elsewhere, Hitler deposed the Danish king, instituted military rule, and disarmed the tiny Danish Army. He decided now to include the Jews of Denmark in the Final Solution. The dates chosen for the round-up were the High Holy Days, when most Jewish families, at worship in the synagogues, would be easily accessible. Four large ships were prepared for the mass deportation, two of which, however, were blown up by saboteurs.

15   What followed was high drama. The German attaché for shipping affairs was Captain Georg Ferdinand Dukwitz, a member of the German Legation in Denmark since 1939. He had close friends in the Danish Jewish community and was on good terms with the Chief Rabbi, Marcus Melchior. He risked his life and well-being when he secretly revealed the Nazi plans to the Danish leadership.[4] He was later asked what inspired his hazardous action. "It was not impetuous," he responded. "I did not think my life was more important than the lives of 7,000 Jews."[5]

---

[4]Leni Yahil, *The Rescue of Danish Jewry*, pp. 148–151.

[5]Aage Bertelsen, Address at World Jewish Congress, 1971, cited in Bejski, *Proceedings of the Second International Conferences, Yad Vashem,* pp. 640–642.

16   Dukwitz's warning spread quickly through Copenhagen and the few other communities where there were Jewish citizens. Overnight, as it were, a rescue organization came into being. Common folk went knocking on their Jewish neighbors' doors to offer shelter in their own homes until transport to Sweden was made ready. The motto was: "Where there's room in the heart, there's room in the house." Teams of young Danes reverently carried off about a hundred Torahs from synagogues and stored them in Protestant churches. The medical profession was especially cooperative. Copenhagen's famed Baspeberg Hospital became a staging area through which the doctors processed about 2,000 Jews for escape. There was no halt in rescue operations, even when the Gestapo brought their machine guns into an operating room when they suspected that the patient on the table was a Jew. Nurses openly kept collection boxes at their stations for small donations to aid the Jewish flight.

17   Meanwhile, a remarkable armada was being outfitted, not unlike the naval gallimaufry that had evacuated tens of thousands of trapped British soldiers at Dunkirk in 1940. Fishing smacks, rowboats, skiffs, yachts, ferries, anything that could float were placed at the disposal of the rescue committees by their owners. No one underestimated the enormous risks of the exodus. The Kattegat, between Elsinore in the north of Denmark and Hälsingborg in Sweden, is only two and a half miles wide, but there are fifteen miles of choppy seas between Copenhagen and the nearest Swedish landfall, Malmö. Nor were some of the Swedish political leaders enchanted with the prospect that the country's precarious neutrality would be jeopardized if they gave refuge to the Danish Jews. But these soon found that they had to deal with a Danish Nobel Laureate, Niels Bohr, considered one of the world's outstanding authorities in atomic science.

18   Bohr's Jewish identity had, until this moment of crisis, been quite nominal; but with 7,000 Jewish lives threatened, his latent loyalties came to life. He and his brother were in Stockholm for a planned stopover on the way to London, and eventually to the United States, for collaboration in the Manhattan atomic project. When word reached Bohr that some of the Swedish political leaders hesitated to offer asylum to the Danish Jews, he notified the Allied command that he would "sit on his duff" in Stockholm unless there was an immediate guarantee that the Danish Jews would be given sanctuary in Sweden. The Manhattan Project had become the most crucial secret weapon in the victory plans of the Allies and Bohr was among the half dozen scientists upon whom its successful completion depended. Churchill or Roosevelt may have expressed their concern to the Swedish embassies, for the guarantee that Bohr demanded came quickly.

19   The rescue operation was a kind of mini-Dunkirk. Nazi patrol boats were everywhere. Some small rescue crafts were sunk and their human cargo drowned; other people were shot in flight. But practically the entire Jewish population of Denmark, excepting those children who undoubtedly were more safely housed in the homes of Danish clergymen, reached the Swedish shores. A courageous Lutheran teacher, Aage Bertelson, and his family, super-

vised one rescue mission that saved about seven hundred Jews. When the Nazis moved in with their 2,000 Gestapo deportation specialists on the High Holy Days (October 1 and 2, 1943), they learned with chagrin that all but about 500 elderly and sick Jews, too weak to escape, had disappeared.[6] For these helpless relics there was no compassion, and they were shipped off to Theresienstadt. That most of them survived was due in largest measure to the continued concern of the Danish government. The king sent to the camp a committee of hand-picked, high-ranking Danes under the aegis of the Danish Red Cross, to observe and report on the condition of Danish prisoners there. . . . [T]he committee was duped about the procedures in the camp, but the requirement by the Danish government for frequent reports may have had some restraining influence. . . .

. . .

20   An as yet unsolved mystery of the postwar world concerns Raoul Wallenberg, the Swedish nobleman who undertook a mission of mercy in Hungary by means of a modern equivalent of an underground railroad and saved tens of thousands of lives. After more than thirty-five years there is still no reliable evidence as to Wallenberg's ultimate fate, despite the many investigators who have written books about him. He was last seen leaving the Swedish Legation in Budapest on the morning of January 17, 1945, in the company of a Russian officer, en route to an appointment with General Malinovski, whose troops had driven the Nazis from the Hungarian capital.

21   Wallenberg was of impressive lineage. One of his grandfathers, scion of an old Lutheran family, was a prominent banker and had been minister to Japan and Turkey. Wallenberg's father had been a naval officer and, later, part of the family's banking empire. Raoul had ranged far in the course of acquiring an education, studying architecture and engineering at the University of Michigan in the United States and law in France, before returning to Stockholm to enter a leading import-export firm. His partner in the firm, Kalmen Lauer, was a Hungarian Jew. During the last months of the war, Lauer's wife and members of her family were stranded in Budapest. It was known in Stockholm that the Nazis were stepping up their extermination of Hungarian Jews, many of whom had maintained a precarious security because of shifting Hungarian political alliances. Wallenberg, who had considerable diplomatic and financial leverage, volunteered to go to Budapest to transport Lauer's relatives and whatever other Jewish families—he had a list—he could salvage. The American War Refugee Board was also eager to have a representative in Budapest to help in the release of Jews from the doomed city.

22   Wallenberg, then thirty-three years old, arrived in Budapest in July 1944 and quickly sized up the chaotic situation, brought on by simultaneous civil war and the collapse of the municipal administration. He decided to expand his modest family-plan mission into a full-scale rescue operation. The stakes

[6]Yahil, *The Rescue of Danish Jewry*, pp. 223–285.

were high. The prewar Jewish population had been slightly more than 400,000, but this figure had risen to more than 800,000 by the annexation of Polish territory and some provinces of the former Austro-Hungarian Empire. The war and deportations had taken a ghastly toll; but in 1944 there were still about 180,000 Jews left, mainly in Budapest.

23   Wallenberg established a special department, Section C, in the Swedish Embassy. The staff of twenty soon grew to more than six hundred, who, along with their families, were placed under the protection of the Swedish flag. Then Wallenberg began to supply Swedish identities even to those who had only the slightest family or business connection with his homeland. Section C printed "protective" passports, impressively emblazoned with Swedish stamps and signatures. Within days of his arrival, Wallenberg had taken more than a thousand families into "Swedish custody." His stratagems were soon part of an effort by other neutral countries, including Switzerland, Portugal, and Spain. The papal nuncio and the Budapest director of the International Red Cross also issued protective papers and the number of those who were covered by new identities grew to the thousands. Unfortunately, while passports and other documents strengthened protection, they did not authorize a right to emigrate.

24   Wallenberg did not confine himself to issuing counterfeit documents. He cooperated fully with Zionist youth movement members, helping them to buy or rent thirty-two buildings that were draped, by his authorization, with Swedish flags, giving them the status of "safehouses." When Wallenberg learned that a large contingent of Jews was being taken by truck to the railroad station for deportation east, he appeared, flourishing what seemed valid credentials, demanding release for them all. His voice and tone exuded command, no doubt buttressed by the knowledge that no junior German officer could be expected to understand either Hungarian or Swedish, and that obedience to an authoritative presence was built into German military training. Wallenberg's half sister, Nina Lengergren, noted in a later interview: "Raoul was a great actor. He could imitate brilliantly. If he wanted to, he could be more German than a Prussian general."

25   In October 1944, barely four months after Wallenberg's arrival, the puppet chief of Hungary, Admiral Horthy, repudiated the imposed alliance with Germany and announced that he would sue for peace with the Allies. The Germans poured back, in full strength, into Budapest. Horthy was arrested, to be replaced by one of Eichmann's own men, Ferenz Szalasi. In the next weeks the Nazis seemed to give equal priority to the destruction of the remaining Jews and resistance to the Russians. No homes, whatever flags they flew, no persons, whatever documents they carried, were spared. Szalasi's underlings went on a spree of killing, burning, looting, flogging, raping. Thousands of mutilated corpses floated in the waters of the Danube.

26   Wallenberg continued fighting for time in the knowledge that the Russians were advancing inexorably. He was assisted by a friendship with a powerful cabinet member of the notorious Arrow Cross, the Hungarian neo-Nazi party, who had so far successfully concealed his Jewish ancestry. From him Wallen-

berg learned that the the Arrow Cross planned a pogrom to liquidate the Jews who still remained in the desolated ghetto. Wallenberg was able to wind up his mission with another dramatic rescue. He contrived an audience with the German commander and warned him that, if the order were not canceled, he would use all his influence to have the commander tried as a war criminal. With the Russians on the outskirts of the city, their bombs already exploding nearby, the general was impressed and he canceled the order for the pogrom. Seventy thousand Jewish lives had hung on this last-minute intercession.[7]

. . .

27 The Nazis were driven from Budapest early in 1945, preceded by hordes of collaborators they had themselves enlisted. Wallenberg did not, as he might well have done, leave Budapest at once. He lingered on for several days hoping to obtain assurances from the Soviet general, Malinovski, that the Jews who had survived would come to no further peril. On the morning of January 17, accompanied by a Soviet motorcycle escort, he left the safety of the Swedish Legation for his fateful interview with the Russians. What happened on the way or immediately after has remained a mystery.

28 Over the years, the Wallenberg family and the government of Sweden have continuously appealed to Soviet authorities to explain Wallenberg's disappearance. Invariably, they received the frustrating response that he had indeed been expected at the Russian headquarters on that January morning. Period. In 1947 the Soviet Foreign Minister, Andre Vishinsky, informed the Swedish government that Wallenberg was not in the Soviet Union and was unknown to Soviet authorities. In February 1957, more than twelve years after Wallenberg's disappearance, the Soviet Foreign Minister, Andrei Gromyko, issued an official statement indicating that Wallenberg had died of a heart attack in Lubyanka Prison on July 17, 1947. The surname was misspelled. No first name was given. No explanation was offered other than that a record had come to light in the prison archives attesting to Wallenberg's death.

29 Despite the Russian disclaimer, hope persisted in the succeeding decades that Raoul Wallenberg had survived. One of those saved by Wallenberg, now Mrs. Thomas Lantos, who had settled in California, and several other survivors, refused to accept the Russian statement of 1957, and they kept up a persistent campaign to learn the fate of their courageous Swedish redeemer.

30 In May 1980, the Swedish Foreign Minister met with Andrei Gromyko, his Soviet counterpart, to urge the Russians to clear up the long-drawn-out case with its conflicting explanations and its insulting silences. What were the Russians hiding that they could not frankly reveal the events that had taken place from the time of Wallenberg's disappearance through the years that followed?

---

[7]F. E. Werbell and T. Clarke (eds.), *The Lost Hero: The Mystery of Raoul Wallenberg*, pp. 138–140.

Gromyko stared into space, whether listening or not, and ended the interview with the laconic statement: "We stand by our 1957 memorandum."

31   In the winter of 1981, an international panel headed by Ingrid Widemann, a Justice of the Swedish Supreme Court, called on the Soviet Union to reopen the case, alleging that "the original Russian statement had been based on tragic misinformation." There were nineteen sworn testimonies in Swedish hands from former cellmates of Wallenberg who had seen him in prison in Lubyanka.

32   Also in 1981 a bill was filed in the U.S. Congress to confer honorary citizenship on Wallenberg. The legislation was sponsored by Mrs. Lantos' husband Thomas, a concentration camp victim who was admitted to the United States after the war period on a student visa which I had obtained for him. He remained in the United States after receiving his degree, and became an American citizen. A successful political career followed, and he was the first Holocaust survivor to serve in Congress as a representative. The legislation to confer honorary citizenship on Wallenberg was unanimously adopted in September 1981. It now became possible for the American government to make official representations to the Soviet Union about Wallenberg's fate.[8]

33   Wallenberg was responsible for the direct rescue of many thousands of Hungarian Jews. Most of them are now dead or have migrated. To the younger generation, Wallenberg became a legend. There is a small building in Budapest still bearing marks of the bullets of 1945 when the Nazis were routed, and of 1956 when the freedom fighters fought the Soviet tanks to regain the liberty that had been lost under communism. A modest plaque on the house front bears the inscription in Hungarian: "To the memory of Raoul Wallenberg, Swedish diplomat whose heroic deeds saved tens of thousands of Hungarians from the final days of Nazi terror. Raoul Wallenberg disappeared during the siege of Budapest." And in the heart of Budapest there is a street named for him.

34   In Jerusalem, the Yad Vashem several times suggested that a tree be planted in Wallenberg's memory in the Grove of the Righteous. But for Wallenberg's family to accept the appreciated honor would be tantamount to signing the death certificate. Until 1980, Raoul Wallenberg's aged mother therefore steadfastly refused permission for the memorial. After her death in that year, the rest of the family conceded that all hope was gone. A carob tree, which will not bear its fruit for another generation, has now been planted.

. . .

35   As one walks up the Avenue of the Righteous, each tree that lines the road tells its story of sacrificial Christian courage. The deeds that are gratefully

---

[8]It was widely noted that honorary citizenship had been conferred only once before, on Sir Winston Churchill. This is not accurate. After the American Revolution, Congress, at the behest of George Washington, granted honorary American citizenship to the Marquis de Lafayette and his descendants in perpetuity. [Sachar's note.]

acknowledged through the plantings saved many families, often whole communities. To be sure, in the dark world of Hitler, only a tiny minority could be counted on for redemptive service. But these kept the hope alive that rainbows would follow every storm. Sholom Asch, the dean of Jewish writers in the Holocaust generation, who was not daunted nor discouraged because there were so few Christians whose compassion outweighed their prudence, wrote:

> On the flood of sin, hatred, and blood, let loose by Hitler upon the world, there was a small ark which preserved intact the common heritage of a Judaeo-Christian outlook, an outlook which is founded on the double principle of love of God and love of one's fellow man. The demonism of Hitler had sought to overturn and overwhelm it in the floods of hate. It was saved by the heroism of a handful of saints.[9]

POST-READING QUESTIONS:

1) Did the thoughts or feelings that you discussed in your response to the first pre-reading question affect your understanding of or help shape your reactions to the material that Sachar presents? Did this material cause you to reexamine your reasons for having these thoughts and feelings?

2) Are the "Righteous Gentiles" referred to in this reading selection the sorts of people whom you consider heroes and heroines? If so, in what ways are their acts heroic? Are they both heroic and nonheroic? After having read Sachar's text, do you want to amend or otherwise rethink your responses to the second and third pre-reading questions?

3) Does this reading selection help you to understand why some individuals act courageously and morally and why others don't?

4) Elsewhere in the chapter from which this reading selection is excerpted, Sachar notes that the ordinary Christian rescuers, who displayed such compassion towards Jews, "influenced no national policy, nor did they turn the tide of events." He continues: "These were men and women who rose above self to follow a vision of Christian duty. Asked why they risked so much when they had no personal stake in the result, they invariably responded that they did have a stake: they were reacting to what gave significance to their being" (96). In your view, is Sachar's commentary apt? Does it, perhaps, also help us to understand why most people did nothing to help Jewish victims of the Nazis, or why many people actively victimized Jews? Finally, does Sachar's commentary have any bearing on your own actions or nonactions?

5) Did Sachar's material meet the pre-reading expectations that you discussed in your response to the fourth pre-reading question? Do you think that you might have responded differently to the facts presented here had they been related in a historical account such as that which Browning offers (see p. 107)? How about if they were

---

[9] Aage Bertelsen. *October '43*, Preface, pp. vii–viii, pp. 223–282.

narrated by Holocaust survivors who had been saved by the people whose stories of rescue Sachar tells?

6) How would you compare the ordinary people whom Christopher Browning describes to those whom Sachar describes? Do you think that Just (compare the excerpt from *Shoah*, p. 92) might have been an ordinary person? How do you think that Wiesel or Katz might answer this question? How do you think that they might respond to Sachar's piece?

HANDS-ON ACTIVITY:

If you are interested in furthering your own understanding of the Holocaust while also doing something practical to help fellow or younger students understand how this tragedy occurred and how a similar one might be averted in the future, call your local chapter of the Anti-Defamation League to see how you might become involved in educational or other activities related either to the Holocaust or to other group tragedies, especially present-day ones. You might also see whether or not your area has any battered women's shelters, rape hot line centers, or other sorts of crisis intervention centers or organizations that respond to victims' needs and that could use your help. Surely our studies of the Holocaust have taught us that the world's being either a realm of hope or a globe of despair depends upon the actions or inactions of its inhabitants. By taking your place among those individuals who dare to improve the lives of our planet's citizens, you'll make your mark on a world that sorely needs your help.

5

"*It* is deeply satisfying to believe that we are not locked into our original statements, that we might start and stop, erase, use the delete key in life, and be saved from the roughness of our early drafts. Words can be retracted; souls can be reincarnated."

NANCY SOMMERS
Between the Drafts

Ideas and Strategies for Revising and Moving Beyond the First Draft

T HE PREWRITING TECHNIQUES highlighted and modeled in the previous chapter in no way represent an exhaustive list of predrafting strategies, nor are they necessarily the best techniques for you to use at all times. Rather easily learned and used, they represent merely some of the component parts that make up the predrafting phase of the writing process—component parts that you can slightly or radically embellish or, if need be, even completely abandon as you develop your own writing style(s). If they help you generate ideas for a first, rough, working draft of your paper, then they will have served their purpose.

The key words here are "first," "rough," "working," and "draft." Far from finished, your first draft represents writing and thinking that is very much work-in-progress. This need not mean that the work is bad or without value; in fact, in the world of academics, work-in-progress often constitutes business-as-usual. A first draft gives the writer a chance to see how her ideas are shaping up in essay form: Should she keep everything that she has written? Should she add more details and delete others? Even if she decides to toss everything that she has written, at least she will have written something—which means that, in all likelihood, she can write some more.

Creating a Second Draft

Ideally, you'll want to **revise** your thinking and writing so that you achieve a well-organized final draft containing fully developed and coherent points couched in polished prose. But don't worry about creating such a draft immediately after you've created your first draft. Instead, throughout the writing process, let your writing itself both shape the direction and narrow the focus of your still-forming thoughts. Remember that writing is a fluid, not a formulaic, process; more like a flowing stream than a pool of stagnant water, writing frequently leads to more (and sometimes to vastly different) writing. By its very nature, writing tends to be a great organizer, sifter, and sometimes even leveler of ideas. However many ideas you might have in your head, you can only write them down one at a time, and you can only form them into a paper one draft (or one part of a draft) at a time. Letting your own writing lead the way, as you begin to move from a first to a second draft, concentrate merely on creating a more complete, more tightly focused blueprint of your written ideas. (Here's a tip: since you will be trying to write progressively better reader-based drafts, you might find it helpful to get some feedback on your drafts-in-progress from an intended reader or from someone else sensitive to the needs of your intended audience.)

To help you begin seeing how you might move beyond the writing of a first draft, let's take another look at the sample first draft sketched in the previous chapter, in which Eddy informs his parents of his decision not to join the family on this year's family vacation:

Dear Mom and Dad,

I want to thank you for your generous and tempting offer to take me with you and the family to Tahiti. I always wanted to go there, and I don't know when I'll have the chance to go—if ever—if I don't go there with you in October. Such a beautiful place! And a free vacation (just kidding—not really, though). But, unfortunately, I'm going to have to say no. As much as I'd like to go, I just can't afford to miss that many classes. Besides, I have exams that week, and my profs. won't let us make up missed exams. "Too bad," they said. "If you're that bad off that you have to miss an exam, you should probably drop out of school." Nice folks, huh? Anyway, if I miss my exams, then I'll fail my courses, and my GPA will be ruined—and you will have wasted your money.

You see, I'm beginning to realize that in college you're expected to attend classes or take your lumps. One of those lumps is that we can't make up missed exams. And if I miss my exams, then I probably can kiss med school good-bye. Besides, my profs. won't write letters for me if I flake off in their classes, which is how they'll judge me if I miss their stupid exams.

Sorry, Mom and Dad! I know how into family vacations you are, but I also know how much you want me to do well in school. So, I'm hoping that you'll understand my decision. If you don't, I'm sure you'll let me know.

Anyway, gotta go now. Give my love to Susie, and tell her that I'll write to her soon—the little squirt!

Love,
Eddy

To be sure, this letter gets Eddy's main point across. But, considering his **audience**, should he send the letter as is or send a revised version of it? If he decides to revise the letter, should he change his tone of voice, making it a bit more formal? Should he adopt a different persona—the "serious student" persona, perhaps, or the "loving son" persona, the "guilt-ridden student-beggar" persona, or maybe the "real me" persona? Also, though in this case he probably knows his audience well, can he assume that they know enough about his present circumstances to respect and accept his decision, if not also to approve of it? Might Eddy's parents feel bad when they read his letter? If so, will he feel guilty? Is he perhaps secretly hoping that his parents will reject his decision and thus leave him "no choice" but to go with them? Conversely, is it possible that they don't really want him to travel with them this year? Should his speculations about their possible reaction influence the way in which he argues his case?

In short, if Eddy were to rework this letter, how might he revise it so that it adequately meets the needs of the "assignment," accounts for both his writing needs and his parents' reading needs, coherently and convincingly presents his case, and displays a smooth link between the letter's form and content?

Let's say that Eddy's parents are very understanding people, the sort who would never consider their financial support of their son's education a waste of money and who want to make sure that he receives a good education so that he can reach his goal of becoming a physician. In light of this fact, Eddy might very well decide to delete his comment about his parents' money and expand on the significance of his not missing classes and exams. In addition, to show them how serious he is about his work, he might decide to change the tone of his letter from one of rather complete informality to something on the order of congenial formality. All in all, he might come up with a next draft that looks something like this:

Dear Mom and Dad,

I want to thank you for your generous—and tempting—offer to have me join you and the family on this year's vacation. I've always wanted to go to Tahiti, and this seems such a perfect opportunity to do so. Unfortunately, though, I'm going to have to say no.

As you know, I'll still be in school in October. That means that I'd have to miss a lot of class time, which really would be harmful to me, since I'm beginning to realize that in college you're expected to attend classes or take the consequences of missing them. One of those consequences is that we can't make up missed exams—and, you guessed it, I have exams during the time that you'll be on vacation! Needless to say, if I miss my exams, then I'll fail my courses, and if I fail my courses, then I'll hurt my GPA. And given how tough it is to get into med school these days, I really need to maintain a strong GPA (I also need strong letters of recommendation from my profs, which I'm not likely to get if I appear to be a flake).

I know how important it is for you to have the family together during vacations, but I also know how important it is for you that I do well in school (I can still hear you telling Grandma, "My son, the doctor!"). So, I'm hoping that you'll understand my decision. Maybe during Thanksgiving break we can take a quick trip to Beaver Falls; that way, we can have at least *some* family vacation where everyone is together. If that's a problem, I'm sure that we can work something else out later.

Anyway, thanks again for asking, and sorry that I can't go with you. But I know that you'll understand. I'll talk with you soon. Give my love to Susie, and tell her that I'll write to her soon.

Love,
Eddy

Perhaps Eddy will revise this letter further, perhaps not. If he has to mail his letter soon because the deadline for his response is approaching, he might simply have to mail the letter in its once-revised form and hope for the best. Since he is writing reader-based prose, maybe he'll have his roommate read it; as a fellow student living away from home, Eddy's roommate probably understands enough about the needs of Eddy's intended audience to be able to offer Eddy good advice on what to add or change here and leave out there. Perhaps Eddy will also read his letter aloud, either to himself or to his roommate; in the course of reading it aloud, he himself might discover further changes that he wants or needs to make. And if he sends this or a subsequently revised version of his letter and his parents respond by saying that, in fact, they *don't* understand his decision, that they're very hurt by his rejection, and so on, he might compose and revise subsequent letters to them differently, in accordance with what he will have learned about both their needs and their reading practices. Whatever he decides to do *now*, at least he will have created a revised, second draft that clearly and carefully states his case and that takes into account the needs of his audience, his reason for writing the letter, his knowledge of the subject, and other related matters. Everything else being equal, there's not much more that any writer can be expected to do.

Four Principles of Good Reader-Based Writing

All that we have just said about Eddy's decisions and choices concerning this letter-writing experience applies to the decisions and choices that you'll have to make when you work on your college writing assignments. You'll have deadlines to meet, you'll probably ask your friends and classmates to read and comment upon your work, and you'll need to revise your papers in light of audience expectations, your purpose for writing, and your instructor's feedback. And though you'll never write the perfect paper (no one ever does), you should be able to write a fairly decent paper if you heed the following four principles, which are offered to help you see how you can keep your reader-based ideas on track. In short, try to write and revise a reader-based paper so that it

1) best accounts for the particular needs of the writing task;

2) takes into account the needs of your intended audience;

3) indicates that you have derived a main point after having closely examined pertinent evidence; and

4) accounts for and explains the significance of enough germane information and evidence to prove or support this main point.

Though not a panacea, these principles will underlie all or nearly all of your college-level, reader-based writing assignments.

The particular needs of the writing task. No one writes in a vacuum, and all writing has a purpose. Whether you are taking notes during lectures, writing an opinion piece for your college newspaper, letting your creative and intellectual juices flow in completely unstructured freewriting, putting the final touches on an academic essay, or writing just for fun, you will greatly aid your writing efforts by keeping in mind why you are writing in the first place and what the particular writing task that you are performing requires of you. If, for instance, you are writing a letter to a friend, you might very well employ an informal tone of voice, use slang, and the like. On the other hand, if you are writing a letter to a dean at your school, you'll probably use more formal language. The same applies when, writing a formal essay, you are working at different points in the writing process. At the beginning of the process, when you are concentrating on freeing up your ideas, you need not worry about writing grammatically correct sentences; during a later phase of the writing process, however, you will want to scrutinize your sentences to see whether or not they are grammatically accurate.

To help yourself account for the particular needs of a given writing task, you might try asking yourself the following sorts of questions before you begin writing: "What is the nature of the assignment?" "What does the assignment specifically ask me to do?" "Why am I bothering to write this paper [or this letter, memo, poem, or short story]?" "What do I hope to gain by writing it? In other words, what is my ultimate purpose for or goal in constructing it?" Even if your goal is nothing more than to pass the class or receive a good grade in it, you can always find a reason to write when you want or need to write. By consciously thinking about the purpose of your writing, you should increase your chances of recognizing the particular needs of your writing task and thus of seeing what you need to say and revise in your work.

Ultimately, you yourself will have to decide what you want to write and how much you want your readers to see. In a personal essay, for example, especially one in which you write about personal experiences nearest your heart, you'll often find that the needs of the writing assignment are intimately bound up with your own interests or needs. You might also find, though, that you don't want to let your reader in on some of your thoughts and feelings, however pertinent they might be to the essay. If you feel that you really want or need to express these thoughts and feelings, then you might view your writing-in-progress as a diary or personal journal entry so that you can both keep writing and say what you feel the need to say. You might then have two papers in progress: one, meant for your eyes only, whose prose you would revise only if doing so would serve the needs of your writer-based writing task; and the other, meant for the eyes of your intended readers, whose prose you would revise if doing so would help the paper reach its reader-based goal. Simply put, different writing tasks have different needs; the wise writer knows this and writes accordingly.

Taking into account the needs of your intended audience. Just as one always writes with a purpose, so one always writes for an intended audience. As your own intended reader of your writer-based prose, you are the best judge of what you need to say or omit from saying in your work. The intended readers of your reader-based prose, though, and not you alone, have the charge as well as the authority to judge your work.

The famous writer E. B. White (the author of *Charlotte's Web*) once commented on the "concern for the bewildered reader" held by William Strunk, Jr., White's former English teacher whose book *The Elements of Style* White eventually coauthored. Having a "deep sympathy for the reader[,]" Strunk "felt that the reader was in serious trouble most of the time, a man floundering in a swamp, and that it was the duty of anyone attempting to write English to drain this swamp quickly and get his man up on dry ground, or at least throw him a rope" (*The Elements of Style* xvi). Even though your readers might not be in quite as much trouble as is the hypothetical reader depicted here, like all readers, yours are going to be given the task of following you from point to point in your papers without having the benefit of being inside your head. If your verbal road signs (to change the metaphor) help them see where they are going, then they should arrive at the appropriate destination with few or no frustrating stories to tell about discouraging detours and dead ends that they had encountered along the way. If your signs send them hither and yon, however, then you can hardly expect them to want to continue on their journey or, should they finally complete the journey, to arrive in good spirits at the intended destination.

To help your readers reach the destination of your ideas, try incorporating into your paper the same landmarks and signs that help *you* know both where you are and where you are going. If from time to time you find yourself becoming a bit lazy (all writers do) and think that you can get away with omitting important information, just remind yourself of how *you* feel when *you* are traveling along unfamiliar highways with unclear road signs posted along the way or when *you* come upon a detour concerning which you received no advance warning. Just as the makers of road signs need to pursue their work with a traveler's eyes, so, too, writers need to write their reader-based prose with the eyes of a reader. Remember: *You* are responsible for whatever you say in your papers—and, sometimes, for what you needed to have said but omitted from saying in them. The more reader-friendly you can make your writing, the more likely your readers will be able to follow you to the points that you want them to reach.

In trying to guide your readers carefully from point to point so that they know where they are going and why they are going there, you are attempting to help them understand your ideas. It usually doesn't matter if readers other than those who comprise your intended audience fail to understand your work, since you aren't writing for them in the first place. The adequacy of your lab report for your physics class is not necessarily in doubt if your roommate, who knows nothing about physics, doesn't understand what you are saying, nor is the adequacy of your composition paper assured just because some of your friends, who know little or nothing about the matters that you are learning in your composition class, read the paper and really like it. But if you load your English paper, say, with unexplained terms from physics and your intended readers—your English instructor and the members of your English class—don't understand what these terms mean and thus don't understand what you've written, then you do have something to worry about. In this case, you haven't adequately fulfilled the needs of the assignment precisely because you have failed to meet the needs of your intended readers. Since, as mentioned above, the writer is always responsible for whatever he or she writes, *you* are responsible either for fixing this problem or, if it's too late for that, trying to insure that you don't make this sort of mistake in your future papers.

On the other hand, you need to accept the fact that, even if you successfully account for your readers' needs, at least some of your intended readers won't understand everything that you've written. If perchance you know your intended readers (such as your instructor, classmates, or parents), you might try to find out—before writing your paper, that is—what their needs are and how you can best meet these needs; by taking this extra step in the writing process, you'll increase the chances that your paper will receive a favorable reading even among those of your readers who might not share your views. As might be expected, readers feel frustrated when they sense that the writer is insensitive to or neglectful of their needs but feel appreciative when they sense that the writer is working hard to account for their needs. In particular, they like knowing that the writer is trying hard to make her or his work *understandable*. If for no other reason, for the sake of your arguments you should try concentrating at least as much on making sure that your readers understand what you are attempting to say as you do on convincing them that you are right. For, if you are right but your readers cannot know that because they cannot comprehend your ideas, then of what value is your reader-based work?

If you don't have the benefit of knowing or meeting with (all of) your intended readers and therefore must settle for anticipating your audience's needs—as would be the case, for example, were you to write an opinion piece for your college newspaper—you can still help insure that you present your intended audience with reader-friendly prose if you think and write *as a reader*, that is, as someone who wants or needs to know certain information in order to make sense of that which he or she is reading. If you ask yourself what *you* would need to know in order to make sense of your paper—in other words, if you ask yourself what landmarks would help *you* find your way—and then attempt to answer that question as honestly and fully as possible, you should be well on your way to discovering how you might account for the needs of your intended audience, whether or not you'll ever meet (everyone in) this audience.

Ask yourself, too, who your intended readers are and what they are likely to expect from your paper. How much might they already know about the subject matter under discussion? How much (more) will they likely need to know to make sense of what you are saying? Which important ideas might you need to explain to them? What assumptions will they likely accept or reject? (Be careful here, though: sometimes, you'll need to provide proof or support for assumptions regardless of whether or not your audience accepts them.) Should you use technical or more generic terms? Should you employ an informal or a formal tone of voice (or both)? And so on. Though you'll likely never say *everything* that needs to be said in your paper or account for *all* of your intended readers' needs, you will serve your writing well if you constantly and consciously try to present your readers with enough pertinent information to allow them to understand your position. To paraphrase a point made earlier: you cannot legitimately expect your readers to respect (let alone accept) your point of view if they can't figure out what it is because you've not explained it to them clearly.

One way that you might help yourself meet your intended readers' needs is to try writing not just as a student who is driven to learn, but also as a teacher who is intent upon helping *others* learn. As you draft and redraft your essays, ask yourself the following kinds of "teacherly" questions:

- Do I understand my points because I'm quite familiar with the material? Might others who are less familiar with the material have trouble understanding these points? If the latter is the case, how can I clarify and develop my ideas so that I can help my intended audience gain some valuable insights into the subject matter?

- Have I, in fact, taught my readers anything in this paper? After reading my paper, will they have a better grasp of the subject matter discussed in the paper than they had before they read my essay?

- If next semester the students taking this class are asked to read my paper before doing this same writing assignment, will they likely benefit from reading what I've written here?

If nothing else, writing for others will help you learn more about the reaches and limitations of your own knowledge concerning the subject matter. As the old saying goes, "to teach is to learn twice."

Deriving your main point from your close examination of evidence. Just as every piece of writing has a purpose and is written for an intended audience, so every paper has—or at least should have—a main point, however widely or narrowly focused that main point is. Indeed, for all of your reader-based work, you should always be able to answer the question "So, what *is* my main point, my main assertion, about all of this material?"

We call the central, unifying, main point of an essay—that is, the main assertion or contention around which the rest of the essay revolves—the paper's **thesis**. The actual statement articulating the thesis is called the **thesis statement**, and the paragraph containing the thesis statement is called the **thesis paragraph**. In short compositions, the thesis is usually *stated* rather than *implied*, the thesis statement is ordinarily one or two sentences long and normally occurs at the beginning or end of the thesis paragraph, and the thesis paragraph is often the first or, less often, the second paragraph of the essay. Be aware, though, that these descriptive facts represent *conventions* rather than *rules*.

A thesis has three characteristics. First, as previously mentioned, it is the paper's *main* point. Second, though it can answer and thus be turned into a question, it itself can never *be* a question; it must be an assertion (indeed, a question is not an assertion). The sentence "What's the greatest country in the world?" is not an assertion, but the sentence "Oz is the greatest country in the world" is. Notice that we can easily turn this second sentence *into* a question ("*Is* Oz the greatest country in the world?"), the answer to which might be a thesis. (Hint: Pay attention to any questions posed in your writing assignments, for the answers to these questions might be possible theses.)

Third, a thesis is not a statement of fact. Rather, it is an arguable point of view about either a fact (or facts) or an inference (or inferences). "Oz is the greatest country in the world" is clearly not a fact, though it is an assertion presumably stemming from a comparative analysis of the world's various countries (Never-never land, Atlantis, Wonderland, Disneyland, and so on). Just as clearly, the assertion "Oz is the greatest country in the world" calls for an explanation and requires proof; hence, it is *arguable*.[1] Whether you attempt to *support* a thesis by trying to show that it *most likely* follows from certain premises or provides the best possible explanation or theory concerning whatever issue is at stake, or whether you attempt to *prove* a thesis by trying to show that it *must* follow from certain true or clearly acceptable premises, you'll always need to argue for the merits of your thesis and not just boldly assert it.

Whatever other reasons you have for writing your paper, in a sense *the* reason that you write your essay is to show your reader why your thesis must be taken seriously. Everything else that you write in the paper should directly or indirectly serve the interests of your thesis. If any information in the paper does not, then you'll need to think about whether you want to change the paper's focus or main assertion to account for this information or omit the information from the paper. However, if you come upon data that *challenge* the claims that your thesis makes or rests upon, then you'll *have* to revaluate your thesis in light of these new pieces of evidence.

You always want the best thesis possible, whether or not you feel personally comforted by it. Indeed, as mentioned in Chapter Two (p. 21), keeping a flawed but comfortable perspective at the expense of a sound but uncomfortable one is a poor bargain. As someone committed to being a careful thinker, you are obligated to derive your main point from evidence, to prove or support it reasonably, and to revise or discard it in the face of evidence or reasoning that forces you to rethink it. Otherwise, you might find yourself doing little more than engaging in rhetorical posturing—a good way to sell products or win an election, perhaps, but a bad way to go about the business of careful thinking.

When you offer your thesis, you enter into a contract with your reader. In effect, you are saying to your reader, "If you act in good faith in your attempts to see whether or not I'm right, I'll act in good faith to prove or support my main contention." If you offer material which in and of itself might be interesting but which does not directly or indirectly advance the cause of your main point, you might be breaking the terms of the contract and needlessly confusing the reader. Similarly, you will fail to live up to the terms of the thesis contract if you fail to prove or support your thesis even though you present relevant material. But don't feel that you are doing something wrong if in the course of revising your paper

---

[1] Sometimes, the **context** of your paper will determine whether or not your thesis is a statement of fact. For example, taken out of context, the statement "California is part of the United States" might seem purely factual. But if offered in response to the question "Does Mexico have a legitimate historical claim to the territory known as California?" this statement is clearly arguable and hence in need of proof.

you discover that you need to change your thesis. In fact, as intimated earlier in this chapter, good writers not infrequently find that the writing process itself forces them to rethink their ideas. In this case, they simply draw up a new contract and then see if they can or should live by *its* terms.

At any stage of the writing process, you should feel free to test a reasonable **hypothesis,** a temporary, educated guess, if you already know enough about an issue to do so. Like a good scientist, you'll want to try to disprove or undermine your hypothesis; for, if it fails, you'll want to reject it. Then, you might test another one that seems reasonable. If eventually you come up with one that you cannot disprove or undermine, see if you can verify it so that you'll know whether or not it might work as a thesis. Always be willing to be wrong, and never simply decide in advance what the truth is and then pretend to discover it.

This last point bears emphasizing: You should always derive your thesis after having carefully examined the nature and quantity of pertinent evidence rather than decide upon a given point of view in advance and then seek evidence to prove or support it. Taking this latter route, you'll run the risk of manipulating the data, misrepresenting the facts or the nature of germane evidence, excluding or ignoring other, pertinent information or evidence that you should account for—in short, you'll risk stacking the deck or fixing the game. If you've ever been judged harshly by someone who, disregarding good evidence to the contrary, already had his mind made up about you, then you understand the dangers connected with the sorts of critical thinking errors alluded to here. To help yourself avoid making these sorts of errors, keep in mind that, although you may and sometimes even should speculate about issues and ideas, you should always be confident or skeptical of your views to the extent that you can or cannot substantiate these views with verifiable evidence. In other words, the more that you can substantiate your views, the more confident you should be of them; the less that you can substantiate your views, the more suspicious you should be of them.

You can help yourself avoid putting the cart (thesis) before the horse (evidence pulling the thesis along) by (1) trying to be in control of as much relevant information as possible, (2) remaining honest about what you know and don't know concerning the material that you are analyzing and writing about, and (3) writing about subject matter concerning which you know enough to write intelligently. If you happen to know that a given thesis is true, clearly acceptable, or strongly probable, you are not necessarily obligated to prove or support it in the course of writing your paper; whether or not you need to do so will depend upon the nature of the assignment, the composition of your audience, and the like. Nevertheless, even a thesis that you know "works" should have been derived from a careful evaluation of evidence in the first place. But be careful: If you are writing a paper that attempts to defend a clearly self-evident thesis—for example, "Nuclear war is awful"—your intended readers might wonder why you are bothering to write the paper at all. In other words, if they are not likely to demand that you prove or support your point, then you might be offering them a point that is not really arguable and hence does not technically qualify as a thesis.

Before moving on, take a look at the following statements, as well as at the accompanying explanations, to see why some of these sentences are theses and why some are not. Assume that each of the sentences in question is meant to constitute a paper's main point.

1) "Shakespeare's plays were written by more than one person." Technically, this statement constitutes a thesis because it makes an arguable assertion. Whether or not the thesis holds up depends upon whether or not it can be proved.

2) "Shakespeare wrote his plays in English." This statement is simply a fact, and thus it does not qualify as a thesis.

3) "So, after examining the relevant data, can we reach any reasonable conclusions concerning whether or not Mary Quitecontrary enjoys gardening?" Since this sentence is written in the form of a question, it cannot qualify as a thesis. The *answer* to this question might very well constitute a thesis, though.

4) "Phil Ibuster is probably a well-spoken gentleman." As was the case with statement #1, statement #4 constitutes a thesis because it, too, makes an arguable assertion. Similarly, however, we do not know whether or not *this* thesis holds up, since we have yet to evaluate an argument that attempts to support it.

Accounting for and explaining the significance of enough germane information and evidence to prove or support your main point. If you have derived your thesis after having examined the evidence before you, then theoretically you should know what you need to say to prove or support your main point. In your essay, you would merely document and explain the evidence that led you to your thesis. Often, of course, this procedure is easier said than done. But it can be done. There's no trick here. All you need to do is make a concerted effort to examine pertinent evidence carefully and to write honestly about a conclusion that follows from this evidence, even if you'd rather not have to write in defense of this particular conclusion.

In deciding what evidence you need to cite and explain, you'll be trying to determine what actually happened, what people really said, what someone's view really is, and so on. Since most of your college instructors will want you to **analyze** rather than simply **summarize** such data (concerning some assignments, they might even explicitly tell you not to summarize the data), be sure that you can distinguish between these two activities. When you summarize, you tell what happened and what was said. When you analyze, you explain *why* something happened, what the consequences are of someone's having said what she said, and the like. To be sure, sometimes the line between summary and analysis is rather thin. All summaries are analytical insofar as they offer interpretive perspectives by highlighting certain features and downplaying or ignoring others.

And all analyses involve at least some degree of overt or tacit summation; if they didn't, we could hardly understand them. Nevertheless, if you are basically telling your readers nothing more than what happened or what was said, you are summarizing; if you are telling them what you *make* of this information, you are analyzing.

Whether or not you decide to include summaries in your writing, you must be able to summarize data accurately in order to analyze them cogently, for you can't very well analyze something whose nature or function you misunderstand or, even worse, misrepresent. Your ability to establish yourself as an informed writer hinges upon your ability to demonstrate a reasonable understanding of relevant evidence. But what kind of evidence constitutes relevant evidence, and how much relevant evidence will you need to cite and explain in order to produce a good analysis? This is a good question, especially since, in your writing, you'll often deal with lots of gray areas and find yourself having to evaluate more than one promising interpretation of the data. Also, you'll often discover that your analytical endeavors are limited by the current state of knowledge about the subject matter in question, as well as, sometimes, by your own inability to explore other relevant interpretive possibilities.

Given this state of affairs, you'll thus need to refrain from dogmatically advancing your own positions when you are operating on difficult interpretive terrain, lest you keep yourself from seeing other promising interpretive possibilities that you might need to account for, if not also embrace. Although, like everyone else, you have no choice *but* to analyze data (even the view that you or anyone can read a literary text merely for pleasure, for example, is an analytical position), you do have some control over how well or badly you analyze them.

When you are writing and revising your papers, keep in mind that analyses are often, if not always, context-specific and that data are often more relative than absolute (remember the example concerning whether or not California is part of the United States?). A person who has lost the sight in one eye is indeed worse off than is someone who has the use of both eyes. On the other hand, as the old saying goes, "[i]n the land of the blind, the one-eyed man is king."

On a case-by-case basis, you'll need to determine which details you should focus on interpreting and which you can ignore without endangering your analysis. Quite often, you'll discover that different people analyzing the same issue, problem, or phenomenon will differ on how they see the very same data (literary analyses often work this way, for example). Sometimes, such differences are so pronounced that the same data don't even seem to be the same data. Any confirmed pessimist will tell you, for instance, that seeing a half-empty glass is certainly not the same as seeing a half-filled glass. And whereas you might have heard Joe *scream pitifully,* your friend might have heard him *yell gratingly.*

Commonly, different people will focus on the same general issue, problem, or phenomenon but will narrow their views to a study of different details or aspects of the issue, problem, or phenomenon and thereby treat the material under investigation quite differently. Analyzing a particular magazine ad for radial tires, for example, Gunther might try to prove that the ad is troublesome because it features a woman in a bikini with a mismatched top and bottom. Cyleste might also try to prove that the ad is troublesome, not, as does Gunther, by trying to demonstrate its aesthetic inadequacies, but, rather, by trying to demonstrate its moral failure, which results from its representing female beauty in a problematically stereotypical way. You, too, might try to prove that the ad is troublesome, but you might do so by attempting to show that, in and of itself, the ad's use of a bikini-clad woman to sell tires constitutes a sexist act. And your friend Toni might try to prove that, in fact, the ad is troublesome only if it fails to convince consumers that they ought to buy the advertised tires.

Clearly, the four of you don't see eye-to-eye on how to interpret this ad. Does this mean that each of your views is on a par with the others? In a word, no. You and Cyleste, for instance, have presented views that seem to merit serious consideration. On the other hand, the views presented by Gunther and Toni lack the analytical acumen displayed by your view and Cyleste's view. Gunther's view is simply nonsense. And though Toni's view might be readily acceptable among some businesspeople, it commits the "ends-justify-the-means" fallacy and thus is illogical and ought to be given up in favor of better views, such as yours and Cyleste's. At the very least, people interested in arriving at the most reasonable analysis of this ad are not obligated to weigh Toni's or Gunther's view equally with yours and Cyleste's.

In short, though we want to consider as many reasonable positions on an issue or a topic as we are able to consider, we also want to avoid assuming that all points of view concerning an issue should therefore be accorded equal weight, notwithstanding everyone's right to have an opinion on the issue (see pp. 23–25 of Chapter Two for a discussion of this point). Concerning the sort of writing that you'll be doing in college, the question isn't whether or not you and everyone else in your class *have* points of view, or whether or not you all agree on what point of view to hold. The question, rather, is whether or not any of you presents a point of view worth holding. If you yourself do, you will do so because you will have successfully made points that needed to be made—the composition of your audience notwithstanding—and because you will have cited and explained enough pertinent information and evidence to prove or support these points.

In sum, people will indeed differ in how they see things and in what they consider relevant and important data. As long as you derive a reasonable thesis from a careful evaluation of pertinent evidence and then present your case as best you can in your essay, you shouldn't worry if you and others offer different interpretations of the same data. You *should* begin to worry, however, if you become intransigent about rethinking your position in the face of cogent criticism of your views. Remember: Whether you are writing a personal narrative or an analytical essay, your obligation as a thinker and writer is to make a good-faith attempt at deriving a thesis from a careful evaluation of evidence and then, in your paper, account for and explain pertinent evidence in the service of proving or supporting your thesis. To the extent that writing reflects your ideas, and to the extent that writing is always writing-in-progress, those of your ideas that you express in your writing are always in progress, too—which means, in effect, that you are not obligated to stick by any of your views simply because you have expressed them in your drafts. In fact, if you maintain views that you know have proved suspect or unworkable, you'll be acting in bad faith.

. . .

Whether or not you are always aware of doing so, you are analyzing data almost all of the time. However, like all skills, analytical skills can always use improvement. To sharpen *your* analytical skills, try consciously analyzing as much data in the everyday world as you can manage to think about without driving yourself crazy. For example, try interpreting the details that you find in store window displays, magazine and television ads, the menu items in your dormitory's dining hall, and items on grocery store shelves (and try analyzing the arrangements of these items on the shelves, as well as the arrangements of the shelves themselves). See what you make of the details that you discover on a cereal box, a rock album cover, a bumper sticker, a T-shirt, a bulletin board in the student center, or a billboard along the highway. Try to determine the sorts of subtle or blatant messages that you have uncovered in your analyses. See whether or not you find similar messages elsewhere, whether or not other people analyze the items in question as you do, whether or not your and their analyses seem culturally specific—and what all of this might mean. Since you cannot help but analyze the data around you, you might as well become as proficient as possible at analyzing them.

Some Words about Paragraphing

Thus far, we have been talking primarily about the *ideas* underlying good reader-based writing. Before we end this chapter, let's take a moment to discuss some *structural* aspects of your writing. Specifically, we'll be discussing the nature and function of your essays' **paragraphs**, which showcase the individual groups of ideas that together form the sum and substance of your entire essay.

Paragraphs are individual units of writing containing a number of *thematically related* sentences, that is, sentences relating to a single, specific theme or idea. Indeed, a good paragraph contains *one main idea*. That main idea might be implied by the paragraph as a whole, but often it is expressed in a single sentence, which is commonly known as the **topic sentence** or **theme sentence.** Somewhat analogously, the topic sentence is to the paragraph what the thesis statement is to the entire paper: The topic sentence articulates the main idea that you are obligated to elaborate on in the paragraph, just as the thesis statement articulates the main idea that you are obligated to prove or support in the paper.

Though space does not permit a discussion of many other important paragraphing matters—such as how you might construct good **transitions** between sentences and paragraphs, how you might create effective **introductions** and **conclusions,** and how you might organize a given paper's **body paragraphs** for greatest logical and rhetorical effect (in all likelihood, you'll go over these and other, related matters in class)—we can say a few words about the three essential, basic elements of all good paragraphs: **unity**, **coherence**, and **development**. After we investigate the nature and function of these elements, we'll take a look at a sample paragraph that, in my view, is unified, coherent, and well developed; of course, if you think that my analysis is faulty, you should feel free to offer an analysis of this paragraph that is different from mine.

Paragraph Unity

In a unified paragraph, all of the paragraph's sentences directly or indirectly relate to the paragraph's main idea. If a paragraph contains even one sentence whose idea is not in line with the main, overarching idea controlling the paragraph, then the paragraph is not entirely unified. A paragraph that lacks unity tends to confuse the reader, who isn't sure what main idea to focus on (remember that a paragraph should contain one main idea only). On the other hand, a unified paragraph helps keep the reader focused on the paragraph's main idea and thus helps her to analyze the strengths and/or weaknesses of the writer's points.

To see whether or not your paragraphs are unified, try reading each paragraph's sentences one at a time, asking yourself if each sentence roughly or clearly talks about the same idea. Or, read through each paragraph, find the topic sentence (or determine what the implied topic of the paragraph is), and then reread the paragraph with an eye towards discovering whether or not all of the sentences either directly or indirectly relate to the main idea expressed in the topic sentence, which, by definition, contains the paragraph's main idea. To correct paragraph unity problems, you might need to omit, add, or revise a sentence or two; in severe cases, you might need to revise most or all of the paragraph.

Paragraph Coherence

Paragraph coherence (sometimes called paragraph continuity) has to do with the extent to which a paragraph's sentences follow each other logically; in other words, the sentences in a coherent paragraph are in sync with each other. Even a unified paragraph that is incoherent will likely make the reader feel disoriented. In effect, such a paragraph resembles a puzzle whose pieces are out of place. A coherent paragraph, on the other hand, is like a puzzle whose pieces have been arranged correctly. (If pieces *in* the puzzle don't *go* with the puzzle, then the puzzle lacks unity. If any of the puzzle's pieces is missing, then the puzzle lacks proper "development"; see below.) Giving your reader a coherent paragraph will aid him in his attempts to understand your points and thus to judge the substantive quality of your work.

Checking for paragraph coherence is rather easy. As perhaps you did when you checked for paragraph unity, start from the beginning of the paragraph and read one sentence at a time, pausing at the end of each sentence to ask yourself what that particular sentence is trying to say; then, read the next sentence, stopping to ask yourself what *it* means and whether or not *it* coherently follows the previous one(s). (If you must spend an inordinate amount of time trying to figure out a sentence's meaning, you probably should think about rewriting that sentence before continuing to check for paragraph coherence.) Use this procedure until you have finished checking the entire paragraph. Then, make any necessary changes, test the paragraph again, and so on until you feel confident that the paragraph is coherent. As you become proficient at using this technique, you might find yourself able to evaluate your paragraphs simultaneously for unity and coherence, since for both evaluations you'll be reading a paragraph's sentences to determine their relation to the other sentences in the paragraph. If, however, you don't reach that point, don't worry; it's more important that you do each technique well than that you do both together.

Paragraph Development

Paragraph development has to do with the amount of explanatory information that a paragraph contains. If a paragraph contains too much information, then it is overdeveloped. If it contains too little information, then it is underdeveloped. And if it contains just enough information, then it is well-developed. An overdeveloped paragraph can make the reader feel overburdened with information. An underdeveloped paragraph can leave the reader feeling cheated out of knowing "the rest of the story." A particularly well-developed paragraph can provoke in the reader a response similar to that which Goldilocks gave when she ate Baby Bear's porridge: "Ah, now that's just right!"

Even if you have already taken into account your intended readers' familiarity with the subject matter, the nature of the assignment, and other relevant matters, from time to time you might find yourself a bit stumped when you are trying to decide whether or not your paragraphs are well-developed. To have a general sense of their development, try eyeballing them to see how developed they actually look, just as you would eyeball your car's tires to see how inflated they look and how their tread is wearing. Often—but certainly not always—if your paragraphs look skimpy, then they probably are skimpy, and if they appear overblown, then they might very well be overblown. Generally, if you have used standard margins (roughly an inch to an inch-and-a-half on all sides) and double-spaced your typing, you should expect to see no more than three well-developed paragraphs per page, and often only two or one-and-a-half per page. If you find that you've written more than three complete paragraphs per page, then you might have found a page containing underdeveloped paragraphs. If you find only one complete paragraph on a given page, then you might have discovered an overdeveloped paragraph, even though the paragraph might be unified. You can easily fix this latter problem by finding a convenient place to split the paragraph into two paragraphs, though you might also need to revise the writing a bit at this breakpoint to insure a smooth transition between paragraphs.

If you think that you might have created an underdeveloped paragraph, and thus that you might have understated your explanation, try adding something more—a further detail, perhaps, or a further clarification. If you discover that you are merely repeating yourself or otherwise spinning your wheels, then possibly you have indeed said enough and are ready to move on. If, on the other hand, the extra material works to make the paragraph that much more fully developed, so much the better. Try adding even more material to the paragraph, narrowing and sharpening your paper's focus more and more. As suggested elsewhere in this book, you'll almost always serve your essay's needs better if you try saying more about less rather than trying to say less about more.

. . .

Now that we know something about paragraph unity, coherence, and development, let's take a look at a paragraph that I've written and that I think contains all three of these essential ingredients:

I like patronizing small, local businesses rather than big ones, even if the latter are in my community. Shopping at a small, local business gives me the feeling that I'm part of the community and that I've helped a friend make it in this world of tough economic times. It also gives me the feeling that the world isn't such a big place after all, that one can still do business with someone who knows one's name and who cares about one's life. On the other hand, when I shop in a big department store, even one that is close to my house, I often have the feeling that the person waiting on me (if he ever does) really couldn't care less whether or not I'm a satisfied customer. Sometimes, in fact, when I ask him for help, I'm made to feel as if I'm keeping him from doing some important work of his own—such as talking with other employees about their plans for the weekend! I never experience such rudeness when I walk into a small store in my community, though. There, I'm made to feel as if my entrance has made the owner's day—a feeling that I leave the store with, too, even if I haven't bought anything.

I have written this paragraph's first sentence as its topic sentence, which means that I've announced the paragraph's main theme in the first sentence. In my attempt to elaborate upon this theme, I've tried to unify the rest of the paragraph's sentences with respect to the paragraph's main idea. I've also tried to arrange these sentences logically so that they form a coherent set of ideas having to do with the contrast between my not liking to shop at big, even if local, department stores and the pleasure that I take in patronizing small, local businesses. Finally, I have tried to develop the paragraph fully by adequately explaining why "I like patronizing small, local businesses rather than big ones, even if the latter are in my community."

If I have written a decent paragraph concerning my attitudes towards shopping, then I have provided you with an understandable set of ideas to analyze. Whether or not you feel that my views have merit is another matter altogether, of course.

. . .

If you feel overwhelmed by having studied all of the preceding material, relax—and be patient. You are probably in command of some of this material already; eventually, with practice, you'll master (or mistress) enough of the rest of it that proves useful to your work. To get a sense of how a fellow student synthesizes and puts into practice a good deal of this material, spend some time studying the works of Shehla Yamani, this chapter's contributing author. As you read through her drafts, note the progress that she makes in developing her ideas. See, for example, how, expanding upon her initial ideas, she fills in, clarifies, and organizes details in an attempt to build a coherent and compelling case. Watch as she creates better and better paragraphs, which contain her developing, ever more focused ideas. Keep in mind that, rather than worrying about whether or not she had to produce a first draft that resembled a finished product, she concentrated from beginning to end on the *process* of writing her paper, patiently and conscientiously working through this process until she reached its end point. This is not to say that the process *always* works, because, truth to tell, all writers, from the most to the least experienced, rightly or wrongly give up on writing projects from time to time. On the other hand, as Yamani's work helps to demonstrate, the likelihood that any given writing project will succeed increases when one lets the process take its course—and even, sometimes, its toll.

READING AND WRITING

This chapter's reading selections deal with the thorny issue of sexual orientation. To be sure, many people, whatever their sexual orientations, face difficulties such as the pressure to marry, date, have children, or have sex. But many nonheterosexuals also face economic discrimination, as well as social stigmatization and ostracism, solely on account of their sexual orientations. Indeed, heterosexism— "the view that heterosexuality is the 'norm' for all social/sexual relationships" (Moraga, "We Fight Back with Our Families" 105)—continues to predominate in many cultures to such an extent that nonheterosexual couples often fear doing even the simplest things that heterosexual partners do without reflection (such as engaging in public displays of affection), lest they be attacked for doing so.

Besides forcing the reader to examine his or her notions concerning both sexual orientation *per se* and people whose sexual orientations differ from his/hers, as a group the reading selections that follow make the reader wonder whether or not people can live peaceably among others who are different from them, or, to ask the question another way, whether or not "we" can live peaceably among others from whom *we* are different. Moreover, besides helping us to understand our judgments of others, these pieces ultimately help all of us discover some important insights into ourselves, whatever else we discover about people whose sexual orientations differ from our own. This latter assistance might constitute these readings' most profound and enduring contribution to our entire study of this issue.

FEATURED ASSIGNMENT

Part I: Write at least two drafts of an essay in which you describe and comment upon your own experiences as an outsider, or as someone who might have made life difficult for a person or people who seemed "different" from you, or both. (If you ever kept silent in the face of oppression or injustice, you might prefer to write about the extent to which your silence was a contributing factor to the oppression or injustice.) To bolster your points, cite and explain specific examples from your own personal experiences and, at various points throughout your paper, either refer to passages in Crew's essay or somehow demonstrate that you understand Crew's main ideas.

Part II: Write a brief reflective commentary on what you experienced, thought, and/or felt while doing this assignment.

FEATURED READING

Thriving As An Outsider, Even As An Outcast, In Smalltown America

LOUIE CREW

Louie Crew (1936–), also known as Li Min Hua, currently is a professor in the English department at Rutgers: The State University of New Jersey, and co-chairs the deputation of his diocese to the legislature of the Episcopal Church. He has authored more than a thousand publications. Among his book-length writings are *Sun Spots* (1976), *Midnight Lessons* (1987), and *Quean Lutibelle's Pew* (1991), all collections of poetry; *The Gay Academic* (1978), a collection of essays; *Electronic Matter from Quean Lutibelle* (1992), a collection of electronic discourse on gay and lesbian correspondence; and a volume that he edited entitled *A Book of Revelations: Lesbian and Gay Episcopalians Tell Their Own Stories* (1991).

Quite committed to his religious faith, Crew was formally recognized in 1992 for his efforts on behalf of the church; in January of that year, at the 118th Convention of Diocese of Newark, New Jersey, he was awarded the Bishop's Outstanding Service Award. Presenting the award, the Right Reverend John S. Spong said that Professor Crew "has exercised an absolutely amazing leadership throughout the entire Anglican communion. . . . I suspect[,]" Spong continued, "that no lay person in the last ten years in the United States has so effectively moved his faith community beyond its prejudices as has Dr. Crew." One final note: On February 2, 1994, Louie Crew and his spouse, Ernest Clay, celebrated the twentieth anniversary of their marriage.

PRE-READING QUESTIONS:

1) Do you have any thoughts or feelings about people whose sexual orientations differ from yours? If you do, keep these thoughts and feelings in mind as you read Crew's essay, watching to see whether or not—and, if so, how, why, and to what extent—they affect your understanding of or reactions to his ideas.

2) Do you have any expectations concerning the featured reading selection that are based on your knowledge that the selection is an essay, is about a gay couple, is about an interracial couple, is written by one of the partners in this couple, and so on? Might your pre-reading expectations be different were any of these facts other than what they are—for example, were the author a heterosexual journalist, the piece a short story, or the partners two same-race lesbians?

3) Have you ever considered yourself an outsider or been made to feel like one? Have you ever made life difficult for someone who seemed "different"? (If so, did you do so on your own, as part of a group, or both?) Finally, did you ever keep silent when you knew that someone or some group who was (considered) different was being treated unfairly?

4) Consider the following statements:

"No one wanted him; he was outcast from life's feast." (Joyce, "A Painful Case," p. 117)

"Anyone who lives inside the United States can never be considered an outsider anywhere within its bounds." (from Martin Luther King, Jr.'s "Letter from Birmingham Jail"; see Chapter Seven, p. 312)

"You shall not wrong a stranger or oppress him, for you were strangers in the land of Egypt." (*Exodus* 22:20)

"'And the King will answer them, "Truly, I say to you, as you did it to one of the least of these my brethren, you did it to me."'" (*Matthew* 25:40)

In your view, what does each of these statements mean?

CLOSE-READING TIP

Crew tries to explain not only how he and his partner attempted to change people's attitudes about nonheterosexuals, but also how their attempts affected both themselves and others. See whether or not your understanding of Crew's explanations helps influence your understanding of and reactions to his essay. Take a look, for example, at what Crew says in paragraphs 9–14, 31, 35, 36, and 40.

CREW

SELECTION

**Thriving As An Outsider,
Even As An Outcast,
In Smalltown America**

1   From 1973 to 1979, my spouse and I lived in Fort Valley, a town of 12,000 people, the seat of Peach County, sixty miles northeast of Plains, right in the geographic center of Georgia. I taught English at a local black college and my spouse was variously a nurse, hairdresser, choreographer for the college majorettes, caterer, and fashion designer.

2   The two of us have often been asked how we survived as a gay, racially integrated couple living openly in that small town. We are still perhaps too close to the Georgia experience and very much caught up in our similar struggles in central Wisconsin to offer a definite explanation, but our tentative conjectures should interest anyone who values the role of the dissident in our democracy.

3   Survive we did. We even throve before our departure. Professionally, my colleagues and the Regents of the University System of Georgia awarded me tenure, and the Chamber of Commerce awarded my spouse a career medal in cosmetology. Socially, we had friends from the full range of the economic classes in the community. We had attended six farewell parties in our honor before we called a halt to further fetes, especially several planned at too great a sacrifice by some of the poorest folks in the town. Furthermore, I had been away only four months when the college brought me back to address an assembly of Georgia judges, mayors, police chiefs, and wardens. We are still called two to three times a week by scores of people seeking my spouse's advice on fashion, cooking, or the like.

4   It was not always so. In 1974 my spouse and I were denied housing which we had "secured" earlier before the realtor saw my spouse's color. HUD documented that the realtor thought that "the black man looked like a criminal." Once, the town was up in arms when a bishop accused the two of us of causing a tornado which had hit the town early in 1975, an accusation which appeared on the front page of the newspaper. "This is the voice of God. The town of Fort Valley is harboring Sodomists. Would one expect God to keep silent when homosexuals are tolerated? We remember what He did to Sodom and Gomorrah" (*The Macon Herald*, March 20, 1975: 1). A year later my Episcopal vestry asked me to leave the parish, and my own bishop summoned me for discipline for releasing to the national press correspondence related to the vestry's back-room maneuvers. Prompted in part by such officials, the local citizens for years routinely heckled us in public, sometimes threw rocks at our apartment, trained their children to spit on us from their bicycles if we dared to jog, and badgered us with hate calls on an average of six to eight times a week.

5   One such episode offers a partial clue to the cause of our survival. It was late summer, 1975 or 1976. I was on my motorcycle to post mail at the street-side box just before the one daily pickup at 6:00 P.M. About fifty yards away, fully audible to about seventy pedestrians milling about the court house and other

public buildings, a group of police officers, all men, began shouting at me from the steps of their headquarters: "Louise! Faggot! Queer!"

6   Anyone who has ever tried to ease a motorcycle from a still position without revving the engine knows that the feat is impossible: try as I did to avoid the suggestion, I sounded as if I were riding off in a huff. About half-way up the street, I thought to myself, "I'd rather rot in jail than feel the way I do now." I turned around, drove back—the policemen still shouting and laughing—and parked in the lot of the station. When I walked to the steps, only the lone black policeman remained.

7   "Did you speak to me?" I asked him.

8   "No, sir," he replied emphatically.

9   Inside I badgered the desk sergeant to tell her chief to call me as soon as she could locate him, and I indicated that I would press charges if necessary to prevent a recurrence. I explained that the police misconduct was an open invitation to more violent hoodlums to act out the officers' fantasies with impunity in the dark. Later, I persuaded a black city commissioner and a white one, the latter our grocer and the former our mortician, to threaten the culprits with suspension if ever such misconduct occurred again.

10   Over a year later, late one Friday after his payday, a black friend of my spouse knocked at our door to offer a share of his Scotch to celebrate his raise—or so he said. Thus primed, he asked me, "You don't recognize me, do you?"

11   "No," I admitted.

12   "I'm the lone black policeman that day you were heckled. I came by really because I thought you two might want to know what happened inside when Louie stormed up to the sergeant."

13   "Yes," we said.

14   "Well, all the guys were crouching behind the partition to keep you from seeing that they were listening. Their eyes bulged when you threatened to bring in the F.B.I. and such. Then when you left, one spoke for all when he said, 'But sissies aren't supposed to do things like that!'"

15   Ironically, I believe that a major reason for our thriving on our own terms of candor about our relationship has been our commitment to resist the intimidation heaped upon us. For too long lesbians and gay males have unwillingly encouraged abuses against ourselves by serving advance notice to any bullies, be they the barnyard-playground variety, or the Bible-wielding pulpiteers, that we would whimper or run into hiding when confronted with even the threat of exposure. It is easy to confuse sensible nonviolence with cowardly nonresistance.

16   In my view, violent resistance would be counter-productive, especially for lesbians and gays who are outnumbered 10 to 1 by heterosexuals, according to Kinsey's statistics. Yet our personal experience suggests that special kinds of creative nonviolent resistance are a major source of hope if lesbians and gay males are going to reverse the physical and mental intimidation which is our daily portion in this culture.

17   Resistance to oppression can be random and spontaneous, as in part was my decision to return to confront the police hecklers, or organized and sustained,

as more typically has been the resistance by which my spouse and I have survived. I believe that only organized and sustained resistance offers much hope for long-range change in any community. The random act is too soon forgotten or too easily romanticized.

18   Once we had committed ourselves to one another, my spouse and I never gave much thought for ourselves to the traditional device most gays have used for survival, the notorious "closet" in which one hides one's identity from all but a select group of friends. In the first place, a black man and a white man integrating a Georgia small town simply cannot be inconspicuous. More importantly, the joint checking account and other equitable economies fundamental to the quality of our marriage are public, not private acts. Our denial of the obvious would have secured closet space only for our suffocation; we would have lied, "We are ashamed and live in secret."

19   All of our resistance stems from our sense of our own worth, our conviction that we and our kind do not deserve the suffering which heterosexuals continue to encourage or condone for sexual outcasts. Dr. Martin Luther King used to say, "Those who go to the back of the bus, deserve the back of the bus."

20   Our survival on our own terms has depended very much on our knowing and respecting many of the rules of the system which we resist. We are not simply dissenters, but conscientious ones.

21   For example, we are both very hard workers. As a controversial person, I know that my professionalism comes under far more scrutiny than that of others. I learned early in my career that I could secure space for my differences by handling routine matters carefully. If one stays on good terms with secretaries, meets all deadlines, and willingly does one's fair share of the busy work of institutions, one is usually already well on the way towards earning collegial space, if not collegial support. In Georgia, I routinely volunteered to be secretary for most committees on which I served, thereby having enormous influence in the final form of the groups' deliberations without monopolizing the forum as most other molders of policy do. My spouse's many talents and sensibilities made him an invaluable advisor and confidante to scores of people in the community. Of course, living as we did in a hairdresser's salon, we knew a great deal more about the rest of the public than that public knew about us.

22   My spouse and I are fortunate in the fact that we like the enormous amount of work which we do. We are not mere opportunists working hard only as a gimmick to exploit the public for lesbian and gay issues. Both of us worked intensely at our professional assignments long before we were acknowledged dissidents with new excessive pressures to excel. We feel that now we must, however unfairly, be twice as effective as our competitors just to remain employed at all.

23   Our survival has also depended very much on our thorough knowledge of the system, often knowledge more thorough than that of those who would use the system against us. For example, when my bishop summoned me for discipline, I was able to show him that his own canons give him no authority to discipline a lay person except by ex-communication. In fact, so hierarchical have

the canons of his diocese become, that the only laity who exist worthy of their mention are the few lay persons on vestries.

24 Especially helpful has been our knowledge of communication procedures. For example, when an area minister attacked lesbians and gays on a TV talk show, I requested equal time; so well received was my response that for two more years I was a regular panelist on the talk show, thereby reaching most residents of the entire middle Georgia area as a known gay person, yet one speaking not just to sexual issues, but to a full range of religious and social topics.

25 When I was occasionally denied access to media, as in the parish or diocese or as on campus when gossip flared, I knew the value of candid explanations thoughtfully prepared, xeroxed, and circulated to enough folks to assure that the gossips would have access to the truthful version. For example, the vestry, which acted in secret, was caught by surprise when I sent copies of their hateful letters to most other parishioners, together with a copy of a psalm which I wrote protesting their turning the House of Prayer into a Court House. I also was able to explain that I continued to attend, not in defiance of their withdrawn invitation, but in obedience to the much higher invitation issued to us all by the real head of the Church. In January, 1979, in the first open meeting of the parish since the vestry's letter of unwelcome three years earlier, the entire parish voted to censure the vestry for that action and to extend to me the full welcome which the vestry had tried to deny. Only three voted against censure, all three of them a minority of the vestry being censured.

26 My spouse and I have been very conscious of the risks of our convictions. We have viewed our credentials—my doctorate and his professional licenses—not as badges of comfortable respectability, but as assets to be invested in social change. Dr. King did not sit crying in the Albany jail, "Why don't these folks respect me? How did this happen? What am I doing here?" When my spouse and I have been denied jobs for which we were the most qualified applicants, we have not naively asked how such things could be, nor have we dwelt overly long on self-pity, for we have known in advance the prices we might have to pay, even if to lose our lives. Our realism about danger and risk has helped us to preserve our sanity when everyone about us has seemed insane. I remember the joy which my spouse shared with me over the fact that he had just been fired for his efforts to organize other black nurses to protest their being treated as orderlies by the white managers of a local hospital.

27 Never, however, have we affirmed the injustices. Finally, we simply cannot be surprised by any evil and are thus less likely to be intimidated by it. Hence, we find ourselves heirs to a special hybrid of courage, a form of courage too often ignored by the heterosexual majority, but widely manifest among sexual outcasts, not the courage of bravado on battlegrounds or sportsfields, but the delicate courage of the lone person who patiently waits out the stupidity of the herd, the cagey courage that has operated many an underground railway station.

28 Our survival in smalltown America has been helped least, I suspect, by our annoying insistence that potential friends receive us not only in our own right, but also as members of the larger lesbian/gay and black communities of which we are a part. Too many whites and heterosexuals are prepared to single us out as "good queers" or "good niggers," offering us thereby the "rewards" of their friendship only at too great a cost to our integrity. My priest did not whip up the vestry against me the first year we lived openly together. He was perfectly happy to have one of his "clever queers" to dress his wife's hair and the other to help him write his annual report. We became scandalous only when the two of us began to organize the national group of lesbian and gay-male Episco-palians, known as INTEGRITY; then we were no longer just quaint. We threatened his image of himself as the arbiter of community morality, espe-cially as he faced scores of queries from brother priests elsewhere.

29 Many lesbians and gay males are tamed by dependencies upon carefully selected heterosexual friends with whom they have shared their secret, often never realizing that in themselves alone, they could provide far more affirma-tion and discover far more strength than is being cultivated by the terms of these "friendships." Lesbians and gay males have always been taught to survive on the heterosexuals' terms, rarely on one's own terms, and almost never on the terms of a community shared with other lesbians and gay males.

30 Heterosexuals are often thus the losers. The heterosexual acquaintances close to us early on when we were less visible who dropped us later as our notoriety spread were in most cases folks of demonstrably much less character strength than those heterosexuals who remained our friends even as we asserted our difference with thoughtful independence.

31 My spouse and I have never been exclusive nor aspired to move to any ghetto. In December, 1978, on the night the Macon rabbi and I had success-fully organized the area's Jews and gays to protest a concert by Anita Bryant, I returned home to watch the videotape of the march on the late news in the company of eight house guests invited by my spouse for a surprise party, not one of them gay (for some strange reason nine out of ten folks are not), not one of them obligated to be at the earlier march, and not one of them uneasy, as most of our acquaintances would have been a few years earlier before we had undertaken this reeducation together.

32 Folks who work for social change need to be very careful to allow room for it to happen, not to allow realistic appraisals of risks to prevent their cultiva-tion of the very change which they germinate.

33 Our survival has been helped in no small way by our candor and clarity in response to rumor and gossip, which are among our biggest enemies. On my campus in Georgia, I voluntarily spoke about sexual issues to an average of 50 classes per year outside my discipline. Initially, those encounters sharpened my wits for tougher national forums, but long after I no longer needed these occa-sions personally for rehearsal, I continued to accept the invitations, thereby reaching a vast majority of the citizens of the small town where we continued to live. I used to enjoy the humor of sharing with such groups facts which

would make my day-to-day life more pleasant. For example, I routinely noted that when a male student is shocked at my simple public, "Hello," he would look both ways to see who might have seen him being friendly with the gay professor. By doing this he is telling me and all other knowledgeable folks far more new information about his own body chemistry than he is finding out about mine. More informed male students would reply, "Hello" when greeted. With this method I disarmed the hatefulness of one of their more debilitating weapons of ostracism.

34 All personal references in public discussions inevitably invade one's privacy, but I have usually found the invasion a small price to pay for the opportunity to educate the public to the fact that the issues which most concern sexual outcasts are not genital, as the casters-out have so lewdly imagined, but issues of justice and simple fairness.

35 Resistance is ultimately an art which no one masters to perfection. Early in my struggles, I said to a gay colleague living openly in rural Nebraska, "We must stamp on every snake." Wisely he counseled, "Only if you want to get foot poisoning." I often wish I had more of the wisdom mentioned in *Ecclesiastes*, the ability to judge accurately, "The time to speak and the time to refrain from speaking." Much of the time I think it wise to pass public hecklers without acknowledging their taunts, especially when they are cowardly hiding in a crowd. When I have faced bullies head-on, I have tried to do so patiently, disarming them by my own control of the situation. Of course, I am not guaranteed that their violence can thus be aborted every time.

36 Two major sources of our survival are essentially very private—one, the intense care and love my spouse and I share, and the other, our strong faith in God as Unbounding Love. To these we prefer to make our secular witness, more by what we do than by what we say.

37 I am not a masochist. I would never choose the hard lot of the sexual outcast in smalltown America. Had I the choice to change myself but not the world, I would return as a white male heterosexual city-slicker millionaire, not because whites, males, heterosexuals, city-slickers, and millionaires are better, but because they have it easier.

38 Yet everyone faces a different choice: accept the world the way you find it, or change it. For year after year I dissented, right in my own neighborhood.

39 America preserves an ideal of freedom, although it denies freedom in scores of instances. My eighth-grade civics teacher in Alabama did not mention the price I would have to pay for the freedom of speech she taught me to value. I know now that the docile and ignorant dislike you fiercely when you speak truth they prefer not to hear. But I had a good civics class, one that showed me how to change our government. I rejoice.

40 Sometimes I think a society's critics must appreciate the society far more than others, for the critics typically take very seriously the society's idle promises and forgotten dreams. When I occasionally see them, I certainly don't find many of my heterosexual eight-grade classmates probing much farther than the issues of our common Form 1040 headaches and the issues as

delivered by the evening news. Their lives seem often far duller than ours and the main adventures in pioneering they experience come vicariously, through television, the movies, and for a few, through books. In defining me as a criminal, my society may well have hidden a major blessing in its curse by forcing me out of lethargy into an on-going, rigorous questioning of the entire process. Not only do I teach *The Adventures of Huckleberry Finn*, my spouse and I have in an important sense had the chance to be Huck and Jim fleeing a different form of slavery and injustice in a very real present.

POST-READING QUESTIONS:

1) Did any of the thoughts or feelings that you discussed in your responses to the first two pre-reading questions affect your understanding of or help shape your reactions to Crew's ideas? Do you think that your responses to these pre-reading questions would have been the same had you read Crew's essay prior to answering these questions?

2) Were you surprised that Crew would take the position that he takes in paragraph 15? Does he seem to be speaking for all victims of oppression? Do you think that he is blaming those victims who don't resist or condemning victims who seem unable to recover from their ordeals?

3) What do you make of Crew's claim that he and his partner had to "be twice as effective as [their] competitors just to remain employed at all" (paragraph 22)? Does this statement seem applicable to the struggles faced by other people, too—including you yourself, perhaps?

4) What do you make of both the confession that Crew offers in paragraph 37 and his attempts to explain his position? Were you surprised that Crew would say what he says in this paragraph, especially in light of what he says elsewhere in his essay? Do any of your responses to the pre- or post-reading questions help you answer this post-reading question?

5) After having read Crew's essay, do you want to revise any of your answers to any of the pre-reading questions?

The Dilemma

SHEHLA YAMANI

Shehla Yamani was born in Karachi, Pakistan, in 1969. She received her education in Karachi, where she earned her bachelor's degree in mathematics, economics, and statistics from the St. Joseph's College for Women. At 21, she immigrated to the United States with her family. Her arrival in Irvine, California, in June 1990 marked her first encounter with the West. Soon after arriving here, she started working as a cashier at a photocopying establishment in Irvine and taking classes at Irvine Valley College. Though initially she had intended to pursue a second bachelor's degree, this one in computer science, after enjoying a tremendous experience in a writing class at Irvine Valley College she felt that perhaps she ought to study the humanities. In the fall of 1992, she transferred to UC Irvine, where she is currently enrolled in the undergraduate comparative literature program. Planning to be graduated from UCI in 1995 and to pursue further studies in colonial/post-colonial literature, Shehla hopes to teach college and to write.

Shehla also plays an active role in the Muslim community both on and off campus. She helped found the Muslim Students' Association at Irvine Valley College and is active in the Muslim Students' Union at UCI. In April 1992, Shehla began working to raise public awareness of the atrocities being committed against Bosnian Muslims. She organized presentations at her school and, there and elsewhere, organized meetings and participated in demonstrations. She is now the secretary and director of a nonprofit, California-based organization called The American Bosnia-Herzegovina Association, which she also helped to establish.

RESPONSE

PART I   **First Draft**

I was born in a Muslim family in Pakistan. I recieved Islamic education in school and at home. My parents laid emphasis on prayers and fasting, while at school I learned about the basic teachings of Islam, a Muslim's duties and rights in Islam. I learned about the concept of Jihad but was never tested on it except in school. At the age of twenty one, I emigrated to America. This was my first encounter with the west.

January 15, 1991 was my very first day in an American college. It was an English Writing class. America invaded Iraq that day. My teacher asked the students to talk about their views on the war. Some said that America had no other choice but to attack Iraq, some said it was a waste of lives, someone behind me expressed his opinion about Islam. He said that war was a part of Islamic culture. I felt as if I was stabbed in the back. I said, "No, that is not true." I had to defend my religion. This was my first real test on Jihad. Some students turned around to look at me. They probably didn't know that I was a Muslim. I told them that Islam was a very peaceful religion. That Jihad means struggle and not Holy War, that war was allowed only as a defence and not as an offence to acquire land or power. While I was talking about Jihad, I was doing Jihad. Jihad against ignorance and misinformation.

Iraq was bombed into the Middle Ages. Here, the Americans celebrated the destruction of Iraq, under the label of victory for the Americans.

Second Draft

It is not easy to be different. It takes a lot of courage and determination to survive in a culture that is different from your own and sometimes hostile to you. I was born in a Muslim family in Pakistan. I recieved Islamic education in school and at home. My parents laid emphasis on prayers and fasting, while at school I learned about the basic teachings of Islam; a Muslim's duties and rights in Islam. At the age of twenty one, I emigrated to America. This was my first encounter with the west.

January 15, 1991 was my very first day in an American college. It was an English Writing class. America invaded Iraq that day. My teacher asked the students to talk about their views on the war. Some said that America had no other choice but to attack Iraq, some said it was a waste of lives, someone behind me expressed his opinion about Islam. He said that war was a part of Islamic culture. I felt as if I was stabbed in the back. I said, "No, that is not true." I had to defend my religion. This was my first real test on Jihad. Some students turned around to look at me. They probably didn't know that I was a Muslim. I told them that Islam was a very peaceful religion. That Jihad means struggle and not Holy War, that war was allowed only as a defence and not as an offence to acquire land or power. While I was telling people about Jihad, I was performing Jihad. Jihad against ignorance and misinformation.

Iraq was bombed into the Middle Ages. Here, the Americans celebrated the destruction of Iraq, under the label of victory for the Americans. Arab and non-Arab Muslims were beaten up and harrassed. My very good friend, Aminah Assilmi, who is an American convert was beaten up by a woman on the campus of The Metropolitan State College in Denver Colorado. A Saudi man was beaten up in Texas and his wife was raped. The couple went back to Saudi Arabia immediately. These people were being punished for being Muslims. I used to hear people at work and on the bus talk about supporting the troops and the war. I wasn't pro-Saddam but I was against the war. I couldn't say anything against the war since I didn't have many people to support me and anyone who was against the war was called unpatriotic and pro-Saddam. I couldn't believe that people could be so callous to human sufferings.

I hear about children dying in Iraq due to hunger and diseases and I cannot believe that people can still be blind to those people's suffering. There is a general misinformation and mistrust among the people about Islam, Muslims and Arabs. When I read articles about Arabs or Muslims in newspapers or magazines, I find that there is a certain bias against the Arabs and Muslims. They are portrayed as terrorists or blood-thirsty fanatics. I wrote a letter to a newspaper, protesting an article in the newspaper that was clearly unjust towards Muslims. The letter was never published. [Editor's note: In her third draft, Yamani added information to this paragraph. See p. 158.]

There was a time when I kept silent in the face of racial hatred. A girl at work was telling an employee that she would like to have a baby but she didn't want to get married. The other person told her that she could adopt a baby. Perhaps an Asian baby. She expressed utter disgust at the idea of adopting an Asian baby. I was the only Asian there. I didn't know what to say. I kept silent. Later, when I thought about this incident, I realised the racist nature of the girl's comment. I decided not to keep silent anymore.

Some time later, we had a new employee. He was from Peru and could not speak English very well. The people at work, who were mostly whites, did not treat him very well. Once, a cash drawer was short and he was suspected of stealing money. He felt very uncomfortable working there, but he needed the money. Once he called in sick. The manager was very rude with him and threatened to fire him if he didn't call earlier the next time. The store opens at eight o' clock, he had called just about eight. People usually call in around this time and nobody raises an eyebrow. He called me later, and told me what had happened. I told the owner that I didn't like the way this employee was being treated. All the owner could say was that the employee has no reason to take us to court.

Even though I am treated in a better way than the employee from Peru, maybe because I can speak better English, I do feel his pain. Maybe I feel guilty for being treated differently. Perhaps that is why I feel that I should take a stand. I don't wear the "Hijab", which is a scarf that Muslim women wear to cover their head. That is why strangers cannot recognize me as a Muslim. If I wear the "Hijab" I know people will treat me differently as many Muslim women, who choose to wear the "Hijab", are treated. Sometimes they are treated with respect, while sometimes they are forced to leave a job because they choose to be different. I do feel the obligation to speak for these brave women who choose to be different. I certainly do not want to pose as a victim, but I do want to speak for those who are victimised.

Material Added to the Third Draft

I hear about children dying in Iraq due to hunger and diseases and I cannot believe that people can still be blind to those people's suffering. There is a general misinformation and mistrust among the people about Islam, Muslims and Arabs. When I read articles about Arabs or Muslims in newspapers or magazines, I find that there is a certain bias against the Arabs and Muslims. They are portrayed as terrorists or blood-thirsty fanatics. I wrote a letter to a newspaper, protesting an article in the newspaper that was clearly unjust towards Muslims. The article was about British Muslims who are demanding the right to establish a Muslim Parliament in Britain. Muslim leaders have asked British Muslims to defy any laws that are against Islamic teachings. A member of the British Parliament told the Muslims that if they could not assimilate they should emigrate. The writer of the article wsed the word Muslim militants to describe the British Muslims who are, in my opinion fighting against racism and oppression. I took objection to the use of the term "militant" in describing Muslims, who are fighting for a just cause. The right to practice their religion. I objected to the double standards of the western media in the case of Muslims. If non-Muslims are fighting for a similar cause in Poland, Czechoslovakia, China or in any other country, they are hailed as freedom fighters and are given full support. Not that I am against their very legitimate and honourable cause, but there should be justice and equity for all communities in a true democracy. I questioned the justice of the western democracy, especially the media. The letter was never published.

The Dilemma

It is not easy to be different in this society. It takes a lot of courage and determination to survive in a culture that is different from your own and sometimes hostile to you. I was born in a Muslim family in Pakistan. I received Islamic education in school and at home. My parents laid emphasis on prayers and fasting, while at school I learned about the basic teachings of Islam. I learned about a Muslim's duties and rights in Islam, which include struggling for justice and freedom from oppression. At the age of twenty-one, I emigrated to America. This was my first encounter with the West.

January 15, 1991 was my very first day in an American college. It was an English writing class. America invaded Iraq that day. My teacher asked the students to talk about their views on the war. Some said that America had no other choice but to attack Iraq, while some said that it was a waste of lives. A person behind me expressed his opinion about Islam. He said that war was a part of Islamic culture. I felt as if I were stabbed in the back. I said, "No, that is not true." I had to defend my religion. This was my first real test on Jihad. Some students turned around to look at me. They probably didn't know that I was a Muslim. I told them that Islam was a very peaceful religion. I said that Jihad means struggle and not Holy War, that war was allowed only as a defense and not as an offense to acquire land or power. While I was telling people about Jihad, I was performing Jihad, Jihad against ignorance and misinformation.

Iraq was bombed into the Middle Ages. Here, the Americans celebrated the destruction of Iraq, as a victory for the Americans. Arab and non-Arab Muslims were beaten up and harassed. My good friend, Aminah Assilmi, who is an American convert, was beaten up by a woman on the campus of the Metropolitan State College in Denver, Colorado. A Saudi man was beaten up in Texas and his wife was raped. The couple returned to Saudi Arabia immediately. These people were being punished for being Muslims. I used to hear people at work and on the bus talk in support of the troops and the war. I wasn't pro-Saddam, but I was against the war. I couldn't say anything against the war, since I didn't have many people to support me and anyone who was against the war was called unpatriotic and pro-Saddam. I couldn't believe that people could be so callous to human sufferings. Children are dying in Iraq due to hunger and diseases and I cannot believe that people can still be blind to these people's sufferings.

There is a general misinformation and mistrust among the Americans about Islam, Muslims and Arabs. When I read articles about Arabs or Muslims in newspapers or magazines, I find that they are biased against the Arabs and Muslims. They are portrayed as terrorists or bloodthirsty fanatics. I wrote a letter to a newspaper, protesting against one of its articles that was clearly unjust towards Muslims. The article was about British Muslims who are demanding the right to establish a Muslim Parliament in Britain. Muslim leaders have asked British Muslims to defy any laws that are against Islamic teachings. A member of the British Parliament told the Muslims that if they did not want to integrate they should emigrate. The writer of the article used the word "Muslim militants" to describe the British Muslims, who, in my opinion, are fighting against racism and oppression. I objected to the use of the term "militant" in describing Muslims, who are fighting for a just cause: the right to practice their religion. I objected to the double standards of the Western media. If non-Muslims are fighting for a similar cause in Poland, Czechoslovakia, China or in any other country, they are hailed as freedom fighters and are given full support. Not that I am against their very legitimate and honorable cause, but there should be justice and equity for all communities in a true democracy. I questioned the justice of western democracy, and especially the justice of its media. The letter was never published.

There was a time when I kept silent in the face of racial hatred. A girl at work was telling another employee that she would like to have a baby but she didn't want to get married. The other person told her that she could adopt a baby, perhaps an Asian baby. She expressed utter disgust at the idea of adopting an Asian baby. I was the only Asian there. I didn't know what to say. I kept silent. Later, when I thought about this incident, I realized the seriousness of the racist nature of the girl's comment. I decided not to keep silent anymore.

Some time later, a new employee was hired. He was from Peru and could not speak English very well. The people at work treated him badly. Once, a cash register was short and he was suspected of theft. He felt very uncomfortable working under such humiliation, but he needed the money. Once he called in sick. The manager was very rude with him and threatened to fire him if he didn't call earlier the next time. The store opens at eight o'clock; he had called just about eight. People usually call in around this time and nobody raises an eyebrow. He called me later and told me what had happened. I told the owner that I didn't like the way this employee was being treated and I told him about the employee's feelings. All the owner could say was that the employee has no reason to take us to court.

Even though I am treated in a better way than the employee from Peru, maybe because I can speak better English, I do feel his pain. Maybe I feel guilty for being treated differently. Perhaps that is why I feel that I should take a stand. I wasn't harassed or beaten up because I am a Muslim. I don't wear the Hijab, a scarf that a Muslim woman wears to cover her head. That is why strangers cannot recognize me as a Muslim. If I wear the "Hijab" I know that people will treat me as differently as they treat many Muslim women who choose to wear the "Hijab". Sometimes they are treated with respect; however, sometimes they are targeted because they choose to be different. Though I am not brave enough to do what they are doing, I do feel the obligation to speak for these brave women who choose to celebrate their values openly. I certainly do not mean to pose as a victim, but I do believe that I must speak for those who are victimized.

PART II   Commentary

As I was reading and annotating Crew's essay, I was trying to extract its essence. To perceive the tenor of Crew's essay and to catch a glimpse of his world, or to speculate on what he was experiencing, I had to assimilate his thoughts and expressions as much as possible. Reading Crew's essay, I began thinking about how to resolve the thesis of my own essay. For one week I struggled with questions like: "What is my position?", "Am I a victim? If I am a victim, how was I victimized?" and so on. I recalled situations that I had encountered at work and every day, especially during the Persian Gulf War. Eventually, my readings of Crew's essay and my annotations of it laid down the stage for my own writing performance. I started to concentrate on composing my thoughts to begin writing.

During the course of writing my essay, I experienced some difficulty in transferring my thoughts to the essay. In the beginning, I had difficulty in finding the correct words to express my ideas; hence, I just wrote my thoughts without worrying about the sentence structure, correct vocabulary, or directness of my speech. Instead, I let my thoughts lead me to write. I was writing with the intention of writing a formal essay, but I was also just writing my thoughts down in just the way as they were coming to me. I articulated my thoughts on paper and from there my essay evolved.

After I had done some initial writing, I read what I had written and revised it to make the sentences more organized and to improve my style. In general, before I had revised my first draft, my writing was confusing and did not have a flow to it. This confusion reflected in my own thoughts as I tried to read my essay and found difficulty in conceptualizing further. However, as I revised my initial draft, my writing became more comprehensible; this new writing reflected on my thoughts as I found it easier, almost natural to go on further with my essay.

As I revised my drafts, I made a number of reader-based changes to them in order to make my writing organized and coherent. For example, since I thought that the reader might find it very hard to understand some of my feelings, in my third draft I added information about the newspaper article and my letter to the newspaper. In my second draft, I added the sentence "It is not easy to be different" in an attempt to sympathize with my readers who might have experienced situations in which they felt alienated from their surroundings. I felt that adding this sentence would help me attract the reader to read my essay. By sympathizing with her I have at once formed a connection with my reader. Hence, through sentences such as this one, I found a common ground to evoke a common sentiment from my readers.

I did run into one very serious problem, though. After I had written the first draft, I could not write any further. I did not know my position. I could not figure out whether I was a victim in the true sense of the word or not. And if I were not a victim, then where did I belong? Facing an inner conflict, I realized that I was caught in a dilemma: I was somewhere between a victim and a member of the victimizing culture. By writing from this perspective, I was not only able to solve my writing problem, but I was also able to understand my own situation and my inner conflicts to some extent. However, even though I was able to write this essay, my questions still remain unresolved.

R E L A T E D   R E A D I N G S

The Sexual Aberrations[1]

SIGMUND FREUD

Sigmund Freud (1856–1939), the often eccentric Viennese neurologist turned psychologist, has come to be known as the "father of psychoanalysis." One of our century's greatest and most controversial theorists, Freud has profoundly influenced our thinking in fields as diverse as medicine, psychology, philosophy, literature, art, film studies, biology, anthropology, sociology, education, and religious studies. The late philosopher Michel Foucault called Freud an "'initiator[] of discursive practices,'" that is, one of those rare individuals whose thinking was so powerfully influential that, in effect, they might be considered inventors of new languages (132 and *passim*). The author of more than 20 volumes of published writing, including now-classic works such as *Beyond the Pleasure Principle, Civilization and Its Discontents, Three Essays on the Theory of Sexuality* (from which the following reading selection is taken), and *The Interpretation of Dreams*, Freud proved to be a dedicated and seemingly tireless researcher, thinker, and writer whose widely influential theories and concepts concerning human behavior have helped revolutionize the ways in which we think about ourselves and others. Indeed, as the eminent historian Peter Gay has argued about this man who "transformed out of all recognition, forever" the entirety of Western culture's "sense of itself," "It is a commonplace that we all speak Freud today whether we recognize it or not" (xix, xvii). And, as Freud's critics might have us add, whether we *like* it or not!

---

[1]The information contained in this . . . essay is derived from the well-known writings of Krafft-Ebing, Moll, Moebius, Havelock Ellis, Schrenck-Notzing, Löwenfeld, Eulenburg, Bloch and Hirschfeld, and from the *Fahrbuch für sexuelle Zwischenstufen*, published under the direction of the last-named author. . . . [*Added* 1910:] The data obtained from the psycho-analytic investigation of inverts are based upon material supplied to me by I. Sadger and upon my own findings. [Freud's note.]

Whether you end up agreeing or disagreeing with Freud's controversial ideas about sexual orientation, after reading his work you should be able to see why his notions continue to underlie and help us understand so many of our own ideas about ourselves and others. At the very least, you should see why most serious thinkers who have studied Freud's work argue that, our agreement or disagreement with his theories notwithstanding, one ignores this man's ideas at one's own peril.

PRE-READING QUESTIONS:

1) What are your opinions or feelings about psychology, psychological therapy, or psychological theorizing? Do you have any special opinions or feelings about Freud's work? As you read the following selection, try to keep tabs on your thoughts and feelings, watching to see whether or not—and, if so, how, why, and to what extent—they affect your understanding of or reactions to Freud's ideas.

2) Do you think that there is such a thing as a "sexual instinct"? If so, how would you describe it and its purpose(s)?

3) What does the word "aberration" mean? Can you give some examples of what you would consider aberrations or aberrant behavior?

4) In your view, is sexual orientation a matter of choice? Of biology? Of something else? What evidence do you think supports your view?

5) What do you make of the following incident concerning a male homosexual's having been physically and sexually brutalized while he was riding on a train to a Nazi concentration camp? "The whole time," the narrator says, the victim's two assailants "spoke obscenely and contemptuously of [him] and other 'filthy queers'." Additionally, "it didn't bother them that as murderers, they were certainly even more rejected by society [than he was]. They emphasized, however, that they were at least 'normal men'" (Heger 28–29).

CLOSE-READING TIP

As suggested in the biographical comments, Freud's ideas continue both to influence the thinking of and to generate controversy among his readers. As you read through this selection, note those of Freud's ideas that seem particularly important and/or controversial. Try to determine whether or not these ideas make sense within the context of Freud's discussion concerning sexual orientation and, if applicable, within a larger context, too. Consider, for example, what Freud says in paragraphs 4 and 10–11, and in note 7, paragraphs 1 and 2.

1   The fact of the existence of sexual needs in human beings and animals is expressed in biology by the assumption of a 'sexual instinct', on the analogy of the instinct of nutrition, that is of hunger. Everyday language possesses no counterpart to the word 'hunger', but science makes use of the word 'libido' for that purpose.

2   Popular opinion has quite definite ideas about the nature and characteristics of this sexual instinct. It is generally understood to be absent in childhood, to set in at the time of puberty in connection with the process of coming to maturity and to be revealed in the manifestations of an irresistible attraction exercised by one sex upon the other; while its aim is presumed to be sexual union, or at all events actions leading in that direction. We have every reason to believe, however, that these views give a very false picture of the true situation. If we look into them more closely we shall find that they contain a number of errors, inaccuracies and hasty conclusions.

3   I shall at this point introduce two technical terms. Let us call the person from whom sexual attraction proceeds the *sexual object* and the act towards which the instinct tends the *sexual aim*. Scientifically sifted observation, then, shows that numerous deviations occur in respect of both of these—the sexual object and the sexual aim. The relation between these deviations and what is assumed to be normal requires thorough investigation.

(1) DEVIATIONS IN RESPECT OF THE SEXUAL OBJECT

4   The popular view of the sexual instinct is beautifully reflected in the poetic fable which tells how the original human beings were cut up into two halves—man and woman—and how these are always striving to unite again in love.[2] It comes as a great surprise therefore to learn that there are men whose sexual object is a man and not a woman, and women whose sexual object is a woman and not a man. People of this kind are described as having 'contrary sexual feelings', or better, as being 'inverts', and the fact is described as 'inversion'. The number of such people is very considerable, though there are difficulties in establishing it precisely.

(A) INVERSION

5   **Behaviour of Inverts.** Such people vary greatly in their behaviour in several respects.

6   (*a*) They may be *absolute* inverts. In that case their sexual objects are exclusively of their own sex. Persons of the opposite sex are never the object of their sexual desire, but leave them cold, or even arouse sexual aversion in them. As a consequence of this aversion, they are incapable, if they are men, of carrying out the sexual act, or else they derive no enjoyment from it.

---

[2][This is no doubt an allusion to the theory expounded by Aristophanes in Plato's *Symposium*.] [Ed note: James Strachey edited the Standard Edition of Freud's works, from which this excerpt is taken.]

7   (*b*) They may be *amphigenic* inverts, that is psychosexual hermaphrodites. In that case their sexual objects may equally well be of their own or of the opposite sex. This kind of inversion thus lacks the characteristic of exclusiveness.

8   (*c*) They may be *contingent* inverts. In that case, under certain external conditions—of which inaccessibility of any normal sexual object and imitation are the chief—they are capable of taking as their sexual object someone of their own sex and of deriving satisfaction from sexual intercourse with him.

9   Again, inverts vary in their views as to the peculiarity of their sexual instinct. Some of them accept their inversion as something in the natural course of things, just as a normal person accepts the direction of *his* libido, and insist energetically that inversion is as legitimate as the normal attitude; others rebel against their inversion and feel it as a pathological compulsion.[3]

10   Other variations occur which relate to questions of time. The trait of inversion may either date back to the very beginning, as far back as the subject's memory reaches, or it may not have become noticeable till some particular time before or after puberty.[4] It may either persist throughout life, or it may go into temporary abeyance, or again it may constitute an episode on the way to a normal development. It may even make its first appearance late in life after a long period of normal sexual activity. A periodic oscillation between a normal and an inverted sexual object has also sometimes been observed. Those cases are of particular interest in which the libido changes over to an inverted sexual object after a distressing experience with a normal one.

11   As a rule these different kinds of variations are found side by side independently of one another. It is, however, safe to assume that the most extreme form of inversion will have been present from a very early age and that the person concerned will feel at one with his peculiarity.

12   Many authorities would be unwilling to class together all the various cases which I have enumerated and would prefer to lay stress upon their differences rather than their resemblances, in accordance with their own preferred view of inversion. Nevertheless, though the distinctions cannot be disputed, it is impossible to overlook the existence of numerous intermediate examples of every type, so that we are driven to conclude that we are dealing with a connected series.

---

[3]The fact of a person struggling in this way against a compulsion towards inversion may perhaps determine the possibility of his being influenced by suggestion [*added* 1910:] or psycho-analysis. [Freud's note.]

[4]Many writers have insisted with justice that the dates assigned by inverts themselves for the appearance of their tendency to inversion are untrustworthy, since they may have repressed the evidence of their heterosexual feelings from their memory. [*Added* 1910:] These suspicions have been confirmed by psycho-analysis in those cases of inversion to which it has had access; it has produced decisive alterations in their anamnesis by filling in their infantile amnesia. [Freud's note.]—[In the first edition (1905) the place of this last sentence was taken by the following one: 'A decision on this point could be arrived at only by a psycho-analytic investigation of inverts.'] [Strachey's note.]

13   **Nature of Inversion.** The earliest assessments regarded inversion as an innate indication of nervous degeneracy. This corresponded to the fact that medical observers first came across it in persons suffering, or appearing to suffer, from nervous diseases. This characterization of inversion involves two suppositions, which must be considered separately: that it is innate and that it is degenerate.

14   **Degeneracy.** The attribution of degeneracy in this connection is open to the objections which can be raised against the indiscriminate use of the word in general. It has become the fashion to regard any symptom which is not obviously due to trauma or infection as a sign of degeneracy.... [But] it seems wiser only to speak of [degeneracy] where

(1) several serious deviations from the normal are found together, and

(2) the capacity for efficient functioning and survival seem to be severely impaired.

15   Several facts go to show that in this legitimate sense of the word inverts cannot be regarded as degenerate:

16   (1) Inversion is found in people who exhibit no other serious deviations from the normal.

17   (2) It is similarly found in people whose efficiency is unimpaired, and who are indeed distinguished by specially high intellectual development and ethical culture.[5]

18   (3) If we disregard the patients we come across in our medical practice, and cast our eyes round a wider horizon, we shall come in two directions upon facts which make it impossible to regard inversion as a sign of degeneracy:

19   (*a*) Account must be taken of the fact that inversion was a frequent phenomenon—one might almost say an institution charged with important functions—among the peoples of antiquity at the height of their civilization.

20   (*b*) It is remarkably widespread among many savage and primitive races, whereas the concept of degeneracy is usually restricted to states of high civilization...; and, even amongst the civilized peoples of Europe, climate and race exercise the most powerful influence on the prevalence of inversion and upon the attitude adopted towards it.[6]

21   **Innate Character.** As may be supposed, innateness is only attributed to the first, most extreme, class of inverts, and the evidence for it rests upon assurances given by them that at no time in their lives has their sexual instinct shown any sign of taking another course. The very existence of the two other

---

[5]It must be allowed that the spokesmen of 'Uranism' are justified in asserting that some of the most prominent men in all recorded history were inverts and perhaps even absolute inverts. [Freud's note.]

[6]The pathological approach to the study of inversion has been displaced by the anthropological. The merit for bringing about this change is due to Bloch (1902–3), who has also laid stress on the occurrence of inversion among the civilizations of antiquity. [Freud's note.]

classes, and especially the third [the 'contingent' inverts], is difficult to reconcile with the hypothesis of the innateness of inversion. This explains why those who support this view tend to separate out the group of absolute inverts from all the rest, thus abandoning any attempt at giving an account of inversion which shall have universal application. In the view of these authorities inversion is innate in one group of cases, while in others it may have come about in other ways.

22   The reverse of this view is represented by the alternative one that inversion is an acquired character of the sexual instinct. This second view is based on the following considerations:

23   (1) In the case of many inverts, even absolute ones, it is possible to show that very early in their lives a sexual impression occurred which left a permanent after-effect in the shape of a tendency to homosexuality.

24   (2) In the case of many others, it is possible to point to external influences in their lives, whether of a favourable or inhibiting character, which have led sooner or later to a fixation of their inversion. (Such influences are exclusive relations with persons of their own sex, comradeship in war, detention in prison, the dangers of heterosexual intercourse, celibacy, sexual weakness, etc.)

25   (3) Inversion can be removed by hypnotic suggestion, which would be astonishing in an innate characteristic.

26   In view of these considerations it is even possible to doubt the very existence of such a thing as innate inversion. It can be argued. . . that, if the cases of allegedly innate inversion were more closely examined, some experience of their early childhood would probably come to light which had a determining effect upon the direction taken by their libido. This experience would simply have passed out of the subject's conscious recollection, but could be recalled to his memory under appropriate influence. In the opinion of these writers inversion can only be described as a frequent variation of the sexual instinct, which can be determined by a number of external circumstances in the subject's life.

27   The apparent certainty of this conclusion is, however, completely countered by the reflection that many people are subjected to the same sexual influences (e.g. to seduction or mutual masturbation, which may occur in early youth) without becoming inverted or without remaining so permanently. We are therefore forced to a suspicion that the choice between 'innate' and 'acquired' is not an exclusive one or that it does not cover all the issues involved in inversion.

28   **Explanation of Inversion.** The nature of inversion is explained neither by the hypothesis that it is innate nor by the alternative hypothesis that it is acquired. In the former case we must ask in what respect it is innate, unless we are to accept the crude explanation that everyone is born with his sexual instinct attached to a particular sexual object. In the latter case it may be questioned whether the various accidental influences would be sufficient to explain the acquisition of inversion without the co-operation of something in the sub-

ject himself. As we have already shown, the existence of this last factor is not to be denied.

29   **Bisexuality.** A fresh contradiction of popular views is involved in the considerations put forward by [several theorists] in an endeavour to account for the possibility of sexual inversion. It is popularly believed that a human being is either a man or a woman. Science, however, knows of cases in which the sexual characters are obscured, and in which it is consequently difficult to determine the sex. This arises in the first instance in the field of anatomy. The genitals of the individuals concerned combine male and female characteristics. (This condition is known as hermaphroditism.) In rare cases both kinds of sexual apparatus are found side by side fully developed (true hermaphroditism); but far more frequently both sets of organs are found in an atrophied condition.

30   The importance of these abnormalities lies in the unexpected fact that they facilitate our understanding of normal development. For it appears that a certain degree of anatomical hermaphroditism occurs normally. In every normal male or female individual, traces are found of the apparatus of the opposite sex. These either persist without function as rudimentary organs or become modified and take on other functions.

31   These long-familiar facts of anatomy lead us to suppose that an originally bisexual physical disposition has, in the course of evolution, become modified into a unisexual one, leaving behind only a few traces of the sex that has become atrophied. . . .

32   [It seems, then, that] a bisexual disposition is somehow concerned in inversion, though we do not know in what that disposition consists, beyond anatomical structure. [Also], we have to deal with disturbances that affect the sexual instinct in the course of its development. . . .

33   **Sexual Object of Inverts.** There can be no doubt that a large proportion of male inverts retain the mental quality of masculinity, that they possess relatively few of the secondary characters of the opposite sex and that what they look for in their sexual object are in fact feminine mental traits. If this were not so, how would it be possible to explain the fact that male prostitutes who offer themselves to inverts—to-day just as they did in ancient times—imitate women in all the externals of their clothing and behaviour? Such imitation would otherwise inevitably clash with the ideal of the inverts. It is clear that in Greece, where the most masculine men were numbered among the inverts, what excited a man's love was not the *masculine* character of a boy, but his physical resemblance to a woman as well as his feminine mental qualities—his shyness, his modesty and his need for instruction and assistance. As soon as the boy became a man he ceased to be a sexual object for men and himself, perhaps, became a lover of boys. In this instance, therefore, as in many others, the sexual object is not someone of the same sex but someone who combines the characters of both sexes; there is, as it were, a compromise between an impulse that seeks for a man and one that seeks for a woman, while it remains a para-

mount condition that the object's body (i.e. genitals) shall be masculine. Thus the sexual object is a kind of reflection of the subject's own bisexual nature.[7]

34   The position in the case of women is less ambiguous; for among them the active inverts exhibit masculine characteristics, both physical and mental, with peculiar frequency and look for femininity in their sexual objects—though here again a closer knowledge of the facts might reveal greater variety.

35   **Sexual Aim of Inverts.** The important fact to bear in mind is that no one single aim can be laid down as applying in cases of inversion. Among men, intercourse *per anum* by no means coincides with inversion; masturbation is quite as frequently their exclusive aim, and it is even true that restrictions of sexual aim—to the point of its being limited to simple outpourings of emotion—are commoner among them than among heterosexual lovers. Among women, too, the sexual aims of inverts are various: there seems to be a special preference for contact with the mucous membrane of the mouth.

36   **Conclusion.** It will be seen that we are not in a position to base a satisfactory explanation of the origin of inversion upon the material at present before us. Nevertheless our investigation has put us in possession of a piece

---

[7][This last sentence was added in 1915.] [Strachey's note.] [*Footnote added* 1910:] It is true that psycho-analysis has not yet produced a complete explanation of the origin of inversion; nevertheless, it has discovered the psychical mechanism of its development, and has made essential contributions to the statement of the problems involved. In all the cases we have examined we have established the fact that the future inverts, in the earliest years of their childhood, pass through a phase of very intense but short-lived fixation to a woman (usually their mother), and that, after leaving this behind, they identify themselves with a woman and take *themselves* as their sexual object. That is to say, they proceed from a narcissistic basis, and look for a young man who resembles themselves and whom *they* may love as their mother loved *them*. Moreover, we have frequently found that alleged inverts have been by no means insusceptible to the charms of women, but have continually transposed the excitation aroused by women on to a male object. They have thus repeated all through their lives the mechanism by which their inversion arose. Their compulsive longing for men has turned out to be determined by their ceaseless flight from women....

[*Added* 1915:] Psycho-analytic research is most decidedly opposed to any attempt at separating off homosexuals from the rest of mankind as a group of a special character. By studying sexual excitations other than those that are manifestly displayed, it has found that all human beings are capable of making a homosexual object-choice and have in fact made one in their unconscious. Indeed, libidinal attachments to persons of the same sex play no less a part as factors in normal mental life, and a greater part as a motive force for illness, than do similar attachments to the opposite sex. On the contrary, psycho-analysis considers that a choice of an object independently of its sex—freedom to range equally over male and female objects—as it is found in childhood, in primitive states of society and early periods of history, is the original basis from which, as a result of restriction in one direction or the other, both the normal and the inverted types develop. Thus from the point of view of psycho-analysis the exclusive sexual interest felt by men for women is also a problem that needs elucidating and is not a self-evident fact based upon an attraction that is ultimately of a chemical nature. A person's final sexual attitude is not decided until after puberty and is the result of a number of factors, not all of which are yet known; some are of a constitutional nature but others are accidental. No doubt a few of these factors may happen to carry so much

of knowledge which may turn out to be of greater importance to us than the solution of that problem. It has been brought to our notice that we have been in the habit of regarding the connection between the sexual instinct and the sexual object as more intimate than it in fact is. Experience of the cases that are considered abnormal has shown us that in them the sexual instinct and the sexual object are merely soldered together—a fact which we have been in danger of overlooking in consequence of the uniformity of the normal picture, where the object appears to form part and parcel of the instinct. We are thus warned to loosen the bond that exists in our thoughts between instinct and object. It seems probable that the sexual instinct is in the first instance independent of its object; nor is its origin likely to be due to its object's attractions. . . .

---

weight that they influence the result in their sense. But in general the multiplicity of determining factors is reflected in the variety of manifest sexual attitudes in which they find their issue in mankind. In inverted types, a predominance of archaic constitutions and primitive psychical mechanisms is regularly to be found. Their most essential characteristics seem to be a coming into operation of narcissistic object-choice and a retention of the erotic significance of the anal zone. There is nothing to be gained, however, by separating the most extreme types of inversion from the rest on the basis of constitutional peculiarities of that kind. What we find as an apparently sufficient explanation of these types can be equally shown to be present, though less strongly, in the constitution of transitional types and of those whose manifest attitude is normal. The differences in the end-products may be of a qualitative nature, but analysis shows that the differences between their determinants are only quantitative. Among the accidental factors that influence object-choice we have found that frustration (in the form of an early deterrence, by fear, from sexual activity) deserves attention, and we have observed that the presence of both parents plays an important part. The absence of a strong father in childhood not infrequently favours the occurrence of inversion. Finally, it may be insisted that the concept of inversion in respect of the sexual object should be sharply distinguished from that of the occurrence in the subject of a mixture of sexual characters. In the relation between these two factors, too, a certain degree of reciprocal independence is unmistakably present....

During the last few years work carried out by biologists...has thrown a strong light on the organic determinants of [homosexuality] and of sexual characters in general. By carrying out experimental castration and subsequently grafting the sex-glands of the opposite sex, it was possible in the case of various species of mammals to transform a male into a female and vice versa. The transformation affected more or less completely both the somatic sexual characters and the psychosexual attitude. . . . It appeared that the vehicle of the force which thus acted as a sex-determinant was not the part of the sex-gland which forms the sex-cells but what is known as its interstitial tissue (the 'puberty-gland'). In one case this transformation of sex was actually effected in a man who had lost his testes owing to tuberculosis. In his sexual life he behaved in a feminine manner, as a passive homosexual, and exhibited very clearly-marked feminine sexual characters of a secondary kind (e.g. in regard to growth of hair and beard and deposits of fat on the breasts and hips). After an undescended testis from another male patient had been grafted into him, he began to behave in a masculine manner and to direct his libido towards women in a normal way. Simultaneously his somatic feminine characters disappeared. . . .

It would be unjustifiable to assert that these interesting experiments put the theory of inversion on a new basis, and it would be hasty to expect them to offer a universal means of 'curing' homosexuality. [One theorist] has rightly insisted that these experimental findings do not invalidate the theory of the general bisexual disposition of the higher animals. On the contrary, it seems to me probable that further research of a similar kind will produce a direct confirmation of this presumption of bisexuality. [Freud's note.]

POST-READING QUESTIONS:

1) Did any of the opinions or feelings that you discussed in your response to the first pre-reading question influence your reading of Freud's work? In light of your understanding of his ideas, do you want to rethink any of these opinions or feelings? Do you want to rethink any of your responses to the second, third, or fourth pre-reading questions in light of this understanding?

2) How do you think that Freud would analyze the incident discussed in the fifth pre-reading question? (See especially paragraphs 8, 24, and 26, and note 7, paragraph 2.) Would he likely agree or disagree with your analysis of this incident? Do you want to revise your analysis given what you've learned from having read this reading selection?

3) Do Freud's major views concerning sexual orientation result in a new way for you to understand the issues under discussion? Do they ever seem to conflict with one another? How might Freud analyze your understanding of his ideas, and how would you analyze his analysis?

4) Does this selection seem to be male-centered and/or slanted against women? If so, does its bias undermine Freud's objectivity (or his ability to be objective) with respect to the matters that he investigates?

5) How do you think that Louie Crew might respond to Freud's views concerning sexual orientation, and how might Freud respond to Crew's response? Can you cite textual evidence to support your speculations?

Evaluating the "Unnaturalness Argument" Concerning Homosexuality

BURTON M. LEISER

Born and raised in Denver, Colorado, Burton M. Leiser (1930–) received his B.A. from the University of Chicago in 1951. Having decided that he wanted to know more about Judaism than he already knew, he hitchhiked to New York, hoping to enter Yeshiva University. Lacking the intensive background that he needed to have in order for him to be a student at this prestigious university, he instead enrolled in the Bobover Yeshiva, a Hasidic institution that had recently been transplanted to the United States by some survivors of the Holocaust. Starting off in a class of seven-year-olds, Leiser studied at this institution for two years. Two years later, he was accepted at Yeshiva University, where he earned a degree of Master of Hebrew Literature. Simultaneously, he enrolled in the philosophy department in the graduate school of New York University, where he studied under Sidney Hook, Milton Munitz, William Barrett, and Paul Edwards, among others. Eventually, he ended up at Brown University, from where, in 1968, he received his Ph.D. in philosophy.

The recipient of an endowed chair at Pace University, Leiser is currently Distinguished Professor of Philosophy and adjunct professor of law there. Prior to accepting this position, he taught at Fort Lewis College in Durango, Colorado; the New York State University College at Buffalo; Sir George Williams University, in Montreal, Canada; and Drake University, in Des Moines, Iowa. While at Drake, he started attending classes at the law school and eventually compiled enough credits to receive the J.D. degree. He passed the Iowa bar exam, was admitted to the bar (later, he was also admitted to the New York Bar), and became clerk to the chief judge of the Iowa Court of Appeals.

Leiser's writings—which have appeared in philosophical, legal, and general magazines and journals, as well as in numerous books—range from articles on ancient archaeological finds and biblical interpretation to articles on art law, copyright, terrorism, and the legalization of narcotics. Leiser has also published the books *Custom, Law, and Morality* (1969), *Liberty, Justice, and Morals* (1973), and *Values in Conflict* (1981). The following reading selection is taken from the second of these three texts.

PRE-READING QUESTIONS:

1) How would you characterize or describe either the field of philosophy or, if you don't know much about that field, people's attempts to discuss issues "philosophically"? As you read Leiser's philosophical treatment of homosexuality and the unnaturalness argument, see if your pre-reading notions concerning philosophy or philosophical discussions affect your understanding of or reactions to the author's points. Also, see if the author's way of writing *per se* is that which you would expect to find in a philosophical discussion.

2) How many different definitions of the words "natural" and "unnatural" can you think of? What examples can you cite to illustrate how these words are used in different contexts?

3) Among the objects or behaviors that you consider unnatural, which do you think are bad, evil, or harmful, and which do you think are good or helpful? Explain your reason(s) for holding your views.

CLOSE-READING TIP

Leiser tries to demonstrate that the "arguments from nature" (so to speak) fail to prove that homosexuality is "unnatural." As you read his piece, think about whether or not he has represented these arguments fairly, evaluated them carefully and adequately, and accounted for all of the major arguments concerning this matter.

1 [The suggestion of the "unnaturalness" of homosexuality] raises the question of the meaning of *nature, natural*, and similar terms. Theologians and other moralists have said they violate the "natural law," and that they are therefore immoral and ought to be prohibited by the state.

2   The word *nature* has a built-in ambiguity that can lead to serious misunderstandings. When something is said to be "natural" or in conformity with "natural law" or the "law of nature," this may mean either (1) that it is in conformity with the descriptive laws of nature, or (2) that it is not artificial, that man has not imposed his will or his devices upon events or conditions as they exist or would have existed without such interference.

3   1. *The descriptive laws of nature.* The laws of nature, as these are understood by the scientist, differ from the laws of man. The former are purely descriptive, whereas the latter are prescriptive. When a scientist says that water boils at 212° Fahrenheit or that the volume of a gas varies directly with the heat that is applied to it and inversely with the pressure, he means merely that as a matter of recorded and observable fact, pure water under standard conditions always boils at precisely 212° Fahrenheit and that as a matter of observed fact, the volume of a gas rises as it is heated and falls as pressure is applied to it. These "laws" merely *describe* the manner in which physical substances *actually behave*. They differ from municipal and federal laws in that they *do not prescribe behavior*. Unlike manmade laws, natural laws are not passed by any legislator or group of legislators; they are not proclaimed or announced; they impose no obligation upon anyone or anything; their "violation" entails no penalty, and there is no reward for "following" them or "abiding by" them. When a scientist says that the air in a tire "obeys" the laws of nature that "govern" gases, he does *not* mean that the air, having been informed that it *ought* to behave in a certain way, behaves appropriately under the right conditions. He means, rather, that as a matter of fact, the air in a tire *will* behave like all other gases. In saying that Boyle's law "governs" the behavior of gases, he means merely that gases do, as a matter of fact, behave in accordance with Boyle's law, and the Boyle's law enables one to predict accurately what will happen to a given quantity of a gas as its pressure is raised; he does *not* mean to suggest that some heavenly voice has proclaimed that all gases should henceforth behave in accordance with the terms of Boyle's law and that a ghostly policeman patrols the world, ready to mete out punishments to any gases that "violate" the heavenly decree. In fact, according to the scientist, it does not make sense to speak of a natural law being violated. For if there were a true exception to a so-called law of nature, the exception would require a change in the description of those phenomena, and the "law" would have been shown to be no law at all. The laws of nature are revised as scientists discover new phenomena that require new refinements in their descriptions of the way things actually happen. In this respect they differ fundamentally from human laws, which are revised periodically by legislators who are not so interested in *describing* human behavior as they are in *prescribing* what human behavior *should* be.

4   2. *The artificial as a form of the unnatural.* On occasion when we say that something is not natural, we mean that it is a product of human artifice. My typewriter is not a natural object, in this sense, for the substances of which it is composed have been removed from their natural state—the state in which they existed before men came along—and have been transformed by a series of chemical and physical and mechanical processes into other substances. They have been rearranged into a whole that is quite different from anything found in nature. In short, my typewriter is an artificial object. In this sense, the clothing that I wear as I lecture before my students is not natural, for it has been transformed considerably from the state in which it was found in nature; and my wearing of clothing as I lecture before my students is also not natural, in this sense, for in my natural state, before the application of anything artificial, before any human interference with things as they are, I am quite naked. Human laws, being artificial conventions designed to exercise a degree of control over the natural inclinations and propensities of men, may in this sense be considered to be unnatural.

5   Now when theologians and moralists speak of homosexuality, contraception, abortion, and other forms of human behavior as being unnatural, and say that for that reason such behavior must be considered to be wrong, in what sense are they using the word *unnatural*? Are they saying that homosexual behavior and the use of contraceptives are contrary to the scientific laws of nature, are they saying that they are artificial forms of behavior, or are they using the terms *natural* and *unnatural* in some third sense?

6   They cannot mean that homosexual behavior (to stick to the subject presently under discussion) violates the laws of nature in the first sense, for, as we have pointed out, in *that* sense it is impossible to violate the laws of nature. Those laws, being merely descriptive of what actually does happen, would have to *include* homosexual behavior if such behavior does actually take place. Even if the defenders of the theological view that homosexuality is unnatural were to appeal to a statistical analysis by pointing out that such behavior is not normal from a statistical point of view, and therefore not what the laws of nature require, it would be open to their critics to reply that any descriptive law of nature must account for and incorporate all statistical deviations, and that the laws of nature, in this sense, do not *require* anything. These critics might also note that the best statistics available reveal that about half of all American males engage in homosexual activity at some time in their lives, and that a very large percentage of American males have exclusively homosexual relations for a fairly extensive period of time; from which it would follow that such behavior is natural, for them, at any rate, in this sense of the word *natural*.

7   If those who say that homosexual behavior is unnatural are using the term *unnatural* in the second sense, it is difficult to see why they should be fussing over it. Certainly nothing is intrinsically wrong with going against nature (if that is how it should be put) in this sense. That which is artificial is often far better than what is natural. Artificial homes seem, at any rate, to be more

suited to human habitation and more conducive to longer life and better health than caves and other natural shelters. There are distinct advantages to the use of such unnatural (i.e. artificial) amenities as clothes, furniture, and books. Although we may dream of an idyllic return to nature in our more wistful moments, we would soon discover, as Thoreau did in his attempt to escape from the artificiality of civilization, that needles and thread, knives and matches, ploughs and nails, and countless other products of human artifice are essential to human life. We would discover, as Plato pointed out in the *Republic*, that no man can be truly self-sufficient. Some of the by-products of industry are less than desirable; but neither industry itself, nor the products of industry, are intrinsically evil, even though both are unnatural in this sense of the word.

8   Interference with nature is not evil in itself. Nature, as some writers have put it, must be tamed. In some respects man must look upon it as an enemy to be conquered. If nature were left to its own devices, without the intervention of human artifice, men would be consumed with disease, they would be plagued by insects, they would be chained to the places where they were born with no means of swift communication or transport, and they would suffer the discomforts and the torments of wind and weather and flood and fire with no practical means of combating any of them. Interfering with nature, doing battle with nature, using human will and reason and skill to thwart what might otherwise follow from the conditions that prevail in the world, is a peculiarly human enterprise, one that can hardly be condemned merely because it does what is not natural.

9   Homosexual behavior can hardly be considered to be unnatural in this sense. There is nothing "artificial" about such behavior. On the contrary, it is quite natural, in this sense, to those who engage in it. And even if it were not, even if it were quite artificial, this is not in itself a ground for condemning it.

10   It would seem, then, that those who condemn homosexuality as an unnatural form of behavior must mean something else by the word *unnatural*, something not covered by either of the preceding definitions. A third possibility is this:

11   3. *Anything uncommon or abnormal is unnatural.* If this is what is meant by those who condemn homosexuality on the ground that it is unnatural, it is quite obvious that their condemnation cannot be accepted without further argument. For the fact that a given form of behavior is uncommon provides no justification for condemning it. Playing viola in a string quartet is no doubt an uncommon form of human behavior. I do not know what percentage of the human race engages in such behavior, or what percentage of his life any given violist devotes to such behavior, but I suspect that the number of such people must be very small indeed, and that the total number of manhours spent in such activity would justify our calling that form of activity uncommon, abnormal (in the sense that it is statistically not the kind of thing that people are ordinarily inclined to do), and therefore unnatural, in this sense of the word. Yet there is no reason to suppose that such uncommon, abnormal

behavior is, by virtue of its uncommonness, deserving of condemnation or ethically or morally wrong. On the contrary, many forms of behavior are praised precisely because they are so uncommon. Great artists, poets, musicians, and scientists are "abnormal" in this sense; but clearly the world is better off for having them, and it would be absurd to condemn them or their activities for their failure to be common and normal. If homosexual behavior is wrong, then, it must be for some reason other than its "unnaturalness" in this sense of the word.

12   4. *Any use of an organ or an instrument that is contrary to its principal purpose or function is unnatural.* Every organ and every instrument—perhaps even every creature—has a function to perform, one for which it is particularly designed. Any use of those instruments and organs that is consonant with their purposes is natural and proper, but any use that is inconsistent with their principal functions is unnatural and improper, and to that extent, evil or harmful. Human teeth, for example, are admirably designed for their principal functions—biting and chewing the kinds of food suitable for human consumption. But they are not particularly well suited for prying the caps from beer bottles. If they are used for the latter purpose, which is not natural to them, they are liable to crack or break under the strain. The abuse of one's teeth leads to their destruction and to a consequent deterioration in one's overall health. If they are used only for their proper function, however, they may continue to serve well for many years. Similarly, a given drug may have a proper function. If used in the furtherance of that end, it can preserve life and restore health. But if it is abused, and employed for purposes for which it was never intended, it may cause serious harm and even death. The natural uses of things are good and proper, but their unnatural uses are bad and harmful.

13   What we must do, then, is to find the proper use, or the true purpose, of each organ in our bodies. Once we have discovered that, we will know what constitutes the natural use of each organ, and what constitutes an unnatural, abusive, and potentially harmful employment of the various parts of our bodies. If we are rational, we will be careful to confine our behavior to our proper functions and to refrain from unnatural behavior. According to those philosophers who follow this line of reasoning, the way to discover the "proper" use of any organ is to determine what it is peculiarly suited to do. The eye is suited for seeing, the ear for hearing, the nerves for transmitting impulses from one part of the body to another, and so on.

14   What are the sex organs peculiarly suited to do? Obviously, they are peculiarly suited to enable men and women to reproduce their own kind. No other organ in the body is capable of fulfilling that function. It follows, according to those who follow the natural-law line, that the "proper" or "natural" function of the sex organs is reproduction, and that strictly speaking, any use of those organs for other purposes is unnatural, abusive, potentially harmful, and therefore wrong. The sex organs have been given to us in order to enable us to maintain the continued existence of mankind on this earth. All perversions—including masturbation, homosexual behavior, and heterosexual intercourse

that deliberately frustrates the design of the sexual organs—are unnatural and bad. As Pope Pius XI once said, "Private individuals have no other power over the members of their bodies than that which pertains to their natural ends."

15   But the problem is not so easily resolved. Is it true that every organ has one and only one proper function? A hammer may have been designed to pound nails, and it may perform that particular job best. But it is not sinful to employ a hammer to crack nuts if I have no other more suitable tool immediately available. The hammer, being a relatively versatile tool, may be employed in a number of ways. It has no one "proper" or "natural" function. A woman's eyes are well adapted to seeing, it is true. But they seem also to be well adapted to flirting. Is a woman's use of her eyes for the latter purpose sinful merely because she is not using them, at that moment, for their "primary" purpose of seeing? Our sexual organs are uniquely adapted for procreation, but that is obviously not the only function for which they are adapted. Human beings may—and do—use those organs for a great many other purposes, and it is difficult to see why any *one* use should be considered to be the only proper one. The sex organs, for one thing, seem to be particularly well adapted to give their owners and others intense sensations of pleasure. Unless one believes that pleasure itself is bad, there seems to be little reason to believe that the use of the sex organs for the production of pleasure in oneself or in others is evil. In view of the peculiar design of these organs, with their great concentration of nerve endings, it would seem that they were designed (if they *were* designed) with that very goal in mind, and that their use for such purposes would be no more unnatural than their use for the purpose of procreation.

16   Nor should we overlook the fact that human sex organs may be and are used to express, in the deepest and most intimate way open to man, the love of one person for another. Even the most ardent opponents of "unfruitful" intercourse admit that sex does serve this function. They have accordingly conceded that a man and his wife may have intercourse even though she is pregnant, or past the age of child bearing, or in the infertile period of her menstrual cycle.

17   Human beings are remarkably complex and adaptable creatures. Neither they nor their organs can properly be compared to hammers or to other tools. The analogy quickly breaks down. The generalization that a given organ or instrument has one and only one proper function does not hold up, even with regard to the simplest manufactured tools, for, as we have seen, a tool may be used for more than one purpose—less effectively than one especially designed for a given task, perhaps, but "properly" and certainly not *sinfully*. A woman may use her eyes not only to see and to flirt, but also to earn money—if she is, for example, an actress or a model. Though neither of the latter functions seems to have been a part of the original "design," if one may speak sensibly of *design* in this context, of the eye, it is difficult to see why such a use of the eyes of a woman should be considered sinful, perverse, or unnatural. Her sex organs have the unique capacity of producing ova and nurturing human embryos, under the right conditions; but why should any other use of those

organs, including their use to bring pleasure to their owner or to someone else, or to manifest love to another person, or even, perhaps, to earn money, be regarded as perverse, sinful, or unnatural? Similarly, a man's sexual organs possess the unique capacity of causing the generation of another human being, but if a man chooses to use them for pleasure, or for the expression of love, or for some other purpose—so long as he does not interfere with the rights of some other person—the fact that his sex organs do have their unique capabilities does not constitute a convincing justification for condemning their other uses as being perverse, sinful, unnatural, or criminal. If a man "perverts" himself by wiggling his ears for the entertainment of his neighbors instead of using them exclusively for their "natural" function of hearing, no one thinks of consigning him to prison. If he abuses his teeth by using them to pull staples from memos—a function for which teeth were clearly not designed—he is not accused of being immoral, degraded, and degenerate. The fact that people *are* condemned for using their sex organs for their own pleasure or profit, or for that of others, may be more revealing about the prejudices and taboos of our society than it is about our perception of the true nature or purpose or "end" (whatever that might be) of our bodies.

18   To sum up, then, the proposition that any use of an organ that is contrary to its principal purpose or function is unnatural assumes that organs *have* a principal purpose or function, but this may be denied on the ground that the purpose or function of a given organ may vary according to the needs or desires of its owner. It may be denied on the ground that a given organ may have more than one principal purpose or function, and any attempt to call one use or another the only natural one seems to be arbitrary, if not question-begging. Also, the proposition suggests that what is unnatural is evil or depraved. This goes beyond the pure description of things, and enters into the problem of the evaluation of human behavior, which leads us to the fifth meaning of "natural."

19   5. *That which is natural is good, and whatever is unnatural is bad.* When one condemns homosexuality or masturbation or the use of contraceptives on the ground that it is unnatural, one implies that whatever is unnatural is bad, wrongful, or perverse. But as we have seen, in some senses of the word, the unnatural (i.e., the artificial) is often very good, whereas that which is natural (i.e., that which has not been subjected to human artifice or improvement) may be very bad indeed. Of course, interference with nature may be bad. Ecologists have made us more aware than we have ever been of the dangers of unplanned and uninformed interference with nature. But this is not to say that *all* interference with nature is bad. Every time a man cuts down a tree to make room for a home for himself, or catches a fish to feed himself or his family, he is interfering with nature. If men did not interfere with nature, they would have no homes, they could eat no fish, and, in fact, they could not survive. What, then, can be meant by those who say that whatever is natural is good and whatever is unnatural is bad? Clearly, they cannot have intended merely to reduce the word *natural* to a synonym of *good, right*, and *proper*, and

unnatural to a synonym of *evil, wrong, improper, corrupt*, and *depraved*. If that were all they had intended to do, there would be very little to discuss as to whether a given form of behavior might be proper even though it is not in strict conformity with someone's views of what is natural; for *good* and *natural* being synonyms, it would follow inevitably that whatever is good must be natural, and vice versa, by definition. This is certainly not what the opponents of homosexuality have been saying when they claim that homosexuality, being unnatural, is evil. For if it were, their claim would be quite empty. They would be saying merely that homosexuality, being evil, is evil—a redundancy that could as easily be reduced to the simpler assertion that homosexuality is evil. This assertion, however, is not an argument. Those who oppose homosexuality and other sexual "perversions" on the ground that they are "unnatural" are saying that there is some objectively identifiable quality in such behavior that is unnatural; and that that quality, once it has been identified by some kind of scientific observation, can be seen to be detrimental to those who engage in such behavior, or to those around them; and that *because* of the harm (physical, mental, moral, or spiritual) that results from engaging in any behavior possessing the attribute of unnaturalness, such behavior must be considered to be wrongful, and should be discouraged by society. "Unnaturalness" and "wrongfulness" are not synonyms, then, but different concepts. The problem with which we are wrestling is that we are unable to find a meaning for *unnatural* that enables us to arrive at the conclusion that homosexuality is unnatural or that if homosexuality is unnatural, it is therefore wrongful behavior. We have examined four common meanings of *natural* and *unnatural*, and have seen that none of them performs the task that it must perform if the advocates of this argument are to prevail. Without some more satisfactory explanation of the connection between the wrongfulness of homosexuality and its alleged unnaturalness, the [unnaturalness] argument. . . must be rejected. . . .

POST-READING QUESTIONS:

1) Did your pre-reading notions concerning either philosophy or philosophical discussions influence your understanding of or help shape your reactions to Leiser's work? Did his work cause you to reexamine any of these notions?

2) Might you have reacted differently to Leiser's ideas had Leiser couched them in, say, a short story or a personal diary entry?

3) Do you agree with Leiser that the arguments from nature that he analyzes must be rejected? Whether or not you find Leiser's arguments and analyses convincing, would you say that they have affected your own thinking about the issue of sexual orientation?

4) Has Leiser accounted for all of the (significant) arguments from nature? If not, would you consider this omission a weakness in his writing? Is the omission weighty enough to jeopardize the status of his overall analysis?

5) Based on your careful evaluation of Leiser's points, would you say that Leiser expresses the opinion that any given sexual orientation is natural? Does he preclude the possibility that homosexuality is unnatural?

6) Do you think that you might have answered any of the pre-reading questions differently from the ways in which you did answer them had you read Leiser's piece prior to responding to those questions?

Born or Bred?

DAVID GELMAN, ET AL.

The following article appeared in the February 24, 1992, issue of *Newsweek*. Senior writer David Gelman wrote the piece, with help from correspondents Donna Foote, Todd Barrett, and Mary Talbot. *Newsweek* has provided the following information on Gelman: "David Gelman [was] a Senior Writer for *Newsweek* [from] 1978 [to 1994], concentrating on stories for the Ideas and Life/Style sections of the magazine. In June 1988, he helped create a new department called 'The Mind' [the following reading selection was published in that department]. Gelman has covered a variety of topics for *Newsweek*[,] including how to calm children's fears about war, how former hostages are coping with post-traumatic stress, [and] the causes of homosexuality and serial killers [*sic*]. . . . He has also contributed to a number of cover stories for the magazine[,] including 'The Mind of the Rapist' (7/23/90) and 'Prozac' (3/26/90). He was also a major contributor to *Newsweek*'s special issue, 'The New Teens: What Makes Them Different,' which received [quite a bit] of media attention. . . . Gelman shares many *Newsweek* awards, including an American Psychiatric Association Media Award for 'Body and Soul' (November 7, 1988 cover story) and a Media Achievement Award from the National Alliance for the Mentally Ill and a Certificate of Commendation from the American Psychiatric Association for [his article] 'Depression' (May 4, 1987 cover story). . . . Before coming to *Newsweek*, Gelman worked for . . . *Newsday* . . . [and] the *New York Post*. . . . [He also worked] for the Peace Corps in Washington, D.C. . . . [He is a] native of Brooklyn, [New York]."

PRE-READING QUESTIONS:

1) In general, how do you feel about journalism or the media? Do you think that journalistic reporting is usually more or less fair or unfair, in-depth or superficial, careful or careless? Do you think that your thoughts and feelings about journalism and the media might influence your reading of the following selection? Would you approach this selection with different pre-reading expectations were the selection an article from a scholarly journal?

2) Do you think that everyone is born with a particular sexual orientation? If researchers were to prove that everyone *is* in fact born with a particular sexual orientation, do you think that this discovery would likely change many

heterosexuals' views on nonheterosexuality, their attitudes towards nonheterosexuals, or their reactions to nonheterosexual lifestyles?

3) Do you find any significance in the use of the terms "gay" and "straight" to refer to one's sexual orientation? Also, are there any derogatory terms equivalent to "fag," "dyke," or "queer" that refer to heterosexuals? Finally, does it matter whether or not people who use any of the terms cited above are themselves either heterosexual or nonheterosexual?

CLOSE-READING TIP

Though they don't always achieve it, many (if not most) journalists strive for objectivity in their reporting. As you read this piece, note those moments when you think that the authors are trying to be objective, and watch for clues to their own biases (concerning the latter, see, for example, paragraphs 9 and 34). If you find biases in the article, try to determine whether or not any of these biases negatively affects the authors' reporting. (By the way, as you read this article, note how often key points are contained in the first sentences of paragraphs.)

*Science and psychiatry are struggling to make
sense of new research that suggests that
homosexuality may be a matter of genetics, not
parenting*

1   Until the age of 28, Doug Barnett* was a practicing heterosexual. He was vaguely attracted to men, but with nurturing parents, a lively interest in sports and appropriate relations with women, he had little reason to question his proclivities. Then an astonishing thing happened: his identical twin brother "came out" to him, revealing he was gay. Barnett, who believed sexual orientation is genetic, was bewildered. He recalls thinking, "If this is inherited and we're identical twins—what's going on here?" To find out, he thought he should try sex with men. When he did, he says, "The bells went off, for the first time. Those homosexual encounters were more fulfilling." A year later both twins told their parents they were gay.

2   Simon LeVay knew he was homosexual by the time he was 12. Growing up bookish, in England, he fit the "sissy boy" profile limned by psychologists: an aversion to rough sports, a strong attachment to his mother, a hostile relationship with his father. It was, LeVay acknowledges, the perfect Freudian recipe for homosexuality—only he was convinced Freud had cause and effect back-

---

*Not his real name. [Gelman's note.]

ward: hostile fathers didn't make sons gay; fathers turned hostile because the sons were "unmasculine" to begin with.

3   Last year, LeVay, now a neuroscientist at the Salk Institute in La Jolla, Calif., got a chance to examine his hunch up close. What he found is still reverberating among scientists and may have a profound impact on how the rest of us think about homosexuality. Scanning the brains of 41 cadavers, including 19 homosexual males, LeVay determined that a tiny area believed to control sexual activity was less than half the size in the gay men than in the heterosexuals. It was perhaps the first direct evidence of what some gays have long contended— that whether or not they choose to be different, they are born different.

4   Doug Barnett, meanwhile, got an opportunity to make his own contribution to the case. Two years ago he was recruited for an ambitious study of homosexuality in twins, undertaken by psychologist Michael Bailey, of Northwestern University, and psychiatrist Richard Pillard, of the Boston University School of Medicine. Published last December, only months after LeVay's work, the results showed that if one identical twin is gay, the other is almost three times more likely to be gay than if the twins are fraternal—suggesting that something in the identical twins' shared genetic makeup affected their sexual orientation.

5   In both studies, the implications are potentially huge. For decades, scientists and the public at large have debated whether homosexuals are born or made— whether their sexual orientation is the result of a genetic roll of the dice or a combination of formative factors in their upbringing. If it turns out, indeed, that homosexuals are born that way, it could undercut the animosity gays have had to contend with for centuries. "It would reduce being gay to something like being left-handed, which is in fact all that it is," says gay San Francisco journalist and author Randy Shilts.

6   But instead of resolving the debate, the studies may well have intensified it. Some scientists profess not to be surprised at all by LeVay's finding of brain differences. "Of course it [sexual orientation] is in the brain," says Johns Hopkins University psychologist John Money, sometimes called the dean of American sexologists. "The real question is, when did it get there? Was it prenatal, neonatal, during childhood, puberty? That we do not know."

7   Others are sharply critical of the Bailey-Pillard study. Instead of proving the genetics argument, they think it only confirms the obvious: that twins are apt to have the same sort of shaping influences. "In order for such a study to be at all meaningful, you'd have to look at twins raised apart," says Anne Fausto Stirling, a developmental biologist at Brown University, in Providence, R.I. "It's such badly interpreted genetics."

8   In the gay community itself, many welcome the indication that gayness begins in the chromosomes. Theoretically, it could gain them the civil-rights protections accorded any "natural" minority, in which the legal linchpin is the question of an "immutable" characteristic. Moreover, it could lift the burden of self-blame from their parents. "A genetic component in sexual orientation says, 'This is not a fault, and it's not your fault'," says Pillard.

9   Yet the intimation that an actual gene for gayness might be found causes some foreboding. If there is a single, identifiable cause, how long before some nerdy genius finds a "cure"? Many scientists say it's naive to think a single gene could account for so complex a behavior as homosexuality. Yet at least three research projects, one of them at the National Institutes of Health, are believed to be searching for a "gay gene" or group of genes. LeVay, for one, thinks a small number of sex genes may be isolated, perhaps within five years: "And that's going to blow society's mind."

10   For some people, it is not too great a leap from there to Nazi-style eugenics. In the nightmare scenario, once a gay fetus is detected in utero, it is aborted, or a genetic switch is "flipped" to ensure its heterosexuality. The gay population simply fades away. Would mothers permit such tampering? Even parents who've come to terms with their child's homosexuality might. "No parent would choose to have a child born with any factor that would make life difficult for him or her," says Laurie Coburn, program director of the Federation of Parents and Friends of Lesbians and Gays (ParentsFLAG).

11   On this subject, feelings are seldom restrained. But cooler voices can be heard, mainly those of lesbians. Many of them say their choice of lesbianism was as much a feminist statement as a sexual one, so the fuss over origins doesn't interest them. "It's mostly fascinating to heteros," says one gay activist. On the whole, lesbians are warier of the research, and their conspicuous absence from most studies angers them. "It's part of the society's intrinsic sexism," says Penny Perkins, public-education coordinator for Lambda Legal Defense and Education Fund, which works to promote lesbian and gay men's rights. Frances Stevens, editor in chief of Deneuve, a lesbian news magazine, admits her personal history supports biological causes; although she came from a wholesome "Brady Bunch" family, she knew she was gay "from day one." But she is skeptical of the studies, she says. "My response was: if the gay guy's [hypothalamus] is smaller, what's it like for dykes? Is it the same size as a straight male's?" That's something researchers still have to find out.

12   Gay men have their own reasons to be irate: as they see it, looking for a "cause" of homosexuality implies it is deviant and heterosexuality is the norm. When John De Cecco, professor of psychology at San Francisco State University and editor of the Journal of Homosexuality, began one of his classes recently by suggesting students discuss the causes of homosexuality, someone called out, "Who cares?" and the class burst into applause.

13   All the same, homosexuals must care deeply about how the straight world perceives them. History has taught them that the consequences of those perceptions can be deadly. Over the centuries they have been tolerated or reviled, enfranchised or oppressed. According to John Boswell's 1980 book, "Christianity, Social Tolerance and Homosexuality," things didn't turn truly nasty until the 13th century, when the church, on the heels of a diatribe from Saint Thomas Aquinas, began to view gays as not only unnatural but dangerous.

14   In our own century of *sex et lux*, beginning with Sigmund Freud, psychiatrists ascribed male homosexuality to unconscious conflicts and fixations that have their roots in early childhood. (Freud was always foggier on female sexuality.) But that view was officially dropped in 1973, when more stringent diagnostic standards—and the lobbying of gay activists—persuaded the American Psychiatric Association to expunge homosexuality from the list of emotional disorders. The decision was bitterly disputed; 37 percent of APA members voted against it in a 1974 referendum. But younger psychiatrists now are taught that rather than trying to "cure" homosexuals, they should help them feel more comfortable about themselves.

15   LeVay resolved to look for sex differences in the brain after the slow, wrenching death from AIDS of his companion of 21 years (box). He'd been impressed by a study done by a UCLA graduate student, Laura Allen, working with biologist Robert Gorski, showing that a portion of the hypothalamus in the brains of males was more than twice as large as that of women. LeVay's report, published in the journal Science on Aug. 30, 1991, was based on his own yearlong study of the hypothalamus in 41 cadavers, including 19 self-avowed homosexual men, 16 heterosexual men and 6 heterosexual women. All the homosexuals had died of AIDS, as had seven of the heterosexuals—including one of the women. What emerged with almost startling clarity was that, with some exceptions, the cluster of neurons known as INAH 3 (the third interstitial nucleus of the anterior hypothalamus, which LeVay calls "the business end as far as sex goes") was more than twice as large in the heterosexual males as in the homosexuals, whose INAH 3 was around the same size as in the women. In the sensation that greeted the report, its cautious wording was all but ignored. "What I reported was a difference in the brain structure of the hypothalamus," says LeVay. "We can't say on the basis of that what makes people gay or straight. But it opens the door to find the answer to that question."

16   One of the major criticisms of the study was that AIDS could have affected the brain structure of the homosexual subjects. LeVay has been able to field that one by pointing out that he found no pathology suggesting such damage either in gay or straight men who died of the disease. Later, in fact, he examined the brain of a homosexual who died of lung cancer, and again found INAH 3 much smaller.

17   The trickier question is whether things might work the other way around: could sexual orientation affect brain structure? Kenneth Klivington, an assistant to the president of the Salk Institute, points to a body of evidence showing that the brain's neural networks reconfigure themselves in response to certain experiences. One fascinating NIH study found that in people reading Braille after becoming blind, the area of the brain controlling the reading finger grew larger. There are also intriguing conundrums in animal brains. In male songbirds, for example, the brain area associated with mating is not only larger than in the female but varies according to the season.

18   Says Klivington: "From the study of animals, we know that circulating sex hormones in the mother can have a profound effect on the organization of the brain of the fetus. Once the individual is born, the story gets more complex because of the interplay between the brain and experience. It's a feedback loop: the brain influences behavior, behavior shapes experience, experience affects the organization of the brain, and so forth."

19   LeVay knows he is somewhat vulnerable on that score. Because his subjects were all dead, he knew "regrettably little" about their sexual histories, besides their declared or presumed orientation. "That's a distinct shortcoming of my study," he concedes. Did the gay men play the passive or aggressive roles in sex? Were some bisexual, another variable, and could that have affected their neuron clusters? To find answers, LeVay plans next to study living subjects with the new MRI (magnetic resonance imaging) technology. But he remains convinced that biology is destiny. "If there are environmental influences," he says, "they operate very early in life, at the fetal or early-infancy stage, when the brain is still putting itself together. I'm very much skeptical of the idea that sexual orientation is a cultural thing."

20   The Bailey-Pillard twin study had its own shortcomings. The numbers alone were impressive. The researchers found that of 56 identical twins, 52 percent were both gay, as against 22 percent of fraternal twins, who have somewhat weaker genetic bonds. (Of the adoptive, nongenetically related brothers in the study, only 11 percent were both gay.) The suggestion of a shared genetic destiny is strong, but many critics have wondered: what about the discordant twins—those where only one was homosexual? Many in the study were not only discordant, but dramatically different.

21   Most sexuality studies use the Kinsey scale, which rates orientation on a seven-point spectrum from strictly heterosexual to exclusively homosexual. The study found that most of the discordant identical twins were at opposite ends of the Kinsey spectrum. How could two individuals with identical genetic traits and upbringing wind up with totally different sexual orientation? Richard Green, a noted UCLA researcher of homosexuality, says he believes research should focus on that finding, which he deems "astounding." Although Pillard and Bailey are certain that biology plays the dominant role, Bailey acknowledges: "There must be something in the environment to yield the discordant twins."

22   What that might be is uncertain. None of the usual domineering-mother, distant-father theories has been conclusively shown to determine sexuality. Meanwhile the case for biology has grown stronger. "If you look at all societies," says Frederick Whitam, who has researched homosexuality in cultures as diverse as the United States, Central America and the Philippines, "homosexuality occurs at the same rates with the same kinds of behavior. That suggests something biological going on. The biological evidence has been growing for 20 or more years."

23 "Something in the environment," "something biological"—the truth is, the nature-nurture argument is no longer as polarized as it once was. Scientists are beginning to realize there is a complex interplay between the two, still to be explored. June Reinisch, director of the Kinsey Institute, prefers to think we are only "flavored, not programmed." Genetics, she says, only give us "a range of outcomes."

24 Should it really matter to gays what makes them gay? Whitam says it does matter. In a 1989 study of attitudes toward gays in four different societies, those who believed homosexuals "were born that way" represented a minority but were also the least homophobic. Observes Whitam: "There is a tendency for people, when told that homosexuality is biological, to heave a sigh of relief. It relieves the families and homosexuals of guilt. It also means that society doesn't have to worry about things like gay teachers."

25 For the most part, gays remain doubtful that even the strongest evidence of biological origins will cut much ice with confirmed homophobes. Many find the assumption naive. "Our organization considers the studies useless," says Dr. Howard Grossman, a gay doctor who heads New York Physicians for Human Rights. "It's just like the military—you can show them a thousand studies that show gay soldiers aren't a security risk and they still don't care."

26 The doctor's pessimism is not unwarranted. Jacquelyn Holt Park, author of a moving novel about the sorrows of growing up lesbian in the sexually benighted 1940s and '50s, is just back from a 9,000-mile book tour where she was astonished to find how little has changed. "There are talk shows," says Park, "where fundamentalists and the like still say [homosexuality] is an abomination, it's vile. They said, 'You're not black, blacks can't change their color, but you can change.' I guess these new studies might address some of those feelings."

27 Even within the enlightened ranks of the American Psychoanalytic Association there is still some reluctance to let homosexual analysts practice. As arrested cases themselves, the argument goes, they are ill equipped to deal with developmental problems. The belief that homosexuality can and should be "cured" persists in some quarters of the profession.

28 Others are exasperated by that view. Richard Isay, chairperson of the APA's Committee on Gay, Lesbian and Bisexual Issues, is convinced analysis can be more damaging than beneficial to gays. "I still see many gay men who come to me after they've been in analysis where the therapist has been trying to change their orientation," he says. "That's extremely harmful to the self-esteem of a gay man." Isay thinks the approach, instead, should be to try to clear away "roadblocks" that may interfere with a gay's ability to function.

29 Perhaps the most voluble spokesman for the "fix it" school is Charles Socarides, a New York City analyst who claims a flourishing practice in turning troubled homosexuals into "happy, fulfilled heterosexuals." To Socarides, the only biological evidence is "that we're anatomically made to go in male-female pairs." Thus he "reconstructs" patients' lives to learn why they can't

mate with opposite-sex partners. There can be many reasons, he says: "abdicating fathers, difficult wives, marital disruptions." From there, he "opens up the path" to hetero-happiness, for which, he says, one gratified customer cabled him recently: "The eagle has landed."

30 Some psychiatrists still see the removal of homosexuality from the official list of emotional disorders as a mistake. (Instead, it was innocuously identified as "sexual orientation disturbance.") "Psychology and psychiatry have essentially abandoned a whole population of people who feel dissatisfied with their feelings of homosexuality," says psychologist Joseph Nicolosi, author of "Reparative Therapy of Male Homosexuality" (*Jason Aronson, 1991*). In graduate school, says Nicolosi, he found the stance was that if a client came in complaining about his gayness, the therapist's job was to teach him to accept it. "It was like the old joke of the patient who tells the doctor his arm hurts when he bends it and the doctor advises him not to bend it."

. . .

31 Nicolosi tries to do more than that for his patients, most of them men in their 20s and 30s who are unhappy with their homosexuality. As director of the Thomas Aquinas Psychology Clinic in Encino, Calif., he tries to bolster his patients' sense of male identity, which he sees as crucial to their orientation. The biological evidence is inconclusive, Nicolosi says; there is much more proof for familial causes of homosexuality. "Research has shown repeatedly that a poor relationship with a distant, aloof father and an overpossessive, domineering mother could cause homosexuality in males," he says.

32 In fact, some of that research, dating back to the 1950s, has been discredited because of faulty techniques, among other problems. Nicolosi is at any rate modest in his own claims. No cures as such, but "a diminishment of homosexual feelings" to the point where some patients can marry and have families. How long is treatment? "Probably a lifetime process," he says.

33 With the debate over origins still going strong, comes one more exhibit in evidence. Recently, Bailey and Pillard divulged just a tidbit from their not-yet-published study of lesbian twins. Finding enough females for the study took twice as long as their earlier project, says Bailey, but apparently it was worth the effort. "If there are genes for homosexuality, they're not gender blind," he says. Lesbians in the study had more lesbian sisters than they did gay brothers.

34 Nature? Nurture? Perhaps the most appropriate answer comes from Evelyn Hooker, who showed in an important 1950s study that it is impossible to distinguish heterosexuals from homosexuals on psychological tests. Hooker takes the long view of the search for origins. "Why do we want to know the cause?" she asks. "It's a mistake to hope that we will be able to modify or change homosexuality. . . If we understand its nature and accept it as a given, then we come much closer to the kind of attitudes which will make it possible for homosexuals to lead a decent life in society." The psychiatric profession heeded Hooker when it stopped calling homosexuality an illness. At 84, her voice has grown fainter, but the rest of us could do worse than to listen to her now.

APPENDIX to Born or Bred

SIMON LEVAY
A grieving scientist's labor of love convinces him that biology is destiny

In the long-running debate over whether homosexuality begins in the genes or the nursery, Simon LeVay was an unlikely champion for the genetic side. As a homosexual himself (with a homosexual brother), he seemed a textbook-perfect product of nurture. "When I look back," he says, "I definitely see things that went along with being gay: not liking rough sports, preferring reading, being very close with my mother." And the classic clincher—"I hated my father as long as I can remember." By Freudian lights, that should have made an open-and-shut case for nurture. But LeVay believed even then that nature comes first. "My point would be that gays are extremely different when they're young and as a *result* they can develop hostile relationships with their fathers. It's just a big mistake to think it's the other way around and the relationships are causative."

An Englishman with a Ph.D. in neuroanatomy, LeVay spent 12 years at Harvard before moving on to the Salk Institute to pursue his field of research—which, ironically, included the influence of environment on development. But when his lover of 21 years, Richard Hersey, died of AIDS, LeVay went into a deep depression. Hospitalized for two weeks, he began reevaluating his goals. "It makes you think what your life is about," he says. Around that time, a UCLA lab announced its finding that a portion of the male hypothalamus that regulates sex was more than twice as large as women's. Suddenly, it seemed to LeVay there was a thesis to pursue: was it also larger than that of gays? "I felt if I didn't find anything, I would give up a scientific career altogether."

After nine months' work, LeVay did find that in at least one group of gays, the sex-regulating area was smaller than in straight men. The work brought him instant fame and a round of talk shows, where he's often obliged to contend with the unconvinced. But he thinks it's worth it, if it promotes the idea that homosexuality is a matter of destiny, not choice. "It's important to educate society," he says. "I think this issue does affect religious and legal attitudes." From here on he'll be spreading the word as codirector of the West Hollywood Institute for Gay and Lesbian Education, on leave from Salk. The new institute opens in September as one of the first free-standing schools for homosexual studies. LeVay may have to abandon research. But he's still on the compassionate course he set out on after the death of his lover.

ANNETTE BRENNER
For parents, a child's 'coming out' can lead to painful episodes of soul-searching

Annette E. Brenner remembers joking when her oldest son was 4 that she'd approve his marrying outside the family's faith as long as he married a woman. When he "came out" to her and her husband at 17, one of her first reactions was to try to "negotiate" him out of his gayness. She offered him a car, a house, if only he would wait and try marriage. He was at boarding school in Connecticut at the time, and she was convinced it was "just a stage." She remembers thinking, "Sure, this week you're a homosexual. Enjoy the experiment, have fun. Next week you'll be a Hare Krishna." Then she became enraged. "What is this kid doing to me?" she'd ask herself. What was he doing to his grandparents, his brother and sister?

Years of gay activism haven't made coming out much easier on parents. At the Chicago-area office of ParentsFLAG (Parents and Friends of Lesbians and Gays), the national support organization Brenner joined, parents often call in tears. Some, she says, have had nervous breakdowns over the news of their child's homosexuality. Brenner had a terrible time accepting her son's revelation. For a while she wondered about the Freudian explanation. "We replayed his whole life" looking for some environmental reason, she says. She wondered whether she had been too domineering. They sent him to a therapist, only to be told he was comfortable with his gayness. Finally, they came to terms with it, too—her husband more easily than she did. She understands now why her son had such a poor self-image at school, why he endured falling grades and bouts of depression.

Her son is 28 now, and he brings his lover home for visits. "He's happy because his family accepts him," says Brenner. Still, she frets about AIDS, and she knows he hasn't been tested. He's been "bashed" a couple of times—and she worries about his physical safety. Even seeing how content her son is, Brenner says, "Had I known that I was to have a gay child, I would probably not want to have a gay child."

At FLAG, parents are firmly behind any research that implicates biology as the source of gayness. It assuages the raging guilt some of them feel that they might be responsible. "Especially if my child gets AIDS," says Brenner, "can you imagine what that would be like?" Probably, it would be shattering. Gays may come out and get on with their lives, often happily. But for parents, the doubts and the dread never seem to stop.

MIKE

Through therapy, a gay widower seeks an end to a lifestyle of cruising

"Mike" is a 49-year-old widower who was married for 18 years and has a teenage son. Although he says he loved his wife, he was secretly cruising gay bars during his marriage and engaging in short-term homosexual encounters. After his wife died, he found his way to Dr. Joseph Nicolosi, whom he consulted for eight months.

"I went on binges, just like an alcoholic would do. [After my wife died] Saturday nights were terrible. I'd go to a heterosexual bar and end up jumping in my car and going to some bath or gay bar. I was at a point in my life where either I was a homosexual and I was going to be open and public about it, or I was not going to be a homosexual and be otherwise. I was in the pits. Whatever I was doing was not making me happy. I was not going to continue living the lie that I was living.

"I kept searching for somebody to help me, but you always heard that nothing could be done about this and anybody who came to your attention was usually a gay therapist. I was more than in a closet, I was in a coffin. I had never revealed this to anybody before. I never trusted anybody. In the very first session [with Dr. Nicolosi], I realized we were on the same wavelength.

"I never had a man in my life who taught me how to be a man. I never had a role model. I realize how my dad's failure to be present for me screwed me up. I was very angry toward my dad. And I never knew why. I [also] felt I'd been castrated by women. When I got into therapy, the resentment toward my mother was far greater than toward my dad. There was a lot of anger, a lot of deep feeling at not having your mother accept your maleness. When I started loving myself, when I started to know who I was, my maleness came with it." *(Six months after completing therapy, Mike says he has not had any homosexual encounters. Does he feel "cured"?)*

"I would have to answer, yes, I still do sometimes have homosexual feelings. But I don't get upset if I get them because I understand them now. Now Saturday night comes and goes and I don't even think about it."

POST-READING QUESTIONS:

1) Did any of your pre-reading thoughts or feelings about journalism, the media, or journalistic reporting affect your reading of this article? Does this piece cause you to want to examine your reasons for having any of these pre-reading thoughts or feelings? Does it cause you to want to rethink your pre-reading comparative analysis of journalistic and scholarly writing?

2) Do you agree with the authors that, "instead of resolving the debate, the studies [cited in the article] may well have intensified it" (paragraph 6)?

3) What do you make of the comment by one "gay [lesbian?] activist" that the issue concerning choice and sexual orientation is "'mostly fascinating to heteros. . . '" (paragraph 11)? If you read the featured reading selection, how do you think that Louie Crew would respond to this claim?

4) What do you make of both the authors' comments about lesbians and their treatment of lesbians' comments concerning the issues under consideration? Take an especially close look at paragraph 11.

5) Can you determine the authors' stance on any of the issues that they address? If so, can you determine whether or not the authors' biases interfere with their ability to be objective?

6) After having read this article, do you want to amend anything that you say in response to the second or third pre-reading question?

The Tables Need Turning

JAN PARKER

Jan Parker's essay appeared in a book entitled *Heterosexuality* (1987), edited by Gillian E. Hanscombe and Martin Humphries; a collection of pieces by various authors, the book was published in Great Britain. The following biographical sketch appears in the "Notes on the Contributors" section of the book: "Jan

Parker was born in London in 1957 and was sparked into political activity by the student Left in 1976. She is an independent socialist, a feminist and (need it be said in this context?) a lesbian—not necessarily in that order. She was a member of NUS Women's Committee 1977–79 and then office worker for the Campaign Against the Corrie Bill and the National Abortion Campaign. A former member of the Spare Rib collective, she still writes and harbours a fantasy about being a singer. She worked until 1986 in the GLC Women's Committee Support Unit. Destination unknown: no doubt la lotta continua" (174).

PRE-READING QUESTIONS:

1) Have you ever thought much about the nature and function of mainstream ideas or practices such as capitalism, monogamy, heterosexuality, meat eating, or theocentricity? How do you feel when you hear someone criticize or attack these or other mainstream ideas or practices? Have you yourself ever criticized or attacked any of them? Think about your responses as you read Parker's essay, watching to see whether or not—and, if so, how, why, and to what extent—they affect your understanding of or reactions to her ideas.

2) Having thought about some relevant data, would you infer that heterosexuality is not only compulsory, but also, perhaps, oppressive?

3) Do you see any relationship between the struggles for women's rights and the struggles for gay/lesbian rights?

4) How do you feel when you notice nonheterosexuals calling attention to their sexual orientations? How about when you notice *heterosexuals* calling attention to *their* sexual orientation?

5) Do you think that gays and lesbians ought be in or out of the closet? Should they be both in *and* out of it? How about heterosexuals?

CLOSE-READING TIP

Parker's essay is something of a mix between personal writing and more traditionally academic writing. And, like Crew, Parker often addresses "the personal" in the context of discussing a group (as opposed to addressing it within a more or less purely personal context). As you read her work, note those aspects of her writing that reflect her personal feelings, those that reflect her identification with particular groups, those that seem more traditionally academic, and those that seem to combine two or more of the above characteristics. Try to determine whether or not—and, if so, how—her essay gains or loses anything when she uses first-person narrative, when she uses third-person narrative (the type of narrative, most commonly found in academic writing), or when she combines these two approaches. Compare, for example, relevant passages in paragraphs 4, 5, 11, and 14.

1   The idea that heterosexuality is of itself oppressive to women and tailored to men's needs and interests is not new in circles familiar with feminist debate and, some may say, not particularly controversial either. The idea of 'compulsory heterosexuality' is newer and makes many more hackles rise. Despite the fact that compulsory heterosexuality was named as one of the 'crimes against women' by the Brussels Tribunal on Crimes Against Women in 1976—one of the first 'official' acknowledgements of its existence that has since been joined by others—it is still mostly dismissed as a loony idea. Yet many features of oppression that have been attributed to sexism are attributable to heterosexism. This may be hard even for some feminists to swallow, but the idea is gaining ground and in this lies a direction that needs pursuing.

2   [The] book [in which this essay appears], called *Heterosexuality* and written by lesbians and gay men, is further evidence that an important shift in focus is slowly happening. It is far more pertinent and clarifying for questions—and the finger—to be pointed at heterosexuality than at lesbianism and homosexuality. The effort of finding and defining our identity and then surviving is a long slog, so it's not surprising that a lot of lesbian and gay energy has gone into this. We're forced into, at best, a corner; and at worst, the closet (cells, psychiatric units). We've been so pathologised that it's still hard to break out of their image of us however much one's guts reject this pressure. We can break through this block by demanding that heterosexuals explain their sexuality rather than accept being forced to constantly explain ours to them.

3   Heterosexuality is a subject it's difficult not to be knowledgeable about. We're bombarded by it, with information about how heterosexuals should and do behave towards their own and the other gender. From a lesbian viewpoint heterosexuality often strikes me as peculiar, if not downright weird, these days. It's easy to feel like an anthropologist spending an evening in the local pub—watching the heterosexual signals, the codes of behaviour and appearance—and to let my mind dwell on the rituals involved, the most obvious example and glaring symbol of institutionalization being the wedding, with all the fantastic hetiquette and paraphernalia that the occasion conjures. There's a minefield of material waiting for anthropologists who don't want to go abroad. There's no way that all this heterosexual palaver is 'natural' and 'normal', as its participants are convinced it is. If I stuck rigidly to my convictions I would devote this chapter to some sort of 'behavioural study'. When I thought about heterosexuality, however, what struck me most was how my attitude towards it has changed since I became a lesbian and through my lesbian experience of ten years. Several episodes came to mind.

4   I remember very well the day I read Adrienne Rich's pamphlet *Compulsory Heterosexuality and Lesbian Existence*. After several years' engagement with lesbian politics it was one of those days when the clouds lifted and the light shone more strongly. I was deeply impressed and was an immediate, albeit easily won, convert. Her idea that heterosexuality is a sys-

tem, a political institution that is imposed, managed, organized, propagandized and maintained by force is not a purely rhetorical case; it is researched, strongly argued and sensitively written. Aspects of male power that feminists have seen as 'only' producing sexual inequality, Rich interpreted as specifically enforcing heterosexuality. In short, it made me feel like a hyperactive fruit machine: lots of pennies fell into place. Though these ideas are the core of my thinking now, they're not widely available ones. Most heterosexuals don't see their sexuality as constructed and organized in very detailed ways, but simply as the way they are, the way the world is. It's a 'personal' and 'private' matter, not a political one in any way and terms such as 'sexual preference' are used in order to 'explain' it all. Those who don't fit in are seen as victims of deviancy who must explain, justify and defend themselves. One reason why I welcome a shift in focus that turns the tables of discussion is that I remember that frame of mind well. Rich, where were you in 1975?

5   Eleven years ago I had my first lesbian relationship. Ten years ago I 'became a lesbian' and soon after this 'came out'. In between and—significantly—before an involvement with the women's movement, I put myself and especially my brain cells through the wringer. It's no coincidence that a lot of lesbian and gay writing has been about 'coming out'. First you have to feel good about being a lesbian yourself, then you have to prepare for the reaction and taking the world on. 'Why, why, why am I this way?' I asked myself. 'What's the cause, the explanation?' I felt very isolated. I read voraciously. Stopping work as a librarian (no helpful books to be found there, needless to say) and moving into the more liberal environment of a university sped up the process. I opted for a course called 'The Biological and Interpersonal Basis of Sex Differences' taught, as luck would have it, by a lesbian and feminist biologist who made sure that tackling heterosexual myths and prejudices was as integral a part of an anti-sexist approach as it should be. By the time I came out I was well equipped for arguments that I wouldn't bother with now and cringe to overhear. Heterosexuals would set the terms of discussion and I'd be able to witter away at length about hormones, genes, the animal kingdom, Sappho, Rome, the family and throw in the odd philosophical comment on human nature. As the task wore me down I began to develop one-off lines that were attempts to stop the conversation.

6   'What do you do in bed?'

7   'Sleep, read, talk, make love—what do you do?'

8   Such ploys were also an attempt to stop exposing myself to such scrutiny. These sorts of conversations are ridiculous but they still go on. It's difficult, impossible, not to feel resentment and anger that heterosexuals rarely, never, are subjected to this sort of questioning or have to explain themselves. Is it unreasonable, given Joe or Jill Public's general level of understanding, to stop engaging in these kind of discussions, answering often offensive questions? It may increase knowledge and 'understanding', but does it fundamentally change anything?

9   As I became more involved in Left, and especially feminist political activity, my tack slowly began to change. When the 'Sex Differences' course was run the next year, right-wing scientists took over the lectures and began teaching-preaching misogyny, homophobia and anti-lesbianism. In response the student women's group, gay society and Communist Party demanded control of three lectures and, to our amazement, succeeded. I never saw a fuller lecture hall in my whole time at university. It was packed with attentive and potentially sympathetic students. From the organizers' point of view things didn't run so smoothly. A lesbian (me) and a gay man (who was a neighbour and friend) were to address one of the lectures. We couldn't agree on a common approach, to the extent that we had a huge argument about it. 'Don't put their backs up,' he said, 'we don't get this sort of chance very often.' I pulled out and sat in the audience. Off he went, talking about his family background, how he came to terms with being gay and how good he felt about it, what sort of relationships he had. Most people looked convinced that he wasn't a bogeyman or a threat to the campus. It was a congenial atmosphere and it all seemed very easy for them. The moment one lesbian, echoed by another, chipped in with how we saw our sexuality as also political discomfort set in and the attacks began. The whole issue had been viewed purely as a question of who went to bed with whom and what did politics have to do with that? We however were seen as feminist crusaders who weren't really interested in pleasure and as perverts who were merely trying to justify politically our sexual desires. What strikes me now is that we were still only saying that lesbianism was political; not that heterosexuality was political too. It was a revealing incident and left me thinking, as always, that there was more homework to be done.

10   The idea of 'political lesbianism' was not a new one, in that it had been fermenting in America since the early 1970s. It burst into profile in a big way in Britain in 1979 when the Leeds Revolutionary Feminist group wrote a conference paper called 'Political Lesbianism: The Case Against Heterosexuality'.[1] When this was published in *WIRES* (the internal national newsletter of the women's movement) the debate raged, literally, for over a year. It caused a furore in the women's movement which was avidly followed by thousands. It shook things up and it changed lives. Many a guilty lesbian became a lesbian feminist and there were heterosexuals who became lesbians, as well as those who defensively stood their ground. The reaction was such that many are still recovering. This paper began to turn the tables and received a lot of criticism, much of which was anti-lesbian. It talked a lot about 'fucking', i.e. heterosexual penetration. Many saw the paper as an attack on heterosexual feminists rather than on heterosexuality and understood withdrawal of sexual services from men as the sum total of its strategy. One of its effects was to make heterosexual feminists feel guilty and very, very defensive. There has been so much more feminist debate about sexuality since this episode that it would be easy to

---

[1] Published, with the ensuing correspondence, as *Love Your Enemy? The debate between heterosexual feminism and political lesbianism* by Onlywomen Press, 1981. [Author's Notes]

forget its impact. It was the *beginning* of an analysis of how heterosexuality is central to women's oppression. It didn't explain *how* it worked but wordsmith Rich, bless her, did. It's all relative, but life's been easier since.

11   Despite the stereotype of lesbians, changing your sexual/political identity is not like changing your clothes or getting your hair cut. Most of us who are/have become lesbians have been through a difficult, complex and often painful process of change that doesn't suddenly stop. Often the nature of this process only becomes clear very gradually as time goes on. This race through my lesbian years traces how my attitude to heterosexuality has changed. I began as a 19-year-old with the attitude that most heterosexuals still hold, but I had to *fit in* to it as a lesbian. It was all about saying I was normal *too* and asking for tolerance, acceptance and peaceful coexistence. I fell straight into the hole dug by the heterosexual tactic of 'sexual preference' and also fell for the line that it's an *equal* choice between heterosexuality and lesbianism. But anything was then better than being an out-and-out pervert.

12   It goes without saying that I have no motivation to fit in any more. I prefer sanity. I know I'm still judged by heterosexuals but fortunately I take it as an irritant rather than a pressure to conform. I now want heterosexuals to hear the ideas of compulsory heterosexuality and make understanding *their* sexuality a priority. In her foreword Rich writes:

> heterosexual feminists will draw political strength for change from taking a critical stance towards the system of coercion which demands heterosexuality; lesbians cannot assume we are untouched by that institution. There is nothing about such a critique that requires us to think of ourselves as victims, as having been brainwashed or totally powerless.[2]

I understand that it's not very helpful, in any situation, to have a 'victim' approach, but confess that I often find that easier said than done. I still have enough heterosexual friends to know that they're not Stepford Wife robots, but I still see a lot of Pavlovian women and men around. I find it hard not to see heterosexual women as a combination of oppressor (by virtue of their actions, attitudes and heterosexual 'privileges') and victims. The tables turn indeed.

13   I recall a scene in the film *The Killing of Sister George* when George and Childie arrange to meet heterosexual Mercy Croft at the Gateways, knowing Mercy would be unaware that it was a lesbian club. A friend once nicknamed Mercy 'the woman with the performing eyebrows' because of her reaction to all the sights before her; most peculiar if not disturbing. I rarely go to hetty rave-ups, but when a recent holiday occasioned an inquisitive visit, 'for a laugh', to a hetty tea dance on the sea front, I remembered Mercy. The cruising

---

[2]*Compulsory Heterosexuality and Lesbian Experience* by Adrienne Rich. Foreword in reprint by Antelope Publications, USA. Available in Britain and published by Onlywomen Press.
Both of the above from Sisterwrite, 190 Upper Street, London N1; and hopefully most 'radical' bookshops at least.

and behaviour were extraordinary. I did my best to keep my eyebrows under control and found it all fascinating and bizarre.

14   Many heterosexual feminists are offended by the notion that they are victims of compulsory heterosexuality. After all, doesn't it deny the principle that every woman's experience is valid and real and that women have the capacity and the right to make their own choices? I can do without listening to how good and different their man is, but don't think there's any harm in heterosexuals being under pressure to assert their happiness after we've been pushed into years of shouting almost banal slogans such as 'Glad to be Gay'. In the main, their offence at having their experiences denied is blinkered. If a woman is taking it on a purely personal level and is a woman who is familiar with the issues and debates, perhaps she has made a *real* choice (?) but this can hardly be said to be the situation for women in general. There's more to a choice than the simple awareness of an alternative. Heterosexuality is a coercive system and although ideology plays a huge role, it's by no means the only factor.

15   Lesbians and gay men are, by our existence, a resistance movement. Whilst I'm all for swelling the ranks, it's about time the idea that sleeping with our own sex is a revolutionary act that—on its own—reaps great changes, was knocked on the head. Some of my favourite lines are from Robin Morgan's poem 'Monster':

I want a woman's revolution like a lover,
I lust for it, I want so much this freedom,
this end to struggle and fear and lies
we all exhale, that I could die just
with the passionate uttering of that desire.[3]

It's ironic enough that Robin Morgan has returned to heterosexuality, has even married. A further irony is that most of us, especially gay men, continue to desire the lover but have stopped lusting for the revolution. Where are we going?

16   Compulsory heterosexuality is not a sexual civil rights sidekick doomed to remain on the bottom of the agenda. It is a fact of life, a major oppression. *That's* the way the world is and nobody except us is going repeatedly to assert this in these times. We've been arguing on heterosexuality's terms and barking up the wrong tree too often, too long. What's in a statistic for example? The line about us being 10 per cent of the population has had its tactical uses, one example being a way of justifying an appropriate (though it never is) allocation of resources from sympathetic Labour local government authorities. Going along with the arguments that see us as a fixed percentage of the population smacks of the genes and hormones routine to me and offers no progress in the long term. It deflects attention away from the amount of energy and force that is put into keeping the vast majority on the heterosexual track. It is what these

---

[3]'Monster' by Robin Morgan, from her first collection *Monster*, published by Random House, but restricted to the U.S. market owing to the legal controversy concerning the poem 'Arraignment'.

practices are, how they operate and how they can be changed that we've got to concentrate on.

17   I don't mean by this that the current functions and activities of lesbians and gay men are insignificant at all. It's vital to have our own resources: centres, switchboards, publications, archives, police monitoring groups, and it's vital to have a culture: theatre, bars, clubs, exhibitions and so on. The impact of an uncloseted life forces us to confront a new, more whole, but still very difficult reality and all this helps isolation and survival and has an impact. But we have to go beyond our own needs and beyond civil rights.

18   'Out of the Closets' was the rallying cry of gay liberation, but it has proved to be inadequate as a total political statement or way of life for gay men and especially lesbians. Yet movement men are still flogging this horse, are still stuck in 1969. Denis Lemon wasted the opportunity of a 30-minute TV programme (*Diverse Reports*, 5 December 1984) and made a call to 'come out' his stunning conclusion after talking to several sacked gay employees and visiting Rugby Council, which had just officially banned employing lesbians and gay men by removing that horrible expression 'sexual orientation' from its equal opportunities policy. Brian Kennedy made the same mistake by concluding a feature in *City Limits* magazine (18 January 1985) with:

> the single most effective way of contending the rampant prejudice and
> homophobia around is by 'coming out' to family and friends. Some may not
> like it, but at least they are meeting the real you and not the alien creature that
> they have been led to believe the homosexual is.

Encouraging people to put their neck on the line with an increasing likelihood of it being chopped off is not an adequate guide to action. It speaks volumes for the advancement of male gay theory. What chance do people have of finding the real you/me when there's such a retreat into conventionality and Victorian values going on?

19   The need to shift focus, turn the tables and talk about compulsory heterosexuality is becoming all the more urgent. The pressure to conform in a society that is becoming increasingly right-wing has become more intense. The Right's message to women is that we are the emotional and sexual property of men, and the institutions by which women are traditionally controlled are being strengthened by legislation, the media, censorship and many other means. We've no choice but to change tack and raise this issue if we want the resistance movement to strengthen rather than be forced underground.

POST-READING QUESTIONS:

1) Did any of the thoughts or feelings that you expressed in response to the first prereading question manifest themselves in your analysis of or reactions to Parker's essay? Does her essay cause you to want to reexamine your reasons for having these thoughts and feelings? Does it make you want to rethink your responses to any of the other pre-reading questions?

2) In light of your overall analysis of her essay, how do you evaluate the points about heterosexuality that Parker makes in paragraph 3?

3) Many minority women and lesbians have felt that, historically, the women's movement in the United States has catered to the needs of white, middle- to upper-class, heterosexual women. In your view, would Parker likely agree or disagree with this charge? If appropriate, reflect on your response to the third pre-reading question.

4) Do you think that you might have responded differently to Parker's ideas were they couched in a work of fiction, such as a poem?

5) Do you find Parker's writing style effective? How would you compare the effectiveness of her writing style with (or to) the effectiveness of Louie Crew's, Elie Wiesel's, Black Elk's, Sandra Cisneros', Maya Angelou's, and/or Barbara Cameron's? What factors are you taking into account in your comparative analysis, and why do you consider these factors important? Are you purposely omitting certain factors? If so, why?

HANDS-ON ACTIVITY:

Though perhaps "the nature-nurture argument [concerning sexual orientation] is no longer as polarized as it once was" ("Born or Bred?," paragraph 23), many heterosexuals consider themselves poles apart from nonheterosexuals, and vice versa. To help bridge this gap, if only to reach a common sense of human understanding with others, talk with your friends about this issue and then see if you might be able to organize an informal colloquium (in your dorm, perhaps) in which people with different sexual orientations can share their thoughts—and even fears—with each other. Set a modest goal for yourself, such as establishing a dialogue or simply having a one-time get-together. For help in organizing such a colloquium, talk with representatives from your school's gay and lesbian student union (if your school has one) or from your area's local chapter of Parents and Friends of Lesbians and Gays (if there is a local chapter in your area). Also talk with clergymen in your area, faculty who have an interest in this issue (check, especially, with faculty in the social and behavioral sciences), and anyone else who shares your desire to create a common understanding among people of goodwill who nevertheless might not see eye-to-eye on some or even any matters pertaining to this topic. If nothing else, hopefully this chapter's readings convincingly intimate that, whether or not people share the same views concerning controversial matters, they often gain a great deal by talking with one another about these matters and lose far too much when they refuse to enter into such a dialogue.

"*Most people think of language as something we use* after *we have thought, but writers use language to think.*"

DONALD M. MURRAY
The Craft of Revision

Developing and Proving/ Supporting a Thesis for a Personal Essay

I F YOU DID the featured writing assignments (or closely approximate versions of them) for Chapters One, Four, and Five, you engaged in a type of writing commonly referred to as "writing from experience." Whether or not you knew it, you were probably doing more than merely summarizing your experiences. If you commented upon them or the consequences that followed from them, then you also engaged in *analytical* writing. And if you did *that*, then you had a point to make in your paper—which is to say that you advanced and tried to prove or support a thesis.[1] Perhaps, after analyzing your material, you were able to derive, develop, and prove or support a thesis fairly early in, or at least fairly easily during, the writing process. On the other hand, maybe for a while you either didn't know what your thesis was or only vaguely knew what it was but didn't know quite how to express it. Many writers face this problem, whether they are engaged in personal or academic writing. Indeed, as this chapter's epigraph asserts, writers use writing itself as a way to think and rethink the subject matter, waiting (sometimes, to be sure, rather impatiently) for a thesis to develop out of their predrafting and draft material. Not uncommonly, *writers often write their way into a thesis.*

Different writers—and even the same writer—might experience difficulties in deriving or recognizing a thesis at different times and for different reasons. Sometimes, a writer simply hasn't thought about the analytical stakes of an experience that he nevertheless can summarize or describe in great detail. Occasionally, there's not much *to* analyze; as even the psychoanalyst Sigmund Freud once suggested, sometimes a cigar is just a cigar. At times, the writer simply doesn't know what to do with the material that he has uncovered and presented. At other times, the writer cannot see a thesis already implied in his paper.

Of course, writers composing papers having little or nothing to do with their own personal experiences also face these and similar dilemmas. However, when the subject matter is personal, and particularly when it hits close to home, the dilemma of what we might call "the delayed thesis" often seems especially pronounced, even when the writer is drafting a traditionally academic paper whose subject matter nevertheless touches a nerve in her. As intimated in Chapter Five (p. 132), this problem becomes even more complex when the writer discovers that the needs of a particular writing assignment are intimately bound up with her own needs to come to terms with a personal experience that is quite near her heart.

To begin understanding the nature of this particular problem, try doing the following little exercise that undoubtedly will seem quite silly at first but that, nonetheless, should help clarify the issue at stake. When you have finished doing this exercise, continue reading.

Place your index finger in front of your face and about a foot from your eyes. If you can do so without becoming sick or dizzy, watch the tip of your finger

---

[1] If you are unfamiliar with the concept of a thesis, please see Chapter Five, pp. 135–138, where this concept is discussed in detail.

as you move it slowly towards you until it rests against the bridge of your nose, which should mean that it rests squarely between your eyes; if you cannot do this second part of the exercise, then just place your fingertip against the bridge of your nose after first having placed your finger in front of your face and about a foot from your eyes.

If you watched the tip of your finger as you moved it closer and closer to its final resting point, you probably began to lose your ability to focus clearly and easily on what you were seeing. And whether you slowly moved your fingertip towards you until it rested on the bridge of your nose or simply placed it against the bridge of your nose, when your fingertip touched the bridge of your nose it was as close as it could be to your eyes without actually touching or being in them. At that moment, you should have been unable to see your fingertip at all. Too close to the subject matter under investigation—in this case, subject matter that you had been looking at quite directly— you quite literally could not "see the point."

To help yourself see how you might overcome this sort of difficulty, should it occur in your own writing experiences, imagine that, in response to this chapter's featured assignment (see p. 207), you write an essay about a situation, moment, or experience from your childhood in which, in your view, a parent, parent figure, or some other influential adult had invalidated your feelings—an unfortunately rather common phenomenon in adult-child interactions. If you are like many of my own students who have written such an essay in response to this assignment, you might find yourself able to discuss in great detail interesting— and often moving and painful—childhood memories, but then, curiously, discover that you cannot (or cannot easily) explain the meaning that your experience holds for you. In fact, you might do what many of my students end up doing—and what many other people probably would do were they to write a similar kind of paper: Abruptly shifting the tone of your narrative, you might begin protecting and defending the parent or the adult in question; embark on a too self-assured explanation of how the experience has made you (in this case) a better person; present general (and analytically evasive) homilies about the nature of the world, goodness, parental responsibilities, and the like; or, in some other way, sidestep the issues at stake.

Revising your paper in order to help it meet the needs of the assignment, you'll need to think about what you have learned both from what you have written and from what you have not written. Concerning the latter, you'll want to discover why you can't or don't (want to) discuss certain ideas. Perhaps you simply don't know what else to do with your material. But, as many of my students have come to discover about their own work, maybe you'll find that you don't want to pay the high price that is exacted when one directly confronts the significance of reopened wounds or of wounds that have never been closed, but merely patched over. We don't need to be psychologists to know that, if we admit that our parents or other influential adults in our lives are fallible or have the ability to hurt us, then we have to deal with some rather uncomfortable truths about ourselves, others, the people we most love and trust, and the world at large. Understandably, like many other people, you yourself might (unconsciously?) try to avoid dealing with such truths.

However, as mentioned in the previous chapter (p. 133) and alluded to above, you are responsible for whatever you write or, in some cases, need to but don't write. Thus, if you choose to write about painful childhood memories in response to the featured assignment, then you have obligated yourself to confront at least some of these truths in your paper and, moreover, to derive, develop, and support or prove an analytical, explanatory thesis concerning these truths—that is, a thesis which explains the data under consideration. In other words, in order to fulfill the requirements of the assignment, you'll have to confront (at least minimally) rather than evade some painful issues at stake. If all goes well, this confrontation should yield you both a thesis and some additional evidence that you'll need to produce in order to prove or support this thesis (in all likelihood, you already will have produced other evidence in your previous drafts).

Not uncommonly, like the tip of your index finger in the exercise that you did a few moments ago, the sought-after main point in the kind of personal essay described above is right in front of your eyes, though it is so close to you that you cannot see it clearly. To help yourself gain enough distance from your own insights to enable you to see them clearly, ask yourself and then try to answer questions that will allow you to begin revising your paper with an eye towards addressing *the significant analytical issues before you*—issues that already had begun surfacing in your previous draft(s). For an idea of the kinds of questions that you might ask, consider the following sample questions, which are relevant to the particular personal essay discussed above: "Am I trying to convince myself that this experience really wasn't so bad after all? If so, then why did I write about it, and why, in the process of writing about it, did I rather suddenly stop talking about the feelings that I experienced at the time?" "In this paper, am I trying to get my mother (or father) off the hook? If so, why?" "Why did I choose to write about this experience? Do I *really* want to know the answer to this question?" "Should I choose to write about something else entirely—such as, perhaps, why I can't or would rather not pursue this paper further?"

Trying to answer such questions, you might discover that your thesis has been inside of you all along. You might find, for example, that in your paper you do indeed try to get your mother off the hook, preferring, or so it seems, to absolve her of any wrongdoing rather than face the fact that she failed to acknowledge your needs at a moment when you really needed her to acknowledge them. In a revised draft, you might offer and then—by citing and explaining the significance of pertinent evidence that you've already uncovered—try to prove or support a thesis similar to one of the following: "Though she might not have meant to do so—after all, she *was* busy trying to get ready for work—

my mother nevertheless badly hurt my feelings when she ignored my request that she help me with my school coloring project"; or "Though initially I thought that this paper was a simple descriptive essay, when I look back at what I've written I can see that this essay presents a rather elaborate (and clever) attempt on my part to keep my mother from taking any blame for hurting my feelings"; or "I think that I am trying to protect my mother because I find it too difficult to blame her."

As suggested in the previous chapter (p. 132), concerning any assignment calling for you to write from personal experience, ultimately you yourself will have to decide what you want (or need) to write and how much you want your readers to see. Nevertheless, you'll want to make such choices with as much information at your disposal as possible. If you work hard at revising your work, remembering that writing is indeed a process and keeping in mind that, to some degree, all papers, including final drafts, are works-in-progress, you should be able to distance yourself from your material enough to see what main point you need to make, how this main point is derived from the material that you already have produced, and how you should focus your discussions so that your thesis is either supported or proved. In other words, if the writing process works, it should enable you eventually to pull your fingertip away from your eyes far enough for you to discover what you are really looking at, what sort of point is really staring you in the face.

Even so, don't worry if initially you don't know precisely what your thesis is, how best to state it, or where to place it. As you'll see from reading her commentary, Mahshid Hajir, this chapter's contributing author, had similar difficulties. Though she seems to have known that all of the scenes which she had been describing were related and that all had to do with a central point, a main idea, and though she sensed that her successive drafts were leading her to discover this main idea, not until late in the writing process was she able to articulate this main point (as you'll see, she presents something like a cross between an implied and a stated thesis). Patiently, she kept working with and thinking about the evidence that she knew was driving her personal writing, allowing it to lead her towards her thesis, which she finally states at the end of her paper.

In other words, as she wrote, Hajir knew that eventually she would have to imply or state a position that would answer the question "So, what *is* my main point?" Rather than believing that writing only follows from and never precedes thinking, she allowed her thinking to lead her to write and her writing to lead her to think. Having approached her paper in this way, she escaped being stuck in that paralyzing state of affairs so commonly expressed by students who feel that they know what they want to say in their papers but can't figure out how to say it—and who don't use writing itself as a way both to help them formulate their ideas and to organize their thoughts around one main point. If in any given personal essay of your own you already know what your thesis is, you might not have to worry about this problem. If, however, you find yourself facing the problem of the delayed thesis, take comfort in the fact that you are not alone. But don't stop there: roll up your sleeves and, like other writers, give yourself permission to write and revise your way into a thesis.

Whatever the themes of your personal essays, hopefully you will write so that your words do justice to the significance of your life. Who knows what insights you might hit upon if, when you are called upon to write a personal essay, you are willing to look closely at the meaning(s) of important episodes from your life and to be patient enough not only to let evidence lead you to a thesis that accurately addresses the substantive concerns of your writing, but also to let your writing lead you to think and rethink your points so that the honesty of your revisions matches the good faith of your visions? Writing and rewriting your way into a thesis, you ought to produce a paper that does justice to the importance of your personal struggles and achievements. Whether or not your own writing experiences are similar to anyone else's, if you always approach writing not as a task with a fixed, immovable agenda, but rather as a sustained and yet free-flowing (if sometimes arduous) activity reflecting a process of continual rethinking and revising, then more often than not you should find yourself drafting your way into personal insights and the greater truths to which these insights point.

READING AND WRITING

What Charles Dickens said about the period of the French Revolution could apply equally well to the periods of childhood and young adulthood: that they were (and still are) both "the best of times" and "the worst of times." This chapter's readings help to confirm this observation. Arranged to take the reader on a journey from early childhood to young adulthood, these pieces illustrate a range of childhood experiences, from those that are almost entirely carefree, to those that are marked by rather constant unrest, to those that lie somewhere between these two extremes. As you attempt to understand the childhood experiences of the people or characters who are the subjects of these pieces, think about the ways in which your own childhood experiences might have helped you determine what you now think of yourself and others, the degree to which they might have taught you something about the private and public worlds that you inhabited when you were young, and the extent to which they prepared you for your arrival into those worlds that you inhabit now. None of us began life as an adult, of course, nor do adults respond to the world as if they have no past. Perhaps, by trying to analyze the meanings of the childhood joys and sorrows that we find in this chapter's readings, we can discover something about our own past and its influence on our present (and future?) lives. At the very least, we ought to find that this chapter's readings bear witness to the truth of the poet William

Wordsworth's famous claim that "The Child is father of the Man"—or, we should add, mother of the Woman.

FEATURED ASSIGNMENT

Part I: Taking your cue from Maya Angelou, write an essay in which you describe a situation, moment, or experience from your childhood that involved you and a parent, parent figure, or some other influential older person and that affected you (positively or negatively) at the time. Explain the effect that this situation, moment, or experience had on you then, and, if it has had a lasting impact on you, explain why and how this impact continues to affect your thoughts, feelings, and behavior. Cite and explain the importance of specific, relevant examples and details to prove or support your thesis. If appropriate, incorporate into your paper relevant points from the featured reading selection and, perhaps, from one or more of the related readings.

Part II: Write a brief reflective commentary on what you experienced, thought, and/or felt while doing this assignment.

FEATURED READING

---

from I Know Why the Caged Bird Sings

MAYA ANGELOU

Maya Angelou (1928–), who was born Marguerita Johnson, "spent [her child-hood] shuttling between rural, segregated Stamps, Arkansas, where her devout grandmother ran a general store, and St. Louis, where her worldly, glamorous mother lived" (*Contemporary Authors, New Revision Series,* vol. 19, p. 22). She is the author of *many* writings, including plays, screenplays, and television plays, as well as several outstanding collections of poetry, such as *And Still I Rise* (1978) and *Shaker, Why Don't You Sing?* (1983), and exceedingly moving autobiographical works, such as *The Heart of a Woman* (1981) and the highly acclaimed *I Know Why the Caged Bird Sings* (1970), from which the featured reading selection is taken. "[H]ailed as one of the great voices of contemporary black literature and as a remarkable Renaissance woman" (*Contemporary Authors,* op. cit., p. 22), Angelou "studied music privately, dance with Martha Graham, Pearl Primus, and Ann Halprin, and drama with Frank Silvera and Gene Frankel" (ibid.). She has been a singer, actress, and civil rights activist (ibid.), and is well-known for her dynamic lectures and poetry readings; indeed, she captivated the crowd at President Clinton's 1992 presidential inauguration when she read one of her poems during that event.

Though her talents range widely, she is probably best known for her autobiographical writings. Praising the narrative excellence in *I Know Why the Caged Bird Sings*, one critic says that Angelou's "'genius as a writer is her ability to recapture the texture of the way of life in the texture of its idioms, its idiosyncratic vocabulary and especially in its process of image-making. . .'" (*Contemporary Authors, op. cit.,* p. 23). Commenting upon her autobiographical writings as a whole, another critic writes that "'it is clear. . . that Angelou is in the process of becoming a self-created Everywoman. In a literature and a culture where there are many fewer exemplary lives of women than of men, black or white,'" this critic continues, "'Angelou's autobiographical self, as it matures through successive volumes, is gradually assuming that exemplary stature'" (ibid.). No doubt that, in the eyes of a good many of her readers, Angelou has already assumed this stature.

PRE-READING QUESTIONS:

1) In your view, why do some children make racist remarks or engage in racist practices? In general, do you consider children's and adults' displays of racism equally serious and troublesome?

2) Do you think that racism generally affects child victims as much as, more than, or less than it affects adult victims?

3) Do you tend to trust what you read in autobiographies? In general, do you expect the material in an autobiography to be more accurate than, less accurate than, or as accurate as the material in a biography, historical document, diary entry, poem, or work of historical fiction?

4) What do you make of the following lines from Paul Laurence Dunbar's poem "Sympathy"? Dunbar (1872–1906) was the son of former slaves.

I know why the caged bird sings,
     ah me,
  When his wing is bruised and
     his bosom sore,—
When he beats his bars and he
     would be free;
It is not a carol of joy or glee,
  But a prayer that he sends from
     his heart's deep core,
But a plea, that upward to Heaven
     he flings—
I know why the caged bird sings!

CLOSE-READING TIP

Angelou is a first-rate writer who chooses her words with the utmost care. Her clear descriptions of people, places, objects, and situations are sometimes searing, sometimes peacefully lulling, and often poetic. Often, these descriptions defy paraphrasing, which, however accurately accomplished, seems to diminish their worth. As you read the following excerpt, watch for those moments in which Angelou creates meanings that seem so intimately and inextricably bound to the language that she uses that you find paraphrasing her ideas nearly impossible, if not also somewhat unforgivable. Consider, for example, representative passages in paragraphs 7, 13, 18, and 21.

SELECTION

MAYA ANGELOU

from **I Know Why the Caged Bird Sings**

1 . . . "Thou shall not be dirty" and "Thou shall not be impudent" were the two commandments of Grandmother Henderson upon which hung our total salvation.

2 Each night in the bitterest winter we were forced to wash faces, arms, necks, legs and feet before going to bed. She used to add, with a smirk that unprofane people can't control when venturing into profanity, "and wash as far as possible, then wash possible."

3 We would go to the well and wash in the ice-cold, clear water, grease our legs with the equally cold stiff Vaseline, then tiptoe into the house. We wiped the dust from our toes and settled down for schoolwork, cornbread, clabbered milk, prayers and bed, always in that order. Momma was famous for pulling the quilts off after we had fallen asleep to examine our feet. If they weren't clean enough for her, she took the switch (she kept one behind the bedroom door for emergencies) and woke up the offender with a few aptly placed burning reminders.

4 The area around the well at night was dark and slick, and boys told about how snakes love water, so that anyone who had to draw water at night and then stand there alone and wash knew that moccasins and rattlers, puff adders and boa constrictors were winding their way to the well and would arrive just as the person washing got soap in her eyes. But Momma convinced us that not only was cleanliness next to Godliness, dirtiness was the inventor of misery.

5 The impudent child was detested by God and a shame to its parents and could bring destruction to its house and line. All adults had to be addressed as Mister, Missus, Miss, Auntie, Cousin, Unk, Uncle, Buhbah, Sister, Brother and a thousand other appellations indicating familial relationship and the lowliness of the addressor.

6   Everyone I knew respected these customary laws, except for the powhite-trash children.

7   Some families of powhitetrash lived on Momma's farm land behind the school. Sometimes a gaggle of them came to the Store, filling the whole room, chasing out the air and even changing the well-known scents. The children crawled over the shelves and into the potato and onion bins, twanging all the time in their sharp voices like cigar-box guitars. They took liberties in my Store that I would never dare. Since Momma told us that the less you say to whitefolks (or even powhitetrash) the better, Bailey and I would stand, solemn, quiet, in the displaced air. But if one of the playful apparitions got close to us, I pinched it. Partly out of angry frustration and partly because I didn't believe in its flesh reality.

8   They called my uncle by his first name and ordered him around the Store. He, to my crying shame, obeyed them in his limping dip-straight-dip fashion.

9   My grandmother, too, followed their orders, except that she didn't seem to be servile because she anticipated their needs.

10   "Here's sugar, Miz Potter, and here's baking powder. You didn't buy soda last month, you'll probably be needing some."

11   Momma always directed her statements to the adults, but sometimes, Oh painful sometimes, the grimy, snotty-nosed girls would answer her.

12   "Naw, Annie. . . "—to Momma? Who owned the land they lived on? Who forgot more than they would ever learn? If there was any justice in the world, God should strike them dumb at once!—"Just give us some extry sody crackers, and some more mackerel."

13   At least they never looked in her face, or I never caught them doing so. Nobody with a smidgen of training, not even the worst roustabout, would look right in a grown person's face. It meant the person was trying to take the words out before they were formed. The dirty little children didn't do that, but they threw their orders around the Store like lashes from a cat-o'-nine-tails.

14   When I was around ten years old, those scruffy children caused me the most painful and confusing experience I had ever had with my grandmother.

15   One summer morning, after I had swept the dirt yard of leaves, spearmint-gum wrappers and Vienna-sausage labels, I raked the yellow-red dirt, and made half-moons carefully, so that the design stood out clearly and mask-like. I put the rake behind the Store and came through the back of the house to find Grandmother on the front porch in her big, wide white apron. The apron was so stiff by virtue of the starch that it could have stood alone. Momma was admiring the yard, so I joined her. It truly looked like a flat redhead that had been raked with a big-toothed comb. Momma didn't say anything but I knew she liked it. She looked over toward the school principal's house and to the right at Mr. McElroy's. She was hoping one of those community pillars would see the design before the day's business wiped it out. Then she looked upward to the school. My head had swung with hers, so at just about the same time we saw a troop of the powhitetrash kids marching over the hill and down by the side of the school.

16   I looked to Momma for direction. She did an excellent job of sagging from her waist down, but from the waist up she seemed to be pulling for the top of the oak tree across the road. Then she began to moan a hymn. Maybe not to moan, but the tune was so slow and the meter so strange that she could have been moaning. She didn't look at me again. When the children reached halfway down the hill, halfway to the Store, she said without turning, "Sister, go on inside."

17   I wanted to beg her, "Momma, don't wait for them. Come on inside with me. If they come in the Store, you go to the bedroom and let me wait on them. They only frighten me if you're around. Alone I know how to handle them." But of course I couldn't say anything, so I went in and stood behind the screen door.

18   Before the girls got to the porch I heard their laughter crackling and pop-ping like pine logs in a cooking stove. I suppose my lifelong paranoia was born in those cold, molasses-slow minutes. They came finally to stand on the ground in front of Momma. At first they pretended seriousness. Then one of them wrapped her right arm in the crook of her left, pushed out her mouth and started to hum. I realized that she was aping my grandmother. Another said, "Naw, Helen, you ain't standing like her. This here's it." Then she lifted her chest, folded her arms and mocked that strange carriage that was Annie Henderson. Another laughed, "Naw, you can't do it. Your mouth ain't pooched out enough. It's like this."

19   I thought about the rifle behind the door, but I knew I'd never be able to hold it straight, and the .410, our sawed-off shotgun, which stayed loaded and was fired every New Year's night, was locked in the trunk and Uncle Willie had the key on his chain. Through the fly-specked screen-door, I could see that the arms of Momma's apron jiggled from the vibrations of her humming. But her knees seemed to have locked as if they would never bend again.

20   She sang on. No louder than before, but no softer either. No slower or faster.

21   The dirt of the girls' cotton dresses continued on their legs, feet, arms and faces to make them all of a piece. Their greasy uncolored hair hung down, uncombed, with a grim finality. I knelt to see them better, to remember them for all time. The tears that had slipped down my dress left unsurprising dark spots, and made the front yard blurry and even more unreal. The world had taken a deep breath and was having doubts about continuing to revolve.

22   The girls had tired of mocking Momma and turned to other means of agi-tation. One crossed her eyes, stuck her thumbs in both sides of her mouth and said, "Look here, Annie." Grandmother hummed on and the apron strings trembled. I wanted to throw a handful of black pepper in their faces, to throw lye on them, to scream that they were dirty, scummy peckerwoods, but I knew I was as clearly imprisoned behind the scene as the actors outside were con-fined to their roles.

23   One of the smaller girls did a kind of puppet dance while her fellow clowns laughed at her. But the tall one, who was almost a woman, said something very quietly, which I couldn't hear. They all moved backward from the porch, still

watching Momma. For an awful second I thought they were going to throw a rock at Momma, who seemed (except for the apron strings) to have turned into stone herself. But the big girl turned her back, bent down and put her hands flat on the ground—she didn't pick up anything. She simply shifted her weight and did a hand stand.

24 Her dirty bare feet and long legs went straight for the sky. Her dress fell down around her shoulders, and she had on no drawers. The slick pubic hair made a brown triangle where her legs came together. She hung in the vacuum of that lifeless morning for only a few seconds, then wavered and tumbled. The other girls clapped her on the back and slapped their hands.

25 Momma changed her song to "Bread of Heaven, bread of Heaven, feed me till I want no more."

26 I found that I was praying too. How long could Momma hold out? What new indignity would they think of to subject her to? Would I be able to stay out of it? What would Momma really like me to do?

27 Then they were moving out of the yard, on their way to town. They bobbed their heads and shook their slack behinds and turned, one at a time:

28 "'Bye, Annie."

29 "'Bye, Annie."

30 "'Bye, Annie."

31 Momma never turned her head or unfolded her arms, but she stopped singing and said, "'Bye, Miz Helen, 'bye, Miz Ruth, 'bye, Miz Eloise."

32 I burst. A firecracker July-the-Fourth burst. How could Momma call them Miz? The mean nasty things. Why couldn't she have come inside the sweet, cool store when we saw them breasting the hill? What did she prove? And then if they were dirty, mean and impudent, why did Momma have to call them Miz?

33 She stood another whole song through and then opened the screen door to look down on me crying in rage. She looked until I looked up. Her face was a brown moon that shone on me. She was beautiful. Something had happened out there, which I couldn't completely understand, but I could see that she was happy. Then she bent down and touched me as mothers of the church "lay hands on the sick and afflicted" and I quieted.

34 "Go wash your face, Sister." And she went behind the candy counter and hummed, "Glory, glory, hallelujah, when I lay my burden down."

35 I threw the well water on my face and used the weekday handkerchief to blow my nose. Whatever the contest had been out front, I knew Momma had won.

36 I took the rake back to the front yard. The smudged footprints were easy to erase. I worked for a long time on my new design and laid the rake behind the wash pot. When I came back in the Store, I took Momma's hand and we both walked outside to look at the pattern.

37 It was a large heart with lots of hearts growing smaller inside, and piercing from the outside rim to the smallest heart was an arrow. Momma said, "Sister, that's right pretty." Then she turned back to the Store and resumed, "Glory, glory, hallelujah, when I lay my burden down. . . . "

POST-READING QUESTIONS:

1) How do you think that Angelou might evaluate the ideas that you put forth in your responses to the first two pre-reading questions? Did her narrative cause you to rethink what you said in those responses?

2) Did Angelou's narrative meet your pre-reading expectations concerning autobiographical writing? Does it make you want to reconsider those expectations?

3) What do you think that Angelou means when she says that she "knew [she] was as clearly imprisoned behind the scene as the actors outside were confined to their roles" (paragraph 22)?

4) Is there any significance to the grandmother's "[singing] on" without changing the tempo of the hymn (or song) or the volume of her voice (paragraph 20)? Does this part of the narrative help us to understand the nature of the victory that Angelou says her grandmother had achieved (see paragraph 35)? And what *is* that victory?

5) Does this excerpt from Angelou's work help you understand why Angelou might have titled her book after a line from Dunbar's poem "Sympathy"? Does her narrative help you to understand the meanings of the verse reprinted in the fourth pre-reading question?

The Lesson

MAHSHID HAJIR

Mahshid Hajir was born in 1965, in a very small town in southern Iran. When she was three, her family moved to Tehran, the capital of Iran, where they lived for the next ten years. During that time, Mahshid studied English and Farsi (the dominant language in Iran) at an international school. In 1979, however, their lives changed. In the midst of the Iranian revolution, which radically altered the lives of many Iranians, Mahshid's family moved to the United States. Never having traveled outside of Iran, Mahshid found herself apprehensive, yet excited, as she and her family started their new life in America. In 1984, she was graduated from Columbia High School in Maplewood, New Jersey. Four years later, she received a Bachelor of Arts degree in psychology from the University of Maryland. One year after college graduation, unsatisfied with her full-time job at a tax credit department in a large corporation, she moved to Irvine, California, where her cousins live. Shortly after this move, she began working at Irvine Valley College as the Facilitator for the Extended Opportunity Program and Services (EOPS) Department, a state-funded program that provides support services to economically and educationally disadvantaged students. She still holds this position. Note: for "reducing barriers encountered by IVC's highest-risk students, and thereby contributing to the successful completion of their studies," Mahshid received Irvine Valley College's 1993–94 Outstanding Service Award (the quotation is included in the formal commendation, made by the college's Board of Trustees [*ETS Test Administration Highlights,* Vol. VIII/No. 1, p. 4]).

RESPONSE

PART I   **Essay**

"Come on azeezam, we are going to miss the bus."

"I'm coming madarjoon."

Madarjoon, that's what I called my maternal grandmother which means dear mom and in return she called me azeezam which means my dearest. It was another hot, humid Friday in Ahvaz (Southern Iran), and I was visiting from Tehran for two weeks during our school's winter break. Every Friday, my grandmother took the one hour trip on the bus to the local bazaar—outdoor market—to purchase groceries and other necessary items. This time, however, she was taking me with her. I was seven years old and extremely excited because she always made these excursions to the market alone. I grabbed my grandmother's hand and squeezed real tight to show how happy I was to be going with her.

The bus came late as usual and my shoes were sticking to the melting asphalt. As I was pulling my sticky shoes off the ground, I looked up at my grandmother. She looked beautiful. She was wearing her bright blue scarf around her head, which made her pretty blue eyes shine. "Madarjoon, where are we going?" "First, we are going to buy some vegetables, and then we're going to see the butcher and get some fresh chicken so that I can make your favorite dish—chicken and rice—for dinner tonight." The thought of my grandmother cooking my absolutely favorite thing made me even more anxious about going on our shopping trip.

The bus finally arrived and it was packed with tons of people. My grandmother handed money (I didn't see exactly how much) to the bus driver and he said "Salaam" (Hello) with a deep voice. The only two seats that were next to each other were way in the back and we had to push our way through to get them. Luckily, the seats were next to the window and since it was so hot all the windows of the bus were open. But, even the open windows did not make it much cooler in the bus.

"Madarjoon, how long is it gonna take? I'm hot." She gently touched my forehead, "I know azeezam, it is very hot today. When we get to the bazaar I will get us some juice okay?" "Okay. Madarjoon, can we go to the jewelry store today? Aunt Shahin says that there are lots of beautiful jewels in the bazaar." My grandmother replied, "We can't go today. We have more important things to do today." I became a little disappointed. My Aunt Shahin wore the most beautiful gold bracelets and I was hoping that I would get to see some more and maybe see if my grandmother would buy some for me. What can be more important than buying bracelets for me?

Oh well, I guess I couldn't get everything I wanted. The ride to the bazaar seemed so much longer than one hour. It was so hot and noisy on this bus. A fat man sitting next to me with a thick, black mustache kept coughing. A child sitting in the front of the bus would not stop crying. I put my head on my grandmother's lap and started dreaming of my Aunt Shahin's beautiful bracelets. After what seemed forever, the bus came to a stop. "We are here azeezam." It seemed like everyone else was going to the bazaar too.

We got off the bus and started walking. What a strange place! So many people! Why is that man shouting? Oh, he's selling something—fruit, I think. It smelled so good. All the shops were next to one another in a row. So many people! I held on tightly to my grandmother's arm. Then, I saw him – an older man with a gray and white beard. He looked so dirty. He was wearing torn brown pants and a brown and grey shirt. I squeezed my grandmother's hand tighter. I wish she didn't walk so close to him. He did not have any shoes on, just bare feet. I couldn't wait until we passed by him. But then, my grandmother stopped right in front of this man. She spoke to him, "Salaam, how are you today?" "Thank you Mrs. Moradi. God bless you, Mrs. Moradi" I can't believe it! She knows him! My clean, beautiful grandmother is talking to this dirty, smelly person.

"Come on, madarjoon; let's go," I begged my grandmother. "In a minute azeezam. I haven't finished talking to Mohammad." Mohammad—she knew his name! "Is this your granddaughter?" he asked timidly, looking at me with a crooked smile. "Yes. This precious one is my only granddaughter. I have five grandsons and this beauty." "Madarjoon, I'm thirsty." "Okay, azeezam, we'll go in a minute." "Here, Mohammad. Take care of yourself until next week." My eyes grew wide because my grandmother reached into her pocket and gave him two bills. "Thank you Mrs. Moradi. You always think of me. May Allah (God) always be with you. I pray for you and your beautiful granddaughter. May she get your kindness." As soon as he said those words, he looked at me. His eyes surprised me. They were so gentle. Why was my grandmother giving him money? Why didn't he work? I didn't know how to ask my grandmother these questions. Anyway, maybe he was an old friend who has had some bad luck. So, I just kept quiet.

We walked a few more steps when she stopped again, this time in front of a younger man asleep on the ground. His clothes were also filthy, and he was asleep on what I think used to be a white blanket. He was wearing an old blue shirt and dirty black pants. I thought to myself, "How come one of his legs looks so skinny?" "Oh my God! He's missing a leg!" I looked at my grandmother, but she did not say anything. She just placed a couple of bills in his tin can, which was next to him, and mumbled something that I didn't catch. I think she said something about peace.

I still did not dare to ask her why she was giving him money too. I was still thirsty, and we had not been in even one shop! I wondered to myself, "Maybe that was the last stop, and now we can continue." But, I was wrong because she stopped again, this time for a lady who was sitting on the ground. Her eyes were strange looking; it looked as if she was rolling her eyes back in her head! "Oh, she can't see me! Or maybe she's pretending." I told myself. I moved my hand gently in front of her face. No, she really couldn't see. My grandmother scowled at me for that move. I just smiled. "How are you?" my grandmother asked this older lady. "Is that you, Mrs. Moradi?" "Yes, it is me and my granddaughter Mahshid." "Salaam, Mrs. Moradi; Salaam, Mahshid." My grandmother asked her, "Please give me your hand." The lady listened and put out her hand. As she had done with the two men, my grandmother gently placed two bills in her palms while saying "God bless you." The lady thanked my grandmother and said, "Can you stay and talk to me?" My grandmother gently shook her head and said, "I'm sorry

Homaira, but this is Mahshid's first time in the bazaar and I want to show her everything." The lady smiled and said, "Okay. Maybe next time. May Allah always be with you. Goodbye, Mahshid." "Goodbye," I said very softly.

As we started walking towards the vegetable stand, I finally got the courage to ask my grandmother, "Madarjoon, do you give these people money every week?" She looked at me with her soothing eyes and said, "Yes, every week. Sometimes the same people aren't here and sometimes I don't have as much to give. Sometimes I bring food instead of money. But, this time your grandfather received a bonus and gave me the money to use however I pleased." "Madarjoon, I don't understand. My dad always says not to give money to beggars because they'll just use it for bad stuff, and some don't even need it." As soon as I said this she stopped and, gently grabbing my shoulders and pulling me towards her, said, "Azeezam, what your father says may be true. But, look around you. What do you see?" I looked around and as I turned my head I saw Homaira sitting, eating an apple. A short distance away from her was a young lady with two children, all of whom were sitting on the ground and staring at the people who walked by. One of the children had long brown hair like mine. She had a red dress—it was so pretty—which was torn on the shoulder. I couldn't stop looking at her sad face. "I see a sad, little girl with her mom and brother," I told my grandmother. My grandmother was about to say something. But, before my grandmother could say a word I grabbed her hand and said, "Madarjoon, do we have any food left over from last night?" My grandmother said, "Yes, we have some beef kebabs and saffron rice." As soon as she said that, I smiled and squeezed her hand. "Oh, great! So, we don't have to buy chicken or vegetables and we can give this extra money to that little girl." "Are you sure, Mahshid?" my grandmother asked. I nodded my head yes. As we were walking towards this family that I didn't know, I realized that I wasn't thirsty anymore.

The bus ride home seemed so much shorter than the ride to the bazaar. I hadn't realized that we were gone so long, but it was almost dark by the time we reached home. As we were walking towards our home, I asked, "Madarjoon, how come I am so happy even though we're going home empty-handed?" My beautiful, wise grandmother squeezed my hand and said, "Azeezam, we're not going home empty-handed. Helping somebody in need is more valuable than all the groceries and jewels in this world." At that moment I smiled, remembering the look of joy on the little girl's face when we stopped to talk to her.

"Madarjoon, can I come with you to the bazaar next week?"

"Yes, azeezam."

In writing a personal essay, I usually try and look back at my life and find an experience that others might be interested in reading about. Then, I just start writing by reliving the experience and tell the story without focusing on a thesis or title. Usually my first draft is very primitive but I am able to use this first draft as my base and write a personal essay complete with thesis and title. I usually focus on global revisions first—does this essay support my thesis? Have I obtained my objective of writing the essay?—then I go back and complete local revisions (involving sentence structure, paragraphing, etc.).

When I chose to write about the experience with my grandmother, I knew that I had learned something from that experience, something valuable that I cherish and have incorporated into my own being. I knew that this experience significantly had changed how I feel about and treat the poor, but I did not know exactly how and when to present my thesis. Whenever I have a difficult time in thinking of or presenting a thesis, I just start writing and I use the writing process in helping me create and present the thesis. Therefore, I used this same approach with "The Lesson." When I finished the paper I was surprised that the thesis appeared at the end since I was taught to write the thesis at the beginning of the paper. However, as I reread "The Lesson" I realized that I liked the final product and decided not to revise the paper and to keep the thesis at the end.

My understanding of Angelou's experience with her grandmother helped me with remembering my own grandmother and the impact this one day had on me. Although my story is not a tragic one, I also wanted to capture the audience's attention and emotion in the same manner which Angelou had. Therefore, I wanted the audience to feel every moment of the story and identify with the seven-year-old. To achieve this I used a "double narrative" approach: I tried to write in a seven-year-old's voice and relive the experience as it happened; also, similar to Angelou, I tried to capture the voice and wisdom of my grandmother.

During the rewrites of drafts for this essay, I was not only concentrating on the writing process but also about my audience. Since I was writing about an experience that happened in a country where many readers might not be familiar with, I tried to include as much detail as possible. Especially since some parts of the paper specifically refers to my religion, Islam, I tried to write the meaning of the foreign words in parentheses so as not to confuse the reader. In one instance, on my draft I had written that the indigent Mohammad "had the name of our prophet", however, in my final draft I decided to delete that statement. It is true that Mohammad was the name of our Prophet and that many Muslims out of love and respect name their sons Mohammad. But, when I reread the draft I decided that this statement might confuse readers who did not know about Prophet Mohammad so I decided to delete this statement.

In writing this essay, I learned about myself as a writer. Before this essay, I had never been given the opportunity to analyze my own reading and writing process. I learned that I rely mostly on the rewriting rather than prewriting to find the thesis and title and that the more rewriting I did the more satisfied I was with the final product. In many different ways, writing this paper was also a cathartic experience for me. First, it allowed me to relive a cherished experience with my wonderful grandmother who I have not seen in fourteen years. Second, I was able to analyze the roots of my desire to help those in need. Third, I was able to understand my grandmother's passion for helping the poor. In addition to being very kind and generous, my grandmother is also very religious. One of the duties of a Muslim is almsgiving or helping those in need. If a Muslim is financially unable to give money then this duty can be fulfilled by other acts of charity such as volunteer work or other acts of kindness. When I look at this information, I realize that my grandmother truly fulfills this duty and I hope that I am able to follow her footsteps and be as kind and charitable as her.

RELATED READINGS

Reminiscences of Childhood

DYLAN THOMAS

A master storyteller and poet, Welsh writer Dylan Thomas (1914–1953) wrote powerful and widely anthologized verse such as "Do Not Go Gentle into That Good Night," "Fern Hill," and "The Force That Through the Green Fuse Drives the Flower," as well as, among other sorts of works, superb short stories and personal narratives. Some of the latter, such as "A Child's Christmas in Wales," are among the best works of literature that we have dealing with the memories and experiences of youth. Yet, sadly, for all of his talent and accomplishments, and despite his having enjoyed an apparently happy and nearly carefree childhood, this superbly talented writer became an often overworked and, eventually, not infrequently ill adult who "had grown increasingly aware of a constant feeling of terror that he could escape only by drinking, yet this means of escape was now beginning to fail him, for he could not drink without becoming sick. He was at the point of physical collapse" (Korg 24). Eventually, Thomas "in effect. . . killed himself" by taking a "massive dose of alcohol" which "caused cerebral poisoning" (ibid.).

Despite Thomas' adulthood troubles and tragic end, many of his stories— such as "Reminiscences of Childhood"—paradigmatically capture the feelings, attitudes, and gestures of carefree youthful innocence, though sometimes, indeed, this vision is marked by a nostalgia tinged with (and tempered by) a degree of melancholy, bitterness, or cynicism. Nevertheless, stories such as this one remain a testament to the freeing power of the imagination, to which we all have access, as well as to the love of language, learning, curiosity, and adventure that, hopefully, the child within each of us stubbornly refuses to abandon.

PRE-READING QUESTIONS:

1) Do you have any thoughts or feelings about the nature of your childhood? If you do, keep these thoughts and feelings in mind as you read Thomas' narrative, watching to see whether or not—and, if so, how, why, and to what extent—they affect your understanding of or reactions to his ideas.

2) How would you describe the city or town in which you grew up? In answering this question, try to reconstruct your *childhood* vision of this place.

3) When you were growing up, did you frequent one particular place more than you frequented others—a park or playground, maybe, or a school yard? If so, describe

this place and discuss how you felt about it then and what sorts of feelings you have as you think about it now. Be as detailed, creative, and sentimental as you wish.

4) How would you describe the nature and inner workings of one club, group, team, or clique to which you belonged when you were in elementary or junior high school? Why did you think that this particular club, group, team, or clique was so special? If by and large you were a loner during those years, explain why you lived this sort of life.

5) In your hometown, was there an individual or family who seemed different or unusual to you and perhaps received special attention or treatment, good or bad, from you or others? If so, describe your reactions to and possible dealings with this individual or family and indicate how you feel now about your former thoughts and behavior.

6) Have you ever been told (or advised) not to use the pronoun "I" in your essays? If so, what did/do you think of this command (or advice)? Did you feel then and/or do you feel now that the writer's need to use certain pronouns and to avoid using others seems to depend upon the context of the particular writing project that he or she is pursuing?

CLOSE-READING TIP

As suggested in the biographical comments, in his writings dealing with children, Dylan Thomas sometimes creates images that simultaneously capture the purity of the child's innocent perceptions of the world and present a retrospective reflection of these perceptions through the filtering lens of the adult's mature—and sometimes melancholy, bitter, or cynical—vision. As you read this excerpt, look carefully at those passages in which you find Thomas employing, sometimes quite poetically and economically, such narrative double visions; try to determine the effect of such passages on the story's overall meaning(s). See, for example, representative passages in paragraphs 3, 6, 11, and 12.

1 I like very much people telling me about their childhood, but they'll have to be quick or else I'll be telling them about mine.

2 I was born in a large Welsh town at the beginning of the Great War—an ugly, lovely town (or so it was and is to me), crawling, sprawling by a long and splendid curving shore where truant boys and sandfield boys and old men from nowhere, beachcombed, idled and paddled, watched the dock-bound

ships or the ships steaming away into wonder and India, magic and China, countries bright with oranges and loud with lions; threw stones into the sea for the barking outcast dogs; made castles and forts and harbours and race tracks in the sand; and on Saturday summer afternoons listened to the brass band, watched the Punch and Judy, or hung about on the fringes of the crowd to hear the fierce religious speakers who shouted at the sea, as though it were wicked and wrong to roll in and out like that, white-horsed and full of fishes.

3   One man, I remember, used to take off his hat and set fire to his hair every now and then, but I do not remember what it proved, if it proved anything at all, except that he was a very interesting man.

4   This sea-town was my world; outside a strange Wales, coal-pitted, moun-tained, river-run, full, so far as I knew, of choirs and football teams and sheep and storybook tall hats and red flannel petticoats, moved about its business which was none of mine.

5   Beyond that unknown Wales with its wild names like peals of bells in the darkness, and its mountain men clothed in the skins of animals perhaps and always singing, lay England which was London and the country called the Front, from which many of our neighbours never came back. It was a country to which only young men travelled.

6   At the beginning, the only "front" I knew was the little lobby before our front door. I could not understand how so many people never returned from there, but later I grew to know more, though still without understanding, and carried a wooden rifle in the park and shot down the invisible unknown enemy like a flock of wild birds. And the park itself was a world within the world of the sea-town. Quite near where I lived, so near that on summer evenings I could listen in my bed to the voices of older children playing ball on the sloping paper-littered bank, the park was full of terrors and treasures. Though it was only a little park, it held within its borders of old tall trees, notched with our names and shabby from our climbing, as many secret places, caverns and forests, prairies and deserts, as a country somewhere at the end of the sea.

7   And though we would explore it one day, armed and desperate, from end to end, from the robbers' den to the pirates' cabin, the highwayman's inn to the cattle ranch, or the hidden room in the undergrowth, where we held beetle races, and lit the wood fires and roasted potatoes and talked about Africa, and the makes of motor cars, yet still the next day, it remained as unexplored as the Poles—a country just born and always changing.

8   There were many secret societies but you could belong only to one; and in blood or red ink, and a rusty pocketknife, with, of course, an instrument to remove stones from horses' feet, you signed your name at the foot of a terrible document, swore death to all the other societies, crossed your heart that you would divulge no secret and that if you did, you would consent to torture by slow fire, and undertook to carry out by yourself a feat of either daring or endurance. You could take your choice: would you climb to the top of the tallest and most dangerous tree, and from there hurl stones and insults at grown-up passers-by, especially postmen, or any other men in uniform? Or

would you ring every doorbell in the terrace, not forgetting the doorbell of the man with the red face who kept dogs and ran fast? Or would you swim in the reservoir, which was forbidden and had angry swans, or would you eat a whole old jam jar full of mud?

9   There were many more alternatives. I chose one of endurance and for half an hour, it may have been longer or shorter, held up off the ground a very heavy broken pram we had found in a bush. I thought my back would break and the half hour felt like a day, but I preferred it to braving the red face and the dogs, or to swallowing tadpoles.

10   We knew every inhabitant of the park, every regular visitor, every nurse-maid, every gardner, every old man. We knew the hour when the alarming retired policeman came in to look at the dahlias and the hour when the old lady arrived in the Bath chair with six Pekinese, and a pale girl to read aloud to her. I think she read the newspaper, but we always said she read the *Wizard*. The face of the old man who sat summer and winter on the bench looking over the reservoir, I can see clearly now and I wrote a poem long long after I'd left the park and the sea-town called:

THE HUNCHBACK IN THE PARK

The hunchback in the park
A solitary mister
Propped between trees and water
From the opening of the garden lock
That lets the trees and water enter
Until the Sunday sombre ball at dark

Eating bread from a newspaper
Drinking water from the chained cup
That the children filled with gravel
In the fountain basin where I sailed my ship
Slept at night in a dog kennel
But nobody chained him up.

Like the park birds he came early
Like the water he sat down
And Mister they called Hey mister
The truant boys from the town
Running when he had heard them clearly
On out of sound

Past lake and rockery
Laughing when he shook his paper
Hunchbacked in mockery
Through the loud zoo of the willow groves
Dodging the park-keeper
With his stick that picked up leaves.

And the old dog sleeper
Alone between nurses and swans
While the boys among willows
Made the tigers jump out of their eyes
To roar on the rockery stones
And the groves were blue with sailors

Made all day until bell-time
A woman figure without fault
Straight as a young elm
Straight and tall from his crooked bones
That she might stand in the night
After the locks and the chains

All night in the unmade park
After the railings and shrubberies
The birds the grass the trees and the lake
And the wild boys innocent as strawberries
Had followed the hunchback
To his kennel in the dark.

11   And that park grew up with me; that small world widened as I learned its
secrets and boundaries, as I discovered new refuges and ambushes in its
woods and jungles; hidden homes and lairs for the multitudes of imagination, for cowboys and Indians, and the tall terrible half-people who rode on
nightmares through my bedroom. But it was not the only world—that world
of rockery, gravel path, playbank, bowling green, bandstands, reservoir,
dahlia garden, where an ancient keeper, known as Smoky, was the whiskered
snake in the grass one must keep off. There was another world where with
my friends I used to dawdle on half holidays along the bent and Devon-fac-
ing seashore, hoping for gold watches or the skull of a sheep or a message in
a bottle to be washed up with the tide; and another where we used to wander
whistling through the packed streets, stale as station sandwiches, round the
impressive gasworks and the slaughter house, past by the blackened monu-
ments and the museum that should have been in a museum. Or we scratched
at a kind of cricket on the bald and cindery surface of the recreation ground,
or we took a tram that shook like an iron jelly down to the gaunt pier, there
to clamber under the pier, hanging perilously on to its skeleton legs or to run
along to the end where the patient men with the seaward eyes of the dock-
side unemployed capped and mufflered, dangling from their mouths pipes
that had long gone out, angled over the edge for unpleasant tasting fish.

12   Never was there such a town as ours, I thought, as we fought on the sand-
hills with rough boys or dared each other to climb up the scaffolding of half-
built houses soon to be called Laburnum Beaches. Never was there such a town,
I thought, for the smell of fish and chips on Saturday evenings; for the Saturday
afternoon cinema matinees where we shouted and hissed our threepences away;

for the crowds in the streets with leeks in their hats on international nights; for the park, the inexhaustible and mysterious, bushy red-Indian hiding park where the hunchback sat alone and the groves were blue with sailors. The memories of childhood have no order, and so I remember that never was there such a dame school as ours, so firm and kind and smelling of galoshes, with the sweet and fumbled music of the piano lessons drifting down from upstairs to the lonely schoolroom, where only the sometimes tearful wicked sat over undone sums, or to repeat a little crime—the pulling of a girl's hair during geography, the sly shin kick under the table during English literature. Behind the school was a narrow lane where only the oldest and boldest threw pebbles at windows, scuffled and boasted, fibbed about their relations—

13   "My father's got a chauffeur."

14   "What's he want a chauffeur for? He hasn't got a car."

15   "My father's the richest man in the town."

16   "My father's the richest man in Wales."

17   "My father owns the world."

18   And swapped gob-stoppers for slings, old knives for marbles, kite strings for foreign stamps.

19   The lane was always the place to tell your secrets; if you did not have any, you invented them. Occasionally now I dream that I am turning out of school into the lane of confidences when I say to the boys of my class, "At last, I have a real secret."

20   "What is it—what is it?"

21   "I can fly."

22   And when they do not believe me, I flap my arms and slowly leave the ground only a few inches at first, then gaining air until I fly waving my cap level with the upper windows of the school, peering in until the mistress at the piano screams and the metronome falls to the ground and stops, and there is no more time.

23   And I fly over the trees and chimneys of my town, over the dockyards skimming the masts and funnels, over Inkerman Street, Sebastopol Street, and the street where all the women wear men's caps, over the trees of the everlasting park, where a brass band shakes the leaves and sends them showering down on to the nurses and the children, the cripples and the idlers, and the gardeners, and the shouting boys: over the yellow seashore, and the stone-chasing dogs, and the old men, and the singing sea.

24   The memories of childhood have no order, and no end.

POST-READING QUESTIONS:

1) Did you find that any of your thoughts or feelings about the nature of your childhood affected your understanding of or helped shape your reactions to Thomas' ideas? Did his narrative cause you to reexamine your reasons for having these thoughts and feelings?

2) How would you compare the description of your hometown to/with the narrator's description of his hometown?

3) How would you compare your and the narrator's feelings about the special places that each of you frequented when you were children? If when trying to answer the third pre-reading question you could not think of any special haunt, can you think of one now?

4) What might the narrator in Thomas' essay say about the club, group, team, or clique that you described in your answer to the fourth pre-reading question? If you were a loner during your childhood and early adolescence, do you think that you might have liked to have been part of a group such as the one that the narrator describes?

5) How would you describe the narrator's attitude concerning the hunchback in the park? If applicable, see your response to the fifth pre-reading question.

6) In your view, is Thomas' use of the pronoun "I" justified? Might you have responded to his essay differently had Thomas used third-person narration?

The Vicious Circle of Contempt

ALICE MILLER

An outspoken champion of children's rights, Alice Miller, one of the foremost psychoanalytic theorists currently writing, has spent the greater part of her career both trying to help patients who had been abused as children and trying to teach the rest of us about the nature, causes, and consequences of childhood victimization, particularly intra-familial childhood victimization (such as incest). Her published works, which contain lengthy analyses of this problem, include *The Drama of the Gifted Child: The Search for the True Self* (1979; formerly *Prisoners of Childhood*), from which the following reading selection is taken; *For Your Own Good: Hidden Cruelty in Child-Rearing and the Roots of Violence* (1980); *Thou Shalt Not Be Aware: Society's Betrayal of the Child* (1981); and *The Untouched Key: Tracing Childhood Trauma in Creativity and Destructiveness* (1988).

Influenced by Freud's work, Miller nevertheless strongly takes issue with a number of Freud's ideas, especially his notion that most patient recollections of childhood incest involve fantasized rather than real abuse. Though Freud never intended to suggest that analysts should treat such fantasizing lightly, Miller argues that, by casting doubt on the truth of such stories, Freud has helped both analysts and the culture at large re-victimize already victimized people. Critical of what she saw as Freud's and others' knowing or unknowing attempts to vindicate abusers and blame victims, until recently Miller nonetheless felt that psychoanalysis contained the means by which this wrong could be righted. In 1988, however, she "officially broke away" from both the Swiss and the International Psychoanalytical associations, having come to the conclusion "that psychoanalytic theory and practice obscure—that is, render unrecognizable—the causes and consequences of child abuse by (among other things) labeling facts as fantasies. . . " ("Vantage Point 1990," in *The Drama of the Gifted Child* vii). Although she has resigned from these psychoanalytic associations, Miller continues to teach us about the psychological causes and ramifications of childhood victimization and—as the following excerpt demonstrates—to give a voice to those victims who otherwise might remain silenced.

PRE-READING QUESTIONS:

1) What are your thoughts or feelings about the ways in which parents either respond or should respond to their children's needs and wants? Keep these thoughts and feelings in mind as you read Miller's piece, watching to see both whether or not they affect your understanding of or reactions to her ideas and whether or not her ideas affect your thoughts and feelings.

2) Do you feel that an infant's needs and wants are indistinguishable, but that, as a child matures, her or his needs and wants become discrete entities? Can you cite some examples to prove or support your claims?

3) Can you think of any examples, either from your own life or from the lives of others, that would either lend support or give trouble to the following view that Miller advances in another of her texts?

> Almost everywhere we find the effort, marked by varying degrees of intensity and by the use of various coercive measures, to rid ourselves as quickly as possible of the child within us—i.e., the weak, helpless, dependent creature—in order to become an independent, competent adult deserving of respect. When we reencounter this creature in our children, we persecute it with the same measures once used on ourselves. And this is what we are accustomed to call "child-rearing." (*For Your Own Good* 58)

4) Do you generally trust or otherwise give credence to psychological explanations of events or behaviors? Why do you feel or think as you do?

CLOSE-READING TIP

A longtime champion of children's rights, Miller has worked hard to give a voice to silenced child victims as well as to the victimized child who still resides within many adults. As you read this piece, pay attention to those moments when Miller tries to present information from the child's perspective. See if you can determine whether or not her attempts to do so help, hurt, or in some other way affect her overall argument, in which she tries to champion children's rights in a way that also accounts for the complex needs of the hurt and hidden child within the adult.

Would not God find a way out, some superior
deception such as the grownups and the powerful
always contrived, producing one more trump card
at the last moment, shaming me after all, not
taking me seriously, humiliating me under the
damnable mask of kindness?

—Herman Hesse—
"A Child's Heart"

Humiliation for the Child, Contempt for the
Weak, and Where It Goes from There

. . . Everyday Examples

1 While away on a vacation, I was sorting out my thoughts on the subject of "contempt" and reading various notes on this theme that I had made about individual analytic sessions. Probably sensitized by this preoccupation, I was more than usually affected by an ordinary scene, in no way spectacular or rare. I shall describe it to introduce my observations, for it illustrates some of the insights I have gained in the course of my analytic work, without any danger of indiscretion.

2 I was out for a walk and noticed a young couple a few steps ahead, both tall; they had a little boy with them, about two years old, who was running alongside and whining. (We are accustomed to seeing such situations from the adult point of view, but here I want to describe it as it was experienced by the child.) The two had just bought themselves ice-cream bars on sticks from the kiosk and were licking them with enjoyment. The little boy wanted one, too. His mother said affectionately, "Look, you can have a bite of mine, a whole one is too cold for you." The child did not want just one bite but held out his hand for the whole ice, which his mother took out of his reach again. He cried in despair, and soon exactly the same thing was repeated with his father: "There you are, my pet," said his father affectionately, "you can have a bite of mine." "No, no," cried the child and ran ahead again, trying to distract himself. Soon he came back again and gazed enviously and sadly up at the two grown-ups, who were enjoying their ice creams contentedly and at one. Time and again he held out his little hand for the whole ice-cream bar, but the adult hand with its treasure was withdrawn again.

3 The more the child cried, the more it amused his parents. It made them laugh a lot and they hoped to humor him along with their laughter, too: "Look, it isn't so important, what a fuss you are making." Once the child sat down on the ground and began to throw little stones over his shoulder in his mother's direction, but then he suddenly got up again and looked around anxiously, making sure that his parents were still there. When his father had com-

pletely finished his ice cream, he gave the stick to the child and walked on. The little boy licked the bit of wood expectantly, looked at it, threw it away, wanted to pick it up again but did not do so, and a deep sob of loneliness and disappointment shook his small body. Then he trotted obediently after his parents.

4   It seemed clear to me that this little boy was not being frustrated in his "oral drives," for he was given ample opportunity to take a bite; it was his narcissistic needs that were constantly being wounded and frustrated. His wish to hold the ice-cream stick in his hand like the others was not understood, worse still, it was laughed at: they made fun of his needs. He was faced with two giants who were proud of being consistent and also supported each other, while he, quite alone in his distress, obviously could say nothing beyond "no," nor could he make himself clear to his parents with his gestures (which were very expressive). He had no advocate.*

5   Why, indeed, did these parents behave with so little empathy? Why didn't one of them think of eating a little quicker or even of throwing away half his ice cream and giving the child his stick with a bit of edible substance? Why did they both stand there laughing, eating so slowly and showing so little concern about the child's obvious distress? They were not unkind or cold parents; the father spoke to his child very tenderly. Nevertheless, at least at this moment, they displayed a lack of empathy. We can only solve this riddle if we manage to see the parents, too, as insecure children—children who have at last found a weaker creature, and in comparison with him they now can feel very strong. What child has never been laughed at for his fears and been told, "You don't need to be afraid of a thing like that." And what child will then not feel shamed and despised because he could not assess the danger correctly, and will that little person not take the next opportunity to pass on these feelings to a still smaller child. Such experiences come in all shades and varieties. Common to them all is the sense of strength that it gives the adult to face the weak and helpless child's fear and to have the possibility of controlling fear in another person, while he cannot control his own. . . .

6   No doubt, in twenty years' time, or perhaps earlier, if he has younger siblings, our little boy will replay this scene with the ice cream, but then *he* will be in possession and the other one will be the helpless, envious, weak little creature, whom he then no longer has to carry within himself, but now can split off and project outside himself.

7   Contempt for those who are smaller and weaker thus is the best defense against a breakthrough of one's own feelings of helplessness: it is an expression of this split-off weakness. The strong person who knows that he, too, carries this weakness within himself, because he has experienced it, does not need to demonstrate his strength through such contempt.

---

*What an unfair situation it is, by the way, when a child is opposed by two big, strong adults, as by a wall; we call it "consistency in upbringing" when we refuse to let the child complain about one parent to the other. [Miller's note.]

8   Many adults first become aware of their Oedipal feelings of helplessness, jeal-
ousy, and loneliness through their own children, since they had no chance to
acknowledge and experience these feelings consciously in their childhood. . . . I
spoke of the patient who was obsessively forced to make conquests with women,
to seduce and then to abandon them, until he was at last able to experience in his
analysis how he himself had repeatedly been abandoned by his mother. Now he
remembered how he had been caught at night outside the locked door of his
parents' bedroom and laughed at. Now, in the analytic session, is the first time
that he consciously experiences the feelings of humiliation and mortification
that were then aroused.

9   The Oedipal suffering that was not lived out can be got rid of by delegating
it to one's own children—in much the same way as in the ice cream scene I
have just described: "You see, we are big, we may do as we like, but for you it
is 'too cold.' You may only enjoy yourself as we do when you get to be big
enough." So, in the Oedipal area, too, it is not the instinctual frustration that is
humiliating for the child, but the contempt shown for his instinctual wishes. It
may well be that the narcissistic component of Oedipal suffering is commonly
accentuated when the parents demonstrate their "grown-upness" to revenge
themselves unconsciously on their child for their own earlier humiliation. In
the child's eyes they encounter their own humiliating past, and they must ward
it off with the power they now have achieved.

10   In many societies, little girls suffer additional discrimination because they
are girls. Since women, however, have control of the new-born and the infants,
these erstwhile little girls can pass on to their children at the most tender age
the contempt from which they once had suffered. Later, the adult man will
idealize his mother, since every human being needs the feeling that he was
really loved; but he will despise other women, upon whom he thus revenges
himself in place of his mother. And these humiliated adult women, in turn, if
they have no other means of ridding themselves of their burden, will revenge
themselves upon their own children. This indeed can be done secretly and
without fear of reprisals, for the child has no way of telling anyone, except perhaps in the form of a perversion or obsessional neurosis, whose language is suf-
ficiently veiled not to betray the mother.

11   Contempt is the weapon of the weak and a defense against one's own
despised and unwanted feelings. And the fountainhead of all contempt, all
discrimination, is the more or less conscious, uncontrolled, and secret exercise
of power over the child by the adult, which is tolerated by society (except in
the case of murder or serious bodily harm). What adults do to their child's
spirit is entirely their own affair. For the child is regarded as the parents'
property, in the same way as the citizens of a totalitarian state are the property
of its government. Until we become sensitized to the small child's suffering,
this wielding of power by adults will continue to be a normal aspect of the
human condition, for no one pays attention to or takes seriously what is
regarded as trivial, since the victims are "only children." But in twenty years'
time these children will be adults who will have to pay it all back to their own

children. They may then fight vigorously against cruelty "in the world"—and yet they will carry within themselves an experience of cruelty to which they have no access and which remains hidden behind their idealized picture of a happy childhood.

12   Let us hope that the degree to which this discrimination is persistently transmitted from one generation to the next might be reduced by education and increasing awareness—especially in its more subtle manifestations. Someone who slaps or hits another or knowingly insults him is aware of hurting him. He has some sense of what he is doing. But how often were our parents, and we ourselves toward our own children, unconscious of how painfully, deeply, and lastingly we injured a child's tender, budding self? It is very fortunate when our children are aware of this situation and are able to tell us about it, for this may enable them to throw off the chains of power, discrimination, and scorn that have been handed on for generations. When our children can consciously experience their early helplessness and narcissistic rage they will no longer need to ward off their helplessness, in turn, with exercise of power over others. In most cases, however, one's own childhood suffering remains affectively inaccessible and thus forms the hidden source of new and sometimes very subtle humiliation for the next generation. Various defense mechanisms will help to justify this: denial of one's own suffering, rationalization (I owe it to my child to bring him up properly), displacement (it is not my father but my son who is hurting me), idealization (my father's beatings were good for me), and more. And, above all, there is the mechanism of turning passive suffering into active behavior. The following examples may illustrate how astonishingly similar the ways are in which people protect themselves against their childhood experiences, despite great differences in personality structure and in education.

13   A thirty-year-old Greek, the son of a peasant and owner of a small restaurant in Western Europe, proudly described how he drinks no alcohol and has his father to thank for this abstinence. Once, at the age of fifteen, he came home drunk and was so severely beaten by his father that he could not move for a week. From that time on he was so averse to alcohol that he could not taste so much as a drop, although his work brought him into constant contact with it. When I heard that he was soon to be married, I asked whether he, too, would beat his children. "Of course," he answered, "beatings are necessary in bringing up a child properly: they are the best way to make him respect you. I would never smoke in my father's presence, for example—and that is a sign of my respect for him." This man was neither stupid nor uncongenial, but he had little schooling. We might therefore nurse the illusion that education could counteract this process of destroying the spirit.

14   But how does this illusion stand up to the next example, which concerns an educated man?

15   A talented Czech author is reading from his own works in a town in Western Germany. After the reading there follows a discussion with the audience, during which he is asked questions about his life, which he answers ingenuously. He

reports that despite his former support of the Prague Spring he now has plenty of freedom and can frequently travel in the West. He goes on to describe his country's development in recent years. When he is asked about his childhood, his eyes shine with enthusiasm as he talks about his gifted and many-sided father who encouraged his spiritual development and was a true friend. It was only to his father that he could show his first stories. His father was very proud of him, and even when he beat him as punishment for some misdemeanor reported by the mother, he was proud that his son did not cry. Since tears brought extra blows, the child learned to suppress them and was himself proud that he could make his admired father such a great present with his bravery. This man spoke of these regular beatings as though they were the most normal things in the world (as for him, of course, they were), and then he said: "It did me no harm, it prepared me for life, made me hard, taught me to grit my teeth. And that's why I could get on so well in my profession."

16 Contrasting with this Czech author, the film director Ingmar Bergman spoke on a television program with great awareness and far more understanding of the implications about his own childhood, which he described as one long story of humiliation. He related, for example, that if he wet his trousers he had to wear a red dress all day so that everybody would know what he had done and he would have to be ashamed of himself. Ingmar Bergman was the younger son of a Protestant pastor. In this television interview he described a scene that often occurred during his childhood. His older brother has just been beaten by the father. Now their mother is dabbing his brother's bleeding back with cotton wool. He himself sits watching. Bergman described this scene without apparent agitation, almost coldly. One can see him as a child, quietly sitting and watching. He surely did not run away, nor close his eyes, nor cry. One has the impression that this scene did take place in reality, but at the same time is a covering memory for what *he himself* went through. It is unlikely that only his brother was beaten by their father.

17 It sometimes happens that patients in analysis are convinced that only their siblings suffered humiliation. Only after years of analysis can they remember, with feelings of rage and helplessness, of anger and indignation, how humiliated and deserted they felt when they were beaten by their beloved father.

18 Ingmar Bergman, however, had other possibilities, apart from projection and denial, for dealing with his suffering—he could make films. It is conceivable that we, as the movie audience, have to endure those feelings that he, the son of such a father, could not experience overtly but nevertheless carried within himself. We sit before the screen confronted, the way that small boy once was, with all the cruelty "our brother" has to endure, and hardly feel able or willing to take in all this brutality with authentic feelings; we ward them off.

When Bergman speaks regretfully of his failure to see through Nazism before 1945, although as an adolescent he often visited Germany during the Hitler period, we may see it as a consequence of his childhood. Cruelty was the familiar air that he had breathed from early on—and so, why should cruelty have caught his attention?

19 And why did I describe these three examples of men who had been beaten in their childhood? Are these not borderline cases? Do I want to consider the effects of beatings? By no means. We may believe that these three cases are crass exceptions. However, I chose these examples partly because they had not been entrusted to me as secrets but had already been made public, but, above all, I meant to show how even the most severe ill-treatment can remain hidden, because of the child's strong tendency to idealization. There is no trial, no advocate, no verdict; everything remains hidden in the darkness of the past, and should the facts become known, then they appear in the name of blessings. If this is so with the crassest examples of physical ill-treatment, then how is mental torment ever to be exposed, when it is less visible and more easily disputed anyway? Who is likely to take serious notice of subtle discrimination, as in the example of the small boy and the ice cream?. . .

20 There are other ways of seducing the child, apart from the sexual, for instance, with the aid of indoctrination, which underlies both the "antiauthoritarian" and the "strict" upbringing. Neither form of rearing takes account of the child's needs at his particular stage of development. As soon as the child is regarded as a possession for which one has a particular goal, as soon as one exerts control over him, his vital growth will be violently interrupted.

21 It is among the commonplaces of education that we often first cut off the living root and then try to replace its natural functions by artificial means. Thus we suppress the child's curiosity, for example (there are questions one should not ask), and then when he lacks a natural interest in learning he is offered special coaching for his scholastic difficulties.

22 We find a similar example in the behavior of addicts, in whom the object relationship has already been internalized. People who as children successfully repressed their intense feelings often try to regain—at least for a short time—their lost intensity of experience with the help of drugs or alcohol.

23 If we want to avoid the unconscious seduction and discrimination against the child, we must first gain a conscious awareness of these dangers. Only if we become sensitive to the fine and subtle ways in which a child may suffer humiliation can we hope to develop the respect for him that a child needs from the very first day of his life onward, if he is to develop emotionally. There are various ways to reach this sensitivity. We may, for instance, observe children who are strangers to us and attempt to feel empathy for them in their situation—or we might try to develop empathy for our own fate. For us

as analysts, there is also the possibility of following our analysand into his past—if we accept that his feelings will tell us a true story that so far no one else knows. . . .

POST-READING QUESTIONS:

1) Did any of the thoughts or feelings that you expressed in your responses to the first and fourth pre-reading questions affect your understanding of or help shape your reactions to Miller's ideas? Did this excerpt cause you to reexamine your reasons for having these thoughts and feelings?

2) How did you feel when you read about the scene involving the ice-cream cones? Might you have responded differently to this scene had you heard or read about it elsewhere without also having read Miller's piece? Finally, does your view of this scene coincide or conflict with the views that you present in your response to the second pre-reading question?

3) Do you feel that some of the points that Miller makes in paragraphs 5, 6, 7, and 11 help confirm or call into question her view that is cited in the third pre-reading question? Do you want to rethink your response to that question in light of what you've learned from having read Miller's piece?

4) Does Miller have an overall, controlling thesis? If so, is it stated or implied? How well is it developed? Is it clearly proved or well supported?

5) In your view, does Miller's personal investment in her work help or hinder her analytical efforts? Does it do both or neither? Would you answer these questions differently were you to consider Miller's piece a personal essay, at least insofar as it reflects her own personal feelings and experiences?

Grandmother's Garden

KATHLEENE WEST

Kathleene West (1947–) grew up on a farm three miles west of Genoa, Nebraska. She holds an M.A. from the University of Washington and a Ph.D. from the University of Nebraska at Lincoln. A rather prolific writer, she has published seven volumes of prose and poetry, including *Water Witching* (1984) and *The Farmer's Daughter* (1988). Her poems have also appeared in a number of anthologies and periodicals, including *All My Grandmothers Could Sing: Poems by Nebraska Women*, from which the following reading selection is taken. She is also listed in *Who's Who in Writers, Editors and Poets: United States and Canada, 1989–1990*. West also has studied abroad rather extensively. A Fulbright fellowship, for example, enabled her to live for two years in Iceland, where she studied Icelandic language and literature. The recipient of several travel grants to Cuba, Mexico, and Central America, West also traveled to Vietnam and Cambodia, where she spent part of her 1993 sabbatical leave. Currently, she is associate professor of English at New Mexico State University at Las Cruces.

PRE-READING QUESTIONS:

1) Do you have any special feelings towards your grandparents—feelings that perhaps you don't have towards anyone else? As you read West's poem, see whether or not your feelings affect your reading of her work.

2) What thoughts and images come to mind when you read the words "grandmother's garden"?

3) How would you describe your grandparents' relationship to each other? How would you compare your relationship with either or both of them to their relationship with each other?

4) In your experience, do many men and women believe in "the myth that men have fragile egos which need protecting" (Schaef 55)? If they do, what do you see as the consequences of their belief?

5) Generally, do you like reading poetry? Do you think that your pre-reading experiences with poetry might affect your ability to understand and enjoy the following selection? Would you have different pre-reading feelings and expectations were you about to read a short story or a work of nonfiction?

CLOSE-READING TIP

Poets often try to create meaning in their poems by using poetic devices such as word images, symbolism, metaphors, and the like. As you read West's poem, note and think about the variety of ways in which West uses particular poetic devices to help create meaning; ask yourself if the meanings that she creates would change were she to have used different poetic devices to achieve her ends. Consider, for example, her use of anaphora in ll. 1–4, her use of a simile in l. 7, her use of alliteration in ll. 12–14, and her use of metaphor in ll. 29–31.

As she loved harvest when the final ear hit the bangboard
as she loved the exquisite snip and tie of huck embroidery
as she loved her children quiet in Sunday best
as she loved all beauty and the reward of rest after work
    she loved her flowers.   5

And when he took a hacksaw
and cut wide swaths, like a scythe through grain,
slicing high the stems of tulip and iris
to make impossible even a salvaged bouquet,
she turned back to the house   10
and busied herself with some kitchen task

to wait for the child, who ran from the shattered blooms,
her small fists clenched on a few ripped petals,
her breath lost in the flattened bed of bouncing betts.

"Grandma, he's killing your flowers!"   15

And Grandmother winked,
                yes,
                    winked
as if to say:

I'm not angry   20
but don't let on to Grandpa.
If he saw I didn't mind
it'd hurt him more
than whatever hurt it gives to me.
Not that he regrets the farm,   25
but with nothing to resist him,
he misses the zest to fight.
You see a cruel act
but you'll play out your part
in dreams cut down, arranged for another's delight,   30
the dry whiff of long-pressed hopes.

The plants still live.
He knows they grip the earth tough and stubborn as weather
or himself.
You won't catch him   35
pushing up the mazes of their roots
or kicking destruction into their plucky stems.
Even this violence is a masque of harvest.
Dry your tears and remember.
Plant flowers, child,   40
plant flowers and tell this story.

POST-READING QUESTIONS:

1) Did any of the thoughts or feelings that you expressed in your responses to the first and fifth pre-reading questions influence your reading of West's poem? Did reading her poem cause you to want to reexamine any of these thoughts or feelings?

2) Do you want to revise any of the views that you expressed in your responses to the second, third, and fourth pre-reading questions in light of your understanding of West's poem?

3) Does there seem to be a relationship between the child in the poem and the poem's narrator? If West had used first-person narration throughout her poem, would the poem's meanings change?

4) Did you find that the poetic devices employed by the poet enhanced or detracted from the poem's meanings? Do you think that this poem's effects on you, the reader, would be heightened or lessened were the episode in question described in prose—in a short story or an expository essay, for example? More generally, how would you evaluate the relationship among the poem's form, content, and meanings?

5) Though we don't normally talk about a poem's having a thesis, do you find any sort of implied or stated main assertion in West's poem, which the rest of the poem tries to develop and either support or prove?

Summer, 1945

LORRAINE DUGGIN

Lorraine Duggin (1941–) earned a B.A. and an M.A. in English from the University of Nebraska at Omaha and a Ph.D. in English/Creative Writing from the University of Nebraska at Lincoln. Granted a number of awards and honors, she received the John Vreeland Award for Writing (1981), an Academy of American Poets Award (1982), the Mari Sandoz Prairie Schooner Fiction Award (1984), a Pushcart Prize nomination for fiction (1984), a Maude Hammond Fling Fellowship (1986), a Stanislav Serpan Scholarship for studies in Czech language (1987), and a Nebraska Arts Council Individual Artist's Fellowship in Poetry (1991). Her poetry, fiction, essays, and memoirs have been published in numerous periodicals and anthologies, including *Prairie Schooner, North American Review, Looking For Home: Women Writing About Exile, Boundaries of Twilight: Czech-Slovak Writing From the New World,* and *All My Grandmothers Could Sing: Poems by Nebraska Women* (from which the following poem is taken). She currently lives in Omaha, Nebraska, and teaches writing at Iowa Western Community College, in Council Bluffs, Iowa.

PRE-READING QUESTIONS:

1) What are your thoughts or feelings about the nature of your childhood? As you read Duggin's poem, compare your thoughts and feelings with those of the poem's persona. (If applicable, before taking a look at Duggin's poem, take another look at your responses to the first pre- and post-reading questions concerning the Dylan Thomas selection [p. 220, 225].)

2) Do you have a childhood memory that, for you, encapsulates the notion of "childhood innocence"? Is there an incident from your childhood that marks the beginning of the end of this innocence?

3) How would you characterize your relationships to your parents and grandparents? Have these relationships changed over the years? If so, how?

4) Do you ever consciously decide to use certain verb tenses rather than others when you write your diary or personal journal entries, essays about personal experience, "impersonal" essays, lab reports, and so on? What factors do you take into account when you make your decisions?

CLOSE-READING TIP

Poets often use the technique of repetition to let readers know that particular points or themes are central to the poems' meanings. As you read Duggin's poem, pay close attention to her use of repetition, seeing if you can sense the ways in which she creates some thematic unity to her piece by her use of this technique. Then, reread the poem to see if you can catch glimpses of foreshadowing achieved through the use of repetition.

May

Four years old, my first birthday party,
I hold wooden pins waist high, drop them
one by one headfirst, the bottle's small mouth
my target. I listen for the loud plunk
against glass bottom to tell me I've won.   5
Bullseye! A helium balloon my prize, it flies
upward, but before I'm home, it's out of my hands,
snags a treelimb, bursts.

June

Visiting Grandpa's farm, I collect henhouse
eggs, lift each from its nest, trembling   10
not to drop a single one. Success!
With bedtime comes reward: he says finally
I'm big enough to use the outhouse, decrepit dark
pit with wooden sides whitewashed by birds,
two dark holes the cover for a target   15
deeper than I'll ever care to look.

July

In the grass beneath our backyard elm,
handing clothespins to my mother
who strings laundry on the line, I find
a robin egg intact. As I decide to climb   20
the tree to replace it in its nest,
a black grackle divebombs Mother's shining sheets
with mulberry stains, and gets me too.

August

Nagasaki and Hiroshima are words
too big for my small mouth. Though I know   25
what a target is, I have to ask
my mother if atom bombs are like balloons.
I'm old enough to know what's meant
by flight, have learned what winning is,
am better at understanding the depth of fear.   30

POST-READING QUESTIONS:

1) If you and the poem's persona met at a restaurant to discuss your retrospective visions of childhood, what would the two of you say to each other? Feel free to be as creative as possible here!

2) How might Duggin's poem be considered the persona's response to the second pre-reading question? How does her response compare with yours?

3) How would you describe the persona's relationships to her mother and grandfather, and how would you compare these relationships with those that you discussed in your response to the third pre-reading question?

4) Why do you think that the poet uses verbs in the present tense? Do you think that the poem would gain or lose any meaning were the poet to vary the tenses of the verbs or consistently use verbs in a tense other than the present tense?

5) Do you find the poet's repetition of certain ideas or imagery helpful, distracting, or both? Does her use of repetition constitute an attempt to present variations on a theme? If so, what is that theme?

6) How would you compare the narrative voice in Kathleene West's poem "Grandmother's Garden" with the narrative voice in Duggin's poem? (If applicable, see your response to the third post-reading question concerning Kathleene West's poem [p. 237].)

Elethia

ALICE WALKER

Like Dylan Thomas, Alice Walker (1944–) is an exceptionally talented story-teller. Perhaps most famous for her book *The Color Purple,* she has written widely in the areas of both fiction and nonfiction. A few of her more recent works include *Finding the Green Stone*, a children's book containing paintings by Catherine Deeter (1991); a collection of essays entitled *Living By The Word* (1988); and her novel *Possessing the Secret of Joy* (1992). Instrumental in helping us rethink our ideas about sensitive, complex, and often interconnected issues such as gender, race, and class, Walker remains one of the dominant forces on both the feminist and the American literary scenes.

Walker is well known for her willingness to "approach[] the forbidden in content as well as form" (Christian 470). "Elethia," for example, is written entirely in italics and contains the sort of prose that we've come to expect from this Pulitzer Prize-winning author: sentimental without also being maudlin; compellably subtle and piercingly acute without also being overblown. And, like Celie, in *The Color Purple,* Elethia, the title character in the following reading selection, seems to have inherited the strength of her collective mothers and grandmothers who "dreamed dreams that no one knew—not even themselves, in any coherent fashion—and saw visions no one could understand." But unlike those of her precursors who "mov[ed] to music not yet written. . . [a]nd. . . waited[,]" Elethia, like others in her generation of young African American women, can wait no more (A. Walker, "In Search of Our Mothers' Gardens" 232).

PRE-READING QUESTIONS:

1) What are your opinions about the relationship between the perpetrators and victims of racism or about race relations in general? As you read Walker's story, see if these opinions influence your interpretation of her work.

2) Do you think that it's morally aboveboard for a shop owner to display a wooden Indian in front of his shop or for anyone to display a black lawn jockey on her front lawn?

3) What images come to mind when you think of African American slaves, both male and female, and when you think of the succeeding generations of African Americans? How about when you think of White racists?

4) Have you ever been told (or advised) to avoid using the pronoun "you" in your writing? If so, what did you think of this command (or advice)? Have your thoughts on this matter changed?

5) When you choose or are asked to read accounts of racism, sexism, or other social problems, do you generally prefer reading fictional or nonfictional accounts? Does one type of account tend to affect you more than does the other?

6) If you thought that you were about to read either the work of a writer who was other than Black and female or an anonymous work, might you have different pre-reading expectations from those that you have now?

CLOSE-READING TIP

Like all great storytellers, Alice Walker often tells the reader precisely what is going on without also giving the entire game away, as it were. Sometimes, for example, she writes poetic prose whose literal significance is enhanced by its metaphorical connotations. At other times, she creates rather subtle foreshadowings that loom large in retrospect. Whatever techniques she uses, she controls her prose so well that the reader who pays close attention to narrative detail will find in Walker's work a rich store of information both in the first reading and in subsequent readings. As you peruse "Elethia," note evidence that you feel reflects Walker's storytelling expertise, try to characterize or describe the nature of this evidence, and see if you can determine the extent to which the story's content and meaning are connected to its form and writing style.

1   *A certain perverse experience shaped Elethia's life, and made it possible for it to be true that she carried with her at all times a small apothecary jar of ashes.*

2   *There was in the town where she was born a man whose ancestors had owned a large plantation on which everything under the sun was made or grown. There had been many slaves, and though slavery no longer existed, this grandson of former slave-owners held a quaint proprietary point of view where colored people were concerned. He adored them, of course. Not in the present—it went without saying—but at that time, stopped, just on the outskirts of his memory: his grandfather's time.*

3   *This man, whom Elethia never saw, opened a locally famous restaurant on a busy street near the center of town. He called it "Old Uncle Albert's." In the window of the restaurant was a stuffed likeness of Uncle Albert himself, a small brown dummy of waxen skin and glittery black eyes. His lips were intensely smiling and his false teeth shone. He carried a covered tray in one hand, raised level with his shoulder, and over his other arm was draped a white napkin.*

4   *Black people could not eat at Uncle Albert's, though they worked, of course, in the kitchen. But on Saturday afternoons a crowd of them would gather to look at "Uncle Albert" and discuss how near to the real person the dummy looked. Only the very old people remembered Albert Porter, and their eyesight was no better*

than their memory. Still there was a comfort somehow in knowing that Albert's likeness was here before them daily and that if he smiled as a dummy in a fashion he was not known to do as a man, well, perhaps both memory and eyesight were wrong.

5   *The old people appeared grateful to the rich man who owned the restaurant for giving them a taste of vicarious fame. The could pass by the gleaming window where Uncle Albert stood, seemingly in the act of sprinting forward with his tray, and know that though niggers were not allowed in the front door, ole Albert was already inside, and looking mighty pleased about it, too.*

6   *For Elethia the fascination was in Uncle Albert's fingernails. She wondered how his creator had got them on. She wondered also about the white hair that shone so brightly under the lights. One summer she worked as a salad girl in the restaurant's kitchen, and it was she who discovered the truth about Uncle Albert. He was not a dummy; he was stuffed. Like a bird, like a moose's head, like a giant bass. He was stuffed.*

7   *One night after the restaurant was closed someone broke in and stole nothing but Uncle Albert. It was Elethia and her friends, boys who were in her class and who called her "Thia." Boys who bought Thunderbird and shared it with her. Boys who laughed at her jokes so much they hardly remembered she was also cute. Her tight buddies. They carefully burned Uncle Albert to ashes in the incinerator of their high school, and each of them kept a bottle of his ashes. And for each of them what they knew and their reaction to what they knew was profound.*

8   *The experience undercut whatever solid foundation Elethia had assumed she had. She became secretive, wary, looking over her shoulder at the slightest noise. She haunted the museums of any city in which she found herself, looking, usually, at the remains of Indians, for they were plentiful everywhere she went. She discovered some of the Indian warriors and maidens in the museums were also real, stuffed people, painted and wigged and robed, like figures in the Rue Morgue. There were so many, in fact, that she could not possibly steal and burn them all. Besides, she did not know if these figures—with their valiant glass eyes—would wish to be burned.*

9   *About Uncle Albert she felt she knew.*

10 *What kind of man was Uncle Albert?*

11   *Well, the old folks said, he wasn't nobody's uncle and wouldn't sit still for nobody to call him that, either.*

12   *Why, said another old-timer, I recalls the time they hung a boy's privates on a post at the end of the street where all the black folks shopped, just to scare us all, you understand, and Albert Porter was the one took 'em down and buried 'em. Us never did find the rest of the boy though. It was just like always—they would throw you in the river with a big old green log tied to you, and down to the bottom you sunk.*

13   *He continued:*

14   *Albert was born in slavery and he remembered that his mama and daddy didn't know nothing about slavery'd done ended for near 'bout ten years, the boss man*

kept them so ignorant of the law, you understand. So he was a mad so-an'-so when he found out. They used to beat him severe trying to make him forget the past and grin and act like a nigger. (Whenever you saw somebody acting like a nigger, Albert said, you could be sure he seriously disremembered his past.) But he never would. Never would work in the big house as head servant, neither— always broke up stuff. The master at that time was always going around pinching him too. Looks like he hated Albert more than anything—but he never would let him get a job anywhere else. And Albert never would leave home. Too stubborn.

15   *Stubborn, yes. My land, another one said. That's why it do seem strange to see that dummy that sposed to be ole Albert with his mouth open. All them teeth. Hell, all Albert's teeth was knocked out before he was grown.*

16 *Elethia went away to college and her friends went into the army because they were poor and that was the way things were. They discovered Uncle Alberts all over the world. Elethia was especially disheartened to find Uncle Alberts in her textbooks, in the newspapers and on t.v.*

17   *Everywhere she looked there was an Uncle Albert (and many Aunt Albertas, it goes without saying).*

18   *But she had her jar of ashes, the old-timers' memories written down, and her friends who wrote that in the army they were learning skills that would get them through more than a plate glass window.*

19   *And she was careful that, no matter how compelling the hype, Uncle Alberts, in her own mind, were not permitted to exist.*

POST-READING QUESTIONS:

1) After having read Walker's story, do you still hold the opinions that you expressed in your response to the first pre-reading question? Does her story cause you to want to rethink your response to the sixth pre-reading question?

2) While reading Walker's story, did you find yourself wanting to rethink any part of your response to the second pre-reading question?

3) How would you describe the younger and older African Americans and White racists represented in this story? After having read "Elethia," do you want to amend your response to the third pre-reading question?

4) What is the significance of the jar of ashes, or of the names "Uncle Albert" or "Albert Porter"?

5) In your view, would Walker's story have lost or gained anything had Walker made her points in a different writing form—perhaps, for example, in an expository essay?

6) In your view, how does the pronoun "you" function in Walker's story? Do you think that Walker's use of this pronoun is justified?

Theme for English B

LANGSTON HUGHES

The author of nearly 30 books, Langston Hughes (1902–1967) is considered one of the greatest writers in American literary history. For years an enormous influence on African American poets, Hughes was a leading figure in the Harlem Renaissance, "[t]he first major, self-conscious literary movement of American black writers" (Holman 208). An author with a range of writing talents, he is known primarily for his verse, some of which continues to be widely anthologized.

"Theme for English B" typifies much of Hughes' poetry, capturing the thoughts and experiences of an African American who has both assimilated into and remained outside of the dominant White culture. Indeed, readers of Hughes' poetry should find the voice of this poem's persona a familiar one. Speaking with a quiet, reflective passion about the pleasures, struggles, disillusionments, and dreams of many African Americans, the voice in "Theme for English B" is in part the quietly powerful, rhythmic, melodic voice heard in "The Negro Speaks of Rivers"; in part the sad, painfully nostalgic, somewhat disembodied voice heard in "Afro-American Fragment"; in part the embittered but finally hopeful and assured voice heard in "Epilogue" ("I, too, sing America") and in "Let America Be America Again"; and in part the upbeat, energetic, often playful voice heard in any number of Hughes' Harlem-centered poems. For all people who feel both connected to and isolated from the worlds in which they live, this poem's voice embodies a simultaneously hopeful and desperate remembrance of things unfortunately not past.

PRE-READING QUESTIONS:

1) What are your thoughts or feelings about issues concerning diversity on campus (diversity in student population, reading materials for class, and so on)? Are these thoughts and feelings based on your own personal experiences, especially those from your childhood? Keep your thoughts and feelings in mind as you read Hughes' poem, watching to see whether or not—and, if so, how, why, and to what extent—they affect your understanding of or reactions to the persona's ideas.

2) How do you feel about being a student at your college and in your particular classes? Do you consider yourself more or less the same as your fellow students or quite different from them (or somewhere in between)?

3) What comes to mind when you think of the phrase "class assignment"? Does each word in this phrase also have a significance of its own?

4) How would you feel about being given a writing assignment for which you are free to write anything that you want to write, as long as what you write comes from the heart?

5) When you are given a writing assignment calling for you to write from personal experience, do you ever find that, although you have important things to say, you aren't sure whether or not, or even how, you should say them? Do you ever feel that you have nothing important to say?

CLOSE-READING TIP

As suggested in the biographical comments, in a number of his poems Hughes articulates the thoughts and feelings of many African Americans who find themselves displaced by an American/western culture with which they also affiliate. This theme figures prominently in "Theme for English B," a poem that explores, among other things, the persona's search for identity and understanding. Watch for those moments when the persona directly or indirectly alludes to this search to see how each allusion functions both on its own and in relation to the poem's overarching theme of inclusion/exclusion.

The instructor said,

> *Go home and write*
> *a page tonight.*
> *And let that page come out of you—*
> *Then, it will be true.*   5

I wonder if it's that simple?

I am twenty-two, colored, born in Winston-Salem.
I went to school there, then Durham, then here
to this college on the hill above Harlem.
I am the only colored student in my class.   10
The steps from the hill lead down into Harlem,
through a park, then I cross St. Nicholas,
Eighth Avenue, Seventh, and I come to the Y,
the Harlem Branch Y, where I take the elevator
up to my room, sit down, and write this page: 15

It's not easy to know what is true for you or me
at twenty-two, my age. But I guess I'm what
I feel and see and hear. Harlem, I hear you:
hear you, hear me—we two—you, me, talk on this page.
(I hear New York, too.) Me—who?   20

Well, I like to eat, sleep, drink, and be in love.
I like to work, read, learn, and understand life.
I like a pipe for a Christmas present,
or records—Bessie, bop, or Bach.
I guess being colored doesn't make me *not* like   25
the same things other folks like who are other races.

So will my page be colored that I write?
Being me, it will not be white.
But it will be
a part of you, instructor.   30
You are white—
yet a part of me, as I am a part of you.
That's American.
Sometimes perhaps you don't want to be a part of me.
Nor do I often want to be a part of you.   35
But we are, that's true!
As I learn from you,
I guess you learn from me—
although you're older—and white—
and somewhat more free.   40

This is my page for English B.

POST-READING QUESTIONS:

1) Did any of your thoughts or feelings about issues concerning diversity on campus affect your understanding of or help shape your reactions to the ideas put forth by the persona in Hughes' poem? Did Hughes' poem cause you to reexamine your reasons for having these thoughts and feelings?

2) How would you compare your response to the second pre-reading question with relevant statements that the persona makes in this poem?

3) Does Hughes' poem constitute the sort of response to a "class assignment" that you had in mind when you answered the third pre-reading question?

4) If you were given the assignment that the students in the persona's class were given, do you think that you might respond to it similarly to or differently from the way in which the persona responded to it?

5) How do you think that the persona might answer the pre-reading questions? How do you think that he might respond to *your* responses to these questions, and how, in turn, would you respond to his response?

6) What significance do you find in the poem's details—especially those concerning the persona's search for identity and understanding—both in and of themselves and in relation to the poem as a whole?

7) If the authors of this chapter's reading selections met to discuss the ideas that they put forth in their pieces, what points in each other's work might particularly interest them? On which points would they likely agree? On which points might they take issue with each other? Be sure to cite and explain textual and other pertinent evidence to support or prove your claims. (Note: If applicable, feel free to bring into this group discussion authors whose works are reprinted in other chapters of this book.)

8) Concerning the different forms of writing (short stories, poems, and essays) that you came across in this chapter's reading selections, did you find that some forms of writing—and perhaps that certain writing styles—were easier, more difficult, or more effective than others? Having read some or all of this chapter's readings, can you draw any general conclusions about the relationship between form and content in writing?

HANDS-ON ACTIVITY:

Discuss the issues that you studied in this chapter with a counselor who works at your college's counseling center, with the director of or a facilitator at your college's special services or equal opportunities offices, or with trained personnel from all of these organizations. Then, find out from these people how you might be of help either to their organizations or to similar ones on campus and/or in your community. You might also see about joining or starting a club or association on your campus whose purpose would be to address concerns having to do with multiculturalism, race relations, children's rights, and the like. If you want to pursue your interests in these areas academically, talk with your instructor about the sorts of relevant individual or group projects that you could pursue (perhaps you could write or coauthor a paper dealing with these interests). Whatever you end up doing, you might be surprised to discover not only the extent to which you and other students are interested in and commited to understanding the issues at stake here, but also the degree to which you and they—sometimes working together, perhaps— want to take this individual and collective learning beyond the classroom.

> "... [T]eachers are not looking for students merely to absorb information and parrot it back. They want students to analyze and evaluate what they study, to take it apart, to examine it piece by piece, to weigh it, judge it, perhaps (who knows?) to doubt or reject it—perhaps even to improve on it, add to it, develop it further. Teachers want students... going after knowledge with a pick and shovel and then putting everything they unearth to the acid test—not to be captious and negative but in the restless search for True Gold."
>
> CHRIS M. ANSON AND
> LANCE E. WILCOX
> *A Field Guide to Writing*

Writing the Traditional Academic Essay

TO THE EXTENT that all of your writing bears the imprint of your thinking, all of your writing is personal. Indeed, whatever you write, you cannot help but have your papers reflect your opinions, your points of view, your biases; for, like a photographer shooting a scene "as it is" or a filmmaker putting together a documentary film, you the writer decide what to focus on in your work, what information to include in or exclude from your papers, how to interpret the data before you, how much to emphasize the significance of some data over the significance of others, and so on. In short, then, all writing, including supposedly "objective" writing, is subjective or personal to the degree that it is marked, created, and informed by the person who writes it.

On the other hand, there certainly are differences between personal narratives or other forms of writing from experience and what we might call the "more traditionally academic" sort of paper that you'll be writing in many of your college courses. For one thing, much of the writing that you'll be expected to produce in your work inside or outside of college will not involve your discussing how the material that you are studying affects you personally, even if you have a high personal stake in the subject matter about which you are writing. For instance, a novice pediatrician might be deeply moved at seeing her first case of a particularly serious disease in an infant, and she might feel a personal mission to cure the baby of this disease. It is unlikely, however, that she'll mention her personal feelings when she writes about this case in her patient's chart; instead, she'll probably document only her diagnosis and other relevant data. Of course, were she to write in her personal journal that night, she might very well decide to focus her attention on how she feels about having seen her first case of this disease in an infant and, perhaps, on how she feels about having helped the baby get well. In this personal writing, she might glide over or even omit saying anything at all about the very medical data that she needed to record in her patient's chart.

To some degree, then, the major difference between a personal essay and a traditional academic one—and the major difference between their corresponding theses (that is, their main assertions)—is that the personal essay (and usually its thesis) is personal, whereas the traditional academic essay (and *its* thesis) often is not.[1] Though many of your college instructors will ask you to include your personal thoughts, feelings, and reflections in the papers that you'll be writing for their classes, many of their writing assignments will require you to analyze data concerning subject matter for which you might have little passion and in which you might also have little interest. For example, you might need to write about the nature of specific textual evidence in a short story that you don't find very exciting, or to determine whether or not certain psychological studies that you find dull are nevertheless reliable and valid, or to interpret the results of a rather uninspiring and routine lab experiment in your biology class. If in carrying out such assignments you *can* find a way to combine your personal interests and your

---

[1] If you are unfamiliar with the concept of a thesis, please see Chapter Five, pp. 135–138, where this concept is discussed in detail.

academic requirements, so much the better; however, even if you cannot, you'll want to execute these assignments well. For the nature and function of a traditional academic essay is to document a (more or less) compelling understanding of the subject matter under investigation, regardless of the writer's own interest in or commitment to the project.

Meaning and Significance

Let's say that, in your psychology class, you need to write a paper in which you are to summarize and evaluate two or three articles concerning gender bias in the classroom. Though you might be free to choose which articles to summarize and evaluate and which angles to pursue in your analyses, you probably cannot get away with summarizing and evaluating articles having to do with a topic far removed from the one under investigation—such as rainfall patterns in Brazil—unless you can show that these articles contain information relevant to the subject matter that you are studying. If your assignment doesn't state or imply that you have the liberty to make such an analytical leap, then you probably should be wary about making it.

But what if, while reading some articles on gender bias in the classroom, you do in fact find yourself thinking about the rainfall in Brazil? At a purely personal level, you would be right to argue that this information is relevant to your analytical work. However, since its relevance is not obvious, you will probably need to do quite a bit of explaining before your reader will grant the appropriateness of your argument. Otherwise, as noted literary critic E. D. Hirsch might say, in making your argument you could easily end up unintentionally sabotaging your project by confusing the "significance" of your reading experience with the article's "meaning" (*Validity in Interpretation* 8 and *passim*).

In a Hirschean schema, the article's "significance" concerns any values that the article might hold for you personally, or any thoughts that come to mind or feelings that are aroused in you as you study this article *and that you somehow attach to the article itself,* whether or not such values, thoughts, or feelings are or conceivably can be verified by the textual evidence in the article. The article's "meanings," on the other hand, have to do with what the article says or implies; interpretations of the article's meanings should be based upon careful analyses of relevant evidence—especially evidence which is contained within the article itself. Even if they don't agree with your analysis of this evidence, other readers familiar with the article ought to be able to see—without having to make extraordinarily great analytical leaps—how the textual evidence in question *could legitimately* lead to your interpretation of it, and, hence, how your interpretation *could legitimately* be considered one that speaks to the article's meanings.

To have a clearer understanding of the major difference between meaning and significance, consider the following interpretations that I offer concerning Shakespeare's famous "Sonnet 73," as well as my explanations of these interpretations. Here is the full text of Shakespeare's poem:

That time of year thou mayst in me behold
When yellow leaves, or none, or few, do hang

Upon those boughs which shake against the cold,
Bare ruined choirs where late the sweet birds sang.
In me thou seest the twilight of such day
As after sunset fadeth in the west,
Which by and by black night doth take away,
Death's second self, that seals up all in rest.
In me thou seest the glowing of such fire
That on the ashes of his youth doth lie,
As the deathbed whereon it must expire,
Consumed with that which it was nourished by.
This thou perceiv'st, which makes thy love more strong,
To love that well which thou must leave ere long.

If after studying this poem I conclude that the poem is valuable because it reminds me (1) that I need to sweep out the fireplace and (2) that, if I fail to do so, I should not lie to others who might later ask me why ashes remain in the fireplace, I can certainly claim that the poem holds this *significance* for me. I might even say that I find verification for my ideas in the lines "In me thou seest the glowing of such fire,/That on the ashes of his youth doth lie. . . " (ll.9–10). However, unless I can show that the *context* in which Shakespeare uses the words "fire" and "lie" substantiates the view that the poem itself "means" something along the lines of that which I find personally *significant* about it, I cannot very easily claim that the significance which the poem holds for me constitutes an acceptable reading (that is, interpretation) of the poem's *meanings*.

However, I would be accounting for some of the poem's meanings were I to offer and then support the thesis that the poem's persona uses metaphors for aging and dying seemingly in order to make his friend "seize the day" by loving the persona as strongly as possible.[2] (A metaphor is an "implied analogy which imaginatively identifies one object with another and ascribes to the first object one or more of the qualities of the second or invests the first with emotional or imaginative qualities associated with the second" [Holman 264]. If you call your friend a "beast" or an "angel," for example, you are speaking metaphorically.) For verification of my interpretation, I can point to the fact that, throughout the poem, the persona uses metaphors having to do with old age and death: the lines quoted above, for example, depict the dying stage of a fire and explicitly connect this stage to a stage in the persona's life. In the poem's opening four lines, the persona suggests that his friend sees in the persona the autumn or early winter of the persona's life. In lines five and six, the persona suggests that the friend sees in the persona "the twilight" of the persona's life, the sort of twilight that one sees "[a]s after a sunset fadeth in the west"; in poetry, "west" is a common metaphor for

---

[2]"Sonnet 73" is part of a collection of thematically related poems, written by Shakespeare, known as a "sonnet sequence" (the collection contains 154 poems in all). The context of the entire sonnet sequence makes it clear that the "thou" whom the persona addresses in "Sonnet 73" is the persona's friend.

death. In the poem's final two lines, the persona in effect says to his friend, "Once you see that I'm not getting any younger, you'll love me even more strongly."

Ultimately, whether or not I like this poem or find it personally significant, my job as an analytical writer calls for me to convince my readers that my interpretation falls within an acceptable range of interpretations concerning the poem's meanings. The more evidence that I can marshal in defense of my thesis, the greater the possibility that I can demonstrate that my reading of the poem strongly accounts for relevant textual evidence and thus constitutes a strong reading of the poem. I'll help myself achieve this goal if as I work on shaping my analysis I remember that, whereas all *significance* which I attribute to the poem is valid, the *meanings* which I uncover in or place upon the poem may or may not be.

If you find yourself utterly confused by this distinction between meaning and significance, don't despair. Actually, many of your college instructors will use the words meaning and significance interchangeably, sometimes even asking you to write about what something means to you personally. Usually, though, if they are interested in having you include in your papers your own personal thoughts, feelings, or attitudes concerning material that you are studying, they'll say as much in their assignments or in-class comments. However, unless they specifically ask you to comment upon what a poem, genetic pool, or rock stratification (for example) means to you personally, you should assume that their assignments call for you to demonstrate your ability to arrive at good, verifiable analyses of the data and to convey your interpretations in clear, coherent prose. Though important, your personal interest or disinterest in the material—and the rewards that you gain from your studies—might finally be beside the point.

Demonstrating Your Analytical Competency

After you have spent some time thinking about the material that you are trying to analyze, and after you have focused your attention on some meaningful and relevant details concerning the subject matter, you must next decide what you make of the material under investigation. As always, you should be guided in this task by an honest evaluation of what you know and don't know, by your thorough appraisal of the evidence under consideration, by your careful consideration of what your instructor expects you to demonstrate in your paper, and by the needs of your intended readers.

Let's examine a test case to see how you might demonstrate your analytical competence in a traditional academic essay. Imagine that your class has just finished studying Stanley Milgram's essay "The Perils of Obedience" (pp. 276). This essay documents and attempts to explain the behavior of experimental subjects who, thinking that they were participating in an experiment concerning the possible relationship between punishment and learning, found themselves forced to choose between obeying their own moral dictates not to cause harm to another human being and obeying the experimenter—an authority figure—who directed them to administer electric shocks to this other human being. As it turns out, unbeknownst to the experimental subjects, the person who was supposed to have received the shocks never did receive them. He was an accomplice in the experiment.

Following your final class discussion of this essay, your instructor gives your class an assignment in which she asks everyone to explain the role of responsibility in the experimental subjects' decisions to obey or disobey the authority figure in question. Though there are no absolute rules governing how you should carry out this assignment, you might reasonably begin by noting (perhaps in your marginal comments) when Milgram directly or indirectly discusses the concept of responsibility. Then, you might engage in some prewriting to help yourself have a better understanding of what seem to be Milgram's ideas concerning this concept. Eventually, you should accumulate enough relevant data to present and analyze in your paper.

As you pursue your interpretive work, you will probably notice that a number of the subjects in Milgram's experiment reached a point at which they wanted to discontinue giving the shocks. They decided to continue with the experiment, however, when the experimenter told them that he took responsibility for their actions. Milgram himself comments that "[t]he essence of obedience is that a person comes to view himself as the instrument for carrying out another person's wishes, and he therefore no longer regards himself as responsible for his actions. Once this critical shift of viewpoint has occurred," Milgram continues, "all of the essential features of obedience follow" (paragraph 50). Seemingly disturbed by what he sees as the far-reaching consequences of his experimental data, Milgram concludes his article by stating that what he found in his experiment ". . . may illustrate a dangerously typical arrangement in a complex society: it is easy to ignore responsibility when one is only an intermediate link in a chain of action" (paragraph 58). And, he adds, ". . . there is a fragmentation of the total human act; no one is confronted with the consequences of his decision to carry out the evil act. The person who assumes responsibility has evaporated. Perhaps this is the most common characteristic of socially organized evil in modern society" (paragraph 60).

After having examined the meanings of these and other relevant statements from the text, you wouldn't want to offer a thesis such as, "Milgram's study demonstrates that the question of responsibility has little if anything to do with whether or not a person will commit evil acts if he or she is ordered to do so by an authority figure," for such a thesis clearly is at odds with the textual evidence. Milgram's study demonstrates quite evidently that the question of responsibility is at the heart of our decisions to obey or disobey an authority figure who orders us to carry out evil acts. Perhaps you could get away with saying that the thesis offered above bespeaks what for you is the *significance* of Milgram's article, but you couldn't very well defend this thesis as one that accounts for the article's *meanings*.

Instead, after carefully examining the data, you might legitimately offer a thesis such as, "Milgram's experiments demonstrate that a person's decision to carry out or refrain from carrying out the order of an authority figure depends not on whether or not the order will result in the person's committing an evil act, but, rather, on whether or not this individual accepts or rejects personal responsibility for his or her actions." Obligated to prove this thesis, you now need to decide how to arrange, present, and explain the nature of the textual evidence that led you to your conclusion. Perhaps, after presenting an introductory/thesis paragraph, in which you set up the general nature of your analytical project, outline the focus of your paper, and announce the main point that you'll try to prove in the paper, you'll want to explain in some detail the nature of the difficult dilemma in which the experimental subjects found themselves. Then, you might decide to explain the ways in which the subjects' attitudes towards responsibility affected their handling of this dilemma. Throughout your analyses, you'll need to cite and explain the meanings of pertinent textual evidence (such as that cited above) in order to support or prove your points. Finally, in your conclusion, you might indicate why an understanding of Milgram's experiment helps us to understand our own relationships not just to authority figures, but also to the subjects whom Milgram tested.

In trying to determine how you should **organize** your paper for maximum effect, think about (1) whether you want to present your strongest evidence first, last, or throughout the paper; (2) where you might want to articulate (and perhaps repeat) key ideas from Milgram's essay; (3) whether you should present textual evidence and then explain this evidence, explain the evidence and then cite it, interweave textual citations and your own ideas, or use all three methods; (4) whether or not (and, if so, where) you should include extra-textual evidence (concerning the massacres in Bosnia, for instance) that you feel highlights the strong relevance of Milgram's ideas to contemporary acts of violence and cruelty; and so on.

To help insure that you **develop** your thoughts as fully as possible and keep your essay's **focus** as tight as possible, you might try both presenting more (relevant) ideas than you think you'll need and saying more about less rather than attempting to say less about more. For instance, you might try to see how much mileage you can get out of analyzing what the experimental subjects thought and felt just prior to and immediately following their discussing the question of responsibility with the experimenter. Or, you might see how much interpretive insight you can glean from Milgram's attempts to use the results of his experiments to explain larger but related societal problems. If you find that, when all is said and done, you have enough material for more than one essay, don't assume that you've necessarily done something *wrong*. Good writers usually accumulate more material than they can use in a given writing project.

There is one final issue that we need to address concerning your attempts to demonstrate your analytical competency in your papers: the needs of your intended readers, the audience for whom you are writing. Though you usually can assume that your intended readers are familiar with the material, you don't want to assume that they will be eager to fill in important interpretive blanks that you leave empty. Especially when you are doing traditionally academic assignments, keep in mind that you are obligated to show both what you know about the material concerning which you are writing and why you think that your analysis makes sense. If in your essay you take too much for granted, you might lose your intended readers or otherwise undermine the success of your paper.

Although it is highly unlikely that for any given paper you will accurately assess all of the needs of all of your intended readers, with a little forethought, you should be able to pinpoint at least some of their major needs. For example, let's say that your sociology instructor asks you to write an essay in which you use the sociological concept of a "cultural lag" to explain why so many African Americans continue to experience racial discrimination in the workplace, even though they are supposed to be protected by civil rights legislation (a cultural lag is "[t]he time lag between adoption of an innovation and accomplishment of the social and cultural adjustments which the innovation makes necessary" [Horton and Hunt 554]). If your primary audience for this paper is your sociology instructor, you probably don't have to explain *what* a cultural lag is, though you'll certainly be expected to explain *how* this concept applies to the problem under consideration.

If, however, your intended readers for this paper were your composition instructor and your classmates in your composition class, then you probably would need to explain what a cultural lag is before you attempted to show how an understanding of this concept could help us better understand the problem in question (you might even want to give an example or two of how sociologists use this term to explain sociological data). Otherwise, the readability of your essay might suffer—so much so, possibly, that your essay will not have accomplished the goals that you had set for it. For, chances are that, unlike your sociology professor, neither your composition instructor nor your peers in your composition class know much, if anything, about the concept of a cultural lag, unless they've studied sociology. Thus, if in your paper you use such jargon (even correctly) without explaining its meaning to readers unfamiliar with this sort of technical language, for all intents and purposes you will be talking to your intended readers in a foreign language that they don't understand. A brilliant analysis of ancient Greek architecture will be lost on an intended reader if the analysis is written in Greek and the reader doesn't understand Greek; indeed, it will be Greek to him.

Thesis—and Antithesis?—and Synthesis?

You'll likely help your efforts to write a good academic paper if at various points throughout the writing process you ask yourself and then attempt to answer the following sorts of questions:

- Have I derived a thesis after having analyzed pertinent evidence?

- Does my thesis adequately address the nature of this evidence, regardless of my own personal feelings about the evidence?

- Does my thesis constitute the best possible theory, or at least a respectable theory, with respect to the evidence before me?

- Have I clarified my thesis carefully enough and developed both it and my arguments fully enough so that my readers can understand precisely what main point I'm trying to prove or support in my paper?

- Have I cited and explained enough pertinent data?

- Have I, in fact, proved or supported my thesis?

If the answer to all of these questions is "yes"—such as would be the case were you to prove that "Milgram's experiments demonstrate that a person's decision to carry out or refrain from carrying out the order of an authority figure depends not on whether or not the order will result in the person's committing an evil act, but, rather, on whether or not this individual accepts or rejects personal responsibility for his or her actions"—then one cannot imagine how any intended readers acting in good faith could reject your position outright, if at all, even if they don't share your point of view about the matter under investigation. On the other hand, were you to use the above questions to test the strength of a paper in which you argue that "Milgram's study demonstrates that the question of responsibility has little if anything to do with whether or not a person will commit evil acts if he or she is ordered to do so by an authority figure," surely you would find yourself having to go back to the drawing board. Though you probably would not be overjoyed to discover that you need to revise your thesis and analysis, undoubtedly you will always prefer to straighten out your paper's difficulties rather than face the consequences of your having left troublesome matters unattended.

If you produce a good analytical paper but your intended readers still don't buy your argument, don't worry. Experienced, secure writers usually are not threatened by their readers' good-faith disagreements with their ideas; at times, in fact, such writers expect—and even welcome—such disagreements. With this perhaps odd-sounding thought in mind, try to pursue your academic work not with the intent that you, your instructor, and your classmates will all arrive at the same interpretation of any given data, but, rather, with the hope that you all will engage yourselves in good-faith efforts to derive, develop, and prove or support reasonable points of view about these data. Even if, for example, it turns out that everyone in your class disagrees with everyone else concerning the main theme of a short story that your class is studying—a state of affairs that might indicate a good deal of interpretive sophistication on everyone's part—all of you should be able to take seriously each legitimate perspective that is offered, that is, each perspective that accounts for relevant evidence and is reasonable. After you all begin sensing the range of interpretive possibilities concerning the material that your class is studying, everyone ought to be able to see how a matter under investigation (such as the meanings of a poem, for example, or the ramifications of a sociological experiment) often both encompasses and transcends anyone's individual views on that matter.

As you prepare to engage in the work for this chapter, see if you, your classmates, and your instructor can reach agreement on how to approach the analytical thinking and writing explicitly called for in this chapter's featured assignment and implicitly alluded to in the chapter's pre- and post-reading questions and close-reading tips. Use your understanding of these discussions to try to see whether or not—and, if so, how and where—your own interpretations of the chapter's reading selections fall within a range of acceptable analyses. Then, see if everyone can agree to disagree with each other (should such disagreement become necessary) without also having to invalidate anyone's *good* analytical efforts. If you and your classmates accomplish nothing more than the goals alluded to in these last two paragraphs, all of you might very well discover that working on a traditional academic paper is indeed more *personally* rewarding than initially any of you might have thought.

READING AND WRITING

Few issues are as central to everyone's life as is the issue of obedience to authority, whether the authority is a deity, a group of deities, a parent, a teacher, or a tribal, religious, or political leader. And few issues have raised so many questions whose answers we often feel uncomfortable contemplating. For example, why, in the name of obedience to authority, do people behave towards others in ways in which they might never even consider behaving otherwise? Should we always obey the commands of someone or some entity (a supreme being or a government, for example) who presumably has power over us, even if our acts of obedience sometimes exact a high moral price from us or others? And what are we to make of someone or some entity in a position of authority who commands people to commit immoral acts? What are we to make of people who acquiesce to her or his demands? What of those who *don't* acquiesce to them?

Is it necessarily true that chaos will ensue if we don't obey the law? If so, might chaos ever be preferable to law and order? In the final analysis, to whom are we ultimately responsible for our acts, and can we ever be held *entirely* responsible for *any* of our acts? Can the excuse that we were "just following orders" ever suffice to absolve us from the guilt of our having committed a misdeed, especially one that hurts others? Does obedience to authority have its good points, or is it always and only problematic? Collectively, the authors of this chapter's reading selections wrestle with these and similar questions.

Of course, fervently wishing to avoid dealing with the unpleasantness evoked by these questions, we might be tempted to suggest that all we ever need do is obey our conscience. Unfortunately, though, as this chapter's readings will attest, obeying one's conscience is often easier said than done; and besides, not everyone's conscience is so admirable. In his memoirs, Rudolph Höss, for example—the Commandant of Auschwitz—talks about the "many heartbreaking scenes [concerning the gassings at Auschwitz]. . . which affected all who were present" (159).

Only a few pages later, however, he tells us, "I had to continue to carry out the process of destruction. . . . I had to watch it all with cold indifference. . . . And yet, I really had no reason to complain about being bored at Auschwitz" (163).

FEATURED ASSIGNMENT

Part I: Write an essay in which you evaluate Alice Miller's analysis of the Abraham and Isaac story. Carefully explain why you think that her analysis does or does not make sense, either in part or in whole. Though in the course of analyzing Miller's work you may cite and explain relevant experiences of your own, your discussion should focus on the strengths and weaknesses of Miller's essay. In your response, be sure to cite and comment upon important passages in Miller's text, and be sure that your citations of her work are contextually sound and are quoted accurately.

Part II: Write a brief reflective commentary on what you experienced, thought, and/or felt while doing this assignment.

F E A T U R E D   R E A D I N G

When Isaac Arises from the Sacrificial Altar
ALICE MILLER

For biographical information on Alice Miller, please see Chapter Six, p. 226. The following reading selection is taken from *The Untouched Key: Tracing Childhood Trauma in Creativity and Destructiveness* (1988).

PRE-READING QUESTIONS:

1) What do you think of the proposition that people should obey God and God's laws? How do you *feel* when you think about this proposition? Keep your thoughts and feelings in mind as you read Miller's piece, watching to see whether or not—and, if so, how, why, and to what extent—they affect your understanding of or reactions to her ideas.

2) In general, should children obey their parents or other authority figures? Are they *obligated* to do so? Can you cite and explain the meanings of specific examples that illustrate the positive aspects of such obedience, as well as specific examples that illustrate the negative aspects of it?

3) In general, should people obey higher authorities? Are they *obligated* to do so? Can you cite some examples of what you would consider positive and negative acts of obedience to authority? How would you characterize people who carry out such acts? How would you characterize the authority figures?

4) Do you enjoy reading analytical texts, such as, perhaps, Sigmund Freud's "The Sexual Aberrations" (p. 163) or Fred E. Katz's "A Sociological Perspective to the Holocaust" (p. 95)? Do you prefer reading analytical texts to reading other sorts of texts, such as personal narratives or works of fiction?

CLOSE-READING TIP

In a number of her writings, Miller tries to show that we cannot fully understand the nature of interpersonal, communal, international, or global conflict unless we understand that the roots of such conflict are in child-rearing practices in particular and parent-child relations in general. This theory underlies Miller's understanding of the Abraham and Isaac story, too. As you read her piece, note those moments when Miller tacitly or clearly tries to use her understanding of the Abraham and Isaac story to explain what she sees as the larger stakes of blind obedience to authority. Try to determine which of her speculations you think are warranted and which, to you, seem unwarranted.

SELECTION

MILLER

When Isaac Arises from the Sacrificial Altar

1   I had been searching for an illustration for the jacket of the British edition of *Thou Shalt Not Be Aware;* I didn't want to leave the selection to chance but thought it important that I myself find an appropriate visual representation of the work's underlying theme. Two Rembrandt depictions of the sacrifice of Isaac—one in Leningrad, the other in Munich—came to mind. In both, the father's hand completely covers the son's face, obstructing his sight, his speech, even his breathing. The main concerns expressed in my book (victimization of the child, the Fourth Commandment admonishing us to honor our parents, and the blindness imposed on children by parents) seemed to find a central focus in Abraham's gesture. Although I was resolved to recommend this detail of Rembrandt's printings to my publisher for the cover, I went to an archive to look at other portrayals of Abraham and Isaac as well. I found thirty in all, done by very dissimilar artists, and with growing astonishment I looked through them one by one.

2   I had been struck by the fact that in both of the Rembrandt versions I already knew, Abraham is grasping his son's head with his left hand and raising a knife with his right; his eyes, however, are not resting on his son but are turned upward, as though he is asking God if he is carrying out His will correctly. At first I thought that this was Rembrandt's own interpretation and that there must be others, but I was unable to find any. In all the portrayals of this scene that I found, Abraham's face or entire torso is turned away from his son

*Rembrandt van Rijn, The
Sacrifice of Isaac Archiv für Kunst
und Geschichte, Berlin*

and directed upward. Only his hands are occupied with the sacrifice. As I looked at the pictures, I thought to myself, "The son, an adult at the peak of his manhood, is simply lying there, quietly waiting to be murdered by his father. In some of the versions he is calm and obedient; in only one is he in tears, but not in a single one is he rebellious." In none of the paintings can we detect any questioning in Isaac's eyes, questions such as "Father, why do you want to kill me, why is my life worth nothing to you? Why won't you look at me, why won't you explain what is happening? How can you do this to me? I love you, I trusted in you. Why won't you speak to me? What crime have I committed? What have I done to deserve this?"

3   Such questions can't even be formulated in Isaac's mind. They can be asked only by someone who feels himself on equal footing with the person being questioned, only if a dialogue is possible, only if one can look the other in the eye. How can a person lying on a sacrificial altar with hands bound, about to be slaughtered, ask questions when his father's hand keeps him from seeing or speaking and hinders his breathing? Such a person has been turned into an *object*. He has been dehumanized by being made a sacrifice; he no longer has a

right to ask questions and will scarcely even be able to articulate them to himself, for there is no room in him for anything besides fear.

4   As I sat in the archive looking at the pictures, I suddenly saw in them the symbolic representation of our present situation. Inexorably, weapons are being produced for the obvious purpose of destroying the next generation. Yet those who are profiting from the production of these weapons, while enhancing their prestige and power, somehow manage not to think of this ultimate result. Like Abraham, they do not see what their hands are doing, and they devote their entire attention to fulfilling expectations from "above," at the same time ignoring their feelings. They learned to deny their feelings as children; how should they be able to regain the ability to feel now that they are fathers? It's too late for that. Their souls have become rigid, they have learned to adapt. They have also forgotten how to ask questions and how to listen to them. All their efforts are now directed toward creating a situation—war—in which their sons too will be unable to see and hear.

5   In the face of mobilization for war—even a conventional one, a nonnuclear war—the questions of the younger generation are silenced. To doubt the wisdom of the state is regarded as treason. Any discussion or consideration of alternative possibilities is eliminated at a single stroke. Only practical questions remain: How do we win the war? How do we survive it? Once the point of asking these questions has been reached, the young forget that prosperous and prominent old men have been preparing for war for a long time. The younger generation will march, sing songs, kill and be killed, and they will be under the impression that they are carrying out an extremely important mission. The state will indeed regard highly what they are doing and will reward them with medals of honor, but their souls—the childlike, living, feeling part of their personality—will be condemned to the utmost passivity. They will resemble Isaac as he is always depicted in the sacrificial scene: hands tied, eyes bound, as if it were the most natural thing in the world to wait unquestioningly in this position to be slaughtered by one's father. (In my German translation of the Bible the verb used in this passage is *schlachten,* which refers to the butchering of animals.)

6   Neither does the father ask any questions. He submits to the divine command as a matter of course, the same way his son submits to him. He must—and wants to—prove that his obedience is stronger than what he calls his love for his child, and as he prepares to carry out the deed his questions vanish. He doesn't ask God for mercy or look for a way out, and if the angel didn't intervene at the last moment, Abraham would become the murderer of his son simply because God's voice demanded it of him. In the pictures I examined, there is no pain to be seen in Abraham's face, no hesitation, no searching, no questioning, no sign that he is conscious of the tragic nature of his situation. All the artists, even Rembrandt, portray him as God's obedient instrument, whose sole concern is to function properly.

7   It is astonishing at first glance that not one of the artists, each with his own distinct and independent personality, was tempted to give this dramatic scene an individual, personal stamp. Of course the dress, the colors, the surroundings, and the positions of the bodies vary, but the numerous depictions of the scene reveal a remarkably uniform psychological content. An obvious explanation is that all the artists were following the Old Testament text, but we are still justified in asking why. Why wasn't there room in the psyche of these artists for doubt? Why did they all take it for granted that the Bible passage could not be questioned? Why did all of these artists accept the story as valid? The only answer I can think of is that the situation involves a fundamental fact of our existence, with which many of us become familiar during the first years of life and which is so painful that knowledge of it can survive only in the depths of the unconscious. Our awareness of the child's victimization is so deeply rooted in us that we scarcely seem to have reacted at all to the monstrousness of the story of Abraham and Isaac. The moral expressed in the story has almost been accorded the legitimacy of natural law, yet if the result of this legitimacy is something as horrifying as the outbreak of nuclear war, then the moral should not be passively accepted like a natural law but must be questioned. If we love life more than obedience and are not prepared to die in the name of obedience and our fathers' lack of critical judgment, then we can no longer wait like Isaac, with our eyes bound and our hands tied, for our fathers to carry out the will of their fathers.

8   How, then, can a condition that has endured for millennia be changed? Would it change if the young were to kill off the old so as not to have to go to war? Wouldn't that simply be a forerunner to the horrible war we are trying to prevent, and wouldn't the old situation then be reinforced, the difference being that Abraham's knife would now be in Isaac's hands and the old man would become the victim of the young man? Wouldn't the same cruelty be perpetuated?

9   But what would happen if Isaac, instead of reaching for the knife, were to use every ounce of his strength to free his hands so that he could remove Abraham's hand from his face? That would change his situation altogether. He would no longer lie there like a sacrificial lamb but would stand up; he would dare to use his eyes and see his father as he really is: uncertain and hesitant yet intent on carrying out a command he does not comprehend. Now Isaac's nose and mouth would be free too, and he could finally draw a deep breath and make use of his voice. He would be able to speak and ask questions, and Abraham, whose left hand could no longer keep his son from seeing and speaking, would have to enter into a dialogue with his son, at the end of which he might possibly encounter the young man he had once been himself, who was never allowed to ask questions.

10   And now that the scenario has changed and Isaac can no longer be counted on to be a victim, there will have to be a confrontation between the two, a confrontation that has no conventional precedent but that nevertheless, or perhaps

for this very reason, offers a golden opportunity. Isaac will ask, "Father, why do you want to kill me?" and will be given the answer "It is God's will." "Who is God?" the son will ask. "The great and benevolent Father of us all, Whom we must obey," Abraham will answer. "Doesn't it grieve you," the son will want to know, "to have to carry out this command?" "It is not for me to take my feelings into account when God orders me to do something." "Then who are you," Isaac will ask, "if you carry out His orders without any feeling, and Who is this God, Who can demand such a thing of you?"

11 It may be that Abraham is too old, that it is too late for him to perceive the message of life his son is bringing him, that he will say, "Keep quiet! You understand nothing of all this." But it may be that he is open to Isaac's questions because they are his own questions as well, which he has had to suppress for decades. Even in the former case, however, the encounter is not doomed to failure as long as Isaac is unwilling to shut his eyes again but is determined to endure the sight of his father as he really is. If Isaac refuses to allow himself to be bound and blinded again for the sake of preserving the illusion of a strong and wise and benevolent father but instead finds the courage to look his fallible father in the eye and hear his "Keep quiet" without letting himself be silenced, the confrontation will continue. Then young people will not have to die in wars to preserve the image of their wise fathers. Once young men see what is actually happening, once they become aware that their fathers are steadfastly, unwaveringly, and unthinkingly developing a gigantic weapons system that they hope will not destroy them, although it may their children, then the children will refuse to lie down voluntarily like lambs on the sacrificial altar. But for this to be possible, the children first must be willing to stop obeying the commandment "Thou shalt not be aware."

12 The commandment itself provides the explanation of why it is so difficult to take that step to awareness. Yet the decision to take it is the first requirement for change. We can still avert our probable fate, provided we do not wait to be rescued by the angel who rewarded Abraham for his obedience. More and more people are refusing to go on playing Isaac's sacrificial role with all its consequences for the future. And perhaps there are also people who reject Abraham's role, who refuse to obey orders that strike them as absurd because they are directed against life. Their ability to ask questions and their refusal to accept senseless answers may signal the beginning of a long overdue reorientation that will help reinforce our Yes to life and No to death. The new Isaac—with his questions, with his awareness, with his refusal to let himself be killed—not only saves his own life but also saves his father from the fate of becoming the unthinking murderer of his child.

POST-READING QUESTIONS:

1) Did any of your thoughts or feelings concerning whether or not people should obey God and God's laws affect your understanding of or help shape your reactions to Miller's ideas? Did this excerpt cause you to reexamine your reasons for having these thoughts and feelings?

2) Do you and Miller have the same reading of the Abraham and Isaac story? In your view, does Miller present a cogent understanding of this story? Should readers apply their understanding of this story to an analysis of issues that lie beyond the story's own biblical context?

3) Do you think that Miller accurately interprets Rembrandt's painting? Does his painting accurately reflect what is going on in *Genesis* 22? Has his pictorial representation of the Abraham and Isaac story affected your interpretation of this story?

4) What do you make of Miller's analogy between children's obeying their parents and soldiers' obeying their governments? Has your understanding of her ideas caused you to rethink your responses to the second and third pre-reading questions?

5) Criticizing the behavior of those European nations that actively took part in the First World War, Sigmund Freud says that the state ". . . absolves itself from the guarantees and treaties by which it was bound to other states, and confesses shamelessly to its own rapacity and lust for power, which the private individual has then to sanction in the name of patriotism" ("The Disillusionment of the War," *S.E.*: 14:280). How might Miller respond to this idea? How do *you* respond to it? (By the way, you might find it interesting to look up the etymology of the word "patriot.")

6) Did you enjoy reading Miller's work, whether or not you found yourself agreeing with some or all of her views? Does Miller's writing seem to be a model of good analytical writing? How would you compare it with the writing in other analytical works that you've read?

Evaluating Alice Miller's analysis of the Abraham and Isaac story

JOHN VERBECK

John Walter Verbeck, III, was born in 1968 in Santa Monica, California. He spent most of his early years living in Torrance, California, except for a brief period when he lived in Bremen, Germany. In 1986, he was graduated from high school and started his collegiate studies at the University of California at Irvine, where he majored in information and computer science. To fulfill his lower-division writing requirement, he enrolled in a writing course at Irvine Valley College. Although he had read two of Alice Miller's books prior to taking this class, in this course he first studied the text by Miller which he analyzes in his essay reprinted below. He brings to this essay the knowledge that he has gained from many years of studying and reading about topics related to biblical history and tradition (from an early age, he has had a great interest in biblical studies).

Currently, John owns and operates his own computer systems integration and consulting company in Irvine, California. He enjoys spending his spare time with his wife and children. Although he has some long-term goals, he prefers to focus on the present and to live his life one day at a time. He knows that living life each day will provide for the completion of his goals or for the insight into how he ought to change them.

PART I   Essay

For many years, Dr. Alice Miller, a renowned psychoanalyst from Switzerland, has focused her talents on writing about child victimization. Many ideas in her writing stem from analyzing case histories of victimized children. The results of her analysis show how adults, through their destructive behavior patterns, cause serious damage to children. In her work "The Untouched Key: Tracing Childhood Trauma in Creativity and Destructiveness", Alice Miller provides psychoanalytic biographies of people including Picasso, Buster Keaton, Nietzsche, and Hitler. The creativity or destructiveness of each person examined is connected to childhood abuse and/or trauma.

Included in "The Untouched Key" is an analysis of *Genesis 22*, the Biblical story of Abraham and Isaac. Through this analysis, Miller attempts to strengthen her message about the harmful effects of physical and emotional abuse by adults on children. While she is successful in strengthening her message, she makes many problematic assumptions along the way. Alice Miller does not directly analyze the story of Abraham and Isaac. Her evaluation is based on an incomplete understanding of the story. Alice Miller's analysis of the *Akedah* is based on an interpretation of the story that cannot be relied upon as factual and is not supported by the original Hebrew text. In evaluating Alice Miller's analysis, I will directly compare it with the original Biblical text found in *Genesis 22*. The unreasonableness of her examination can be established through this comparison.

Miller's first problematic assumption stems from her use of another representation of the Biblical story. Miller examines a number of famous paintings in order to find a suitable one that shows her theme of child abuse. Miller writes, "I had been searching for an illustration for the jacket of the British edition of 'Thou Shalt Not Be Aware'; I didn't want to leave the selection to chance but thought it important that I myself find an appropriate visual representation of the work's underlying theme." While examining these paintings, she notices a recurrent theme in each painter's interpretation. She asserts that all paintings of the Biblical event contain the same interpretation of the original story. Her research was limited, and she found only paintings that illustrated and supported a theme of child abuse. Perhaps because she found what she was looking for, she neglected to look further.

The similarity of the paintings that Miller examined, including Rembrandt's rendering, indicates a tradition of interpretive thought regarding the Abraham and Isaac story not based on the Biblical text. Alice Miller writes ". . . the numerous depictions of the scene reveal a remarkably uniform psychological content. An obvious explanation is that all the artists were following the Old Testament text . . ." Since the original text does not include the details for this psychological depiction, clearly the "obvious explanation" is that the artists were exercising their artistic license while painting the event. Moreover, Miller does not recognize the possibility of an incorrect interpretation of the Biblical story, nor does she quote the original text as a reference. The original text does not use descriptive detail about the interaction between Abraham and Isaac. It says:

"And Isaac spoke to Abraham his father and said, "My father!" And he said, "Here I am, my son." And he said, "Behold, the fire and the wood, but where is the lamb for the burnt offering?" And Abraham said, "God will provide for Himself the lamb for the burnt offering, my son." So the two of them walked on together. Then they came to the place of which God had told him; and Abraham built the altar there, and arranged the wood, and bound his son Isaac, and laid him on the altar on top of the wood." [Ed. note: Verbeck is quoting from *The New American Standard Bible, Study Edition,* and not from the text used in the related readings section.]

The extensive detail used as evidence in Miller's analysis is found in Rembrandt's painting of the event, not in the original story. Rembrandt's painting is not problematic. However, the way in which Miller uses the painting is. Rembrandt captured the offering of Isaac into a single picture. He took a story that had its roots in an oral tradition and basically retold it on canvas with paint. Usually, when a story is retold, the storyteller adds in his own nuances to the original story, as well as leaving out other details. In the case of Rembrandt's painting, the context and extent of the original story are limited, but the graphic detail of the interaction between Abraham and Isaac is significantly embellished. For example, Miller focuses her attention on Abraham's actions in Rembrandt's painting. She says, "the father's hand completely covers the son's face, obstructing his sight, his speech, even his breathing." "How can a person lying on a sacrificial altar with hands bound, about to be slaughtered, ask questions when his father's hand keeps him from seeing or speaking and hinders his breathing? Such a person has been turned into an object." While this is a very good point, we do not know that this happened, except maybe in the mind of Rembrandt. Nowhere in the original text is there a reference to Abraham's covering Isaac's face. The original story only tells us that he, Abraham, bound his son, Isaac. By accepting Rembrandt's painting as an accurate pictorial representation of the *Akedah*, without using the original text for comparison, Miller has chosen to accept that the event happened the way Rembrandt painted it. The original event has now become limited in scope and significantly embellished. While this interpretation works to illustrate her thesis, it reduces the original story into a single instant, captured on canvas by Rembrandt.

According to Miller, psychological detailed information is now available through Rembrandt's interpretation. While this might be true, doesn't the detailed psychological information reveal more about Rembrandt and his tradition, than Abraham's and Isaac's? To be fair, the original sparse story does support the idea of Abraham's victimizing his son. Abraham is portrayed as the blindly obedient servant of God. But, Miller doesn't focus on God's role. She is more concerned with the relationship between Abraham and Isaac. This is another problematic mistake. The incident in *Genesis 22* is part of a larger story. The context in which it exists needs to be understood. God is an integral part of the story. Throughout the Bible there is a recurrent theme. This motif is brought out by the use of these stories. The theme is that God's plan and promise will be brought to fruition, despite the stupidity and intervention of man. In the story of Abraham and Isaac, this is a key to understanding the story's meaning.

Furthermore, the idea of a god that would ask his child to kill the favorite son is worth examination. Miller takes issue with this concept. She imagines a confrontational dialog between Abraham and a "new" Isaac. "Isaac will ask, 'Father, why do you want to kill me?' and will be given the answer 'It is God's will.' 'Who is God?' the son will ask. 'The great and benevolent Father of us all, Whom we must obey,' Abraham will answer. 'Doesn't it grieve you,' the son will want to know, 'to have to carry out this command?' 'It is not for me to take my feelings into account when God orders me to do something.' 'Then who are you' Isaac will ask, 'if you carry out His orders without any feeling, and Who is this God, Who can demand such a thing of you?'" The fact that Miller imagines this dialog shows her lack of understanding of the original story. The story of Isaac's offering, not sacrifice, was originally written in Hebrew. Examining this story in Hebrew gives a better understanding of the story's meaning, context, and intent.

In the original Hebrew story, the request for the "sacrifice" is given by Elohim, a generic Hebrew term for gods or god. This is interesting because at that time in history other gods in other religions were asking their followers to sacrifice children. Child sacrifice was a common occurrence. But when the time came for Abraham to actually kill his son, Adonai does not allow Isaac to die. Adonai is the name of Abraham's God in Hebrew. (This difference in translation is directly addressed in several Hebrew commentaries that discuss the difference between Adonai and Elohim, as well as the context and meaning of the original story. Gerhard von Rad / Haftarah Vayera) The story is certainly one of unconditional obedience, but most importantly the story is anti-sacrificial. The *Akedah* sets a precedent and shows the people of Abraham's God that the physical death of their children at the hands of the parents is not acceptable as an offering to God. The motif of God's promise being fulfilled despite Abraham's foolishness is displayed. Alice Miller's analysis is based on an incomplete understanding and thus a misunderstanding of the Hebrew story.

Another interesting question that Miller does not address is the absence of descriptive detail in the original story about the interaction between Abraham and Isaac. (Alice Miller ignores this problem by using Rembrandt's painting for detailed evidence.) Could the answer simply be that the author of the original story was trying to make his point by focusing on the interaction between a confused Abraham and his God, a God who was all knowing and all loving? It is this same God who ordered his people to love and not kill their children, a God who was willing to show to his people the way from victimization through words and also through the actions of Abraham. That this man, Abraham, is thought to be the father of an entire race of people is surely noteworthy in this case. If Abraham was capable of making the mistake of victimizing his own son, then any of Abraham's people were just as capable of making the same mistake. God took an opportune moment thousands of years ago to show the correct way. The decision to follow or not was left up to man.

The conclusions drawn by Alice Miller based on her hypothetical exchange between Isaac and Abraham are correct but unnecessary. The resolution and redemption of the original Hebrew story shows how God and not the "new" Isaac "not only saves [Isaac's] life but also saves [Abraham] from the fate of becoming the unthinking murderer of [Isaac]." This original theme is ignored by Alice Miller. She decides, instead, that the story should turn out a different way, claiming that the victim must rise up and question the victimizer. This hypothetical ending is unnecessary. The original story is resolved by God. The "misunderstood" issue is over and Isaac is not killed. Isaac does arise from the sacrificial altar to fulfill his role in the remainder of the story, but again Miller ignores the complete story, substituting her own version of it for that found in the Hebrew Bible.

The Biblical text does not support her assumptions due to its paucity of detail. This is not to say that her analysis is unfounded. Rather, her analysis is merely based upon perceptions that cannot be relied upon as factual. Quite possibly Alice Miller simply misunderstood the original Hebrew text. Interestingly enough, her analysis resulted in almost the same outcome, portrayed by the "new" Isaac, as the outcome provided for by God in the *Akedah*.

PART II	Commentary

Alice Miller's analysis was part of a larger work. The story was extracted from her book, "The Untouched Key". I felt it necessary to provide some insight into Alice Miller's work, before attacking her analysis and claiming that she misunderstood the original story. I have great respect for most of Alice Miller's early work and because of her status I felt it necessary to start off the paper in a generous tone. Once that tone was established, I then felt comfortable about taking issue with her analysis.

Without question, my ideas were sharpened during the course of my writing. Some ideas became redundant or less important to proving my point as my writing progressed. Thus I felt it necessary to omit certain items from some drafts. Later I realized that some of the omitted items helped to support other larger ideas and so I re-introduced them into the paper. The example relating to my comments about Alice Miller's omitting any reference to God's mercy was taken out of the third draft because I thought that it was an obvious point. In the final draft I did try to address God's role in the original story. He is a key character in the text.

Writing this essay forced me to derive a newer format for academic pieces. I was placed in a difficult position. I had previous knowledge of Alice Miller's work as well as experience in Biblical study. While I knew that the original story in *Genesis 22* did not support Alice Miller's piece from "The Untouched Key", I did know that Alice Miller had written many excellent, well supported pieces about child victimization. When I first read her piece from "The Untouched Key" I turned to read the following page and thought I had missed something in the transition from Biblical examination to weapons proliferation. It was then that I knew her analysis had some problems. At first I felt upset at her use of this story. I wondered about the implications of her interpretation. I thought about the anti-Semitic overtones. However, knowing that I was well supported by Hebrew scholars and Biblical commentaries about the meaning and context of the original story of Abraham and Isaac, I was convinced by the instructor that using a generous tone would be better served. Quite possibly, Alice Miller misunderstood the story, which I'm sure she didn't read in Hebrew. Furthermore, she is a psychoanalyst not a Hebrew scholar, so I had to allow some latitude for an incorrect interpretation. I honestly believe that Alice Miller was genuine in her motivation for writing this piece. She clearly wanted to show how deep the roots for victimization ran. Unfortunately, she was too "quick on the draw." I feel that she just misunderstood the original story. This is not hard to believe when you examine the original Hebrew text and compare it to the English translations. Once I finally reconciled Alice Miller's intent in writing this piece, I was able to follow my normal conventions of revision to finish the remaining drafts. However, I spent several drafts venting my frustration. The way I tackled and dealt with the task of writing this paper was simple. I sat down and wrote the first draft and then continually rewrote and revised. Many times I threw out the draft completely and started over. If this had been a personal essay, the approach would have been more relaxed. I would definitely have had a different approach for a personal essay.

From writing this paper, I learned several things as a writer. About myself, I realized that my critical writing tone needs to be squelched. I learned not to quickly prejudge another person's ideas, especially when that person is a well respected, articulate psychoanalyst. I learned how to write with restraint. I came to the conclusion that Alice Miller's analysis was an honest misunderstanding of the original Hebrew text. I would suggest that the students take the time to evaluate as much information regarding the subject as time permits. By that I mean that it was beneficial to have a knowledge of Hebrew, Biblical literature, and the previous work of Alice Miller. When I read "The Untouched Key" in its entirety, I found that the significance of her analysis of the *Akedah* was less important. The book as a whole was very interesting and mostly factual.

R E L A T E D   R E A D I N G S

Genesis 22: "The *Akedah*"[1]

The translation of this famous and controversial story from the Hebrew Bible is that used in *The Torah: A Modern Commentary* (edited by W. Gunther Plaut), which closely follows the Hebrew text. Included with this translation are Plaut's excellent explanatory footnotes.

PRE-READING QUESTIONS:

1) Do you have any thoughts or feelings about religion in general or Judaism in particular? If you do, keep these thoughts and feelings in mind as you read *Genesis 22*, watching to see if they affect your reading of this biblical excerpt.

---

[1]Ed. note: The Hebrew word *akedah* means "binding." Literally, then, this story has to do with the binding of Isaac, not with his sacrifice (which never occurs).

2) In general, should children obey their parents or other authority figures? Should adults obey authority figures? Are either children or adults *obligated* to obey authority figures? Can you cite some examples of what you would consider positive acts of obedience to authority, as well as some that you would consider negative acts of obedience to authority? (If applicable, take another look at your response to the fourth post-reading question concerning the featured reading selection; see p. 265.)

3) In your view, is the allusion to God as a father figure and to human beings as God's children apt? Does this allusion do justice both to God and to human beings? Does it diminish either's stature or worth?

4) The word "family" is often applied to many nonfamilial groups, such as a network of employers and employees working for the same company, collections of students, faculty, staff, and administrators from the same school, social clubs consisting of similarly minded members, and the like. Do you find such widespread use of this word appropriate? Does it make sense for people to refer to all or part of the human race as a "family" (as in the old epithet "family of Man")?

5) Do you tend to read religious texts similarly to or differently from the ways in which you tend to read other kinds of texts?

CLOSE-READING TIP

As the contributing author suggests, the textual details concerning the binding of Isaac are sparse. Nevertheless, careful readers should find a number of the text's details quite telling—especially when they reread the story—whether or not they agree on how to interpret these details. As you peruse *Genesis 22*, note those passages that immediately strike you as being weighty with meaning. Then, upon rereading the story, note any passages that *initially* had seemed insignificant but that take on meaning retrospectively. Consider, for example, 22:8, 14, and 18.

1 Some time afterward, God put Abraham to the test. He said to him, "Abraham," and he answered, "Here I am."

2 And He said, "Take your son, your favored one, Isaac, whom you love, and go to the land of Moriah, and offer him there as a burnt offering on one of the heights which I will point out to you."

3 So early next morning, Abraham saddled his ass and took with him two of his servants and his son Isaac. He split the wood for the burnt offering, and he set out for the place of which God had told him.

4 On the third day Abraham looked up and saw the place from afar.

5 Then Abraham said to his servants, "You stay here with the ass. The boy and I will go up there; we will worship and we will return to you."

6   Abraham took the wood for the burnt offering and put it on his son Isaac. He himself took the firestone and the knife; and the two walked off together.

7   Then Isaac said to his father Abraham, "Father!" And he answered, "Yes, my son." And he said, "Here are the firestone and the wood; but where is the sheep for the burnt offering?"

8   And Abraham said, "God will see to the sheep for His burnt offering, my son." And the two of them walked on together.

9   They arrived at the place of which God had told him. Abraham built an altar there; he laid out the wood; he bound his son Isaac; he laid him on the altar, on top of the wood.

10   And Abraham picked up the knife to slay his son.

11   Then an angel of the Lord called to him from heaven: "Abraham! Abraham!" And he answered, "Here I am."

12   And he said, "Do not raise your hand against the boy, or do anything to him. For now I know that you fear God, since you have not withheld your son, your favored one, from Me."

13   When Abraham looked up, his eye fell upon a ram, caught in the thicket by its horns. So Abraham went and took the ram and offered it up as a burnt offering in place of his son.

14   And Abraham named that site Adonai-yireh, whence the present saying, "On the mount of the Lord there is vision."

15   The angel of the Lord called to Abraham a second time from heaven,

16   and said, "By Myself I swear, the Lord declares: because you have done this and have not withheld your son, your favored one,

17   I will bestow My blessing upon you and make your descendants as numerous as the stars of heaven and the sands on the seashore; and your descendants shall seize the gates of their foes.

18   All the nations of the earth shall bless themselves by your descendants, because you have obeyed My command."

19   Abraham then returned to his servants, and they departed together for Beer-sheba; and Abraham stayed in Beer-sheba.

20   Some time later, Abraham was told, "Milcah too has borne children to your brother Nahor:

21   Uz the first-born, and Buz his brother, and Kemuel the father of Aram;

22   and Chesed, Hazo, Pildash, Jidlaph and Bethuel"—

23   Bethuel being the father of Rebekah. These eight Milcah bore to Nahor, Abraham's brother.

24   And his concubine, whose name was Reumah, also bore children: Tebah, Gaham, Tahash, and Maacah.

PLAUT'S NOTES

22:1 *Some time afterward.* According to the Rabbis, Isaac was thirty-seven years old. However, the story should be read not in chronological order but rather as an unrelated unit; here Isaac is a mere boy.

/The Rabbis took the death of Sarah (Gen. 23:1) to be immediately related to the Akedah (see Gleanings to Gen. 23:1–20, "Why Sarah Died"); therefore, with Sarah dying at 127 years of age, Isaac would be 37, having been born when his mother was 90 [1]./

2 *Moriah.* The original name is obscure and the actual location unknown. Subsequent biblical tradition, however, has suggested that it refers to the Temple mount in Jerusalem (II Chron. 3:1) [2]. It is believed that the city's famed Dome of the Rock is built over the rock on which Abraham bound his son.

/The Vulgate relates Moriah to [*mah-reh*, the Hebrew word for (vision)]; the Septuagint to "high" or "lofty"—two word plays rather than etymologies./

9 Note the staccato phrases that heighten the tension. Abraham seems to move "like a sleepwalker" [3].

13 *Ram.* The ram occupied an important place in ancient Israel's sacrificial cult (e.g., Lev. 5–15, 18; 19:21; Num. 5:8; 6:17). The image of a ram caught in the thicket was known in Ur of the Chaldees, where archeologists have found two Sumerian statues depicting the animal tied to a bush [4]. A similar substitutional offering is portrayed in Greek mythology [5].

The above translation is based, following ancient versions, on the reading [*ah-yeel echad*, Hebrew for (a ram)], while the Masoretic text has [*ah-chad*, which is Hebrew for (after or afterward)].

14 *Adonai-yireh.* "The Lord will see," an allusion to verse 8.

There is vision. Another assonance: *Adonai yera-eh.*

17 *Seize the gates of their foes.* Whereby they will possess the city.

20 *Milcah too.* Like Sarah. The names listed represent twelve tribes or princes. They parallel the twelve tribes of Israel and illustrate a duodecimal principle of tribal organization found also in extra-biblical sources.

/Others have suggested that these tribes were all Arameans [6]./

21 *Uz.* The name occurs several times in Genesis (10:23; 36:28). Job comes from "the land of Uz" (Job 1:1).

/Hence the talmudic tradition that Job lived in the days of Abraham [7]./

22 *Chesed.* Probably related to *Casdim,* Chaldeans.

24 *Concubine.* The institution of multiple marriage, with first-rank and second-rank wives, was widespread in the Fertile Crescent.

---

1. Gen. R. 56:8.

2. See Josephus, *Antiquities,* I, 13:2; Jubilees 18:13.

3. Speiser.

4. Reproduced in *From Adam to Daniel,* ed. G. Cornfeld (New York: Macmillan, 1962), p. 75.

5. Compare Euripides' play, *Iphigenia at Aulis.* On the use of the Akedah in ancient decorations, see Bernard Goldman, *The Sacred Portal* (Detroit: Wayne State University Press, 1966), pp. 53 ff.

6. Eduard Meyer, *Die Israeliten und ihre Nachbarstämme* (Halle: M. Niemeyer, 1906), p. 241.

7. Jer. Sotah 5:8, 20C. This was, however, a minority opinion. The majority held that Job was a contemporary of Moses; see B. B. 14b.

POST-READING QUESTIONS:

1) Did any of the thoughts or feelings that you addressed in your response to the first pre-reading question influence your reading of *Genesis* 22? Did this excerpt from the Hebrew Bible confirm the validity of any of these thoughts and feelings, cause you to want to rethink some or all of them, or affect you in both of these ways?

2) What are your thoughts and feelings about the story presented in *Genesis* 22? Who is answering this question? The child within you? You as an adult? Both? Neither? Is the person/Are the people responding to this post-reading question the same one/ones who answered any or all of the pre-reading questions?

3) Do you agree with John Verbeck, the contributing author, that the story in *Genesis* 22 differs from the story that Alice Miller analyzes (see p. 259)?

4) Reminding us that "[t]he practice of human sacrifice, which was well-known to the ancients and central to the cults of Israel's neighbors, stands as a backdrop to [*Genesis*] 22[,]" W. Gunther Plaut argues that, "[i]n the framework of his time and experience, Abraham [thus] could have considered the command to sacrifice his son entirely legitimate. . . . God's demand must have struck Abraham as harsh and bitter but not as ungodly" (149). Do you agree with Plaut's interpretation? Do your interpretation of and reaction to the story affect your understanding of the story's historical context?

The Perils of Obedience

STANLEY MILGRAM

Social psychologist Stanley Milgram (1933–1984) had a wide-ranging and long-standing interest in experimental research. "During his youth," one biographical source records, Milgram "was, in his [own] words, 'always doing experiments.' As he told one interviewer, 'It was as natural as breathing, and I tried to understand how everything worked'" (*Current Biography Yearbook 1979* 258). As a professional, Milgram investigated matters as diverse (and yet similar) as problems in urban living, the relationship between psychology and geography, and the possible effects of television violence on viewers' behavior. This last investigation culminated in a jointly published book entitled *Television and Antisocial Behavior: Field Experience* (1973), in which Milgram and coauthor R. Lance Shotland argue that "there was no proved connection between exposure to television violence and an individual's propensity to commit violent acts" (*Current Biography Yearbook 1979* 259).

Besides writing numerous articles, Milgram also wrote *Obedience to Authority: An Experimental View* (1974)—an outgrowth of his obedience experiments conducted when he was an assistant professor of psychology at Yale University in the early 1960s (he also taught at Harvard University and the City University of New York)—and *The Individual in a Social World: Essays and Experiments* (1977). Also artistically talented, he "won a silver medal at the International Film and Television Festival of New York for his collaborative work on the documentary film, *The City and Self* [1972]" (*Current Biography Yearbook 1979* 260). But for all of his other achievements, Milgram remains best known for his extremely influential—and controversial—studies of obedience to authority. In light of the depressingly ominous conclusions about human behavior that Milgram draws from these studies (see the reading selection that follows), there is more than a tinge of sad irony in his having been so consistently "fascinated by 'what is' as 'a band on the broader perspective of what might have been'" (ibid.). [Other sources of information for this biographical sketch are *Current Biography Yearbook 1985* 470–471 and *American Men & Women of Science: Social and Behavioral Sciences*, 13th. ed., p. 827.]

PRE-READING QUESTIONS:

1) Do you think that an ordinary person would inflict pain on someone else simply because someone in a position of authority ordered him or her to do so? What evidence can you cite to prove or support your claim?

2) Have you ever been asked to do something that you knew conflicted with your moral values? If so, what were you asked to do, how did you respond to this request, and why did you respond as you did? Would you respond now as you did then? If you've never been in such a situation, how do you think that you *might* react were you in one?

3) Do you feel that everyone is more or less responsible for her or his actions and behaviors? Can you cite and explain the meaning and significance of some examples to prove or support your position?

4) Imagine that, on the orders of an authority figure, someone electrocutes someone else. Would you react similarly to this piece of datum regardless of where you read it—for example, regardless of whether you read it in a poem, an academic essay, a prison warden's logbook, the *New York Times,* the *National Enquirer,* or a pre-reading question in your composition book?

CLOSE-READING TIP

An understanding of the notion of "responsibility" is central to an understanding of both the data produced by Milgram's experiments and Milgram's analyses of these data. As you read the following essay, note those moments when Milgram implicitly or explicitly links an experimental subject's acceptance or rejection of responsibility to her/his decision to disobey or obey the experimenter. Also, see if you agree with Milgram that an understanding of the experimental data concerning the relationship between responsibility and obedience to authority sheds light on the nature and consequences of what Milgram calls "socially organized evil in modern society" (paragraph 60). Attempting to accomplish these two tasks, consider, for example, what Milgram writes in paragraphs 13–16, 21, 45, 50, 52, and 60.

1   Obedience is as basic an element in the structure of social life as one can point to. Some system of authority is a requirement of all communal living, and it is only the person dwelling in isolation who is not forced to respond, with defiance or submission, to the commands of others. For many people, obedience is a deeply ingrained behavior tendency, indeed a potent impulse overriding training in ethics, sympathy, and moral conduct.

2   The dilemma inherent in submission to authority is ancient, as old as the story of Abraham, and the question of whether one should obey when commands conflict with conscience has been argued by Plato, dramatized in *Antigone*, and treated to philosophic analysis in almost every historical epoch. Conservative philosophers argue that the very fabric of society is threatened by disobedience, while humanists stress the primacy of the individual conscience.

3   The legal and philosophic aspects of obedience are of enormous import, but they say very little about how most people behave in concrete situations. I set up a simple experiment at Yale University to test how much pain an ordinary citizen would inflict on another person simply because he was ordered to by an experimental scientist. Stark authority was pitted against the subjects' strongest moral imperatives against hurting others, and, with the subjects' ears ringing with the screams of the victims, authority won more often than not. The extreme willingness of adults to go to almost any lengths on the command of an authority constitutes the chief finding of the study and the fact most urgently demanding explanation.

4   In the basic experimental design, two people come to a psychology laboratory to take part in a study of memory and learning. One of them is designated as a "teacher" and the other a "learner." The experimenter explains that the study is concerned with the effects of punishment on learning. The learner is conducted into a room, seated in a kind of miniature electric chair; his arms are strapped to prevent excessive movement, and an electrode is attached to his wrist. He is told that he will be read lists of simple word pairs, and that he will then be tested on his ability to remember the second word of a pair when he hears the first one again. Whenever he makes an error, he will receive electric shocks of increasing intensity.

5   The real focus of the experiment is the teacher. After watching the learner being strapped into place, he is seated before an impressive shock generator. The instrument panel consists of thirty lever switches set in a horizontal line. Each switch is clearly labeled with a voltage designation ranging from 15 to 450 volts. The following designations are clearly indicated for groups of four switches, going from left to right: Slight Shock, Moderate Shock, Strong Shock, Very Strong Shock, Intense Shock, Extreme Intensity Shock, Danger: Severe Shock. (Two switches after this last designation are simply marked XXX.)

6   When a switch is depressed, a pilot light corresponding to each switch is illuminated in bright red; an electric buzzing is heard; a blue light, labeled

"voltage energizer," flashes; the dial on the voltage meter swings to the right; and various relay clicks sound off.

7   The upper left-hand corner of the generator is labeled shock generator, type zlb, dyson instrument company, waltham, mass. output 15 volts–450 volts.

8   Each subject is given a sample 45-volt shock from the generator before his run as teacher, and the jolt strengthens his belief in the authenticity of the machine.

9   The teacher is a genuinely naíve subject who has come to the laboratory for the experiment. The learner, or victim, is actually an actor who receives no shock at all. The point of the experiment is to see how far a person will proceed in a concrete and measurable situation in which he is ordered to inflict increasing pain on a protesting victim.

10   Conflict arises when the man receiving the shock begins to show that he is experiencing discomfort. At 75 volts, he grunts; at 120 volts, he complains loudly; at 150, he demands to be rel ased from the experiment. As the voltage increases, his protests become more vehement and emotional. At 285 volts, his response can be described only as an agonized scream. Soon thereafter, he makes no sound at all.

11   For the teacher, the situation quickly becomes one of gripping tension. It is not a game for him; conflict is intense and obvious. The manifest suffering of the learner presses him to quit; but each time he hesitates to administer a shock, the experimenter orders him to continue. To extricate himself from this plight, the subject must make a clear break with authority.[1]

12   The subject, Gretchen Brandt,[2] is an attractive thirty-one-year-old medical technician who works at the Yale Medical School. She had emigrated from Germany five years before.

13   On several occasions when the learner complains, she turns to the experimenter coolly and inquires, "Shall I continue"? She promptly returns to her task when the experimenter asks her to do so. At the administration of 210 volts, she turns to the experimenter, remarking firmly, "Well, I'm sorry, I don't think we should continue."

EXPERIMENTER: The experiment requires that you go on until he has learned all the word pairs correctly.

BRANDT: He has a heart condition, I'm sorry. He told you that before.

EXPERIMENTER: The shocks may be painful but they are not dangerous.

BRANDT: Well, I'm sorry, I think when shocks continue like this, they are dangerous. You ask him if he wants to get out. It's his free will.

EXPERIMENTER: It is absolutely essential that we continue. . .

BRANDT: I'd like you to ask him. We came here of our free will. If he wants to continue I'll go ahead. He told you he had a heart condition. I'm sorry. I don't

---

[1]The ethical problems of carrying out an experiment of this sort are too complex to be dealt with here, but they receive extended treatment in the book from which this article is adapted [Milgram's note].

[2]Names of subjects described in this piece have been changed [Milgram's note].

want to be responsible for anything happening to him. I wouldn't like it for me either.

EXPERIMENTER: You have no other choice.

BRANDT: I think we are here on our own free will. I don't want to be responsible if anything happens to him. Please understand that.

14 She refuses to go further and the experiment is terminated.

15 The woman is firm and resolute throughout. She indicates in the interview that she was in no way tense or nervous, and this corresponds to her controlled appearance during the experiment. She feels that the last shock she administered to the learner was extremely painful and reiterates that she "did not want to be responsible for any harm to him."

16 The woman's straightforward, courteous behavior in the experiment, lack of tension, and total control of her own action seem to make disobedience a simple and rational deed. Her behavior is the very embodiment of what I envisioned would be true for almost all subjects.

. . .

17 Before the experiments, I sought predictions about the outcome from various kinds of people—psychiatrists, college sophomores, middle-class adults, graduate students and faculty in the behavioral sciences. With remarkable similarity, they predicted that virtually all subjects would refuse to obey the experimenter. The psychiatrists, specifically predicted that most subjects would not go beyond 150 volts, when the victim makes his first explicit demand to be freed. They expected that only 4 percent would reach 300 volts, and that only a pathological fringe of about one in a thousand would administer the highest shock on the board.

18 These predictions were unequivocally wrong. Of the forty subjects in the first experiment, twenty-five obeyed the orders of the experimenter to the end, punishing the victim until they reached the most potent shock available on the generator. After 450 volts were administered three times, the experimenter called a halt to the session. Many obedient subjects then heaved sighs of relief, mopped their brows, rubbed their fingers over their eyes, or nervously fumbled cigarettes. Other displayed only minimal signs of tension from beginning to end.

19 When the very first experiments were carried out, Yale undergraduates were used as subjects, and about 60 percent of them were fully obedient. A colleague of mine immediately dismissed these findings as having no relevance to "ordinary" people, asserting that Yale undergraduates are a highly aggressive, competitive bunch who step on each other's necks on the slightest provocation. He assured me that when "ordinary" people were tested, the results would be quite different. As we moved from the pilot studies to the regular experimental series, people drawn from every stratum of New Haven life came to be employed in the experiment: professionals, white-collar workers, unemployed

persons, and industrial workers. *The experimental outcome was the same as we had observed among the students.*

20   Moreover, when the experiments were repeated in Princeton, Munich, Rome, South Africa, and Australia, the level of obedience was invariably somewhat *higher* than found in the investigation reported in this article. Thus one scientist in Munich found 85 percent of his subjects obedient.

. . .

21   Fred Prozi's reactions, if more dramatic than most, illuminate the conflicts experienced by others in less visible form. About fifty years old and unemployed at the time of the experiment, he has a goodnatured, if slightly dissolute, appearance, and he strikes people as a rather ordinary fellow. He begins the session calmly but becomes tense as it proceeds. After delivering the 180-volt shock, he pivots around in his chair and, shaking his head, addresses the experimenter in agitated tones:

PROZI: I can't stand it. I'm not going to kill that man in there. You hear him hollering?

EXPERIMENTER: As I told you before, the shocks may be painful, but . . .

PROZI: But he's hollering. He can't stand it. What's going to happen to him?

EXPERIMENTER: (his voice is patient, matter-of-fact): The experiment requires that you continue, Teacher.

PROZI: Aaah, but, unh, I'm not going to get that man sick in there—know what I mean?

EXPERIMENTER: Whether the learner likes it or not, we must go on, through all the word pairs.

PROZI: I refuse to take the responsibility. He's in there hollering!

EXPERIMENTER: It's absolutely essential that you continue, Prozi.

PROZI: (indicating the unused question): There's too many left here, I mean, Jeez, if he gets them wrong, there's too many of them left. I mean, who's going to take the responsibility if anything happens to that gentleman?

EXPERIMENTER: I'm responsible for anything that happens to him. Continue, please.

PROZI: All right. (Consults list of words.) The next one's "Slow—walk, truck, dance, music." Answer, please. (A buzzing sound indicates the learner has signaled his answer.) Wrong. A hundred and ninety-five volts. "Dance." (Zzumph!)

LEARNER (YELLING): Let me out of here! My heart's bothering me! (Teacher looks at experimenter.)

EXPERIMENTER: Continue, please.

LEARNER (SCREAMING):Let me out of here! You have no right to keep me here! Let me out of here, my heart's bothering me, let me out!

PROZI (SHAKES HEAD, PATS THE TABLE NERVOUSLY): You see, he's hollering. Hear that? Gee, I don't know.

EXPERIMENTER: The experiment requires . . .

PROZI (INTERRUPTING): I know it does, sir, but I mean—hunh! He don't know what he's getting in for. He's up to 195 volts! (Experiment continues, through 210 volts, 225 volts, 240 volts, 255 volts, 270 volts, at which point Prozi, with evident relief, runs out of word-pair questions.)

EXPERIMENTER: You'll have to go back to the beginning of that page and go through them again until he's learned them all correctly.

PROZI: Aw, no. I'm not going to kill that man. You mean I've got to keep going up with the scale? No sir. He's hollering in there. I'm not going to give him 450 volts.

EXPERIMENTER: The experiment requires that you go on.

LEARNER: Ohhh. I absolutely refuse to answer anymore. (Shouting urgently now.) Let me out of here! You can't hold me here! Get me out. Get-me-out-of-here!

EXPERIMENTER: Continue. The next word is "Green," please.

PROZI: "Green—grass, hat, ink, apple." (Nothing happens. No answering buzz. Just gloomy silence.)

PROZI: I don't think he is going to answer.

EXPERIMENTER: If the learner doesn't answer in a reasonable time, about four or five seconds, consider the answer wrong. And follow the same procedures you have been doing for wrong answers. Say, "Wrong," tell him the number of volts, give him the punishment, read him the correct answer. Continue, please.

PROZI: "Green—grass, hat, ink, apple." Answer, please. (More silence. Subject just sits there.)

EXPERIMENTER: Go on with the procedure, please.

PROZI: Three hundred and fifteen volts. The answer is "ink." (Zzumph!)

LEARNER: Ohh. Oooohh.

PROZI (relieved to hear response): Next one . . .

LEARNER: I absolutely refuse to answer.

PROZI: You got to. You get a shock if you don't answer. (Experiment continues with learner refusing to answer, and, finally, failing even to grunt or groan. At 375 volts, the subject stands up.)

PROZI: I think something's happening to that fellow in there. I don't get no answer. He was hollering at less voltage. Can't you check in and see if he's all right, please?

EXPERIMENTER (with same detached calm): Not once we've started. Please continue, Teacher.

PROZI (sits down, sighs deeply): "Cool—day, shade, water, paint." answer, please. Are you all right in there? Are you all right?

EXPERIMENTER: Please continue, Teacher. Continue, please. (Subject pushes lever. Zzumph!)

PROZI (swiveling around in his chair): Something's happened to that man in there. (Swiveling back.) Next one. "Low—dollar, necklace, moon, paint."

(Turning around again.) Something's happened to that man in there. You better check in on him, sir. He won't answer or nothing.

EXPERIMENTER: Continue. Go on, please.

PROZI: You accept all responsibility?

EXPERIMENTER: The responsibility is mine. Correct. Please go on. (Subject returns to his list, starts running through words as rapidly as he can read them, works through to 450 volts.)

PROZI: That's that.

EXPERIMENTER: Continue using the 450 switch for each wrong answer. Continue, please.

PROZI: But I don't get anything!

EXPERIMENTER: Please continue. The next word is "white."

PROZI: Don't you think you should look in on him, please?

EXPERIMENTER: Not once we've started the experiment.

PROZI: What if he's dead in there? (Gestures toward the room with the electric chair.) I mean, he told me he can't stand the shock, sir. I don't mean to be rude, but I think you should look in on him. All you have to do is look in on him. All you have to do is look in the door. I don't get no answer, no noise. Something might have happened to the gentleman in there, sir.

EXPERIMENTER: We must continue. Go on, please.

PROZI: You mean keep giving him what? Four-hundred-fifty volts, what he's got now?

EXPERIMENTER: That's correct. Continue. The next word is "white."

PROZI (now at a furious pace): "White—cloud, horse, rock, house." Answer, please. The answer is "horse." Four hundred and fifty volts. (Zzumph!) Next word, "Bag—paint, music, clown, girl." The answer is "paint." Four hundred and fifty volts. (Zzumph!) Next word is "Short—sentence, movie . . . "

EXPERIMENTER: Excuse me, Teacher. We'll have to discontinue the experiment.

. . .

22   Morris Braverman, another subject, is a thirty-nine-year-old social worker. He looks older than his years because of his bald head and serious demeanor. His brow is furrowed, as if all the world's burdens were carried on his face. He appears intelligent and concerned.

23   When the learner refuses to answer and the experimenter instructs Braverman to treat the absence of an answer as equivalent to a wrong answer, he takes his instruction to heart. Before administering 300 volts he asserts officiously to the victim, "Mr. Wallace, your silence has to be considered as a wrong answer." Then he administers the shock. He offers halfheartedly to change places with the learner, then asks the experimenter. "Do I have to follow these instructions literally?" He is satisfied with the experimenter's answer that he does. His very refined and authoritative manner of speaking is increasingly broken up by wheezing laughter.

24   The experimenter's notes on Mr. Braverman at the last few shocks are:

25 *Almost breaking up now each time gives shock. Rubbing face to hide laughter.*
26 *Squinting, trying to hide face with hand, still laughing.*
27 *Cannot control his laughter at this point no matter what he does.*
28 *Clenching fist, pushing it onto table.*

29 In an interview after the session, Mr. Braverman summarizes the experiment with impressive fluency and intelligence. He feels the experiment may have been designed also to "test the effects on the teacher of being in an essentially sadistic role, as well as the reactions of a student to a learning situation that was authoritative and punitive." When asked how painful the last few shocks administered to the learner were, he indicates that the most extreme category on the scale is not adequate (it read EXTREMELY PAINFUL) and places his mark at the edge of the scale with an arrow carrying it beyond the scale.

30 It is almost impossible to convey the greatly relaxed, sedate quality of his conversation in the interview. In the most relaxed terms, he speaks about his severe inner tension.

EXPERIMENTER: At what point were you most tense or nervous?
MR. BRAVERMAN: Well, when he first began to cry out in pain, and I realized this was hurting him. This got worse when he just blocked and refused to answer. These was I. I'm a nice person, I think, hurting somebody, and caught up in what seemed a mad situation . . . and in the interest of science, one goes through with it.

31 When the interviewer pursues the general question of tension, Mr. Braverman spontaneously mentions his laughter.

32 "My reactions were awfully peculiar. I don't know if you were watching me, but my reactions were giggly, and trying to stifle laughter. This isn't the way I usually am. This was a sheer reaction to a totally impossible situation. And my reaction was to the situation of having to hurt somebody. And being totally helpless and caught up in a set of circumstances where I just couldn't deviate and I couldn't try to help. This is what got me."

33 Mr. Braverman, like all subjects, was told the actual nature and purpose of the experiment, and a year later he affirmed in a questionnaire that he had learned something of personal importance: "What appalled me was that I could possess this capacity for obedience and compliance to a central idea, i.e., the value of a memory experiment, even after it became clear that continued adherence to this value was at the expense of violation of another value, i.e., don't hurt someone who is helpless and not hurting you. As my wife said, 'You can call yourself Eichmann.' I hope I deal more effectively with any future conflicts of values I encounter."

. . .

34 One theoretical interpretation of this behavior holds that all people harbor deeply aggressive instincts continually pressing for expression, and that the experiment provides institutional justification for the release of these impulses. According to this view, if a person is placed in a situation in which he has complete power over another individual, whom he may punish as much as he

likes, all that is sadistic and bestial in man comes to the fore. The impulse to shock the victim is seen to flow from the potent aggressive tendencies, which are part of the motivational life of the individual, and the experiment, because it provides social legitimacy, simply opens the door to their expression.

35 It becomes vital, therefore, to compare the subject's performance when he is under orders and when he is allowed to choose the shock level.

36 The procedure was identical to our standard experiment, except that the teacher was told that he was free to select any shock level on any of the trials. (The experimenter took pains to point out that the teacher could use the highest levels on the generator, the lowest, any in between, or any combination of levels.) Each subject proceeded for thirty critical trials. The learner's protests were coordinated to standard shock levels, his first grunt coming at 75 volts, his first vehement protest at 150 volts.

37 The average shock used during the thirty critical trials was less than 60 volts—lower than the point at which the victim showed the first signs of discomfort. Three of the forty subjects did not go beyond the very lowest level on the board, twenty-eight went no higher than 75 volts, and thirty-eight did not go beyond the first loud protest at 150 volts. Two subjects provided the exception, administering up to 325 and 450 volts, but the overall result was that the great majority of people delivered very low, usually painless, shocks when the choice was explicitly up to them.

38 This condition of the experiment undermines another commonly offered explanation of the subjects' behavior—that those who shocked the victim at the most severe levels came only from the sadistic fringe of society. If one considers that almost two-thirds of the participants fall into the category of "obedient" subjects, and that they represented ordinary people drawn from working, managerial, and professional classes, the argument becomes very shaky. Indeed, it is highly reminiscent of the issue that arose in connection with Hannah Arendt's 1963 book, *Eichmann in Jerusalem*. Arendt contended that the prosecution's effort to depict Eichmann as a sadistic monster was fundamentally wrong, that he came closer to being an uninspired bureaucrat who simply sat at his desk and did his job. For asserting her views, Arendt became the object of considerable scorn, even calumny. Somehow, it was felt that the monstrous deeds carried out by Eichmann required a brutal, twisted personality, evil incarnate. After witnessing hundreds of ordinary persons submit to the authority in our own experiments, I must conclude that Arendt's conception of the banality of evil comes closer to the truth than one might dare imagine. The ordinary person who shocked the victim did so out of a sense of obligation—an impression of his duties as a subject—and not from any peculiarly aggressive tendencies.

39 This is, perhaps, the most fundamental lesson of our study: ordinary people, simply doing their jobs, and without any particular hostility on their part, can become agents in a terrible destructive process. Moreover, even when the destructive effects of their work become patently clear, and they are asked to

carry out actions incompatible with fundamental standards of morality, relatively few people have the resources needed to resist authority.

40 Many of the people were in some sense against what they did to the learner, and many protested even while they obeyed. Some were totally convinced of the wrongness of their actions but could not bring themselves to make an open break with authority. They often derived satisfaction from their thoughts and felt that—within themselves, at least—they had been on the side of the angels. They tried to reduce strain by obeying the experimenter but "only slightly," encouraging the learner, touching the generator switches gingerly. When interviewed, such a subject would stress that he had "asserted my humanity" by administering the briefest shock possible. Handling the conflict in this manner was easier than defiance.

41 The situation is constructed so that there is no way the subject can stop shocking the learner without violating the experimenter's definitions of his own competence. The subject fears that he will appear arrogant, untoward, and rude if he breaks off. Although these inhibiting emotions appear small in scope alongside the violence being done to the learner, they suffuse the mind and feelings of the subject, who is miserable at the prospect of having to repudiate the authority to his face. (When the experiment was altered so that the experimenter gave his instructions by telephone instead of in person, only a third as many people were fully obedient through 450 volts.) It is a curious thing that a measure of compassion on the part of the subject—an unwillingness to "hurt" the experimenter's feelings—is part of those binding forces inhibiting his disobedience. The withdrawal of such deference may be as painful to the subject as to the authority he defies.

· · ·

42 The subjects do not derive satisfaction from inflicting pain, but they often like the feeling they get from pleasing the experimenter. They are proud of doing a good job, obeying the experimenter under difficult circumstances. While the subjects administered only mild shocks on their own initiative, one experimental variation showed that, under orders, 30 percent of them were willing to deliver 450 volts even when they had to forcibly push the learner's hand down on the electrode.

43 Bruno Batta is a thirty-seven-year-old welder who took part in the variation requiring the use of force. He was born in New Haven, his parents in Italy. He has a rough-hewn face that conveys a conspicuous lack of alertness. He has some difficulty in mastering the experimental procedure and needs to be corrected by the experimenter several times. He shows appreciation for the help and willingness to do what is required. After the 150-volt level, Batta has to force the learner's hand down on the shock plate, since the learner himself refuses to touch it.

44 When the learner first complains, Mr. Batta pays no attention to him. His face remains impassive, as if to dissociate himself from the learner's disruptive behav-

ior. When the experimenter instructs him to force the learner's hand down, he adopts a rigid, mechanical procedure. He tests the generator switch. When it fails to function, he immediately forces the learner's hand onto the shock plate. All the while he maintains the same rigid mask. The learner, seated alongside him, begs him to stop, but with robotic impassivity he continues the procedure.

45 What is extraordinary is his apparent total indifference to the learner; he hardly takes cognizance of him as a human being. Meanwhile, he relates to the experimenter in a submissive and courteous fashion.

46 At the 330-volt level, the learner refuses not only to touch the shock plate but also to provide any answers. Annoyed, Batta turns to him, and chastises him: "You better answer and get it over with. We can't stay here all night." These are the only words he directs to the learner in the course of an hour. Never again does he speak to him. The scene is brutal and depressing, his hard, impassive face showing total indifference as he subdues the screaming learner and gives him shocks. He seems to derive no pleasure from the act itself, only quiet satisfaction at doing his job properly.

47 When he administers 450 volts, he turns to the experimenter and asks, "Where do we go from here, Professor?" His tone is deferential and expresses his willingness to be a cooperative subject, in contrast to the learner's obstinacy.

48 At the end of the session he tells the experimenter how honored he has been to help him, and in a moment of contrition, remarks, "Sir, sorry it couldn't have been a full experiment."

49 He has done his honest best. It is only the deficient behavior of the learner that has denied the experimenter full satisfaction.

50 The essence of obedience is that a person comes to view himself as the instrument for carrying out another person's wishes, and he therefore no longer regards himself as responsible for his actions. Once this critical shift of viewpoint has occurred, all of the essential features of obedience follow. The most far-reaching consequence is that the person feels responsible *to* the authority directing him but feels no responsibility *for* the content of the actions that the authority prescribes. Morality does not disappear—it acquires a radically different focus: the subordinate person feels shame or pride depending on how adequately he has performed the actions called for by authority.

51 Language provides numerous terms to pinpoint this type of morality: *loyalty, duty, discipline* all are terms heavily saturated with moral meaning and refer to the degree to which a person fulfills his obligations to authority. They refer not to the "goodness" of the person per se but to the adequacy with which a subordinate fulfills his socially defined role. The most frequent defense of the individual who has performed a heinous act under command of authority is that he has simply done his duty. In asserting this defense, the individual is not introducing an alibi concocted for the moment but is reporting honestly on the psychological attitude induced by submission to authority.

52   For a person to feel responsible for his actions, he must sense that the behavior has flowed from "the self." In the situation we have studied, subjects have precisely the opposite view of their actions—namely, they see them as originating in the motives of some other person. Subjects in the experiment frequently said, "If it were up to me, I would not have administered shocks to the learner."

53   Once authority has been isolated as the cause of the subject's behavior, it is legitimate to inquire into the necessary elements of authority and how it must be perceived in order to gain his compliance. We conducted some investigations into the kinds of changes that would cause the experimenter to lose his power and to be disobeyed by the subject. Some of the variations revealed that:

54   • *The experimenter's physical presence has a marked impact on his authority.* As cited earlier, obedience dropped off sharply when orders were given by telephone. The experimenter could often induce a disobedient subject to go on by returning to the laboratory.

55   • *Conflicting authority severely paralyzes action.* When two experimenters of equal status, both seated at the command desk, gave incompatible orders, no shocks were delivered past the point of their disagreement.

56   • *The rebellious action of others severely undermines authority.* In one variation, three teachers (two actors and a real subject) administered a test and shocks. When the two actors disobeyed the experimenter and refused to go beyond a certain shock level, thirty-six of forty subjects joined their disobedient peers and refused as well.

57   Although the experimenter's authority was fragile in some respects, it is also true that he had almost none of the tools used in ordinary command structures. For example, the experimenter did not threaten the subjects with punishment—such as loss of income, community ostracism, or jail—for failure to obey. Neither could he offer incentives. Indeed, we should expect the experimenter's authority to be much less than that of someone like a general, since the experimenter has no power to enforce his imperatives, and since participation in a psychological experiment scarcely evokes the sense of urgency and dedication found in warfare. Despite these limitations, he still managed to command a dismaying degree of obedience.

58   I will cite one final variation of the experiment that depicts a dilemma that is more common in everyday life. The subject was not ordered to pull the level that shocked the victim, but merely to perform a subsidiary task (administering the word-pair test) while another person administered the shock. In this situation, thirty-seven of forty adults continued to the highest level on the shock generator. Predictably, they excused their behavior by saying that the responsibility belonged to the man who actually pulled the switch. This may illustrate a dangerously typical arrangement in a complex society: it is easy to ignore responsibility when one is only an intermediate link in a chain of action.

59   The problem of obedience is not wholly psychological. The form and shape of society and the way it is developing have much to do with it. There was a time, perhaps, when people were able to give a fully human response to any situation because they were fully absorbed in it as human beings. But as soon as there was a division of labor things changed. Beyond a certain point, the breaking up of society into people carrying out narrow and very special jobs takes away from the human quality of work and life. A person does not get to see the whole situation but only a small part of it, and is thus unable to act without some kind of overall direction. He yields to authority but in doing so is alienated from his own actions.

60   Even Eichmann was sickened when he toured the concentration camps, but he had only to sit at a desk and shuffle papers. At the same time the man in the camp who actually dropped Cyclon-b into the gas chambers was able to justify *his* behavior on the ground that he was only following orders from above. Thus there is a fragmentation of the total human act; no one is confronted with the consequences of his decision to carry out the evil act. The person who assumes responsibility has evaporated. Perhaps this is the most common characteristic of socially organized evil in modern society.

POST-READING QUESTIONS:

1) In light of your understanding of Milgram's essay, do you want to reconsider your responses to the first two pre-reading questions?

2) Do you agree with the ideas that Milgram puts forth in the final sentence of paragraph 58? Having read Milgram's essay, do you want to amend your response to the third pre-reading question?

3) What do you make of Morris Braverman's post-experiment comments, which he offers in paragraphs 29–33? Would Milgram likely agree with your evaluation of these comments?

4) Does Milgram present a stated or implied thesis? Does he offer several theses? Does he cite weighty enough evidence to support or prove his thesis/theses? Are his analyses of this evidence sufficient?

5) If you were the editor of a paper such as the *National Enquirer,* would you publish Milgram's article? If so, would you make any changes to it?

6) If Stanley Milgram, Christopher R. Browning (see p. 107), and Fred E. Katz (see p. 95) met to discuss the topic of obedience to authority, what might they tell each other? Would they always agree with each other's views concerning this topic? What examples from their own and from each other's work might they cite to prove or support their points?

Early Years

RUDOLPH HÖSS

Rudolph Höss (1900–1947) was the commandant of the infamous concentration camp complex at Auschwitz, which at his war crimes trial in Nuremberg he called "'the greatest human extermination center of all time'" (Sachar 24). No one knows for certain how many people died in Auschwitz, but even conservative estimates put the figure in the millions (at Auschwitz-Birkenau, where people were deliberately gassed to death, the vast majority of the exterminated vicims were Jews). In his memoirs, which he wrote between 1946 and 1947, Höss claims that, although he is "responsible for [everything that took place at Auschwitz] because according to camp regulations: the camp Kommandant is *fully responsible* for everything that happens in his camp[,]" he "never personally mistreated a prisoner, or even killed one" (*Death Dealer* 184 and 183; author's italics).

How does one describe Höss? The philosopher Bertrand Russell describes him as "'a very ordinary little man' who, nonetheless, was 'perhaps the greatest executioner of all time'" (Katz 282). This characterization may or may not be entirely accurate. Höss grew up in a religious household, "took up farming[,] and married. He had five children, two of whom were born during [his] service in concentration camps." However, he also "joined a reactionary organization after [the First World War]. . . [and] was imprisoned for a political murder in 1923" (ibid.). And he "regarded his family life at Auschwitz to be exceedingly happy—a 'paradise,' he called it—that was only occasionally visited by the realities of his monstrous work. . . . There were bucolic joys of quiet walks in the woods, not far from the electric fences and the chimneys" (ibid. 290).

Ordinary or not, Höss says towards the end of his life that "[w]ithout realizing it, [he] became a cog in the wheel of the huge extermination machine of the Third Reich." He continues: "The machine is smashed, the motor has perished, and I must perish with it. The world demands it" (*Death Dealer* 186). Having been found guilty initially by the Nuremberg Tribunal and subsequently by a Polish war crimes tribunal, Höss was hanged on April 16, 1947, "for his participation in the greatest crime in history. His body was cremated and his ashes scattered. So ended the Death Dealer of the Third Reich. . . " (Paskuly, in *Death Dealer* 197).

PRE-READING QUESTIONS:

1) What do you imagine the childhood years of high-ranking Nazis might have been like?

2) Have you ever felt closer to animals than to people?

3) Did you tend to respect, fear, love, or obey one of your parents or parent figures more than you respected, feared, loved, or obeyed the other or others?

4) In general, would you describe your childhood as a normal, happy one? Were you particularly religious? Did you have many friends? Did people generally like you?

5) In general, how would you describe your relationship with your parents and siblings and their relationship with each other?

6) Do you tend to trust what you read in autobiographies or memoirs?

CLOSE-READING TIP

Consciously or unconsciously, Höss gives away quite a bit of telling information about himself as a child, information that seems retrospectively—and ominously—germane to his later role as SS Commandant of Auschwitz. As you read and reread the following excerpt from his memoirs, note those details that, however casually Höss seems to give them, strike you as containing more than just "surface" meaning. Consider, for example, relevant passages in paragraphs 5 and 7–10.

---

1 My family lived in an average home outside of Baden-Baden until I was six. In the surrounding area there were only isolated farmhouses. I had no playmates at all, because all the children in the neighborhood were older, so my social life depended on adults. This wasn't much fun, and I always tried, whenever possible, to escape their supervision and go off exploring by myself. I was often lured into the nearby Black Forest by the tall pine trees. I never went in very far and always kept sight of our valley from the mountain slopes. Actually, I was not allowed to go into the forest alone because when I was much younger some passing Gypsies had found me playing by myself and had taken me with them. Fortunately, a neighboring farmer happened to pass by, recognized me, snatched me from the Gypsies and brought me home.

2 I was especially attracted to the large city water tower. For hours on end I would listen in secret to the rushing water behind its thick walls. I never could understand what this was, even though my parents tried to explain it to me. Most of the time, however, I went to the stables to see the horses. If someone wanted to find me, all he had to do was to go to the stables. I was absolutely fascinated by horses. There simply wasn't enough time for stroking, talking to, and feeding them sweets. If the grooming brushes were handy, I would immediately begin brushing and combing the horses. The farmer was always afraid that I would get hurt as I would creep between the horses' legs as I brushed them. Never did any animal ever hit, bite, or harm me in any way. Even the wildest bull the farmer had was my best friend. I was never afraid of dogs, and they never harmed me either.

3 My favorite trick was to sneak off to the barns when I was supposed to be taking a nap. My mother tried everything to break me of this obsessive love of animals, but it was completely useless because I didn't pay any attention to her. She thought it was too dangerous. I enjoyed playing by myself or finding

things to do alone. I didn't like it when others tried to join in and I didn't like being watched by anybody. I was and would always be a loner.

4   I had an irresistible passion for water. I had to constantly wash and bathe. I would take any opportunity to wash or bathe in a tub or stream that flowed through our garden. I ruined a lot of toys and clothes by doing this. Even today I have this passion for water.

5   When I was six years old, we moved to the Mannheim area, which was outside the city, but to my deepest regret there were no stables and no livestock. My mother often reminisced how for weeks on end I was heartsick for my animals and my forest. My parents did all they could then to help me get over my great love of animals. They didn't succeed because I always found books with pictures of animals, and I would sneak off and dream about my cows and horses.

6   On my seventh birthday, I was given Hans, a coal-black pony with flashing eyes and a long mane. I was exploding with joy. I had finally found my friend. Hans was so faithful that he followed me everywhere, just like a dog. When my parents were away, I would even take him up to my room. I got along well with the servants, and they looked the other way as far as my childish behavior was concerned, and they never told on me. In the area where we now lived there were playmates my age. With the few friends I had, I played the same childish games and all the pranks as children have throughout the ages all over the world. But best of all, I enjoyed going with Hans into the Haardt Forest, where we were all alone, riding for hours on end without a living soul around.

7   Life became more serious once school started. During the first years of elementary school, nothing worth mentioning happened. I studied hard, did my homework as quickly as possible, so that I could have time to play around with Hans. My parents gave me the freedom to do as I wanted because my father had made a vow that I would lead a religious life and become a priest. The way I was raised was entirely affected by this. I was raised in a strong military fashion because of my father. Because of his faith, there was a heavy religious atmosphere in our family. My father was a fanatic Catholic. During our time in Baden-Baden, I seldom saw him because he traveled for months at a time or was busy with other matters. This all changed in Mannheim. My father now took the time every day to give me some attention, whether it was to look over my schoolwork or talk about my future vocation as a priest. I especially liked his stories about his service in East Africa: his descriptions of the battles with the rebellious natives, their culture and work, and their mysterious religious worship. I listened in radiant rapture as he spoke of the blessed and civilizing activities of the missionary society. I resolved that I would become a missionary no matter what, and that I would go into darkest Africa, even venture into the center of the primeval forest. It was especially exciting when one of the old, bearded African fathers who knew my father in

East Africa came to visit. I did not budge from the spot so that I would not miss a single word of the conversation. Yes, I even forgot all about my Hans.

8   My parents constantly had guests at our house so they seldom went to parties. Our house was the meeting place for the religious from all areas. My father became even more devout as the years passed. As time allowed, he would take me on pilgrimages to the holy places of our country, yes, even to the hermitages in Switzerland and Our Lady of Lourdes in France. He fervently prayed for heaven's blessing so I would become an inspired priest. I myself believed deeply, as much as one can as a child, and I took my religious duties seriously. I prayed with the proper childish reverence and was zealous as an altar boy. I was taught to obey all adults, especially older people, and treat them with respect no matter what the circumstances. Most of all, it was essential to be helpful, and this was my highest duty. It was emphatically pointed out again and again that I carry out the requests and orders of parents, teachers, priests, and all adults, even the servants, and that this principle be respectfully obeyed. I was not permitted to leave anything unfinished. Whatever they said was always right. This type of training is in my flesh and blood.

9   I can still recall how my father was a determined opponent of the Kaiser's government because he was such a fanatic Catholic. But in spite of his political views, he constantly reminded his friends that the laws of the government were to be obeyed unquestioningly. Even from childhood on up, I was trained in a complete awareness of duty. Attention to duty was greatly respected in my parent's home, so that all orders would be performed exactly and conscientiously. Each person always had certain responsibilities. My father paid special attention to see that I obeyed all his orders and instructions, which were to be carried out painfully. I can still remember a time when he got me out of bed because I left the saddle blanket hanging in the garden instead of in the barn where he told me to hang it to dry out. I had simply forgotten about it. He repeated over and over that from little things which seemed unimportant carelessness generally develops into great tragedy. I did not understand what he meant at the time; only later would I learn through bitter experience to follow these principles.

10   A warm relationship existed between my parents, full of love, full of respect and mutual understanding. And yet, I never saw them being affectionate to one another. But at the same time, it was very seldom that they exchanged an angry or bad word between them. My two younger sisters were four and six years old. They were around my mother a great deal and loved to cuddle with her, but I refused any open show of affection, even from my early years on, much to the constant regret of my mother and all of my aunts and relatives. A handshake and a few brief words of thanks were the most that one could expect from me. Although both of my parents cared for me very much, I could never find a way to confide in them. I would never share any problems, either big or small, which occasionally depress young people. Inwardly I struggled with all these things by myself. The only one I confided in was my Hans.

He understood me, as far as I was concerned. My two sisters were very attached to me and tried repeatedly to form a good, loving relationship with me. But I never wanted to bother with them. I played with them only when I had to and then annoyed them until they ran crying to mother. I played many pranks on them. In spite of that, they cared deeply for me, and I regret to this day that I could never display a warm feeling for them. They always remained strangers to me.

11   I respected and admired my parents very much, my father as well as my mother. However, love, the kind of love which I came to know later as a parent, I could not pretend to show for them. Why was this? I cannot explain, and even today I can find no reason. I was never what you would call a good boy, or even an ideal child. I played all the pranks which a young mind in those years could invent. I ran with other boys through the wildest games and fights or whatever came along. There were always times when I had to be alone.

12   I always was able to get my way.

13   If someone did something wrong to me, I did not rest until I felt I had gotten even. I was relentless and I was feared by my classmates. Oddly enough, I sat at the same desk during my whole time in high school with a Swedish girl who wanted to become a doctor. During all the years of struggle in school, we understood each other like good buddies, and we never fought. It was customary in our high school for students to spend all of the school years with the same classmate at the same desk. . . .

POST-READING QUESTIONS:

1) Was Höss' childhood similar to that which you had imagined a high-ranking Nazi might have had? Was it similar to yours?

2) In light of your understanding of "Early Years," how would you evaluate the following passage found later in Höss' memoirs? "When something [at Auschwitz] upset me very much and it was impossible for me to go home to my family, I would climb onto my horse and ride until I chased the horrible pictures away. I often went into the horse stables during the night, and there found peace among my darlings" (163).

3) Would you consider Höss an "ordinary" or an "extraordinary" person? How do you think that *he* would answer this question? How do you think that Stanley Milgram, Christopher R. Browning, or Fred E. Katz might answer it (see pp. 276, 107, and 92)?

4) Does this reading selection help you to understand why Höss was able to be Commandant of Auschwitz, one of the most infamous death factories in the history of the world, a place of unspeakable human brutality?

5) Do you believe that Höss is telling the truth in this excerpt? If this excerpt were from a reputable biography of Höss, would you consider it as reliable as, more reliable than, or less reliable than you consider it now?

Crito

PLATO

Along with his teacher, Socrates (470?–399 B.C.E.), and his most famous student, Aristotle (384–322 B.C.E.), Plato (427?–347 B.C.E.) helped shape the course that western philosophy would take for more than two millennia. Besides leaving us with some of the most influential texts in western philosophical history, Plato founded "the Academy" in Athens, "the first permanent institution devoted to philosophical research and teaching, and the prototype of all western universities" (*The Last Days of Socrates* 1). Today, whenever we routinely talk of life in academics or in "the Academy," we are paying tribute to the efforts of this great and pioneering philosopher.

Since for the most part Plato's writings are elaborations of Socrates' teachings (Socrates left no writings that we know of), philosophers often use the names Plato and Socrates interchangeably. In most of his approximately two dozen philosophical dialogues—including well-known works such as the *Symposium,* the *Republic,* and the *Sophist*—Plato presents Socrates engaged (often challenged) in discussions with others concerning pressing philosophical, political, and social issues such as justice, right moral conduct, and the like. Inevitably, Socrates' position turns out to be the dialogue's most compelling position on the issue.

In the *Crito,* for example, an imprisoned Socrates, dialoguing with his old friend Crito, argues for a typically Socratic position of right moral conduct, one that transcends both his own personal interests and, indeed, the value of his own life. Behaving according to his long-standing moral principles, Socrates chooses to die honorably rather than to live ignominiously. Like the *Euthyphro, Apology,* and *Phaedo,* the *Crito* is based on what transpired during Plato's beloved teacher's last days of life, when Socrates was awaiting death as a result of his having been (fraudulently) accused and found guilty of both corrupting the morals of the youth and not believing in the gods. Though Plato surely accepted the argument that Socrates offers in the *Crito,* one wonders if there might not have been at least a little bit of Plato in Crito, who hopes to convince his old friend to escape from prison and thus to remain alive.

In any event, "disgusted by the violence and corruption of Athenian political life, and sickened especially by [Socrates'] execution...," Plato advanced his teacher's high ethical principles by seeking "a cure for the ills of society not in politics but philosophy" (Plato "came from a family that had long played a prominent part in Athenian politics..."). Arguing for the still fascinating notion of philosopher kings, Plato "arrived at his fundamental and lasting conviction that [society's] ills would never cease until philosophers became rulers or rulers philosophers" (*The Last Days of Socrates* 1). Whether or not his prognosis is correct, we in the West would be hard-pressed to deny that Plato—and, because of him, Socrates—continues to have an overwhelming influence on our philosophical-political thinking, even, and perhaps especially, if we are unaware of the presence of his thoughts in our own ideas.

PRE-READING QUESTIONS:

1) In your opinion, are citizens always and necessarily obligated to obey the laws of their state or country? Keep your views in mind as you read Plato's *Crito*, checking to see if they affect your understanding of Socrates' ideas and, in turn, if his ideas make you wonder whether or not you still want to retain your views.

2) Did anyone ever unjustly accuse you of having done something wrong? If so, how did you react? If not, how do you think that you might react if someone were unjustly to accuse you of wrongdoing?

3) Do you believe in anything or anyone so strongly that you would never do anything to harm it or him/her, no matter what?

4) How would you characterize your friends *as* friends, distinguishing them from your acquaintances, from your enemies (if you have any), and from the many people whom you meet more or less fleetingly during the course of a normal day?

5) How would you define "living well"? Should one strive to live well?

6) How would you characterize or describe what you know or imagine to be a "philosophical dialogue"? How would you distinguish this kind of dialogue from other kinds? Do all dialogues have common traits, too?

CLOSE-READING TIP

In his dialogues with friends and students, Socrates often employed a question and answer approach—commonly referred to now as "the Socratic method" and still widely used by educators—which he had hoped would lead him and his audience to the truth concerning whatever topic they were investigating. The path leading to this truth was reason, rational thinking. As Socrates says to his friend Crito, "[I]t has always been my nature never to accept advice from any of my friends unless reflexion shows that it is the best course that reason offers" (paragraph 35). As you read the *Crito*, pay attention to those moments when Socrates alludes to or uses reasoning to make his points; try to determine whether or not his thinking is or seems reasonable and thus whether or not it enhances his position. Consider, for example, some representative passages in paragraphs 27, 35, 69, 93, and 98.

---

*   At Athens sentence of execution was normally carried out at once; but the day before Socrates' trial was also the first day of the annual Mission to Delos: a ceremony intended to commemorate the exploit of Theseus when he delivered Athens from the yearly tribute of sending young men and women as food for the Cretan Minotaur. While the State galley was absent on this mission the death penalty could not be inflicted. This year the mission took so long that Socrates was kept in prison for a month...

[SCENE: *A room in the State prison at Athens in the year 399 B.C. . . .*]*

1   SOCRATES: Here already, Crito? Surely it is still early?

2 CRITO: Indeed it is.

3 SOCRATES: About what time?

4 CRITO: Just before dawn.

5 SOCRATES: I wonder that the warder paid any attention to you.

6 CRITO: He is used to me now, Socrates, because I come here so often; besides, he is under some small obligation to me.

7 SOCRATES: Have you only just come, or have you been here for long?

8 CRITO: Fairly long.

9 SOCRATES: Then why didn't you wake me at once, instead of sitting by my bed so quietly?

10 CRITO: I wouldn't dream of such a thing, Socrates. I only wish I were not so sleepless and depressed myself. I have been wondering at you, because I saw how comfortably you were sleeping; and I deliberately didn't wake you because I wanted you to go on being as comfortable as you could. I have often felt before in the course of my life how fortunate you are in your disposition, but I feel it more than ever now in your present misfortune when I see how easily and placidly you put up with it.

11 SOCRATES: Well, really, Crito, it would be hardly suitable for a man of my age to resent having to die.

12 CRITO: Other people just as old as you are get involved in these misfortunes, Socrates, but their age doesn't keep them from resenting it when they find themselves in your position.

13 SOCRATES: Quite true. But tell me, why have you come so early?

14 CRITO: Because I bring bad news, Socrates; not so bad from your point of view, I suppose, but it will be very hard to bear for me and your other friends, and I think that I shall find it hardest of all.

15 SOCRATES: Why, what is this news? Has the boat come in from Delos—the boat which ends my reprieve when it arrives?

16 CRITO: It hasn't actually come in yet, but I expect that it will be here to-day, judging from the report of some people who have just arrived from Sunium[1] and left it there. It's quite clear from their account that it will be here to-day; and so by to-morrow, Socrates, you will have to—to end your life.

17 SOCRATES: Well, Crito, I hope that it may be for the best; if the gods will it so, so be it. All the same, I don't think it will arrive to-day.

18 CRITO: What makes you think that?

19 SOCRATES: I will try to explain. I think I am right in saying that I have to die on the day after the boat arrives?

20 CRITO: That's what the authorities say, at any rate.

---

*These comments, as well as the explanatory notes that follow *Crito*, are Hugh Tredennick's; they are all taken from Hugh Tredennick, ed., Plato, *The Last Days of Socrates*, the book from which *Crito* is also taken. [Ed. note]

[1] *Sunium:* A headland at the southern extremity of Attica and about thirty miles from Athens.

21   SOCRATES: Then I don't think it will arrive on this day that is just beginning, but on the day after. I am going by a dream that I had in the night, only a little while ago. It looks as though you were right not to wake me up.

22   CRITO: Why, what was the dream about?

23   SOCRATES: I thought I saw a gloriously beautiful woman dressed in white robes, who came up to me and addressed me in these words: 'Socrates, To the pleasant land of Phthia on the third day thou shalt come.'[2]

24   CRITO: Your dream makes no sense, Socrates.

25   SOCRATES: To my mind, Crito, it is perfectly clear.

26   CRITO: Too clear, apparently. But look here, Socrates, it is still not too late to take my advice and escape. Your death means a double calamity for me. I shall not only lose a friend whom I can never possibly replace, but besides a great many people who don't know you and me very well will be sure to think that I let you down, because I could have saved you if I had been willing to spend the money; and what could be more contemptible than to get a name for thinking more of money than of your friends? Most people will never believe that it was you who refused to leave this place although we tried our hardest to persuade you.

27   SOCRATES: But my dear Crito, why should we pay so much attention to what 'most people' think? The really reasonable people, who have more claim to be considered, will believe that the facts are exactly as they are.

28   CRITO: You can see for yourself, Socrates, that one has to think of popular opinion as well. Your present position is quite enough to show that the capacity of ordinary people for causing trouble is not confined to petty annoyances, but has hardly any limits if you once get a bad name with them.

29   SOCRATES: I only wish that ordinary people *had* an unlimited capacity for doing harm; then they might have an unlimited power for doing good; which would be a splendid thing, if it were so. Actually they have neither. They cannot make a man wise or stupid; they simply act at random.

30   CRITO: Have it that way if you like; but tell me this, Socrates. I hope that you aren't worrying about the possible effects on me and the rest of your friends, and thinking that if you escape we shall have trouble with informers for having helped you to get away, and have to forfeit all our property or pay an enormous fine, or even incur some further punishment? If any idea like that is troubling you, you can dismiss it altogether. We are quite entitled to run that risk in saving you, and even worse, if necessary. Take my advice, and be reasonable.

31   SOCRATES: All that you say is very much in my mind, Crito, and a great deal more besides.

32   CRITO: Very well, then, don't let it distress you. I know some people who are willing to rescue you from here and get you out of the country for quite a moderate sum. And then surely you realize how cheap these informers are to buy off; we shan't need much money to settle them; and I think you've got enough of my money for yourself already. And then even supposing that in

---

[2] *To the pleasant land,* etc.: The line is an echo of *Iliad* ix. 363, where Phtia (in eastern Thessaly) is the homeland of Achilles; and probably the suggestion here is simply that Socrates is going home.

your anxiety for my safety you feel that you oughtn't to spend my money, there are these foreign gentlemen staying in Athens who are quite willing to spend theirs. One of them, Simmias of Thebes, has actually brought the money with him for this very purpose; and Cebes[3] and a number of others are quite ready to do the same. So as I say, you mustn't let any fears on these grounds make you slacken your efforts to escape; and you mustn't feel any misgivings about what you said at your trial, that you wouldn't know what to do with yourself if you left this country. Wherever you go, there are plenty of places where you will find a welcome; and if you choose to go to Thessaly, I have friends there who will make much of you and give you complete protection, so that no one in Thessaly can interfere with you.

33   Besides, Socrates, I don't even feel that it is right for you to try to do what you are doing, throwing away your life when you might save it. You are doing your best to treat yourself in exactly the same way as your enemies would, or rather did, when they wanted to ruin you. What is more, it seems to me that you are letting your sons down too. You have it in your power to finish their bringing up and education, and instead of that you are proposing to go off and desert them, and so far as you are concerned they will have to take their chance. And what sort of chance are they likely to get? The sort of thing that usually happens to orphans when they lose their parents. Either one ought not to have children at all, or one ought to see their upbringing and education through to the end. It strikes me that you are taking the line of least resistance, whereas you ought to make the choice of a good man and a brave one, considering that you profess to have made goodness your object all through life. Really, I am ashamed, both on your account and on ours your friends'; it will look as though we had played something like a coward's part all through this affair of yours. First there was the way you came into court when it was quite unnecessary[4]—that was the first act; then there was the conduct of the defence—that was the second; and finally, to complete the farce, we get this situation, which makes it appear that we have let you slip out of our hands through some lack of courage and enterprise on our part, because we didn't save you, and you didn't save yourself, when it would have been quite possible and practicable, if we had been any use at all.

34   There, Socrates; if you aren't careful, besides the suffering there will be all this disgrace for you and us to bear. Come, make up your mind. Really it's too late for that now; you ought to have it made up already. There is no alternative; the whole thing must be carried through during this coming night. If we lose any more time, it can't be done, it will be too late. I appeal to you, Socrates, on every ground; take my advice and please don't be unreasonable!

35   SOCRATES: My dear Crito, I appreciate your warm feelings very much—that is, assuming that they have some justification; if not, the stronger they are, the

---

[3] *Simmias* and *Cebes* conduct most of the discussion with Socrates in the *Phaedo*.

[4] *when it was quite unnecessary:* Socrates might have left the country before the trial came on.

harder they will be to deal with. Very well, then; we must consider whether we ought to follow your advice or not. You know that this is not a new idea of mine; it has always been my nature never to accept advice from any of my friends unless reflexion shows that it is the best course that reason offers. I cannot abandon the principles which I used to hold in the past simply because this accident has happened to me; they seem to me to be much as they were, and I respect and regard the same principles now as before. So unless we can find better principles on this occasion, you can be quite sure that I shall not agree with you; not even if the power of the people conjures up fresh hordes of bogies to terrify our childish minds, by subjecting us to chains and executions and confiscations of our property.

36   Well, then, how can we consider the question most reasonably? Suppose that we begin by reverting to this view which you hold about people's opinions. Was it always right to argue that some opinions should be taken seriously but not others? Or was it always wrong? Perhaps it was right before the question of my death arose, but now we can see clearly that it was a mistaken persistence in a point of view which was really irresponsible nonsense. I should like very much to inquire into this problem, Crito, with your help, and to see whether the argument will appear in any different light to me now that I am in this position, or whether it will remain the same; and whether we shall dismiss it or accept it.

37   Serious thinkers, I believe, have always held some such view as the one which I mentioned just now: that some of the opinions which people entertain should be respected, and others should not. Now I ask you, Crito, don't you think that this is a sound principle?—You are safe from the prospect of dying to-morrow, in all human probability; and you are not likely to have your judgement upset by this impending calamity. Consider, then; don't you think that this is a sound enough principle, that one should not regard all the opinions that people hold, but only some and not others? What do you say? Isn't that a fair statement?

38   CRITO: Yes, it is.

39   SOCRATES: In other words, one should regard the good ones and not the bad?

40   CRITO: Yes.

41   SOCRATES: The opinions of the wise being good, and the opinions of the foolish bad?

42   CRITO: Naturally.

43   SOCRATES: To pass on, then: what do you think of the sort of illustration that I used to employ? When a man is in training, and taking it seriously, does he pay attention to all praise and criticism and opinion indiscriminately, or only when it comes from the one qualified person, the actual doctor or trainer?

44   CRITO: Only when it comes from the one qualified person.

45   SOCRATES: Then he should be afraid of the criticism and welcome the praise of the one qualified person, but not those of the general public.

46 CRITO: Obviously.

47 SOCRATES: So he ought to regulate his actions and exercises and eating and drinking by the judgement of his instructor, who has expert knowledge, rather than by the opinions of the rest of the public.

48 CRITO: Yes, that is so.

49 SOCRATES: Very well. Now if he disobeys the one man and disregards his opinion and commendations, and pays attention to the advice of the many who have no expert knowledge, surely he will suffer some bad effect?

50 CRITO: Certainly.

51 SOCRATES: And what is this bad effect? Where is it produced?—I mean, in what part of the disobedient person?

52 CRITO: His body, obviously; that is what suffers.

53 SOCRATES: Very good. Well now, tell me, Crito—we don't want to go through all the examples one by one—does this apply as a general rule, and above all to the sort of actions which we are trying to decide about: just and unjust, honourable and dishonourable, good and bad? Ought we to be guided and intimidated by the opinion of the many or by that of the one—assuming that there is someone with expert knowledge? Is it true that we ought to respect and fear this person more than all the rest put together; and that if we do not follow his guidance we shall spoil and mutilate that part of us which, as we used to say, is improved by right conduct and destroyed by wrong? Or is this all nonsense?

54 CRITO: No, I think it is true, Socrates.

55 SOCRATES: Then consider the next step. There is a part of us which is improved by healthy actions and ruined by unhealthy ones. If we spoil it by taking the advice of non-experts, will life be worth living when this part is once ruined? The part I mean is the body; do you accept this?

56 CRITO: Yes.

57 SOCRATES: Well, is life worth living with a body which is worn out and ruined in health?

58 CRITO: Certainly not.

59 SOCRATES: What about the part of us which is mutilated by wrong actions and benefited by right ones? Is life worth living with this part ruined? Or do we believe that this part of us, whatever it may be, in which right and wrong operate, is of less importance than the body?

60 CRITO: Certainly not.

61 SOCRATES: It is really more precious?

62 CRITO: Much more.

63 SOCRATES: In that case, my dear fellow, what we ought to consider is not so much what people in general will say about us but how we stand with the expert in right and wrong, the one authority, who represents the actual truth. So in the first place your proposition is not correct when you say that we should consider popular opinion in questions of what is right and honourable and good, or the opposite. Of course one might object 'All the same, the people have the power to put us to death.'

64   CRITO: No doubt about that! Quite true, Socrates; it is a possible objection.

65   SOCRATES: But so far as I can see, my dear fellow, the argument which we have just been through is quite unaffected by it. At the same time I should like you to consider whether we are still satisfied on this point: that the really important thing is not to live, but to live well.

66   CRITO: Why, yes.

67   SOCRATES: And that to live well means the same thing as to live honourably or rightly?

68   CRITO: Yes.

69   SOCRATES: Then in the light of this agreement we must consider whether or not it is right for me to try to get away without an official discharge. If it turns out to be right, we must make the attempt; if not, we must let it drop. As for the considerations you raise about expense and reputation and bringing up children, I am afraid, Crito, that they represent the reflections of the ordinary public, who put people to death, and would bring them back to life if they could, with equal indifference to reason. Our real duty, I fancy, since the argument leads that way, is to consider one question only, the one which we raised just now: Shall we be acting rightly in paying money and showing gratitude to these people who are going to rescue me, and in escaping or arranging the escape ourselves, or shall we really be acting wrongly in doing all this? If it becomes clear that such conduct is wrong, I cannot help thinking that the question whether we are sure to die, or to suffer any other ill effect for that matter, if we stand our ground and take no action, ought not to weigh with us at all in comparison with the risk of doing what is wrong.

70   CRITO: I agree with what you say, Socrates; but I wish you would consider what we ought to *do.*

71   Socrates: Let us look at it together, my dear fellow; and if you can challenge any of my arguments, do so and I will listen to you; but if you can't, be a good fellow and stop telling me over and over again that I ought to leave this place without official permission. I am very anxious to obtain your approval before I adopt the course which I have in mind; I don't want to act against your convictions. Now give your attention to the starting point of this inquiry—I hope that you will be satisfied with my way of stating it—and try to answer my questions to the best of your judgement.

72   CRITO: Well, I will try.

73   SOCRATES: Do we say that one must never willingly do wrong, or does it depend upon circumstances? Is it true, as we have often agreed before, that there is no sense in which wrongdoing is good or honourable? Or have we jettisoned all our former convictions in these last few days? Can you and I at our age, Crito, have spent all these years in serious discussions without realizing that we were no better than a pair of children? Surely the truth is just what we have always said. Whatever the popular view is, and whether the alternative is pleasanter than the present one or even harder to bear, the fact remains that to do wrong is in every sense bad and dishonourable for the person who does it. Is that our view, or not?

74   CRITO: Yes, it is.

75   SOCRATES: Then in no circumstances must one do wrong.

76   CRITO: No.

77   SOCRATES: In that case one must not even do wrong when one is wronged, which most people regard as the natural course.

78   CRITO: Apparently not.

79   SOCRATES: Tell me another thing, Crito: ought one to do injuries or not?

80   CRITO: Surely not, Socrates.

81   SOCRATES: And tell me: is it right to do an injury in retaliation, as most people believe, or not?

82   CRITO: No, never.

83   SOCRATES: Because, I suppose, there is no difference between injuring people and wronging them.

84   CRITO: Exactly.

85   SOCRATES: So one ought not to return a wrong or an injury to any person, whatever the provocation is. Now be careful, Crito, that in making these single admissions you do not end by admitting something contrary to your real beliefs. I know that there are and always will be few people who think like this; and consequently between those who do think so and those who do not there can be no agreement on principle; they must always feel contempt when they observe one another's decisions. I want even you to consider very carefully whether you share my views and agree with me, and whether we can proceed with our discussion from the established hypothesis that it is never right to do a wrong or return a wrong or defend one's self against injury by retaliation; or whether you dissociate yourself from any share in this view as a basis for discussion. I have held it for a long time, and still hold it; but if you have formed any other opinion, say so and tell me what it is. If, on the other hand, you stand by what we have said, listen to my next point.

86   CRITO: Yes, I stand by it and agree with you. Go on.

87   SOCRATES: Well, here is my next point, or rather question. Ought one to fulfil all one's agreements, provided that they are right, or break them?

88   CRITO: One ought to fulfil them.

89   SOCRATES: Then consider the logical consequence. If we leave this place without first persuading the State to let us go, are we or are we not doing an injury, and doing it in a quarter where it is least justifiable? Are we or are we not abiding by our just agreements?

90   CRITO: I can't answer your question, Socrates; I am not clear in my mind.

91   SOCRATES: Look at it in this way. Suppose that while we were preparing to run away from here (or however one should describe it) the Laws and Constitution of Athens were to come and confront us and ask this question: 'Now, Socrates, what are you proposing to do? Can you deny that by this act which you are contemplating you intend, so far as you have the power, to destroy us, the Laws, and the whole State as well? Do you imagine that a city can continue to exist and not be turned upside down, if the legal judgements

which are pronounced in it have no force but are nullified and destroyed by private persons?'—how shall we answer this question, Crito, and others of the same kind? There is much that could be said, especially by a professional advocate, to protest against the invalidation of this law which enacts that judgements once pronounced shall be binding. Shall we say 'Yes, I do intend to destroy the laws, because the State wronged me by passing a faulty judgement at my trial'? Is this to be our answer, or what?

92   CRITO: What you have just said, by all means, Socrates.

93   SOCRATES: Then what supposing the Laws say 'Was there provision for this in the agreement between you and us, Socrates? Or did you undertake to abide by whatever judgements the State pronounced?' If we expressed surprise at such language, they would probably say: 'Never mind our language, Socrates, but answer our questions; after all, you are accustomed to the method of question and answer. Come now, what charge do you bring against us and the State, that you are trying to destroy us? Did we not give you life in the first place? was it not through us that your father married your mother and begot you? Tell us, have you any complaint against those of us Laws that deal with marriage?' 'No, none', I should say. 'Well, have you any against the laws which deal with children's upbringing and education, such as you had yourself? Are you not grateful to those of us Laws which were instituted for this end, for requiring your father to give you a cultural and physical education?' 'Yes', I should say. 'Very good. Then since you have been born and brought up and educated, can you deny, in the first place, that you were our child and servant, both you and your ancestors? And if this is so, do you imagine that what is right for us is equally right for you, and that whatever we try to do to you, you are justified in retaliating? You did not have equality of rights with your father, or your employer (supposing that you had had one), to enable you to retaliate; you were not allowed to answer back when you were scolded or to hit back when you were beaten, or to do a great many other things of the same kind. Do you expect to have such licence against your country and its laws that if we try to put you to death in the belief that it is right to do so, you on your part will try your hardest to destroy your country and us its Laws in return? and will you, the true devotee of goodness, claim that you are justified in doing so? Are you so wise as to have forgotten that compared with your mother and father and all the rest of your ancestors your country is something far more precious, more venerable, more sacred, and held in greater honour both among gods and among all reasonable men? Do you not realize that you are even more bound to respect and placate the anger of your country than your father's anger? that if you cannot persuade your country you must do whatever it orders, and patiently submit to any punishment that it imposes, whether it be flogging or imprisonment? And if it leads you out to war, to be wounded or killed, you must comply, and it is right that you should do so; you must not give way or retreat or abandon your position. Both in war and in the law-courts and everywhere else you must do whatever your city and your country commands,

or else persuade it in accordance with universal justice; but violence is a sin even against your parents, and it is a far greater sin against your country.'— What shall we say to this, Crito?—that what the Laws say is true, or not?

94   CRITO: Yes, I think so.

95   SOCRATES: 'Consider, then, Socrates,' the Laws would probably continue, 'whether it is also true for us to say that what you are now trying to do to us is not right. Although we have brought you into the world and reared you and educated you, and given you and all your fellow-citizens a share in all the good things at our disposal, nevertheless by the very fact of granting our permission we openly proclaim this principle: that any Athenian, on attaining to manhood and seeing for himself the political organization of the State and us its Laws, is permitted, if he is not satisfied with us, to take his property and go away wherever he likes. If any of you chooses to go to one of our colonies, supposing that he should not be satisfied with us and the State, or to emigrate to any other country, not one of us Laws hinders or prevents him from going away wherever he likes, without any loss of property. On the other hand, if any one of you stands his ground when he can see how we administer justice and the rest of our public organization, we hold that by so doing he has in fact undertaken to do anything that we tell him; and we maintain that anyone who disobeys is guilty of doing wrong on three separate counts: first because we are his parents, and secondly because we are his guardians; and thirdly because, after promising obedience, he is neither obeying us nor persuading us to change our decision if we are at fault in any way; and although all our orders are in the form of proposals, not of savage commands, and we give him the choice of either persuading us or doing what we say, he is actually doing neither. These are the charges, Socrates, to which we say that you will be liable if you do what you are contemplating; and you will not be the least culpable of your fellow-countrymen, but one of the most guilty.' If I said 'Why do you say that?' they would no doubt pounce upon me with perfect justice and point out that there are very few people in Athens who have entered into this agreement with them as explicitly as I have. They would say 'Socrates, we have substantial evidence that you are satisfied with us and with the State. You would not have been so exceptionally reluctant to cross the borders of your country if you had not been exceptionally attached to it. You have never left the city to attend a festival or for any other purpose, except on some military expedition; you have never travelled abroad as other people do, and you have never felt the impulse to acquaint yourself with another country or constitution; you have been content with us and with our city. You have definitely chosen us, and undertaken to observe us in all your activities as a citizen; and as the crowning proof that you are satisfied with our city, you have begotten children in it. Furthermore, even at the time of your trial you could have proposed the penalty of banishment, if you had chosen to do so; that is, you could have done then with the sanction of the State what you are now trying to do without it. But whereas at that time you made a noble show of indifference if you had to die, and in fact preferred death, as you said, to banishment, now you show no

respect for your earlier professions, and no regard for us, the Laws, whom you are trying to destroy; you are behaving like the lowest type of menial, trying to run away in spite of the contracts and undertakings by which you agreed to live as a member of our State. Now first answer this question: Are we or are we not speaking the truth when we say that you have undertaken, in deed if not in word, to live your life as a citizen in obedience to us?' What are we to say to that, Crito? Are we not bound to admit it?

96 CRITO: We cannot help it, Socrates.

97 SOCRATES: 'It is a fact, then,' they would say, 'that you are breaking covenants and undertakings made with us, although you made them under no compulsion or misunderstanding, and were not compelled to decide in a limited time; you had seventy years in which you could have left the country, if you were not satisfied with us or felt that the agreements were unfair. You did not choose Sparta or Crete[5]—your favourite models of good government—or any other Greek or foreign state; you could not have absented yourself from the city less if you had been lame or blind or decrepit in some other way. It is quite obvious that you stand by yourself above all other Athenians in your affection for this city and for us its Laws;—who would care for a city without laws? And now, after all this, are you not going to stand by your agreement? Yes, you are, Socrates, if you will take our advice; and then you will at least escape being laughed at for leaving the city.

98 'We invite you to consider what good you will do to yourself or your friends if you commit this breach of faith and stain your conscience. It is fairly obvious that the risk of being banished and either losing their citizenship or having their property confiscated will extend to your friends as well. As for yourself, if you go to one of the neighbouring states, such as Thebes or Megara,[6] which are both well governed, you will enter them as an enemy to their constitution,[7] and all good patriots will eye you with suspicion as a destroyer of law and order. Incidentally you will confirm the opinion of the jurors who tried you that they gave a correct verdict; a destroyer of laws might very well be supposed to have a destructive influence upon young and foolish human beings. Do you intend, then, to avoid well governed states and the higher forms of human society? and if you do, will life be worth living? Or will you approach these people and have the impudence to converse with them? What arguments will you use, Socrates? The same which you used here, that goodness and integrity, institutions and laws, are the most precious possessions of mankind? Do you not think that Socrates and everything about him will appear in a disreputable light? You certainly ought to think so. But perhaps you will retire from this part of the world and go to Crito's friends in

---

[5] *Sparta or Crete:* Socrates admired these states because of their respect for law and order. The fact that they were oligarchies gavee his opponents another political handle.

[6] *Thebes* and *Megara* adjoined Attica on the north-west and south-west respectively. They too were oligarchies; the Laws are being a trifle sarcastic.

[7] *an enemy to their constitution:* Note as being a democrat, but as a law-breaker.

Thessaly? That is the home of indiscipline and laxity, and no doubt they would enjoy hearing the amusing story of how you managed to run away from prison by arraying yourself in some costume or putting on a shepherd's smock or some other conventional runaway's disguise, and altering your personal appearance. And will no one comment on the fact that an old man of your age, probably with only a short time left to live, should dare to cling so greedily to life, at the price of violating the most stringent laws? Perhaps not, if you avoid irritating anyone. Otherwise, Socrates, you will hear a good many humiliating comments. So you will live as the toady and slave of all the populace, literally "roistering in Thessaly",[8] as though you had left this country for Thessaly to attend a banquet there; and where will your discussions about goodness and uprightness be then, we should like to know? But of course you want to live for your children's sake, so that you may be able to bring them up and educate them. Indeed! by first taking them off to Thessaly and making foreigners of them, so that they may have that additional enjoyment? Or if that is not your intention, supposing that they are brought up here with you still alive, will they be better cared for and educated without you, because of course your friends will look after them? Will they look after your children if you go away to Thessaly, and not if you go away to the next world? Surely if those who profess to be your friends are worth anything, you must believe that they would care for them.

99 'No, Socrates; be advised by us your guardians, and do not think more of your children or of your life or of anything else than you think of what is right; so that when you enter the next world you may have all this to plead in your defence before the authorities there. It seems clear that if you do this thing, neither you nor any of your friends will be the better for it or be more upright or have a cleaner conscience here in this world, nor will it be better for you when you reach the next. As it is, you will leave this place, when you do, as the victim of a wrong done not by us, the Laws, but by your fellowmen. But if you leave in that dishonourable way, returning wrong for wrong and evil for evil, breaking your agreements and covenants with us, and injuring those whom you least ought to injure—yourself, your friends, your country, 100and us—then you will have to face our anger in your lifetime, and in that place beyond when the laws of the other world know that you have tried, so far as you could, to destroy even us their brothers, they will not receive you with a kindly welcome. Do not take Crito's advice, but follow ours.'

That, my dear friend Crito, I do assure you, is what I seem to hear them saying, just as a mystic[9] seems to hear the strains of music; and the sound of their arguments rings so loudly in my head that I cannot hear the other side. I

[8] *roistering in Thessaly:* The phrase is semi-proverbial; the Thessalian 'barons' were notorious for their luxury. The constant repetition of the name 'Thessaly' is intended to be scornful.

[9] *a mystic:* The actual reference is to worshippers of the Asiatic goddess Cybele, whose rites were accompanied by exciting music. The point seems to be that in devout ears the music goes on ringing when the playing has ceased. But the main object of the simile, with its religious assocations, is no doubt to suggest that the voice of the Laws is only another expression of the inner voice; which (as the last line of the dialogue makes clear) is the voice of God.

warn you that, as my opinion stands at present, it will be useless to urge a different view. However, if you think that you will do any good by it, say what you like.

101   CRITO: No, Socrates, I have nothing to say.

102   SOCRATES: Then give it up, Crito, and let us follow this course, since God points out the way.

POST-READING QUESTIONS:

1) Did the views that you presented in your response to the first pre-reading question affect your understanding of Socrates' ideas? Did his ideas cause you to rethink your views?

2) What kind of friend does Crito seem to be to Socrates? Do you think that Socrates treats him as a friend? Does he mistreat him? When you reexamine your response to the fourth pre-reading question, do you find that you and Socrates understand the notion of "friendship" similarly or dissimilarly?

3) One of Socrates' central claims is that "one must not even do wrong when one is wronged. . . " (paragraph 77). Do you agree with Socrates on this point?

4) Do you and Socrates define "living well" similarly? Do you agree with Socrates that "the really important thing is not to live, but to live well" (paragraph 65)?

5) What are Socrates' reasons for staying in prison? Is his reasoning sound? How do you know? When all is said and done, do you think that Socrates made the right decision?

6) Does the philosophical dialogue presented in this reading selection resemble the one that you discussed in your answer to the sixth pre-reading question? Do you think that Socrates' position would have been better showcased had Plato presented it in an essay—or, perhaps, in a short story?

Letter from Birmingham Jail

THE REVEREND DR. MARTIN LUTHER KING, JR.

A believer in nonviolent direct action as a means by which disenfranchised citizens can protest their condition and try to gain equality, Martin Luther King, Jr. (1929–1968)—a native Southerner and son of a clergyman—followed in the tradition of such great political figures as Henry David Thoreau and Mahatma Gandhi, the latter of whom was one of King's own heroes. Having achieved national recognition in the mid–1950s for his leadership in the Montgomery bus boycott—which eventuated in the desegregation of buses in Montgomery, Alabama—King went on to become one of the dominant forces in the struggle for civil rights in the United States. His efforts helped ensure such momentous achievements as the passing of the Civil Rights Act of 1964 and the Voting Rights Act of 1965. In 1964, King was twice honored internationally: in January, he was "proclaimed 'Man of the Year' by *Time,* the first black [*sic*] to be so honored" (Gonsior 278); in December, he was awarded the Nobel Peace Prize.

Above all else, King was a deeply spiritual man who believed in the oneness of the human race. He movingly celebrated this belief in his famous "I Have a Dream" speech, which he delivered in front of the Lincoln Memorial in Washington, D.C., in August 1963, during a civil rights march on Washington that turned out to be one of the largest political gatherings in the history of this country. Besides giving many memorable speeches, King also wrote a number of essays and several books, including *Stride Toward Freedom: The Montgomery Story* (1958), *Why We Can't Wait* (1964), and *Where Do We Go from Here: Chaos or Community?* (1967). (See Gonsior 276ff. for a detailed account of King's writings.)

Although throughout his short professional career King had many followers and supporters, including Presidents Kennedy and Johnson, he also had enemies. The F.B.I. secretly tried to bring him down, perhaps because of his opposition to the war in Vietnam, perhaps for other reasons as well (see Graham 304). During the marches and protests that he led, he encountered direct resistance from people hostile to or at least not entirely understanding of his efforts to help bring about racial equality in the United States. (As you'll see when you read "Letter from Birmingham Jail," King met with resistance even from the clergy, though the clergymen to whom he writes his letter were certainly not his enemies.) On April 4, 1968, his enemies succeeded in stopping him, at least physically. While he was on the balcony of his hotel in Memphis, Tennessee, where he had come to help lead a strike by that city's Black sanitation workers, King was assassinated. Though his legacy lives on, the world is surely a poorer place for his absence.

PRE-READING QUESTIONS:

1) What, in your view, is the relationship or difference between what is legal and what is moral? Can you cite and elaborate upon the meanings of some examples to prove or support your ideas?

2) Do you feel that citizens *necessarily* should or are *always obligated* to obey the law? Would you be willing to go to jail for breaking the law if you felt that you needed to engage in an illegal act in order to follow your convictions?

3) What comes to mind when you hear the word "rhetoric"? Can you give some examples of how this word is used—positively and/or negatively?

4) How would you characterize some important similarities and differences between "insiders" and "outsiders"? Cite some examples that you think help to prove or support your contentions.

5) In your view, how is a letter similar to and/or different from other sorts of writing? Do you have any particular pre-reading expectations of King's piece, knowing that it is written in the form of a letter?

CLOSE-READING **TIP**

King is unquestionably one of the greatest orators in American history. Well-schooled in the art of rhetoric, that is, in the art of persuasion, he almost always seemed to know how to control the tempo of his speeches, how to arrange the dynamics of his voice, how to use rhetorical techniques, and, in general, how to use language to its fullest effect to help him make his points. If you are familiar with some of King's speeches—perhaps his famous "I Have a Dream" speech, for example—you are probably familiar with his oratorical mastery. In the reading selection that follows, you'll have an opportunity to see a written equivalent of this mastery. To sense the full impact of his words, try reading his letter aloud, watching and listening for the effect that his language skills have on you (you might even want to record and then play back your own oral delivery of his letter). Consider, for example, his use of comparison and analogy in paragraph 3, his use of catchy epigrammatic expressions and interconnecting series of metaphors in paragraph 4, his appeals to authority and use of a rhetorical question in paragraph 16, his use of anaphora in paragraph 26, and his use of alliteration in paragraph 35. (Using a good college dictionary, look up the meanings of any of these terms with which you are unfamiliar.)

A CALL FOR UNITY
Members of the Birmingham Clergy

April 12, 1963

1 We the undersigned clergymen are among those who, in January, issued "An Appeal for Law and Order and Common Sense," in dealing with racial problems in Alabama. We expressed understanding that honest convictions in racial matters could properly be pursued in the courts, but urged that decisions of those courts should in the meantime be peacefully obeyed.

2 Since that time there had been some evidence of increased forbearance and a willingness to face facts. Responsible citizens have undertaken to work on various problems which cause racial friction and unrest. In Birmingham, recent public events have given indication that we all have opportunity for a new constructive and realistic approach to racial problems.

3 However, we are now confronted by a series of demonstrations by some of our Negro citizens, directed and led in part by outsiders. We recognize the natural impatience of people who feel that their hopes are slow in being realized. But we are convinced that these demonstrations are unwise and untimely.

4 We agree rather with certain local Negro leadership which has called for honest and open negotiation of racial issues in our area. And we believe this

kind of facing of issues can best be accomplished by citizens of our own metropolitan area, white and Negro, meeting with their knowledge and experience of the local situation. All of us need to face that responsibility and find proper channels for its accomplishment.

5   Just as we formerly pointed out that "hatred and violence have no sanction in our religious and political traditions," we also point out that such actions as incite to hatred and violence, however technically peaceful those actions may be, have not contributed to the resolution of our local problems. We do not believe that these days of new hope are days when extreme measures are justified in Birmingham.

6   We commend the community as a whole, and the local news media and law enforcement officials in particular, on the calm manner in which these demonstrations have been handled. We urge the public to continue to show restraint should the demonstrations continue, and the law enforcement officials to remain calm and continue to protect our city from violence.

7   We further strongly urge our own Negro community to withdraw support from these demonstrations, and to unite locally in working peacefully for a better Birmingham. When rights are consistently denied, a cause should be pressed in the courts and in negotiations among local leaders, and not in the streets. We appeal to both our white and Negro citizenry to observe the principles of law and order and common sense.

8   C.C.J. Carpenter, D.D., L.L.D., Bishop of Alabama; Joseph A. Durick, D.D., Auxiliary Bishop, Diocese of Mobile-Birmingham; Rabbi Milton L. Grafman, Temple Emanu-El, Birmingham, Alabama; Bishop Paul Hardin, Bishop of the Alabama-West Florida Conference of the Methodist Church; Bishop Holan B. Harmon, Bishop of the North Alabama Conference of the Methodist Church; George M. Murray, D.D., L.L.D., Bishop Coadjutor, Episcopal Diocese of Alabama; Edward V. Ramage, Moderator, Synod of the Alabama Presbyterian Church in the United States; Earl Stallings, Pastor, First Baptist Church, Birmingham, Alabama.

April 16, 1963

My Dear Fellow Clergymen:[1]

1   While confined here in the Birmingham city jail, I came across your recent statement calling my present activities "unwise and untimely." Seldom do I pause to answer criticism of my work and

---

[1] This response to a published statement by eight fellow clergymen from Alabama (Bishop C. C. J. Carpenter, Bishop Joseph A. Durick, Rabbi Milton L. Grafman, Bishop Paul Hardin, Bishop Holan B. Harmon, the Reverend George M. Murray, the Reverend Edward V. Ramage and the Reverend Earl Stallings) was composed under somewhat constricting circumstances. Begun on the margins of the newspaper in which the statement appeared while I was in jail, the letter was continued on scraps of writing paper supplied by a friendly Negro trusty, and concluded on a pad my attorneys were eventually permitted to leave me. Although the text remains in substance unaltered, I have indulged in the author's prerogative of polishing it for publication. [King's note]

ideas. If I sought to answer all the criticisms that cross my desk, my secretaries would have little time for anything other than such correspondence in the course of the day, and I would have no time for constructive work. But since I feel that you are men of genuine good will and that your criticisms are sincerely set forth, I want to try to answer your statement in what I hope will be patient and reasonable terms.

2   I think I should indicate why I am here in Birmingham, since you have been influenced by the view which argues against "outsiders coming in." I have the honor of serving as president of the Southern Christian Leadership Conference, an organization operating in every southern state, with headquarters in Atlanta, Georgia. We have some eighty-five affiliated organizations across the South, and one of them is the Alabama Christian Movement for Human Rights. Frequently we share staff, educational, and financial resources with our affiliates. Several months ago the affiliate here in Birmingham asked us to be on call to engage in a nonviolent direct-action program if such were deemed necessary. We readily consented, and when the hour came we lived up to our promise. So I, along with several members of my staff, am here because I was invited here. I am here because I have organizational ties here.

3   But more basically, I am in Birmingham because injustice is here. Just as the prophets of the eighth century B.C. left their villages and carried their "thus saith the Lord" far beyond the boundaries of their home towns, and just as the Apostle Paul left his village of Tarsus and carried the gospel of Jesus Christ to the far corners of the Greco-Roman world, so am I compelled to carry the gospel of freedom beyond my own home town. Like Paul, I must constantly respond to the Macedonian call for aid.

4   Moreover, I am cognizant of the interrelatedness of all communities and states. I cannot sit idly by in Atlanta and not be concerned about what happens in Birmingham. Injustice anywhere is a threat to justice everywhere. We are caught in an inescapable network of mutuality, tied in a single garment of destiny. Whatever affects one directly, affects all indirectly. Never again can we afford to live with the narrow, provincial, "outside agitator" idea. Anyone who lives inside the United States can never be considered an outsider anywhere within its bounds.

5   You deplore the demonstrations taking place in Birmingham. But your statement, I am sorry to say, fails to express a similar concern for the conditions that brought about the demonstrations. I am sure that none of you would want to rest content with the superficial kind of social analysis that deals merely with effects and does not grapple with underlying causes. It is unfortunate that demonstrations are taking place in Birmingham, but it is even more unfortunate that the city's white power structure left the Negro community with no alternative.

6   In any nonviolent campaign there are four basic steps: collection of the facts to determine whether injustices exist; negotiation; self-purification; and direct action. We have gone through all these steps in Birmingham. There can be no gainsaying the fact that racial injustice engulfs this community. Birmingham is

probably the most thoroughly segregated city in the United States. Its ugly record of brutality is widely known. Negroes have experienced grossly unjust treatment in the courts. There have been more unsolved bombings of Negro homes and churches in Birmingham than in any other city in the nation. These are the hard brutal facts of the case. On the basis of these conditions, Negro leaders sought to negotiate with the city fathers. But the latter consistently refused to engage in good-faith negotiation.

7   Then, last September, came the opportunity to talk with leaders of Birmingham's economic community. In the course of the negotiations, certain promises were made by the merchants—for example, to remove the stores' humiliating racial signs. On the basis of these promises, the Reverend Fred Shuttlesworth and the leaders of the Alabama Christian Movement for Human Rights agreed to a moratorium on all demonstrations. As the weeks and months went by, we realized that we were the victims of a broken promise. A few signs, briefly removed, returned; the others remained.

8   As in so many past experiences, our hopes had been blasted, and the shadow of deep disappointment settled upon us. We had no alternative except to prepare for direct action, whereby we would present our very bodies as a means of laying our case before the conscience of the local and the national community. Mindful of the difficulties involved, we decided to undertake a process of self-purification. We began a series of workshops on nonviolence, and we repeatedly asked ourselves: "Are you able to accept blows without retaliating?" "Are you able to endure the ordeal of jail?" We decided to schedule our direct-action program for the Easter season, realizing that except for Christmas, this is the main shopping period of the year. Knowing that a strong economic-withdrawal program would be the by-product of direct action, we felt that this would be the best time to bring pressure to bear on the merchants for the needed change.

9   Then it occurred to us that Birmingham's mayoral election was coming up in March, and we speedily decided to postpone action until after election day. When we discovered that the Commissioner of Public Safety, Eugene "Bull" Connor, had piled up enough votes to be in the run-off, we decided again to postpone action until the day after the run-off so that the demonstrations could not be used to cloud the issues. Like many others, we waited to see Mr. Connor defeated, and to this end we endured postponement after postponement. Having aided in this community need, we felt that our direct-action program could be delayed no longer.

10   You may well ask, "Why direct action? Why sit-ins, marches, and so forth? Isn't negotiation a better path?" You are quite right in calling for negotiation. Indeed, this is the very purpose of direct action. Nonviolent direct action seeks to create such a crisis and foster such a tension that a community which has constantly refused to negotiate is forced to confront the issue. It seeks so to dramatize the issue that it can no longer be ignored. My citing the creation of tension as part of the work of the nonviolent resister may sound rather shocking. But I must confess that I am not afraid of the word "ten-

sion." I have earnestly opposed violent tension, but there is a type of constructive, nonviolent tension which is necessary for growth. Just as Socrates felt that it was necessary to create a tension in the mind so that individuals could rise from the bondage of myths and half truths to the unfettered realm of creative analysis and objective appraisal, so must we see the need for nonviolent gadflies to create the kind of tension in society that will help men rise from the dark depths of prejudice and racism to the majestic heights of understanding and brotherhood.

11   The purpose of our direct-action program is to create a situation so crisis-packed that it will inevitably open the door to negotiation. I therefore concur with you in your call for negotiation. Too long has our beloved Southland been bogged down in a tragic effort to live in monologue rather than dialogue.

12   One of the basic points in your statement is that the action that I and my associates have taken in Birmingham is untimely. Some have asked: "Why didn't you give the new city administration time to act?" The only answer that I can give to this query is that the new Birmingham administration must be prodded about as much as the outgoing one, before it will act. We are sadly mistaken if we feel that the election of Albert Boutwell as mayor will bring the millennium to Birmingham. While Mr. Boutwell is a much more gentle person than Mr. Connor, they are both segregationists, dedicated to maintenance of the status quo. I have hoped that Mr. Boutwell will be reasonable enough to see the futility of massive resistance to desegregation. But he will not see this without pressure from devotees of civil rights. My friends, I must say to you that we have not made a single gain in civil rights without determined legal and nonviolent pressure. Lamentably, it is an historical fact that privileged groups seldom give up their privileges voluntarily. Individuals may see the moral light and voluntarily give up their unjust posture; but, as Reinhold Niebuhr has reminded us, groups tend to be more immoral than individuals.

13   We know through painful experience that freedom is never voluntarily given by the oppressor; it must be demanded by the oppressed. Frankly, I have yet to engage in a direct-action campaign that was "well timed" in the view of those who have not suffered unduly from the disease of segregation. For years now I have heard the word "Wait!" It rings in the ear of every Negro with piercing familiarity. This "Wait" has almost always meant "Never." We must come to see, with one of our distinguished jurists, that "justice too long delayed is justice denied."

14   We have waited for more than 340 years for our constitutional and God-given rights. The nations of Asia and Africa are moving with jet-like speed toward gaining political independence, but we still creep at horse-and-buggy pace toward gaining a cup of coffee at a lunch counter. Perhaps it is easy for those who have never felt the stinging darts of segregation to say, "Wait." But when you have seen vicious mobs lynch your mothers and fathers at will and

drown your sisters and brothers at whim; when you have seen hate-filled policemen curse, kick, and even kill your black brothers and sisters; when you see the vast majority of your twenty million Negro brothers smothering in an airtight cage of poverty in the midst of an affluent society; when you suddenly find your tongue twisted and your speech stammering as you seek to explain to your six-year-old daughter why she can't go to the public amusement park that has just been advertised on television, and see tears welling up in her eyes when she is told that Funtown is closed to colored children, and see ominous clouds of inferiority beginning to form in her little mental sky, and see her beginning to distort her personality by developing an unconscious bitterness toward white people; when you have to concoct an answer for a five-year-old son who is asking, "Daddy, why do white people treat colored people so mean?"; when you take a cross-country drive and find it necessary to sleep night after night in the uncomfortable corners of your automobile because no motel will accept you; when you are humiliated day in and day out by nagging signs reading "white" and "colored"; when your first name becomes "nigger," your middle name becomes "boy" (however old you are) and your last name becomes "John," and your wife and mother are never given the respected title "Mrs."; when you are harried by day and haunted by night by the fact that you are a Negro, living constantly at tiptoe stance, never quite knowing what to expect next, and are plagued with inner fears and outer resentments; when you are forever fighting a degenerating sense of "nobodiness"—then you will understand why we find it difficult to wait. There comes a time when the cup of endurance runs over, and men are no longer willing to be plunged into the abyss of despair. I hope, sirs, you can understand our legitimate and unavoidable impatience.

15   You express a great deal of anxiety over our willingness to break laws. This is certainly a legitimate concern. Since we so diligently urge people to obey the Supreme Court's decision of 1954 outlawing segregation in the public schools, at first glance it may seem rather paradoxical for us consciously to break laws. One may well ask: "How can you advocate breaking some laws and obeying others?" The answer lies in the fact that there are two types of laws: just and unjust. I would be the first to advocate obeying just laws. One has not only a legal but a moral responsibility to obey just laws. Conversely, one has a moral responsibility to disobey unjust laws. I would agree with St. Augustine that "an unjust law is no law at all."

16   Now, what is the difference between the two? How does one determine whether a law is just or unjust? A just law is a man-made code that squares with the moral law or the law of God. An unjust law is a code that is out of harmony with the moral law. To put it in the terms of St. Thomas Aquinas: An unjust law is a human law that is not rooted in eternal law and natural law. Any law that uplifts human personality is just. Any law that degrades human personality is unjust. All segregation statutes are unjust because segregation distorts the soul and damages the personality. It gives the segregator a false

sense of superiority and the segregated a false sense of inferiority. Segregation, to use the terminology of the Jewish philosopher Martin Buber, substitutes an "I-it" relationship for an "I-thou" relationship and ends up relegating persons to the status of things. Hence segregation is not only politically, economically, and sociologically unsound, it is morally wrong and sinful. Paul Tillich has said that sin is separation. Is not segregation an existential expression of man's tragic separation, his awful estrangement, his terrible sinfulness? Thus it is that I can urge men to obey the 1954 decision of the Supreme Court, for it is morally right; and I can urge them to disobey segregation ordinances, for they are morally wrong.

17 .Let us consider a more concrete example of just and unjust laws. An unjust law is a code that a numerical or power majority group compels a minority group to obey but does not make binding on itself. This is *difference* made legal. By the same token, a just law is a code that a majority compels a minority to follow and that it is willing to follow itself. This is *sameness* made legal.

18 Let me give another explanation. A law is unjust if it is inflicted on a minority that, as a result of being denied the right to vote, had no part in enacting or devising the law. Who can say that the legislature of Alabama which set up that state's segregation laws was democratically elected? Throughout Alabama all sorts of devious methods are used to prevent Negroes from becoming registered voters, and there are some counties in which, even though Negroes constitute a majority of the population, not a single Negro is registered. Can any law enacted under such circumstances be considered democratically structured?

19 Sometimes a law is just on its face and unjust in its application. For instance, I have been arrested on a charge of parading without a permit. Now, there is nothing wrong in having an ordinance which requires a permit for a parade. But such an ordinance becomes unjust when it is used to maintain segregation and to deny citizens the First Amendment privilege of peaceful assembly and protest.

20 I hope you are able to see the distinction I am trying to point out. In no sense do I advocate evading or defying the law, as would the rabid segregationist. That would lead to anarchy. One who breaks an unjust law must do so openly, lovingly, and with a willingness to accept the penalty. I submit that an individual who breaks a law that conscience tells him is unjust, and who willingly accepts the penalty of imprisonment in order to arouse the conscience of the community over its injustice, is in reality expressing the highest respect for law.

21 Of course, there is nothing new about this kind of civil disobedience. It was evidenced sublimely in the refusal of Shadrach, Meshach, and Abednego to obey the laws of Nebuchadnezzar, on the ground that a higher moral law was at stake. It was practiced superbly by the early Christians, who were willing to face hungry lions and the excruciating pain of chopping blocks rather

than submit to certain unjust laws of the Roman Empire. To a degree, academic freedom is a reality today because Socrates practiced civil disobedience. In our own nation, the Boston Tea Party represented a massive act of civil disobedience.

22 We should never forget that everything Adolf Hitler did in Germany was "legal" and everything the Hungarian freedom fighters did in Hungary was "illegal." It was "illegal" to aid and comfort a Jew in Hitler's Germany. Even so, I am sure that, had I lived in Germany at the time, I would have aided and comforted my Jewish brothers. If today I lived in a Communist country where certain principles dear to the Christian faith are suppressed, I would openly advocate disobeying the country's antireligious laws.

23 I must make two honest confessions to you, my Christian and Jewish brothers. First, I must confess that over the past few years I have been gravely disappointed with the wh te moderate. I have almost reached the regrettable conclusion that the Negro's great stumbling block in his stride toward freedom is not the White Citizen's Counciler or the Ku Klux Klanner, but the white moderate, who is more devoted to "order" than to justice; who prefers a negative peace which is the absence of tension to a positive peace which is the presence of justice; who constantly says, "I agree with you in the goal you seek, but I cannot agree with your methods of direct action"; who paternalistically believes he can set the timetable for another man's freedom; who lives by a mythical concept of time and who constantly advises the Negro to wait for a "more convenient season." Shallow understanding from people of good will is more frustrating than absolute misunderstanding from people of ill will. Lukewarm acceptance is much more bewildering than outright rejection.

24 I had hoped that the white moderate would understand that law and order exist for the purpose of establishing justice and that when they fail in this purpose they become the dangerously structured dams that block the flow of social progress. I had hoped that the white moderate would understand that the present tension in the South is a necessary phase of the transition from an obnoxious negative peace, in which the Negro passively accepted his unjust plight, to a substantive and positive peace, in which all men will respect the dignity and worth of human personality. Actually, we who engage in nonviolent direct action are not the creators of tension. We merely bring to the surface the hidden tension that is already alive. We bring it out in the open, where it can be seen and dealt with. Like a boil that can never be cured so long as it is covered up but must be opened with all its ugliness to the natural medicines of air and light, injustice must be exposed, with all the tension its exposure creates, to the light of human conscience and the air of national opinion, before it can be cured.

25 In your statement you assert that our actions, even though peaceful, must be condemned because they precipitate violence. But is this a logical assertion? Isn't this like condemning a robbed man because his possession of money pre-

cipitated the evil act of robbery? Isn't this like condemning Socrates because his unswerving commitment to truth and his philosophical inquiries precipitated the act by the misguided populace in which they made him drink hemlock? Isn't this like condemning Jesus because his unique God-consciousness and never-ceasing devotion to God's will precipitated the evil act of crucifixion? We must come to see that, as the federal courts have consistently affirmed, it is wrong to urge an individual to cease his efforts to gain his basic constitutional rights because the quest may precipitate violence. Society must protect the robbed and punish the robber.

26   I had also hoped that the white moderate would reject the myth concerning time in relation to the struggle for freedom. I have just received a letter from a white brother in Texas. He writes: "All Christians know that the colored people will receive equal rights eventually, but it is possible that you are in too great a religious hurry. It has taken Christianity almost two thousand years to accomplish what it has. The teachings of Christ take time to come to earth." Such an attitude stems from a tragic misconception of time, from the strangely irrational notion that there is something in the very flow of time that will inevitably cure all ills. Actually, time itself is neutral; it can be used either destructively or constructively. More and more I feel that the people of ill will have used time much more effectively than have the people of good will. We will have to repent in this generation not merely for the hateful words and actions of the bad people, but for the appalling silence of the good people. Human progress never rolls in on wheels of inevitability; it comes through the tireless efforts of men willing to be co-workers with God, and without this hard work, time itself becomes an ally of the forces of social stagnation. We must use time creatively, in the knowledge that the time is always ripe to do right. Now is the time to make real the promise of democracy and transform our pending national elegy into a creative psalm of brotherhood. Now is the time to lift our national policy from the quicksand of racial injustice to the solid rock of human dignity.

27   You speak of our activity in Birmingham as extreme. At first I was rather disappointed that fellow clergymen would see my nonviolent efforts as those of an extremist. I began thinking about the fact that I stand in the middle of two opposing forces in the Negro community. One is a force of complacency, made up in part of Negroes who, as a result of long years of oppression, are so drained of self-respect and a sense of "somebodiness" that they have adjusted to segregation; and in part of a few middle-class Negroes who, because of a degree of academic and economic security and because in some ways they profit by segregation, have become insensitive to the problems of the masses. The other force is one of bitterness and hatred, and it comes perilously close to advocating violence. It is expressed in the various black nationalist groups that are springing up across the nation, the largest and best known being Elijah Muhammad's Muslim movement. Nourished by the

Negro's frustration over the continued existence of racial discrimination, this movement is made up of people who have lost faith in America, who have absolutely repudiated Christianity, and who have concluded that the white man is an incorrigible "devil."

28   I have tried to stand between these two forces, saying that we need emulate neither the "do-nothingism" of the complacent nor the hatred and despair of the black nationalist. For there is the more excellent way of love and nonviolent protest. I am grateful to God that, through the influence of the Negro church, the way of nonviolence became an integral part of our struggle.

29   If this philosophy had not emerged, by now many streets of the South would, I am convinced, be flowing with blood. And I am further convinced that if our white brothers dismiss as "rabble-rousers" and "outside agitators" those of us who employ nonviolent direct action, and if they refuse to support our nonviolent efforts, millions of Negroes will, out of frustration and despair, seek solace and security in black nationalist ideologies—a development that would inevitably lead to a frightening racial nightmare.

30   Oppressed people cannot remain oppressed forever. The yearning for freedom eventually manifests itself, and that is what has happened to the American Negro. Something within has reminded him of his birthright of freedom, and something without has reminded him that it can be gained. Consciously or unconsciously, he has been caught up by the *Zeitgeist,* and with his black brothers of Africa and his brown and yellow brothers of Asia, South America, and the Caribbean, the United States Negro is moving with a sense of great urgency toward the promised land of racial justice. If one recognizes this vital urge that has engulfed the Negro community, one should readily understand why public demonstrations are taking place. The Negro has many pent-up resentments and latent frustrations, and he must release them. So let him march; let him make prayer pilgrimages to the city hall; let him go on freedom rides—and try to understand why he must do so. If his repressed emotions are not released in nonviolent ways, they will seek expression through violence; this is not a threat but a fact of history. So I have not said to my people, "Get rid of your discontent." Rather, I have tried to say that this normal and healthy discontent can be channeled into the creative outlet of nonviolent direct action. And now this approach is being termed extremist.

31   But though I was initially disappointed at being categorized as an extremist, as I continued to think about the matter I gradually gained a measure of satisfaction from the label. Was not Jesus an extremist for love: "Love your enemies, bless them that curse you, do good to them that hate you, and pray for them which despitefully use you, and persecute you." Was not Amos an extremist for justice: "Let justice roll down like waters and righteousness like an ever-flowing stream." Was not Paul an extremist for the Christian gospel:

"I bear in my body the marks of the Lord Jesus." Was not Martin Luther an extremist: "Here I stand; I cannot do otherwise, so help me God." And John Bunyan: "I will stay in jail to the end of my days before I make a butchery of my conscience." And Abraham Lincoln: "This nation cannot survive half slave and half free." And Thomas Jefferson: "We hold these truths to be self-evident, that all men are created equal. . . ." So the question is not whether we will be extremists, but what kind of extremists we will be. Will we be extremists for hate or for love? Will we be extremists for the preservation of injustice or for the extension of justice? In that dramatic scene on Calvary's hill three men were crucified. We must never forget that all three were crucified for the same crime—the crime of extremism. Two were extremists for immorality, and thus fell below their environment. The other, Jesus Christ, was an extremist for love, truth, and goodness, and thereby rose above his environment. Perhaps the South, the nation, and the world are in dire need of creative extremists.

32   I had hoped that the white moderate would see this need. Perhaps I was too optimistic; perhaps I expected too much. I suppose I should have realized that few members of the oppressor race can understand the deep groans and passionate yearnings of the oppressed race; and still fewer have the vision to see that injustice must be rooted out by strong, persistent, and determined action. I am thankful, however, that some of our white brothers in the South have grasped the meaning of this social revolution and committed themselves to it. They are still all too few in quantity, but they are big in quality. Some—such as Ralph McGill, Lillian Smith, Harry Golden, James McBride Dabbs, Ann Braden, and Sarah Patton Boyle—have written about our struggle in eloquent and prophetic terms. Others have marched with us down nameless streets of the South. They have languished in filthy, roach-infested jails, suffering the abuse and brutality of policemen who view them as "dirty nigger-lovers." Unlike so many of their moderate brothers and sisters, they have recognized the urgency of the moment and sensed the need for powerful "action" antidotes to combat the disease of segregation.

33   Let me take note of my other major disappointment. I have been so greatly disappointed with the white church and its leadership. Of course, there are some notable exceptions. I am not unmindful of the fact that each of you has taken some significant stands on this issue. I commend you, Reverend Stallings, for your Christian stand on this past Sunday, in welcoming Negroes to your worship service on a nonsegregated basis. I commend the Catholic leaders of this state for integrating Spring Hill College several years ago.

34   But despite these notable exceptions, I must honestly reiterate that I have been disappointed with the church. I do not say this as one of those negative critics who can always find something wrong with the church. I say this as a minister of the gospel, who loves the church; who was nurtured in its bosom; who has been sustained by its spiritual blessings and who will remain true to it as long as the cord of life shall lengthen.

35   When I was suddenly catapulted into the leadership of the bus protest in Montgomery, Alabama, a few years ago, I felt we would be supported by the white church. I felt that the white ministers, priests, and rabbis of the South would be among our strongest allies. Instead, some have been outright opponents, refusing to understand the freedom movement and misrepresenting its leaders; all too many others have been more cautious than courageous and have remained silent behind the anesthetizing security of stained-glass windows.

36   In spite of my shattered dreams, I came to Birmingham with the hope that the white religious leadership of this community would see the justice of our cause and, with deep moral concern, would serve as the channel through which our just grievances could reach the power structure. I had hoped that each of you would understand. But again I have been disappointed. . . .

37   There was a time when the church was very powerful—in the time when the early Christians rejoiced at being deemed worthy to suffer for what they believed. In those days the church was not merely a thermometer that recorded the ideas and principles of popular opinion; it was a thermostat that transformed the mores of society. Whenever the early Christians entered a town, the people in power became disturbed and immediately sought to convict the Christians for being "disturbers of the peace" and "outside agitators." But the Christians pressed on, in the conviction that they were "a colony of heaven," called to obey God rather than man. Small in number, they were big in commitment. They were too God intoxicated to be "astronomically intimidated." By their effort and example they brought an end to such ancient evils as infanticide and gladiatorial contests.

38   Things are different now. So often the contemporary church is a weak, ineffectual voice with an uncertain sound. So often it is an arch-defender of the status quo. Far from being disturbed by the presence of the church, the power structure of the average community is consoled by the church's silent—and often even vocal—sanction of things as they are.

39   But the judgment of God is upon the church as never before. If today's church does not recapture the sacrificial spirit of the early church, it will lose its authenticity, forfeit the loyalty of millions, and be dismissed as an irrelevant social club with no meaning for the twentieth century. Every day I meet young people whose disappointment with the church has turned into outright disgust.

40   Perhaps I have once again been too optimistic. Is organized religion too inextricably bound to the status quo to save our nation and the world? Perhaps I must turn my faith to the inner spiritual church, the church within the church, as the true *ekklesia* and the hope of the world. But again I am thankful to God that some noble souls from the ranks of organized religion have broken loose from the paralyzing chains of conformity and joined us as active partners in the struggle for freedom. They have left their secure congregations and walked the streets of Albany, Georgia, with us. They have gone down the

highways of the South on torturous rides for freedom. Yes, they have gone to jail with us. Some have been dismissed from their churches, have lost the support of their bishops and fellow ministers. But they have acted in the faith that right defeated is stronger than evil triumphant. Their witness has been the spiritual salt that has preserved the true meaning of the gospel in these troubled times. They have carved a tunnel of hope through the dark mountain of disappointment.

41   I hope the church as a whole will meet the challenge of this decisive hour. But even if the church does not come to the aid of justice, I have no despair about the future. I have no fear about the outcome of our struggle in Birmingham, even if our motives are at present misunderstood. We will reach the goal of freedom in Birmingham and all over the nation, because the goal of America is freedom. Abused and scorned though we may be, our destiny is tied up with America's destiny. Before the pilgrims landed at Plymouth, we were here. Before the pen of Jefferson etched the majestic words of the Declaration of Independence across the pages of history, we were here. For more than two centuries our forebears labored in this country without wages; they made cotton king; they built the homes of their masters while suffering gross injustice and shameful humiliation—and yet out of a bottomless vitality they continued to thrive and develop. If the inexpressible cruelties of slavery could not stop us, the opposition we now face will surely fail. We will win our freedom because the sacred heritage of our nation and the eternal will of God are embodied in our echoing demands.

42   Before closing I feel impelled to mention one other point in your statement that has troubled me profoundly. You warmly commended the Birmingham police force for keeping "order" and "preventing violence." I doubt that you would have so warmly commended the police force if you had seen its dogs sinking their teeth into unarmed, nonviolent Negroes. I doubt that you would so quickly commend the policemen if you were to observe their ugly and inhumane treatment of Negroes here in the city jail; if you were to watch them push and curse old Negro women and young Negro girls; if you were to see them slap and kick old Negro men and young boys; if you were to observe them, as they did on two occasions, refuse to give us food because we wanted to sing our grace together. I cannot join you in your praise of the Birmingham police department.

43   It is true that the police have exercised a degree of discipline in handling the demonstrators. In this sense they have conducted themselves rather "nonviolently" in public. But for what purpose? To preserve the evil system of segregation. Over the past few years I have consistently preached that nonviolence demands that the means we use must be as pure as the ends we seek. I have tried to make clear that it is wrong to use immoral means to attain moral ends. But now I must affirm that it is just as wrong, or perhaps even more so, to use moral means to preserve immoral ends. Perhaps Mr. Connor and his policemen have been rather nonviolent in public, as was Chief Pritchett in Albany, Georgia, but they have used the moral means of

nonviolence to maintain the immoral end of racial injustice. As T. S. Eliot has said, "The last temptation is the greatest treason: To do the right deed for the wrong reason."

44 I wish you had commended the Negro sit-inners and demonstrators of Birmingham for their sublime courage, their willingness to suffer, and their amazing discipline in the midst of great provocation. One day the South will recognize its real heroes. They will be the James Merediths, with the noble sense of purpose that enables them to face jeering and hostile mobs, and with the agonizing loneliness that characterizes the life of the pioneer. They will be old, oppressed, battered Negro women, symbolized in a seventy-two-year-old woman in Montgomery, Alabama, who rose up with a sense of dignity and with her people decided not to ride segregated buses, and who responded with ungrammatical profundity to one who inquired about her weariness: "My feets is tired, but my soul is at rest." They will be the young high school and college students, the young ministers of the gospel and a host of their elders, courageously and nonviolently sitting in at lunch counters and willingly going to jail for conscience' sake. One day the South will know that when these disinherited children of God sat down at lunch counters, they were in reality standing up for what is best in the American dream and for the most sacred values in our Judaeo-Christian heritage, thereby bringing our nation back to those great wells of democracy which were dug deep by the founding fathers in their formulation of the Constitution and the Declaration of Independence.

45 Never before have I written so long a letter. I'm afraid it is much too long to take your precious time. I can assure you that it would have been much shorter if I had been writing from a comfortable desk, but what else can one do when he is alone in a narrow jail cell, other than write long letters, think long thoughts, and pray long prayers?

46 If I have said anything in this letter that overstates the truth and indicates an unreasonable impatience, I beg you to forgive me. If I have said anything that understates the truth and indicates my having a patience that allows me to settle for anything less than brotherhood, I beg God to forgive me.

47 I hope this letter finds you strong in the faith. I also hope that circumstances will soon make it possible for me to meet each of you, not as an integrationist or a civil rights leader but as a fellow clergyman and a Christian brother. Let us all hope that the dark clouds of racial prejudice will soon pass away and the deep fog of misunderstanding will be lifted from our fear-drenched communities, and in some not too distant tomorrow the radiant stars of love and brotherhood will shine over our great nation with all their scintillating beauty.

> Yours in the cause of
> Peace and Brotherhood,
> Martin Luther King, Jr.

POST-READING QUESTIONS:

1) Do you and King have the same view concerning the relationship or difference between what is legal and what is moral? Do you want to reexamine your view in light of your understanding of King's ideas? Do you think that, if he were alive, King should reexamine his view in light of your ideas?

2) Does your understanding of King's letter cause you to want to amend your responses to the third or fourth pre-reading questions?

3) Why does King feel that an individual is not always obligated to obey the law? How might King respond to you if you told him how you answered the second pre-reading question? Do you want to amend your response to that question in light of your understanding of King's ideas on this matter?

4) Are King's views concerning just and unjust laws sound? Should they satisfy King's colleagues that King does not in fact hold a contradictory position concerning whether or not one should obey the law?

5) Analyzing the extraordinarily long periodic sentence in paragraph 14, do you find a relationship among the sentence's meaning, its effect on the reader, and the nature of the particular subordinating conjunction that King uses in each of the sentence's dependent clauses? Would the sentence have gained or lost in rhetorical effectiveness had King tried to make his point by using some other grammatical or stylistic structure?

6) Does King's letter resemble the kinds of letters with which you are familiar? How does it compare, say, to the letter in *Shoah* (see p. 92)? Do you think that King's ideas would be any more or less effective were they couched in a traditional academic essay? Is his letter an epistolary essay, that is, an essay written in letter form?

7) What might King and Socrates say to each other if, finding themselves sharing the same jail cell, they were to engage in a dialogue concerning the question of whether or not a citizen is necessarily obligated to obey the laws of her or his state or country? Have some fun trying to imitate each author's speaking/writing style!

8) In a televised roundtable discussion of the question concerning whether or not an individual should obey people or institutions of authority, what might Martin Luther King, Jr., Morris Braverman, Bruno Batta, Rudolph Höss, and Alice Miller say to each other? (Feel free to revise the membership of this panel in a way that proves to be more workable for you.)

9) If you could speak with the authors of this chapter's readings, would you recommend that any of them make changes to her or his piece in light of how you reacted to it?

HANDS-ON ACTIVITY:

With the exception of the Höss piece, all of this chapter's readings directly or indirectly call for people of conscience to "do the right thing," as we might say today. However, as the readings also make clear, sometimes doing the right thing lands people in deep trouble. Such is especially the case when people of conscience oppose governments that are more or less intolerant of political dissent. To find out more about what happens to such people and how you can help them, speak with someone from your area's (or school's) chapter of Amnesty International, a nonpolitically affiliated organization whose chief purpose is to fight human rights violations, including those of "prisoners of conscience," that is, people jailed simply because of their political views. Whatever you decide to do, keep in mind that, as the philosopher Edmund Burke wrote, "All that is necessary for the triumph of evil is that good men do nothing." On the other hand, as Holocaust survivor Simon Wiesenthal has said, "Hope lives when people remember."

"[O]ne question you should ask at the start of every article or book is: How strong a presence should you be in your presentation of the facts? In my own writing I usually like to be strongly present. To write in the first person — 'I,' 'me,' 'we,' 'us' — is the most natural way of talking to someone else on paper, which is what writing is. . . . But in two [of my] books I discovered . . . that [sometimes] a writer can damage his material if he intrudes himself and his opinions on it."

WILLIAM ZINSSER
On Writing Well

Incorporating the Personal into the Academic Essay

WHEN THINKING ABOUT what to say in an essay, you occasionally might find yourself wondering whether or not you should express or avoid expressing your own thoughts and feelings in the paper. Concerning your personal writing, of course, the answer to this question is rather obvious. But, as suggested in the opening comments to the previous chapter, since nearly every paper that you'll write will bear the imprint of your thinking and feelings in *some* way, you cannot help but express them even in traditional academic writing. Nevertheless, the question is a good one, for the investment of personal thoughts and feelings in other than personal work can indeed be a risky venture. (For many academicians, this problem is often both keen and commonplace, since most, if not all, academicians pursue studies in areas in which they are personally interested.) Let's explore the nature of this problem to see how you might avoid the pitfalls pertaining to it while also pursuing meaningful academic work grounded in your own personal interests.

Distinguishing Between Feelings and Opinions

Let's say that, because of your very strong feelings about abortion, you write an opinion piece for your college newspaper, in which you try to convince your readers to give serious thought to, if not to accept outright, your perspective on abortion. If in fact you present good reasons for holding your point of view, then your argument shouldn't suffer—at least not from the standpoint of logic—simply because you inject your personal feelings into your article. However, your argument *might* suffer were you to confuse the concepts of feelings and opinions and, as a result, end up offering feelings instead of reasons to try to prove or support your views.

To be sure, your feelings are entirely acceptable *as* feelings. If, for example, you express feelings of sadness because you think that abortions involve the taking of innocent lives, or you express feelings of anger because you are convinced that "anti-choice" forces in the culture have succeeded in keeping women from exercising their right to have safe, professionally performed abortions, or you express feelings of happiness because you are persuaded that most people understand that someone can be both "pro-life" and "pro-choice," who among your intended readers could legitimately argue that your *feelings* are wrong? You have a right to your feelings—period. On the other hand, your article might solicit some letters to the editor from readers who, acknowledging the validity of your feelings, nevertheless legitimately question the soundness of your views.

In questioning these views, your readers are questioning not your feelings, but your *opinions*. Unlike feelings, which are always valid, opinions can be valid or invalid to the extent that they are (more or less) informed, uninformed, or misinformed. Their status depends upon whether or not they (more or less) square with evidence relevant to the issue under investigation. To demonstrate to your readers that you have an *informed* opinion about abortion, that is, an opinion that your intended readers should take seriously, you'll need to do more than merely say how you feel about this subject. You'll also need to present and explain the meaning of relevant evidence: for example, evidence having to do with whether or not fetuses constitute living beings; evidence concerning the extent to which women are or are not impeded from having safe, professionally performed abortions; and statistical evidence concerning the number of people who consider themselves both pro-life and pro-choice. (If you have not done so already, see Chapter Five, pp. 135–141, for a detailed discussion concerning the nature and importance of relevant evidence.)

The widely used and perhaps otherwise nonproblematic phrase "personal opinion" might add to the confusion surrounding the concepts of feelings and opinions to the extent that it not only suggests that opinions are personal possessions, but also lends an air of unquestionable acceptability to any opinion that happens to be expressed personally—which is to say, to just about every opinion on the planet. The following passage concerning antisemitic "opinions," taken from Jean-Paul Sartre's book *Anti-Semite and Jew*, highlights the nature of this double-edged problem (the insights articulated here pertain to bigoted views in general, of course):

> If a man attributes all or part of his own misfortunes and those of his country to the presence of Jewish elements in the community, if he proposes to remedy this state of affairs by depriving the Jews of certain of their rights, by keeping them out of certain economic and social activities, by expelling them from the country, by exterminating all of them, we say that he has anti-Semitic *opinions*.
>
> This word *opinion* makes us stop and think. It is the word a hostess uses to bring to an end a discussion that threatens to become acrimonious. It suggests that all points of view are equal; it reassures us, for it gives an inoffensive appearance to ideas by reducing them to the level of tastes. All tastes are natural; all opinions are permitted. Tastes, colors, and opinions are not open to discussion. In the name of democratic institutions, in the name of freedom of opinion, the anti-Semite asserts the right to preach the anti-Jewish crusade everywhere. (7–8; author's italics)

If you have ever heard a bigot or sexist try to defend his or her bigoted or sexist viewpoints not by offering reasons in support of them but instead by saying, simply, "That's just my personal opinion," then perhaps you already understand the nature of the critical thinking dangers that Sartre is addressing. Understanding his point, you can probably easily see why you yourself will want to avoid treating your own opinions as if they were nothing more than personal tastes. (If you have not already done so, see Chapter Two, p. 21 for a detailed discussion of critical thinking.)

Reason Versus Emotion: A False Dichotomy

The above explanation is not meant to imply that emotion and reason are logically incompatible; in fact, the positing of such a dichotomy constitutes a false dilemma, a fallacy in which two alternatives are mistakenly offered as exhaustive, mutually exclusive possibilities. If a condition, circumstance, or proposition admits of only two alternatives, then such a condition, circumstance, or proposition constitutes a *true* dilemma. Consider, for instance, the following set of alternatives that one of my former professors offered as an example of a true dilemma: either a citizen living in Nazi-occupied territory collaborated with the Nazis or he didn't. This statement represents a state of affairs marking a true dilemma because a citizen living under Nazi rule had no other choice but to collaborate with or to resist the Nazis. He could not claim that he didn't collaborate with them on the grounds that he cooperated only slightly. In Nazi-occupied territories, going along with Nazi policy in any way constituted an act of collaboration; not going along with it constituted an act of resistance, an act for which the resister, if caught, was punished by the Nazis, often severely. Thus, the two alternatives in question—that is, to collaborate or to refuse to do so—are exhaustive and mutually exclusive, and therefore the proposition represents a true dilemma.

Now consider the following example of a *false* dilemma: "America—love it or leave it!" (this Vietnam-era slogan articulates the feelings of many Americans who opposed those of their countrymen who were protesting the United States' involvement in the Vietnam War). Though to demonstrate that the thinking implied by this slogan constitutes a false dilemma we need find only *one plausible* alternative to the either/or alternatives that the slogan offers, we can easily find at least two plausible alternatives to these two choices: (1) one can both love *and* leave America or (2) one can both hate it and stay. In other words, the two alternatives implied by the slogan are neither exhaustive nor mutually exclusive, and thus the slogan constitutes a false dilemma.

I offer the above explanations in the hope that they will help you see why the popular view that people cannot be simultaneously emotional and reasonable constitutes a false, not a true, dilemma. People certainly can argue reasonably about an issue concerning which they also show quite a bit of passion. Imagine, for example, that you become highly emotional while offering the following argument, which logicians often use as a classic example of sound reasoning: "All men are mortal; Socrates was a man; therefore, Socrates was mortal." Someone hearing you passionately articulate this argument might very well wonder why you care so much about Socrates' mortality, but he would be responding irrationally were he to say that your conclusion is unreasonable because you argued for it emotionally. Conversely, were you to remain unemotional while arguing that the moon must be made of cheese because you happen to like cheese, your argument would not therefore be a strong one. Again, someone who would say that it is strong *because* you remained calm while offering it would himself be arguing irrationally.

Be that as it may, many people do indeed react negatively to displays of intense emotion and passion. Has anyone ever said to you, for example, "It's not *what* you said that bothered me, but *how you said it*"? Why people seem bothered by someone's mode of delivering a message whose content apparently doesn't bother them is a topic far too complex to discuss here. For now, suffice it to say that you might distance at least some of your intended readers if you express your thoughts and insights in ways that could frighten or offend them. On the other hand, if you are writing about pressing issues, such as the issue of abortion, concerning which you have very strong feelings and about which you can write both objectively and passionately, then you might decide to write objectively and passionately in the hope that, by doing so, you will arouse strong feelings in your readers and thus help motivate them to act. Whether or not they will act as you hope that they will, at least you can feel comforted by the fact that, in your writing, you are true to the integrity of your own thoughts and feelings. You can't make your readers' choices for them, but you can take responsibility for making your own.

Feelings and Critical Thinking: A Sometimes Precarious or Uncomfortable Relationship

All of that having been said, do try to avoid having your personal feelings interfere with your ability to engage in strong analytical thinking. There is a world of difference, for instance, between your arguing, "Though I cannot stand even the thought of abortion, I must conclude that, at least under special circumstances, every pregnant woman has the right to have an abortion," and your arguing, "I cannot stand even the thought of abortion. Abortion is just wrong, wrong, wrong." To be sure, the former position in no way *necessarily* constitutes a position that your intended readers will accept without proof. But were you to cite and explain the meaning of relevant evidence that proves your thesis that "every pregnant woman has the right to have an abortion," your thesis would literally stand to reason, regardless of both your readers' *and* your own personal feelings about abortion. However, were you *not* to argue well for your thesis, then your thesis would remain unproved *even if* your intended readers and you like this thesis.

Occasionally, you might find yourself having to argue for a position that you personally would rather not have. Let me draw from the experiences of some of my own students to help clarify what I mean here. When some of my religious students write personal narratives about their religious beliefs, they revel in the joy that they derive from their faith. However, when writing what we might call a "personally driven academic paper" in which they inject their own feelings about their religion into an analysis of the political and social acts—good or bad—carried out in the name of their religion, many of these students happily document the good deeds carried out by members of their faith and sadly (and sometimes angrily) try to deal with the fact that, in the name of *their own religion*, people and governments have committed many crimes against humanity. Truly, they would rather *not* have to believe that the latter is the case. But, having carefully done their homework—that is, having carefully examined indisputable facts and drawn reasonable inferences from their analyses of these facts—they feel that they cannot conclude otherwise and still engage in good-faith analyses of the evidence confronting them.

The Problem of Poor Sampling

Another critical thinking stumbling block common to personally driven academic papers—though certainly not a stumbling block exclusive to such papers—

has to do with a problem known as "poor sampling." For example, if, having never before seen a cat, I happen to see one with three legs and then conclude that all cats probably have three legs, I will have reasoned weakly. Now, to be sure, you yourself will not likely make such an obvious mistake. But you might make a conceptually similar one if you assume too readily that your own personal experiences bespeak general views or claims. The following example illustrates this not uncommon problem.

One day, while I was working in our college's writing lab, I was helping a student who had written a promising paper in which she had argued that parents need to take more responsibility for their children's lives. At one point in her paper, she mentioned that parents are unaware of the fact that their children face much more difficult problems than the parents themselves had to face when they were young, problems concerning school violence, drugs, and so on. I responded that such a finding flies in the face of *voluminous* evidence to the contrary; indeed, even a cursory glance at this evidence (presented, for example, in academic studies and media specials) should yield me the insight that many parents not only are *well* aware of the problems to which this student was referring, but also feel frustrated that, regardless of their concern, their children have to face such problems. Surprised at hearing such a counter position to her own point of view, this student suggested that, nevertheless, her opinion was legitimate. When I asked how many sets of parents she had spoken to about this issue, she replied, "One." A bright and motivated student, she immediately realized that the evidence which she had garnered in her poor sampling of parental opinion does not outweigh such a massive body of counter evidence, and that this poor sampling had led her to produce an analytically suspicious (if not clearly inaccurate) statement concerning the issue at stake. Though, as it turns out, she didn't have to revise or abandon her thesis (that is, her main assertion)[1] concerning parental responsibility, she learned how opinions derived from poor samplings can lead to trouble.

To see how you might avoid having this problem in your own work, imagine that you are asked to read Sandra Cisneros' short story "My Name" (see p. 46) and then to write a paper in which, drawing partly or largely from some of your own experiences concerning injustice, oppression, and the like, you are to analyze the narrator's attitudes about her name. Analyzing too hastily or unreflectively the meaning or significance of your own experiences, good or bad, you might be tempted to conclude that the narrator is a whiner, a complainer, and that people should just try to deal with their personal problems as best they can and then move on. Or, you might want to conclude that the narrator speaks courageously for all troubled, disenfranchised "outsiders." Either way (and these are but two of the possible conclusions that you might reach), you could be risking the integrity

---

[1]If you are unfamiliar with the concept of a thesis, please see Chapter Five, pp. 135–138, where this concept is discussed in detail.

of your paper were you to reach such conclusions without having carefully examined the relationship between your personal experiences and relevant textual evidence in Cisneros' story.

To help yourself arrive at a fair analysis of the narrator's views, ask yourself and then, as honestly as possible, attempt to answer the following kinds of questions: (1) "Can I accept the fact that the narrator's attitudes are legitimate *for her*, whether or not I or anyone else shares, approves of, or even likes them?" (2) "Do I know what the narrator's attitudes are and understand why she has them?" (3) "Do my own attitudes jibe with hers?" (4) "Can I legitimately say that the status of the narrator's views depends upon whether or not I share, approve of, or like them?"(5) "Do I have a reasonable enough sampling of evidence upon which to draw any general conclusions from my analysis?" If you answer such questions in good faith, you ought to be well on your way to writing a substantively sound, personally oriented academic paper.

Some Final Thoughts

With work, practice, and patience, you should begin sensing how, on a case-by-case basis, you can profitably balance the needs of a writing project that bridges the gap between a personal narrative and a traditional academic essay, a project in which, ultimately, you'll need to decide how much emphasis you should place on the personal elements in your writing and how much you should place on the nonpersonal, academic ones. If, for instance, you do (at least some version of) this chapter's featured assignment, you might decide to subordinate examples concerning your own experiences to an analysis of the points made by Mitsuye Yamada, the author of the featured reading selection. Or, like J. Kehaulani Kauanui, the contributing author, you might decide to use a close reading of the Yamada material as a point of departure for your own analytically driven personal narrative.

Similarly, concerning your paper's structure, you might decide that, as Kauanui did in her essay, you want to deal with points from Yamada's essay at the beginning and end of your paper but use the body of your essay to analyze your own situations, problems, and so forth. Or, you might decide to interweave Yamada's thoughts and yours throughout your paper. Additionally, like Kauanui, you might decide to use explanatory footnotes and to refer to writings other than Yamada's. Or, you might decide that your paper will be better served if you keep all of your explanations in the body of the essay and that you can make your case well enough by focusing your analysis only on Yamada's and your own ideas. Though the possibilities for structuring your personally driven academic essay are probably not endless, they are plentiful enough to allow you to write an essay that more than adequately fulfills the needs of the assignment and proves meaningful to you.

However you decide to structure your paper, you should—as always— allow yourself to be guided by the needs of the assignment, the needs of your intended readers, the nature of the material that you are presenting, and your own knowledge about and personal investments in such material. But remember that, as is the case when you write any sort of essay, writing a personally driven academic paper always involves (what else?) a *process*. Thus, you shouldn't be discouraged if throughout the writing process your ideas develop and take shape slowly—unless, of course, you've begun doing the assignment the night before it is due! Working hard to combine your interconnected acts of close reading, careful thinking and rethinking, and diligent writing and rewriting, you should produce enough clearly written, analytically strong essays that win the respect of conscientious readers, writers, and thinkers of *all* kinds, academic or not.

READING AND WRITING

During the 1960s, when a number of civil rights movements swept across the United States, women began seeing their longtime struggles for equality reach a turning point. And yet, like other historically disenfranchised people, women still face both blatant and subtle forms of cultural oppression that hamper their efforts to achieve full equality in the United States. Indeed, women as a group are blatantly and commonly devalued in our culture, a fact that one can easily verify by taking even a cursory inventory of the sexist images and messages in magazine and television advertisements, television shows, and movies, and on mud flaps, bumper stickers, and billboards. In fact, one would be hard-pressed to find an area of American life in which sexism does not exist blatantly or subtly at some level. In light of the continuing promotion of misogyny in our culture, it isn't surprising that we continue to see a steady stream of violence against women and that women still have difficulty being taken seriously as mothers, executives, physicians, judges, combat soldiers, presidential candidates, and so on.

This chapter's readings deal with a range of issues and problems having to do with sexism, including the roots and consequences of men's sexist attitudes and behaviors towards women; the sadly common problem of female misogyny; the ramifications of nonmainstream women's invisibility within or outright rejection from mainstream women's movements in the United States; and the often complex relationship among sexism, racism, and other forms of bigotry. While perusing this chapter's reading selections, think about how far-reaching your own vision presently is—and, perhaps even more important, how insightful you want that vision to be—with respect to the being and status of the many individuals and groups who have been or who are culturally, socially, politically, religiously, sexually, or in some other way "invisible." Hopefully, your attempts to synthesize the information in this chapter's readings will help you better understand *yourself* by helping you better understand the various types of invisibility felt by disenfranchised people. Don't be surprised, though, if you also discover that the line between the visible and the invisible is often little more than thinly veiled.

FEATURED ASSIGNMENT

Part I: Write a paper in which you either support or take issue with what you consider to be Yamada's view on a central problem that she discusses in her essay, such as her view concerning the racism that she confronts in her personal and professional life, or her perspective on the sexism that she confronts in her family and culture. Your analysis should either directly or indirectly highlight the problem on which you choose to focus and be supported by pertinent, germane evidence from Yamada's essay as well as from your own personal experiences. Though you might decide to try to achieve a balance between personal and traditional academic writing, you are not obligated to do so.

Part II: Write a brief reflective commentary on what you experienced, thought, and/or felt while doing this assignment.

F E A T U R E D   R E A D I N G

Invisibility is an Unnatural Disaster: Reflections of an Asian American Woman

MITSUYE YAMADA

Mitsuye Yamada (1923–) was born in Fukuoka, Japan. In 1926, she came to the United States; and though her parents were already U.S. residents when she was born (they were visiting Japan in 1923), Yamada did not become a naturalized U.S. citizen until 1955. In the intervening years, she received her B.A. from New York University and her M.A. from the University of Chicago. During the Second World War, she was deported to the Minidoka Relocation Center (in Idaho), which was one of the concentration camps for West-Coast Japanese Americans (Yamada and her family had been living in Seattle prior to the outbreak of the war). She writes movingly about her experiences in that camp in a collection of poetry entitled *Camp Notes and Other Poems* (1976). Others of her publications include *Desert Run: Poems and Stories* (1988) and *Sowing Ti Leaves* (1990), an anthology of women writers from a variety of cultures, which she co-edited with Sarie Sachie Hylkema.

Besides continuing to write, Yamada lectures at workshops and women's conferences and gives poetry readings. She also served on the National Board of Amnesty International from 1987–1992. Though in 1989 she retired from her position as a professor of English at Cyprus College (in Cyprus, California), where, during the 1970s, she was also coordinator of the women's program, Yamada has recently been a visiting professor at UCLA and, currently, at San Diego State University, where she teaches in the creative writing program. She is also the founder and coordinator of Multicultural Women Writers, a writers' group based in Irvine, California. While commenting on her own work a number of years ago, she remarked that, as she was becoming older, she found herself "'mov[ing] from writing intensely personal poetry to writing essays on social and political issues. . . [because her] identity as an Asian American and [her] identity as a woman [had begun] to merge within [her] as a singular identity and [she had felt] a missionary zeal to let others know about it'" (*Contemporary Authors*, vols. 77–80, p. 615). The following reading selection manifests the markings of this major emotional and intellectual turning point in Yamada's position concerning her life and work, a position that, as she remarked recently, still basically holds true with respect to the work that she is doing now. [Some of the information for this biographical sketch was obtained from *Contemporary Authors, op. cit.*]

PRE-READING QUESTIONS:

1) Do you have any thoughts or feelings about sexism, racism, and the possible relationship between the two? If you do, keep these thoughts and feelings in mind as you read Yamada's essay, watching to see whether or not—and, if so, how, why, and to what extent—they affect your understanding of or reactions to her ideas concerning these matters.

2) Were you ever verbally attacked for complaining about your problems?

3) Have you ever felt that your ideas were discounted because of who or what you are? Were others who were taken more seriously than you given credit for coming up with ideas that you yourself had voiced?

4) Have you ever tried to overcome an image that others have of you or to become someone other than the person whom they want you to be? If so, how did they react to your desire to change? Were you ever in their shoes?

5) How would you define a "personally driven academic essay"? How would you distinguish this sort of essay from other sorts with which you are familiar? Are there common denominators among all essays?

CLOSE-READING TIP

Yamada's essay is a good example of analytically oriented writing that combines "the personal" and "the academic." Yamada weaves together her attempt to understand and explain her own struggles as a woman and as a member of a minority, the struggles of others with whom she identifies, the ways in which oppression in general functions, the ways in which the metaphors of "visibility" and "invisibility" help us better understand how disenfranchised people respond to oppression, and the ways in which we might begin to rethink our attitudes and actions concerning oppression. As you read and reread her essay, pay attention to those passages in which Yamada directly links the personal and the academic in her attempts to explicate the interrelatedness of these concerns. Consider, for example, relevant passages in paragraphs 4, 9, 13, and 19.

YAMADA

SELECTION

Invisibility is
An Unnatural Disaster

L ast year for the Asian segment of the Ethnic American Literature course I was teaching, I selected a new anthology entitled *Aiiieeeee!* compiled by a group of outspoken Asian American writers. During the discussion of the long but thought-provoking introduction to this anthology, one of my students blurted out that she was offended by its militant tone and that as a white person she was tired of always being blamed for the oppression of all the minorities. I noticed several of her classmates' eyes nodding in tacit agreement. A discussion of the "militant" voices in some of the other writings we had read in the course ensued. Surely, I pointed out, some of these other writings have been just as, if not more, militant as the words in this introduction? Had they been offended by those also but failed to express their feelings about them? To my surprise, they said they were not offended by any of the Black American, Chicano or American Indian writings, but were hard-pressed to explain why when I asked for an explanation. A little further discussion revealed that they "understood" the anger expressed by the Black and Chicanos and they "empathized" with the frustrations and sorrow expressed by the American Indian. But the Asian Americans??

2   Then finally, one student said it for all of them: "It made me angry. *Their* anger made *me* angry, because I didn't even know the Asian Americans felt oppressed. I didn't expect their anger."

3   At this time I was involved in an academic due process procedure begun as a result of a grievance I had filed the previous semester against the administrators at my college. I had filed a grievance for violation of my rights as a teacher who had worked in the district for almost eleven years. My student's remark "Their anger made me angry...I didn't expect their anger," explained for me the reactions of some of my own colleagues as well as the reactions of the administrators during those previous months. The grievance procedure was a time-consuming and emotionally draining process, but the basic principle was too important for me to ignore. That basic principle was that I, an individual teacher, do have certain rights which are given and my superiors cannot, should not, violate them with impunity. When this was pointed out to them, however, they responded with shocked surprise that I, of all people, would take them to task for violation of what was clearly written policy in our college district. They all seemed to exclaim, "We don't understand this; this is so uncharacteristic of her; she seemed such a nice person, so polite, so obedient, so non-trouble making." What was even more surprising was once they were forced to acknowledge that I was determined to start the due process action, they assumed I was not doing it on my own. One of the

337

administrators suggested someone must have pushed me into this, undoubtedly some of "those feminists" on our campus, he said wryly.

4   In this age when women are clearly making themselves visible on all fronts, I, an Asian American woman, am still functioning as a "front for those feminists" and therefore invisible. The realization of this sinks in slowly. Asian Americans as a whole are finally coming to claim their own, demanding that they be included in the multicultural history of our country. I like to think, in spite of my administrator's myopia, that the most stereotyped minority of them all, the Asian American woman, is just now emerging to become part of that group. It took forever. Perhaps it is important to ask ourselves why it took so long. We should ask ourselves this question just when we think we are emerging as a viable minority in the fabric of our society. I should add to my student's words, "because I didn't even know they felt oppressed," that it took this long because we Asian American women have not admitted to ourselves that we *were* oppressed. We, the visible minority that is invisible.

5   I say this because until a few years ago I have been an Asian American woman working among non-Asians in an educational institution where most of the decision-makers were men*; an Asian American woman thriving under the smug illusion that I was *not* the stereotypic image of the Asian woman because I had a career teaching English in a community college. I did not think anything assertive was necessary to make my point. People who know me, I reasoned, the ones who count, know who I am and what I think. Thus, even when what I considered a veiled racist remark was made in a casual social setting, I would "let it go" because it was pointless to argue with people who didn't even know their remark was racist. I had supposed that I was practicing passive resistance while being stereotyped, but it was so passive no one noticed I was resisting; it was so much my expected role that it ultimately rendered me invisible.

6   My experience leads me to believe that contrary to what I thought, I had actually been contributing to my own stereotyping. Like the hero in Ralph Ellison's novel *The Invisible Man*, I had become invisible to white Americans, and it clung to me like a bad habit. Like most bad habits, this one crept up on me because I took it in minute doses like Mithradates' poison and my mind and body adapted so well to it I hardly noticed it was there.

7   For the past eleven years I have busied myself with the usual chores of an English teacher, a wife of a research chemist, and a mother of four rapidly growing children. I hadn't even done much to shatter this particular stereotype: the middle class woman happy to be bringing home the extra income and quietly fitting into the man's world of work. When the Asian American woman is lulled into believing that people perceive her as being different from other Asian women (the submissive, subservient, ready-to-please, easy-to-get-along-with Asian woman), she is kept comfortably content with the state of

---

*It is hoped this will change now that a black woman is Chancellor of our college district. [Yamada's note.]

things. She becomes ineffectual in the milieu in which she moves. The seemingly apolitical middle class woman and the apolitical Asian woman constituted a double invisibility.

8   I had created an underground culture of survival for myself and had become in the eyes of others the person I was trying not to be. Because I was permitted to go to college, permitted to take a stab at a career or two along the way, given "free choice" to marry and have a family, given a "choice" to eventually do both, I had assumed I was more or less free, not realizing that those who are free make and take choices; they do not choose from options proffered by "those out there."

9   I, personally, had not "emerged" until I was almost fifty years old. Apparently through a long conditioning process, I had learned how *not* to be seen for what I am. A long history of ineffectual activities had been, I realize now, initiation rites toward my eventual invisibility. The training begins in childhood; and for women and minorities, whatever is started in childhood is continued throughout their adult lives. I first recognized just how invisible I was in my first real confrontation with my parents a few years after the outbreak of World War II.

10   During the early years of the war, my older brother, Mike, and I left the concentration camp in Idaho to work and study at the University of Cincinnati. My parents came to Cincinnati soon after my father's release from Internment Camp (these were POW camps to which many of the Issei* men, leaders in their communities, were sent by the FBI), and worked as domestics in the suburbs. I did not see them too often because by this time I had met and was much influenced by a pacifist who was out on a "furlough" from a conscientious objectors' camp in Trenton, North Dakota. When my parents learned about my "boy friend" they were appalled and frightened. After all, this was the period when everyone in the country was expected to be one-hundred percent behind the war effort, and the Nisei† boys who had volunteered for the Armed Forces were out there fighting and dying to prove how American we really were. However, during interminable arguments with my father and overheard arguments between my parents, I was devastated to learn they were not so much concerned about my having become a pacifist, but they were more concerned about the possibility of my marrying one. They were understandably frightened (my father's prison years of course were still fresh on his mind) about repercussions on the rest of the family. In an attempt to make my father understand me, I argued that even if I didn't marry him, I'd still be a pacifist; but my father reassured me that it was "all right" for me to be a pacifist because as a Japanese national and a "girl" *it didn't make any difference to anyone.* In frustration I remember shouting, "But can't you see, *I'm* philosophically committed to the pacifist cause," but he dismissed this with "In my col-

---

*Issei—Immigrant Japanese, living in the U.S. [Yamada's note.]

†Nisei—Second generation Japanese, born in the U.S. [Yamada's note.]

lege days we used to call philosophy, foolosophy," and that was the end of that. When they were finally convinced I was not going to marry "my pacifist," the subject was dropped and we never discussed it again.

11   As if to confirm my father's assessment of the harmlessness of my opinions, my brother Mike, an American citizen, was suddenly expelled from the University of Cincinnati while I, "an enemy alien", was permitted to stay. We assumed that his stand as a pacifist, although he was classified a 4-F because of his health, contributed to his expulsion. We were told the Air Force was conducting sensitive wartime research on campus and requested his removal, but they apparently felt my presence on campus was not as threatening.

12   I left Cincinnati in 1945, hoping to leave behind this and other unpleasant memories gathered there during the war years, and plunged right into the politically active atmosphere at New York University where students, many of them returning veterans, were continuously promoting one cause or other by making speeches in Washington Square, passing out petitions, or staging demonstrations. On one occasion, I tagged along with a group of students who took a train to Albany to demonstrate on the steps of the State Capitol. I think I was the only Asian in this group of predominantly Jewish students from NYU. People who passed us were amused and shouted "Go home and grow up." I suppose Governor Dewey, who refused to see us, assumed we were a group of adolescents without a cause as most college students were considered to be during those days. It appears they weren't expecting any results from our demonstration. There were no newspersons, no security persons, no police. No one tried to stop us from doing what we were doing. We simply did "our thing" and went back to our studies until next time, and my father's words were again confirmed: it made no difference to anyone, being a young student demonstrator in peacetime, 1947.

13   Not only the young, but those who feel powerless over their own lives know what it is like not to make a difference on anyone or anything. The poor know it only too well, and we women have known it since we were little girls. The most insidious part of this conditioning process, I realize now, was that we have been trained not to expect a response in ways that mattered. We may be listened to and responded to with placating words and gestures, but our psychological mind set has already told us time and again that we were born into a ready-made world into which we must fit ourselves, and that many of us do it very well.

14   This mind set is the result of not believing that the political and social forces affecting our lives are determined by some person, or a group of persons, probably sitting behind a desk or around a conference table.

15   Just recently I read an article about "the remarkable track record of success" of the Nisei in the United States. One Nisei was quoted as saying he attributed our stamina and endurance to our ancestors whose characters had been shaped, he said, by their living in a country which has been constantly besieged by all manner of natural disasters, such as earthquakes and hurricanes. He said the Nisei has inherited a steely will, a will to endure and hence, to survive.

16   This evolutionary explanation disturbs me, because it equates the "act of God" (i.e. natural disasters) to the "act of man" (i.e., the war, the evacuation). The former is not within our power to alter, but the latter, I should think, is. By putting the "acts of God" on par with the acts of man, we shrug off personal responsibilities.

17   I have, for too long a period of time accepted the opinion of others (even though they were directly affecting my life) as if they were objective events totally out of my control. Because I separated such opinions from the persons who were making them, I accepted them the way I accepted natural disasters; and I endured them as inevitable. I have tried to cope with people whose points of view alarmed me in the same way that I had adjusted to natural phenomena, such as hurricanes, which plowed into my life from time to time. I would readjust my dismantled feelings in the same way that we repaired the broken shutters after the storm. The Japanese have an all-purpose expression in their language for this attitude of resigned acceptance: "Shikataganai." "It can't be helped." "There's nothing I can do about it." It is said with the shrug of the shoulders and tone of finality, perhaps not unlike the "those-were-my-orders" tone that was used at the Nuremberg trials. With all the sociological studies that have been made about the causes of the evacuations of the Japanese Americans during World War II, we should know by now that "they" knew that the West Coast Japanese Americans would go without too much protest, and of course, "they" were right, for most of us (with the exception of those notable few), resigned to our fate, albeit bewildered and not willingly. We were not perceived by our government as responsive Americans; we were objects that happened to be standing in the path of the storm.

18   Perhaps this kind of acceptance is a way of coping with the "real" world. One stands against the wind for a time, and then succumbs eventually because there is no point to being stubborn against all odds. The wind will not respond to entreaties anyway, one reasons; one should have sense enough to know that. I'm not ready to accept this evolutionary reasoning. It is too rigid for me; I would like to think that my new awareness is going to make me more visible than ever, and to allow me to make some changes in the "man made disaster" I live in at the present time. Part of being visible is refusing to separate the actors from their actions, and demanding that they be responsible for them.

19   By now, riding along with the minorities' and women's movements, I think we are making a wedge into the main body of American life, but people are still looking right through and around us, assuming we are simply tagging along. Asian American women still remain in the background and we are heard but not really listened to. Like Musak, they think we are piped into the airwaves by someone else. We must remember that one of the most insidious ways of keeping women and minorities powerless is to let them only talk about harmless and inconsequential subjects, or let them speak freely and not listen to them with serious intent.

20   We need to raise our voices a little more, even as they say to us "This is so uncharacteristic of you." To finally recognize our own invisibility is to finally be on the path toward visibility. Invisibility is not a natural state for anyone.

POST-READING QUESTIONS:

1) Did you find that any of your thoughts or feelings about sexism, racism, and the possible relationship between the two affected your understanding of or helped shape your reactions to Yamada's ideas concerning these matters? Did her essay cause you to reexamine your reasons for having these thoughts and feelings?

2) Does your understanding of Yamada's essay help you to understand the significance of your responses to the second and third pre-reading questions?

3) How might Yamada evaluate your response to the fourth pre-reading question? Concerning the issues at stake here, are you and Yamada essentially on the same side?

4) In your view, does Yamada successfully employ the metaphors of "visibility" and "invisibility" in her analysis of oppression? Does her analysis seem essentially personal, or does it seem to have implications beyond the personal? Does her essay fit your definition of the personally driven academic essay? Do you want to rethink your definition after having read Yamada's piece?

5) Might our understanding of the expression "'Shikataganai'" (paragraph 17) help us to understand either how and why Yamada's ideas concerning oppression are related or how and why they are exclusive of one another (or possibly both)? Would a careful analysis of this expression aid one's understanding of, say, the final sentences in paragraphs 19 and 20?

6) If Langston Hughes (see p. 244) and Louie Crew (see p. 146) were to do this chapter's featured assignment, what ideas and feelings do you think that they might express in their essays? On which of the problems that Yamada discusses might they focus? How might they evaluate and respond to Yamada's views concerning these problems? In your view, would their evaluations be on the mark?

Shifting Identities, Shifting Alliances

J. KEHAULANI KAUANUI

Several years before the controversial term "political correctness" became popular, J. Kehaulani Kauanui was already engaged in *substantively* politically correct thinking and action. For example, in the mid–1980s, when she was a student at Irvine Valley College—which is located in Orange County, California, one of the most important seats of political conservatism in the country—Kehaulani helped found the college's Women's Resource Center (now the Re-Entry and Women's Center), a task that was anything but easy. After completing her studies at Irvine Valley, she transferred to the University of California at Berkeley, where she received her B.A. in women's studies with a minor in ethnic studies, and where she developed a serious commitment to writing. Her work has appeared in *Third Force: Issues and Actions in Communities of Color* (May/June 1993), *Moving the Mountains: Asian American Women's Journal* (Spring 1993), and *Diatribe* (October 1992). In 1994, not long after she had been graduated from Berkeley, she was awarded a Fulbright Fellowship to study Maori and Pacific Island studies at the University of Auckland in Aotearoa (New Zealand). Her past and future research plans include studies of, in her own words, "diasporic Pacific Island communities and their struggles for self-determination, indigenous Pacific women's leadership, and decolonization and postcolonial feminisms." Planning to teach college after receiving her Ph.D., Kehaulani remains committed to continuing her academic and political work on behalf of disenfranchised people.

RESPONSE

PART I   **Essay**

In "Invisibility is an Unnatural Disaster: Reflections of an Asian American Woman," Mitsuye Yamada describes a discussion with her students regarding the "militant voices" expressed in writings by people of color. Yamada remembers the white students' shock at learning about the anger of Asian Americans: "Their anger made me angry. . . . I didn't expect their anger." Yamada recalls some of her experiences with racism and analyzes how she has contributed to her own stereotyping and invisibility. I identify with Yamada, facing those who are puzzled by my own anger, and dealing with my own issues of invisibility regarding race.

Most of Yamada's white students did not feel individually responsible for the oppression of people of color. Understanding that racist oppression is institutionalized—that is, it isn't only expressed on a personal level where one person simply doesn't like another person, but that *it is also structural*—may move white people to feel a collective responsibility and take an anti-racist stance. This stance should include accountability for the white privileges from which most whites benefit to varying degrees depending on their class, gender, and ethnic identification.

The fact that many of Yamada's white students were surprised at the anger of the Asian American writers is very telling. The "ranking" of oppressions is all too common amongst people of color, and is compounded when whites perceive only some of us as "legitimately" militant. The "model minority" stereotyping of Asian

Americans persists. That is, many persons believe that Asian Americans are supposedly not exposed to racism, are economically well-to-do, and are a "fine example" of how "minorities"—with enough hard work and persistence—can overcome what is lightly referred to as "setbacks" of the past.

Although I do not identify with Yamada's white students, I do contend with issues of white privilege. I am perceived as white, although I identify as a woman of color. I am biracial—of Native Hawaiian and mixed European descent. Both whites and people of color, in general, assume that I'm white. My surname, which is Hawaiian, usually signifies that I'm other than white. I was raised by my white mother and her white husband. While growing up with them, in a predominantly white neighborhood, I was conditioned to identify as white. Like Yamada, "I had learned how not to be seen for what I am." Although I would admit that I was Hawaiian, and visited my family in Hawai'i regularly, I still perceived myself as white. I was *expected* to be white. All of this "training" was reinforced by my parents' verbal degradation of people of color. I had internalized this racism (feeling internal conflict but not having the language to *name it*) while living with the everyday privileges my light skin affords me.

It wasn't until I moved away from home to attend college (another privilege) that I started to reevaluate my racial identity. After two years of remembering these various incidents of "training" and a visit back to Hawai'i (after not having travelled there for seven years—*by choice*) I made a conscious effort to identify myself as Native Hawaiian, and more specifically as biracial Native Hawaiian. I also decided to go by my middle name which is Hawaiian, rather than by my first name, "Josette," which is *haole* (a Hawaiian word meaning white). This was a major step in affirming my heritage, "claiming my color," and voicing my political loyalties to Native Hawaiians. It was my way of reminding myself and others that whites do not own me. Curiously, many people have treated me as "ungrateful" for claiming my Hawaiian name. In their view, since I had the choice to "pass" for white I should do so and not hinder myself. While having to confront the fact that on many levels I do have some white privileges, I have rejected this "honorary" white membership.

This "honorary" white membership is historically specific to Native peoples[1] in the United States. The federal government has enforced this white membership by, for example, establishing blood quantum standards.[2] If we cannot furnish such proof, we do not have any political recourse (say, if a land trust relationship is abused), nor can we qualify for any federal so-called benefits. As the great majority of Native peoples are multi-racial this systematic inclusion/exclusion has vast economic and social impacts.[3] Thus my visibility as a Native Hawaiian[4] (although I am not legally recognized as such) is an oppositional stance.

Many people were surprised that there was anything political in my "claiming color." Most people believe that Hawai'i—so beautiful—couldn't possibly have any social or economic problems and that Hawaiians, when not lounging under coconut trees, must be happy to sing and dance for (usually *haole*) tourists. Just as Yamada's students are struck at the anger of Asian Americans, most people also find it hard to accept that Native Hawaiians have something to "complain about."

Yamada names those who are most likely to "have been trained not to expect a response in ways that mattered." Light-skinned people of color are familiar with the resistance from those who feel threatened that we are *naming ourselves* instead of accepting the categories they set for us. "Mixed-race people threaten the core of a racist society."[5] The polarizing "black and white" racial discourse

---

[1] Here I am referring to both Native American Indians, Eskimos, Aleuts, and Native Hawaiians. Native Hawaiians, although we are not federally recognized as a sovereign people—we are defined as wards of the state—we are, under the Religious Freedom Act, Native American Health Care Act, and various educational acts, legally classified as Native Americans.

[2] The federal government, since 1921, legally defines a "Native Hawaiian" as someone who can prove 50% blood quantum (with legal documents, genealogical records, etc.), otherwise they are treated as "part-Hawaiian" (which has little or no legal standing).

[3] It is important to note here how historically this *has not* been the case for other race groups. For example, African Americans have been legally categorized as black even if they are only of 1/32 African descent. So, depending on the motives of those in power, race is defined in various ways for different purposes. African Americans have been denied Civil Rights and representation because of that "one drop" of "negro blood" while for Native peoples we've had to prove that we do have "the blood."

[4] I make the distinction between the use of the term to identify Native indigenous people and the use of the word "Hawaiian" as one might call herself a "Californian" or a "New Yorker."

[5] I thank writer and activist Lani Ka'ahumanu for this line from her poem "Hapa Haole Wahine" which is published in *Bi Any Other Name*, co-edited by Ka'ahumanu. (Alyson Publications, 1991)

can render many of us invisible. With the changing racial demographics in this country, more people of color are realizing that we do have the growing numbers to help make political changes. We must make a difference and become visible, racially and otherwise, for, as Yamada declares, "invisibility is not a natural state for anyone."

This style of "mixing" academic writing with personal narrative is my favorite type of assignment. I bring my "self" and my experiences to the work I do. As I don't believe that there is ever total "objectivity" I signal to the reader the *degree* to which I am subjective. Even in my more "academic" voice I locate myself. For example, when I write a research paper about Hawaiian history and/or politics, I might tell "where I'm coming from" in the introduction. I locate myself (not "explain" myself) to a lesser degree. In this piece where I "mix" the styles, I am subjective to a large degree.

　　I had trouble formulating a thesis though I had an easy time in general writing on Yamada's piece. My thesis is more derived from my work. My thesis: "Although I do not identify with Yamada's white student's, I do contend with issues of white privilege. I am perceived as white, although I identify as a woman of color," is closely linked to Yamada's thesis that she "contributed to her own stereotyping and racism" and that "invisibility is an unnatural disaster." Ultimately, I see this last line as the thesis of Yamada's piece and my own.

　　I definitely sharpened my ideas in the course of writing my paper. In my piece I map out my path from the time and place of experiences and the shift I made in my own racial identity and development. I first marked on Yamada's essay parts which especially moved me. I situated my thesis where it emerged, after I got past simply identifying with Yamada (with her anger, and invisibility), I asserted a thesis about my own life and privileged my own experiences while sometimes drawing parallels between my own experiences, and Yamada's. I also tried to point to larger themes of the interlocking ideologies about race and gender, in this case, Asian Americans and Pacific Islanders, a Japanese woman, and me the biracial Hawaiian woman.

My mode of operation was not formulized at all, writing the piece was a process, and I developed my theory as I worked it. When I read a piece and consider writing I write down notes off the top of my head which strike me from previous recent readings, hence, I don't necessarily confine myself to the one essay about which I'm writing. Another writer's voice may echo as I write and think about my paper, I may bring their work to my piece without "researching" *per se*.

My title is a good example of how my writing is a process. I believe my title reflects the essence of my paper as well as my thesis. And by reading my title alone, one may guess that I subordinated an analysis of Yamada's view to an evaluation of n y own personal experience.

I didn't think too consciously about the task at hand. This essay lent itself to my approach. But I was conscious about the readers' knowledge about the specifics about my story, in this case the self-determination of Native Hawaiians.

R E L A T E D   R E A D I N G S

from Women's Reality

ANNE WILSON SCHAEF

Anne Wilson Schaef (1934–) is a practicing psychotherapist, lecturer, workshop leader, consultant, public speaker, and author. Among her published writings are *Co-Dependence: Misunderstood-Mistreated* (1986), *When Society Becomes an Addict* (1987), *The Addictive Organization* (1990), and *Women's Reality: An Emerging Female System in a White Male Society* (1981), the book from which the following reading selection is taken and for which Schaef might be best known. Arguing from a woman-centered perspective, Schaef tries to demonstrate in this text that what she calls "the White Male System" of thinking and behaving is an abusive, death-oriented system of psychological, religious, political, and social control. She also tries to show women (especially) how they might escape from this system's suffocating grip on them. Curiously, Schaef had not wanted to write *Women's Reality* but felt pressured to do so from people who had heard her lecture on the ideas that would eventually become the substantive matter of this text (*Contemporary Authors,* vol. 118, p. 415). Schaef herself has this to say about her book, which she finally wrote "'in two five-day stretches'": "'I feel that [it] is a book that had to be written. . . . In some ways I do not feel that [it] is *my* book, and I have very little ego tied up in it. I felt that it was some kind of assignment from beyond myself, and I finally just gave up the struggle and wrote it'" (ibid.; author's italics).

PRE-READING QUESTIONS:

1) Knowing that you are about to read the work of a psychotherapist who developed her "approach to psychotherapy. . . from a Female-System approach to healing" (*Contemporary Authors*, vol. 118, p. 416), do you have any pre-reading expectations about the kinds of ideas that you might find in the following reading selection? If you do, see if these expectations play a part in your attempts to understand Schaef's ideas.

2) Can you give some examples of how you use the adjectives "realistic" and "unrealistic"? Do you think that "reality" is fixed, changeable, both, or neither?

3) Drawing from your own experiences and knowledge, how would you characterize male-female relationships? In general, do men seem to like women, and vice versa? In what sorts of circumstances do women seem to enjoy being with men (and vice versa)? Under what circumstances do women prefer being with other women and do men prefer being with other men?

4) What comes to mind when you hear the phrase "White Male System"? Does this phrase provoke feelings of anger or pride in you? Does it seem too general or vague? Does it seem to be a euphemism, an understatement, an overstatement, or something else entirely?

CLOSE-READING TIP

To a great extent, the success or failure of Schaef's analyses in *Women's Reality* hinges upon how well Schaef can justify her ideas concerning what she calls "the White Male System." Curiously, at certain points in her analyses Schaef seems to *personify* this system. As you read the following excerpts, note those moments when the White Male System seems to take on—or be given—a life of its own. Try to determine whether Schaef strengthens or weakens her analyses, or whether she does both or neither, when she animates the White Male System. Consider, for example, relevant passages in paragraphs 30, 31, 47, and 49.

The White Male System and the Way the World Isn't

1 . . . When working with clients, therapists have traditionally taken one of two approaches: the *intrapsychic* or the *interpersonal*. In the former, the therapist focuses on what goes on *inside* the person, emphasizing the importance of dreams, fantasies, defense mechanisms, fixations, and the like. Of special significance are the first five years of a client's life; these are seen as having shaped the person and determined what she or he would be and become in the future.

2 Many practitioners now feel that the intrapsychic approach is sorely lacking. The information gained by that methodology may be useful, but it is just not enough. True, a therapist can work with an individual's insides and make

great strides, but it is also necessary to work with her or his *outsides*—specifically, to become aware of and/or involved with the significant others in the client's life. After all, no one lives in a vacuum! The interpersonal approach, then, focuses on the system in which the client lives *and* on the system which is the client herself or himself.

3   As a practicing psychotherapist, I myself have used both approaches—the intrapsychic and the interpersonal—with my clients, depending on their needs and my perceptions. Both have worked at different times; both have helped people to become living, loving, capable individuals. Still, I have never been entirely satisfied with either approach or the combination of the two. Something is missing from each one—something which I have grown to feel is essential not only to the therapeutic process but also to getting along in the world on a day-to-day basis.

4   What is missing is an understanding and awareness of what I have chosen to call the White Male System. It is crucial to be able to define this system and deal with it simply because it surrounds us and permeates our lives. Its myths, beliefs, rituals, procedures, and outcomes affect everything we think, feel, and do.

5   Let me explain what I mean by the White Male System. It is the system in which we live, and in it, the power and influence are held by white males. This system did not happen overnight, nor was it the result of the machinations of only a few individuals; we all not only let it occur but participated in its development. Nevertheless, the White Male System is just that: a system. We all live in it, but it is not reality. It is not the way the world is. Unfortunately, some of us do not recognize that it is a system and think it *is* reality or the way the world is.

6   The White Male System—and it is important to keep in mind that I am referring to a *system* here and not pointing a finger at specific individuals within it—controls almost every aspect of our culture. It makes our laws, runs our economy, sets our salaries, and decides when and if we will go to war or remain at home. It decides what *is* knowledge and how it is to be taught. Like any other system, it has both positive and negative qualities. But because it is only a system, it can be clarified, examined, and changed, both from within and without.

7   There are other systems within our culture. The Black System, the Chicano System, the Asian-American System, and the Native American System are completely enveloped in and frequently overshadowed by the White Male System. As, of course, is the Female System, which includes women from the other ethnic systems as well as white women.

8   There are a few white men who do not fit into the White Male System. They form a small but growing group which is frequently perceived as a sanctuary by white men who do not want to acknowledge their sexism. Whenever I mention the existence of this group during a lecture, I can almost see the men in the room rushing to crowd into it. If they can just get into that circle, they

can be "different" and not have to face themselves. I wait until they are comfortably crowded in before saying, "Of course, at this point in history that group is largely homosexual." They then quickly rush right out again! I use this statement for effect, and while it is not necessarily accurate, it *does* encourage men to realize that there is more to sexism than meets the eye. This keeps the focus where it should be and is also an amusing process to observe.

9   Saying that you are not sexist—or that you do not want to be, or would rather not admit that you are—is not the same as doing something about your sexism. To give a parallel example, this is much like what many of us white liberals did during the civil rights movement. We needed our Black friends to tell us that we were different. We needed to hear that we were not like everyone else, that we were not discriminatory and racist. Once we heard that, we could avoid having to deal with our racism, which was real no matter how hard we tried to ignore it or cover it up.

10   I had two Black colleagues who simply refused to tell me what I wanted to hear. I finally learned that the issue was not one of *whether* I was racist, but of *how* I was racist. As soon as I was able to acknowledge this—with my friends' help—then and only then could I begin to work on my own racist attitudes and behaviors. Similarly, because we all live in a white male culture, the question is not one of *whether* we are sexist, but of *how* we are sexist. (This is true for women as well as men, by the way.)

11   Before we can deal with our sexism, we must learn to distance ourselves from the White Male System. We must learn to step back, take a long look at it, and see it for what it really is.

Clearing the Air: Pollution vs. Non-Pollution

12   I like to think of the White Male System as analogous to pollution. When you are in the middle of pollution, you are usually unaware of it (unless it is especially bad.) You eat in it, sleep in it, work in it, and sooner or later start believing that that is just the way the air is. You are unaware of the fact that pollution is *not* natural until you remove yourself from it and experience nonpollution.

13   I live in the Colorado mountains where the air is very clear. Whenever I go to the East Coast, I almost immediately start coughing and fighting a postnasal drip. As I choke and sputter, I comment to local residents, "My, the pollution is bad today!" They in turn look startled and ask, "What pollution?" What they are really saying, of course, is this: "Isn't the air always a little thick and yellowish-gray?"

14   When flying into New York—or Los Angeles, for that matter—it is easy enough to look down and say, "Now, that's pollution!" Once you are in it for a while, though, you simply forget all about it and accept polluted air as a given.

15   Native Americans have always recognized the White Male System as pollution. The Blacks were the next group to challenge the system. The Blacks went off by themselves and said, "We have a system of our own—the Black

system. It isn't always right, but it isn't always wrong. Black is beautiful and our system is just fine." Until then, very few groups had stepped away from the White Male System, reflected on it, and declared their own alternatives.

16 It is very difficult to stand back from the White Male System because it is everywhere in our culture. You can get away from pollution by leaving New York City and going to the mountains, but you can not get away from the White Male System as easily as that. It *is* our culture. We all live in it. We have been educationally, politically, economically, philosophically, and theologically trained in it, and our emotional, psychological, physical, and spiritual survival have depended on our knowing and supporting the system. White women believe that they get their identity externally from the White Male System and that the White Male System is necessary to validate that identity. Therefore, challenging the system becomes almost impossible.

17 There is a direct correlation between buying into the White Male System and surviving in our culture. Since white women have bought into the system the most, they have survived better than other groups both economically and physically although they do get battered and raped and mutilated (for example, through unnecessary surgery). They have had to hide and/or unlearn their own system and accept the stereotypes that the White Male System has set up for them.

18 Blacks have accepted the White Male System less wholeheartedly than white women and have not done as well within it. (Of course, white men have not exactly been enthusiastic about welcoming Blacks into their system.) Chicanos and Asian Americans are even further removed. Finally, most Native Americans have generally refused to have anything at all to do with it. When one looks at how Native Americans have fared within this culture, one sees graphic evidence of what happens to those who try to escape or ignore the White Male System. They are either exterminated outright or have to fight every step of the way. Economic and physical survival have been directly related to accepting and incorporating the White Male System.

19 There is also an *inverse* relationship between accepting and incorporating the White Male System and personal survival. The stress of having to be innately superior at all times is more than the human organism can tolerate. Those persons who buy into the system the most and work the hardest to become shining examples of what it means tend to drop dead ahead of their time from heart attacks, strokes, high blood pressure, ulcers, and other physical after effects of unrelenting tension and stress.

20 One unforeseen consequence of the civil rights movement is that more Black males are dying of heart attacks these days. As they move into the White Male System and become part of it, they inherit the unfortunate legacy of stress and early death. The same appears to be true for women who are "making it" in the White Male System. It seems as if high blood pressure goes hand in hand with three-piece suits and attaché cases.

21   This does not have to be so, however. One big problem with the White Male System is that stress is assumed to be an integral part of the system. If one tries to live up to the myths of the system, then one naturally undergoes a great deal of strain. One can choose *not* to live up to these myths. One can choose to remove the causes of stress rather than merely learning how to cope with them. The only really effective way to go about doing this is to challenge the myths of the White Male System and eventually to change the system itself. It can be done; in some cases, it *is* already being done.

22   I am not talking here about women's liberation, or Black liberation, or the liberation of any other single group within our culture. Instead, I am looking forward to a time when we can all become the persons we really are. Blacks and women are learning to tell the difference between pollution and non-pollution. They are showing us that it is possible to stand back and say, "The White Male System is only a system. It is not reality. It is not the way the world is." Blacks have defined their own system, and some of them have tried to communicate this to the rest of us. Unfortunately, many of us have been very slow learners. It is difficult to teach a new concept to someone who already "knows it all" (one of the myths of the White Male System). Some Blacks have not bothered trying to tell others about their system. They have just focused on getting into the White Male System because they know they must in order to survive.

23   I have described the White Male System as it is perceived by Female System women. Similarly, there is a Female System. It is not good or bad. It just is. It is not necessary to choose one system over the other. As the Female System is described, we will see and understand another system. The more systems we know about, the more choices we have. Over time, perhaps, more new—and better—systems, models, and alternatives will emerge.

The Four Great Myths of the White Male System

24   The White Male System has four myths that feed it, sustain it, and (theoretically at least) justify it. These myths have been around for so long that most men are not even conscious of them. Many would deny their existence. Yet to challenge or doubt them is akin to heresy: they are sacred givens.

25   The first myth is that *the White Male System is the only thing that exists.* Because of this, the beliefs and perceptions of other systems—especially the Female System—are seen as sick, bad, crazy, stupid, ugly, and incompetent.

26   This myth is damaging in two ways. It limits women who want to explore their own perceptions and abilities, and it limits men who want to experience and learn from them.

27   Almost every woman has heard these words more than once: "You just don't know how the world is!" implying that the White Male System's view of the world is somehow "right." Women are also told time and again that they do not understand "reality." The White Male System is not reality. It is *a* reality, but it is not *the* reality, and women may very well have a reality all their

own. Neither reality is right. Neither is the way the world is. Each simply *is*. When one is set up as being the only true reality, however, and the other is dismissed as sick, bad, crazy, stupid, etc., then no one is free to explore the possibilities inherent in other realities.

28   There may be one true reality somewhere, but it has not yet been demonstrated that the White Male System can claim it. If we were all given the opportunity to seek out and study other realities, we might come closer to understanding one another. The myth which states that there is one and only one reality limits our search for others.

29   Since the White Male System is so thoroughly convinced that it is the only thing that exists in the world, it lacks what I like to call a "theology of differences." Once someone is sure that the way in which he (or she) sees the world is the way things *are*, then he (or she) perceives any differences of opinion as threatening. This results in a closed system and a rigid approach to life in which all differences must be discounted, disparaged, or destroyed. No one is allowed to explore them or use them as opportunities for new growth because their very existence jeopardizes the most basic myth of the White Male System—that it is the right and only way of life without which there would be nothing.

30   The second myth is that *the White Male System is innately superior*. Note that the first and second myths do not follow logically. If the White Male System is the only thing that exists, then how can it be superior and to what? Unfortunately, this inconsistency is of no concern to the White Male System.

31   At some level, the White Male System has recognized in spite of itself that other realities exist. It has gone on to define itself as superior to them while simultaneously believing that it is the only reality. Anyone who does not belong to this system is by definition innately inferior—and this includes members of all other racial groups, women, and the few white men who do not fit into the White Male System.

32   According to the White Male System, innate superiority and innate inferiority are birthrights which cannot be earned or traded away. Some men would like to give their innate superiority away—it is often too large a burden to bear. It is just plain difficult to be "the best" all of the time. Nor is it good for one's health. Superiority can be a killing gift.

33   The third myth is that *the White Male System knows and understands everything*. This is one reason why women so frequently look to men for advice and direction. Both sexes genuinely believe that men should and do know it all. In contrast to the first two myths, which are diametrically opposed, this myth follows the second one very nicely. If one is innately superior, then by rights one should be omniscient as well.

34   This myth is directly related to racial and sex-role stereotyping. A stereotype is no more than a definition of one group of persons by another who wishes to control it. Taken together, stereotypes support the myths of the White Male System.

35   No one would deny the fact that there are other people in our culture besides white men. Blacks, Chicanos, Native Americans, Asian Americans, and women are not exactly invisible. Precisely because they are different from white men, the White Male System must come to terms with them in some way. So it develops stereotypes that neatly describe and categorize these other groups. As long as the members of these groups go along with the stereotypes, they support the illusion that the White Male System knows and understands everything. If white men say that women are weak, and women behave as if they are weak, then who can argue with the myth?

36   Blacks were the first to defy the stereotypes given them by the White Male System. They started living within their own system. The other racial groups, and women, have done this also to some extent, but at considerable personal expense and threat to their existence.

37   The fourth and final myth of the White Male System is that *it is possible to be totally logical, rational, and objective*. The problem with this myth is that one must constantly do battle with the ways in which one is not all of these things. One must continually overcome and deny any tendencies toward illogical, irrational, subjective, or intuitive thoughts or behaviors.

38   Members of the White Male System spend a lot of time and energy telling women that females are by nature not logical, rational, or objective. Often they do so in highly emotional ways!

39   I once counseled with a couple who had marital problems. Both the man and the woman had thriving businesses of their own. The man was constantly complaining that while he was always logical and rational about their differences of opinion, his wife was always emotional. To support his position, he drafted a twenty-four-page document—on legal-sized paper—explaining the situation as he perceived it. He then presented it to me at the beginning of one session and told me to read it. During his next visit, he asked if I had understood his thesis. I told him that I had read the whole thing, carefully weighed it (literally!), and had come to the conclusion that any outpouring of that size and intensity had to be an emotional statement!

40   One part of psychology is the science of individual differences. Whole fields of study have developed out of the awareness that when two or more persons observe the same event, they are apt to come up with two or more different reports of it. People are simply not capable of being totally logical, rational, and objective.

41   The fourth myth—that this sort of behavior *is* possible—poses an occupational hazard for therapists (and their clients). If one accepts it, then one must neglect the subjective, intuitive resources within oneself. The therapeutic process becomes a problem to be solved in a series of logical, orderly steps rather than a healing experience. And a great deal of valuable data and information are lost along the way.

42   Living according to these myths can mean living in ignorance. For example, the only way to maintain the myth of knowing and understanding everything

is to *ignore* a whole universe of other information. When one clings to the myth of innate superiority, one must constantly overlook the virtues and abilities of others.

43   Nevertheless, the mere thought that these myths might not be truisms terrifies White Male System persons. I have seen proof of this over and over again. Once, when I was lecturing on this subject to a group of professional men and women, I noticed one of the men becoming increasingly agitated. When he could sit still no longer (he started pacing back and forth at the far end of the room), I finally stopped and asked him to tell us what he was experiencing.

44   "If what you are saying is true," he said, "then I am nothing but a piece of shit."

45   "I don't think I was implying that," I answered. "Can you tell us more?"

46   "Well," he went on—and these were his exact words—"if I'm not innately superior and I don't know and understand everything, then I'm nothing but a piece of shit, *just like the rest of you!*"

47   His statement suggests a number of important issues. First, was his overwhelming need to hold on to his sense of superiority and his conviction that he knew and understood everything. Second, was his very real fear that if this turned out not to be true, the only alternative was to be worthless (like the rest of us)! This reveals the dualistic thinking inherent in the White Male System. Things have to be either this way or that. One must be either superior or inferior. One must be either one-up or one-down. What horrible and debilitating options! How limiting and exhausting always to have to be one-up so as not to be one-down. Another assumption that his statement reveals is that the only way the world can be is the way he sees it. If it suddenly became different, then chaos would reign. It is easy to see why men would be frightened by this. To avoid this dreadful possibility, the White Male System must defend itself at all costs and can not risk exploring other alternatives.

48   A professional man became very upset during another group I was leading. He stood up, waved his arms, and said, "Anne, if you ever do get the power, you'll do the same thing to us that we've done to you!" What he was really saying, of course, was that power could only be used as his system has used it—to control, condemn, and stereotype. He was locked into his mythology. It is difficult for others of us to recognize how deeply this belief system penetrates the souls of white males and how frightening it is to have it challenged.

49   The White Male System sees its mythology as all-knowing and all-revealing. In truth, however, it is just the opposite. I realized this most clearly many years ago when I was doing a workshop on racial issues in a Southern state. (This was during the heyday of the civil rights movement, when school districts were required to sponsor workshops on this topic in order to keep their public funding.) The group I was working with was about half Blacks and half whites. Neither side wanted to disturb the tenuous equilibrium they had established thus far, and they invited me in because I was perceived as essentially harmless.

50   I had designed a relatively simple exercise I wanted to try out on the group in order to generate some data. I asked the participants to draw three columns on a sheet of paper. In the first, they were to list those characteristics which they perceived as uniquely Black. In the second, they were to list those they perceived as uniquely white. In the third, they were to list characteristics they saw as common to both groups.

51   After explaining what I wanted the group to do, I sat down to wait. After a while, the anxiety in the room became almost palpable. I decided to find out what was happening.

52   I found that the Blacks had done precisely what I had asked them to do. Because they knew the Black system, they had been able to list characteristics they perceived as uniquely Black. Because they also knew the White Male System—they had to in order to survive—they had been able to list characteristics they saw as uniquely white. They were ready to move on to the third column.

53   The whites were having great difficulty completing the exercise, however. Because they knew nothing about the Black system, they could not do column one. Because they could not see the White Male System for what it is (one has to experience non-pollution before being able to recognize pollution), they could not do column two either. Increasingly frustrated, most of them had gone directly to column three. They had decided to ignore the differences between the two systems ("Let's not look at the differences. Differences separate us!") and focus instead on common characteristics ("Let's look at ways in which we're alike and ignore the experience of being Black in the White Male System!").

54   In addition, as often happens in educational groups, the whole group had started cheating. People were looking at one another's papers. When the whites saw that the Blacks had been able to come up with answers for the first two columns, they became agitated ("What do they know that we don't know—and how can this be?"). When the Blacks saw that the whites had not been able to come up with answers for those two columns, they felt exposed. ("We cannot let them know that *we* know that *they* don't know *more*. We'll lose our jobs if they find that we know they aren't superior.")

55   What the group had just experienced was a full-fledged myth-breaker. The whites were not superior and did not know more than the Blacks. In fact, the Blacks knew more. They had to. They had learned all about the White Male System because they needed to in order to survive in it. Because the whites did not have to know the Black system to survive, the whites had learned little or nothing about the Black system. The only way for them to find out about it would have been for Blacks to teach it to them, and that had not happened. Nor was it likely to happen.

56   Both sides were exhausted by this exercise. The whites were supposed to be innately superior and all-knowing—but they could not come up with answers! The Blacks were trying to support the myth that whites were innately superior and all-knowing—in order to keep their jobs—but they had completed the

exercise. Sometimes it is difficult to remember what one is not supposed to know! The myth was that the whites knew more. The reality was that the Blacks did.

57   Teaching a white man about a system other than his own can be extraordinarily difficult. Even if he is open to learning about other realities, he must constantly do battle with his own feeling of innate superiority and the confidence that he already knows and understands everything. These myths go deep into the core of most white males and are not easily overcome. It requires almost superhuman effort and enormous commitment on both sides. Now that I have been trying to teach the Female System to white men, I find myself appreciating the time, energy, and love my Black friends have put forth in teaching me about their system.

58   All four myths of the White Male System can be summarized by another that is almost always unspoken but nevertheless present and real. This final myth is that *it is possible for one to be God*. If the White Male System is the only system that exists, if white males are innately superior, if they know and understand everything, and if they can be totally logical, rational and objective, then they can be God—at least, the way the White Male System defines God.

59   Being a deity is not easy though. In fact, it can be lethal for White Male System persons to deny their own humanity and fallibility. The human mind and body are not designed to stand up under such stress and strain. White men who finally achieve such high stature in their own minds suffer from heart attacks, strokes, ulcers, and high blood pressure. In the end, godhood can kill. . . .

How Women See Men

60   Most women have a pretty good idea of how men see them, but they are reluctant to verbalize their own ideas on how they see men. This happens for two reasons. First, we frequently distrust our own perceptions, and this makes us hesitant to express them. And second, when we do express them and they are different from the way men see things, we are dismissed and ridiculed.

61   Nevertheless, we cannot help but form opinions of men, even though we must often keep them to ourselves. Some of these opinions are given us by the White Male System and others stem from our own observations and experiences. . . .

62   [W]omen are taught from birth that men are innately superior. As a result, we expect and hope that they will be. We may know inside that they are not, but we try to ignore this because we believe that we need them to absolve us of our Original Sin of Being Born Female. We want them to save us from our birthright of inferiority. Some men do their best to live up to our expectations, but they cannot help wondering what, or who, they are supposed to save us from, and why!

63   We look to men to be superior while simultaneously resenting and hating their birthright. We place men on pedestals, and this, needless to say, makes relaxed, caring relationships almost impossible. We cannot really relate to

someone above us. We do our best to "catch a husband"—and far too frequently discover that we have not caught what we thought.

64 Women also need to see men as all-knowing and all-understanding. Many women feel misunderstood most of the time (as well they might!) and spend much of their lives seeking understanding. When we do not feel as if the men in our lives understand us, we blame ourselves for not communicating properly. We struggle desperately not to accept the awareness that men do not understand us completely because they cannot. They are able to understand little—if anything—beyond the pale of the White Male System unless they take special care to because they do not believe other systems exist.

65 It takes a great deal of strength, patience, and caring for an "inferior" person to teach his or her system to a "superior" person. It also takes about twice as much energy as communicating with a peer does. This is because "superior" system people are often slow learners and are not very motivated to learn about other systems. Why should they? They're already in charge! The Blacks learned this when they tried to communicate their system to the whites; many of them decided that it wasn't worth the effort.

66 Since men have been brainwashed—by their own system and by women—into thinking that they are superior and that they know and understand everything, they assume that they can tell us who we are and what we are like. Not only do they assume that they have the *right* to tell us who we are but also that they are *correct* in their perceptions of us and that we will accept whatever they say. We resent this very much! We want men to say, "Tell me what you are like;" instead we hear them saying, "Let *me* tell you what you are like!" Whenever we try to explain the Female System to them, they reply, "Put this information into the language and concepts of *my* system so I can understand it." It is almost as if they are saying, "It's *your* responsibility to make me understand. If I don't understand, it's *your* fault. It's not up to me to learn another system!"

67 I used to think that it was my sacred duty to help every man "understand" the Female System. I now have a new policy: I explain the concepts I'm trying to get across twice. If men do not appear as if they are beginning to understand what I am saying by then, I tell them that *they* have a problem!

68 Of course confronting them like this goes against another important fact that women are expected to know about men: namely, that their egos are very fragile and need to be "protected." Many women devote their entire lives to caring for the "fragile male ego."

69 They believe the myth that men cannot tolerate the knowledge that they are not always good lovers, that they do not know and understand everything, that they are not always strong, that they do not always have to be "in charge"—in other words, that they are human like the rest of us. However, by believing and fostering the myth that men have fragile egos which need protecting, women assure themselves of being indispensable. If we are the only ones who can protect their egos, then how can they live without us?

70 It is important to look at whom we choose to protect. We *usually* protect those whom we see as weaker and more vulnerable than ourselves. In addition

to assuring us a place of indispensability, this results in keeping the protected person weak and vulnerable. Thus, the cycle continues.

71   Some women have been willing to be honest and risk their position of indispensability with the men in their lives. They have found that men can, indeed, tolerate the knowledge that they are not always good lovers; they can tolerate knowing that they are only human; they can tolerate knowing any number of things when that information is presented in a caring way and not as a weapon of resentment against a "superior" being. They may not like the information but they can tolerate it. This process, in turn, opens the door for more honest and mutually satisfying relationships.

72   A woman once told me, "Oh sure, I know all this, but I hide what I know from my husband. I protect him so he is able to get out front and do the dirty work. What woman in her right mind would want to fool around with finances, economics, and politics?" Yet when men take charge of these areas, we have to live with their decisions whether or not we like them. More and more of us are becoming less willing to do this.

73   There is another aspect of the male ego that is important. Anyone who ever takes an elementary biology course learns about one-celled organisms called amoebas. The amoeba can assume any shape, and its main goal in life is food-gathering. Whenever it comes into contact with a possible food source, it sends out its pseudopods, its false feet, surrounds the food, and takes it into its food vacuole. The amoeba then either absorbs the food—after which it becomes indistinguishable from the amoeba itself—or rejects it.

74   Women experience some men as having "pseudopodic egos." Their egos reach out, pull women into their sphere, incorporate them, and from that time on the women are indistinguishable from them. (This is a special occupational hazard of wives and secretaries.) Once a man "absorbs" a woman, he literally does not perceive that she is a separate being.

75   This is different from the many women who extend their egos by living through their husbands and children. When pressed, these women always know that they are separate from their husbands and children, even when they would prefer this not to be the case. But persons with pseudopodic egos genuinely believe that there is no difference between themselves and others. Women who become involved with men of this type frequently describe their experience as one of having been "devoured" or "swallowed up."

76   Prime examples of pseudopodic egos are often seen during divorce cases. When the time comes to divide up the property, the woman usually knows what she had when she and her husband were married, what he had, and what they acquired jointly. The man, on the other hand, just assumes that everything belongs to him. He literally cannot distinguish between his wife's things and his. It is the old adage corrupted: "What's mine is mine, and what's yours is mine too!"

77   No wonder so many women feel as if they are nothing more than men's possessions! And no wonder men become so upset when their wives—or secretaries—try to claim their own possessions *and* their own beings.

78   Women also see men as unresponsive to their ideas—and this is an accurate observation. Men are very attached to their own ideas. They also appear to be very attached to one another's ideas. Women have long complained that they have difficulty getting their ideas across in professional and staff meetings. We are often left with two choices: we can either propose our ideas ourselves and run the risk of their being rejected, because they came from a woman, or we can give them to men and let them present them as their own. Then, at least, our ideas have *some* chance of being accepted and implemented!

79   Men will fight tenaciously for their ideas. In fact, men defend their ideas like a lioness defends her cubs. On observing this, I realized that men's ideas really *are* their offspring. Perhaps, then, it is easier for a woman to part with her ideas because she has the capacity to produce human offspring, while a man's major production *is* his ideas.

80   The more we model ourselves after men, the more possessive we are becoming of our ideas. We are no longer as willing to turn them over to men. We are demonstrating more willingness to fight for them and to claim what I call "conceptual paternity." (I use the phrase advisedly.) Perhaps, as we pass through the stage of having to "make it" in the White Male System, we will move further to a place where we can give birth to our ideas, nurture them and help them grow, and then turn them over to others for development and finally let them go. . . .

POST-READING QUESTIONS:

1) Did this reading selection meet, fail to meet, or exceed your pre-reading expectations of it? Do you want to revise your pre-reading thinking in light of your understanding of this piece? Might you have responded differently to these two questions if, after having read this selection, you discovered before answering this first post-reading question that, contrary to what you had thought, the piece was written by, say, a white make who is a distinguished professor of science?

2) Having read Schaef's material, do you want to revise any or all of your responses to the second, third, and fourth pre-reading questions?

3) Does it seem to you that, although she clearly recognizes that "the Female System. . . includes women from the other [*sic*] ethnic systems as well as white women" (paragraph 7), Schaef sometimes writes as if there is only *one* Female System? Does she seem to write in similarly reductive ways when she talks about other groups, too? Are these sorts of moves necessarily problematic?

4) Many scholars argue that sexism, racism, heterosexism, speciesism, and other negative ideologies share a common set of underlying assumptions and lead to similarly troublesome consequences. Did you hold a similar point of view prior to reading Schaef's material? Has your understanding of her work caused you to want to strengthen or rethink that point of view? Does her work generally help you see where you stand on this issue?

Tales Out of Medical School

ADRIANE FUGH-BERMAN

Adriane Fugh-Berman (1958–) is medical director of the Taoist Health Institute, an alternative health clinic in Washington, D.C. She is also the medical advisor to the National Women's Health Network, a feminist consumer advocacy organization. Her articles on women's health issues, medical education, alternative medicine, and public health have appeared in, among other sources, *The Lancet, The New England Journal of Medicine, The Nation,* and *The Washington Post*. She is currently working on a book about alternative medicine.

PRE-READING QUESTIONS:

1) Do you think that, in general, professional women do their jobs well? In your experience, how do men's and women's job performances compare?

2) What connotations do the terms "mistress," "spinster," "lady doctor," "lady minister," and "female boss" have? Can you think of any other gender-related terms with particularly telling connotative values?

3) Have any of your courses, textbooks, or teachers tended to favor men over women, or vice versa? If so, how did you feel when that happened? In your view, was the bias in question ever justifiable?

4) Have you ever been ignored or otherwise treated unfairly because of who or what you are? Have you ever ignored or otherwise treated others unfairly because of who or what they are? If in either case the aggrieved party appealed to someone in authority to redress the wrong, what happened?

5) The following reading selection first appeared in *The Nation*, which is a magazine with leftist political leanings. Knowing that fact, do you have any particular pre-reading expectations concerning Fugh-Berman's article?

CLOSE-READING TIP

While attempting to demonstrate the pervasiveness of the sexism that she encountered during her medical school training, Fugh-Berman argues that the implications of her experiences range beyond the parameters of her problematic schooling. As she says at one point, "Depersonalizing our cadaver was good preparation for depersonalizing our patients later" (paragraph 5). As you read her work, note those moments when Fugh-Berman analyzes her personal experiences in the service of making larger claims. Evaluate the extent to which you agree or disagree with her assumptions, conclusions, and (often implied) prognoses.

1   With the growth of the women's health movement and the influx of women into medical schools, there has been abundant talk of a new enlightenment among physicians. Last summer, many Americans were shocked when Frances Conley, a neurosurgeon on the faculty of Stanford University's medical school, resigned her position, citing "pervasive sexism." Conley's is a particularly elite and male-dominated subspecialty, but her story is not an isolated one. I graduated from the Georgetown University School of Medicine in 1988, and while medical training is a sexist process anywhere, Georgetown built disrespect for women into its curriculum.

2   A Jesuit school, most recently in the news as the alma mater of William Kennedy Smith, Georgetown has an overwhelmingly white, male and conservative faculty. At a time when women made up one-third of all medical students in the United States, and as many as one-half at some schools, my class was 73 percent male and more than 90 percent white.

3   The prevailing attitude toward women was demonstrated on the first day of classes by my anatomy instructor, who remarked that our elderly cadaver "must have been a Playboy bunny" before instructing us to cut off her large breasts and toss them into the thirty-gallon trash can marked "cadaver waste." Barely hours into our training, we were already being taught that there was nothing to be learned from examining breasts. Given the fact that one out of nine American women will develop breast cancer in her lifetime, to treat breasts as extraneous tissue seemed an appalling waste of an educational opportunity, as well as a not-so-subtle message about the relative importance of body parts. How many of my classmates now in practice, I wonder, regularly examine the breasts of their female patients?

4   My classmates learned their lesson of disrespect well. Later in the year one carved a tick-tack-toe on a female cadaver and challenged others to play. Another gave a languorous sigh after dissecting female genitalia, as if he had just had sex. "Guess I should have a cigarette now," he said.

5   Ghoulish humor is often regarded as a means by which med students overcome fear and anxiety. But it serves a darker purpose as well: Depersonalizing our cadaver was good preparation for depersonalizing our patients later. Further on in my training an ophthalmologist would yell at me when I hesitated to place a small instrument meant to measure eye pressure on a fellow student's cornea because I was afraid it would hurt. "You have to learn to treat patients as lab animals," he snarled at me.

6   On the first day of an emergency medicine rotation in our senior year, students were asked who had had experience placing a central line (an intravenous line placed into a major vein under the clavicle or in the neck). Most of the male students raised their hands. None of the women did. For me, it was graphic proof of inequity in teaching; the men had had the procedure taught to them, but the women had not. Teaching rounds were often, for women, a spectator sport. One friend told me how she craned her neck to watch a physician teach a minor surgical procedure to a male student; when they were done

the physician handed her his dirty gloves to discard. I have seen a male attending physician demonstrate an exam on a patient and then wade through several female medical students to drag forth a male in order to teach it to him. This sort of discrimination was common and quite unconscious: The women just didn't register as medical students to some of the doctors. Female students, for their part, tended (like male ones) to gloss over issues that might divert attention, energy or focus from the all-important goal of getting through their training. "Oh, they're just of the old school," a female classmate remarked to me, as if being ignored by our teachers was really rather charming, like having one's hand kissed.

7   A woman resident was giving a radiology presentation and I felt mesmerized. Why did I feel so connected and involved? It suddenly occurred to me that the female physician was regularly meeting my eyes; most of the male residents and attendings made eye contact only with the men.

. . .

8   "Why are women's brains smaller than men's?" asked a surgeon of a group of male medical students in the doctors' lounge (I was in the room as well, but was apparently invisible). "Because they're missing logic!" Guffaws all around.

9   Such instances of casual sexism are hardly unique to Georgetown, or indeed to medical schools. But at Georgetown female students also had to contend with outright discrimination of a sort most Americans probably think no longer exists in education. There was one course women were not allowed to take. The elective in sexually transmitted diseases required an interview with the head of the urology department, who was teaching the course. Those applicants with the appropriate genitalia competed for invitations to join the course (a computer was supposed to assign us electives, which we had ranked in order of preference, but that process had been circumvented for this course). Three women who requested an interview were told that the predominantly gay male clinic where the elective was held did not allow women to work there. This was news to the clinic's executive director, who stated that women were employed in all capacities.

10   The women who wanted to take the course repeatedly tried to meet with the urologist, but he did not return our phone calls. (I had not applied for the course, but became involved as an advocate for the women who wanted to take it.) We figured out his schedule, waylaid him in the hall and insisted that a meeting be set up.

11   At this meeting, clinic representatives disclosed that a survey had been circulated years before to the clientele in order to ascertain whether women workers would be accepted; 95 percent of the clients voted to welcome women. They were also asked whether it was acceptable to have medical students working at the clinic; more than 90 percent approved. We were then told that these results could not be construed to indicate that clients did not mind women medical students; the clients would naturally have assumed that "medical student" meant "male medical student." Even if that were true, we asked,

if 90 percent of clients did not mind medical students and 95 percent did not mind women, couldn't a reasonable person assume that female medical students would be acceptable? No, we were informed. Another study would have to be done.

12   We raised formal objections to the school. Meanwhile, however, the entire elective process had been postponed by the dispute, and the blame for the delay and confusion was placed on us. The hardest part of the struggle, indeed, was dealing with the indifference of most of our classmates—out of 206, maybe a dozen actively supported us—and with the intense anger of the ten men who had been promised places in the course.

13   "Just because you can't take this course," one of the men said to me, "why do you want to ruin it for the rest of us?" It seemed incredible to me that I had to argue that women should be allowed to take the same courses as men. The second or third time someone asked me the same question, I suggested that if women were not allowed to participate in the same curriculum as the men, then in the interest of fairness we should get a 50 percent break on our $22,500 annual tuition. My colleague thought that highly unreasonable.

14   Eventually someone in administration realized that not only were we going to sue the school for discrimination but that we had an open-and-shut case. The elective in sexually transmitted diseases was canceled, and from its ashes arose a new course, taught by the same man, titled "Introduction to Urology." Two women were admitted. When the urologist invited students to take turns working with him in his office, he scheduled the two female students for the same day—one on which only women patients were to be seen (a nifty feat in a urology practice).

15   The same professor who so valiantly tried to prevent women from learning anything unseemly about sexually transmitted diseases was also in charge of the required course in human sexuality (or, as I liked to call it, he-man sexuality). Only two of the eleven lectures focused on women; of the two lectures on homosexuality, neither mentioned lesbians. The psychiatrist who co-taught the class treated us to one lecture that amounted to an apology for rape: Aggression, even hostility, is normal in sexual relations between a man and a woman, he said, and inhibition of aggression in men can lead to impotence.

16   We were taught that women do not need orgasms for a satisfactory sex life, although men, of course, do; and that inability to reach orgasm is only a problem for women with "unrealistic expectations." I had heard that particular lecture before in the backseat of a car during high school. The urologist told us of couples who came to him for sex counseling because the woman was not having orgasms; he would reassure them that this is normal and the couple would be relieved. (I would gamble that the female half of the couple was anything but relieved.) We learned that oral sex is primarily a homosexual practice, and that sexual dysfunction in women is

often caused by "working." In the women-as-idiots department, we learned that when impotent men are implanted with permanently rigid penile prostheses, four out of five wives can't tell that their husbands have had the surgery.

17   When dealing with sexually transmitted diseases in which both partners must be treated, we were advised to vary our notification strategy according to marital status. If the patient is a single man, the doctor should write the diagnosis down on a prescription for his partner to bring to her doctor. If the patient is a married man, however, the doctor should contact the wife's gynecologist and arrange to have her treated without knowledge of what she is being treated for. How to notify the male partner of a female patient, married or single, was never revealed.

18   To be fair, women were not the only subjects of outmoded concepts of sexuality. We also received anachronistic information about men. Premature ejaculation, defined as fewer than ten thrusts(!), was to be treated by having the man think about something unpleasant, or by having the woman painfully squeeze, prick or pinch the penis. Aversive therapies such as these have long been discredited.

19   Misinformation about sexuality and women's health peppered almost every course (I can't recall any egregious wrongs in biochemistry). Although vasectomy and abortion are among the safest of all surgical procedures, in our lectures vasectomy was presented as fraught with long-term complications and abortion was never mentioned without the words "peritonitis" and "death" in the same sentence. These distortions represented Georgetown's Catholic bent at its worst. (We were not allowed to perform, or even watch, abortion procedures in our affiliated hospitals.) On a lighter note, one obstetrician assisting us in the anatomy lab told us that women shouldn't lift heavy weights because their pelvic organs will fall out between their legs.

. . .

20   In our second year, several women in our class started a women's group, which held potlucks and offered presentations and performances: A former midwife talked about her profession, a student demonstrated belly dancing, another discussed dance therapy and one sang selections from *A Chorus Line*. This heavy radical feminist activity created great hostility among our male classmates. Announcements of our meetings were defaced and women in the group began receiving threatening calls at home from someone who claimed to be watching the listener and who would then accurately describe what she was wearing. One woman received obscene notes in her school mailbox, including one that contained a rape threat. I received insulting cards in typed envelopes at my home address; my mother received similar cards at hers.

21   We took the matter to the dean of student affairs, who told us it was "probably a dental student" and suggested we buy loud whistles to blow

into the phone when we received unwanted calls. We demanded that the school attempt to find the perpetrator and expel him. We were told that the school would not expel the student but that counseling would be advised.

22   The women's group spread the word that we were collecting our own information on possible suspects and that any information on bizarre, aggressive, antisocial or misogynous behavior among the male medical students should be reported to our designated representative. She was inundated with a list of classmates who fit the bill. Finally, angered at the school's indifference, we solicited the help of a prominent woman faculty member. Although she shamed the dean into installing a hidden camera across from the school mailboxes to monitor unusual behavior, no one was ever apprehended.

23   Georgetown University School of Medicine churns out about 200 physicians a year. Some become good doctors despite their training, but many will pass on the misinformation and demeaning attitudes handed down to them. It is a shame that Georgetown chooses to perpetuate stereotypes and reinforce prejudices rather than help students acquire the up-to-date information and sensitivity that are vital in dealing with AIDS, breast cancer, teen pregnancy and other contemporary epidemics. Female medical students go through an ordeal, but at least it ends with graduation. It is the patients who ultimately suffer the effects of sexist medical education.

POST-READING QUESTIONS:

1) Does Fugh-Berman's essay shed light on why you responded as you did to the first three pre-reading questions? Has her essay caused you to rethink your responses to these questions? Might you have answered these questions as you did had you read her essay *prior* to answering them?

2) If you were to send Fugh-Berman a letter in which you reprinted your response to the fourth pre-reading question and your post-reading analysis of that response, how do you think that she would evaluate your ideas?

3) Does Fugh-Berman's article meet your pre-reading expectations of an article that was first published in *The Nation?* Would you have had different pre-reading expectations of this article had you thought that it was published in, say, the *Christian Science Monitor* or *Playboy?*

4) In your view, does Fugh-Berman's analysis of the discriminatory practices within the field of medicine help us to understand the discriminatory practices in other fields, too? Are you aware of any attempts made within the medical profession or within other professions to eradicate unjustifiable discrimination based on gender, race, or other characteristics?

5) How might Mitsuye Yamada (see p. 335) or Anne Wilson Schaef (see pp. 347) evaluate Fugh-Berman's experiences and her analyses of these experiences?

The Girls in Their Summer Dresses

IRWIN SHAW

By anyone's standards, the American writer Irwin Shaw (1913–1984) wrote prolifically. He wrote 12 novels, including the masterpieces *The Young Lions* (1948) and *The Troubled Air* (1950). *Rich Man, Poor Man* (1970), a work of perhaps lesser quality, nevertheless "was made into the first television mini-series" and "'is generally credited with inspiring the television craze for mini-series based on novels that continues today'" (*Contemporary Authors*, vol. 21, p. 408). In the 1930s, Shaw was a script writer for the "Andy Gump" and "Dick Tracy" radio shows, for which, for three years, "he wrote nine serial episodes" weekly (ibid. 406). He also wrote or collaborated on more than a dozen screenplays, and he wrote ten plays, including *Bury the Dead* (1936), a "searing antiwar play" that remains a masterpiece of theater (*Contemporary Authors*, vol. 21, p. 406). But, in the eyes of a number of critics, it was in the genre of short story writing that Shaw produced his best work. One critic said of Shaw's "storytelling talent," "'Coupled with the narrative gift is the ability to write with an ease and a clarity that only [F. Scott] Fitzgerald had.'" Another critic, comparing Shaw to Charles Dickens, says that Shaw "'has created, prodigally, a crowded gallery of memorable people.'" Yet another critic, writing as if he were referring to the following reading selection, recognizes Shaw's "'attempt to lend common experiences and ordinary people a secular grace'" (ibid. 407). Indeed, despite the mixed reviews that his overall corpus has received, few writers have been able to match Shaw's ability to find in the everyday the extraordinariness of banality.

PRE-READING QUESTIONS:

1) In your view, should partners in a relationship feel free to "notice," and perhaps even to comment upon, other people whom they find attractive? Does it matter whether or not the partners are together at the time that such noticing or commenting occurs? See whether or not your pre-reading ideas affect and, in turn, are affected by the way in which you interpret Shaw's story.

2) Why do you suppose that many women resent being seen or treated as sex objects? Do you think that many men also resent being seen or treated as such? How do you yourself feel about this issue?

3) As you think about the various cultural artifacts with which you come into contact daily—that is, the books, articles, stories, or poems that you read, the advertisements, movies, and television shows that you see, the music that you listen to, and the like—do you sense that you live in a male- or female-dominated world or in a world more or less free of gender bias?

4) Can you cite any examples of works of fiction—for example, Alice Walker's *The Color Purple* or Charles Dickens' *A Tale of Two Cities*—that, in your view, deal with an event, problem, or issue in an especially provocative way? Do the fictional portrayals that you have in mind seem even more realistic than do nonfictional portrayals (with which you are familiar) of the same event, problem, or issue?

CLOSE-READING TIP

Shaw's story is composed almost entirely of dialogue. Yet, within this extended dialogue, as well as within the sparse narration that Shaw provides, Shaw tends to *show* rather than *tell* what is going on in the story. As you read and reread this piece, pay attention to the ways in which the story's meanings seem couched within both the narrator's descriptions and the characters' language and gestures. Note, especially, the use of suggestive words and phrases, the foreshadowing of events, and the repetition of key words, images, and ideas. See, for example, representative passages in paragraphs 1, 3, 8, 29, 35–39, and 62.

1 Fifth Avenue was shining in the sun when they left the Brevoort. The sun was warm, even though it was February, and everything looked like Sunday morning—the buses and the well-dressed people walking slowly in couples and the quiet buildings with the windows closed.

2 Michael held Frances' arm tightly as they walked toward Washington Square in the sunlight. They walked lightly, almost smiling, because they had slept late and had a good breakfast and it was Sunday. Michael unbuttoned his coat and let it flap around him in the mild wind.

3 "Look out," Frances said as they crossed Eighth Street. "You'll break your neck." Michael laughed and Frances laughed with him.

4 "She's not so pretty," Frances said. "Anyway, not pretty enough to take a chance of breaking your neck."

5 Michael laughed again. "How did you know I was looking at her?"

6 Frances cocked her head to one side and smiled at her husband under the brim of her hat. "Mike, darling," she said.

7 "O.K.," he said. "Excuse me."

8 Frances patted his arm lightly and pulled him along a little faster toward Washington Square. "Let's not see anybody all day," she said. "Let's just hang around with each other. You and me. We're always up to our neck in people, drinking their Scotch or drinking our Scotch; we only see each other in bed. I want to go out with my husband all day long. I want him to talk only to me and listen only to me."

9 "What's to stop us?" Michael asked.

10 "The Stevensons. They want us to drop by around one o'clock and they'll drive us into the country."

11 "The cunning Stevensons," Mike said. "Transparent. They can whistle. They can go driving in the country by themselves."

12 "Is it a date?"

13 "It's a date."

14 Frances leaned over and kissed him on the tip of the ear.

15 "Darling," Michael said, "this is Fifth Avenue."

16 "Let me arrange a program," Frances said. "A planned Sunday in New York for a young couple with money to throw away."

17 "Go easy."

18 "First let's go to the Metropolitan Museum of Art," Frances suggested, because Michael had said during the week he wanted to go. "I haven't been there in three years and there're at least ten pictures I want to see again. Then we can take the bus down to Radio City and watch them skate. And later we'll go down to Cavanagh's and get a steak as big as a blacksmith's apron, with a bottle of wine, and after that there's a French picture at the Filmarte that everybody says—say, are you listening to me?"

19 "Sure," he said. He took his eyes off the hatless girl with the dark hair, cut dancer-style like a helmet, who was walking past him.

20 "That's the program for the day ' Frances said flatly. "Or maybe you'd just rather walk up and down Fifth Avenue."

21 "No," Michael said. "Not at all."

22 "You always look at other women," Frances said. "Everywhere. Every damned place we go."

23 "No, darling," Michael said, "I look at everything. God gave me eyes and I look at women and men in subway excavations and moving pictures and the little flowers of the field. I casually inspect the universe."

24 "You ought to see the look in your eye," Frances said, "as you casually inspect the universe on Fifth Avenue."

25 "I'm a happily married man." Michael pressed her elbow tenderly. "Example for the whole twentieth century—Mr. and Mrs. Mike Loomis. Hey, let's have a drink," he said, stopping.

26 "We just had breakfast."

27 "Now listen, darling," Mike said, choosing his words with care, "it's a nice day and we both felt good and there's no reason why we have to break it up. Let's have a nice Sunday."

28 "All right. I don't know why I started this. Let's drop it. Let's have a good time."

29 They joined hands consciously and walked without talking among the baby carriages and the old Italian men in their Sunday clothes and the young women with Scotties in Washington Square Park.

30 "At least once a year everyone should go to the Metropolitan Museum of Art," Frances said after a while, her tone a good imitation of the tone she had used at breakfast and at the beginning of their walk. "And it's nice on Sunday. There're a lot of people looking at the pictures and you get the feeling maybe Art isn't on the decline in New York City, after all—"

31 "I want to tell you something," Michael said very seriously. "I have not touched another woman. Not once. In all the five years."

32 "All right," Frances said.

33 "You believe that, don't you?"

34   "All right."

35   They walked between the crowded benches, under the scrubby city-park trees.

36   "I try not to notice it," Frances said, "but I feel rotten inside, in my stomach, when we pass a woman and you look at her and I see that look in your eye and that's the way you looked at me the first time. In Alice Maxwell's house. Standing there in the living room, next to the radio, with a green hat on and all those people."

37   "I remember the hat," Michael said.

38   "The same look," Frances said. "And it makes me feel bad. It makes me feel terrible."

39   "Sh-h-h, please, darling, sh-h-h."

40   "I think I would like a drink now," Frances said.

41   They walked over to a bar on Eighth Street, not saying anything. Michael automatically helping her over curbstones and guiding her past automobiles. They sat near a window in the bar and the sun streamed in and there was a small, cheerful fire in the fireplace. A little Japanese waiter came over and put down some pretzels and smiled happily at them.

42   "What do you order after breakfast?" Michael asked.

43   "Brandy, I suppose," Frances said.

44   "Courvoisier," Michael told the waiter. "Two Courvoisiers."

45   The waiter came with the glasses and they sat drinking the brandy in the sunlight. Michael finished half his and drank a little water.

46   "I look at women," he said. "Correct. I don't say it's wrong or right. I look at them. If I pass them on the street and I don't look at them, I'm fooling you. I'm fooling myself."

47   "You look at them as though you want them," Frances said, playing with her brandy glass. "Every one of them."

48   "In a way," Michael said, speaking softly and not to his wife, "in a way that's true. I don't do anything about it, but it's true."

49   "I know it. That's why I feel bad."

50   "Another brandy," Michael called. "Waiter, two more brandies."

51   He sighed and closed his eyes and rubbed them gently with his fingertips. "I love the way women look. One of the things I like best about New York is the battalions of women. When I first came to New York from Ohio that was the first thing I noticed, the million wonderful women, all over the city. I walked around with my heart in my throat."

52   "A kid," Frances said. "That's a kid's feeling."

53   "Guess again," Michael said. "Guess again. I'm older now. I'm a man getting near middle age, putting on a little fat, and I still love to walk along Fifth Avenue at three o'clock on the east side of the street between Fiftieth and Fifty-seventh Streets. They're all out then, shopping, in their furs and their crazy hats, everything all concentrated from all over the world into seven blocks—the best furs, the best clothes, the handsomest women, out to spend money and feeling good about it."

54 The Japanese waiter put the two drinks down, smiling with great happiness.

55 "Everything is all right?" he asked.

56 "Everything is wonderful," Michael said.

57 "If it's just a couple of fur coats," Frances said, "and forty-five dollar hats—"

58 "It's not the fur coats. Or the hats. That's just the scenery for that particular kind of woman. Understand," he said, "you don't have to listen to this."

59 "I want to listen."

60 "I like the girls in the offices. Neat with their eyeglasses, smart, chipper, knowing what everything is about. I like the girls on Forty-fourth Street at lunchtime, the actresses, all dressed up on nothing a week. I like the salesgirls in the stores, paying attention to you first because you're a man, leaving the lady customers waiting. I got all this stuff accumulated in me because I've been thinking about it for ten years and now you've asked for it and here it is."

61 "Go ahead," Frances said.

62 "When I think of New York City, I think of all the girls on parade in the city. I don't know whether it's something special with me or whether every man in the city walks around with the same feeling inside him, but I feel as though I'm at a picnic in this city. I like to sit near the women in the theatres, the famous beauties who've taken six hours to get ready and look it. And the young girls at the football games, with the red cheeks, and when the warm weather comes, the girls in their summer dresses." He finished his drink. "That's the story."

63 Frances finished her drink and swallowed two or three times extra. "You say you love me?"

64 "I love you."

65 "I'm pretty, too," Frances said. "As pretty as any of them."

66 "You're beautiful," Michael said.

67 "I'm good for you," Frances said, pleading. "I've made a good wife, a good housekeeper, a good friend. I'd do any damn thing for you."

68 "I know," Michael said. He put his hand out and grasped hers.

69 "You'd like to be free to—" Frances said.

70 "Sh-h-h."

71 "Tell the truth." She took her hand away from under his.

72 Michael flicked the edge of his glass with his finger. "O.K.," he said gently. "Sometimes I feel I would like to be free."

73 "Well," Frances said, "any time you say."

74 "Don't be foolish." Michael swung his chair around to her side of the table and patted her thigh.

75 She began to cry silently into her handkerchief, bent over just enough so that nobody else in the bar would notice. "Someday," she said, crying, "you're going to make a move."

76 Michael didn't say anything. He sat watching the bartender slowly peel a lemon.

77 "Aren't you?" Frances asked harshly. "Come on, tell me. Talk. Aren't you?"

78 "Maybe," Michael said. He moved his chair back again. "How the hell do I know?"

79 "You know," Frances persisted. "Don't you know?"

80 "Yes," Michael said after a while, "I know."

81 Frances stopped crying then. Two or three snuffles into the handkerchief and she put it away and her face didn't tell anything to anybody. "At least do me one favor," she said.

82 "Sure."

83 "Stop talking about how pretty this woman is or that one. Nice eyes, nice breasts, a pretty figure, good voice." She mimicked his voice. "Keep it to yourself. I'm not interested."

84 Michael waved to the waiter. "I'll keep it to myself," he said.

85 Frances flicked the corners of her eyes. "Another brandy," she told the waiter.

86 "Two," Michael said.

87 "Yes, ma'am, yes, sir," said the waiter, backing away.

88 Frances regarded Michael coolly across the table. "Do you want me to call the Stevensons?" she asked. "It'll be nice in the country."

89 "Sure," Michael said. "Call them."

90 She got up from the table and walked across the room toward the telephone. Michael watched her walk, thinking what a pretty girl, what nice legs.

POST-READING QUESTIONS:

1) Did the pre-reading ideas that you discussed in your response to the first pre-reading question influence the way in which you interpreted Shaw's story? Did his story cause you to reexamine these pre-reading ideas?

2) Did Shaw's story confirm or challenge the ideas that you articulated in your response to the second pre-reading question? Did you find yourself identifying or sympathizing more with Frances than with Michael? Did you perhaps identify or sympathize with both or neither of them? Before answering these questions, look again at paragraphs 23 and 53.

3) Is the world portrayed in Shaw's story similar to or different from the world that you described in your response to the third pre-reading question? Is it both similar to and different from that world? Trying not to offer an overly simplified response, do you think that Shaw's story reflects a "male" viewpoint? Might a woman have written this story differently? In answering these questions, be specific—and careful!

4) Might one legitimately argue that Frances' lines in paragraph 28 somehow embody much of the story's overall meaning(s)? Have you yourself ever been in a situation in which you've spoken such lines?

5) If you were to make a film based on Shaw's story, would you make a documentary or a nondocumentary film? How would you arrange the film's scenes? If you were to make a nondocumentary film, what details, if any, would you add to or omit from the story? Whom would you cast in the role of Frances and Michael? Concerning

particularly important scenes, how would you direct the main actor and actress to deliver their lines?

6) At one point in her book *Women's Reality*, Anne Wilson Schaef offers the following description of what she calls "the public Perfect Marriage":

> . . . [T]he man is the parent, and the woman is the child. The man takes care of the woman. He is the one who deals with the outside world, makes the money, decides how the money will be spent, and makes all of the decisions (either subtly or openly.) [*sic*] He gets the car repaired and handles all home maintenance problems. He takes care of the "little woman." (58–59)

In your view, does this portrayal accurately describe Frances and Michael's relationship—at least insofar as we are able to determine the general nature of their relationship from the details that Shaw provides for us in this story? Do Schaef's ideas seem dated, or do they still seem relevant to marriages with which you are familiar? Do they have relevance to love relationships other than those involving married couples?

The Mutes

DENISE LEVERTOV

A teacher, writer, lecturer, editor, and political activist who became a naturalized American citizen in 1956, homeschooled, English-born Denise Levertov (1923–) is one of the most talented poets still writing. Levertov's poetry has appeared in such major anthologies as *The Norton Anthology of Modern Poetry, Penguin Modern Poets IX,* and *New Poets of England and America (Current Biography Yearbook: 1991* [hereafter *CB*], p. 368). Also, besides publishing two works of prose, *The Poet in the World* (1973) and *Light Up the Cave* (1981), Levertov has produced more than 15 volumes of poetry. These collections catalogue Levertov's evolving social, political, and aesthetic attitudes. *Here and Now* (1957), *The Jacob's Ladder* (1961), and *O Taste and See* (1964), for example, reflect the influence of the American poet William Carlos Williams on her work; "Williams emphasized the dailiness—the here and now—of poetic vision: 'no ideas but in things' was his clarion call" (*CB* 365). *The Sorrow Dance* (1967), considered by many to be "her most powerful and enduring book of poems[,]. . . is a forceful and daring sequence of poems in which a strand of mourning for her sister, Olga, who died in 1964, is intertwined with her rage and grief at the [Vietnam] war" (*CB* 366–367). *A Door in the Hive* (1989) contains poems that are "'inspired by the small miracles of the natural world, terrorism in Central America, paintings, and other artists, especially [Rainer Maria] Rilke [an early influence on Levertov's work,]'" as well as "'the mystics [Levertov] often evokes. . . '" (*CB* 367–368).

Among Levertov's ever-evolving views and attitudes concerning her life and work, perhaps none has been as meaningful and enduring as has been her view concerning the relationships between art and politics and, indeed, between art and life. As she herself explains, in a fittingly poetic style, "'Poetry is necessary to a whole man, and that poetry be not divided from the rest of life is necessary to *it*. Both life and poetry fade, wilt, shrink, when they are divorced'" (*CB* 367; author's italics). As you read "The Mutes," see if you can sense this underlying connection between poetry and life, as well as the view "that what is important is one's inward conviction, that inward seeing to which [Levertov] has devoted her art" (*CB* 368).

PRE-READING QUESTIONS:

1) Do you feel that it's okay for men to whistle or gape at women whom they see in public or otherwise to let these women know that the women have been noticed? Is it okay for women to act this way towards men, or for people of one gender to act this way towards others of their gender? Are all of these acts of noticing on a par with all of the others? See if your pre-reading thoughts and feelings affect your understanding of or reactions to the ideas articulated by the poem's persona.

2) Writer Anaïs Nin once sold some pornography to a male "collector," who told her, after having read it, "'It is fine. But leave out the poetry and descriptions of anything but sex. Concentrate on sex'" (*Delta of Venus* ix). Nin sees this man's reaction as manifesting a major difference between the ways in which men tend to view sexuality and the ways in which women tend to view it. She suggests that women, unlike men, "have never separated sex from feeling, from love of the whole man" (ibid.). In your opinion, does Nin provide an accurate comparative analysis of men's and women's views concerning sexuality?

CLOSE-READING TIP

A number of literary critics and theorists feel that works of fiction defamiliarize the everyday world for us, enabling us to see this world as if we had never seen it before. For example, they might say, Alice Walker's *The Color Purple* deals with the problems of sexism and racism in such a unique way that even many people who are already familiar with these problems respond to Walker's treatment of them as if they were hearing about these problems for the first time. In other words, as one noted theorist might say, Walker's fictional account of these problems has given American culture "words that permit it to speak [about sexism and racism] as if for the first time" (Krieger 195). As you read Levertov's poem, note any instances in which the poet's (often unusual) use of everyday language and images helps you to envision anew the complex problems that the poet places before you—problems with which you might already be quite familiar. Consider, for example, ll. 6–12, 30–32, and 36–37.

Those groans men use
passing a woman on the street
or on the steps of the subway

to tell her she is a female
and their flesh knows it,   5

are they a sort of tune,
an ugly enough song, sung
by a bird with a slit tongue

but meant for music?

Or are they the muffled roaring   10
of deafmutes trapped in a building that is
slowly filling with smoke?

Perhaps both.

Such men most often
look as if groan were all they could do,   15
yet a woman, in spite of herself,

knows it's a tribute:
if she were lacking all grace
they'd pass her in silence:

so it's not only to say she's   20
a warm hole. It's a word

in grief-language, nothing to do with
primitive, not an ur-language;
language stricken, sickened, cast down

in decrepitude. She wants to   25
throw the tribute away, dis-
gusted, and can't,

it goes on buzzing in her ear,
it changes the pace of her walk,
the torn posters in echoing corridors   30

spell it out, it
quakes and gnashes as the train comes in.
Her pulse sullenly

had picked up speed,
but the cars slow down and   35
jar to a stop while her understanding

keeps on translating:
'Life after life after life goes by

without poetry,
without seemliness,   40
without love.'

POST-READING QUESTIONS:

1) Did any of the pre-reading thoughts or feelings that you discussed in your response to the first pre-reading question affect your understanding of or help shape your reactions to the ideas articulated by the poem's persona? Did the poem cause you to reexamine your reasons for having these thoughts and feelings? How do you think that the poem's persona might react to what you say in your answers to the first pre- and post-reading questions?

2) How do you think that Anaïs Nin might interpret Levertov's poem? Do you want to amend any aspect of your response to the second pre-reading question in light of your understanding of this poem? (Before answering these questions, reread ll. 38–41.)

3) In your view, does "The Mutes" attest to Levertov's much respected ability to see multifarious complexities concerning whatever problems or issues that she happens to be addressing in a particular poem?

4) Do you find that Levertov's use of everyday language and images helps you to envision anew the complex problems that the poet has placed before you—problems with which you might already be quite familiar?

5) How do you think that Frances and Michael, in Irwin Shaw's "The Girls in Their Summer Dresses" (see p. 367), might interpret or react to Levertov's poem? How do you think that the poem's persona might interpret or react to Shaw's story?

My Brother's Sex Was White. Mine, Brown

CHERRÍE MORAGA

Writer and teacher Cherríe Moraga (1952–) is among the most important and influential non-mainstream writers in the United States. Her works include the plays *Giving Up the Ghost (1986)* and *The Last Generation* (1993) and a collection of poems, stories, and essays entitled *Loving in the War Years: lo que nunca pasó por sus labios* [literally, "that which never passed from your lips"] (1983), from which the following reading selection is taken. In 1986, *This Bridge Called My Back: Writings by Radical Women of Color* (1981)—which Moraga coedited with Gloria Anzaldúa—won the Before Columbus Foundation American Book Award (Ward 382). *Shadow of a Man* (1993), another of Moraga's plays, "won the Fund for New American Plays Award, a project of the John F. Kennedy Center for the Performing Arts" (Ward 382).

   Cuentos: Stories by Latinas (1983), which Moraga coedited with Alma Gómez and Mariana Romo-Carmona and which was published by Kitchen Table: Women of Color Press, a press that Moraga cofounded, "was the first collection of stories by Latina writers in the United States" (Ward 382). The long-awaited reception of such a work was perhaps most movingly expressed by the eminent writer Alice Walker, who said, "'How I have longed to begin to know these Latinas. . . . What a new but comfortingly familiar world opens up through this book: How connected I feel'" (comments reprinted on the back cover of *Cuentos*).

One of Moraga's distinguishing characteristics as a writer is her ability to give us extraordinarily vivid, often painful, and always honest accounts of herself as an "outsider," specifically, as a "mixed-blood, lesbian, intellectual of working-class origins, and feminist cultural nationalist. . . seek[ing] a recuperation of language, reunion with family, and the retribalization of her people" (Ward 381). Though some readers cannot bring themselves to judge such textual matter fairly, Moraga's honesty with respect to her own struggles, uncertainties, and vulnerabilities is so disarming that even readers who might otherwise be uncomfortable hearing about the issues that she raises often find themselves, if not sympathizing with her, at least beginning to understand important aspects of the complex relationship among gender, race, class, and sexuality—a relationship the nature of which Moraga expends much energy and emotion trying to explain. Perhaps ironically, this intensely personal writer has opened up avenues of exploration that take both us and her well beyond herself.

PRE-READING QUESTIONS:

1) In your family, are/were there clearly defined gender-role expectations and responsibilities?

2) Do the men and women in your family participate equally in the making of a major family event, such as a Thanksgiving or Christmas dinner, for example? If not, do most or all of the men and women occupy themselves in stereotypically gender-specific activities? If they do, how do you feel about this pattern of behavior?

3) Do you identify with and (try to) emulate a particular man or woman? If so, has this person played an important role in helping you develop a sense of yourself as a man or woman and in helping you form your attitudes towards members of both your own and the opposite sex?

4) Have you ever envied some or all members of the opposite sex? If so, why?

CLOSE-READING TIP

Moraga is a master (or, rather, a mistress) at the art of personal essay writing. A writer with a superb ability to create poignant poetic prose, she is so genuinely open about her own joys, yearnings, faults, doubts, anger, and vulnerabilities that she often is able to disarm even the most skeptical—and sometimes hostile—of her readers. As you read the following essay, note those moments when you see Moraga displaying her adeptness at personal writing and think about whether or not her skill at writing personal narrative affects your reactions to her ideas and sentiments.

1   If somebody would have asked me when I was a teenager what it means to
be Chicana, I would probably have listed the grievances done me. When
my sister and I were fifteen and fourteen, respectively, and my brother a
few years older, we were still waiting on him. I write "were" as if now, nearly
two decades later, it were over. But that would be a lie. To this day in my
mother's home, my brother and father are waited on, including by me. I do
this now out of respect for my mother and her wishes. In those early years,
however, it was mainly in relation to my brother that I resented providing
such service. For unlike my father, who sometimes worked as much as seventy
hours a week to feed my face every day, the only thing that earned my brother
my servitude was his maleness.

2   It was Saturday afternoon. My brother, then seventeen-years-old, came into
the house with a pile of friends. I remember Fernie, the two Steves, and
Roberto. They were hot, sweaty, and exhausted from an afternoon's basketball
and plopped themselves down in the front room, my brother demanding,
"Girls, bring us something to drink."

3   "Get it yourself, pig," I thought, but held those words from ever forming
inside my mouth. My brother had the disgusting habit on these occasions of
collapsing my sister, JoAnn's and my name when referring to us as a unit: his
sisters. "Cher'ann," he would say. "We're really thirsty." I'm sure it took everything in his power *not* to snap his fingers. But my mother was out in the yard
working and to refuse him would have brought her into the house with a
scene before these boys' eyes which would have made it impossible for us to
show our faces at school that following Monday. We had been through that
before.

4   When my mother had been our age, over forty years earlier, she had waited
on her brothers and their friends. And it was no mere lemonade. They'd come
in from work or a day's drinking. And las mujeres, often just in from the fields
themselves, would already be in the kitchen making tortillas, warming frijoles
or pigs feet, albondigas soup, what-have-you. And the men would get a clean
white tablecloth and a spread of food laid out before their eyes and not a word
of resentment from the women.

5   The men watched the women—my aunts and mother moving with the
grace and speed of girls who were cooking before they could barely see over
the top of the stove. Elvira, my mother, knew she was being watched by the
men and loved it. Her slim hips moved patiently beneath the apron. Her deep
thick-lidded eyes never caught theirs as she was swept back into the kitchen by
my abuelita's call of "Elvirita," her brown hands deepening in color as they
dropped back into the pan of flour.

6   I suppose my mother imagined that Joe's friends watched us like that, too.
But we knew different. We were not blonde or particularly long-legged or
"available" because we were "Joe's sisters." This meant no boy could "make"
us, which meant no boy would bother asking us out. Roberto, the Guatemalan,
was the only one among my brother's friends who seemed at all sensitive to

how awkward JoAnn and I felt in our role. He would smile at us nervously, taking the lemonade, feeling embarrassed being waited on by people he considered peers. He knew the anglo girls they visited would never have succumbed to such a task. Roberto was the only recompense.

7   As I stopped to wait on their yearning throats, "jock itch" was all that came to my mind. Their cocks became animated in my head, for that was all that seemed to arbitrarily set us apart from each other and put me in the position of the servant and they, the served.

8   I wanted to machine-gun them all down, but swallowed that fantasy as I swallowed making the boy's bed every day, cleaning his room each week, shining his shoes and ironing his shirts before dates with girls, some of whom *I* had crushes on. I would lend him the money I had earned house-cleaning for twelve hours, so he could blow it on one night with a girl because he seldom had enough money because he seldom had a job because there was always some kind of ball practice to go to. As I pressed the bills into his hand, the car honking outside in the driveway, his double-date waiting, I knew I would never see that money again.

9   Years later, after I began to make political the fact of my being a Chicana, I remember my brother saying to me, "*I've* never felt 'culturally deprived',," which I guess is the term "white" people use to describe Third World people being denied access to *their* culture. At the time, I wasn't exactly sure what he meant, but I remember in re-telling the story to my sister, she responded, "Of course, he didn't. He grew up male in our house. He got the best of both worlds." And yes, I can see now that that's true. *Male in a man's world. Light-skinned in a white world. Why change?*

10   The pull to identify with the oppressor was never as great in me as it was in my brother. For unlike him, I could never have *become* the white man, only the white man's *woman*.

11   The first time I began to recognize clearly my alliances on the basis of race and sex was when my mother was in the hospital, extremely ill. I was eight years old. During my mother's stay in the hospital, my tía Eva took my sister and me into her care; my brother stayed with my abuela; and my father stayed by himself in our home. During this time, my father came to visit me and my sister only once. (I don't know if he ever visited my brother.) The strange thing was I didn't really miss his visits, although I sometimes fantasized some imaginary father, dark and benevolent, who might come and remind us that we still *were* a family.

12   I have always had a talent for seeing things I don't particularly want to see and the one day my father did come to visit us with his wife/our mother physically dying in a hospital some ten miles away, I saw that he couldn't love us—not in the way we so desperately needed. I saw that he didn't know how and he came into my tía's house like a large lumbering child—awkward and embarrassed out of his league—trying to play a parent when he needed our mother back as much as we did just to keep him eating and protected. I hated

and pitied him that day. I knew how he was letting us all down, visiting my mother daily, like a dead man, unable to say, "The children, honey, I held them. They love you. They think of you." Giving my mother *something*.

13   Years later, my mother spoke of his visits to the hospital. How from behind the bars of her bed and through the tubes in her nose, she watched this timid man come and go daily—going through the "motions" of being a husband. "I knew I had to live," she told us. "I knew he could never take care of you."

14   In contrast to the seeming lack of feeling I held for my father, my longings for my mother and fear of her dying were the most passionate feelings that had ever lived inside my young heart.

15   *We are riding the elevator. My sister and I pressed up against one wall, holding hands. After months of separation, we are going to visit my mamá in the hospital. Mi tía me dice, "Whatever you do, no llores Cherríe. It's too hard on your mother when you cry." I nod, taking long deep breaths, trying to control my quivering lip.*

16   *As we travel up floor by floor, all I can think about is not crying, breathing, holding my breath. "¿Me prometes?" she asks. I nod again, afraid to speak fearing my voice will crack into tears. My sister's nervous hand around mine, sweating too. We are going to see my mamá, mamá, after so long. She didn't die after all. She didn't die.*

17   *The elevator doors open. We walk down the corridor, my heart pounding. My eyes are darting in and out of each room as we pass them, fearing/anticipating my mamá's face. Then as we turn around the corner into a kind of lobby, I hear my tía say to an older woman—skin and bones. An Indian, I think, straight black and grey hair pulled back. I hear my tía say, "Elvira."*

18   *I don't recognize her. This is not the woman I knew, so round and made-up with her hair always a wavy jet black! I stay back until she opens her arms to me—this strange and familiar woman—her voice hoarse, "¡Ay mi'jita!" Instinctively, I run into her arms, still holding back my insides—"Don't cry. Don't cry." I remember. "Whatever you do, no llores." But my tía had not warned me about the smell, the unmistakable smell of the woman, mi mama—el olor de aceite y jabón and comfort and home. "Mi mamá." And when I catch the smell I am lost in tears, deep long tears that come when you have held your breath for centuries.*

19   There was something I knew at that eight-year-old moment that I vowed never to forget—the smell of a woman who is life and home to me at once. The woman in whose arms I am uplifted, sustained. Since then, it is as if I have spent the rest of my years driven by this scent toward la mujer.

when her india makes love
it is with the greatest reverence
to color, texture, smell

by now she knew the scent of earth

could call it up
even between the cracks
in sidewalks

steaming dry
from midday summer
rain

20   With this knowledge so deeply emblazed upon my heart, how then was I supposed to turn away from La Madre, La Chicana? If I were to build my womanhood on this self-evident truth, it is the love of the Chicana, the love of myself as a Chicana I had to embrace, no white man. Maybe this ultimately was the cutting difference between my brother and me. To be a woman fully necessitated my claiming the race of my mother. My brother's sex was white. Mine, brown.

POST-READING QUESTIONS:

1) Did Moraga's descriptions of familial gender-role expectations and responsibilities seem familiar to you? Do her analyses of gender-role expectations and responsibilities seem sound? In your view, is this reading selection a good model of an essay that effectively combines elements of personal and traditional academic writing?

2) How would you compare the nature and consequences of Moraga's identification with her mother with the nature and consequences of the identification that you discussed in your response to the third pre-reading question?

3) How do you think that Moraga might respond to what you wrote in your answers to the second and fourth pre-reading questions?

4) What does Moraga seem to mean when she says that "Roberto was the only recompense" (paragraph 6)? Similarly, how does the title of her essay reflect some of the complexities underlying her discussions of discrimination, including, and perhaps especially, her discussions of in-group discrimination?

5) Does Moraga's essay support and perhaps also challenge the view put forth by Anne Wilson Schaef that many (if not all) women feel "that to be born female means to be born innately inferior, damaged, that there is something innately 'wrong' with [them]" (*Women's Reality* 24)?

"Gee, You Don't Seem Like An Indian From the Reservation"

BARBARA CAMERON

A native of South Dakota, Barbara Cameron describes herself in the following way: "Lakota patriot, Hunkpapa [a band of the Sioux], politically non-promiscuous, born with a caul" (contributor's notes to Moraga and Anzaldúa, *This Bridge Called My Back*). Elsewhere, she remarks that she is "a lesbian" who is "quiet and shy" and who "loves cats" (contributor's notes to Brandt, *A Gathering of Spirit*).

PRE-READING QUESTIONS:

1) Do you have any thoughts or feelings concerning stereotypes or stereotyping? If you do, keep these thoughts and feelings in mind as you read Cameron's essay, watching to see whether or not—and, if so, how, why, and to what extent—they affect your understanding of or reactions to her ideas.

2) To what extent do you consciously identify yourself in terms of your ethnicity? How do you feel about being who you are?

3) Have you ever had experiences so painful or traumatic that they affected your thoughts and behavior whenever you found yourself in circumstances that triggered memories of those experiences?

4) In your view, should Native Americans try to adapt their beliefs, traditions, values, and lifestyles to those of non-Native Americans? Should non-Native Americans try to adapt *their* beliefs, traditions, values, and lifestyles to those of Native Americans? In either case, which beliefs, traditions, values, and lifestyles ought to be privileged? Should any be abandoned entirely?

CLOSE-READING TIP

People derive their sense of who they are largely from their real or imagined interactions with significant others. Thus, we commonly talk about children's following in their parents' footsteps, the partners of long-standing relationships acting and talking in similar ways, and so on. Often, human relationships and one's sense of self involve, among other things, a number of complex *group* dynamics, too (hence the importance of group or peer pressure on an individual or of a community's influence on its individual members). As you read and reread Cameron's essay, pay attention to the many instances in which Cameron talks about various sorts of self-other relationships, especially those involving an individual's identifying with and/or feeling excluded from certain groups. Try to note the ways in which she weaves an understanding of such relationships into an analysis of her own situation, and then think about whether or not her approach to explaining the issues at stake helps us better understand her essay as a whole.

1   One of the very first words I learned in my Lakota language was *wasicu* which designates white people. At that early age, my comprehension of wasicu was gained from observing and listening to my family discussing the wasicu. My grandmother always referred to white people as the "wasicu sica" with emphasis on *sica*, our word for terrible or bad. By the age of five I had seen one Indian man gunned down in the back by the police and was a silent witness to a gang of white teenage boys beating up an elderly Indian

man. I'd hear stories of Indian ranch hands being "accidentally" shot by white ranchers. I quickly began to understand the wasicu menace my family spoke of.

2   My hatred for the wasicu was solidly implanted by the time I entered first grade. Unfortunately in first grade I became teacher's pet so my teacher had a fondness for hugging me which always repulsed me. I couldn't stand the idea of a white person touching me. Eventually I realized that it wasn't the white skin that I hated, but it was their culture of deceit, greed, racism, and violence.

3   During my first memorable visit to a white town, I was appalled that they thought of themselves as superior to my people. Their manner of living appeared devoid of life and bordered on hostility even for one another. They were separated from each other by their perfectly, politely fenced square plots of green lawn. The only lawns on my reservation were the lawns of the BIA officials or white christians. The white people always seemed so loud, obnoxious, and vulgar. And the white parents were either screaming at their kids, threatening them with some form of punishment or hitting them. After spending a day around white people, I was always happy to go back to the reservation where people followed a relaxed yet respectful code of relating with each other. The easy teasing and joking that were inherent with the Lakota were a welcome relief after a day with the plastic faces.

4   I vividly remember two occasions during my childhood in which I was cognizant of being an Indian. The first time was at about three years of age when my family took me to my first pow-wow. I kept asking my grandmother, "Where are the Indians? Where are the Indians? Are they going to have bows and arrows?" I was very curious and strangely excited about the prospect of seeing real live Indians even though I myself was one. It's a memory that has remained with me through all these years because it's so full of the subtleties of my culture. There was a sweet wonderful aroma in the air from the dancers and from the traditional food booths. There were lots of grandmothers and grandfathers with young children running about. Pow-wows in the Plains usually last for three days, sometimes longer, with Indian people traveling from all parts of our country to dance, to share food and laughter, and to be with each other. I could sense the importance of our gathering times and it was the beginning of my awareness that my people are a great and different nation.

5   The second time in my childhood when I knew very clearly that I am Indian occurred when I was attending an all white (except for me) elementary school. During Halloween my friends and I went trick or treating. At one of the last stops, the mother knew all of the children except for me. She asked me to remove my mask so she could see who I was. After I removed my mask, she realized I was an Indian and quite cruelly told me so, refusing to give me the treats my friends had received. It was a stingingly painful experience.

6   I told my mother about it the next evening after I tried to understand it. My mother was outraged and explained the realities of being an Indian in South Dakota. My mother paid a visit to the woman which resulted in their expressing a barrage of equal hatred for one another. I remember sitting in our pick-

up hearing the intensity of the anger and feeling very sad that my mother had to defend her child to someone who wasn't worthy of her presence.

7   I spent a part of my childhood feeling great sadness and helplessness about how it seemed that Indians were open game for the white people, to kill, maim, beat up, insult, rape, cheat, or whatever atrocity the white people wanted to play with. There was also a rage and frustration that has not died. When I look back on reservation life it seems that I spent a great deal of time attending the funerals of my relatives or friends of my family. During one year I went to funerals of four murder victims. Most of my non-Indian friends have not seen a dead body or have not been to a funeral. Death was so common on the reservation that I did not understand the implications of the high death rate until after I moved away and was surprised to learn that I've seen more dead bodies than my friends will probably ever see in their lifetime.

8   Because of experiencing racial violence, I sometimes panic when I'm the only non-white in a roomful of whites, even if they are my closest friends; I wonder if I'll leave the room alive. The seemingly copacetic gay world of San Francisco becomes a mere dream after the panic leaves. I think to myself that it's truly insane for me to feel the panic. I want to scream out my anger and disgust with myself for feeling distrustful of my white friends and I want to banish the society that has fostered those feelings of alienation. I wonder at the amount of assimilation which has affected me and how long my "Indianness" will allow me to remain in a city that is far removed from the lives of many Native Americans.

9   "Alienation" and "assimilation" are two common words used to describe contemporary Indian people. I've come to despise those two words because what leads to "alienation" and "assimilation" should not be so concisely defined. And I generally mistrust words that are used to define Native Americans and Brown People. I don't like being put under a magnifying glass and having cute liberal terms describe who I am. The "alienation" or "assimilation" that I manifest is often in how I speak. There isn't necessarily a third world language but there is an Indian way of talking that is an essential part of me. I like it, I love it, yet I deny it. I "save" it for when I'm around other Indians. It is a way of talking that involves "Indian humor" which I know for sure non-Indian people would not necessarily understand.

10   *Articulate. Articulate.* I've heard that word used many times to describe third world people. White people seem so surprised to find brown people who can speak fluent english and are even perhaps educated. We then become "articulate." I think I spend a lot of time being articulate with white people. Or as one person said to me a few years ago, "Gee, you don't seem like an Indian from the reservation."

11   I often read about the dilemmas of contemporary Indians caught between the white and Indian worlds. For most of us, it is an uneasy balance to maintain. Sometimes some of us are not so successful with it. Native Americans have a very high suicide rate.

12   *When I was about 20, I dreamt of myself at the age of 25–26, standing at a place on my reservation, looking to the North, watching a glorious, many-colored horse galloping toward me from the sky. My eyes were riveted and attracted to the beauty and overwhelming strength of the horse. The horse's eyes were staring directly into mine, hypnotizing me and holding my attention. Slowly from the East, an eagle was gliding toward the horse. My attention began to be drawn toward the calm of the eagle but I still did not want to lose sight of the horse. Finally the two met with the eagle sailing into the horse causing it to disintegrate. The eagle flew gently on.*

13   I take this prophetic dream as an analogy of my balance between the white (horse) and Indian (eagle) world. Now that I am 26, I find that I've gone as far into my exploration of the white world as I want. It doesn't mean that I'm going to run off to live in a tipi. It simply means that I'm not interested in pursuing a society that uses analysis, research, and experimentation to concretize their vision of cruel destinies for those who are not bastards of the Pilgrims; a society with arrogance rising, moon in oppression, and sun in destruction.

14   Racism is not easy for me to write about because of my own racism toward other people of color, and because of a complex set of "racisms" within the Indian community. At times animosity exists between half-breed, full-blood, light-skinned Indians, dark-skinned Indians, and non-Indians who attempt to pass as Indians. The U.S. government has practiced for many years its divisiveness in the Indian community by instilling and perpetuating these Indian vs. Indian tactics. Native Americans are the foremost group of people who continuously fight against pre-meditated cultural genocide.

15   I've grown up with misconceptions about Blacks, Chicanos, and Asians. I'm still in the process of trying to eliminate my racist pictures of other people of color. I know most of *my* images of other races come from television, books, movies, newspapers, and magazines. Who can pinpoint exactly where racism comes from? There are certain political dogmas that are excellent in their "analysis" of racism and how it feeds the capitalist system. To intellectually understand that it is wrong or politically incorrect to be racist leaves me cold. A lot of poor or working class white and brown people are just as racist as the "capitalist pig." We are *all* continually pumped with gross and inaccurate images of everyone else and we *all* pump it out. I don't think there are easy answers or formulas. My personal attempts at eliminating my racism have to start at the base level of those mind-sets that inhibit my relationships with people.

16   Racism among third world people is an area that needs to be discussed and dealt with honestly. We form alliances loosely based on the fact that we have a common oppressor, yet we do not have a commitment to talk about our own fears and misconceptions about each other. I've noticed that liberal, consciousness-raised white people tend to be incredibly polite to third world people at parties or other social situations. It's almost as if they make a point to SHAKE YOUR HAND or to introduce themselves and then run down all the latest right-on third world or Native American books they've just read. On the other

hand it's been my experience that if there are several third world gay people at a party, we make a point of avoiding each other, and spend our time talking to the whites to show how sophisticated and intelligent we are. I've always wanted to introduce myself to other third world people but wondered how I would introduce myself or what would I say. There are so many things I would want to say, except sometimes I don't want to remember I'm Third World or Native American. I don't want to remember sometimes because it means recognizing that we're outlaws.

17   At the Third World Gay Conference in October 1979, the Asian and Native American people in attendance felt the issues affecting us were not adequately included in the workshops. Our representation and leadership had minimal input which resulted in a skimpy educational process about our struggles. The conference glaringly pointed out to us the narrow definition held by some people that third world means black people only. It was a depressing experience to sit in the lobby of Harambee House with other Native Americans and Asians, feeling removed from other third world groups with whom there is supposed to be this automatic solidarity and empathy. The Indian group sat in my motel room discussing and exchanging our experiences within the third world context. We didn't spend much time in workshops conducted by other third world people because of feeling unwelcomed at the conference and demoralized by having an invisible presence. What's worse than being invisible among your own kind?

18   It is of particular importance to us as third world gay people to begin a serious interchange of sharing and educating ourselves about each other. We not only must struggle with the racism and homophobia of straight white america, but must often struggle with the homophobia that exists within our third world communities. Being third world doesn't always connote a political awareness or activism. I've met a number of third world and Native American lesbians who've said they're just into "being themselves", and that politics has no meaning in their lives. I agree that everyone is entitled to "be themselves" but in a society that denies respect and basic rights to people because of their ethnic background, I feel that individuals cannot idly sit by and allow themselves to be co-opted by the dominant society. I don't know what moves a person to be politically active or to attempt to raise the quality of life in our world. I only know what motivates my political responsibility. . . the death of Anna Mae Aquash—Native American freedom fighter—"mysteriously" murdered by a bullet in the head; Raymond Yellow Thunder—forced to dance naked in front of a white VFW club in Nebraska—murdered; Rita Silk-Nauni—imprisoned for life for defending her child; my dear friend Mani Lucas-Papago—shot in the back of the head outside of a gay bar in Phoenix. The list could go on and on. My Native American History, recent and past, moves me to continue as a political activist.

19   And in the white gay community there is rampant racism which is never adequately addressed or acknowledged. My friend Chrystos from the Menom-

inee Nation gave a poetry reading in May 1980, at a Bay Area feminist book-store. Her reading consisted of poems and journal entries in which she wrote honestly from her heart about the many "isms" and contradictions in most of our lives. Chrystos' bluntly revealing observations on her experiences with the white-lesbian-feminist-community are similar to mine and are probably echoed by other lesbians of color.

20   Her honesty was courageous and should be representative of the kind of forum our community needs to openly discuss mutual racism. A few days fol-lowing Chrystos' reading, a friend who was in the same bookstore overheard a white lesbian denounce Chrystos' reading as anti-lesbian and racist.

21   A few years ago, a white lesbian telephoned me requesting an interview, explaining that she was taking Native American courses at a local university, and that she needed data for her paper on gay Native Americans. I agreed to the interview with the idea that I would be helping a "sister" and would also be able to educate her about Native American struggles. After we completed the interview, she began a diatribe on how sexist Native Americans are, fol-lowed by a questioning session in which I was to enlighten her mind about why Native Americans are so sexist. I attempted to rationally answer her inanely racist and insulting questions, although my inner response was to tell her to remove herself from my house. Later it became very clear how I had been manipulated as a sounding board for her ugly and distorted views about Native Americans. Her arrogance and disrespect were characteristic of the racist white people in South Dakota. If I tried to point it out, I'm sure she would have vehemently denied her racism.

22   During the Brigg's Initiative scare, I was invited to speak at a rally to repre-sent Native American solidarity against the initiative. The person who spoke prior to me expressed a pro-Bakke sentiment which the audience booed and hissed. His comments left the predominantly white audience angry and in dis-ruption. A white lesbian stood up demanding that a third world person address the racist comments he had made. The MC, rather than taking responsibility for restoring order at the rally, realized that I was the next speaker and I was also T-H-I-R-D-W-O-R-L-D!! I refused to address the remarks of the previous speaker because of the attitudes of the MC and the white lesbian that only third world people are responsible for speaking out against racism. *It is inappropriate for progressive or liberal white people to expect warriors in brown armor to eradicate racism.* There must be co-responsibility from people of color and white people to equally work on this issue. It is not just MY responsibility to point out and educate about racist activities and beliefs.

23   Redman, redskin, savage, heathen, injun, american indian, first americans, indigenous peoples, natives, amerindian, native american, nigger, negro, black, wet back, greaser, mexican, spanish, latin, hispanic, chicano, chink, ori-ental, asian, disadvantaged, special interest group, minority, third world, fourth world, people of color, illegal aliens—oh yes about them, will the U.S.

government recognize that the Founding Fathers (you know George Washington and all those guys) are this country's first illegal aliens.

24   *We are named by others and we are named by ourselves.*

Epilogue. . .

25   Following writing most of this, I went to visit my home in South Dakota. It was my first visit in eight years. I kept putting off my visit year after year because I could not tolerate the white people there and the ruralness and poverty of the reservation. And because in the eight years since I left home, I came out as a lesbian. My visit home was overwhelming. Floods and floods of locked memories broke. I rediscovered myself there in the hills, on the prairies, in the sky, on the road, in the quiet nights, among the stars, listening to the distant yelps of coyotes, walking on Lakota earth, seeing Bear Butte, looking at my grandparents' cragged faces, standing under wakiyan, smelling the Paha Sapa (Black Hills), and being with my precious circle of relatives.

26   My sense of time changed, my manner of speaking changed, and a certain freedom with myself returned.

27   I was sad to leave but recognized that a significant part of myself has never left and never will. And that part is what gives me strength—the strength of my people's enduring history and continuing belief in the sovereignty of our lives.

POST-READING QUESTIONS:

1) Did you find that any of your thoughts or feelings concerning stereotypes or stereotyping affected your understanding of or helped shape your reactions to Cameron's ideas? Did her essay cause you to reexamine your reasons for having these thoughts and feelings?

2) Do you and Cameron have much in common vis-à-vis your and her feeling a part of and/or apart from your respective ethnic cultures?

3) When you compare what you say in your response to the third pre-reading question with that which Cameron says in paragraph 8, do you find that the two of you have anything in common?

4) Do you want to amend any part of your response to the fourth pre-reading question in light of your understanding of Cameron's essay? Before answering this question, reread paragraphs 9–13.

5) How might the points contained in paragraph 10 form the analytical hub of the entire essay, in terms of both Cameron's analysis of white racist ideas and practices and her analysis of third-world racist ideas and practices, including her own? (Note: take another look at paragraphs 13ff.) Are the points contained in paragraph 10 relevant to an understanding of *all* racist ideas and practices?

6) What seems to be the relationship between the epilogue and the rest of the essay?

7) How would you compare Cameron's experiences as a Native American with those of Black Elk (see p. 52)? How would you compare her experiences as a

disenfranchised person with those of Maya Angelou (see p. 207), Louie Crew (see p. 146), Mitsuye Yamada (see p. 335), or any other writer whose work appears in this book and who discusses her or his experiences as a disenfranchised person?

HANDS-ON ACTIVITY:

Whether or not you agree with all—or any—of the views expressed by the authors of this chapter's readings, hopefully their work has helped you to gain a greater appreciation for women's struggles, however sensitive you already might have been to women's predicaments. But such understanding will be of questionable worth if it is not translated into action of one sort or another. You yourself will have to decide how best to mobilize your feelings into action. If you don't already do so, at the very least you can refrain from telling or, if possible, listening to sexist jokes about women, since the sexist ideas underlying such jokes also underlie real acts of physical violence against women. Though such resistance to sexism is hardly inconsequential (just watch what happens the next time that someone wants to tell you a sexist joke and you refuse to listen to it), you might want to do even more. If that's the case, you might volunteer your efforts on behalf of your college's women's resource center, a local battered women's shelter, or both. Since, for security reasons, the locations of battered women's shelters are kept fairly secret, you'll need to speak with a psychologist or counselor at your school who can help you get in touch with a shelter's director. Whatever you decide to do, keep in mind that much (if not most) of the world's significant social change has resulted from the small efforts of many people, and that, without such efforts, great social change rarely, if ever, occurs.

The following is a bibliographical listing of works that have been cited in this text.

American Men & Women of Science: Social and Behavioral Sciences. 13th ed. Ed. Jaques Cattell Press. New York: R. R. Bowker Co., 1978. 827.

Beck, Evelyn Torton. Rev. of Alice Bloch's *The Law of Return. The News* (Los Angeles), 11 December 1987. Ctd. in Em L. White. Entry for " Alice Bloch." In *Contemporary Lesbian Writers of the United States: A Bio-Bibliographical Critical Sourcebook,* ed. Sandra Pollack and Denise D. Knight. Westport, Conn.: Greenwood Press, 1993. 61–64.

Bloch, Alice. *Lifetime Guarantee: A Journey Through Loss and Survival.* Watertown, Mass.: Persephone Press, Inc., 1981.

Brandt, Beth, ed. *A Gathering of Spirit: Writing and Art by North American Indian Women.* Rockland, Maine: Sinister Wisdom Books, 1984.

Christian, Barbara. "Alice Walker: The Black Woman Artist as Wayward." In *Black Women Writers (1950–1980): A Critical Evaluation,* ed. Mari Evans. Garden City, N.Y.: Anchor Press/Doubleday, 1984. 457–477.

Cisneros, Sandra. *The House on Mango Street.* "About the Author." New York: Vintage Books/Random House, Inc., 1991. 111.

―――. *The House on Mango Street.* "About Sandra Cisneros and *The House on Mango Street.*" Houston: Arte Publico Press, 1986. 103.

Contemporary Authors: A Bio-Bibliographical Guide to Current Writers in Fiction, General Nonfiction, Poetry, Journalism, Drama, Motion Pictures, Television, and Other Fields. Vol. 131. Ed. by Susan M. Trosky. Detroit: Gale Research, Inc., 1991. 109.

―――. Vol. 118. Ed. Hal May, et al. Les Stone, Senior Writer. Detroit: Gale Research Company, 1986. 415–416.

―――. Vols. 77–80. Ed. Frances Carol Locher. Detroit: Gale Research Company, 1979. 615.

―――. *New Revision Series.* Vol. 21. Ed. Deborah A. Straub, et al. Thomas Wiloch, Senior Writer. Detroit: Gale Research Company, 1987. 405–409.

―――. *New Revision Series.* Vol. 19. Ed. Linda Metzger, et al. Thomas Wiloch, Senior Writer. Detroit: Gale Research Company, 1987. 21–24.

Current Biography Yearbook 1991. Ed. Charles Moritz, et. al. New York: The H. W. Wilson Company, 1992. 364–368.

Current Biography Yearbook 1985. Ed. Charles Moritz, et al. New York: The H. W. Wilson Company, 1986. 470–471.

Current Biography Yearbook 1979. Ed. Charles Moritz, et. al. New York: The H. W. Wilson Company, 1980. 257–260.

de Beauvoir, Simone. "Preface." In *Shoah: An Oral History of the Holocaust. The Complete Text of the Film,* by Claude Lanzmann. New York: Pantheon Books, 1985. iii–vi.

ETS Test Administration Highlights, Vol. VIII/No. 1 (Fall 1994), p. 4.

Ferguson, Everett, ed. *Encyclopedia of Early Christianity.* New York: Garland Publishing, Inc., 1990. 588–589.

Foucault, Michel. "What Is an Author?" In *Language, Counter-Memory, Practice: Selected Essays and Interviews,* by Michel Foucault, ed. Donald F. Bouchard, trans. Donald F. Bouchard and Sherry Simon. Ithaca, N.Y.: Cornell University Press, 1981. 113–138.

Fox, Robin Lane. *The Unauthorized Version: Truth and Fiction in the Bible.* New York: Alfred A. Knopf, Inc., 1992.

Freud, Sigmund. "The Disillusionment of the War." In *The Standard Edition of the Complete Psychological Works of Sigmund Freud,* trans. from the German under the general editorship of James Strachey, in collaboration with Anna Freud, assisted by Alix Strachey and Alan Tyson. London: The Hogarth Press and the Institute of Psycho-Analysis, 1953–1986. Vol. 14. 275–288.

Gay, Peter. *Freud: A Life for Our Time.* New York: W. W. Norton & Company, 1988.

Gonsior, Marian. Entry for "Martin Luther King, Jr." In *Contemporary Authors, New Revision Series* [for complete bibliographic details, see the listing for *Contemporary Authors, New Revision Series,* above]. Vol. 27. Ed. Hal May, et al. Thomas Wiloch, Senior Writer. Detroit: Gale Research Company, 1989. 276–281.

Graham, Hugh Davis. Entry for "Martin Luther King, Jr." In *Encyclopedia of African-American Civil Rights: From Emancipation to the Present.* Ed. Charles D. Lowery and John F. Marszalek. Westport, Conn.: Greenwood Press, 1992. 302–305.

Hanscombe, Gillian E. and Martin Humphries. "Notes on the Contributors." In *Heterosexuality,* ed. Gillian E. Hanscombe and Martin Humphries. London: GMP Publishers, Ltd., 1987.

Heger, Heinz. *The Men with the Pink Triangle.* Trans. by David Fernbach. Boston: Alyson Publications, Inc., 1980, 1986.

Hirsch, E. D. Jr. *Validity in Interpretation.* New Haven, Conn.: Yale University Press, 1976.

Holman, C. Hugh. *A Handbook to Literature.* 4th ed. Indianapolis: The Bobbs-Merrill Company, Inc., 1980.

Horton, Paul B. and Chester L. Hunt. *Sociology.* 3rd ed. New York: McGraw Hill, Inc., 1972.

Höss, Rudolph. *Death Dealer: The Memoirs of the SS Kommandant at Auschwitz.* Ed. Steven Paskuly, trans. Andrew Pollinger. Buffalo, N.Y.: Prometheus Books, 1992.

Joyce, James. "A Painful Case." In *Dubliners,* by James Joyce. New York: Penguin Books, 1977. 107–117.

Katz, Fred E. "A Sociological Perspective to the Holocaust." In *Modern Judaism* 2.3 (October 1982): 273–296.

Korg, Jacob. *Dylan Thomas.* New York: Hippocrene Books, Inc., 1972. [Formerly, Twayne Publishers, Inc., 1965.]

Krieger, Murray. "Literature as Illusion, as Metaphor, as Vision." In *Poetic Presence and Illusion: Essays in Critical History and Theory,* by Murray Krieger. Baltimore: The Johns Hopkins University Press, 1979. 188–196.

[The] Last Days of Socrates. Trans. Hugh Tredennick. New York: Viking Penguin, Inc., 1985.

Miller, Alice. "Vantage Point 1990." Trans. Leila Vennewitz. In *The Drama of the Gifted Child: The Search for the True Self,* by Alice Miller. Trans. Ruth Ward. Basic Books/HarperCollins Publishers, 1990. vii–x.

————. *For Your Own Good: Hidden Cruelty in Child-Rearing and the Roots of Violence.* Trans. by Hildegarde and Hunter Hannum. New York: Farrar, Straus, Giroux, 1986.

Moraga, Cherríe. "We Fight Back with Our Families." In *Loving in the War Years: lo que nunca pasó por sus labios,* by Cherríe Moraga. Boston: South End Press, 1983. 105–111.

Moraga, Cherríe and Gloria Anzaldúa, eds. *This Bridge Called My Back: Writings by Radical Women of Color.* New York: Kitchen Table: Women of Color Press, 1981.

Neihardt, John G. *Black Elk Speaks: Being the Life Story of a Holy Man of the Oglala Sioux, as told through John G. Neihardt (Flaming Rainbow).* New York: Pocket Books, 1975.

Nietzsche, Friedrich. "On Truth and Lies in a Nonmoral Sense." In *Philosophy and Truth: Selections from Nietzsche's Notebooks of the Early 1870's,* by Friedrich Nietzsche. Trans. and ed. Daniel Breazeale. Atlantic Highlands, N.J.: Humanities Press, 1979. 79–97.

Nin, Anaïs. *Delta of Venus: Erotica.* New York: Bantam/Harcourt Brace Jovanovich, Inc., 1981.

Paskuly, Steven. "Epilogue." In *Death Dealer: The Memoirs of the SS Kommandant at Auschwitz,* by Rudolph Höss. Ed. Steven Paskuly, trans. Andrew Pollinger. Buffalo, N.Y.: Prometheus Books, 1992. 196–205.

Plato, *Socrates' Defense [Apology].* Trans. Hugh Tredennick. In *The Collected Dialogues of Plato, Including the Letters,* by Plato. Ed. by Edith Hamilton and Huntington Cairns. Princeton: Princeton University Press, 1980. 4–26.

Plaut, W. Gunther. Commentary on *Genesis* 22. In *The Torah: A Modern Commentary.* [Translated by the Jewish Publication Society, 1962, 1967.] Ed. W. Gunther Plaut. New York: The Union of American Hebrew Congregations, 1981. 149–151.

Pope, Alexander. "An Essay on Criticism." In *Critical Theory Since Plato,* ed. Hazard Adams. New York: Harcourt Brace Jovanovich, Inc., 1971. 278–286.

Sachar, Abram L. *The Redemption of the Unwanted: From the Liberation of the Death Camps to the Founding of Israel.* New York: St. Martin's/Marek, 1983.

Salter, Susan. Entry for "Maya Angelou." In *Contemporary Authors, New Revision Series*. Vol. 19 [for complete bibliographic details, see the listing for *Contemporary Authors, New Revision Series*, above].

Sartre, Jean-Paul. *Anti-Semite and Jew.* Trans. George J. Becker. New York: Schocken Books, Inc., 1976.

Schaef, Anne Wilson. *Women's Reality: An Emerging Female System in a White Male Society.* San Francisco: Harper & Row, Publishers, 1981.

Shakespeare, William. "Sonnet 73." In *The Sonnets,* by William Shakespeare. Ed. William Burto. New York: Signet/New American Library, 1964.

Telushkin, Rabbi Joseph. *Jewish Literacy: The Most Important Things to Know About the Jewish Religion, Its People, and Its History.* New York: William Morrow and Company, Inc., 1991.

Van Biema, David H. "Filmmaker Claude Lanzmann Devotes 11 Years of His Life to a Biography of Death." Ir *People Weekly.* February 10, 1986: 65–70.

Walker, Alice. "In Search of Our Mothers' Gardens." In Alice Walker, *In Search of Our Mothers' Gardens: Womanist Prose by Alice Walker.* New York: Harcourt Brace Jovanovich, Inc., 1983. 231–243.

———. "Writing *The Color Purple.*" In Alice Walker, *In Search of Our Mothers' Gardens: Womanist Prose by Alice Walker.* New York: Harcourt Brace Jovanovich, Inc., 1983. 355–360.

———. Comments reprinted on the back cover of *Cuentos: Stories by Latinas.* Ed. Alma Gómez, Cherríe Moraga, and Mariana Romo-Carmona. New York: Kitchen Table: Women of Color Press, Inc. 1983.

Walker, Barbara G. *The Woman's Encyclopedia of Myths and Secrets.* San Francisco: Harper & Row, Publishers, 1983.

Ward, Skye. Entry for "Cherríe Moraga." In *Contemporary Lesbian Writers of the United States: A Bio-Bibliographical Critical Sourcebook,* eds. Sandra Pollack and Denise D. Knight. Westport, Conn.: Greenwood Press, 1993. 379–383.

White, E. B. "Introduction." In William Strunk, Jr., and E. B. White, *The Elements of Style,* 3rd ed. New York: Macmillan Publishing Co., Inc., 1979. xi–xvii.

White, Em L. Entry for "Alice Bloch." In *Contemporary Lesbian Writers of the United States: A Bio-Bibliographical Critical Sourcebook,* eds. Sandra Pollack and Denise D. Knight. Westport, CT: Greenwood Press, 1993. 61–64.

Wiloch, Thomas. Entry for "Irwin Shaw." In *Contemporary Authors, New Revision Series*. Vol. 21 [for complete bibliographic details, see the listing for *Contemporary Authors, New Revision Series*, above].

Zinser, William. *On Writing Well: An Informal Guide to Writing Nonfiction.* New York: HarperCollins Publishers, Inc.: 1990.

Credits

Chapter 5

"Thriving As An Outsider, Even As An Outcast In Small Town America." Copyright © 1981. Proceedings of the Third Annual Conference on the Small City, Vol. 3, 1981. University of Wisconsin/Stevens Point, Center for the Small City.

Excerpt from "Three Essays on The Theory of Sexuality" by Sigmund Freud from *The Standard Edition of the Complete Psychological Works of Sigmund Freud*, translated and edited by James Strachey. Copyright © 1962 by Sigmund Freud Copyrights, Ltd. Reprinted by permission of HarperCollins Publishers, Inc., The Institute of Psycho-Analysis and The Hogarth Press.

"Evaluating the 'Unnaturalness Argument' Concerning Homosexuality" by Burton M. Leiser, reprinted with the permission of Simon & Schuster from the Macmillan College text *Liberty, Justice, and Morals*, 3rd Edition, by Burton M. Leiser. Copyright © 1986 by Burton M. Leiser.

"Born or Bred?" by David Gelman from *Newsweek*, February 24, 1992. Copyright © 1992, Newsweek, Inc. All rights reserved. Reprinted by permission.

"The Tables Need Turning" by Jan Parker from *Heterosexuality,* edited by Gillian E. Hanscombe and Martin Humphries. World copyright © 1987 GMP Publishers Ltd. World copyright © 1987 the respective authors. Reprinted by permission of GMP Publishers Ltd.

Chapter 6

From *I Know Why the Caged Bird Sings* by Maya Angelou. Copyright © 1969 by Maya Angelou. Reprinted by permission of Random House, Inc.

"Reminiscences of Childhood" by Dylan Thomas from *Early One Morning*. Copyright © 1954 by New Directions Publishing Corporation. Reprinted by permission of New Directions Publishing Corporation.

"The Vicious Circle of Contempt" from *The Drama of the Gifted Child* by Alice Miller, translated from the German by Ruth Ward. Copyright © 1979 Suhrkamp Verlag Frankfurt am Main. Reprinted by permission.

"Grandmother's Garden" by Kathleene West as appeared in *All My Grandmothers Could Sing,* edited by Judith Sornberger. Reprinted by permission of Kathleene West.

"Summer, 1945" by Lorraine Duggin as appeared in *All My Grandmothers Could Sing,* edited by Judith Sornberger. Reprinted by permission.

"Elethia" from *You Can't Keep a Good Woman Down*, copyright © 1979 by Alice Walker, reprinted by permission of Harcourt Brace & Company.

"Theme for English B" from *Montage of a Dream Deferred* by Langston Hughes. Reprinted by permission of Harold Ober Associates Incorporated. Copyright © 1951 by Langston Hughes. Copyright renewed 1979 by George Houston Bass.

Chapter 7

"When Isaac Arises form the Sacrificial Altar" from *The Untouched Key* by Alice Miller. Copyright © 1990 by Alice Miller. Used by permission of Doubleday, a division of Bantam Doubleday Dell Publishing Group, Inc.

"The Akedah, Genesis 22" from *The Torah: A Modern Commentary*. The English translation of The Torah, published and copyrighted © 1962, 1967 by the Jewish Publication Society, is used by special permission of the Society.

"The Perils of Obedience" abridged and adapted from *Obedience to Authority* by Stanley Milgram. Reprinted by permission of HarperCollins Publishers, Inc.

"Early Years" from *Death Dealer: The Memoirs of the SS Kommandant at Auschwitz* by Rudolph Höss, edited by Steven Paskuly, translated by Andrew Pollinger. Copyright © 1992 by Steven Paskuly. Reprinted by permission of Prometheus Books.

From *The Last Days of Socrates* by Plato, translated by Hugh Tredennick (Penguin Classics 1954, revised edition 1959) copyright © Hugh Tredennick, 1954, 1959.

"Letter from Birmingham Jail" by Martin Luther King, Jr. Reprinted by arrangement with The Heirs to the Estate of Martin Luther King, Jr., c/o Joan Daves Agency as agent for the proprietor. Copyright © 1963 by Martin Luther King, Jr., copyright renewed 1991 by Coretta Scott King.

Chapter 8

"Invisibility Is An Unnatural Disaster" by Mitsuye Yamada from *This Bridge Called My Back,* edited by Cherríe Moraga and Gloria Anzaldua. Copyright © 1983 by Kitchen Table Press. Used by permission of the author and of Kitchen Table: Women of Color Press, P.O. Box 988, Latham, NY 12110.

Excerpts from *Women's Reality* by Anne Wilson Schaef. Copyright © 1981 by Anne Wilson Schaef. Reprinted by permission of HarperCollins Publishers, Inc.

"Tales Out of Medical School" by Adrian Fugh-Berman from *The Nation*, January 20, 1992. Reprinted with permission from *The Nation* Magazine. © The Nation Company L.P.

"The Girls in Their Summer Dresses" by Irwin Shaw from *Five Decades* by Irwin Shaw. Copyright © 1978 by Irwin Shaw. Used by permission of Dell Books, a division of Bantam Doubleday Dell Publishing Group, Inc.

"The Mute" by Denise Levertov from *Poems 1960–1967*. Copyright © 1964 by Denise Levertov Goodman. Reprinted by permission of New Directions Publishing Corporation.

"My Brother's Sex was White, Mine Brown" from *Loving in the War Years* by Cherríe Moraga. Reprinted by permission of South End Press.

"Gee, You Don't Seem Like An Indian From The Reservation" by Barbara Cameron from *This Bridge Called My Back*, edited by Cherríe Moraga and Gloria Anzaldúa. Copyright © 1983. Used by permission of the author and of Kitchen Table: Women of Color Press, P.O. Box 988, Latham, NY 12110.

Index

Instructor's Manual
to accompany

Careful Reading, Thoughtful Writing

A GUIDE WITH MODELS FOR COLLEGE WRITERS

Richard J. Prystowsky

Irvine Valley College

HarperCollins*College*Publishers

Contents

Introduction

Though I strongly believe that your best teaching moments concerning the material in this reader will derive from your and your students' own, initiatory efforts at dealing with this material, I offer you the following thoughts, comments, questions, and concerns about both this text's instructional material and its readings. Please feel free not only to exploit those of my ideas and suggestions that prove useful to you, but also to discard those that aren't very helpful. Moreover, I urge you to voice both your agreements and your disagreements with my views or pedagogical approaches as part of the work that you do with your students, challenging them and me—and perhaps even yourself—to reach beyond our grasp, as Robert Browning might have said. Further, I invite you and your students to write to me about any concerns that you or they have with either this reader or the issues discussed in this manual, as well as about those aspects of the reader and manual that you or your students particularly like.

For your convenience, I have arranged this manual's material in a consistent pattern. For each chapter, I first briefly discuss some of what I take to be (or have seen to be) the instructional issues at stake. Then, I talk about the chapter's readings, discussing first the featured reading selection, and then the related readings. Concerning the featured reading selection, I discuss "Things to Think About," "The Featured Assignment and the Contributing Author's Model Response," "Corollary Readings," and "Alternate Assignments." Concerning the related readings, I discuss "Things to Think About," "Corollary Readings," "Possible Assignments," and "Individual, Group, and/or Class Activities." (In light of the nature and arrangement of the book's first two chapters, this manual's discussion headings pertaining to these chapters have been modified.)

Although you surely will disagree with at least some of my choices, for brevity's sake (if not also for the sake of your and my sanity!) I decided to suggest no more than about a half-dozen corollary readings per reading selection (not including a chapter's related readings), unless I found it necessary to suggest all of the readings in a chapter other than the one under discussion. Similarly, I decided to limit the suggestions for alternate or possible assignments to four and the ideas for individual, group, and/or class activities to four or five. Concerning the creation of assignments—including prewriting exercises, formal or informal writing activities, and group or class presentations—please note that many other possibilities exist (other than those that I suggest, that is) in the form of the reader's pre- and post-reading questions and close-reading tips. When appropriate, I point out how you might want to amend any of these apparatuses.

Let me end these introductory comments by briefly addressing two matters: the order in which you decide to use the book's material, and the ways in which you might respond to your students' writing. Though I urge you to experiment with tailoring the book to fit your own pedagogical needs (keep in mind, however, that the material contained in the text's final three chapters presupposes that your students already understand something about the substantive matters discussed in the book's first five chapters), I do feel that you'll help your students greatly if in the first weeks of your course you cover the instructional material in the text's second and third chapters, since so much of their college work will involve close reading and critical thinking of one sort or another. However, while your students are learning about close reading and critical thinking, I see no reason that you shouldn't have them study and write about (or simply write in response to) readings from elsewhere in the text, such as Alice Miller's "When Isaac Arises from the Sacrificial Altar" (p. 259) and John Verbeck's "Evaluating Alice Miller's analysis of the Abraham and Isaac story" (p. 265), for example, or one or more of the text's poetry selections.

After using either approach (and these two possibilities are neither exhaustive nor mutually exclusive, of course), you might then have your students concentrate on writing full essays without their having spent much time studying the prewriting instructional material and models in Chapter Four; or, you might decide to have groups of students make class presentations concerning Chapter Four's material as a way of expediting the teaching of that material. My point is that this text ought to contain enough useful material to help you teach your class in whatever ways seem most efficacious.

Concerning the ways in which you might respond to your students' writing, I'll suggest only that you not underestimate the extent to which most of your students will take criticism personally and the degree to which their written and classroom performances might be affected by your adverse criticism of their work. This is not to say that you shouldn't criticize your students' work—indeed, part of your job as their teacher is to do so when necessary—but only to remind you that, like all writers, including you yourself, I would dare say, your students will likely take criticism of their work to heart. Our students *should* be personally concerned about their work; what we, their teachers, need to remember is that this concern is informed in large part by our reactions to their work, and that, in turn, their subsequent work is often affected by our reactions—both positive and negative—to their previous work.[1]

In short, we who teach composition courses—courses known to inspire fear even in bright, gifted, talented writing students—should be sensitive to the complicated relationship between our evaluations of our students' work and our students' present and possibly future written performances. However else we respond to their work, let us always try to be as encouraging and nonpunitive as possible. From time to time, our patience will certainly be tested, and on more

---

[1]Here are some other problems to ponder: Does a teacher's giving high praise to a student's efforts sometimes give that student a false sense of security? Are we possibly rewarding a student for having problematic writing habits by calling to her/his attention the troublesome writing that we see in her/his paper? In trying to help out students with their writing problems, do we sometimes confuse a cognitive difficulty with a behavioral one? Though space does not permit a discussion of these or related issues, I invite instructors interested in talking about these complicated matters to write to me.

occasions than we would like to see we will need to inform students that they aren't doing well in their work. Nevertheless, let us always try to respond to our students' work with the kindness and compassion that we want our own readers to display when they respond to our work. We could do far worse than to encourage our students and criticize their work in a spirit of kindness and compassion, all the while validating them as human beings and helping them take responsibility for their own empowerment.

Chapter One: Thinking About Writing

INSTRUCTIONAL ISSUES

For the past two years or so, I have begun my freshman writing courses with the instructional material (or some version of it) found in this chapter. I have had great success with this material, not because it represents some kind of dazzling performance of my rhetorical skill, but primarily, I think, because it tries to validate students' feelings both about writing and about themselves as writers. What I have found particularly useful is to have students talk in class about their previous experiences with writing and with English classes, as well as about their present expectations, fears, sense of excitement, and so on. I try to have each student speak, but I never like to force a student to do so. Generally, students seem to feel relieved that they are not the only ones who have had problems with writing; and those who happen to like writing sometimes help the others begin to see that, indeed, writing can be a worthwhile activity. (Perhaps not unexpectedly, students seem to hear this message differently when they hear it from a peer than when they hear it from an instructor.) Often, I participate in this discussion, sharing with my students my own joys about and frustrations with writing. Many students are surprised (and relieved) to hear that a "real" writer, besides having produced some work that people praise, also continues to produce work that editors and others reject (they also seem to like knowing that, as they do, I feel bad when my work is rejected and good when it receives praise).

One final matter here: Though I let my students know right from the start of the course that, for the next 16 weeks, I will consider them writers and treat them as such, I also make it clear to them that I refuse to own their responsibility for their attitudes and behavior. To be sure, I often try to help them devise workable writing schedules, for example, or revise their prose for strength and clarity, but I insist that they take responsibility for seeing me or not seeing me during my office hours, working to create or deciding not to schedule effective "writing blocks" (see pp. 4–6), and so on. I have found that co-dependent behavior on my part doesn't mix well with the sum and substance of this chapter's instructional material—or, for that matter, with the sum and substance of the material in this book as a whole.

SHERWOOD ANDERSON
Certain Things Last: A Writer Warms to His Story

THINGS TO THINK ABOUT

Towards the beginning of this piece, Anderson says, "What I am trying to make clear is that, as a writer, I am up against the same things that confront you, as a reader" (paragraph 2). In my view, Anderson not only helps students begin to understand the complex and yet intriguing relationship between a writer and her/his reader-based prose, but also, by directly addressing the reader as "you," includes students as full participants in the reading-writing phenomenon. Moreover, he succeeds in making it clear that he, too, struggles to say the right things, that he isn't always sure why he writes what he writes, and so on—precisely the sorts of concerns that nearly all composition students have. As I intimate above, students seem to feel more at ease with themselves as writers knowing that even professional writers struggle with their work. I try to impress upon them the idea that, in fact, if they are *not* having the sorts of struggles to which Anderson refers, then as writers they might very well be doing something wrong, and that, conversely, if they *are* having these kinds of struggles, then, at least in terms of their being actively engaged writers, they are probably doing something right.

As an opening reading selection, Anderson's story contains other useful ideas that you might capitalize on, too. Anderson suggests, for example, that writing can benefit the writer; he tells himself, "'If I can write everything out plainly, perhaps I will myself understand better what has happened'" (paragraph 4). He demonstrates the narrative technique of showing rather than telling: "My fingers pick up little things on my desk and then put them down" (paragraph 8). He articulates the frustration that writers often feel during the course of their work: "I write again, and again tear up my words" (paragraph 15), he says. And, to allude to but one more feature of his piece, Anderson documents the persistence demonstrated by the committed writer. Despite his continued setbacks, he tells himself that "'[t]he thing to be done . . . is to begin writing my book by telling as clearly as I can the adventures of that certain moment'" (paragraph 35). [Note: if you plan to have your students engage in a close, analytical reading of Anderson's story, you might suggest that they take a look at the instructional material in Chapter Three (p. 41), as well as, in Chapter Seven, the discussion concerning the differences between "meaning" and "significance" (pp. 251–253).]

THE FEATURED ASSIGNMENT AND THE CONTRIBUTING AUTHOR'S MODEL RESPONSE

This chapter's featured assignment has a twofold purpose: one, to allow students the opportunity to vent their frustrations with and/or express their enjoyment of writing; and two, to help students start to become as familiar as possible with their writing voices. To help them in these two tasks, you might think about not grading this first assignment, using it, perhaps, as something of a diagnostic. You might find that, by using the assignment in this way, you'll not only elicit from your students the kinds of honest responses that they might be wary of offering in a paper that is to be graded, but also help alleviate some of their anxiety about writing, as well as about taking a writing course.

Though in the main Kevin Mullen's (that is, the contributing author's) model response to the assignment has proved to be quite valuable, I have found that some of my students are a bit intimidated by this essay. Some students, for example, cannot imagine that they themselves could ever write such a good paper. Fortunately, I seem to allay at least some of their fears once I explain to them that they and Mullen are not the same person, that they are expected to write their own papers, and not his, and that these two points go to the heart of much of this chapter's instructional substance.

COROLLARY READINGS

As a way of helping your students become comfortable engaging in serious college-level reading and writing activities, you might supplement Anderson's piece with any number of this reader's selections. For example, you might want to have your students first read Langston Hughes' "Theme for English B" (p. 244), which documents a student's struggle to write authentically in response to an English assignment, and then do the assignment that is given at the beginning of the poem (when I have students do this, I usually receive some excellent, insightful, creative responses). Since Anderson talks a bit about his childhood, you might also find it useful to have your students read some or all of the other selections in Chapter Six (the Hughes poem is included among these readings). Dylan Thomas' "Reminiscences of Childhood" (p. 220) might be an especially useful reading with which to pair the Anderson story.

ALTERNATE ASSIGNMENT

Besides having good luck using the assignment given in the Langston Hughes poem (alluded to above), I've also had good luck using, as an opening assignment, a version of the featured assignment that appears in Chapter Four (p. 80). If you decide to take this path, you may or may not want to have your students read Elie Wiesel's "Why I Write" (p. 80), which deals with the topic of the Holocaust. In any event, an early assignment asking students to talk about why they (like to) write or don't (like to) write might yield some provocative and promising results.

INDIVIDUAL, GROUP, AND/OR CLASS ACTIVITIES

Though you are not teaching a course in creative writing, you might find that you help your students become better writers by helping them discover the creative writer in them. Concerning the Anderson piece, for example, you might ask them to engage in the following post-reading task: "Imagine that you and Anderson are having dinner at a restaurant. Reflecting on both his and your experiences, you begin discussing the highs and lows of the writing process. What will you likely say to each other? Which of your experiences will likely give him pause to think? Which of his experiences will probably make *you* think? During your conversation with Anderson, do you consciously conceive of yourself as a writer? Why or why not? And how does your self-perception affect not only what you say to Anderson, but also, perhaps, the way in which you interpret what he says to you?" (Note: Given its nature, you might want your students to do this assignment as a reflective commentary.)

Chapter Two: Critical Thinking: An Introduction

INSTRUCTIONAL ISSUES

Since I have found that many of my students are more or less unfamiliar with critical thinking, I often spend at least one or two *early* class sessions going over the material in this chapter before asking my students to incorporate critical thinking concepts into their personal and analytical writing. I also have found it especially helpful—and necessary—to stress both early in and at various times throughout the course that the real litmus test of one's willingness to engage in careful thinking occurs not when one must analyze issues concerning which one has little or no investment, but, rather, when one must analyze issues concerning which one is deeply invested. Sooner or later during the semester—perhaps, for example, when you are talking with a student about her troublesome attempt to support the thesis that abortion is murder, or when you are trying to help a student understand the problematic nature of his thesis that no one ever has the right to tell a woman what she can or cannot do with her body—you will see why I am suggesting that you yourself make this point both early in and throughout the course.

READINGS

AESOP
The Shepherd Boy and the Wolf
and
LEWIS CARROLL
Who Stole the Tarts?

THINGS TO THINK ABOUT

Since some students are frightened merely by the idea of critical thinking, I often like to ease students into this kind of thinking by letting them have some fun using the chapter's principles of critical thinking to analyze relevant aspects of the chapter's two reading selections. If you follow suit, you might ask your students, for example, whether or not the shepherd boy takes serious issues seriously, approaching them humbly and carefully (see critical thinking tip #2, p. 26), or whether or not Aesop's conclusion (the moral of the story) or any of the conclusions articulated in the excerpt from *Alice's Adventures in Wonderland* derives from reasons and squares with pertinent evidence (see critical thinking tip #6, p. 27)[2]

The excerpt from *Alice's Adventures in Wonderland* provides many other opportunities for your students to practice their critical thinking skills. For example, they might try to analyze the reasoning in Alice's statement "'That's the judge . . . because of his great wig'" (paragraph 2), or the King's reasoning that the Hatter's hat is stolen seemingly because the Hatter's hat doesn't belong to him (that is, to the Hatter) (paragraphs 22–23). Perhaps the *pièce de résistance* for your students' critical thinking test occurs in paragraph 95ff., wherein we find the famous trial of the Knave of Hearts.

COROLLARY READINGS

Though every reading selection in this book provides opportunities for your students to practice their critical thinking skills, the readings in Chapter Seven might prove especially helpful. You might also consider using Fred E. Katz's "A Sociological Perspective to the Holocaust" (p. 95), Christopher R. Browning's "Ordinary Men" (p. 107), Sigmund Freud's "The Sexual Aberrations" (p. 163), Burton M. Leiser's "Evaluating the 'Unnaturalness Argument' Concerning Homosexuality" (p. 172), Alice Miller's "The Vicious Circle of Contempt" (p. 226), and Mitsuye Yamada's "Invisibility is an Unnatural Disaster: Reflections of an Asian American Woman" (p. 335).

ALTERNATE ASSIGNMENTS

Although there is no featured assignment for this chapter, in light of the end-of-chapter comments, you might ask your students to write about their impressions of the characters' and narrator's reasoning in Aesop's tale, in the process explaining how they themselves might have reasoned and what they might have done had they been the narrator or one of the characters. If you ask them to evaluate some of the thinking that they find in the excerpt from Lewis Carroll's book, you might have them discuss and evaluate the ways in which the characters deal with evidence. You can make this assignment playful by asking your students to explain whether or not, if they were on trial, they would want any of these characters representing them, serving on the jury, or acting as judge. Those of your

---

[2]To prepare your students to deal with a theme that they'll likely come across in this book's other reading selections, you might also want to have them discuss the ways in which Aesop's fable helps us to understand the relationship between reason and action. You might prompt this discussion by asking your students what they make of the fact that, concluding that the shepherd boy was up to his old tricks, the villagers "paid no heed to his cries, and the wolf devoured the sheep" (p. 32).

students who are knowledgeable about arguments *per se* (perhaps because they have taken or are taking a logic course) might find it interesting to evaluate some of the arguments that they find in this chapter's two readings. If they are particularly good in logic, these students might also enjoy comparing these arguments *as arguments* with those arguments that they find in one or more of the corollary readings listed above.

INDIVIDUAL, GROUP, AND/OR CLASS ACTIVITIES

1) Discuss and/or write about the extent to which fables offer us what the philosopher Aristotle would say are types, that is, likenesses to human nature in general. To help make your points, talk about the particular sorts of likenesses represented (in Aesop's fable) by the villagers, sheep, a wolf, and a shepherd who is also a boy. [Note: Before you have your students do this activity, you might need to have them read and discuss appropriate excerpts from Aristotle's *Poetics*.]

2) Discuss and/or write about some of the ways in which Aesop's fable helps us to understand both our world and the people who inhabit it. If appropriate, compare the didactic nature of Aesop's story with that of the excerpt from Maya Angelou's *I Know Why the Caged Bird Sings* (p. 207), Langston Hughes' "Theme for English B" (p. 244), or Alice Walker's "Elethia" (p. 240).

3) Comparing the excerpt from Lewis Carroll's book with Aesop's fable, discuss the extent to which each work effectively teaches, entertains, or otherwise moves you, the reader(s). If appropriate, compare the effectiveness (of the sort noted above) of works of fiction such as Aesop's fable, the excerpt from Lewis Carroll's book, and Denise Levertov's poem "The Mutes" (p. 373) with the effectiveness of works of nonfiction such as Plato's *Crito* (p. 295) or Martin Luther King, Jr.'s "Letter from Birmingham Jail" (p. 308).

Chapter Three: Careful Reading

INSTRUCTIONAL ISSUES

Although Chapter Three offers a number of ideas and tips concerning textual annotation, I highly suggest that you not be dogmatic about any of these (or other) ideas and tips. Do help your students see how their textual annotations can aid their reading and writing efforts and how they can facilitate these efforts further by using personal journals to record their thoughts about that which they read; but don't try to control their annotations and journal writing. I would especially caution you against having them use their journals to record formulaic reader-response questions and answers. From what I have observed, such reader-response work soon turns into manneristic busy work, the sort that, unfortunately, kills the joy of reading and impedes the progress of the reader.

FEATURED READING

SANDRA CISNEROS
My Name

THINGS TO THINK ABOUT

Although I have generally had good luck teaching this story, I have found that some of my students have difficulty sympathizing with the story's narrator. Some, seeing her as something of a complainer, don't seem to understand that her feelings are valid for *her*, whether or not they might also be valid for others. If your students react similarly, they might find it helpful to read about the problem of poor sampling (Chapter Eight, pp. 331–333) and then use their understanding of this problem to analyze their reaction to the narrator in Cisneros' story.

THE FEATURED ASSIGNMENT AND THE CONTRIBUTING AUTHORS' MODEL RESPONSES

Let me suggest that, rather than insisting that your students use any given technique of textual annotation, you encourage them to begin discovering the annotation techniques that work or don't work for *them*. If for no other reason, have them study Ellen K. Miles' and Susan McKenzie's markedly different model responses to the assignment (pp. 48 and 51) so that they can begin having a sense of the range of annotating methods.

To help your students see where within this range their own responses to the featured assignment situate themselves, you might ask them, for example, whether or not they, Miles, and McKenzie consider the same passages important or especially noteworthy, whether or not they, Miles, and McKenzie make similar sorts of marginal comments, structurally as well as thematically, whether or not, in general, their, Miles', and McKenzie's annotations help to indicate the extent to which everyone understands or reacts to various aspects of Cisneros' story similarly or differently, and so on. You might also ask your students to comment upon the sorts of similarities and/or differences that they see in the relationship between their own summary comments about the story and annotations of it and the summary comments and annotations made by Miles and McKenzie. You might ask them, for example, "Does a comparative examination of your and the contributing authors' comments and annotations help clarify the similarities and/or differences between your and their points of view? If so, how?"

COROLLARY READINGS

The Cisneros piece is short enough that students can reread it many times, a quality that I think you will want any reading selection to have that you are using as part of an introduction to close reading. Among this text's readings that would serve your purposes in this regard and that are thematically related to the Cisneros piece, you might consider using (aside from using this chapter's other readings) the excerpt from Alice Bloch's *The Law of Return* (p. 60), Alice Walker's "Elethia" (p. 240), Langston Hughes' "Theme for English B" (p. 244), and, perhaps, Cherríe Moraga's "My Brother's Sex Was White. Mine, Brown" (p. 376).

ALTERNATE ASSIGNMENTS

If your students will be answering the third pre-reading question, you might find it helpful to have them reflect on the following sorts of questions: "Have your parents' or relatives' last names changed over the years? Does your first name say anything about you personally? Does your surname indicate anything about your family's history or social status?" Reflecting on such questions might help your students make discoveries that they might not have made otherwise concerning the origin, meaning, or significance of their names in terms of their culture, family, and/or ethnic group.

Here are some other ideas for assignments:

1) Write a story of your own that is modeled on Cisneros' story. Or, write an essay in response to the question, "If you were to write a story about your own name, would it be similar to or different from Cisneros' story?" In either case, review your responses to the pre-reading questions and think about the nature of any changes that you made to these responses in light of your having read and reread Cisneros' story.

2) Compose a letter to Cisneros, telling her what you liked or disliked about her story and, if appropriate, how your own story or essay would differ from or be similar to hers (see the above assignment). In a follow-up assignment (perhaps in a reflective commentary), write about how you would have constructed this piece of writing differently were you to have written it as a formal essay, either for Cisneros' eyes only, or for your teacher and perhaps your classmates, or for other intended readers. Comment, too, on whether or not doing this assignment has helped you to learn anything about the relationship between form and content, as well as about the relationship among writer, the written work *per se*, and the writer's intended audience.

R E L A T E D   R E A D I N G S

BLACK ELK, AS TOLD THROUGH JOHN G. NEIHARDT
from Black Elk Speaks

THINGS TO THINK ABOUT

Unfortunately, many students continue to stereotype Native Americans as bloodthirsty savages, rich and greedy casino owners, romanticized versions of noble savages, great and insightful spiritual guides who never mistreat nature, and so on. And many students speak about Native Americans or about Native American values, beliefs, and lifestyles as if all Native Americans have the same values, beliefs, and lifestyles—in short, as if all Native Americans were one being or belonged to one tribe.

To help your students either avoid falling into these kinds of traps or escape such traps if they are already in them, you might ask them to read one or more of the following texts: the entirety of *Black Elk Speaks*, excerpts from Jack D. Forbes' *The Indian in America's Past* and Dee Brown's *Bury My Heart at Wounded Knee*, and selected poems from Wendy Rose's *The Halfbreed Chronicles and Other Poems* and Joy Harjo's *She Had Some Horses*. You might also consider reading aloud to your class excerpts from *American Indian Myths and Legends*, selected and edited by Richard Erdoes and Alfonso Ortiz, and having your students read (and perhaps even write about) Ignatia Broker's *Night Flying Woman: An Ojibway Narrative*. The latter text is an excellent narrative concerning both the Ojibway's displacement from their land and the strength of an Ojibway medicine woman, one of whose descendants is the book's narrator. Finally, I would recommend that, if possible, you use some good documentary films (such as *Hopi*) and an audio tape or two (*Fools Crow—Holy Man* is particularly good), and that you bring in guest speakers, preferably Native Americans who know about or are trying to recapture the ways of their people.

COROLLARY READINGS

Having your students read Barbara Cameron's "'Gee, You Don't Seem Like An Indian From the Reservation'" (p. 381) along with the excerpt from *Black Elk Speaks* might do much to help them see complexity rather than superficiality concerning Native Americans and Native American culture and history. Aside from using this chapter's other readings in conjunction with your using the Black Elk selection, you might also consider having your students read one or more of the following readings, each of which is more or less thematically related to the Black Elk selection: Louie Crew's "Thriving As An Outsider, Even As An Outcast, In Smalltown America" (p. 146); Shehla Yamani's "The Dilemma" (p. 154); the excerpt from Maya Angelou's *I Know Why the Caged Bird Sings* (p. 207); Alice Walker's "Elethia" (p. 240); and Langston Hughes' "Theme for English B" (p. 244). Additionally, you might consider having your students read and talk about Martin Luther King, Jr.'s "Letter from Birmingham Jail" (p. 308) either before or after they have studied and discussed the issues at stake in the Black Elk selection.

POSSIBLE ASSIGNMENTS

If you are having your students answer the second pre-reading and the fourth post-reading questions (pp. 53 and 56), you might also ask that they discuss events, holidays, or places that are important to them and whose names have special interpretive significance. If appropriate, they might also discuss the significance of the names of the days and months both in western culture and, if they know, in other cultures.

In addition to asking your students to answer the second question in post-reading question #4, you might ask them to discuss the similarities and/or differences between their narrative concerning events, holidays, or places that are important to them and whose names have special interpretive significance and Black Elk's descriptions of or references to important dates, events, and places.

Here's one additional assignment that you might want to try: How might a close reading of the excerpt from *Black Elk Speaks* and Barbara Cameron's essay "'Gee, You Don't Seem Like An Indian From the Reservation'" help readers understand why they shouldn't stereotype Native Americans or Native American values, beliefs, and lifestyles?

MATTHEW

from The Gospel According to Matthew

THINGS TO THINK ABOUT

Though many of my students fully appreciate the sacred nature of the texts and stories from their own spiritual traditions, more than a few sometimes have trouble appreciating the sacred nature of texts and stories from other spiritual traditions. At best, some of these students show respect for these other texts and stories while maintaining that these texts and stories are not up to spiritual (or religious) par with the texts and stories from their own tradition. At the other end of the spectrum are those students who find all so-called sacred texts and stories suspect to such a degree that they cannot appreciate much, if anything, that these texts and stories have to offer. Not infrequently, I have students who see common ground among various sacred texts and stories and who don't privilege one culture's or people's beliefs over another.

If you find that similar views surface during your class discussions of the chapter from *Matthew* and you want to keep class conflicts to a minimum, concentrate on staying focused on the issues discussed in the text *per se*, relating them, perhaps, to the chapter's theme of naming. If, on the other hand, you don't mind seeing some tensions surface in your class discussions, then you might try asking your students to discuss the relationship between texts and (constructions of) truth, as well as the ability or inability of people in the same community (such as a college classroom) to disagree with each other and yet respect each other's views and live together peacefully (you might even ask them to discuss the relationship between these two discussion themes). Personally, I believe that a college classroom should be a place where students test and challenge both their and others' ideas, and thus I often encourage students to raise and discuss controversial concerns. Moreover, I have found that most students struggling to live meaningful lives and acting in good faith handle sometimes tense class discussions (concerning religious texts, for example) quite well and gain a fair amount of insight from engaging in such discussions.

COROLLARY READINGS

In terms of the issue of naming, the other readings in this chapter serve as excellent corollaries to the excerpt from *Matthew*. In addition, using *Genesis* 22: "The *Akedah*" (p. 272) along with the *Matthew* excerpt might provoke some interesting discussions concerning how readers interpret sacred texts from different cultures and traditions (the chapter from the Hebrew Bible also contains important passages having to do with naming and names). To this end, you might also ask your students to read Alice Miller's "When Isaac Arises from the Sacrificial Altar" (p. 259) and John Verbeck's "Evaluating Alice Miller's analysis of the Abraham and Isaac story" (p. 265).

In various ways, the following other readings might prove to correlate well with the chapter from *Matthew*: Elie Wiesel's "Why I Write" (p. 80); the excerpt from Claude Lanzmann's *Shoah* (p. 92); Denise Levertov's "The Mutes" (p. 373); and Abram L. Sachar's "The Carob Tree Grove: Christian Compassion" (p. 113).

POSSIBLE ASSIGNMENTS

1) Use your understanding of the Matthew text as a point of departure for an essay in which you analyze other instances in the Bible in which a change of name indicates, if not also constitutes, a clear or apparent change in identity or destiny.

2) Trace your own family's genealogy. Discuss in some detail the life and character of anyone on your family tree who is particularly important to your family's history or reputation. Also, be sure to talk about any unusual events within or outside of your family that bear significantly on your family's history.

3) After doing a bit of research, write a paper in which you discuss whether or not the story of Jesus' birth is unique in religious or mythological lore. Be sure that you provide details in order to clarify your ideas and to prove or support your claims.

4) Discuss what you make of this excerpt's nongenealogical details, both in and of themselves and in relation to the genealogical history presented by Matthew.

ALICE BLOCH

from **The Law of Return**

THINGS TO THINK ABOUT

This brief excerpt ought to yield you quite a bit of teaching material. For one thing, it should help your students come to some interesting insights concerning themes and issues that probably concern a number of them: sexism, male-female relationships, antisemitism (compare racism), cultural identity, and problems involving inclusion in and exclusion from groups and from society at large. Additionally, it might help disabuse those of your Christian students who, though probably without malice, nevertheless mistakenly continue to believe that the Hebrew Bible is an "old" testament, that is, an incomplete document in need of improvement. Implicitly countering this claim, the narrator in Bloch's story says that "[t]o use Biblical words everyday [*sic*] made everyday life holy, made [her] want to acknowledge every day's holiness through [her] people's ancient religious practices, in [her] people's ancient city [Jerusalem], in [her] people's ancient tongue" (paragraph 7). If the Bloch selection does no more than disabuse students of their misconceptions about Judaism, then it will have accomplished quite a lot.

COROLLARY READINGS

This chapter's other reading selections should provide good supplemental material for your students. In addition, Elie Wiesel's "Why I Write" (p. 80) might help them understand some aspects of the social, political, and religious contexts within which a modern Jewish writer writes. Abram L. Sachar's "The Carob Tree Grove: Christian Compassion" (p. 113) might prove a useful antidote to tensions between Christians and Jews that might surface during class discussions of Jewish-Christian relations. Louie Crew's "Thriving As An Outsider, Even As An Outcast, In Smalltown America" (p. 146), Shehla Yamani's "The Dilemma" (p. 154), the excerpt from Maya Angelou's *I Know Why the Caged Bird Sings* (p. 207), Langston Hughes' "Theme for English B" (p. 244), and all of the readings in Chapter Eight might give your students additional insights into the problems faced by outsiders or other disenfranchised people, as well as giving them insights into various other complex problems raised in Bloch's text.

POSSIBLE ASSIGNMENTS

1) Discuss the ways in which and the extent to which issues concerning gender play a role in the Bloch excerpt and, perhaps, in this chapter's readings. Do these issues seem central to the texts' meanings? Do the chapter's readings treat these issues similarly, differently, or both?

2) Imagine that Cisneros, Black Elk, Matthew, and Bloch meet to talk about both the significance of names and naming and the relationship among personal names, personal identity, and cultural identity. Based on your understanding of their views expressed in this chapter's reading selections, write a paper in which you discuss what you think they might say to each other about these topics. Are there particular points on which you think that they would clearly agree or disagree? Use examples from their texts to help prove or support your claims.

INDIVIDUAL, GROUP, AND/OR CLASS ACTIVITIES

1) Take a look at a poem entitled "Please Call Me by My True Names," written by the eminent Zen Buddhist Monk Thich Nhat Hanh and found in *Call Me by My True Names: The Collected Poems of Thich Nhat Hanh*. Then, compare the ways in which Thich Nhat Hanh treats the theme of names/naming with (or to) the ways in which the authors of this chapter's reading selections treat this theme. More generally, examine the meanings of this poem in the context of what you have learned from studying this chapter's readings and participating in relevant class discussions. (Thich Nhat Hanh's poem, accompanied by commentary, is also

included in his book *Peace Is Every Step: The Path of Mindfulness in Everyday Life*, in a section entitled "Call Me by My True Names.")

2) Do some writing in which you note the observations that you would make about some or all of this chapter's readings if you were responsible for teaching your classmates these readings. In particular, discuss what you think would help your fellow students better understand the issues, problems, and themes with which these pieces deal. You might also ask yourself how other students might benefit from studying both your annotations of these readings and your responses to the pre- and post-reading questions.

3) Take another look at your response to the fifth post-reading question concerning the Bloch piece (p. 65). Then, test your creativity by setting up a round-table discussion, or a panel discussion (maybe you can be the moderator?), in which Cisneros, Black Elk, Matthew, and Bloch elaborate upon their own ideas and evaluate each other's ideas concerning both the significance of names and naming and the relationship among personal names, personal identity, and cultural or ethnic identity. Have them draw from both their own and each other's work in order to help prove or support their claims.

4) Before coming to class, make a copy of your annotated version of one of the chapter's readings and distribute this copy to some of your classmates; they should do the same with their annotated versions of the reading. Then, concentrating on the similarities and differences among everyone's annotations and summary comments, try to determine why people highlighted and commented upon particular passages and left others alone, as well as why they said what they did in their summary comments. See whether or not, in the final analysis, you and your classmates agree that sometimes one can tell a great deal about how active readers read—that is, interpret—a text just by studying their annotations of the text (their marginal comments, end comments, highlighting, check marks, exclamations points, question marks, and the like). See, too, whether or not your and your classmates' annotations help to support or counter everyone's interpretive claims.

5) Photocopy your responses to selected pre- and post-reading questions and distribute these photocopies to members of your class; your classmates should do the same with their responses to these (or, perhaps, other) questions. After everyone has had a chance to read each other's responses, discuss the similarities and differences among everyone's reading and writing experiences.

Chapter Four: Prewriting Your Way to a First Draft

INSTRUCTIONAL ISSUES

Although I have found that the vast majority of my students grasp the instructual material in this chapter fairly easily, I also have found that, during class discussions and office visits, I need to stress the fact that the process of writing is not straight-forward, and thus that students should use the instructional material in this and the next chapter as guidelines meant to help them prewrite, write, and rewrite at *various* phases of the writing process. Also, given that prewriting and writing techniques are only as good as they are helpful, I never force my students to use any technique that they themselves find counterproductive. Though indeed I want to help my students come into their own as writers, I don't want to control their writing efforts or own their responsibility to take the lead in their own learning. I hope that instructors using this text feel similarly about their relationship to their students' writing and learning and thus use this chapter's instructional material (as well as the instructional material in the rest of the text) accordingly.

FEATURED READING

ELIE WIESEL
Why I Write

THINGS TO THINK ABOUT

In my teaching experience, I have found that most students are fascinated by the subject matter of the Holocaust, and that some produce their most authentic writing in response to Holocaust-related material that we are studying. However, since for various reasons very few of my students are adequately prepared to deal with this complex subject, I find that I must spend some time helping them both understand and come to terms with a number of crucial issues related to the Holocaust, lest they end up producing frustratingly inadequate work.

Though you'll probably find yourself needing to do similar work with your students, fortunately you have at your disposal Elie Wiesel's essay, which provides a very good, brief introduction to the Holocaust. Wiesel writes with feeling, passion, and compassion; most of my students take to him immediately, even if they don't understand everything that he is saying. To help your students have a better understanding of Wiesel's life and work, including those aspects of his life and work that he talks about in "Why I Write," you might show them an excellent PBS documentary entitled *A Portrait of Elie Wiesel: In the Shadow of Flames*. Also, you might think about having your students read *Night*, which is Wiesel's account of his Holocaust experiences; a classic in the field of Holocaust Studies, this book is short and filled with emotion. Those of my students who have read it and who have read "Why I Write" have found much grist for their interpretive mills.

I would also suggest that, prior to teaching any of this chapter's readings, you show your students a film on the Holocaust. *Genocide*, produced by the Simon Wiesenthal Center, provides an excellent overview of events. Other good documentaries are *Night and Fog, Hitler: The Whole Story*, and *Mein Kampf*. (Also, for an excellent printed chronology of events, take a look at David A. Adler's *We Re-*

member the Holocaust.) You might also see about arranging for Holocaust survivors to address your class (a local chapter of the Anti-Defamation League might be able to arrange for speakers to visit your class). If that's not possible, you might want to show clips from Claude Lanzmann's *Shoah*, especially those scenes in which Lanzmann interviews survivors (you might also want to show the scene in which a voice-over narrator reads the letter that is reprinted as one of this chapter's related readings). Finally, keep in mind that the Holocaust involves more questions than answers and more paradoxes than resolutions. Encourage your students to voice their questions, frustrations, anger, concerns, and curiosity; help them to understand that, if they feel unsettled by what they are studying, then they are doing something right. And remember that such feelings are often the seeds of their continuing moral development.

THE FEATURED ASSIGNMENT AND THE CONTRIBUTING AUTHOR'S MODEL RESPONSE

Although I wrote this assignment with an eye towards capturing the sum and substance of the chapter's instructional material, and though I think you'll agree that Jay Julos, the contributing author, did a wonderful job in his response to the featured assignment, I don't want you to feel hemmed in by either the assignment or Jay's work. The assignment can be easily revised to meet your and your students' needs. For example, you could have your students submit nothing more than their freewrites or, perhaps, the first drafts of their essays. The point is, after studying the contributing author's models of three prewriting techniques and a first draft, your students ought to learn enough about how prewriting functions to see how they might incorporate it into their own writing, whether or not they choose to use the same prewriting techniques that Jay uses, and they ought to see how their own first drafts might function as blueprints for their essays, whether or not their first drafts look like Jay's first draft. Besides, in the next chapter, they'll have a chance to see another first draft. For now, Jay Julos' work should serve more than adequately as an imitable model of good initial-phase writing from which your students might learn some substantive lessons.

COROLLARY READINGS

Besides using this chapter's related readings to supplement the Wiesel piece, as well as some of the suggested texts that I list as corollary readings for the chapter's related reading selections, you might find it interesting to pair Wiesel's essay with *Genesis* 22: "The *Akedah*" (p. 272), if only because elsewhere Wiesel considers Isaac the first Holocaust survivor. Though this idea might initially seem odd, it becomes less so when one recalls that the term holocaust has to do with a burning of the whole; rooted in religious contexts, its meaning has to do with sacrifice—or, in Isaac's case, with a survivor of a potential sacrifice. If nothing else, using this piece from the Hebrew Bible should generate discussion concerning terminology (*is* the term "Holocaust" an appropriate term to use to talk about the attempted destruction of European Jewry?), a discussion that I think you'll discover will yield many possibilities for your students' further study of the issues at stake here.

Additionally, given Wiesel's struggles to produce meaningful writing about events that encapsulate but also transcend his own experiences, you might find it very helpful to supplement his essay with the following readings, which overtly or tacitly manifest similar struggles: Kevin Mullen's "Writing: A Leap of Faith" (p. 17); the various drafts of Shehla Yamani's "The Dilemma" (p. 154); Mahshid Hajir's "The Lesson" (p. 213); J. Kehaulani Kauanui's "Shifting Identities, Shifting Alliances" (p. 342); and Langston Hughes' "Theme for English B" (p. 244).

ALTERNATE ASSIGNMENTS

1) Do some prewriting and/or a first draft for an essay to be written in response to Chapter One's featured assignment (p.12). If you've already done that assignment, do some prewriting and/or a first draft for an essay to be written in which you expand upon some of your ideas from your previous essay in an attempt to explain either why you (like to) write or why you don't (like to) write.

2) Compare the writing in "Why I Write" with the writing in *Night*, paying careful attention to (what you see as) the relationship between form and content. Hint: watch for clipped sentences in each piece of writing.

3) Feeling very strongly that art and Auschwitz don't mix, Wiesel has suggested, for example, that if a book is a novel, then it isn't about Auschwitz, and if it's about Auschwitz, then it isn't a novel. Write the first draft of an essay in which you explain the ways in which "Why I Write" seems either to confirm or to contradict this view (or to do both). When you turn in this draft, submit samples of any prewriting that you might have done, too.

4) Do some prewriting in which you speculate about the things that Langston Hughes, Kevin Mullen, and Elie Wiesel might say to each other concerning each other's work. What might they say, for example, concerning each other's attempts to write that which is both personal and meaningful, as well as that which, though still meaningful, transcends the personal?

RELATED READINGS

CLAUDE LANZMANN
from **Shoah**

THINGS TO THINK ABOUT

Given the Nazis' extensive use of language to conceal the true nature of their deeds, deceive their victims, and, perhaps, help themselves deny the reality of their own involvement in evil (they referred to planned mass killings as "actions," for example, and to the deportations of Jews to concentration, labor, and death camps as "resettlement"), prior to and/or after you have your students study this document from Lanzmann's *Shoah*, you might ask them to think about (and possibly to write in response to) the following passage in Sam Keen's *Faces of the Enemy: Reflections of the Hostile Imagination* (San Francisco: Harper & Row, Publishers, 1986): "Confucius claimed we could have harmony in society if we named things accurately. Peace begins with the rectification of terms" (96).

Also, you might consider using the excerpt from Lanzmann's book to help teach your students some of the substantive differences between active and passive voice. Afterwards, ask your students whether or not there are any circumstances under which one of these verb forms seems more suitable than the other, and then ask them what Just (the letter writer) seems to accomplish by using passive rather than active voice, and whether or not he gets away with anything by not using active voice. I often find that students grasp the importance of their choosing carefully between using active and using passive voice constructions in their own writing when they see the stakes of such a choice contextualized in writings such as the letter reprinted here.

COROLLARY READINGS

Wiesel's essay pairs quite provocatively with this excerpt from Lanzmann's book, as do this chapter's other readings. Langston Hughes' "Theme for English B" (p. 244) and Denise Levertov's "The Mutes" (p. 373) might also prove to be interesting supplemental material, as might be the excerpt from Alice Bloch's *The Law of Return* (p. 60).

POSSIBLE ASSIGNMENTS

1) If you read the excerpt from *Black Elk Speaks* (p. 52), you might recall that you were asked to think about Black Elk's verb choices (see the close-reading tip on p. 54). Compare the verb choices that you found in that excerpt with those that you find in this letter. Does the question of *context* come into play in your comparative analysis?

2) Discuss how your knowing something about the name "Saurer" helps you to understand more about the scope of the Holocaust, particularly in terms of the range of people and *companies* (there's your clue) implicated as perpetrators.

3) Analyze what you make of the euphemisms used in this letter. Are they effective or appropriate? Would you answer this question differently if you or someone you know was referred to as "merchandise" or part of a "load"—or, to cite some common euphemisms, a "fifth wheel" or "extra baggage"? If you wish, incorporate into your response appropriate aspects of your answers to the second and third post-reading questions.

FRED E. KATZ
A Sociological Perspective to the Holocaust

THINGS TO THINK ABOUT

Since the Katz piece is a work of scholarship, you might need to prepare your students to read academic prose. As part of this preparation, you might remind them that writers write for intended readers, a point covered in some detail in Chapter One and again in Chapter Five.

Also, you'll probably help your students have a better contextual understanding of Katz's ideas if you explain to them that Katz is trying to help us take a different interpretive path in our investigations of the Holocaust, a path that diverges from the one taken by people such as Elie Wiesel, who have argued that the Holocaust is finally incomprehensible. Katz suggests precisely the opposite. He outlines here that which he tries to show in greater detail in his recent book, *Ordinary People and Extraordinary Evil: A Report on the Beguilings of Evil*: to wit, that the monstrous deeds committed during the Holocaust were committed for the most part by ordinary people, and that the commission of these deeds not only *can* be understood and explained, but also *must* be understood and explained if we are to prevent the commission of other evil deeds.

COROLLARY READINGS

As the above comments intimate, Elie Wiesel's "Why I Write" (p. 80) pairs extremely well with Katz's essay. This chapter's other readings also should prove to be useful supplements to Katz's essay, especially Christopher R. Browning's "Ordinary Men" (p. 107) and Abram L. Sachar's "The Carob Tree Grove: Christian Compassion" (p. 113). Of this book's other selections, the following might also prove to be valuable corollary readings: Kevin Mullen's "Writing: A Leap of Faith" (p. 17); Shehla Yamani's "The Dilemma" (p. 154); Mahshid Hajir's "The Lesson" (p. 213); Stanley Milgram's "The Perils of Obedience" (276); Alice Miller's "The Vicious Circle of Contempt" (p. 226) and "When Isaac Arises from the Sacrificial Altar" (p. 259) (if you use the latter Miller piece, you might also want to use John Verbeck's "Evaluating Alice Miller's analysis of the Abraham and Isaac story" [p. 265]); and Rudolph Höss' "Early Years" (p. 290).

POSSIBLE ASSIGNMENTS

1) Keeping in mind any relevant information that you've picked up from reading or any attitudes or feelings that you've begun to form as a result of your having read the Wiesel and Lanzmann material, explain why you agree or disagree with Katz's view that "evil can be *routinized*[,] . . . [that] 'ordinary' human behavior can be harnessed in the service of 'extraordinary,' and monstrous objectives" (paragraph 35; author's italics).

2) Do you know anything about Adolf Eichmann? If so, how would you describe him? If not, look up his name in an encyclopedia and read about him. Then, discuss whether or not the Eichmann described by Katz is similar to or different from the one about whom you have just read.

3) If you've read Stanley Milgram's "The Perils of Obedience," how do you think that Katz would analyze the attitudes and behavior of Morris Braverman (see paragraphs 22–33)? In particular, how might he analyze what Braverman says in para-

graphs 32 and 33? Are there other subjects in Milgram's experiment concerning whom a Katzian analysis might yield some interesting and provocative insights?

CHRISTOPHER R. BROWNING
Ordinary Men

THINGS TO THINK ABOUT

As I suggest both previously and later, Browning's text and Katz's text form an exceptionally good pair of readings; I would highly recommend that you use both texts if you decide to use either. What Katz attempts to help us understand sociologically, Browning tries to help us understand historically. Both authors focus on the problem of ordinary people's carrying out extraordinarily bad deeds, Katz situating his analysis within a context of sociological hermeneutics, and Browning situating his on a shifting terrain of historical methodology.

Ultimately, both authors are interested in understanding why, how, and to what extent ordinary people can perform monstrous deeds. And Browning shares Katz's view (expressed in *Ordinary People and Extraordinary Evil*, cited above) that all of us have the potential to be very kind or very cruel (see Browning, paragraphs 7–8). But Browning's text introduces a matter that you won't find in Katz's work, simply because each author is focusing on a different aspect of the process of destruction. Unlike the incremental destruction to which Katz refers, the destruction to which Browning refers is more or less sudden. It occurs after January 1942, when, during the Wannsee conference, top-ranking Nazi officials outlined the plan for the "Final Solution to the Jewish Question." After that point, the destruction of European Jewry increased dramatically. As Browning notes, "In mid-March 1942 some 75 to 80 percent of all victims of the Holocaust were still alive, while 20 to 25 percent had perished. A mere eleven months later, in mid-February 1943, the percentages were exactly the reverse" (paragraph 1). Whether or not Browning is right to suggest that "[a]t the core of the Holocaust was a short, intense wave of mass murder" (ibid.), the historical phenomenon that contextualizes his analysis is weighty enough to be the subject of a good deal of class discussion.

COROLLARY READINGS

Besides using Katz's essay, you should find it very useful to supplement the Browning selection with this chapter's other readings, as well as with any of the readings in Chapter Seven, especially Stanley Milgram's "The Perils of Obedience" (p. 276), Rudolph Höss' "Early Years" (p. 290), and Martin Luther King, Jr.'s "Letter from Birmingham Jail" (p. 308). Also useful might be Kevin Mullen's "Writing: A Leap of Faith" (p. 17); Shehla Yamani's "The Dilemma" (p. 154); Mahshid Hajir's "The Lesson" (p. 213); Alice Miller's "The Vicious Circle of Contempt" (p. 226); and Lorraine Duggin's "Summer, 1945" (p. 237).

POSSIBLE ASSIGNMENTS

If you use the close-reading tip as a prompt for some prewriting, you might want to append the following question to that apparatus: Think and write about whether or not, in your view, any historical record can escape either the historian's or the reader's judgments.

If you have your students respond to the second pre-reading question (p. 107), as a prompt either for prewriting or for other forms of informal writing, you might want to amend that question either before or after they write to include the following (kinds of) questions: Did (or would) your decision to comply or not to comply with this other person's request depend upon the nature of the task, the particular circumstances of the situation, the sort of person making the request, and so on? Or, did/would you feel that, no matter what, right is right, wrong is wrong, and one should always act accordingly? Have any of this chapter's readings influenced your present thoughts concerning this dilemma? (If appropriate, review your responses to the third and fourth post-reading questions.)

Here are some ideas for other assignments:

1) Discuss whether or not your understanding of this chapter's other readings has influenced your answers to the first three pre-reading questions and the fourth post-reading question concerning the Browning selection (see pp. 107 and 113). Do you think that you might have answered these questions differently had you not read these other selections?

2) Browning says that "the German attack on the Jews of Poland was not a gradual or incremental program stretched over a long period of time . . ." (paragraph 1). Compare this attack with the bureaucratic "attacks" (so to speak) that comprise the incremental process of destruction described by Katz.

3) Discuss whether or not you think that the authors of this chapter's reading selections (including Just, who wrote the bureaucratic letter) would agree with Browning that, "in the same situation [in which the men of Reserve Police Battalion 101 found themselves], [anyone] could have been either a killer or an evader—both were human . . ." (paragraph 8).

4) Browning says that Major Wilhelm Trapp, the battalion commander of Reserve Police Battalion 101, "made an extraordinary offer: if any of the older men among them did not feel up to the task that lay before him, he could step out" (paragraph 12). Discuss why you think that Browning sees this offer as extraordinary. Would Katz likely agree with your or Browning's assessment? How about Wiesel, Sachar, Just, and, perhaps, your classmates?

ABRAM L. SACHAR

The Carob Tree Grove: Christian Compassion

THINGS TO THINK ABOUT

In that period of barbarism and darkness that we call the Holocaust, there were some beacons of light, however rare, some glimmers of a humanity seemingly all but lost and forgotten. Among these beacons of light were those people who risked their lives to save Jews; their actions proved an antidote to the evil that surrounded them, an antidote weak in comparison to the large-scale destruction of human lives that they couldn't stop, but strong in its message of hope and in its delivery of real salvation for the few lives that were saved. Though a few of these rescuers, such as Oskar Schindler, were rather well connected with officials of the Nazi party, most of the rescuers were ordinary citizens, who carried out their missions often at great risk to themselves and their families. To be sure, some of these rescuers helped in order to earn some money from their victims; the vast majority, however, seem to have helped simply because, as one rescuer whom I interviewed suggested to me, it was the morally right thing to do. As Abram L. Sachar notes, "Asked why they risked so much when they had no personal stake in the result, [these ordinary rescuers] invariably responded that they did have a stake: they were reacting to what gave significance to their being" (96). Though comparatively few in number, these rescuers demonstrate that the ordinary citizen can indeed rise to great heights of heroism in the service of helping her or his fellow human being.

Although you certainly should encourage your students to acknowledge these acts of heroism, you should also, if necessary, help them avoid reaching the conclusion that these stories represent a balance between good and evil in the Holocaust. During the Holocaust, there was a plethora of evil and a sprinkling of good, a fact that doesn't diminish the acts of the rescuers, but that does help to contextualize these acts accurately. (A related misconception might be held by some of your students who, having read or seen the movie version of *Schindler's List*, imagine that there was something of a balance between good Nazis and bad Nazis. The fact of the matter is that the vast majority of Nazis had anything but the Jews' interest at heart.)

Also, keep in mind that, although the stories that Sachar chronicles put a good face on Jewish-Christian relations, these relations have been quite strained since, and to a large degree because of, the Holocaust. As Elie Wiesel (a man who greatly respects Christianity and who is greatly admired by many Christians) says in his book *A Jew Today* (New York: Vintage Books, 1979), "[A]s surely as the [Jewish] victims [of the Holocaust] are a problem for the Jews, the killers are a problem for the Christians" (14). Bewildered and saddened, he wonders why so few Christians "came to the aid of Jews," and, perhaps more important, how "the Christian in [the killers] did not make their arms tremble as they shot at children or their conscience bridle as they shoved their naked, beaten victims into the factories of death" (ibid.). In an interview, he says quite bluntly that "the sincere Christian knows that what died in Auschwitz was not the Jewish people but Christianity" (Harry James Cargas, "What is a Jew? Interview of Elie Wiesel," in Harry James Cargas, ed., *Responses to Elie Wiesel*. [New York: Persea Books, 1978], p. 152). He goes on to say that Pope John XXIII, whom he greatly admires,

understood . . . that Auschwitz represented a failure, a defeat for 2000 years of Christian civilization. . . . The commandoes were the worst of the criminals. . . .

They were shooting thousands and thousands of Jews—entire communities, with machine guns, directly. There was a direct contact. And they had Ph.D.s and some of them were theologians, and some of them, many of them, went to the priest, to confession and so forth. . . . [W]hat happened in Auschwitz. . . marked an end to orthodox Christianity. (152–153)

Although these charges might not seem to be borne out by the excerpts from Sachar's book reprinted in this reader, if one considers Pope Pius XII's silence in the face of Jewish destruction, as well as the many, many examples of Christian antisemitism displayed during the Holocaust, one realizes that, indeed, Wiesel might have a point.

Unfortunately, I cannot suggest any easy ways for you to handle this difficult topic, should it come up during class discussions or in your students' papers. However, speaking from the perspective of someone who does some work in the area of Jewish-Christian relations, I feel confident that, if you encourage your students to remain in good faith in their struggles to deal with the issues at stake here and to respect each other's views concerning these issues, you'll find yourself in the midst of some very instructive, indeed, some very enlightening—even if very emotional—class discussions.

COROLLARY READINGS

All of the readings in this chapter are good companion pieces to be used along with the Sachar material. Though you'll want to guard against the danger of relativizing historical, political, and social phenomena, you can give your students a wider interpretive context within which to view the Sachar material by suggesting that they also read widely among the readings in Chapter Seven; Martin Luther King, Jr.'s "Letter from Birmingham Jail" (p. 308) should prove an especially useful corollary reading. Also useful as thematically similar supplements to the Sachar text are Kevin Mullen's "Writing: A Leap of Faith" (p. 17), Shehla Yamani's "The Dilemma" (p. 154), and Mahshid Hajir's "The Lesson" (p. 213). Rudolph Höss' "Early Years" (p. 290) might serve as a useful thematic counter-text, so to speak, and Alice Miller's "The Vicious Circle of Contempt" (p. 226) might provide your students with some promising opportunities for insight into the psychological dimensions of both the problems at stake here and the cures for these problems.

POSSIBLE ASSIGNMENTS

1) In an omitted portion of the excerpt that appears in this reader, Sachar says that "immediately following the war and for a long time thereafter there was no distinction in a reputation for saving Jews." Discuss what you think Sachar means here and whether or not his essay supports or refutes this claim (or does both). Also, does his claim apply to other people's attempts to save victims of other tragedies, too—victims such as, for example, the Vietnamese Boat People, the Haitian refugees, the Bosnian Muslims, or the starving Somalis?

2) If you have read, or seen the movie version of, *Schindler's List*, analyze the actions and attitudes of Oskar Schindler within the context of your understanding of the Sachar material presented in this reader. Or, if you prefer, analyze the actions and attitudes of one or more Christian rescuers whose stories are told by Sachar, comparing, perhaps, these actions and attitudes with Schindler's.

3) In light of your understanding of the Katz and/or Browning material, compare Raoul Wallenberg or Martin Niemöller to Adolf Eichmann and/or the men in Reserve Police Battalion 101. If you wish, include your thoughts about Oskar Schindler at appropriate moments in your analyses.

4) If you worked with the excerpt from *Matthew* (p. 57), discuss whether or not your study of, reaction to, and, perhaps, writing about that excerpt has influenced your understanding of and reaction to the historical relationship between Judaism and Christianity or between individual (or groups of) Jews and Christians. Then, discuss your understanding of and reaction to the historical relationship between Judaism and Christianity or between individual (or groups of) Jews and Christians in light of your understanding of and reaction to the material contained in the Sachar excerpt. Has reading Sachar's text caused you to want to rethink any of your views concerning the significance of the excerpt from *Matthew* and/or the historical relationship between Judaism and Christianity or between individual (or groups of) Jews and Christians?

INDIVIDUAL, GROUP, AND/OR CLASS ACTIVITIES

1) Discuss whether or not—and, if so, how, why, and to what extent—your thoughts and feelings about human beings and their relations to each other have changed as a result of your having read some or all of this chapter's readings. If you've had changes of mind and heart, can these changes be charted in your responses to any of this chapter's pre- or post-reading questions or in any of your textual annotations, formal or informal writing, or comments made during group or class discussions?

2) Throughout his essay, Abram L. Sachar alludes to individuals who defied orders, undermined bureaucratic procedures, or used other bureaucratic procedures to save victims of Nazi persecution. In his narrative concerning the Danish resistance, he shows us how successful such resistance could be, suggesting that Werner Best, the German ambassador to Denmark, mistakenly thought that he could "rely upon the normal machinery of government" (paragraph 35). Explain how, in your view, Elie Wiesel, Christopher R. Browning, Fred E. Katz, and, possibly, Stanley Milgram and Martin Luther King, Jr., would evaluate or respond to the issues at stake in this aspect of Sachar's work. How do *you* respond to or evaluate these issues, especially in light of what you've learned about the Christian rescuers?

3) In a section of his essay excluded from the version reprinted in this reader, Katz says the following: "In their everyday life many (perhaps most) people knowingly participate in activities that are damaging and obnoxious, alongside activities that are wholesome and benign." Discuss whether or not any examples from this chapter's readings seem to bear out this claim. Do any seem to refute it?

4) Katz wonders "how it is that persons may carry out, indeed enthusiastically embrace, 'radical evil'[3] while their faculties are intact. While they are able to distinguish good from evil they engage in evil of a level that is wholly unassimilatable by ordinary canons of moral conduct." Discuss how this chapter's readings might help us to understand this state of affairs. Also, talk about whether or not you fully agree with Katz on this point. Finally, if you have read Stanley Milgram's "The Perils of Obedience," speculate upon how you think that Milgram might evaluate these ideas or, for that matter, anything else presented in this chapter—including, perhaps, your and your classmates' views concerning this chapter's material.

5) If you are interested in investigating the effects of the Holocaust on both the children of survivors and the children of perpetrators, take a look at Helen Epstein's *Children of the Holocaust* and Peter Sichrovsky's *Born Guilty*. Reading these two texts should give you deep insight into the tragic burden carried by those children whose parents have been emotionally scarred by the Holocaust and should help you appreciate the onerous legacy inherited by other children who, to paraphrase a biblical passage, are visited by their families' iniquities.

Chapter Five: Ideas and Strategies for Revising and Moving Beyond the First Draft

INSTRUCTIONAL ISSUES

Though you should find that the instructional material in this chapter works well, I would suggest that, when you give your students some suggestions concerning how they might articulate and where they might place a thesis statement, you remind them of the differences between *conventions* and *rules*. See my comments to this effect on pp. 135–138.

Also, when discussing with your students ways that they might derive, develop, and prove or support a thesis, you might need to remind them that a thesis should be derived *after*, and *not prior to*, an investigation of the matter under study. Some of your students who think (or are led to believe) that they should come up with a point of view first and then try to defend it might need extra help in understanding that a good researcher carefully examines her or his data before drawing a conclusion concerning these data. Other students who misunderstand matters here might be confusing the notion of a hypothesis with that of a thesis; in this case, you'll need to help them understand that a hypothesis isn't (necessari-

---

[3]Katz notes that this phrase is derived from K.R. Seeskin's essay "The Reality of Radical Evil," in *Judaism* 29.4 (Fall 1980): 440-453.

ly) the same as a wild guess, that it needs to be tested, that the person testing it should try both to falsify or undermine it and to verify it, and that it should be discarded if it proves unworkable and kept only if it stands to reason and accounts for enough verifiable evidence.

FEATURED READING

LOUIE CREW

Thriving As An Outsider, Even As An Outcast, In Smalltown America

THINGS TO THINK ABOUT

I have found that the essay by Louie Crew, like the writing of Cherríe Moraga (see p. 376), tends to work well with students, including those who are initially reluctant to read material on or even think about the topic of homosexuality. In a word, Crew disarms suspicious and even hostile students. He comes across as being (and I see no reason to doubt that he is) sincere, honest, hardworking, religious, and monogamous—precisely those qualities that some of your students might uphold as standards of moral excellence in a person's character. In fact, some of my students find themselves so much on Crew's side that they become genuinely angry at him for saying what he says in paragraph 37 of his essay. They feel that he should be proud of who he is. (The sincerity and passion of their comments led me to create the fourth post-reading question [p. 154].) Whether or not your students respond as many of my students do to the ideas that Crew articulates in paragraph 37, I think that I can say that, for those students who might feel squeamish about this topic, Crew's essay should prove to be a very safe point of departure (and, perhaps, a very controversial starting point precisely because it is safe).

To help prepare your students to study this chapter's readings, you might try showing them the excellent PBS programs entitled *Before Stonewall* and *Silent Pioneers*. These programs present some very useful historical information and clarify the nature of some important political and social climates in which this topic has been addressed and debated.

Also, before you have any class discussions on the issue of sexual orientation or have your students do any reading on this topic, you might try the following in-class exercise: Ask your students to make three columns on a sheet of paper and then to list in the appropriate columns those characteristics that they would describe as being uniquely heterosexual, those that they would say are uniquely homosexual, and those that they see as being common to both categories. Ask them to be as specific as possible. These questions are inspired by similar ones found in

Anne Wilson Schaef's book *Women's Reality*, excerpts from which constitute the first related reading selection in Chapter Eight (see p. 347).

THE FEATURED ASSIGNMENT AND THE CONTRIBUTING AUTHOR'S MODEL RESPONSE

As is the case with the featured assignment for Chapter Four, this chapter's featured assignment can be altered without impeding your students' chances to learn from the work of the chapter's contributing author. Whether or not you decide to change the assignment's theme, your students ought to be able to gain much from seeing how Shehla Yamani, a very good student-writer, moves from a first draft to a final one. So, even if you customize the featured assignment, Yamani's work should still prove to be admirably useful to your students.

Before I move on, I would like to mention that, at first, I was worried that the contributing author's first draft, which is quite short, might be troublesome as a model, despite my also having seen how nicely Shehla had developed her thoughts in her subsequent drafts. However, this draft has proved to be quite useful indeed. Many of my students seem stunned that such a truncated first draft could help lead a writer to produce a final draft that is as good as Shehla's essay "The Dilemma." They seem genuinely relieved to know that they themselves don't have to produce a good final draft right away. It's one thing for them to read in a textbook that they don't have to write their final draft as their first draft, and quite another thing for them to see in the work of another student that such is the case.

Moreover, using Shehla's work in class has kept me honest. When I see how useful my students find her work, I am reminded that, although I should indeed offer my students help when they need *and ask* for it, I should also try to stay out of their way as they attempt to lead themselves through the writing process, and I should trust that most of them will eventually produce a more or less satisfactory final draft. The work that Shehla produced for this chapter should help all of us who use it keep in mind that the best writing is authentic, not formulaic, and that most of our students working in good faith will eventually produce good (or at least satisfactory) work, even if they have trouble doing so at various points along the way. At those moments when you have your own doubts concerning the quality of your students' papers, maybe you can recall my initial, mistaken doubt about Shehla's first draft and decide to trust both your students' and your own efforts to help them grow as writers.

COROLLARY READINGS

This chapter's related readings provide excellent informational and interpretive contexts for Louie Crew's essay; I strongly recommend that you supplement the Crew reading with as many of these pieces as possible. Additionally, you might find it helpful for your students to read selections that treat both the theme of the outsider and the theme of discrimination. Many of the readings in Chapter Eight should work well for this purpose, especially Cherríe Moraga's "My Brother's Sex Was White. Mine, Brown" (p. 376) and Barbara Cameron's "'Gee, You Don't Seem Like An Indian From the Reservation'" (p. 381), both of which deal with the issue of sexual orientation. Other good corollary readings are Sandra Cisneros' "My Name" (p. 46), the excerpt from *Black Elk Speaks* (p. 52), Alice Bloch, from *The Law of Return* (p. 60), Langston Hughes' "Theme for English B" (p. 244), and Martin Luther King, Jr.'s "Letter from Birmingham Jail" (p. 308).

ALTERNATE ASSIGNMENTS

1) Before reading Crew's essay, do some informal writing concerning what you are expecting, hoping, or fearing to read in an essay on a biracial gay couple. Then, after reading Crew's essay, write an essay in which you compare your pre-reading feelings to (or with) your post-reading reactions to Crew, his lifestyle, his essay, and so on. Concentrate on proving or supporting your thesis by offering and explicating germane evidence from your own experiences, Crew's text, and, if necessary, other sources. Submit at least a first and a revised draft of your essay.

2) Before reading Crew's essay, write a "coming out" letter, in which you announce to someone (or to some people) that you are gay or lesbian. (I obtained the idea for this assignment from one of this book's reviewers. Having had very good luck using this assignment, I feel confident telling you that, from the moment that you announce this assignment until your final discussions of the issues at stake, you should find that this assignment yields your students much material to analyze, much self-enlightenment, and a greater understanding of disenfranchised people than they initially might have had—and you should find that such is the case even for those of your students who are nonheterosexual. [Note: This assignment might prove to be a useful prelude to the featured assignment.]

3) Think about Crew's comment that "the issues which most concern sexual outcasts are not genital, as the casters-out have so lewdly imagined, but issues of justice and simple fairness" (paragraph 34). Then, write about whether or not you agree with Crew's assessment. In your attempts to make your case, try answering questions such as the following: What does Crew mean when he refers to the claims made by the "casters-out" as being "lewdly imagined"? Does Crew's position on this matter help us to understand what he means when he says, just one paragraph earlier, that the student who "would look both ways to see who might have seen him being friendly with the gay professor . . . is telling [Crew] and all other knowledgeable folks far more new information about his own body chemistry than he is finding out about [Crew's]"?

R E L A T E D   R E A D I N G S

SIGMUND FREUD

The Sexual Aberrations

THINGS TO THINK ABOUT

Unfortunately, though many people have opinions about Freud and his work—often negative or in some other way condescending—few of these people seem to have read much (if anything at all) either by or about him. Indeed, when pressed to tell the truth, many of my own students admit that they "heard" such and such from friends or professors or read in an introductory psychology book a few paragraphs or a page or two about Freud and his work. Given its level of verbal and, for its time, at least, theoretical sophistication, "The Sexual Aberrations" tends to humble Freud's unreflective detractors in their attitudes about Freud and his work, showing them that there is more to this person and his ideas than they had initially imagined (it also tends to humble Freud's unreflective supporters, showing them that they need to avoid offering facile support of Freud's ideas). None of this is to say that your goal in using the Freud material should be to make Freudians out of your students, but, rather, that this specimen of Freud's work ought to help your students gain some intellectual humility even as it helps them to gain insight into the thematic issues at stake in this chapter.

To help your students understand both Freud and his ideas, you might try showing them the *Nova* special on Freud that aired sometime in the 1980s. You yourself might find it helpful to take a look at the following books, portions of which you might decide to share with your students: J. Laplanche and J.-B. Pontalis, *The Language of Psycho-Analysis*; Octave Mannoni's *Freud: The Theory of the Unconscious*; Carrie Lee Rothgeb, ed., *Abstracts of the Standard Edition of the Complete Psychological Works of Sigmund Freud*; Peter Gay, *The Freud Reader* and *Freud: A Life for Our Time*; and Sigmund Freud, *An Autobiographical Study*.

COROLLARY READINGS

The Freud piece should help establish a context within which your students can read the other selections in this chapter and discuss the various issues raised in these other readings. The Freud selection might also pair usefully with Cherríe Moraga's "My Brother's Sex Was White. Mine, Brown" (p. 376) and Barbara Cameron's "'Gee, You Don't Seem Like An Indian From the Reservation'" (p. 381). You might ask your students both to read these essays in light of what Freud says about homosexuality and to read Freud's theories in light of what Moraga and Cameron have to say about their being lesbians. Due cautions here are probably obvious, though.

To the extent that the Freud selection deals in rather sophisticated ways with questions concerning ordinariness, normalcy, and other aspects of psycho-social behavior, it might be usefully and interestingly paired with Fred E. Katz's "A Sociological Perspective to the Holocaust" (p. 95), Christopher R. Browning's "Ordinary Men" (p. 107), Stanley Milgram's "The Perils of Obedience" (p. 276), and Mitsuye Yamada's "Invisibility is an Unnatural Disaster: Reflections of an Asian American Woman" (p. 335). (Burton M. Leiser's "Evaluating the 'Unnaturalness Argument' Concerning Homosexuality," which is one of this chapter's readings, should also be counted among those works that, dealing sophisticatedly with questions concerning ordinariness, normalcy, and other aspects of psycho-social behavior, might be usefully paired with the Freud selection.)

POSSIBLE ASSIGNMENTS

1) Explain how you think that Freud might analyze Louie Crew's comment that "the issues which most concern sexual outcasts are not genital, as the casters-out have so lewdly imagined, but issues of justice and simple fairness" (paragraph 34), as well as Crew's observation that the student who "would look both ways to see who might have seen him being friendly with the gay professor . . . is telling [Crew] and all other knowledgeable folks far more new information about his own body chemistry than he is finding out about [Crew's]" (paragraph 33). If you wish, include in your analysis any relevant points from this chapter's (or book's) other reading selections.

2) Discuss whether or not you think that Freud's ideas help us to understand any of the issues at stake in this chapter's other readings, and whether or not these other readings, in turn, shed light on Freud's ideas.

3) Evaluate Freud's appeals to science. Would you characterize Freud's writing as scientific? Why or why not? (In trying to answer these questions, you might find it helpful to refer to your responses to the first pre- and post-reading questions.)

4) Imagine that you are lying (!) on Freud's famous couch, talking freely to him about whatever comes into your mind. In the course of your free-associating, begin to discuss your thoughts and feelings concerning those of his views that you read in the excerpt of his work reprinted in this reader. Feel free to create a dialogue, in which, at appropriate intervals, you have Freud respond to your thoughts and feelings. Here's a variation on this assignment's theme: After freewriting in response to some of Freud's ideas, discuss how you think that Freud might respond to the thoughts and feelings that you express in your freewrite.

BURTON M. LEISER

Evaluating the "Unnaturalness Argument" Concerning Homosexuality

THINGS TO THINK ABOUT

Though your students should be able to gain quite a bit by reading the Leiser (pronounced LEE-ZER) piece without also knowing something about logic, they would surely gain even more were they to know at least some basic principles of logic. If you yourself can teach them these principles, so much the better. If you cannot, at least try to help them understand the following three points from the Leiser piece. One, because people often use the terms "natural" and "unnatural" quite ambiguously when they are talking about sexual orientation, their arguments are often unclear (and problematic). Two, even if we grant that homosexuality is unnatural, we would have to conclude that people who argue that homosexuality is bad or immoral because it is unnatural are presenting an invalid argument, because something unnatural is not necessarily bad or immoral (many people who make this argument also seem to choose their examples quite arbitrarily). Three, even if we grant that homosexuality is unnatural, the conclusion doesn't necessarily follow that homosexuality ought to be prohibited on the grounds that it is unnatural. (Note: In Leiser's treatment of them, these three points often intersect.)

COROLLARY READINGS

Your students should gain some significant insights into the topic under discussion if they read the Leiser piece in conjunction with their reading this chapter's other selections. You might also try pairing Leiser's essay with pieces that, like his, present material in orderly, methodical, intellectually challenging ways (see the Freud selection, for example). To this end, you might consider using Fred E. Katz's "A Sociological Perspective to the Holocaust" (p. 95), Alice Miller's "The Vicious Circle of Contempt" (p. 226), Stanley Milgram's "The Perils of Obedience" (p. 276), Plato's *Crito* (p. 295), Martin Luther King, Jr.'s "Letter from Birmingham Jail" (p. 308), and Mitsuye Yamada's "Invisibility is an Unnatural Disaster: Reflections of an Asian American Woman" (p. 335). For a humorous contrast, you might also pair Leiser's essay with Lewis Carroll's "Who Stole the Tarts?" (p. 32).

POSSIBLE ASSIGNMENTS

1) Use your understanding of the Leiser piece to analyze the substantive points in Crew's or Parker's essay. Or, if you wish, speculate on how you think that Freud would evaluate Leiser's arguments, especially, perhaps, the argument concerning descriptive laws of nature. By the same token, how do you think that Leiser would evaluate Freud's arguments? Use germane textual evidence to prove or support your points.

2) In sections four and five of his essay (paragraphs 12–19), Leiser talks about "the rights of some other person" and the putative "detrimental" or "harm[ful]" aspects of sexuality. Discuss how well you think that Leiser argues his case with respect to these two points. Cite and explain evidence to prove or support your claims.

3) On p. 24 of Chapter Two, you'll find a discussion of the "democratization of ideas fallacy." After (re)reading that section carefully, write about whether or not, in your view, Leiser helps us to understand why we shouldn't accord equal weight to all opinions about morality and immorality. Be sure to discuss what distinguishes good opinions about morality and immorality from bad ones. Also, try to answer the following questions: Should one's opinions about morality and immorality always be backed up by reasons? If not, why not? If so, should all reasons offered to (help) prove or support people's views on (im)morality be given equal weight? If so, why? If not, why not?

DAVID GELMAN, ET AL.
Born or Bred?

THINGS TO THINK ABOUT

Whatever else it accomplishes, this article should help your students understand that different kinds of writing have different requirements. You might explain to your students that the majority of this article's paragraphs might be considered underdeveloped, for example, were these paragraphs presented in an essay for a composition class. But, you might hasten to add, since journalists need to worry that "gray" not appear in an article—that is, they don't want to create such a long paragraph in a narrow column that the column becomes an eyesore—they would probably balk at the idea of lengthening this article's paragraphs so that the paragraphs contain something on the order of, say, six or eight sentences apiece.

Studying this article should also help students understand that writing is always audience-specific. Journalists writing for *Newsweek*, for example, need to consider a wider audience than do scholars writing for a particular academic crowd (see your students' responses to the first pre- and post-reading questions [pp. 181 and 191], perhaps) or students writing for their classmates or instructor. To help your students better understand the issues at stake here, you might have them do the first assignment listed below.

COROLLARY READINGS

Aside from having your students read each of this chapter's reading selections in conjunction with their reading the Gelman piece, you might want to have them read Adriane Fugh-Berman's "Tales Out of Medical School" (p. 361), this book's only other journalistic reading selection. If you have them read Fugh-Berman's article, you might ask them to compare Fugh-Berman's writing style with Gelman's and to analyze, comparatively, the relationship between form and content in each article, as well as each author's attempt to write for a given audience.

Your students might also enjoy seeing how the narratives in nonjournalistic writings sometimes read journalistically. To this end, have them first take a look at paragraphs 9–20 in Christopher R. Browning's "Ordinary Men" (p. 107) and then compare the narrative in these paragraphs with that in the first eight paragraphs of the Browning selection. Finally, have them compare Browning's piece in its entirety with Gelman's. (In this interpretive context, Abram L. Sachar's "The Carob Tree Grove: Christian Compassion" [p. 113] might also pair usefully with the Gelman selection, as well as, perhaps, with the Browning piece.)

POSSIBLE ASSIGNMENTS

1) After doing some prewriting concerning the changes that you might make were you to try to turn Gelman's magazine article into a formal essay—perhaps an essay for your composition class—write a first and second draft of this essay. Here are some variations on this assignment's theme: (A) Write an opinion piece for your school newspaper concerning any of the issues discussed in this chapter's (or in this book's) readings. (B) Turn the excerpt from *Matthew* (p. 57), the Freud selection, Milgram's "The Perils of Obedience" (p. 276), or Alice Walker's "Elethia" (p. 240) into a journal article.

2) According to Gelman, et al., gays by and large "remain doubtful that even the strongest evidence of biological origins will cut much ice with confirmed homophobes" (paragraph 25). Frederick Whitam and, apparently, the authors of the article (see paragraph 5) don't agree, whereas Dr. Howard Grossman and novelist Jacquelyn Holt Park do seem to agree. Explain your view concerning this issue, carefully elucidating the reasons for your position. If you wish, include (and perhaps expand upon) relevant points that you made in your responses to the second pre-reading question and the sixth post-reading question.

3) Explain how Leiser might respond to Gelman's point that, "[t]heoretically," a biological basis for homosexuality "could gain [gays] the civil-rights protections accorded any 'natural' minority, in which the legal linchpin is the question of an 'immutable' characteristic" (paragraph 8). How might he respond to Thomas Aquinas' influential views on homosexuality (see paragraph 13)? What might Leiser say about Evelyn Hooker's notion concerning our accepting the nature of homosexuality as a given (paragraph 34)? Do you think that, as someone who clearly relies on logic in his analyses, he would have found Joseph Nicolosi's being the director of the Thomas Aquinas Psychology Clinic relevant to the status of Nicolosi's arguments?

4) Talk about how you think that Louie Crew might respond to those parts of this *Newsweek* article concerning whether or not people would choose to be homosexual. Compare, for example, paragraphs 10 and 11 in this article (and the information about Annette Brenner and her son) with the last four paragraphs of Crew's essay, especially paragraphs 37 and 38.

JAN PARKER

The Tables Need Turning

THINGS TO THINK ABOUT

I find Parker's essay useful in a number of ways, two of the most important of which are the following. First, Parker helps us to understand something about the nature of our assumptions concerning discourses of normalcy and power, not only in terms of the issue of sexual orientation, but also in terms of various aspects of dominance and disenfranchisement. In asking why nonheterosexuals always seem to have to justify their lives as nonheterosexuals and what might happen were we to turn the tables here and demand that, instead, *heterosexuals* offer a similar justification, Parker is tacitly asking us to think about what might happen were mainstream people in general, rather than nonmainstream people, asked or forced to justify their existence, beliefs, lifestyles, and so on. If we follow these interrogative leads, we might learn much about our assumptions concerning who we (think we) are and who (we think) others are. (See the points made in this chapter's section entitled "Reading and Writing" [p. 145].)

Second, Parker does a wonderful job in helping us to see that the question of sexual orientation cannot be separated from the question of gender. In particular, she helps to demonstrate the interrelatedness of the struggle for women's rights and the struggle for gay/lesbian rights. To help my students better understand this latter point, I try to help them see that, the more that women gain politically and socially, the more, it seems, that lesbianism is taken seriously—usually, as a threat. In the United States, for example, where women hold far more political and social power than they used to hold (though they hold far less than they ought to hold), we commonly find overt hostility displayed towards lesbians by some contemporary American radio talk show hosts, politicians, and ordinary citizens. In Nazi Germany, on the other hand, where women were considered to be inferior to men and thus were not considered threatening, lesbianism was apparently considered so unworthy of consideration that, even in the expanded version of Paragraph 175 of the German Penal Code, lesbians were not included among homosexuals, who were targeted for imprisonment and the loss of their civil rights. This paragraph, by the way, predated the Nazis' reign of power and terror. For a complete text of the paragraph, see Richard Plant, *The Pink Triangle: The Nazi War Against Homosexuals* [New York: A New Republic Book/Henry Holt and Company, 1986], p. 206.) (See, too, pp. 10–11 of David Fernbach's introduction to the first edition of Heinz Heger's *The Men with the Pink Triangle* [Boston: Alyson Publications, Inc., 1980.) For some excellent insights into some of the larger issues at stake here, see Rose Weitz's "What Price Independence? Social Reactions to Lesbians, Spinsters, Widows, and Nuns," in Gary Colombo, Robert Cullen, and Bonnie Lisle, eds., *Rereading America: Cultural Contexts for Critical Thinking and Writing* (Boston: Bedford Books of St. Martin's Press, 2nd ed., 1992), pp. 257–270.

COROLLARY READINGS

Aside from using this chapter's other readings in connection with your using Parker's essay, you might also have your students take a look at any of the readings in Chapter Eight, especially Cherríe Moraga's "My Brother's Sex Was White. Mine, Brown" (p. 376) and Barbara Cameron's "'Gee, You Don't Seem Like An Indian From the Reservation'" (p. 381). The excerpt from Alice Bloch's

The Law of Return (p. 60) might also prove to be a useful corollary to the Parker essay. Alice Miller's "The Vicious Circle of Contempt" (p. 226) might add an interesting analytical context to your class discussions, as might Kathleene West's "Grandmother's Garden" (p. 234), Alice Walker's "Elethia" (p. 240), and Langston Hughes' "Theme for English B" (p. 244).

POSSIBLE ASSIGNMENTS

If you want to use the fourth and fifth pre-reading questions (p. 192), you might try combining them and then adding the following questions to them: "If you think that gays and lesbians ought to live openly *as* gays and lesbians, do you feel that they should not call *too* much attention to themselves *as* gays and lesbians? Do you feel the same way about heterosexuals' living openly as heterosexuals and/or calling attention to themselves as heterosexuals?" Also, if you use the fifth post-reading question, you might think about either amending it as follows or using what follows as a second option for your students: "In general, do you find Parker's essay effective, particularly from the standpoint of its writing style? If you read Crew's essay, would you say that his is more or less effective than Parker's? Does it matter that Crew is male and that Parker is female, or that Crew is American and that Parker is British? All in all, do you feel that you are judging these two pieces strictly in terms of their substantive details? If not, on what basis are you making your comparative judgment, and how do you evaluate your judgment?"

Here are some other ideas for assignments:

1) Write about how you think that Parker and Shehla Yamani might evaluate each other's analysis of oppression. If you feel particularly creative, you might try to imagine what each author would say to the other during a phone conversation or in an exchange of letters. Creatively or not, try to prove or support your claims by drawing from textual evidence found in each author's work, as well as from any other pertinent sources and, perhaps, from your own germane personal experiences.

2) Parker says that "[h]eterosexuality is a subject it's difficult not to be knowledgeable about. We're bombarded by it, with information about how heterosexuals should and do behave towards their own and the other gender" (paragraph 3). Evaluate this view, drawing from textual evidence as well as, perhaps, from your own personal experiences.

3) Compare what is said in paragraph 11 of "Born or Bred?" with what Parker says about the relationship among lesbianism, choice, and politics. In your view, does the same relationship seem to hold among male homosexuality, choice, and politics? If not, do you think that the gay man's gender is a significant factor here?

4) Consider the following analysis of the relationship between the Nazi ideology concerning gender and the Nazi ideology concerning sexual orientation:

> [I]t was quite fundamental to Nazi ideology that men were to be properly 'masculine', and women properly 'feminine', and that homosexuality went diametrically against this 'Nordic' tradition. . . . [W]hen male homosexuality disguises itself as a cult of 'manliness' and virility, it is less obnoxious from the

fascist standpoint than is the softening of the gender division that
homosexuality invariably involves when it is allowed to express itself freely.
(Fernbach, in Heger 11)

Supporting or proving your points by drawing from and explaining pertinent textual evidence and your own or others' germane experiences, discuss how you think that Parker would evaluate this analysis, as well as how you evaluate it. Can you think of any present-day examples that would either confirm or contradict Fernbach's claims?

INDIVIDUAL, GROUP, AND/OR CLASS ACTIVITIES

1) Discuss whether or not—and, if so, how, why, and to what extent—you felt personally implicated in or untouched by the views put forth by the authors of this chapter's reading selections. Did you have any particular favorites among the readings? Were any of the readings particularly offensive? Did any piece make you particularly angry or sad, whether or not it also offended and/or enlightened you? Did your feelings about a reading selection either interfere with or aid your ability to judge the issues under discussion fairly? Have your thoughts and feelings about the issue of sexual orientation changed as a result of your having read some or all of this chapter's readings? If you could speak with the authors of these readings, would you recommend that any of them revise his or her essay in light of your views, as well as in light of your reaction to his or her piece?

2) All of the readings in this chapter have something to say about whether or not we can—and, if we can, how we ought to—use terms such as "normal," "abnormal," "natural," and "unnatural" when we discuss the issue of sexual orientation. Compare the ways in which two or more pieces treat this question, incorporating into your analysis, your own views on the matters at stake here. Did any of the readings help you change your thinking?

3) Discuss the different writing styles that you came across in this chapter's reading selections. Were any styles particularly effective, more so than others, perhaps? In your view, would the impact of any selection change were that selection written in a different form or had the selection employed a different narrative tone of voice? In general, what seems to be the relationship between each selection's form and content?

4) Discuss what you think that Crew, Freud, Leiser, Parker, and the authors of "Born or Bred?" would say to each other if they met to discuss the ideas that they put forth in this chapter's readings. What points of each other's work might particularly interest them, for example? What points might they take issue with? How, for example, might Freud react to the scientific discoveries discussed in "Born or Bred?" or evaluate Doug Barnett's experimentation with men ("Born or Bred?," paragraph 1)? Might Freud pay more attention to or give more credence to Leiser's discussion than to Parker's? What might Leiser say to Freud about the latter's use of terms such as "inversion" or "normal"? What might Parker say to Crew about the latter's feelings concerning nonviolent resistance? What might Crew say to Parker about her point that "[e]ncouraging people to put their neck on the line

with an increasing likelihood of it being chopped off is not an adequate guide to action[,] [though] it speaks volumes for the advancement of male gay theory" ("The Tables Need Turning," paragraph 18)? What might Parker say to Freud about Freud's ideas concerning women? More generally, how do the chapter's authors address issues or notions concerning gender? Can you draw any general conclusions from this comparison? [To help your students deal with this last issue, you might want to refer them to the Fernbach quote, cited above.] And so on.

Chapter Six: Developing and Proving/Supporting a Thesis for a Personal Essay

INSTRUCTIONAL ISSUES

Though the instructional material for Chapter Six should work fairly well, you might need to remind students of the points (concerning a thesis and concerning thesis statements) that I mention in my comments pertaining to the instructional issues in Chapter Five. You might also find it necessary to remind your students of their need to ask the following sorts of questions at the beginning of and, perhaps, throughout the writing process, questions which should help them account for the particular needs of a given writing task: "Why am I bothering to write this paper (or this letter, memo, poem, or short story)?" "What do I hope to gain by writing it?" "In short, what is my purpose for or ultimate goal in constructing it?" Your students might also find it helpful to read or reread Elie Wiesel's essay "Why I Write" (p. 80), as well as the section entitled "Four Principles of Good Reader-Based Writing," in Chapter Five, pp. 131–141.

FEATURED READING

MAYA ANGELOU
from I Know Why the Caged Bird Sings

THINGS TO THINK ABOUT

Although I usually find that Angelou's material works very well on its own, I have often discovered that my students appreciate her work even more if, before having them read it, I show them a video such as *Ethnic Notions*, a PBS special on the history of stereotypes pertaining to African Americans. Also, to supplement her work, I sometimes have found it helpful to use some of the poetry to which she refers; Paul Laurence Dunbar's "Sympathy," which contains the line "I know why the caged bird sings," is an obvious choice. In addition to or instead of using these approaches, you might find it helpful to play for your students an audio tape of Angelou reading from her own work. Finally, after they have read the featured reading selection, you might show your class the video *I Know Why the Caged Bird Sings*; if you decide to do this, have your students discuss, prior to seeing this video, how they hear the voices and see the images in the featured reading selection and then, after they see the video, ask them to compare their pre- and post-viewing interpretations of the scene represented in the featured reading selection. Whatever you do with her material, you should find that this Angelou selection continually opens up wonderful possibilities for teaching and learning.

THE FEATURED ASSIGNMENT AND THE CONTRIBUTING AUTHOR'S MODEL RESPONSE

Perhaps because of the nature of its thematic focus, few assignments that I have used have yielded so many provocative, intriguing student papers than has the assignment featured in this chapter. I hope that you have similar luck with this assignment.

To help prepare your students to do the featured assignment, and, if appropriate, to help them weave the Angelou material into their essay, you might ask them to prewrite in response to the following two pre-reading questions:

1) Did you have a childhood relationship either with an adult member of your family or with an adult from outside of your family who made you feel special— who made you feel that you really counted? Were there particularly memorable moments or experiences that you had with this person?

2) Is there a particular incident or event—good or bad—from your childhood that had or continues to have a powerful effect on you? Did this incident or event involve you and the person whom you discuss in your answer to the above question?

You might also find it worthwhile to ask your students to write in response to the following two post-writing questions:

1) Does your work reflect a close reading of Angelou's narrative? Does Mahshid Hajir's? Are you able to determine whether or not you and Hajir understand and react to Angelou's ideas in the same way?

2) Did your understanding of Angelou's narrative help or hinder your efforts to develop ideas for your paper, and, in turn, did writing your paper help you sharpen your ideas about her piece? If your understanding of her narrative helped your own efforts, in what ways and to what extent is this understanding represented in your paper? For example, in the featured selection, Angelou captures and presents both a child's perspective and the wisdom of an adult who nevertheless still seems to feel the pain of the child within her. Did you yourself try to achieve this sort of "double narrative," as it were? Were you trying to do something else entirely? In terms of the issues addressed in these questions, how does your work compare to the work of Mahshid Hajir, the contributing author?

COROLLARY READINGS

Aside from this chapter's related readings, the following selections pair very well with the Angelou selection: Sandra Cisneros' "My Name" (p. 46), Black Elk, from *Black Elk Speaks* (p. 52), Shehla Yamani's "The Dilemma" (p. 154), Martin Luther King, Jr.'s "Letter from Birmingham Jail" (p. 308), and to some extent Cherríe Moraga's "My Brother's Sex Was White. Mine, Brown" (p. 376) and Barbara Cameron's "'Gee, You Don't Seem Like An Indian From the Reservation'" (p. 381). You might also find it provocative and interesting to use Rudolph Höss' "Early Years" in conjunction with the Angelou selection.

ALTERNATE ASSIGNMENTS

1) Discuss any literal significance in or symbolic value to the scenes in which the narrator rakes and rerakes the dirt yard. Whether or not you find these scenes especially important, do you think that the narrative's final paragraph is particularly significant?

2) Discuss whether or not you feel that the featured reading selection is more or less self-contained, even though it is excerpted from a longer narrative. If you feel that it is self-contained, do you think that it states or implies a governing, controlling assertion—that is, a *thesis*? If it does contain a thesis, is the thesis derived from evidence? Does the thesis adequately explain this evidence? Put differently, does the evidence support or prove the thesis?

3) Elsewhere in her book, Angelou writes:

> What sets one Southern town apart from another, or from a Northern town or hamlet, or city high-rise? The answer must be the experience shared between the unknowing majority (it) and the knowing minority (you). All of childhood's unanswered questions must finally be passed back to the town and answered there. Heroes and bogey men, values and dislikes, are first encountered and labeled in that early environment. In later years they change faces, places and maybe races, tactics, intensities and goals, but beneath those penetrable masks they wear forever the stocking-capped faces of childhood.

Discuss what you think this passage means. Then, talk about whether or not—and, if so, how—this passage sheds light on the featured reading selection and, perhaps, whether or not (and, if so, how) the featured reading selection sheds light on *it*.

4) Discuss what you imagine that Maya Angelou, Louie Crew, Jan Parker, and Martin Luther King, Jr., might say to each other were they to have a roundtable discussion concerning the topic of victimization. Use evidence from their texts to prove or support your claims.

RELATED READINGS

DYLAN THOMAS
Reminiscences of Childhood

THINGS TO THINK ABOUT

One would almost think that Maya Angelou, Alice Walker, and Dylan Thomas wrote prose in order to show college writing students how to write exceptionally good narratives. To help students use Thomas' work as a model for their own writing, I have found it useful to have them study Thomas' ability "simultaneously [to] capture the purity of the child's innocent perceptions of the world and [to] present a retrospective reflection of these perceptions through the filtering lens of the adult's mature—and sometimes melancholy, bitter, or cynical—vision" (close-reading tip, p. 221). Also, I have discovered that students benefit from hearing and enjoy listening to recordings of Thomas reading from his own works; he was, as you might know, a captivating, engaging reader. Though I've not found a recording of "Reminiscences of Childhood," I have used with a great deal of success recordings of Thomas reading "A Child's Christmas in Wales" and selected poems.

COROLLARY READINGS

Besides supplementing the Thomas reading with this chapter's other reading selections, you might try pairing it with one of more of the following: Aesop's "The Shepherd Boy and the Wolf" (p. 31); Lewis Carroll's "Who Stole the Tarts?" (p. 32); Sandra Cisneros' "My Name" (p. 46); Rudolph Höss' "Early Years" (p. 290); and Cherríe Moraga's "My Brother's Sex Was White. Mine, Brown" (p. 376). Mitsuye Yamada's "Invisibility is an Unnatural Disaster: Reflections of an Asian American Woman" (p. 335) and J. Kehaulani Kauanui's "Shifting Identities, Shifting Alliances" (p. 342) might also pair well with Thomas' essay, though probably to a lesser degree than do these other readings.

POSSIBLE ASSIGNMENTS

If you want your students to respond to the second post-reading question, you might add the following to that question: "Pay attention to each description's *tone*, and not just to its actual *details*. Ask yourself whether or not each description invites readers inside the writer's memories so that, in a way, we feel a part of them. Does each description's tone allow us virtually to *see* and *feel* what the writer is describing?"

The following are some other ideas for assignments:

1) Immediately following the poem "The Hunchback in the Park," Thomas says, "And that park grew up with me" (p. 224). Explain what you think this line seems to mean. Do the surrounding words—particularly those which immediately precede and follow this line—provide a context for understanding it? And why, in your view, does Thomas begin the sentence with the coordinating conjunction "and"?

2) Explain why you think that Thomas included a poem in his prose narrative. Would it have made any difference had he merely related, perhaps rather casually, a point or two about the particular figure represented in this poem? In general, do you find a relationship between form and content in Thomas' personal narrative?

3) Discuss whether or not you think that Thomas states or implies a thesis. If you feel that Thomas states or implies a thesis, write a paper in which you 1)

identify his thesis, 2) explain why you think that the assertion which you cite *is* his thesis, and 3) discuss how well you think that he develops and proves or supports his main point.

4) Compare your childhood to Thomas'. If you read Rudolph Höss' "Early Years," you might also (or instead) want to compare Höss' childhood to Thomas'. Would you say that both Thomas' narrative and Höss' narrative provide any hints as to the kinds of adults Thomas and Höss were to become?

ALICE MILLER
The Vicious Circle of Contempt

THINGS TO THINK ABOUT

For a number of reasons, I find this reading selection a quite useful way to help students begin to discover for themselves some significant meanings in their childhood experiences and to begin understanding the possible effects of these experiences on their psycho-social development. My intention is not to psychoanalyze my students, nor is it to have them accept Miller's views. (In fact, a number of my students reject her views; but sometimes even their rejection, and our subsequent discussions of it, proves to be a useful writing prompt.) My purpose, rather, is to give my students some tools by means of which they can make some valuable self-discoveries that, in turn, could help them generate ideas for meaningful writing.

In my own classes, I often couple this excerpt with Roald Dahl's *James and the Giant Peach*. You might consider giving this pedagogical move a try. If you've never used children's literature in a writing class, you might be surprised to discover how much your students gain from both studying such material and directly or indirectly incorporating it into their written work.

COROLLARY READINGS

Given its analytical underpinnings, the Miller selection provides some good theoretical grounding for a study of the chapter's other readings. You might also consider pairing this selection with the other Miller piece contained in this reader, namely, "When Isaac Arises from the Sacrificial Altar" (p. 259). If you take this route, you might also want to have your students read *Genesis* 22: "The *Akedah*" (p. 272) and John Verbeck's "Evaluating Alice Miller's analysis of the Abraham and Isaac story" (p. 265). Other promising corollary readings include Aesop's "The Shepherd Boy and the Wolf" (p. 31), Stanley Milgram's "The Perils of Obedience" (p. 276), Rudolph Höss' "Early Years" (p. 290), Plato's *Crito* (p. 295), and Cherríe Moraga's "My Brother's Sex Was White. Mine, Brown" (p. 376).

POSSIBLE ASSIGNMENTS

1) Earlier in *The Drama of the Gifted Child*, the text from which the Miller excerpt is taken, Miller talks about the phenomenon of parents' projecting onto their chil-

dren the fears and anxieties from their own childhood that they had introjected (that is, internalized) as children. She tells us that "unconsciously the parents' childhood tragedy is continued in their children." Analyze the ways in which this explanation of projection might help us to understand the analytical ideas that Miller puts forth in "The Vicious Circle of Contempt." To help yourself in this endeavor, you might want to review your responses to the third and fourth pre-reading and the first and third post-reading questions. Also, you might want to do some prewriting in which you note any examples, from your own life or from the lives of others, which would seem to support or, perhaps, contradict (or cause trouble for) Miller's contention.

2) Write an essay in which you explain why you identify with—or, perhaps, why you can't identify with—the father, the mother, the child, the narrator, or someone else in this piece. Do you perhaps identify with some or all of these persons, or maybe with none of them? Before attempting to answer these questions, you might want to reexamine your responses to appropriate pre- and post-reading questions and then do some prewriting based on this reexamination.

3) If you read Sigmund Freud's "The Sexual Aberrations" (p. 163), explain how you think that Freud would evaluate the quality of Miller's psychoanalytic theorizing. How might Miller evaluate the quality of Freud's?

4) Explain how you think that Miller might analyze the actions and attitudes of the children and adults portrayed in either the excerpt from Maya Angelou's *I Know Why the Caged Bird Sings* or Kathleene West's poem "Grandmother's Garden." How might she analyze the relationship between the children and their adult family members?

KATHLEENE WEST
Grandmother's Garden

THINGS TO THINK ABOUT

As a friend of mine who is a poet and prose fiction writer suggests, writing poetry is a way for a writer to keep track of and to take control over her or his words. It is an especially useful activity for writers who feel, as my friend sometimes does, that their words are getting away from them. Among its other uses, Kathleene West's poem should help you show your students how a careful writer uses words carefully, wasting nothing in her composition. During your class discussions of this matter, you might also find it convenient and useful to talk with your students about the relationship between form and content, as well as about the relationship between a given piece of writing's purpose and the probable expectations of the writer's intended audience.

Thematically, this poem is rich in interpretive possibilities. If you're not used to using poetry in a writing class, let me suggest that you give your students some lee-way in interpreting the poem's details. You might ask them to read, in preparation for their work here, the section in Chapter Seven entitled "Meaning and Significance" (pp. 251–253). Or, you might simply help guide their close-reading efforts, taking them through the interpretive meaning and significance of, for example, the grandfather's attempted destruction of his wife's garden, the grandmother's seeming understanding of the grandfather's action and her seeming lack of anger at him, the image of the granddaughter as bystander who "see[s] a cruel act/but . . . [will] play out [her] part/in dreams cut down, arranged for another's delight, /the dry whiff of long-pressed hopes" (ll. 28–31), the allusion to "this violence" as "a masque of harvest" (l. 38), and the command that the granddaughter "plant flowers and tell this story" (l. 41).

COROLLARY READINGS

Aside from this chapter's other readings, Sandra Cisneros' "My Name" (p. 46) and any of the readings in Chapter Eight, especially the excerpt from Anne Wilson Schaef's *Women's Reality* (p. 347) and Cherríe Moraga's "My Brother's Sex Was White. Mine, Brown" (p. 376), should prove to be interesting corollary readings. Given its articulations of close family bonds, the excerpt from *Black Elk Speaks* (p. 52) might also pair nicely with this poem. In terms of family identity, the excerpt from Alice Bloch's *The Law of Return* (p. 60) could yield some interesting results were it used in conjunction with the West selection. Rudolph Höss' "Early Years" could provide some interesting points of comparison. Finally, as a way of helping them to become familiar with different poetic discourses, you might also find it useful to have your students read Langston Hughes' "Theme for English B" (p. 244) or Denise Levertov's "The Mutes" (p. 373). (Lorraine Duggin's "Summer, 1945," one of this chapter's readings, should prove useful for this purpose, too.)

POSSIBLE ASSIGNMENTS

If you are going to have your students respond to the third pre-reading question (p. 235), you might want to have them answer the following post-reading questions, too: Are the family constellations that you discussed in your response to the third pre-reading question similar to or different from those presented in West's poem? Are they both similar to and different from—or perhaps neither similar to nor different from—the ones described in this poem?

If you plan to use the fourth pre-reading question (p. 235), you might want to have your students answer the following post-reading questions as well: Does the grandmother in Kathleene West's poem seem to subscribe to the "myth" referred to in the fourth pre-reading question? If so, what, if any, consequences do you see resulting from her belief, and are these consequences the same as those that you discussed in your response to the fourth pre-reading question? If not, then how would you describe the grandmother's reaction to her husband's violent act?

Other ideas for possible assignments include the following:

1) To test your understanding of the relationship between form and content, as well as your ability to let your creative juices flow, turn West's poem into a differ-

ent form of writing, such as a short story, an essay, a diary entry, or a newspaper article. Then, in a reflective commentary, talk about the kinds of changes that you had to make in transforming the poem into this new piece of writing and whether or not these changes work for the better.

2) Compare Kathleene West's "Grandmother's Garden" with Lorraine Duggin's "Summer, 1945" in terms of the ways in which each poem focuses on the dual theme of childhood joys and sorrows. Whatever else you write, you might find it helpful to discuss the ways in which both works help to clarify how an adult's perceptions of herself and others are rooted (to a large extent, at least) in her childhood familial contexts.

3) In "My Brother's Sex Was White. Mine, Brown," Cherríe Moraga talks about a troubling manifestation of sexism, in which women turn against themselves, a move that they are taught to make at a very early age, often by their mothers and other female role models. Discuss the ways in which West's poem documents, critiques, and, perhaps, supplies an antidote to this problem.

4) Compare the thoughts and images that you came up with in your answer to the second pre-reading question with those that you find in West's poem. Does this comparative analysis yield insight into the similarities and differences between you and the poem's characters, including the narrator? Do the adjectives and verbs that West uses in her poem give you any insight into the underlying meanings of the thoughts and images portrayed in the poem? In your response to the second pre-reading question, do you use similar adjectives to describe the thoughts and images that you discuss?

LORRAINE DUGGIN

Summer, 1945

THINGS TO THINK ABOUT

Among this poem's many themes, one of the most disturbing has to do with the relationship between childhood and violence. I have found that one useful way to help students understand this theme is to explain it according to what I call the continuum theory (I didn't originate the thinking behind this theory, of course). This theory suggests that violence, for example, occurs on a continuum of severity: some acts of violence are more severe than others, some are less severe than others, and most are somewhere in between. According to this theory, acts of violence differ in degree, but not necessarily in kind. Further, an act of violence is understood not simply in terms of the particular context (political or social, for example) in which it occurred, nor only in terms of its own characteristics (for instance, the characteristics of an act of murder differ from those of an act of verbal abuse), but also in relation to other acts of violence, including instigative acts of violence (such as incitement to riot or, as was the case in the rape of the young woman portrayed in the movie *The Accused*, incitement to rape).

You yourself might find this theory a useful prompt for stimulating class discussion of Duggin's poem. If you do explain this theory to your students, you might try using an example such as the relationship between sexist jokes and acts of rape to help your students better understand how the continuum theory works (sexist jokes are the verbal equivalent of physical acts of rape, which themselves represent the verbal abuse of women taken to its logical conclusion). You might then ask your students to apply this theory to an understanding of the various images and allusions of bombing in Duggin's poem. Of course, the object here is not to have all of your students agree on how to interpret the poem, but, rather, to give them an interpretive tool that might help them arrive at a provocative and promising analysis of the poem.

COROLLARY READINGS

Aside from supplementing Duggin's poem with this chapter's other reading selections and, perhaps, with the poetry selections mentioned in my comments concerning corollary readings for West's poem, you might want to supplement Duggin's poem with Alice Miller's "When Isaac Arises from the Sacrificial Altar" (p. 259), as well as, perhaps, the attendant commentary by John Verbeck (p. 265) and the excerpt from *Genesis* (p. 272). Miller's discussion of the cycles of violence that she sees portrayed in (and encouraged by?) the Abraham and Isaac story might provide a useful, even if controversial, context within which to discuss Duggin's poem.

The images and messages in Rudolph Höss' "Early Years" (p. 290) might provide some provocative similarities and contrasts to the images and messages in Duggin's poem. If you use the Höss piece, you might also consider using Christopher R. Browning's "Ordinary Men" (p. 107), a work that helps to document the fact that ordinary people can carry out extraordinarily bad deeds (see the third assignment, below).

POSSIBLE ASSIGNMENTS

If you decide to use the fifth post-reading question (p. 231), you might want to add the following words to the last query within that question (which is "If so, what is that theme?"): "and where in the poem do you see it reflected?"

Here are some ideas for other assignments:

1) Discuss the ways in which the pronoun "I" functions in Duggin's poem. Explain whether or not you think that Duggin should have avoided using this pronoun in her poem. If appropriate, see your response to the third post-reading question concerning Kathleene West's poem (see p. 237).

2) Compare the ways in which Duggin treats a particular theme concerning childhood with the ways in which other authors whose work appears in this book treat this same theme.

3) The reserve policemen to whom Christopher R. Browning refers in "Ordinary Men" were "middle-aged family men mostly of working-class background" (p. 110, paragraph 9). Discuss whether you see these men as being similar to, different from, or both similar to and different from the men who dropped the atom bombs to which Duggin refers in her poem's final stanza. In your discussion,

comment upon the meaning or significance of the persona's line "Though I know/what a target is, I have to ask/my mother if atom bombs are like balloons" (ll. 25–27).

4) Take a look at Shakespeare's "Sonnet 73," which is reprinted in the next chapter (p. 251), examining in particular Shakespeare's use of the poetic/rhetorical technique known as anaphora to help showcase what in music would be called a variation on a theme (you might recall that we studied this technique when we read and discussed Kathleene West's poem). Notice how, in each of his poem's quatrains, which are four-line stanzas having particular rhyme and metrical patterns, Shakespeare has the persona explain, in different ways, that the latter is growing old.

After you have studied Shakespeare's use of repetition, reread Duggin's poem, trying to analyze the nature and function of repetition in *it*. Then, commit your analysis to writing, discussing, among other things, whether or not Duggin's use of repetition helps to create both foreshadowing in and thematic unity to her poem. Here are some representative stanzas for you to consider:

Stanza 1: ". . . I . . . drop [wooden pins]/one by one headfirst, the bottle's small mouth/my target. I listen for the loud plunk/against glass bottom to tell me I've won./Bullseye!"

Stanza 2: ". . . I collect henhouse/eggs, lift each from its nest, trembling/not to drop a single one. Success!/ . . . the outhouse, decrepit dark/pit with wooden sides whitewashed by birds,/two dark holes the cover for a target. . . . " [By the way, do you notice any metaphors here?]

Stanza 3: ". . . handing clothespins to my mother/ . . . I find/a robin egg intact. . . ./a black grackle divebombs Mother's shining sheets. . . . "

Stanza 4: ". . . I know/what a target is. . . . /I'm old enough to know what's meant/by flight, have learned what winning is. . . . "

ALICE WALKER
Elethia

THINGS TO THINK ABOUT

Like the works of other great writers, Alice Walker's works lend themselves easily to provocative discussions. Unless I have a class of students who seem to have taken a vow of silence for the semester, I generally find that I need do little more than serve as moderator for class discussions of Walker's material. When I add my own views to those of my students, I often find it helpful to supplement their points by discussing themes and issues from others of Walker's works, especially themes and issues that might not surface, or that might be only indirectly manifest, in the work that we're studying—"Elethia," in this case. For example, a not uncommon feature in Walker's stories is the presence and development of a strong female character who initially might have appeared weak but who ends up "saving the day," as it were. Celie, in *The Color Purple*, is one such character, as is the wife in the short story "Coming Apart."

If you travel this analytical route with your students, you might ask them whether or not Elethia is such a character. In addition, you might want to introduce your students to and have them discuss, in relation to "Elethia," Walker's notion of a "womanist," a term that Walker defines in a footnote to the version of "Coming Apart" published in *Take Back the Night: Women on Pornography*, edited by Laura Lederer (New York: William Morrow and Company, Inc., 1980). In that note, Walker says that the term womanist "encompasses 'feminist' as it is defined in Webster's, but also means *instinctively* pro-woman" (100; author's italics). Moreover, Walker says, this word "has a strong root in Black women's culture. It comes (to me) from the word 'womanish,' a word our mothers used to describe, and attempt to inhibit, strong, outrageous or outspoken behavior when we were children" (ibid.). Walker goes on to say that this "labeling . . . failed, for the most part, to keep us from acting 'womanish' whenever we could, that is to say, like our mothers themselves, and like other women we admired" (ibid.). (See, too, Walker's definition of "womanist" that appears on p. xi of her book *In Search of Our Mothers' Gardens*, the full bibliographical details concerning which are provided in the "Works Cited" section of this reader, p. 393.) Note: Unfortunately, not all of Walker's readers admire (or seem to understand) her concept of a womanist or the use of this concept in her stories. See, for example, George Stade's "Womanist Fiction and Male Characters," in *Partisan Review* 52.3 (1985): 264–270.

COROLLARY READINGS

Aside from supplementing "Elethia" with the chapter's other readings, you might want to pair this story with Aesop's "The Shepherd Boy and the Wolf" (p. 31). Doing so could yield some interesting discussions concerning a comparative analysis that accounts for the boy's attitudes and actions, the villagers' attitudes and actions, the attitudes and actions of the young people in "Elethia," and those of the old(er) people in this story. You might also want to use Lewis Carroll's "Who Stole the Tarts?" (p. 32) as a way to help make the point that our interpretations of actions (such as stealing) are almost always context-specific.

Of this book's many other readings that could pair well with "Elethia," the following might prove to be especially useful: Sandra Cisneros' "My Name" (p. 46); the excerpt from Claude Lanzmann's *Shoah* (p. 92); Louie Crew's "Thriving As An Outsider, Even As An Outcast, In Smalltown America" (p. 146); Martin Luther King, Jr.'s "Letter from Birmingham Jail" (p. 308); Adriane Fugh-Berman's "Tales Out of Medical School" (p. 361); and Barbara Cameron's "'Gee, You Don't Seem Like An Indian From the Reservation'" (p. 381).

POSSIBLE ASSIGNMENTS

If you use the fourth post-reading question (p. 243), you might want to append the following questions to it: Also, why do you think that this story is titled

"Elethia"? Would the story's meaning(s) or significance change were the piece titled, say, "Uncle Albert" or "Albert Porter"? [As suggested earlier, you might want to have your students read, in Chapter Seven, the section entitled "Meaning and Significance" (pp. 251–253).]

Here are some other ideas for possible assignments:

1) A number of literary critics and theorists feel that works of fiction defamiliarize the everyday world for us, enabling us to see this world as if we had never seen it before. For example, they might say, Alice Walker's *The Color Purple* deals with the problems of sexism and racism in such a unique way that even many people who are already familiar with these problems respond to Walker's treatment of them as if they were hearing about these problems for the first time. In other words, as one noted theorist might say, Walker's fictional account of these problems has given American culture "words that permit it to speak [about sexism and racism] as if for the first time" (Krieger 195; for full bibliographical details, see "Works Cited," p. 392).

In an essay focusing on this issue, discuss the ways in which Walker's use of everyday language and images in "Elethia" helps us to envision anew the complex problems that Walker places before us—problems with which we might already be quite familiar. If applicable, include in your essay any relevant information contained in your response to the fifth post-reading question. [This assignment uses material from the close-reading tip for Denise Levertov's "The Mutes" (p. 373); you might want to amend this assignment to include material relevant to a comparative analysis of Walker's story and Levertov's poem.]

2) Like Shakespearean comedies, a number of Walker's stories move from impending gloom to redemptive resolution. Write an essay in which you discuss whether or not, in your view, "Elethia" follows such a pattern. Be sure to cite textual evidence to prove or support your claims.

3) The philosopher Jean-Paul Sartre has written that, "[f]ar from experience producing [the antisemite's] idea of the Jew, it was the latter which explained his experience. If the Jew did not exist," Sartre goes on to say, "the anti-Semite would invent him" (13; for full bibliographical details, see "Works Cited," p. 393.) Apply Sartre's notion to a close reading of Walker's story, explaining as carefully as possible how Sartre's theory accounts for the ideas and experiences of the bigots discussed in Walker's story as well as, perhaps, the ideas and experiences of bigots in general. Of course, feel free to take issue with Sartre if and when you think that you should.

4) Discuss some possible meanings in Walker's having interwoven two sets of narratives in this story, the first set consisting of the main narrative *per se*, and the second set consisting of a "written down" retelling of "the old-timers' memories" that Elethia has in her possession. In your view, what is each narrative's relationship to the other? Are they different, similar, both, neither, or something else altogether? Is it significant that Walker groups together these memories, the jar of ashes, and Elethia's friends (see paragraph 18)? Explain your readings (that is, your interpretations) of her text as carefully as possible, citing and elucidating textual evidence to prove or support your claims.

LANGSTON HUGHES

Theme for English B

THINGS TO THINK ABOUT

Having had nothing but good luck using "Theme for English B" in both writing and literature classes, and being a big fan of Hughes' work, I never tire of teaching this interpretively and affectively rich piece of literature. Let me tell you a few aspects of the poem that I usually cover in class and that normally engage my students' interest, though I want to encourage you both to work with the poem in ways that make it yours, as it were, and to help your students work with it in ways that make it theirs.

Hughes presents a number of images having to do with up and down movements. These images strike me as being quite important to the poem's meanings, since they concern such matters as the persona's move from the South to the North and his travels between Harlem and Columbia University. Many of my students seem to find this aspect of the poem very useful for their own readings, whether or not their readings agree with mine.

Hughes masterfully uses subtle and blatant details to indicate both the complexities underlying the persona's being caught between Black and White America and the persona's frustration at his having to live in something akin to what Paula Gunn Allen calls a bicultural bind. With only a bit of prompting, students begin to find and offer good interpretations of these details, such as those found in ll. 21–26.

Finally (to offer but one more pedagogical leaning of mine), I find that Hughes' poem presents an exceptionally fine illustration of the complexities underlying self-other relationships. Take a close look, for example, at what Hughes writes in ll. 16–20 and 27–40.

Good luck in teaching this poem. And have fun!

COROLLARY READINGS

Hughes' poem pairs wonderfully with the other readings in this chapter. If you use it along with any or all of these other readings, you should find that your students have a wealth of good material to work with and write about. Thematically, Kevin Mullen's "Writing: A Leap of Faith" (p. 17) also pairs nicely with Hughes' poem, as do Sandra Cisneros' "My Name" (p. 46), the excerpt from Alice Bloch's *The Law of Return*, Elie Wiesel's "Why I Write" (p. 80), Jay Julos' "Why I Write" (p. 86), Shehla Yamani's model rough drafts and final version of "The Dilemma," as well as her commentary on her writing experiences (p. 154), Martin Luther King, Jr.'s "Letter from Birmingham Jail" (p. 308), and all of the readings in Chapter Eight, with the possible exceptions of Irwin Shaw's "The Girls in Their Summer Dresses" (p. 367) and Denise Levertov's "The Mutes" (p. 373), though even these pieces offer some interesting insights into self-other relations, insights which you might find useful in discussions concerning Hughes' poem.

POSSIBLE ASSIGNMENTS

If you use the sixth post-reading question (p. 246), you might want to include the following information as part of your directions or prompts: Take a look again at the following details in this poem: the moods of the verbs and the specific sorts of verbs used throughout the poem; the use of directional and geographical imagery in ll. 7–15; the use of colons and dashes throughout the poem; and the alliterative references to "Bessie, bop, [and] Bach" in l. 24 (by the way, in *Montage of a Dream Deferred*, the book of Hughes' poems in which this poem appears, "Theme for English B" is the first of the poems contained in the section entitled "Vice Versa to Bach").

Perhaps you'll want to consider using one or more of the following assignments:

1) Do the assignment that is articulated at the beginning of Hughes' poem. Then, in a reflective commentary, imagine that you are having a discussion with the persona about both your response and his response to the assignment. How would the two of you talk about the ways in which your responses compare? What questions would you ask him about his response, what questions might he ask you about your response, and what answers would each of you offer? How would you explain to him your reaction to what he writes in response to the assignment, and what do you imagine that he would say to you in explaining his reaction to what *you* write in response to the assignment? What do you think that he might ask you about your answers to some of the pre-reading questions, and how would you respond to his questions? [In an alternate version of this assignment, you might want your students to respond to the fourth and fifth pre-reading questions (pp. 244 and 245) prior to reading Hughes' poem and doing this assignment and then to respond to the fourth and *possibly* to the fifth post-reading questions (p. 246), or amended versions of them, after reading his poem and doing this assignment.]

2) Discuss how you think that Martin Luther King, Jr., might interpret Hughes' poem. How might he characterize the poem's persona? Cite and explain the meaning or significance of pertinent textual evidence to help prove or support your contentions.

3) Do a close reading of this poem, concentrating on analyzing one or two aspects of the poem to help make your case. Among the elements in Hughes' poem ripe for analysis, the following ought to prove especially promising (though you are not obligated to analyze any of them): the poem's images having to do with up and down movements; the poem's subtle and blatant details having to do with the persona's being caught between Black and White America; and the poem's treatment of self-other relationships. Whatever thematic focus you choose for your essay, be sure that you read pertinent lines closely, explaining their importance both in and of themselves and to the poem as a whole.

4) Consider the following lines from Paul Laurence Dunbar's late nineteenth century poem entitled "Accountability":

> We is all constructed diff'ent,
>   d'ain't no two of us de same;
> We cain't he'p ouah likes an' dis-
>   likes, ef we'se bad we ain't to
>   blame.

Write an essay in which you discuss the ways in which these lines might serve as a useful commentary on, or perhaps be better understood in light of, Hughes' poem.

INDIVIDUAL, GROUP, AND/OR CLASS ACTIVITIES

1) Unless we had particularly harsh childhoods, most of us probably smooth over or have forgotten many of the rough times that we had and remember our childhoods more or less fondly. For some people, of course, this memory is accurate: their childhoods seemed to have been rather happy, save for the usual difficulties and dilemmas that all children face from time to time. For others, though, this memory is not so accurate. Psychoanalyst Sigmund Freud describes well the conflict that these latter people have between their memories and experiences, a conflict which he sees as universal: "When an adult recalls his childhood it seems to him to have been a happy time. . . . But if children themselves were able to give us information earlier they would probably tell a different story. It seems that childhood is not the blissful idyll into which we distort it in retrospect . . . " (*S.E.*: 11:126; for full bibliographical details concerning the *Standard Edition* of Freud's work, see this reader's "Works Cited" section, p. 391).

Discuss one or more of this chapter's readings in light of Freud's comment. In particular, talk about whether or not, in your view, the authors of this chapter's readings describe the best and worst aspects of childhood without "distort[ing] it in retrospect."

2) Compare the ways in which two or more of this chapter's readings treat similar issues. If you discover theses in the works under investigation, how would you compare the authors' arguments that attempt to prove or support these theses? Can you draw any general conclusions from your comparative analysis of these works? Also, where do you now stand with respect to the issues discussed by these authors? Did any of the readings help change your thinking? Did any make you particularly angry or sad? Be sure that you cite and explain textual and other relevant evidence to help support or prove your claims.

3) In one way or another, each of this chapter's readings deals with the status and feelings of children. In your school's library, see if you can locate Jeremiah Abrams' *Reclaiming the Inner Child*. Containing some enlightening and intriguing perspectives on adults and children, this book presents readings that concentrate particularly on explaining the complex and profoundly influential relationships between the adult and the child who lives within her or him. If you find this book, take a look at some of its selections, and then see if you can apply your understanding of them to an analysis of one or more of this chapter's readings.

4) During the next two weeks, pay close attention to the ways in which children and childhood are portrayed in movies, on television, in advertisements, and so on. Then, write a report entitled something to the effect of "The State of Our Children," in which you present and defend a thesis that derives from your careful analysis of your observations.

Chapter Seven: Writing the Traditional Academic Essay

INSTRUCTIONAL ISSUES

If your students are like mine, many will harbor doubts about their ability to analyze data, despite your best teaching efforts. To help my own students gain some confidence in this area, I sometimes have them engage in group-level projects similar to the individual projects to which I allude at the end of Chapter Five (p. 199). The following description ought to give you a good idea of what the students do in this regard. Feel free to use either this exact approach or a modified version of it, which might better fit your own pedagogical needs.

I divide students into four or five groups, each of which is given a particular task to complete; in a week or two, the groups report their findings to the class. One group might be asked to spend the day at a local mall, looking carefully at store window displays for clues to any patterns of messages concerning male-female relationships, sexual orientation, and so on. Another group might watch television programs to see whether or not these programs incorporate verbal or physical violence into their plots, and, if they do, to determine the kind of violence that is portrayed, its frequency of portrayal, and its severity. Another group might be assigned to visit a few supermarkets in order to investigate where certain products are shelved, whether or not there are any color patterns to labels, and so on. Still another group might be asked to investigate messages on license plate holders or bumper stickers, or perhaps on people's t-shirts. Sometimes, we add or alter tasks so that we can take advantage of the analytical opportunities presented by an important current event.

Generally, the students seem to enjoy doing these projects. More important, during their class presentations many students demonstrate both to the class and to themselves that they can indeed analyze data fairly well. I must tell you, though, that there *are* pitfalls to having students engage in such activities. Several years ago, for example, one of my students, whose group had studied violence in television programming, told the class that, among the many programs that his group had analyzed, only *M*A*S*H* promoted an antiwar message (by the way, his group had treated news programs as television programs). When I asked him how he accounted for this phenomenon, he talked about the antiwar sentiment that pervaded the culture "back then"—that is, in the 1970s, when *M*A*S*H* was originally aired! Back then. Oh, well, I guess some of us just have to get used to the fact that, semester after semester, our students are younger and younger.

FEATURED READING

ALICE MILLER
When Isaac Arises from the Sacrificial Altar

THINGS TO THINK ABOUT

Though I myself find this particular essay troubling, I use it as this chapter's featured reading because it is a gold mine of analytical possibilities. Whether they end up agreeing or disagreeing with Miller's views, my own students have gained much from analyzing this piece; I am assuming that your students will have a similar experience.

One of the problems that I see with this essay is that, like many other works grounded in psychoanalytic theory, it tacitly assumes that psychoanalytic insight necessarily takes precedence over other interpretive possibilities. Making this assumption, more than a few psychoanalytic critics have demonstrated carelessness with their data. In the eyes of a number of people—including those who, as I do, otherwise support Miller's views, especially those contained in works such as "The Vicious Circle of Contempt," for example, in which we find theoretically careful and analytically sound ideas—Miller has fallen into this very trap in "When Isaac Arises from the Sacrificial Altar." In this essay, they see rather careless, unreflective thinking. For instance, one of my colleagues, a humanities scholar, finds in Miller's analysis of the Abraham and Isaac story perhaps unwitting, but nevertheless real and problematic, antisemitism. Another colleague, an art historian, has suggested that Miller presents us here with good psychoanalysis but bad art history. Similarly, this chapter's contributing author feels that Miller articulates some sound psychological insights but some rather sloppy biblical criticism.

On the other hand, more than a few of my students feel that Miller's analysis concerning the problematic nature of the Abraham and Isaac story is quite cogent. A number of these students, themselves victims of child abuse, feel that they have a strong advocate in Miller, who gives voice to the pain and trauma that they themselves have or have had trouble articulating. Still other students, who have problems with the underlying patriarchal ideologies of male-centered religions, find in Miller's analysis support for their own critiques.

In short, whatever their own views concerning this essay, many students studying and writing about it find more than enough fodder for close reading and critical analysis. Moreover, in the best of circumstances, they seem to gain a deep understanding of the need for a community of thinkers (such as those taking a college class together) to accept each other's good-faith efforts to come to terms with some troubling issues and, if necessary, to agree to disagree with each other.

THE FEATURED ASSIGNMENT AND THE CONTRIBUTING
AUTHOR'S MODEL RESPONSE

Although the featured assignment is a straightforward, traditionally academic one that most of your students should be able to execute with at least a fair degree of success, you might find that you need to spend some class time and office hours working with at least some students whose predisposed views threaten to undermine their analytical efforts. In my own teaching experience, I have had students whose hostility to psychological therapy ran so deep that they wanted to write off Miller's views in advance. On the other end of the spectrum, I've had students who suffered such terrible child abuse that they couldn't understand how anyone could see Abraham as anything other than a cruel, blindly obedient victimizer and Isaac as anything other than an innocent victim. Between these two extremes, I've had a number of students whose theoretical presuppositions endangered their analyses of Miller's work—and, by extension, of others' work, as well.

To some degree, the pre- and post-reading questions are meant to help students become reflective readers of their own predisposed views. Nevertheless, as I suggest above, you might find, as I often find in my own teaching, that you need to spend some extra time talking with at least some of your students about this matter.

Though John Verbeck, the contributing author, didn't have the problem alluded to above, in my view he did need to curb his criticism of Miller, which I thought undermined his otherwise good analysis of her work. He refers to this problem in his commentary, in which he openly discusses his struggles to write a well-conceived analysis of Miller's work. You and your students will surely notice, too, that John's commentary is written in more or less relaxed, informal prose, rather than in the sophisticated prose displayed in his paper—an excellent paper that John reached only after he had written many previous drafts. Given its subject matter and writing style, this particular reflective commentary should prove to be one of the most useful apparatuses in this book. If you have your students read and discuss John's paper, then you really should have them read and discuss his commentary, too.

COROLLARY READINGS

You might want your students to read the first related reading, *Genesis* 22: "*The Akedah*," before they read Miller's essay or John Verbeck's critique of Miller's essay, so that they have an understanding of the text that Miller is analyzing—or, in the eyes of the contributing author, *not* analyzing. In their own ways, this chapter's other readings should prove to be useful corollary readings, too.

Given Miller's advocacy of children and children's rights, you might also find it useful to have your students read most, if not all, of the readings in Chapter Six. The following selections, too, might prove useful as corollary readings to the Miller text, even though some of them do not treat themes concerning children or childhood: Shehla Yamani's "The Dilemma" (p. 154); Mitsuye Yamada's "Invisibility is an Unnatural Disaster: Reflections of an Asian American Woman" (p. 335); the excerpt from Anne Wilson Schaef's *Women's Reality* (p. 347); Cherríe Moraga's "My

Brother's Sex Was White. Mine, Brown" (p. 376); and Barbara Cameron's "'Gee, You Don't Seem Like An Indian From the Reservation'" (p. 381). Also useful might be the excerpt from Claude Lanzmann's *Shoah* (p. 92), which documents the consequences of the objectification of human beings, and Abram L. Sachar's "The Carob Tree Grove: Christian Compassion" (p. 113), which provides documentation concerning the antidote to interpersonal conflict.

ALTERNATE ASSIGNMENTS

As preparation for anything that they write or present concerning Miller's work, if they haven't already done so your students might find it helpful to answer an appropriately revised version of the first pre-reading question concerning the Sigmund Freud reading selection in Chapter Five (p. 164) and the fourth pre-reading question concerning the Alice Miller reading selection in Chapter Six (p. 227), as well as appropriate post-reading questions of your own devising, which ask your students whether or not they want to revaluate their responses to these two pre-reading questions in light of their views concerning Alice Miller's "When Isaac Arises from the Sacrificial Altar."

  Some additional possibilities for assignments follow:

  1) Though many people would agree that, in the best case scenarios, obedience to authority leads to an orderly and socially just society, well-run, ethically-minded businesses, and so on, they would probably also agree that, in the worst case scenarios, obedience to authority can lead to devastating political, psychological, and social consequences. Basing your views primarily on your analysis of Alice Miller's views, write a well-focused essay concerning the problem of obedience to authority. Try to address this problem as honestly and authentically as possible, using examples from this chapter's other readings and from any other pertinent sources to help you make your points.

  2) In one of his critiques of religion, Sigmund Freud says that, "by forcibly fixing [people] in a state of psychical infantilism and by drawing them into a mass-delusion, religion succeeds in sparing many people an individual neurosis[,] [b]ut hardly anything more" (*S.E.*: 21:84–85; for full bibliographical details concerning the *Standard Edition* of Freud's works, see, in this reader's "Works Cited" section, p. 391). Write an essay in which you not only explain what you think that Freud means here, but also agree or disagree with his view in light of reliable data. Include in your analysis (or, perhaps, in a different paper) an explanation concerning both whether or not Freud's view helps us to understand Miller's position with respect to the Abraham and Isaac story and whether or not Miller's view helps to confirm or shed light on Freud's idea. If appropriate, also discuss whether or not either Freud's or Miller's theorizing seems anti-Christian or antisemitic.

  3) As you saw, Miller tries to demonstrate that the significance of the Abraham and Isaac story ranges far beyond the theological context in which the story is couched. Evaluating her analysis, explain whether or not Miller adequately makes her case. Does she show or fail to show the close relationship between the actions and attitudes of Abraham and Isaac and those of other people (or other

types of people) to whom she refers in her essay? Does she perhaps both succeed and fail in this regard?

4) Write an essay in which you compare your analysis of Miller's essay with that of John Verbeck. What similarities and differences do you see between your and his attempts to derive, develop, and prove or support a thesis? Does your work reflect a close reading of Miller's essay? Does his? Are you always able to determine whether or not you and Verbeck understand and react to Miller's ideas similarly or differently? If you wrote a commentary on the work that you did for the featured assignment, is it similar to or different from Verbeck's commentary? Is it perhaps both similar to and different from his?

R E L A T E D   R E A D I N G S

GENESIS 22: "THE *AKEDAH*"

THINGS TO THINK ABOUT

Many of your Christian students might bring to their reading of *Genesis* 22 the notion that the Hebrew Bible is an "old" testament in need of completion by the "new" testament of Christianity. Accordingly, many, if not all, will see in Isaac a prefiguration of Jesus.[4] If you have any Islamic students in your class, you might find that some or most of them will see in Isaac something of a usurper; Abraham's first-born son, after all, is Ishmael, the disinherited offspring who, as legend has it, is to the Arabs what Isaac is to the Jews (hence, the sibling rivalry that has plagued Arab-Jewish relations for millennia?). One of my Islamic students even told me that, when Muslims read *Genesis* 22, they substitute Ishmael for Isaac; unfortunately, I've never discovered whether or not this reading practice is common.

Personally, I feel the need to try to help students understand that *Genesis* 22 is a Jewish text, not a Christian or Islamic one, even though both Christianity and Islam have the right to claim it as part of the textual roots of their own faiths. In other words, I try to help students understand that, however else they see the story of Abraham and Isaac, they should also try to see it in the context of Jewish history and culture if they want to understand it on its own terms, as it were (in making this effort, I sometimes remind my students that the phrases "Old Testament" and "New Testament" are Christian phrases; what Christians call the Old Testament Jews simply call the Bible.) Though sometimes emotionally trying, such discussions do students a great service, in my view, by helping them to understand that *no* religious beliefs are necessarily universal, nor do any necessarily represent absolute, inviolable interpretive norms or standards.

---

[4]For a good understanding for some of the diferent ways in which Jewish and Christian theologians read the Bible, take a look at Andrew M. Greeley and Jacob Neusner's *The Bible and Us: A Priest and a Rabbi Read Scripture Together* (New York: Warner Books, Inc., 1990); pages 86-115 are germane to the Abraham and Isaac story.

As if such concerns weren't enough for instructors teaching *Genesis* 22, teachers of this work are also faced with the problem of trying to help their students understand a text that is very short on detail, very long on controversy, and very deeply rooted in ancient history and ancient social practices. The first two difficulties are indeed challenging, but they need not impede class discussions; in fact, I find that they often prove to be fodder for good class discussions. To deal as effectively as possible with the last pedagogical burden, I have found it quite useful to spend some time discussing with my students the information contained in the fourth post-reading question (p. 276). Nevertheless, the text in question, one of the most controversial and important texts in the Hebrew Bible, eludes even our best critical efforts to understand or, ultimately, contain it. For many readers, perhaps this fact alone underscores the essence of the text's continued and intriguing allure.

COROLLARY READINGS

As I have suggested, you might want to have your students study this text prior to having them read either Alice Miller's analysis of it or John Verbeck's analysis of Miller's interpretation. Be that as it may, this text should help illuminate a number of the issues in the chapter's other readings, and they, in turn, should help illuminate a number of issues in it. However, during class discussions, you might want to help your students exercise some caution in using *Genesis* 22 with these other readings, lest they end up eliding crucial differences by too easily pairing ideas. For example, were they to suggest, without first establishing a careful analytical context within which to make this point, that the ideas underlying Abraham's obedience to God also underlie the problematic gestures of obedience to authority shown by Rudolph Höss, the Commandant of Auschwitz, they might be rightfully accused of engaging in sloppy thinking, if not also of articulating antisemitic ideas. Abraham and Höss are not parallel types merely because each displays obedience to authority any more than bottles of red wine and human beings are the same simply because each needs to breathe.

With similar due caution, you might want to supplement the *Genesis* selection with the following other readings, too: Fred E. Katz's "A Sociological Perspective to the Holocaust" (p. 95); Christopher R. Browning's "Ordinary Men" (p. 107); Abram L. Sachar's "The Carob Tree Grove: Christian Compassion" (p. 113); and all of the readings in Chapter Six (since they have to do with adult-child relationships). Also useful might be Mitsuye Yamada's "Invisibility is an Unnatural Disaster: Reflections of an Asian American Woman" (p. 335), the excerpt from Anne Wilson Schaef's *Women's Reality* (p. 347), Cherríe Moraga's "My Brother's Sex Was White. Mine, Brown" (p. 376), and Barbara Cameron's "'Gee, You Don't Seem Like An Indian From the Reservation'" (p. 381).[5]

---

[5] To the extent that Elie Wiesel finds Isaac to be the first Holocaust survivor, Wiesel's "Why I Write" (p. 80) might also prove to be an interesting supplement to *Genesis* 22. However, before using Wiesel's text in this way, you probably should read Zev Garber and Bruce Zucherman's essay "Why Do We Call the Holocaust 'The Holocaust?' An Inquiry Into the Psychology of Labels," in *Modern Judaism* 9.2 (May 1989): 197-211; the authors discuss Wiesel's views on p. 202ff.

POSSIBLE ASSIGNMENTS

If you use the third post-reading question (p. 276), you might want to supplement it with the first question in the second post-reading question (p. 276), which is "What are your thoughts and feelings about the story presented in *Genesis* 22?" You might also ask your students whether or not their responses would alter were they to hold different views about religion from those that they now hold.

Here are two other assignment options, the second of which is a version of the second assignment option for Miller's "When Isaac Arises from the Sacrificial Altar" (see p. IM-56):

1) Study the photograph of the Rembrandt painting "The Sacrifice of Isaac," which is reprinted on p. 261. Then, write an essay in which you discuss whether or not, in your opinion, Rembrandt accurately portrays what is going on in Genesis 22. If you have read Alice Miller's "When Isaac Arises from the Sacrificial Altar" and John Verbeck's "Evaluating Alice Miller's analysis of the Abraham and Isaac story," feel free to include your views of their work in your response. If you wish, write a different essay, one in which you evaluate Rembrandt's, Miller's, and Verbeck's analyses. In either case, keep your analysis well focused, and draw from good, reliable data to help prove or support your points.

2) In one of his critiques of religion, Sigmund Freud says that, "by forcibly fixing [people] in a state of psychical infantilism and by drawing them into a mass-delusion, religion succeeds in sparing many people an individual neurosis[,] [b]ut hardly anything more" (*S.E.*: 21:84–85; for full bibliographical details concerning the *Standard Edition* of Freud's works, see, in this reader's "Works Cited" section, p. 391). Write an essay in which, using reliable data to help prove or support your views, you explain whether or not Freud's view is germane to an understanding of *Genesis* 22. If you wish, include in your analysis (or, perhaps, in a different paper) an explanation concerning both whether or not Freud's view helps us to understand Miller's position with respect to the Abraham and Isaac story and whether or not Miller's view helps to confirm or shed light on Freud's idea. If appropriate, also discuss whether or not either Freud's or Miller's theorizing seems anti-Christian or antisemitic.

STANLEY MILGRAM
The Perils of Obedience

THINGS TO THINK ABOUT

Milgram caused quite a stir when he published the results of his famous obedience experiments. Some researchers were concerned about the study's possibly damaging effects on the experiment's subjects, who discovered that they had the capacity to harm and maybe even kill an innocent human being in the interest of science and on the orders of a stranger who, in his combined capacity of scientist-authority, commanded them to administer electric shocks to this other human being (of course, unbeknownst to the subjects, this other human being never did receive any electric shocks). Milgram had his own concerns: he wondered, probably rhetorically, what governments might be able to exact from their citizens by way of obedience if in a university lab setting he could exact such a high degree of obedience from ordinary people. One shouldn't forget that Milgram published his book on these experiments not quite 30 years after the end of the Second World War.

When I teach Milgram's essay, I conduct my own small experiment. Either before or after they read Milgram's article, I ask my students whether or not they think that they would cause harm to another human being on the orders of an authority figure if they could choose to disobey with impunity. Semester after semester, the results are the same, whether I ask this question as a pre-reading or as a post-reading question: out of the entire class, only a handful of students (at the *most*) admit that, even if they could disobey with impunity, they probably would obey the authority figure even if doing so meant that they would have to go against their own moral values. At this point, I ask how it is possible that, semester after semester, my students suggest that they are an exception to a rule of behavior concerning obedience to authority that Milgram (and others, subsequently) have repeatedly documented. In other words, I ask why so many of them imagine that, unlike the majority of people, they themselves would not obey an authority figure who asks or demands that they hurt another person. We then begin having some very useful discussions concerning denial, personal responsibility, self-other relations, political and social pressures, and so on.

One final matter. The results of Milgram's experiments are often used to explain the *situational* dynamics of obedience to authority. In other words, so the theory goes, when the conditions of a given situation are right, ordinary people can commit evil deeds that, under other circumstances, they would not or might not commit. Opposing or complementing this theory is one suggesting that some people are *dispositionally* bad; such people commit (or can commit) evil deeds regardless of the situation in which they find themselves. For a better understanding of these two theories, as well as for an understanding of a third theory, the "interactional approach," which attempts to combine and move beyond these other two theories, see Thomas Blass' "Psychological Perspectives on the Perpetrators of the Holocaust: The Role of Situational Pressures, Personal Dispositions, and Their Interaction," in *Holocaust and Genocide Studies* 7.1 (Spring 1993): 30–50.

COROLLARY READINGS

Concerning this chapter's other readings, the Milgram piece should provide a good analytical context within which to study Rudolph Höss' "Early Years," but it should be used with caution as an analytical source for the material from *Genesis*. The way in which you decide to use Alice Miller's essay (and perhaps John Verbeck's) as a corollary to Milgram's article will depend, I would think, on the way in which you pair the Milgram and *Genesis* material. Finally, pairing Milgram's essay with Plato's *Crito* and Martin Luther King, Jr.'s "Letter from Birmingham Jail" ought to produce some interesting interpretive results.

Given their various thematic emphases on humanity, the following student essays ought to pair nicely with Milgram's piece: Kevin Mullen's "Writing: A Leap of Faith" (p. 17), Shehla Yamani's "The Dilemma" (p. 154), and Mahshid Hajir's "The Lesson" (p. 213). Since all of the readings in Chapter Four have to do with the Holocaust, and since Milgram's work has so much bearing on that event, using these readings, too, along with the Milgram piece should yield excellent results; Fred E. Katz's "A Sociological Perspective to the Holocaust" (p. 95), Christopher R. Browning's "Ordinary Men" (p. 107), and Abram L. Sachar's "The Carob Tree Grove: Christian Compassion" (p. 113) ought to work especially well. Other readings that might also prove useful are Alice Miller's "The Vicious Circle of Contempt" (p. 60), Alice Walker's "Elethia" (p. 240), Mitsuye Yamada's "Invisibility is an Unnatural Disaster: Reflections of an Asian American Woman" (p. 335), and Cherríe Moraga's "My Brother's Sex Was White. Mine, Brown" (p. 376).

POSSIBLE ASSIGNMENTS

If you use the second post-reading question (p. 289), you might want to append the following line to that assignment: "Cite and explain the significance of examples from your own or others' experiences to support or prove your claims."

Especially if you use the class experiment to which I refer in my previous comments, you might want to use the following either in addition to or as part of the fourth pre-reading question: If you were a participant in an experiment in which you were told by the scientist in charge to administer electric shocks to a subject each time that the subject answered one of the experimental questions incorrectly, would you administer the shocks? Why or why not?

If you decide to use the first pre-reading question, you might want to append the following to that question: If you read Fred E. Katz's "A Sociological Perspective to the Holocaust" (p. 95) and thus have gained some insight into how one social scientist investigates and tries to explain the ways in which ordinary people can end up committing evil acts, you might try using your newfound insight to help you gain some understanding of Milgram's approaches to and analyses of this same problem.

Here are some other possibilities for assignments:

1) In extreme cases, unreflective obedience to authority can result in mass tragedies such as the slaughtering of civilians in Bosnia and Cambodia and the attempted destruction of European Jewry during the Holocaust. Indeed, as social scientist Thomas Blass says, the results of Milgram's experiments imply "that anyone—not just the Nazis and their collaborators—would have been a willing participant in the destruction of European Jewry during World War II." In a well-focused essay, discuss whether or not you agree with these views (perhaps you both agree and disagree with them). To help prove or support your claims, feel free to use material from Christopher R. Browning's "Ordinary Men" (p. 107),

Fred E. Katz's "A Sociological Perspective to the Holocaust" (p. 95), Rudolph Höss' "Early Years" (p. 290), or any other reading selection in this book.

2) [After explaining to your class the distinctions among the "dispositional," "situational," and "interactional" approaches to the problem of obedience to authority (see my comments, above), you might ask your students to do the following assignment.] For Milgram, a study of the "situational" aspects of obedience to authority demonstrates what he argues is "perhaps . . . the most fundamental lesson" of the study (paragraph 39): that, under the right circumstances, "ordinary people, simply doing their jobs, and without any particular hostility on their part, can become agents in a terrible destructive process" (ibid.). Discuss whether or not, in your view, the situational approach can help us to understand the issues at stake in any of this chapter's other readings, too. Might a dispositional or interactional approach to these issues yield better interpretive results? Is none of these approaches applicable to a study of these important issues? To help prove or support your claims, feel free to use material from Christopher R. Browning's "Ordinary Men" (p. 107), Fred E. Katz's "A Sociological Perspective to the Holocaust" (p. 95), Rudolph Höss' "Early Years" (p. 290), or any other reading selection in this book.

3) Evaluate your response to the fifth post-reading question concerning the featured reading selection (p. 265) in light of what you have learned from having studied Milgram's essay. Also, discuss how you think that Milgram might respond to Freud's view and how Freud might read (that is, interpret) Milgram's findings. Finally, discuss whether or not you might have responded differently to Freud's view had you read Milgram's essay prior to seeing or knowing about that view.

4) Analyze Milgram's descriptions of Gretchen Brandt (paragraph 12), Fred Prozi (paragraph 21), Morris Braverman (paragraph 22), and Bruno Batta (paragraph 43). Is Milgram perhaps doing more here than merely *describing* these people? If so, does his language affect his interpretations of the data corresponding to these subjects' responses? Are there any other instances in which Milgram's language *per se* is food for thought?

RUDOLPH HÖSS
Early Years

THINGS TO THINK ABOUT

I find this excerpt from Höss' autobiography frightening. It forces us to ask some very probing and difficult questions about the relationship between child-rearing practices and adult behavior, and it presents a sobering view of what are at least the *appearances* of normalcy (concerning individuals, families, cultural values, and so on). The only recommendation that I want to give you here is that, although you certainly could teach the Höss piece by itself, you probably will help your students understand it more fully if you pair it with one or more of the corollary selections listed below, especially the selection by Alice Miller. Whatever you do, be patient, and proceed cautiously with your students—and be prepared for them to resist, deny, or in some other way try to avoid dealing with the larger implications of the Höss piece, especially those that directly affect them, their families, their religious beliefs and practices, their cultural values, and so on. I would think that very few of your students are likely to admit *with full sincerity* that they themselves have the capability to be another Höss, which is to say, that they have the capability to be the supervisor of a death camp. And yet, the philosopher Bertrand Russell, observing Höss during the latter's war crimes trial, described the former Commandant of Auschwitz as "'a very ordinary little man'" (Katz, *Ordinary People and Extraordinary Evil: A Report on the Beguilings of Evil* [Albany, New York: State University Press of New York, 1993], p. 17).

COROLLARY READINGS

In my comments concerning the corollary readings for the *Genesis* material, I caution against a facile pairing of that material with the Höss reading. With respect to the comments that I make in the previous section, I would like to add that, although you should find it useful to pair the Höss selection with the Alice Miller material in this chapter, as well as with her piece "The Vicious Circle of Contempt" (p. 226), you'll want to exercise some caution when doing so. Höss was an ordinary man, yes; but his actions were anything but ordinary, and the explanations of those actions are anything but simple. As we engage our students in some intellectually challenging tasks here, let's remember to help them understand that quick and easy answers to difficult problems often prove to be well off the mark.

These cautions notwithstanding, the Höss excerpt does work well with this chapter's other readings, as it does to varying degrees and in various ways with many, and perhaps even most, of the book's other reading selections. You should find especially useful corollary material in Kevin Mullen's "Writing: A Leap of Faith" (p. 17), all of the readings in Chapter Four, with the exception of Jay Julos' "Why I Write" (p. 86), and all of the readings in Chapter Six. However, given the haunting ability of the themes in the Höss excerpt to correlate with so many of the other themes that your students will be studying, I would highly recommend that you encourage your students to roam freely among this book's various reading selections in their search for corollary—including, and perhaps especially, their search for disturbingly corollary—material.

POSSIBLE ASSIGNMENTS

If your students have read Dylan Thomas' "Reminiscences of Childhood" (p. 220) and you are using the fourth pre-reading question concerning the Höss piece (p. 290), you might want to append the following to this pre-reading question: Keep your thoughts about Thomas' essay in mind as you read the Höss material. Then, after you have read this material, compare Höss' childhood to the childhood that Thomas describes. Do you trust one author's narrative more than you trust the other's? If so, why? If not, why not?

Here are some other ideas for possible assignments:

1) Write a character analysis of the Rudolph Höss whom you meet in this reading selection. Is he similar to or different from you or from people you know personally? Do you find it significant or ironic that, despite his having to "carry out the requests and orders of parents, teachers, priests, and all adults, even the servants" (paragraph 8), Höss would "sneak off to the barns when [he] was supposed to be taking a nap" (paragraph 3), or, "[w]hen [his] parents were away, . . . would take [his pony] up to [his] room" (paragraph 6)? Feel free to incorporate into your essay any relevant material from your responses to the pre- and post-reading questions concerning "Early Years."

2) Based on your understanding of what Höss says in "Early Years," evaluate the following remarks that he makes later in his memoirs, remarks concerning Hitler's order to kill all of the Jews of Europe. To help prove or support your claims, feel free to cite and explain the meaning or significance of evidence from any of this book's other readings.

> It goes without saying that the Hitler order was a firm fact for all of us, and also that it was the duty of the SS to carry it out. However, secret doubts tormented all of us. Under no circumstances could I reveal my secret doubts to anyone. I had to convince myself to be like a rock when faced with the necessity of carrying out this horribly severe order, and I had to show this in every way, in order to force all those under me to hang on mentally and emotionally. (161)

3) Write an essay in which you analyze how Alice Miller or Stanley Milgram might evaluate what Höss says 1) in "Early Years," 2) in those of his remarks cited in the second post-reading question, and 3) in those of his remarks that I [that is, that you, the instructor] have brought to your attention.

4) Write an essay in which you imagine Höss as a subject in Milgram's experiment. Using some of the experimenter's lines (which are cited in Milgram's essay), suggest responses, attitudes, and comments by Höss that seem appropriate, given what you know of Höss. Throughout your paper, analyze these responses, attitudes, and comments. At the end of your paper, offer a conclusion that adequately reflects reliable data. To help yourself create a good essay, you might try prewriting in response to the following kinds of questions: Whom among the subjects discussed in Milgram's article does Höss most resemble? Whom does he *least* resemble? How might he respond were he a subject in that variation of the experiment in which his two fellow "teachers" refused to continue with the experiment? If the experimenter were to put Höss in charge of the experiment, what might Höss do? If Höss, in charge of the experiment, instructed *me* to shock the "learner," would I? And how might he analyze my answer to this question?

PLATO

Crito

THINGS TO THINK ABOUT

Though *Crito* is a self-contained text, you might want either to supplement it with the *Apology*, which documents Socrates' defense and provides a good lead-in to *Crito*, or to spend some time summarizing for your students the details of Socrates' trial. In terms of helping my students understand the political context of Socrates' imprisonment, I've not found any appreciable difference in using one or the other of these two approaches.

You may or may not also want to share with your students Hugh Tredennick's speculation (which I don't think is unique) that "[s]ome delay in [Socrates'] execution must have been foreseen[,] and [that] it is possible that Socrates' enemies expected or intended that he should escape and leave the country" (77; for full bibliographical details concerning *The Last Days of Socrates*, from which this quotation is taken, see p. ?? in the "Works Cited" section of the text proper). Unfortunately, I don't know how acceptable Tredennick's speculation is among historians or scholars; however, I have found that this speculation sometimes serves as a useful prompt for class discussions.

Finally, in all likelihood, not all of your students will agree that Socrates made the right decision to remain in prison. During discussions of this issue, students on both sides of the question might very well appeal to the fact that Socrates never doubts the legitimacy of the State's laws. In my own classes, discussions concerning these two matters not only yield excellent interpretations concerning *Crito*, but also help students prepare for a comparative analysis of Plato's dialogue and this chapter's final reading selection, Martin Luther King, Jr.'s "Letter from Birmingham Jail."

COROLLARY READINGS

King's essay, alluded to above, makes for such a good corollary reading with Plato's dialogue that I rarely use the one reading without also using the other. Indeed, though all of this chapter's readings pair well with the Plato selection, none does so as well as does the King essay.

In light of Socrates' deep interest in and commitment to justice and reason, as well as in light of Socrates' having been terribly wronged, I suggest that you also consider using one or more of the following readings as corollary selections: Kevin Mullen's "Writing: A Leap of Faith" (p. 17), Lewis Carroll's "Who Stole the Tarts?" (p. 32), the excerpt from *Black Elk Speaks* (p. 52), Louie Crew's "Thriving As An Outsider, Even As An Outcast, In Smalltown America" (p. 146), Shehla Yamani's "The Dilemma" (p. 154), the excerpt from Alice Walker's "Elethia" (p. 240), and the readings contained in Chapter Eight.

POSSIBLE ASSIGNMENTS

If you have your students do the sixth pre-reading question (p. 296), you might also ask them either to respond to the first pre-reading question and the first (and possibly second) post-reading questions concerning the Burton M. Leiser reading selection (p. 180) or to review the responses that they made to these questions.

Here are some ideas for other possible assignments:

1) Before reading Plato's *Crito*, look up the word "patriot" in your dictionary, paying particular attention to this word's etymology (that is, its root). Then, read *Crito*. In light of your understanding of Plato's dialogue, write an essay in which you analyze the ways in which this piece sheds light on the concept of patriotism. Does Plato's dialogue also shed light on what is at stake in any of this chapter's (or book's) other readings having to do with issues concerning the relationship (or simply the analogy) between families and governments? Do your understandings of these other readings (and of the denotative and connotative meanings of the word patriot) shed light on what is at stake in Plato's work? (If appropriate, review your responses to the fourth and fifth post-reading questions concerning the featured reading selection; see p. 265.)

2) Write an essay in which you analyze whether or not Socrates' asking "rhetorical questions" enhances or undermines the effectiveness of his points (or does both). (A rhetorical question is a non-open-ended question that a person asks in order to achieve a certain effect; the person asking the question already has an answer in mind.) Or, if you prefer, analyze the relationship between the substantive matter in Socrates' rhetorical questions and his views concerning right moral conduct, especially in terms of how these views affect his decision to remain in prison.

3) Compare Socrates' and Martin Luther King, Jr.'s views concerning whether or not an individual is obligated to obey the laws of the State. To help prove or support your points, cite and, if necessary, elucidate pertinent textual evidence.

MARTIN LUTHER KING, JR.

Letter from Birmingham Jail

THINGS TO THINK ABOUT

To help your students gain the most from their study of this exceptionally fine and eminently provocative essay, you might want to show them, before they read this essay, a good documentary covering King's life and work (*I Have a Dream* is a very good film to use for this purpose). Also useful is the *Eyes on the Prize* series; the video that highlights important events in Albany, Georgia, includes a brief segment in which King reads aloud from his "Letter from Birmingham Jail."

Though few people can match King's rhetorical abilities, you will probably help your students appreciate King's oratorical prowess if you read to them from his letter. I have had particularly good luck reading the entirety of paragraph 14, a performance that I set up by lecturing at some length on some of the crucial issues at stake (see paragraph 13). In paragraph 14, King uses temporal subordinating conjunctions in the longest periodic sentence that I've ever seen, forcing readers/listeners to wait for a long, long time before they discover the sentence's main clause. As they wait, they hear one subordinating clause after another in which King describes with terrible clarity the indignities visited upon Black Americans. Whether or not readers find themselves empathizing with Black Americans after finally reading or hearing the sentence's main clause, in which King tells his readers "then you will understand why we find it difficult to wait" (paragraph 14), King has made his point—rhetorically, emotionally, and, in my mind, soundly.

I'll end these comments by making just one more point. One of the central issues in King's letter has to do with King's proposal that people obey some laws and disobey others. King knows that his ability to make a reasonable case for his position hinges on his ability to demonstrate that his and his followers' views on and actions concerning this matter are not arbitrary. A former student of mine pointed out, in a brilliant paper that she wrote on King's essay, that perhaps the best way for us to understand King's ultimately convincing view on this matter is to understand its solid grounding in the notion that law is a function of justice. In effect, the argument runs, only a just law is a true law, for only a just law squares with natural laws or God's laws. Since an unjust law squares with neither, it is not a true law. Segregation laws don't square with either God's laws or natural laws, and thus they are unjust laws. It follows, then, that people who break segregation laws are not breaking true laws, since segregation laws, which are unjust laws, are not true laws. Moreover, those who break segregation laws are displaying respect for true laws.

To be sure, I've greatly reduced the complexity of King's (and my student's) position here. But I think that you see where this explanation is going. Please feel free to use it if you think that it might help your students appreciate King's intellectual and rhetorical sophistication.

COROLLARY READINGS

As I suggest above in my comments concerning the corollary readings for Plato's *Crito*, Plato's dialogue works extremely well in conjunction with King's essay. To varying degrees and in various ways, the rest of the chapter's readings work well, too, but none, in my view, works as well with King's piece as does the Plato selection. Of the many other readings in this text with which you could profitably pair the King essay, I would suggest the following, each of which, in its own way, treats or responds to the issue of discrimination and injustice in terms of compassion and/or nonviolence: the excerpt from Abram L. Sachar's "The Carob Tree Grove: Christian Compassion" (p. 113); Louie Crew's "Thriving As An Outsider, Even As An Outcast, In Smalltown America" (p. 146); Shehla Yamani's "The Dilemma" (p. 154); the excerpt from Maya Angelou's *I Know Why the Caged Bird Sings* (p. 207); Mahshid Hajir's "The Lesson" (p. 213); Alice Miller's "The Vicious Circle of Contempt" (p. 226); and Kathleene West's "Grandmother's Garden" (p. 234).

POSSIBLE ASSIGNMENTS

If you use the seventh post-reading question (p. 324), you might want to append the following to it: Would King and Socrates share the same point of view concerning this issue? Might their different social positions bear on how they might respond to the question of whether or not a citizen is necessarily obligated to obey the laws of his or her state or country? To help make your scenario credible, base your script on what each author actually says in his own work as well as on your understanding of both authors' views concerning the relevant issues at stake.

Here are some additional ideas for possible assignments:

1) Prior to redefining his group of demonstrators as "insiders," King says that he came to Birmingham to take part in "nonviolent direct-action program[s] . . . because [he] was invited [there]" (paragraph 2). Write an essay in which you explain whether or not King's reason legitimizes his actions. More generally, to what extent do you feel that the excuse "we were asked to come here" legitimizes actions taken by "outsiders" on territory belonging to "insiders"? How do you think that King might answer this question? Can you cite instances of outside intervention concerning which you approve and instances concerning which you disapprove?

2) Write an essay in which you discuss how you think that King might interpret Langston Hughes' poem "Theme for English B" (p. 244). How might he characterize the poem's persona? Cite and explain the significance of pertinent textual evidence from both King's essay and Hughes' poem to prove or support your contentions.

3) King argues that "an individual who breaks a law that conscience tells him is unjust, and who willingly accepts the penalty of imprisonment in order to arouse the conscience of the community over its injustice, is in reality expressing the highest respect for law" (paragraph 20). Evaluate this perspective from the standpoint of King's attempts to distinguish just from unjust laws. At some point in your evaluation, you might want to answer questions such as the following: If someone whose conscience is awry breaks a just law, is that person still "in reality expressing the highest respect for the law"? Could a segregationist legitimately appeal to the principle that King articulates in order to justify her or his attempts to stop desegregation from occurring in her or his community? (To prepare for this assignment, you might find it helpful to read [or reread] Burton M. Leiser's comments concerning "laws of nature"; see p. 174.)

4) As you read in Chapter Five, writers never write in a vacuum, and they always write for an intended audience. For this assignment, write an essay in which you offer, develop, and then try either to prove or to support a thesis that answers the following question: Is King's essay limited because King writes it (at least ostensibly) in order to convince his fellow clergymen that his and his followers' actions are moral and legitimate and that, moreover, the clergy ought to support the cause of civil rights far more actively than they have supported it thus far? (Here's a shorter version of this question: Does King's essay reach beyond the limits of its intended purpose and speak to readers beyond those few to whom it is

[again, ostensibly] written?) Clarify and develop your ideas as fully as possible, drawing evidence from King's essay and, if appropriate, from other readings in this book to prove or support your points.

INDIVIDUAL, GROUP, AND/OR CLASS ACTIVITIES

1) Discuss whether or not—and, if so, to what extent—any of your views concerning the issue of obedience to authority has changed as a result of your having studied this chapter's readings. Are your views concerning this issue aligned with those of any of the authors of this chapter's reading selections? In your opinion, which of the views presented in this chapter's readings were the strongest? Which were the weakest? Which were somewhere in between? Be sure to cite and explain the meaning or significance of pertinent evidence to show that your opinion is informed.

2) In a self-critical reference to one of the top Nazi officials in charge of carrying out the "Final Solution to the Jewish Question," Morris Braverman, a subject in Stanley Milgram's obedience experiments, said, "'As my wife said, "You can call yourself Eichmann"'" (paragraph 33). In a section of his memoirs not reprinted in this chapter, Rudolph Höss says, ". . . I have to confess openly that after [certain] conversations with Eichmann [concerning the carrying out of the 'Final Solution'] [my] human emotions seemed almost like treason against the Führer. There was no escaping this conflict as far as I was concerned. I had to continue to carry out the process of destruction" (163). Talk about how the authors of this chapter's readings (including Höss himself) might respond to these two statements. Cite and explain the significance of pertinent textual evidence from their work to prove or support your claims.

3) Discuss what three or more of the authors whose works appear in this chapter—including, if you wish, the chapter's contributing author—might say to each other in a televised roundtable discussion of the question concerning whether or not (and, if so, the conditions under which) an individual should obey authority figures or be loyal to religious, governmental, educational, or other kinds of institutions of authority. Citing relevant passages from the authors' works, be specific not only about the issues that each of the authors would raise concerning religion, the power of the father, patriarchy, patriotism, loyalty, and the like, but also about the authors' views on these issues. What points in each other's work might particularly interest all of these authors, for example? On which points would they likely agree? On which points might they take issue with each other? As a way to start the discussion, you might pose the following questions for them to answer: "In your view, what qualities must an authority have to be considered an authority? Does it matter whether the authority in question is a recognizable member of the family, a deity, a member of a respectable profession, or that nebulous construct which we call 'the State'? Are all authorities to be obeyed *as* authorities simply by virtue of their *being* authorities? Could someone or some group *reasonably* assert that some authorities must always be obeyed but that others need not always be obeyed? If so, would you please give specific examples to help the audience understand your points? They would be especially grateful if you would

draw at least some of your examples from your work or from the work of your fellow panelists."

4) Discuss the different forms of writing and the different writing styles that you came across in this chapter's reading selections. Were some forms and styles more effective than others? Having read some or all of this chapter's readings, can you draw any general conclusions about the relationship between form and content in writing?

Chapter Eight: Incorporating the Personal into the Academic Essay

INSTRUCTIONAL ISSUES

Like J. Kehaulani Kauanui, this chapter's contributing author, many of your students might enjoy writing the kind of paper discussed in this chapter (to the degree that they enjoy writing any kind of paper, that is). Nevertheless, despite your best teaching efforts, some probably will remain uncertain about the extent to which they should try to prove or support their points by means of personal data and the extent to which they should try to prove or support them by means of other than personal data. When my own students find themselves grappling with these issues, I tell them that having such a concern is the mark of a careful writer, and not of a careless one. Then, I try to help them see why writers need to make decisions concerning this matter on a case by case basis. Using the instructional material in this chapter to help them with their own work, and giving them quite a bit of leeway to make the decisions that are right for them, I usually discover that most of my students eventually produce a good, or at least a satisfactory, personally driven academic paper. Hopefully, this chapter's instructional material will help you have similar luck with your own students.

FEATURED READING

MITSUYE YAMADA

Invisibility is an Unnatural Disaster: Reflections of an Asian American Woman

THINGS TO THINK ABOUT

Though Yamada's essay tends to be challenging for all students, it is especially challenging for those who have only a superficial or unreflective understanding of the issues that Yamada addresses and the views that she espouses. Interestingly, I have found this to be the case for both liberal and conservative students, for both males and females, for both foreign students and U.S. citizens, and for both minority and nonminority students.

I often find a particularly high incidence of this problem among my younger female students. If your younger female students display this problem, too, you might try to help them overcome it by helping them to see the extent to which they are engaged in acts of what I call "intra-victimization," that is, victimization that turns inward (either between/among victims or with respect to an individual victim). Using Yamada's essay as your guide, you might try to help them understand the extent to which their misogynist discourse is deeply rooted in the anti-female discourse of historical and current patriarchies, a discourse that encourages men to distance themselves from women and that encourages women to distance themselves from each other. Though tragic, female misogyny need not be a permanent state of affairs, a point that I've learned from watching a number of my female students begin to overcome this problem in themselves. A very bright, young female student of mine, for example, once confessed to me that she disliked feminism, and that she found both a source and support for her dislike in Rush Limbaugh's views on feminism! Fortunately, she allowed herself to question her own attitudes. If memory serves me correctly, Yamada's essay was an impetus for both her confession to me and her change in attitude.

THE FEATURED ASSIGNMENT AND THE CONTRIBUTING AUTHOR'S MODEL RESPONSE

To help your students produce a good paper in response to the featured assignment, you might want to offer them the following advice (or a modified version of this advice, one that matches the tone of your own pedagogical voice): "To help yourself generate some ideas for writing, think about an issue that Yamada discusses which grabbed your attention. Then, think about whether or not, with respect to this issue, you've had any experiences similar to hers and whether the two of you reacted to and analyzed your respective experiences similarly, differently, or both. Once you've begun organizing your thoughts along these lines, consider whether you want to (1) subordinate an analysis of your personal experiences to an analysis of whichever of Yamada's views that you decide to highlight, (2) subordinate an analysis of her view to an evaluation of your own personal experiences, or (3) maintain a balance between these two approaches.

"For rhetorical effect, you might want to ease into your analysis by recounting the opening scene in Yamada's essay and then explaining whether you identify with Yamada, her students, both, or neither. Or, you might want to begin your essay by devising an opening scene of your own, by citing and explaining the significance of a relevant, provocative quotation (perhaps from one of the reading selections contained in this book), or by simply plunging right into your own analysis. Whatever organizational procedure you adopt for your paper, be sure that your approach meets the needs of your essay and that your essay fulfills the needs of the assignment."

J. Kehaulani Kauanui's model paper is substantively strong and personally honest—a strong mix of the two thematic ingredients in a personally driven academic paper. The relaxed, more or less informal writing in her commentary provides a useful contrast to the formal prose in her essay. If nothing else, seeing this contrast ought to help your students better understand how writers write with an eye towards the particular needs of a writing project, how they try to take their intended audiences into account, and the like. All in all, you should find, as I have found, that Kehaulani's work stands as a good model response to the featured assignment.

COROLLARY READINGS

Aside from this chapter's related readings, the following readings might correlate well with Yamada's essay; in its own way, each documents or at least tacitly deals with more than one of the inter- and intrapersonal struggles to which Yamada refers in her own piece: Sandra Cisneros' "My Name" (p. 46); the excerpt from Alice Bloch's *The Law of Return* (p. 60); Kathleene West's "Grandmother's Garden" (p. 234); Louie Crew's "Thriving As An Outsider, Even As An Outcast, In Smalltown America" (p. 146); the excerpt from Maya Angelou's *I Know Why the Caged Bird Sings* (p. 207); Alice Walker's "Elethia" (p. 240); and Langston Hughes' "Theme for English B" (p. 244).

ALTERNATE ASSIGNMENTS

If you have your students answer the third pre-reading question (p. 336), you might want them to append the following to that apparatus: If you respond "yes" to either question, explain the nature of the circumstances under which the incident(s) took place. As you reflect on this incident (or on these incidents), do you experience any of the same feelings that you experienced at the time that the incident(s) occurred?

You might also want to amend this pre-reading question to include the following two queries: Have you ever discounted someone else's ideas because of who or what she/he is? Did you accept these same (or similar) ideas when they were expressed by someone whom you respected? Did you ever find yourself in the middle rather than on either side of this sort of conflict?

The following are ideas for other assignments:

1) Compare the ways in which Mitsuye Yamada's essay and one other reading selection from this chapter (including the essay by the chapter's contributing author) address the multidimensional aspects of sexism and oppression. How do the two readings document and comment upon the problems of women's invisibility and female intra-victimization, for example? Does each essay end on an uplifting note—a note of redemptive promise, perhaps?

2) Write an essay in which you describe what happened when you tried to defend a seemingly controversial point of view in a discussion with someone who, no matter what kind of evidence you presented, simply would not listen to reason. Or, write an essay in which you describe what happened when *you* acted in-

tractably towards someone who, in a discussion with you, tried to defend what you considered a controversial point of view. In either case, compare your experiences with relevant ones that Yamada discusses (for example, with those that she discusses concerning her confrontations with her parents). Also, discuss whether or not her views have affected your thinking, perhaps making you feel the need to rethink your attitudes and feelings concerning the issues at stake here.

3) Explain what you think is meant by the expression "seen but not heard." Clarify your ideas by citing and explaining the significance of pertinent examples. If you've never heard this expression, explain what you think that it might mean and in what circumstances you think that it might be used. Given your understanding of Yamada's essay, would you argue that she and you probably have a similar understanding of this expression?

RELATED READINGS

ANNE WILSON SCHAEF
from Women's Reality

THINGS TO THINK ABOUT

Although I have used Schaef's material with much success, I have also found it necessary to deal with two problems in *Women's Reality*. The first problem is methodological. To be sure, Schaef admits that her research "is generally classified under the heading, 'soft research'" (*Women's Reality* xvi). Nevertheless, as many of my students have rightly noted (though in different words from those that I'm about to use), too often she engages in the kind of unreflective interpretive practices that, as she herself correctly argues, help to ground misogynistic discourse. On the other hand, as I try to argue in class, whether or not she presents corresponding data to prove or support her contentions, she almost always seems to be right.

Concerning the second problem, though, Schaef cannot be so easily let off the hook, I'm afraid. As a student of mine noted in a brilliantly written analysis of her text, although Schaef does acknowledge that not all women are the same, she often speaks of women as if they were. Whether or not this problem is troubling in and of itself, when it is evaluated in the context of legitimate complaints that the women's movements in the United States have spoken mostly for White, middle- to upper-class, heterosexual women, this problem takes on a very troubling aspect indeed. As my student asked in his paper, how many of Schaef's clients are poor or are otherwise socially disadvantaged women? How many poor, disenfranchised women attend her group therapy retreats? Despite her sincere attempts to recognize the differences among different groups of people, Schaef seems to base many of her conclusions about male-female relationships and about women's ways of thinking and behaving on the data that she collects from working with her clients, who seem to be, more or less, in the class of privileged women.

Having said all of this, I want to repeat that I have used Schaef's material with much success. Many of my female students feel that Schaef has voiced their concerns quite well. And, after reading Schaef's work, a number of my male students find themselves admitting that Schaef has made enough good cases to force them to rethink at least some of their views. Both male and female students seem to find that Schaef's work helps them generate some very good ideas for writing. Whatever its faults, then, an instructor could want little more from a reading selection, especially one used in a writing class.

COROLLARY READINGS

This chapter's other readings pair very well with the Schaef material, sometimes providing support for her views, and sometimes providing counter-views to her positions. Other useful corollary readings are Sandra Cisneros' "My Name" (p. 46), the excerpt from *Black Elk Speaks* (p. 52), Louie Crew's "Thriving As An Outsider, Even As An Outcast, In Smalltown America" (p. 146), Jan Parker's "The Tables Need Turning" (p. 191), Kathleene West's "Grandmother's Garden" (p. 234), and Alice Walker's "Elethia" (p. 240).

POSSIBLE ASSIGNMENTS

1) Consider the following line that you might have seen on buttons and bumper stickers: "The best man for the job is a woman." Explain what, in your view, this saying means, both denotatively and connotatively. How do you feel when you hear such a line, and why do you feel this way? To help clarify your ideas, cite and explain the significance of specific examples that seem relevant to your points, and explain why you think that these examples help to prove or support your claims. When possible, refer to the Schaef material to help make your case.

2) In his introduction to Heinz Heger's *The Men with the Pink Triangle*, David Fernbach writes the following:

> [I]t was quite fundamental to Nazi ideology that men were to be properly
> 'masculine', and women properly 'feminine', and that homosexuality went
> diametrically against this 'Nordic' tradition. . . . [W]hen male homosexuality
> disguises itself as a cult of 'manliness' and virility, it is less obnoxious from the
> fascist standpoint than is the softening of the gender division that
> homosexuality invariably involves when it is allowed to express itself freely.
> (Fernbach, in Heger 11)

Explain how you think that Schaef might evaluate this analysis. How do *you* evaluate it? Can you think of any present-day examples that would either confirm or contradict Fernbach's claims? (Before doing this assignment, you might want to take another look at paragraph 8 of Schaef's work.)

3) Write an essay in which you explain whether, in general, you find Schaef's analyses to be more or less deep and full or rather superficial and oversimplified (or something in between). In your attempts to be fair, keep in mind that, in the introduction to her book, Schaef acknowledges that her research "is generally

classified under the heading, 'soft research'" and that "[b]y no means does [her] book present the complete picture" (xvi and xviii).

4) Explain how you think that Schaef might analyze any of this chapter's readings other than her own. Explain, too, how you think that the author of the piece in question might analyze Schaef's analysis. To help prove or support your claims, use examples from the texts in question, as well as, perhaps, from your own experiences.

ADRIANE FUGH-BERMAN
Tales Out of Medical School

THINGS TO THINK ABOUT

If it is successful, Fugh-Berman's essay should cause a stir in your class. Don't be surprised if your students' interpretations of her piece group themselves according to gender or political affinities. And don't be surprised if a number of your students either question the ubiquity of the problems that Fugh-Berman addresses or in some other way try to discredit her. Why the possibility that your class will react to her essay in extreme ways? Because in her trenchant critique of the sexist attitudes in and practices of the medical profession, Fugh-Berman brings to the surface a number of the problematic ideological underpinnings of some of our most trusted (or at least revered) institutions. In all likelihood, many of your students, like many people in general, would rather deny than face the existence or severity of the problems that Fugh-Berman's essay forces us to confront. If you don't mind having controversy enter your class discussions, or, better yet, if you encourage your students to discuss controversial topics because you know the benefits to their thinking and writing that derive from their having such discussions, then you couldn't ask for a better "prompt" than Fugh-Berman's essay.

COROLLARY READINGS

Aside from using this chapter's other readings to supplement the Fugh-Berman essay, you might consider using one or more of the following selections, which, when paired with the Fugh-Berman essay and interpreted within a context of a comparative analysis, ought to yield some interesting and provocative results: Sandra Cisneros' "My Name" (p. 46); Alice Bloch, from *The Law of Return* (p. 60); Claude Lanzmann, from *Shoah* (p. 92); Sigmund Freud's "The Sexual Aberrations" (p. 163); Jan Parker's "The Tables Need Turning" (p. 191); Alice Walker's "Elethia" (p. 240); and Martin Luther King, Jr.'s "Letter from Birmingham Jail" (p. 308).

POSSIBLE ASSIGNMENTS

If you use the first pre-reading question (p. 361), you might want to append the following to it: For example, do you think that, as a general rule, female physicians are as qualified and capable as their male counterparts? In general, do you prefer having an appointment with a male physician or with a female physician? Are there particular circumstances under which you would prefer to see a female physician rather than a male one (or vice versa)?

If you use the third pre-reading question (p. 361), you might want to amend it by adding the following to it: Did you notice other sorts of biases, too—say, cultural or political ones? If so, do some or all of these biases seem grounded in similar assumptions?

Here are some ideas for other possible assignments:

1) Early in her article, Fugh-Berman says that "Georgetown built disrespect for women into its curriculum" (paragraph 1). Discuss whether or not you think that she adequately proves this claim. Does her claim (and her attempts to prove it) correspond to anything that you said in your answer to the third pre-reading question? Do you want to amend that answer in light of your understanding of Fugh-Berman's analysis?

2) Explain how one might argue that an understanding of the information presented in paragraphs 11–13 of Fugh-Berman's essay is essential to an understanding of both Fugh-Berman's experiences and her analysis of those experiences. As you prepare to answer this question, think about the nature and consequences of *indifference* and *blaming the victim*.

3) Some readers of this article might be tempted to ask, "If the author didn't like the way that she was treated in medical school, then why didn't she leave? Why didn't she try to transfer to a different medical school? Or, if she was that unhappy with the medical profession (at least as she perceived it), why didn't she choose to enter another profession?" Write an essay in which you explain how you think that the author might respond to these questions. Include in your essay comments concerning how you think that Mitsuye Yamada, Anne Wilson Schaef, or Louie Crew (see pp. 335, 347, and 146) might respond to it, too.

4) Perform a close reading of an important line or passage from Fugh-Berman's essay, showing the line's interpretive meaning and/or significance both in and of itself and to the essay as a whole. Try to prove or support your contentions by drawing from and explicating examples from Fugh-Berman's essay, from this book's other readings, from your own experiences, and/or from other relevant sources. The following are some possible passages for you to consider analyzing in detail:

> Teaching rounds were often, for women, a spectator sport. One friend told me how she craned her neck to watch a physician teach a minor surgical procedure to a male student; when they were done the physician handed her his dirty gloves to discard. (paragraph 6)

> Such instances of casual sexism are hardly unique to Georgetown, or indeed to medical schools. But at Georgetown female students also had to contend with outright discrimination of a sort most Americans probably think no longer exists in education. (paragraph 9)

> Only two of the eleven lectures [on human sexuality] focused on women; of the two lectures on homosexuality, neither mentioned lesbians. The psychiatrist

who co-taught the class treated us to one lecture that amounted to an apology for rape: Aggression, even hostility, is normal in sexual relations between a man and a woman, he said, and inhibition of aggression in men can lead to impotence. (paragraph 15)

IRWIN SHAW

The Girls in Their Summer Dresses

THINGS TO THINK ABOUT

I have found that Shaw's story always generates excellent class discussions. Of the many issues and topics that surface during these discussions, none seems to provoke more emotion from both male and female students than do those concerning Frances' responses to Michael's attitude about and behavior towards other women and, conversely, Michael's reactions to Frances' responses to his rather overt interest in (nay, his rather clear desire for) other women. The most heated debates concerning Michael that I've heard among students have to do with whether or not he himself is or could be seen as a victim. Concerning Frances' responses to Michael's attitude and behavior, students often talk passionately about what Frances does or doesn't do and about whether or not they think she is at least partly responsible for her husband's attitudes and behavior (if your students discuss this issue, you might find it helpful to take them through a close reading of paragraphs 28–40 and 57–62).

Clearly, Shaw's story contains much fodder for good class discussions, meaningful student papers, and reflective post-reading and post-writing commentaries. However you and your students handle this story, I think that you'll find it eminently teachable and that both you and they will find it wonderfully provocative. (One more note: if your students are like mine, they might have some fun talking about the fact that this story, published more than 40 years ago, is quite contemporary.)

COROLLARY READINGS

Aside from this chapter's readings, the following selections should correlate well with Shaw's story: Sherwood Anderson's "Certain Things Last: A Writer Warms to His Story" (p. 12); Sandra Cisneros' "My Name" (p. 46); the excerpt from Alice Bloch's *The Law of Return* (p. 60); the excerpt from Claude Lanzmann's *Shoah* (p. 92); and Kathleene West's "Grandmother's Garden" (p. 234).

POSSIBLE ASSIGNMENTS

1) Reread paragraphs 28–40 and 57–62. Then, in a carefully focused essay, perform a close reading of either of these sets of paragraphs, indicating the importance of the paragraph's details in and of themselves and to the story as a whole. If you prefer, you may choose other sets of paragraphs to analyze closely.

2) Characters in a story, like people in real life, rarely talk in a monotone. In an essay whose thesis concerns the relationship between tone and meaning in Shaw's story, explain how you would expressively read key lines in this story—for example, Frances' lines in paragraphs 3, 4, 22, 36, 40, 59, and 61. Do you use different narrative tones while reading her different lines here? Do your choices of narrative tones reflect the thematic meaning that you find in the lines in question and in the story as a whole?

3) In *Women's Reality*, Anne Wilson Schaef writes the following:

> Women . . . experience an inner space[,] . . . [which] is almost always in the solar plexus. Women use various words and phrases to name it—hole, pit, nothingness, void, "black" space, cavern. We are fearful of it and vulnerable to it. In strange, unfamiliar, or threatening situations, we will often stand with our arms folded over our solar plexus—our *cavern*. Women have also developed body postures that "sink in" and protect this area. We often cover it with fat.
>
> Our cavern is central to our identity and wholeness. . . . It is related to our Original Sin of Being Born Female and our need to look outside ourselves for validation and approval. When we begin to determine who we are from inside, our cavern begins to get smaller. (34; author's italics)

Write an essay in which you explain how you might apply the ideas contained in this passage to an understanding of Frances' own dilemmas, difficulties, and anxieties. Might Schaef's ideas also be applicable to an understanding of Michael's troubles? Do you yourself find Schaef's ideas convincing, or at least provocative? (Note: In her book, Schaef critiques rather than accepts the notion of what she calls women's "Original Sin of Being Born Female.")

DENISE LEVERTOV
The Mutes

THINGS TO THINK ABOUT

I often pair Levertov's poem with Shaw's story, using ideas from the one to highlight or explicate ideas from the other. As is the case with Shaw's story, "The Mutes" tends to generate lots of good class discussion. Among the more hotly debated issues that come up during these discussions is one concerning whether or not there is anything wrong with men's whistling at or in some other way "noticing" women who are walking down the street, sitting in a bar, and the like. As you'll see, Levertov's persona responds to this question ambivalently. So do a number of my students, both male and female. Unfortunately, though, some of the men in my classes feel that there is nothing at all wrong with a man's whistling at or in some other way noticing a woman who is walking down the street and can't understand why women would be offended by such gestures. Sometimes, when a female student challenges male students holding this view, asking them something to the effect of, "How would *you* feel if *women* whistled at *you*," the male students respond with something on the order of barely suppressed glee at the thought of such an occurrence.

After this exchange occurs, I try to help all of my students see that, in general, men and women occupy different power bases in the culture, and that, given that fact, a man's whistling at a woman is not the same gesture *substantively* (though it is the same gesture *superficially*) as is a woman's whistling at a man. (I feel that, if they understand this point, then they'll have a better understanding of some of the poem's meanings.) The latter act, I explain, does not carry the weight of cultural history that the former act does, a history that includes real aggression by men against women. This aggression, I explain further, is symbolized by or at least tacitly present in the act of a man's whistling at a woman (sometimes, I also try to explain this point by talking about it in terms of the continuum theory of violence; see p. ??).

At this point, I usually find that most of my female students understand both explicitly and implicitly what I am saying but that at least a few of my male students still harbor doubts. To help clarify matters, I ask my male students who had expressed their glee at being the object of a woman's gaze and whistle to imagine that they are soldiers on a foreign battlefield, alone, at night, having lost their company. Trying to find their way back to their unit, they hear a voice in broken English say, "Hey, Yankee, I see you, and you die tonight." I then ask these students how they feel now. Are they turned on? Do they want to see fulfilled the promised act of violence and violation? Would they find this act fulfilling? Is this act, perhaps, what they themselves secretly want, what they truly desire? "In other words," I ask them, "when you put yourself in at least a *somewhat* analogous position to that of women who are the objects of men's gazes and whistles, do you still want to be in the position of the vulnerable, potential victim of violation and violence?" Though some men still hold out (or so they make it seem) against my attempts to help them understand the issues at stake here, most, I've discovered, seem to see what I'm driving at by this point in our discussion.

COROLLARY READINGS

Though all of this chapter's other readings pair well with "The Mutes," Shaw's "The Girls in Their Summer Dresses," as suggested above, pairs especially well with it. I would also recommend your considering as corollary readings Sandra Cisneros' "My Name" (p. 46), the excerpt from Alice Bloch's *The Law of Return* (p. 60), and Louie Crew's "Thriving As An Outsider, Even As An Outcast, In Smalltown America" (p. 146).

POSSIBLE ASSIGNMENTS

If you ask your students to answer the third post-reading question (p. 376), you might want to append the following questions to that apparatus: Can you cite and explain the meaning or significance of textual evidence from "The Mutes" attesting to such insight on her part? If you were to ascribe a thesis to this poem, what would that thesis be? Would the evidence that you just cited help to prove or support this thesis?

Here are two ideas for other possible assignments:

1) [If you use this assignment, you should probably have your students answer the second pre- and post-reading questions (pp. 374 and 376).] Many scholars distinguish between the concepts "erotica" and "pornography." For example, in "Erotica and Pornography: A Clear and Present Difference," Gloria Steinem explains that the word "'erotica' is rooted in 'eros' or passionate love, and thus in the idea of positive choice, free will, the yearning for a particular person. (Interestingly, the definition of erotica leaves open the question of gender.) [On the other hand, the word] '[p]ornography' begins with a root 'porno,' meaning 'prostitution' or 'female captives,' thus letting us know that the subject is not mutual love, or love at all, but domination and violence against women. (Though, of course, homosexual pornography may imitate this violence by putting a man in the 'feminine' role of victim.)" (Qtd. in *Take Back the Night*, edited by Laura Lederer [New York: William Morrow and Company, Inc., 1980], p. 37.)

Write an essay in which you explain how your understanding of Levertov's poem influences your evaluation of, or at least helps you to understand, the "clear and present difference" between erotica and pornography to which Gloria Steinem refers. By the same token, explain how your understanding of Steinem's point influences or facilitates your reading of Levertov's poem. Are your feelings about and reactions to the issues that Steinem and the poem's persona raise similar to or different from those that you had (concerning these issues) prior to your having been made aware of Steinem's view (which isn't uniquely hers, by the way) and before you read "The Mutes"?

2) Many women feel vulnerable or afraid when a man whistles or gapes at them; on the other hand, many men say that they would very much enjoy having women whistle or gape at *them*. Given these different reactions, one might suspect that the gestures—that is, a man's gaping or whistling at a woman and a woman's gaping or whistling at a man—are superficially the same but substantively different. Explain whether or not you think that this claim has merit. What evidence might be offered in support of such a claim? What evidence might prove troublesome for it? As much as possible, base your analysis on your understanding of Levertov's poem, other readings in this book, and/or your own or other people's personal experiences.

CHERRÍE MORAGA

My Brother's Sex Was White. Mine, Brown

THINGS TO THINK ABOUT

I would like to cite here a portion of my biographical sketch of Moraga, for the ideas contained in this portion bespeak a crucial aspect of Moraga's work that I think any teacher teaching this work should address: ". . . Moraga's honesty with respect to her own struggles, uncertainties, and vulnerabilities is so disarming that even readers who might otherwise be uncomfortable hearing about the issues that she raises often find themselves, if not sympathizing with her, at least beginning to understand important aspects of the complex relationship among gender, race, class, and sexuality—a relationship the nature of which Moraga expends much energy and emotion trying to explain. Perhaps ironically, this intensely personal writer has opened up avenues of exploration that take both us and her well beyond herself" (p. 377).

I would add to this comment only the point that, the more I teach Moraga's work, the more knowledge I gain about the issues that she raises, and the more humbled I feel in the presence of a truly gifted—indeed, in the presence of a great—writer. If you've never taught her work, I think (and hope) that both you and your students will discover what I discover whenever I use her material in class: nothing short of excellent teaching and learning opportunities, and a wellspring of possibilities for interpretive insight and personal growth.

COROLLARY READINGS

Though Moraga's essay correlates well with the other readings in this chapter, especially Barbara Cameron's "'Gee, You Don't Seem Like An Indian From the Reservation,'" you might consider using, either instead of or in addition to these other readings, Sandra Cisneros' "My Name" (p. 46), the excerpt from Alice Bloch's *The Law of Return* (p. 60), and any of the readings in Chapters Five, Six, and Seven, with the possible exceptions of the student essays in Chapters Six and Seven (though even these pieces might prove useful). Indeed, this reader contains no shortage of pairings for Moraga's essay.

POSSIBLE ASSIGNMENTS

1) Write an essay in which you discuss whether or not you think that, despite environmental influences, men and women *naturally* think and act differently from each other. Does your opinion influence your sense of the efficacy of men's and women's liberation movements? If so, how? Finally, how do you think that Moraga might respond to your views concerning this issue? When possible, cite and explain the significance of pertinent data to prove or support your claims.

2) Introducing one of his most well-known and controversial theories concerning infantile sexuality, Sigmund Freud says that "[l]ittle girls . . . are overcome by envy for the penis—an envy culminating in the wish, which is so important in its consequences, to be boys themselves" (*S.E.*: 7:195). Some people argue that, if we interpret Freud's idea to be a comment on innate male privilege, we'll find much to recommend his claim. Write an essay in which you explain whether or not, in your view, Moraga would likely go along with this sort of interpretation of Freud's idea. Cite and explain the meaning or significance of specific textual evidence that seems pertinent to this discussion and that you think confirms your view. Is there any germane textual evidence that might undermine your view?

Does Freud's view shed light on or make you want to reconsider your response to the fourth pre-reading question?

3) In a well-focused paper, explain the ways in which Moraga's essay teaches us something about the nature and complexities of what we might call intra-victimization, that is, victimization that turns inward, a phenomenon in which we discover members of one disenfranchised group turning against members of another, members of one disenfranchised group turning against members of their own group, or an individual victim turning against himself/herself. To help prove or support your claims, cite and explain the meaning or significance of specific, pertinent textual evidence.

4) Write an essay in which you explain how the author of another of this book's readings might analyze one or more of the following passages from Moraga's essay. When necessary, use textual evidence to prove or support your claims.

> I wanted to machine-gun them all down, but swallowed that fantasy as I swallowed making the boy's bed every day, cleaning his room each week, shining his shoes and ironing his shirts before dates with girls, some of whom *I* had crushes on [author's italics]. I would lend him the money I had earned house-cleaning for twelve hours, so he could blow it on one night with a girl because he seldom had enough money. . . . As I pressed the bills into his hand, the car honking outside in the driveway, his double-date waiting, I knew I would never see that money again. (paragraph 8)

> I have always had a talent for seeing things I don't particularly want to see and the one day my father did come to visit us with his wife/our mother physically dying in a hospital some ten miles away, I saw that he couldn't love us—not in the way we so desperately needed. (paragraph 12)

> In contrast to the seeming lack of feeling I held for my father, my longings for my mother and fear of her dying were the most passionate feelings that had ever lived inside my young heart. (paragraph 14)

BARBARA CAMERON
"Gee, You Don't Seem Like An Indian From the Reservation"

THINGS TO THINK ABOUT

In my comments concerning the excerpt from *Black Elk Speaks* (pp. 10–11), I intimate that many of your students are likely to romanticize or in some other way stereotype Native Americans. Additionally, I imply, many of your students might speak universally or prototypically about Native Americans or about Native American values, beliefs, and lifestyles. As I try to intimate in my comments concerning corollary readings for the Black Elk selection, Barbara Cameron's essay ought to help your students counter (or at least rethink) such problematic interpretive gestures.

But Cameron's essay has more than this utilitarian value. Like Moraga's, it is forthright and honest, emotional and direct, sobering and uplifting. In short, it engages the reader in various ways and at various levels of interest. I find its epilogue a fitting way to end not just the essay, but this entire reader. Indeed, I see in this epilogue an encapsulating of many thematic and instructional issues that this reader has labored hard to articulate. "My sense of time changed," Cameron writes concerning a visit that she had made to her home in South Dakota. As we might hope to hear our students say about their own struggles to reach beyond their grasps, Cameron continues: ". . . my manner of speaking changed, and a certain freedom with myself returned. . . . I was sad to leave but recognized that a significant part of myself has never left and never will. And that part is what gives me strength—the strength of my people's enduring history and continuing belief in the sovereignty of our lives" (paragraphs 26–27).

COROLLARY READINGS

Of this chapter's other readings, all of which can be used to supplement Cameron's essay, the Moraga piece pairs exceptionally well with that essay. Of the book's other reading selections, the excerpt from *Black Elk Speaks* (p. 52) helps to provide a larger historical, political, and social context within which students can interpret Cameron's ideas. Other very useful corollary readings are Sandra Cisneros' "My Name" (p. 46), the excerpt from Alice Bloch's *The Law of Return* (p. 60), Elie Wiesel's "Why I Write" (p. 80), Louie Crew's "Thriving As An Outsider, Even As An Outcast, In Smalltown America" (p. 146), Shehla Yamani's "The Dilemma" (p. 154), the excerpt from Maya Angelou's *I Know Why the Caged Bird Sings* (p. 207), and Langston Hughes' "Theme for English B" (p. 244).

POSSIBLE ASSIGNMENTS

1) Write an essay in which you explain whether Cameron's analysis seems specific to the struggles of this one lesbian Native American feminist or whether it seems to have a wider interpretive application. If your judgment inclines towards the latter, does that judgment affect the essay's impact on you? Does your understanding of Cameron's situation lessen, heighten, or have no effect on your understanding of other people's unfortunate circumstances?

2) Explain the ways in which Anne Wilson Schaef's comments about pollution (see pp. 350–351, paragraphs 12–16) might help us to understand Cameron's point that "[d]eath was so common on the reservation that [Cameron] did not understand the implications of the high death rate until after [she] moved away . . ." (paragraph 7).

3) Explain what Cameron seems to mean when she says, "The easy teasing and joking that were inherent with the Lakota were a welcome relief after a day with the plastic faces" (paragraph 3). Citing and explaining evidence from Cameron's essay to prove or support your claims, discuss the importance of this line both in and of itself and in relation to the essay as a whole.

4) Compare Maya Angelou's narrative to Cameron's, focusing on each author's attempts to explain her experiences with and views on racism. Cite germane textual evidence, as well as, perhaps, evidence from your own life, to help prove or support your points.

INDIVIDUAL, GROUP, AND/OR CLASS ACTIVITIES

1) Discuss the extent to which any of your views concerning the issues discussed in this chapter's readings has changed as a result of your having read these pieces. If you could speak with the authors of these readings, would you try to convince any of them to change her/his views in light of yours? Is there any author who presented views so incompatible with yours or whose material you felt so offended by that you wouldn't even want to speak with her or him? Is there any author with whom you feel a particular affinity?

2) Each of this chapter's readings blatantly or subtly addresses the complicated problem of "invisibility" that many women confront in one form or another. Compare the ways in which *three* of the authors whose works are represented here—including, if you wish, the chapter's contributing author—confront and analyze this problem. Cite and explain the significance of pertinent textual evidence to prove or support your claims. If you want to carry out this task creatively, you might try engaging in some role-playing with other members of your class. Each of you play the part of an author whose work appears in this chapter. In a roundtable discussion, talk about the points in each other's work that particularly interest each of you. On which points would you and your writer colleagues likely agree? On which points might some or all of you disagree?

3) Another, related issue raised in this chapter's readings concerns the extent to which people know, understand, or in some other way see themselves in relation to others. Creatively or not, carry out the task articulated in suggestion #2, focusing your efforts on understanding how at least *three* of the chapter's readings deal with the specific issue of self-other relationships.

4) Discuss the different writing styles and forms of writing that you came across in this chapter's reading selections. Were some styles and forms more effective than others? Having read some or all of this chapter's readings, can you draw any general conclusions about the relationship between form and content in writing?

5) To further your understanding of some of the issues dealt with in this chapter's readings, take a look at just about any issue of the magazine *Woman of Power* (the Spring 1990 issue is particularly useful), as well as at one or more of the following three books: *This Bridge Called My Back: Writings by Radical Women of Color*, edited by Cherríe Moraga and Gloria Anzaldúa; Angela Y. Davis' *Women, Race & Class*; and Maxine Hong Kingston's *The Woman Warrior: Memoirs of a Girlhood Among Ghosts*. Then, compare the ways in which one or more of the authors of these writings and one or more of the authors of the chapter's reading selections deal with similar issues that they address in their work. The following two, related issues might prove useful as interpretive focal points: 1) the issue con-

cerning the extent to which the goals, values, beliefs, and ideas ordinarily associated with mainstream thinking are often assumed to be everyone's goals, values, beliefs, and ideas; and 2) the issue concerning the problem that, more often than not, people outside of the mainstream, and not people in the mainstream, are called upon to explain their differences, justify their behavior (or even their very existence), and the like. If nothing else, after completing this project, you might find that you have come upon a whole new world of understanding that had been awaiting—and that perhaps had already discovered—*you*!